D1207486

PRESIDENTIAL STYLE

A Cass Canfield BOOK

Also by Samuel I. Rosenman

The Public Papers and Addresses of Franklin D. Roosevelt, Vols. 1–13

Working with Roosevelt

Also by Dorothy Rosenman

A Million Homes a Year

PRESIDENTIAL STYLE

Some Giants and a Pygmy in the White House

Samuel and Dorothy Rosenman

INTRODUCTION BY JAMES MACGREGOR BURNS

HARPER & ROW, PUBLISHERS

New York, Evanston, San Francisco, London

FIRST EDITION

Designed by C. Linda Dingler

Library of Congress Cataloging in Publication Data

Rosenman, Samuel Irving, 1896–1973.
   Presidential style.

   (A Cass Canfield book)
   Includes bibliographies and index.
   1. Presidents—United States. I. Rosenman, Dorothy
Reuben, joint author. II. Title.
JK516.R517   1976   353.03′13   74–1850
ISBN 0-06-013669-3

76 77 78 79 10 9 8 7 6 5 4 3 2 1

To our grandchildren
Andy, Robert, Debbie, Lynn and Mary

CONTENTS

AUTHOR'S NOTE

Initially this book was a husband and wife collaboration, Sam—of course—writing it, and I doing the research and editing. With the exception of the final editing, the chapters on Theodore Roosevelt and Franklin D. Roosevelt had been completed before Sam died. In fact, his Theodore Roosevelt had been sent to Cass Canfield two days before Sam suddenly passed away on June 24, 1973. And he had written the first few pages on Woodrow Wilson.

We had spent ten days working at the Roosevelt Library at Hyde Park in the spring of 1972 shortly after the Roosevelt-Churchill Papers had been opened to the public. I was assigned the interesting task of reading them with particular attention to be focused upon whatever material pertained to the Balkans and the "soft underbelly." After I had spent many weeks collating other material dealing with this subject, Sam quite characteristically said, "Now you write it." With misgivings, I did. This time Sam edited my material and sent that section to Mr. Canfield as having been "researched and written by Dorothy Rosenman."

That is probably the reason that I have been given the privilege of finishing what Sam started. I have not "quaked in my boots" while writing because I have been fortified by the confidence which my husband placed in me. He would have been pleased that I have done this; and now I can but hope that others will be.

Mr. Canfield showed more courage than I, and I am thankful to him.

DOROTHY ROSENMAN

ACKNOWLEDGMENTS

I wish to thank most heartily Mr. William J. Stewart, M.A., Assistant Director of the Franklin D. Roosevelt Library, and Mr. Joseph W. Marshall, M.S.L.S., Librarian and Head of the Research Unit of the Franklin D. Roosevelt Library —along with their staff—for the generous contribution of their time in assisting Judge Rosenman and me in our days of research at the Library in the spring of 1972.

This book could not have been completed without the privilege of using the books of The Library of Columbia University. For the helpfulness of Miss Mary Lou Lucy, Head of the Humanistic and Historical Center at the Library, and of Miss Mary Ann Bourke, Head of its Circulation Department, I am most grateful.

Words of thanks must also be given to Mr. Harry H. Schwartz for making available books from his interesting collection.

Mr. Philip C. Brooks, Director of The Harry S. Truman Library, provided guidance to printed material. No research was done at the Library because relevant papers have not yet been open to the public.

Finally, I must say that it has been a pleasure to work with the capable and companionable Harper & Row editor, Ruth Pollack.

INTRODUCTION

This work appears at a time when Americans are re-assessing the Presidency and in a year when the voters will pass judgment on a President who is, one presumes, neither a pygmy nor a giant. In the wake of Watergate and the final Vietnam whimper, the re-assessment has been urgent and searching. One of the several major contributions of Samuel and Dorothy Rosenman's book is to bring direct experience, historical understanding, and a fine contemporary judgment to bear on the workings of this uniquely American institution in the twentieth century.

The Framers of the Constitution established a system of government that, in its broad structure, has lasted almost two centuries. They were able to bring off one of the most brilliant acts of political planning in the western experience because they understood the physiology of power as well as the mechanics of governmental structures and institutions. "Ambition must be made to counteract ambition," wrote James Madison, in defending the essential strategy of the Constitution. By this he meant that power under the new Constitution would be contained and stabilized because—and only if—the rulers of the future were brought into conflict with one another, as a result of the constituencies to which they would appeal—an electoral college, state legislatures, separate congressional district electorates—being arrayed against one another in pursuit of competing goals. This system has been known as the separation of powers, but more properly as the checks and balances.

Within this system the Framers also established the foundations of strong executive power, for these practical men wanted executive efficiency as well as republican representation. Save for the Civil War, when the new Constitution failed in the face of the explosive sectional passions over slavery, the system was not sharply tested during the nineteenth century. But almost from the dawn of the present century the ferment of reform, the projection of the United States into the imperial theatre, the impact of depression, the hypertrophy of the cities, the enormous demands of world wars, and the heightened expectations of the voters combined with the easy promise-making of office-seekers—all combined to put an eighteenth-century constitution under enormous stress.

The Constitution has weathered the storms, in part as a result of some institutional changes. But in two respects at least the hopes of the Framers have been blighted. One is the presidential war power. Vietnam exposed the fragility of the bonds with which the constitution-makers pinned down the power of the Commander in Chief not only to conduct war but to make war, to create war.

The other is the corruption of power. It had been expected that at the very least the Constitution would have the strength of its weaknesses—i.e., one great value in establishing a somewhat negative government was that in setting so many cooks to watching the broth—and watching one another—the broth would not be spoiled. But Watergate demonstrated that even with a strong and sharp-eyed press, a Congress controlled by the opposition party, and a responsible judiciary, presidential authority was abused and perverted to a vast degree before the countervailing pressures, partly owing to a stroke of luck, could be brought to bear.

Already the agony of Vietnam and Watergate has brought some corrective measures, as in the passage of a war powers act and of a campaign finance bill. But one of the paradoxical results of this reformist spirit may be an overreaction to the growth of presidential power, a new call for congressional government, and a repudiation of the essential purpose of the Framers to establish a *balance* of powers. And one reason for this overreaction has been an excessive preoccupation with the Lyndon Johnson and Richard Nixon presidencies at the expense of full understanding of the "strong Presidents" earlier in the century.

By focusing on the two Roosevelts, Wilson, and Truman, the Rosenmans not only provide a vivid panorama of leaders, issues, conflicts, institutions, and policies during some of the most exciting years of our national existence. They also remind us forcefully that power has been both abused and contained, that power has both degraded and healed, that power not only corrupts but power *vacuums* corrupt. Revealing episodes abound in the book: Teddy Roosevelt summoning the Speaker of the House to the White House as a test of strength, and failing; Woodrow Wilson dominating Congress and meeting final defeat at the hands of the Senate; Harding creating a vacuum of power that enabled the most mercenary and banal forces to take over; Franklin Roosevelt managing Congress with supreme skill and yet humbled in his effort to limit judicial power; Truman carefully mobilizing the full strength of the executive leadership in his administration before sacking General MacArthur and thus defying the general's supporters on the Hill. We are reminded of especially significant presidential statements and rationalizations—for example, the first Roosevelt's exposition in a letter to Henry Cabot Lodge of the President's need to know that Oliver Wendell Holmes was "in entire sympathy with our views" before he would feel justified in appointing him to the Supreme Court. The anatomy of these and many other collaborations and conflicts, and their outcomes, has been too varied to permit glib generalities about either presidential despotism or congressional usurpation.

The skill with which Samuel Rosenman, with the assistance and later the full participation of Dorothy Rosenman, have treated these episodes, in the context of the broader social and economic and ideological forces of this century, reminds us of a small phenomenon of American politics. This is the remarkable reportorial and even literary ability of so many of the presidential advisers of recent chief executives. FDR's Raymond Moley, Frances Perkins, Grace Tully, Robert Sherwood, James A. Farley, Jonathan Daniels; John Kennedy's Theodore Sorensen, Arthur Schlesinger, Jr., Evelyn Lincoln, Morris Udall, Lawrence O'Brien, Fred Dutton, Chester Bowles, Richard Neustadt; Lyndon Johnson's Joseph Califano, Douglas Cater, Harry McPherson, George Reedy, Walt Rostow, Jack Valenti are only some of the more notable contributors to an understanding of the administrations they served. Some of these persons had distinguished literary reputations before entering the White House, as in the cases of Schlesinger and Cater, but one wonders whether the White House experience has not only educated these many advisers but lent added force and eloquence to their pens.

Much depends, however, on the qualities an adviser first brings to the White House. Samuel Rosenman will long serve as a kind of exemplar for such literary-minded aides. In this work, and in his earlier *Working with Roosevelt,* he has made a notable contribution to our understanding of the American political experience not only because of the opportunity he had to participate in executive decisionmaking, but even more because he brought to the White House an understanding of the American legal and constitutional background, compassion for the needs of a depression-ridden people, an ear for the right words to help his chief talk to the nation, and an eye for the play of power among the master politicians of his time. These qualities are fully reflected in this volume.

JAMES MACGREGOR BURNS

PREFACE

Hundreds of books have been written on the American presidency and on the Presidents. New books appear each year. The Presidents have been examined, individually and collectively, in the minutest detail. There are descriptions of every public act, reproductions of their letters, messages and statements—and even of many private and personal ones. An admirer of any particular President can find many books to support and even enhance his admiration. Also, in nearly every case, he can find books which tend to diminish his admiration, or to induce him to denounce the authors.

There is plenty of reason for the great interest in the American presidency. It is a unique institution in the history of civilization. There was never anything exactly like it before its creation in 1787 at Philadelphia; and it has not been copied exactly by any of the scores of new political governments which have since come into being. As this nation has assumed its position among the nations of the world, the presidency has grown into the most powerful office of any of the democratic governments. Therefore, it is to be expected that political writers and historians would study and restudy the constitutional powers and functions of the office and the gradual extension by our strong Presidents of those powers in domestic and foreign affairs.

This book will not be a history of the presidency or of any individual administration—except to the extent necessary to demonstrate the style of the strong, great Presidents—the giants—of the twentieth century, and, as contrast, that of the one who was weak and termed by historians a failure—a pygmy.

The thesis of this book is that, in peace or war, in times of crisis and in times of tranquility, each great President has exercised his own individual style of operation. The purpose of the book is, hopefully, to study and analyze that style. Presidential style can be analyzed in many situations, much like style in literature, painting or sculpture. Though each President started with the same explicit constitutional bases of power, some of them found more power implied in the Constitution than did others. Some Presidents were given additional statutory powers of vast magnitude; others were denied them. Crises, foreign and domestic, confronted some; others were spared, and led comparatively tranquil lives in Washington. Great events often determine the powers to be implied and, as a result, have much to do with fixing the President's place in history.

The "great" Presidents in our history never hesitated, in the face of emergencies, to use vast "implied" powers for the first time. Each one in turn thus enhanced Presidential prestige, and his "great" successors built upon this enhanced prestige.

This book will attempt to analyze the style of the four Presidents of the twentieth century who have been rated by scholars, and recognized by most historians, to have been the "great" or "near-great" of our Presidents, and of one of the two Presidents rated in the same way as "failures" in office.

The greatness of Presidents is one of the favorite topics of American conversation. There can be many criteria for rating such greatness, which fluctuate according to the appraiser's own political preference, education, bias, social philosophy, background and personal experiences. Popular polls have been tried in various forms, but they are not reliable. They alter from year to year and even from day to day. There have even been mechanical tests, such as measuring the lines accorded to each President in various biographical compilations. Obviously, these cannot be very reliable.

However, two well-known polls were taken in 1948 and in 1962, which were directed by an American historian and scholar, and addressed only to experts, that is, American historical scholars, historians, political scientists and a few others. In selecting the giants ("great" operators) in the White House for discussion in this book, we have taken the ratings in these two polls—plus another scholarly and more meticulous poll (see Appendix).

By dictionary definition, "style" is "the way in which something is said or done as distinguished from its substance."[1] An analogy of Presidential style may be made with style in the arts. A painter works with specific material objects which have well-known and constant characteristics and properties. For example, oil paint or tempera, canvas or paper, the acids used in etchings, are all subject to the same physical and chemical laws, no matter who uses them. There are certain definite primary colors; the artist can mix them in known proportions to produce any color he wants on a canvas. If the proportions are right, the color will not change no matter when used or by whom.

But two or more artists may use the same materials and the same brushes, and may set up their easels in the same place and paint the same scene, yet what finally emerges are entirely different pictures. The results stem not from the fixed quality and quantity of the materials, but from the artist alone, from his skill, ingenuity, imagination, inspiration—his genius. One of the pictures, using the same materials, the same strokes and composition as the others, may be a masterpiece, while the rest may be disasters. The difference will not depend on the materials with which the artists work, but on the artist himself.

A President, of course, functions and does his job with a very different kind of material. Nothing that he uses is even remotely as fixed and set in its qualities as marble, canvas, paint or brush. The President's job deals essentially with probably the most volatile, unpredictable and uncontrollable material on the face of the earth—human beings.

Human beings falling within his orbit may be friendly or hostile to him, or may change from friendship to hostility, or vice versa. They include his own Cabinet, his staff, the millions of federal employees, his Army and Navy chiefs —all theoretically subject to his command—who may at times, and frequently do, disregard or actually sabotage his orders and policies. Each President has had his own way or style in dealing with the people under his immediate direction, sometimes similar to that of certain other Presidents, sometimes entirely different from all of them.

Human beings include also the members of Congress—consisting of friends and foes—each answerable to a constituency more limited and more homogeneous than the President's, whose sectional interests are often in conflict with the President's policies and even with the national interests. Here, because of the large number of people involved, he often has to rely largely on congressional leaders and committee chairmen, who may themselves be wholly out of sympathy with his own policies. Frequently he has to bypass the leaders of Congress and make direct personal contact with individual congressmen, or do so through his staff, or, at times, through the political leaders back in the congressmen's districts. He must always be aware of one of the truest facts of political life, that no congressman is more likely to get publicity, and often favor back home, than one who publicly attacks the President—the more vitriolic the attack, the greater the publicity. Each of the Presidents also has had his own way or style in dealing with Congress.

And, always, there is the media, frequently hostile, often misinformed, and sometimes even guilty of managing the news. A President must manage to get his messages over to the American people in spite of adverse comment in print or on the air. Often he must appeal to his people directly over the heads of congressional foes and a hostile press.

One of his greatest modern assets (or pitfalls) can be a press conference, where all alone he faces more than a hundred clever, experienced, and often ruthless human beings—most of whom would like to trap him with leading questions—all waiting for some slip of tongue or mind which they can magnify into examples of ignorance or credibility, or worse. All of these contacts involve human beings.

Each of the Presidents had his own way of dealing with the press and (in recent times) with radio and television. Each had his own way of reaching out for the approval of the people, his main source of strength.

Above all, each President had his own way of dealing with the personal problems of people, with the promotion of social justice among them, with what we have come to know as their economic well-being and security.

There are also always likely to be disturbances or conflicts in some part of the globe—again the acts of human beings—which he would like to try to stop, mediate or keep from spreading. That is part of the job as a world leader that the modern President must assume.

A President's style is not as easy to analyze as that of a painter or sculptor. It is quite simple for a person, with just a smattering of knowledge of painting, to recognize at a glance a Picasso or Modigliani, a Rubens or Rembrandt, a Rodin or Giacometti. Obviously, this is not so easy with Presidents; yet there is a distinctive method of operation discernible in each of our great Presidents.

Although this book will be a study only of style and not, in any sense, a history of the administration of any President, it is necessary in order to determine the style of a President that some of his actions, speeches, messages and statements be discussed. It is impossible to present his style in a vacuum; it must be related to something that he did, and particularly to *how* he did it. That is why there will be a discussion of events, speeches, attitudes, and so on, of the President being examined, which will be related to the style with which he conducted his operation in the White House.

Whether you think of the handling of the presidency as an art or a science, essentially what a President does is to run a vast, complex and intricate operation, extending over the entire world—and recently into the immeasurable distances of space itself. A successful President, no matter what his social, political or economic philosophy may be, must above all be a successful operator of such a system.

The word "operator," especially in the jargon of politics, sometimes conveys a connotation of deviousness. The American Heritage Dictionary of the English Language, for example, gives among others these definitions of "operate": "to bring about a desired or proper effect, to function effectively; to conduct the affairs of." And for the word "operator"—or one who operates—in addition to the normal definitions an informal definition, or definition acceptable in conversation, is added, "a cultivated colloquialism" but not suitable in formal writing, as follows: "a shrewd and sometimes unscrupulous person who gets what he wants by devious means."

The implication of deception or dishonesty in this book's use of the word "devious" is emphatically denied. For example, the shocking story of the Pentagon Papers is a story of deception practiced on the American people, by those in high command, including the President himself. These reports and representations were not devious, they were downright false.

There will be many examples of what is meant by deviousness on the part of some of our "great" and "near-great" Presidents. It must be said—with the greatest respect for the office and for the great Presidents who have filled it—that no President today, dealing as he must with so many human beings, friendly and hostile, can be entirely successful without a substantial amount of deviousness as here defined in his conduct and nature.

One of the outstanding Presidential biographies of our day is *Franklin D. Roosevelt, The Lion and the Fox,* by James MacGregor Burns. The subtitle was based on the following statement by Machiavelli, in *The Prince:* "A prince must imitate the fox and the lion, for the lion cannot protect himself from traps, and the fox cannot defend himself from wolves. One must therefore be a fox to recognize traps, and a lion to frighten wolves. Those that wish to be only lions do not understand this. Therefore, a prudent ruler ought not to keep faith when by so doing it would be against his interest, and when the reasons which made him bind himself no longer exist. If men were all good, this precept would not be a good one; but as they are bad, and would not observe their faith with you, so you are not bound to keep faith with them."

Professor Burns points out the incidents in which Franklin D. Roosevelt's style as President showed the qualities of the lion, those in which he showed the qualities of the fox—and those in which he showed a mixture of both. Success often depended upon which qualities were displayed. Roosevelt's choice was not always the correct one, as events proved and as we shall see. But generally, his choice was the successful one.

It is in this sense that the great Presidents came to be known as "operators." George Washington had none of the fox in his actions as President, and he did not need it. But since his time, every President who has achieved outstanding success and greatness has had to play the lion or the fox—and frequently both at the same time. Some of the ratings compiled by historians to assess the greatness of Presidents are concerned in a way with these qualities—often politely referred to as "sincerity," "strength of action," and "practicality."

Let us not lose sight of the fact that even the style of an artist changes. Hang three Picassos on a wall next to each other, one from his Blue period, one from his Cubist period and one from his recent work. Unless the observer knows something of the history and work of this man, he would swear that the three pictures were each the product of a different artist.

In the same way, the style of a President may change. This does not mean merely that he might reverse some of his prior decisions, or even change some policies. It means that his fundamental style itself may change. For example, the Franklin D. Roosevelt style of 1937 and 1938, the years of the Supreme Court fight and of the attempted "purge," and his style of 1939, the year when Congress seemed to hold him at bay, were entirely different from Roosevelt's style in his first term or third term. There are reasons for this, which will be discussed in the chapter dealing with him.

The style of operation of a President flows to a great extent from decisionmaking. Every policy or program is the sum of many decisions, and each President has his own way of arriving at decisions. It is not always easy—in fact, it is very difficult—to analyze the elements that go into decisionmaking by a President. Indeed, the decision cannot always be rationally analyzed; sometimes it is purely "hunch" or intuition.

The style of a President mirrors his manner of functioning. It delineates his personality and influences his achievements and failures. The giants of the twentieth century were markedly different; their personalities, actions, lack of action, reactions, their temperaments and methods differed. However, each of them had courage, imagination, initiative and resolution, which they used according to their own style. Each of them exercised leadership, but the manner differed with the urgencies of their particular times and with the composition of their temperaments. The pygmy had none of these qualities and shirked leadership.

In appraising leadership, it must be remembered that the Constitution of the United States was drawn by delegates to the Constitutional Convention who were forced to make many compromises in order to reach an agreement. The sharpest cleavage of opinion—the one over which most debate flourished, and which was not finally settled until practically the end of the convention—involved the nature and power of the executive branch of government, and most particularly its chief, the President. There were, to be sure, specific provisions. But that which gave our Presidents "executive power" was vague—vague because the delegates could not have reached agreement if it had been made specific. "Executive power" was invested in him, and he was to "take care that the laws be faithfully executed." These elastic phrases were the tools of Presidents who were leaders.

But in this "balanced constitution," there were many limits placed upon his power by the convention through its grants of power to the Congress.

The powers given by the convention to Congress were indeed formidable—and provided the principal checks on the President:

1. The power of the purse, i.e., the sole power to levy taxes and make appropriations without which the executive and his departments could not operate.

2. The power to override his veto.

3. The power of censure.

4. The power of impeachment.

5. Inability of the President to dissolve Congress—which was also given fixed terms.

6. The power to declare war, fix tariffs, borrow money, regulate interstate and international commerce.

7. The power to pass immigration and naturalization acts, bankruptcy laws, to coin money and regulate the value thereof, establish post offices, grant patents and copyrights, and to set up inferior courts.

8. The power to fix the size of the Army and Navy and to provide for their support and control.

9. To provide for organizing, arming, disciplining and calling out the militia.

10. To enact laws to carry out the foregoing powers and all other powers vested by this Constitution in the government of the United States.

It would take a "great" man as President—a man of dedication and determination—to look at this array of powers in the Congress without saying, "How can I ever get anything done in my program?" It was the "great" Presidents who were able to meet these restraints on their office, to overcome them, to persuade the Congress not to exercise them, or to get around them. The weak ones were satisfied to let the Congress use its powers at will without any interference from them. In the White House, the men were soon to be set aside from the boys.

However, the width of Presidential power, as well as congressional power, has been limited from time to time by the judicial branch of government—the Supreme Court. This restraint was implied but not delineated by those who drafted the Constitution.

When the framers were debating about separation of powers and checks and balances, they were primarily—indeed, almost exclusively—concerned with the executive and the legislative branches of government. The judicial or third branch was given scant consideration in its relationship to the other two. And although the doctrine of judicial review of the acts of the other two was mentioned in a desultory way in the debates, nothing was done about it; it never came into actual use until 1827.

Today, the Court often makes the final determination of a disputed constitutional power exercised by the President. The only possibility of changing the viewpoint of a Supreme Court opposed to a President's philosophy to one attuned to it lies either in the hands of God—who may create vacancies which a President can then fill with men of more congenial viewpoints—or in an executive's ability to influence public opinion, which in turn may influence the attitude of some members of the Court.

In selecting the giants in the White House and the pygmy, the authors have not relied upon their own judgment, but upon polls taken by historians among historians. Those polls asked American historical scholars, historians and political scientists to rate the Presidents as Great, Near Great, Average and Failure. The decisions were to be based only on "performance in office, omitting anything before or after." (See Appendix for polls.)

Because it would require more than one volume to treat the performance style of all the Presidents, or even the top eight, and because the presidency of the twentieth century is so different from that of the nineteenth century in range of powers, territory covered, foreign affairs, domestic crises and new administrative management aids, it has been decided to discuss only the four "giants" of this century—the two Roosevelts, Wilson and Truman. In order to show the contrast in style between the "greats" and the failures, the style of Warren G. Harding as President will also be discussed.

1

THEODORE ROOSEVELT

(1858–1919)

President, September 14, 1901, to March 4, 1909

"Anything can happen now that that damn cowboy is in the White House," muttered Mark Hanna, the National Republican political boss, when his friend President McKinley died from an assassin's bullet on September 14, 1901. On that day, Vice President Theodore Roosevelt succeeded to the presidency. Hanna's rueful remark was to be proven in each of the next seven years.

At the Republican National Convention in July the year before, Hanna had had a worried premonition; now it had actually come to pass. When Theodore Roosevelt was suggested to him as the Vice-Presidential candidate to run that year with President McKinley, who had been nominated for re-election, Hanna —violently opposed to the idea—blurted out, "Don't you realize that there's only one life between that madman and the White House?"

That "one life" had been snuffed out.

This changing of the guard on September 14, 1901, was soon to put an end to the seemingly serene system of national laissez-faire toward the economic and social forces in the United States which had been generated by the Industrial Revolution. It was to bring to a close the era of rugged individualism which had marked American life under all the Presidents since Abraham Lincoln. Its most important result—the one which led to all the others—was a substantial shifting of federal power for the first time in thirty-five years, from the Congress of the United States to the White House, a change which was to characterize forty-eight of the following seventy-two years of the twentieth century.

By the time of McKinley's death, the number of corporations in industry, finance and transportation had multiplied, and many were in process of expanding into bigger and more powerful giants. They were popularly known as trusts in those days. Government had watched this movement approvingly as one of natural and beneficent growth, with indifference to any effect it might have on the lives of the millions of ordinary men and women in the United States. In fact, the government often acted as if its chief function was to encourage this development. Certainly no government powers were invoked to stop it, regulate it, adequately tax it, or alleviate any of the financial and industrial evils which had followed in its wake.

It is true that there was on the statute books a law enacted in 1890 designed to prevent monopolies and restraint of trade, called the Sherman Antitrust Act. But enforcement of that law required a determined and courageous Attorney General, backed by a President who believed in its purposes and wanted to see them attained. Before the advent of Theodore Roosevelt, Washington had had neither. In fact, no antitrust prosecution since 1890 had ever emanated from Washington against any business combination. Such cases as had been instituted were begun by zealous United States attorneys in the local United States District Courts. Besides, one of the cases the Supreme Court of the United States decided in 1895 had rendered the statute practically impotent by holding (1) that the statute did not apply to the production of commodities within a state, and (2) that the purchase by the "Sugar Trust" of three other sugar corporations by exchange of stock was not "interstate commerce" within the meaning of the statute. These conclusions were reached even though the result of the merger was to create a monopoly of 98 per cent of the sugar production in the United States, which thereupon did pass in interstate commerce.

Calvin Coolidge's laconic summary in 1924 of this attitude of government to big business, and to the financiers who furnished the means by which big business became bigger, applied even more aptly to the America of McKinley's day than it did to his own: "The business of the United States is business." In McKinley's day, big business by its control of Congress actually controlled the government itself. Big business had the key to the back door of the White House; it also had the key to the front door of the United States Senate. Senators were not elected by the people, but by the legislatures of the various states—most of which were controlled by state political leaders, who in turn were generally subservient to business and financial interests. It was no accident or mere coincidence that the big Republican leaders in Theodore Roosevelt's time were also members of the United States Senate: Hanna, Platt, Spooner, Lodge and Aldrich. There were also many members of Congress who felt no reluctance in furthering their own financial fortunes as well as the interests of big business on the floor and in the committee rooms of Congress. Conflict of interest was no badge of dishonor in those days; it was a commonplace.

"Anything could happen" with respect to all this—and it did.

In the field of foreign affairs also, Hanna's mournful misgivings were to be justified. Under the new "madman," the United States was to leave the walls of isolation and claim its position as a world power equal to the world powers of Europe; it was to carry out its "manifest destiny" and take on its share of the "white man's burden"; it was practically to assume the role of guardian for some parts of Latin America, and to expand the sweep of the Monroe Doctrine to an extent that would have astounded its original promulgator. It was, in Roosevelt's words, even to "take Panama" for purposes of a canal.

The new President, however, lost no time in announcing to all the members of the McKinley Cabinet who were present when he took the oath of office that his style of government was to be the same as that of his predecessor: "I wish to say that it shall be my aim to continue absolutely unbroken, the policy of President McKinley for the peace, the prosperity and the honor of our beloved country."

Roosevelt's conduct as Governor of New York during the preceding two years not only contradicted this promise, but indicated that even as he made it in the emotion of the moment, he must have had no intention of fulfilling it. Perhaps, consistent with his style on many occasions, he was deluding himself as well as his audience rather than deliberately lying about his real intentions. No matter what the reason for this rash pledge, Wall Street knew better. Wall Street, where all the financial and economic power lay, the base of operations of those whom President Theodore Roosevelt was later to castigate as "malefactors of great wealth," was too smart to take this declaration at its face value.

In fact, Wall Street and all big business were—in a word—scared. They knew all about Roosevelt's past, and were frightened about what the new President might do. It was ironically different from the fear which Wall Street was to feel when Franklin D. Roosevelt took his first oath of office. On March 4, 1933, their fear was not for what the President was going to do, but what he might not do. They were in a panic, frantically urging the new President to do something— almost anything—to save the country, to save them *and* to save their ancient privileges, including the privilege of running the government as they had from 1920.[1] Both Roosevelts would take action; for the style of both of them was always one of action and more action. Theodore was to start the first step away from laissez-faire and toward regulation and control; Franklin, a generation later, would take more and longer strides in the same direction.

When Theodore Roosevelt became President at the youngest age in our history—not quite forty-three years—he brought to Washington a vast experience in government: as a member of the legislature of New York; as chairman of the Civil Service Commission of the United States, as chairman of the Police Board of New York City, as Assistant Secretary of the Navy, and finally as Governor of the State of New York. "The White House is no place for amateurs," it has been said; Theodore Roosevelt was no amateur.

He was born a sickly, asthmatic child, at times breathing with great difficulty and much pain. His eyes were weak from birth, one going completely blind before he was fifty, a condition which he concealed from all except a handful of friends. He was always near-sighted. He had difficulty as a boy with his thin pipe-stem legs. These physical defects had much to do with Roosevelt's later life and with his style in government. His sister, Corinne, relates a momentous conversation between Theodore at the age of twelve and his father. His father pointed out to him, "You have the mind, but you have not the body and without the body, the mind cannot go as far as it should." This was a challenge; and the father put it that way intentionally. "Theodore, you must make your body. It is hard drudgery to make one's body, but I know you will do it." The boy, who hated the weakness of his body and the disabilities which it imposed, "threw back his head in characteristic fashion," and, "with a determined flash of his teeth," replied firmly, " 'I'll make my body.' "[2]

It was indeed drudgery, but he *did* make it. He embarked upon a course of boring exercises, first at Wood's Gymnasium in New York City and then in a homemade gymnasium on the open-air back porch of his home in New York City. He began camping, walking, climbing trees and mountains, horseback riding, running—all to build up his muscles. He kept it up with such persistence and patience and singlemindedness that it became an obsession which was to last through life. He did succeed in developing a strong body, but it was only by this constant compulsive effort. He would later feel contempt for anyone who was unwilling to go through the same gruelling process. The "strenuous life" soon became for him the ideal life, and it was one of the ideals which he later repeatedly held before American youth.

During his last spring at Harvard in 1880, he had a physical examination by the university physician, Dr. Dudley A. Sargent. The doctor then took Theodore aside and warned him that his weak point was his heart, that he must give up all the physical exertion which he had conscientiously continued while at Harvard, and that he should not even run upstairs. Theodore, in his ever-blunt style, immediately answered the doctor that he would pay no attention to this kind of medical advice, and that he preferred an early death to that kind of life. He never, until more than thirty years later in 1918, told anyone about this talk, or wrote a word in his diary or letters about it. Carleton Putnam[3] has concluded, after reviewing the kind of life Roosevelt had led up to that point in 1880, that his heart difficulty was functional rather than organic—that it was just "tired" after all the walking, running, tennis, rowing, swimming, riding and hunting. Always remembering his father's challenge, Roosevelt had never let up—except during actual illness in bed—in "making his body." Roosevelt's physical response to the doctor's medical warning was typical of his courage, his persistence and his determination; he immediately went on a tough six-week hunting trip out west with his brother Elliott. Probably to show himself what he thought of the medical advice, he wrote his mother: "I expect to enjoy the western trip greatly as I think it will build me up."

This love of the strenuous life was one of the sources of his later belief and style in advocating measures as President which called upon "those most valuable of all qualities, the soldierly virtues." He was convinced that "all the great masterful races have been fighting races." As a boy he got into some fights with older boys, and was at least once badly beaten and humiliated. He immediately started boxing lessons, and became a boxer of some ability—even making the semi-finals one year at Harvard in the boxing championship. He was not going to let anyone physically beat him again if he could help it. He also learned to ride well, and to hunt. His early interest in natural history took him afield into the fresh air constantly. He almost began to worship strength, for he himself had been able to attain it by effort, determination, patience and single-minded purpose. As President in 1901, he wrote his son, Theodore, "I was very sorry to learn that you had broken your collar bone, but I am glad you played right through the game, and that you seem to have minded it so little."[4] It was not unnatural that this worship of strength would eventually be transferred from strength for an individual to strength for the nation. To make America strong among the nations of the world, to command the respect of the world because of her strength, to continue to show the world the strength which the nation had attained—all were to play an important part in his style as President.

He began to accumulate his vast political experience at the very young age of twenty-two. There was as little in his early environment and social economic status and in his education to indicate the selection by him of a political career as there was to be in Franklin's. He came from the same social and financial background, and naturally followed the same traditional pattern of life. His was a family of substantial wealth. Early education as well as preparation for college came with private tutors; travel abroad was extensive and frequent; there was the gentleman's education at Harvard, with membership in its best clubs. Roosevelt studied law for a year at Columbia Law School but he soon learned that the practice of law would be distasteful to him, and he finally dropped it. He also found incompatible the standards of many successful lawyers—the ablest and the most eminent—who were in the service of great corporations and who were able to find ways for their clients to evade the spirit of the law. This idealism remained with him and grew in later years to influence his style as President in dealing with huge corporate entities. Fortunately for him, he had a sufficient inheritance to avoid the necessity of earning a living.

Roosevelt began to develop some of his later style as President at a very early age, indeed while he was still at Harvard. In his graduating year, he began and wrote one or two chapters of his *Naval War of 1812.* The following year, 1881, he finished the 500-page book, and turned it in to his publisher on December 3. If he had done nothing during 1881 but work on the book, it would have been something of an achievement, for it is an exhaustive study, full of details about guns and armaments of different fighting vessels. But in 1881, besides writing the book, he attended Columbia Law School, was an active socialite, got married, and spent the summer on his wedding trip sightseeing in Europe and writing many letters home about what he had seen.

Undertaking and completing this project in the midst of all his other activities shows the breadth of his growing interest in public affairs, and also an energy, determination and dedication rarely displayed by one of his years. But more significant is the fact that the book shows his conviction, which was to continue throughout life, of the necessity for military preparation and rigorous training of fighting forces. He draws lessons from American lack of preparation and training in 1812, which he bluntly and boldly uses to condemn the pacifist policies of the government of the United States in 1881.

The book is also notable for the beginning of the many statements to be made by Roosevelt on the question of race, especially the superiority over the other races of the English and American "races," which had been infused with the German, Irish and Norse. There was to be more of this in his later *Winning of the West,* and it was to continue during most of his political life. He always was to believe that America and her institutions were largely the result of their North European ancestry, and he had a much lower estimate of the other ethnic components of American culture.

To the surprise of his friends in the high society of New York City—if not to their dismay—he suddenly, in 1880, added another but different kind of club to those he called "clubs of social pretension" to which his family and he already belonged: the Republican Club of the 21st Assembly District. His reasons for this step—so unusual in his circle—taken in spite of the warnings of the big businessmen and lawyers he knew that "political clubs were not controlled by 'gentlemen,'" were prophetic of much of his style in later public office; self-assurance, confidence that he could do things better than anyone else, conviction that the Republican Party was always the party of greater virtue. He later wrote that he had gone into the machine politics of a district club because he would there meet the people who were the "governing class," that the people he knew socially were not, and that "I intended to be one of the governing class." He added that it had to be a Republican club because, in 1880, "a young man of my bringing-up and convictions could join only the Republican Party."

Twenty years later, looking back from his position as Vice President of the United States over all the years he had spent in public life, he expressed the same idea in a letter to a friend: "My whole career in politics is due to the simple fact that when I came out of Harvard, I was firmly resolved to belong to the *governing class,* not to the governed. I found that I could belong to the *governing class* in just one way and that was by taking the trouble to put myself in a position where I could hold my own in the decisive struggles for or against those who really did govern. Accordingly, I joined my district association. . . . The various opportunities that came along passed in my direction. I was always on hand and I gradually acquired what may be called the 'political habit,' and so I went into public life."[5] (Emphasis added)

This lifelong obsession about belonging to the "governing" or "ruling class" explains not only his tremendous urge to move up the political ladder, but also his compulsive and joyous style in the use of executive power in every office where he found himself in the governing class. As long as he was in that class he meant to do his full share of the governing. That style would persist through his presidency, where he would use his executive power as it had never been used since Lincoln.

He had a definite feeling from the beginning, as he later wrote, that politics involved action and fight—especially fight for good government—and that the educated college graduate belonged in the thick of the "hurly-burly." He noted, however, that not all educated men had the same yen for a fight as he did, and he faulted them on this score as lacking the "robuster virtues, which makes them shrink from the struggle and the inevitable contact with rough politicians," as "too delicate to have the element of 'strike back' in their natures, and because they have an unmanly fear of being forced to stand up for their own rights when threatened with abuse or insult." No one would ever accuse Roosevelt of any of these soft traits; and he showed this at the very start of his political career.[6]

The new club which he joined was quite different from his others. Its headquarters consisted of one room above a saloon on the site now occupied by the General Motors building on Fifth Avenue and 59th Street in New York City. It was sparsely furnished with just the bare necessities for holding a meeting: a dais, a table, a number of chairs. It did not have the shining brass of the other clubs; what brass there was, was limited to the huge cuspidors which lined the walls and were well worn. A man's quality was sometimes measured by the members by the accuracy with which he could use the cuspidor from a distance. Its members were different too from the members of his other clubs: day laborers, wardheelers, bartenders, drifters. Of course, women were strictly barred; they could not vote and were therefore considered politically worthless—and clearly not qualified to join the "governing class." The 21st District was what we would today call a "silk stocking" district; it was then called a "diamond back" district because it included many wealthy neighborhoods whose residents were popularly believed to dine on diamond-back terrapin each night. It was safely Republican.

Theodore was quite frank about his lack of idealism in starting into district politics. "When I went into politics at this time, I was not conscious of going in with the set purpose to benefit other people, but of getting for myself the privilege to which I was entitled in common with other people." He also confessed the shortcomings in his own social views in 1880. "Neither Joe Murray nor I, nor any of our associates were alive to the social and industrial problems which we now [1913] all of us recognize."

The members of the club regarded young Roosevelt as an outsider and a dude, who was playing at politics merely for diversion. It is to Roosevelt's great credit, and an example of his common sense, that he chose to begin his political career at the very bottom. He did his best to break down the natural barriers between him and the other club members. As he put it: "I went around there often enough to have the men get accustomed to me and to have me get accustomed to them, so that each could begin to live down in the other's mind what Bret Harte has called 'the defective moral quality of being a stranger.' "

To a degree, he succeeded in this effort; and he soon reached a reasonably good relationship with the district leader, Jake Hess, who, he later wrote, "treated

[him] with rather distant affability." He became an intimate lifetime friend, however, of Joe Murray, the lieutenant leader. A lucky combination of unusual circumstances in 1881 catapulted Roosevelt, one year after joining the club, into active elective politics. There was dissatisfaction with the incumbent assembly-man of the district; Murray wanted to break up Hess's tight control and decided to appeal to the "better" people of the district by tendering the nomination as assemblyman to young Roosevelt. Roosevelt was at first reluctant to accept, but finally did so. His reluctance, according to himself, was based on fear that it would be believed that he had joined the club for the purpose of being nominated. Whether this was an example of his everlasting style of self-righteousness, or of self-delusion, is not clear. Murray did some extensive manipulation, and the nomination followed.

Roosevelt wrote in a letter of explanation to a friend that, "Finding it would not interfere much with my law," he accepted. It was another item—a very big item—to add to everything else he had crowded into that one year. Theodore did, however, try his hand at campaigning even though it was not necessary. His kind of campaigning was not very auspicious as a political beginning, but it showed his future style of political inflexibility and idealism in some matters in later life. His first effort at campaigning was to invade Democratic strongholds in the district. Accompanied by both Jake Hess and Joe Murray, he visited a series of saloons on Sixth Avenue—quite a different kind of neighborhood from the one where his friends and he lived. The saloon in those days was the "poor man's club," and at all times there would be a number of voters sitting around. At election time, the customers expected a local candidate to come in and buy at least one round of drinks for everyone.

In one of those saloons the proprietor, who was always an important man to cultivate in each saloon for he could talk favorably of a candidate to all his customers, took the opportunity of discussing with the young candidate the merits of some legislation involving the saloon business. Among the proprietor's grievances was the very important one that the saloon license fee was too high. After some discussion of the facts and economics of the saloon business, the candidate blurted out that he thought the license fee was too low, and that it should be raised instead of reduced. This caused some consternation in everybody listening, and some fairly rough remarks by the saloonkeeper. Hess and Murray gingerly escorted the young candidate out of the saloon, and in a sidewalk conference advised him to stay out of the saloons at least for the duration of the campaign—indeed, to stay off Sixth Avenue entirely and to concentrate his campaigning to Fifth Avenue, leaving Sixth Avenue to them. This kind of plain talk to his constituent was to be Roosevelt's style on many occasions as President, and was to cause comparable difficulties with political leaders, public administra-tive officials, senators and many others.

Theodore's first appearance in 1882, as the youngest member in the Assembly, was not greeted with enthusiasm. He wore pince-nez eyeglasses on a black silk cord; he was dressed and acted like a "dude," and was so characterized by most of his colleagues and in contemporary cartoons. He was a decided novelty to the rough men of the Assembly, who were for the most part not concerned either with good manners, social graces or correct grammar. What you had to notice first about him was an almost unnaturally large head, with copious and carefully parted sandy-colored hair. His shoulders and chest had been developed by all his persistent exercises, but they seemed dwarfed by this head. When he smiled, his large prominent teeth became unduly visible—and in later years of fame they became the basis of cartoonists' caricatures, as well as his audiences' delight. He still had his Harvard accent; and his expensive and well-fitting clothes contrasted with the "store-bought" clothes used by his farmer and city colleagues. Roosevelt's selection of clothes was always out of the ordinary, and played a part in the self-exhibitionism which remained fixed in his style. He normally had a resonant tenor voice, but when he got excited during a speech (which was frequently) his vehemence would produce a shrill tone—almost a falsetto, which seemed to cry out for attention, a characteristic which remained with him as he realized its effectiveness. He was given to bold gesturing to emphasize the points he was making, gestures of the arms, shoulders, and flexible body movement which added to the effect of his oratory.

One of the major modern qualifications of a Presidential candidate—as well as an influential President—is an effective and attractive television personality. Professor Thomas A. Bailey has written that: "Theodore Roosevelt with his falsetto voice, staccato delivery, clenched teeth, flailing fists and Old Testament dedication, might well draw more laughs than votes."[7] But in all his speeches all during his life he would exude a style of great sincerity. He found most of his new colleagues in the Assembly distasteful, but the "Republicans seem to be of a higher calibre," he wrote in his diary. A significant entry was one which recorded that twenty-five of the Democratic contingent were Irish, and added, "the average Catholic Irishman of the first generation as represented in this Assembly is a low, venal, corrupt and unintelligible brute."

His nomination, election and appearance in Albany had been all so swift and sudden that he had had no time to prepare any program or even any attitude toward lawmaking—except one of independence.

He made his mark in the Assembly, however, at the very beginning of the session. The membership was about equally divided, the Democrats having a majority of only one. The Democratic majority was, however, divided among themselves; there were about six Tammany Hall members and the rest were anti-Tammany. The Tammany Hall members had made their usual "deal" with the Republican leaders, by which the former would nominate a member of their own group for the all-important office of Speaker, and then count on the Republicans to help them elect that candidate. It required a majority vote of all the members to elect the Speaker. The price for this cooperation was to be a division of all the patronage at the Speaker's disposal between the Tammany Hall members and the Republicans. This arrangement, of course, made impossible the election of the candidate of the much larger group of Democratic anti-Tammany members. This sort of deal had been accepted in the past as routine. The brash young Roosevelt rose in his maiden speech to break it up! Not only was he violating the custom of silence among first-year members; he was tackling both Tammany Hall and the Republican leaders at the same time.

He urged as a Republican that the Democrats be allowed to elect the Speaker themselves, since they were in the majority. He also urged the Republicans to stay out of the fight, and not to help the Democrats to break the deadlock. In answer to those who said that the deadlock was delaying the session and preventing much necessary legislation, he drily remarked that he had discussed the deadlock with men in his district who had large commercial interests, and that they did not mind the delay, saying that the absence of legislation relieved them rather than annoyed them. His speech was widely hailed in the press. A "deal" like the one proposed can be worked only in secrecy. Roosevelt by bringing it out into the open foiled it; and the anti-Tammany Hall candidate was elected. This was a remarkably courageous and independent effort; immediately it gave young Roosevelt great stature in the legislature, and also throughout the state.

His most important activity in his first legislative session was to give him the same kind of fame as Franklin later achieved in his first year—opposition to his own political party. He rose on April 5, 1882, to urge the adoption of his resolution that the Assembly investigate reports in the press that T. R. West-brook, a Republican Justice of the Supreme Court, had engaged in collusion with Jay Gould and other financiers to help Gould gain control of the Manhattan Elevated Railway. The speech was indirectly aimed at the legislative bosses of both parties, all of whom wanted to keep the long-simmering charges under cover. Roosevelt, true to his political style of the future, spared nobody's feelings in his speech. The *New York Sun* said it "was made with a boldness that was almost scathing." *Harper's Weekly* commented that he was "a young man . . . who does not know the meaning of fear and to whom the bluster and bravado of party and political bullies are as absolutely indifferent as the blowing of the wind." It aroused civic leaders so much that the political leaders of both parties in the Assembly lost control of their members. The resolution was adopted. It was a great victory for this first-year member, and widely hailed as such. The inquiry itself turned out, however, to be a whitewash, and Westbrook was exonerated. But Roosevelt's reputation had been made. In his own words he thereafter "rose like a rocket." His vigorous attack involved more than the acts of one judge; it was aimed right at the heart of a system which dominated much of the political life of 1882, and one which Roosevelt was to meet on a grander scale in the White House: the conflict between the power of great wealth and the power of the law —with all the odds on the power of great wealth. The legislative inquiry, the later vote in the Assembly confirming the majority report of the committee to exoner-ate and repudiating the minority vote to impeach, involved the type of subservi-ence of legislators and legislatures to the "malefactors of great wealth" which Roosevelt was later to fight so hard on a national front.

It is doubtful whether any man in the history of the New York legislature, which has produced many political giants, has ever in his first year accomplished so much or has created for himself so clear and so widespread an image of courage and independence, if not actual hostility to political bosses.

These early days in the Assembly also opened his eyes to the group in the legislature—a small group—who used legislation as a means of making money, either by taking bribes from corporations to vote for bills by which the corpora-tions would benefit financially, or, in the many more instances, by introducing "strike" bills which corporations would pay money to legislators to vote against. What astounded him most, he wrote in 1913, was that "various men whom [he] had known well socially and had been taught to look up to, prominent business men and lawyers acted in a way . . . which I was quite unable to reconcile with the theories I had formed as to their high standing. . . . I was little more than a year out of college at the time."[8] A lawyer friend of his family took him out to lunch one day, and explained to him that there was an "inner circle—including certain big business men—and politicians, lawyers and judges who were in alli-ance with and to a certain extent dependent on them—and that the successful man had to win his success by the backing of the same forces, whether in law, business or politics." This conversation was always to be remembered by Roosevelt, "for it was the first glimpse [he] had of that combination between business and politics which . . . [he] was in after-years so often to oppose." "In the America of that day," Roosevelt continued, ". . . the successful business man was regarded by everybody as pre-eminently *the* good citizen."

Roosevelt added that the legislative problems with which he dealt were "mostly concerned with honesty and decency, and with legislative and administrative efficiency." He had, however, little interest in reform in other fields. There was nothing in young Roosevelt's first year to show any sense of fair play to labor. On the contrary, as far as his social philosophy was concerned—as differentiated from his passion for administrative efficiency and civic virtue, and his hatred of corruption in public office—it seemed to be limited to the traditional concepts of 1880 conservative Republicanism: low taxes and no great social services at public expense.

Roosevelt's success in his first term in the Assembly, and the uniformly favorable reviews of the *Naval War of 1812* that he received that year from the literary critics, did not clear up his own uncertainties at the time as to his future life. His letters of the period indicate a preference for law or business; but as far as politics was concerned, he did nothing to stop, or even discourage, his renomination for the Assembly.

The elections of 1882 in New York were disastrous for the Republican Party. Democratic Grover Cleveland was elected Governor, and the Democratic majority in the Assembly was increased. In spite of the Democratic landslide, Roosevelt, however, was re-elected by a 2 to 1 majority, even though Grover Cleveland carried the same district. He made only one campaign speech, which was prophetic of the style of many of his speeches in national campaigns. It was mostly a plea for Republican loyalty to the Republican Party and a tirade against the Democratic Party. If re-elected, he promised again to carry "honesty, courage and private morality into public office," and also to tackle an issue of "great importance"—monopoly. As a measure of young Roosevelt's growing reputation, he was nominated as a compliment by his Republican colleagues for the position of Speaker in 1883; but since the Democrats had a majority, he could not be elected. However, by virtue of his nomination, he became ipso facto the minority leader. Such position for so young a man—only in his second year—was unprecedented in New York political history.

His second term in the Assembly, while not as productive of results as his first, did add to his stature. A "strike" bill was introduced to cut the fare on the New York City Elevated Railway system from 10 cents to 5. The only purpose was to get the railway to pay legislators to vote against it. Roosevelt voted for the bill although it was contrary to his general laissez-faire attitude—chiefly because of his hostility to Jay Gould, the most important stockholder.

Governor Grover Cleveland vetoed the bill in a magnificent display of political courage on the ground that it was a breach of contract, insisting that the "State should not only be strictly just, but scrupulously fair." Roosevelt, contrary to his original vote, voted with equal courage to support the veto. He made a very impassioned speech admitting he had "blundered grievously" in supporting the bill, "partly in a vindictive spirit toward the infernal thieves and conscienceless swindlers who have the railway in charge," but mostly because of the popular demand of the people for the bill. He added, apparently in the belief that his action might end his political career also, that he would rather leave politics feeling "that I have done what was right than to stay in . . . knowing in my heart that I had acted as I ought not to." This was one of the very rare instances where he was willing to confess any error on his part. His political style was almost invariably one of dogmatic certitude about his acts and an unshakable conviction that he was right.

Later in the session he made a vitriolic attack on Jay Gould and on the *New York World* which Gould owned. He seemed to have come to a decision within himself—if he ever had any doubts—that he was not going to follow the advice of the family lawyer friend about "playing the game" with the "inner circle." It was a decision which would regulate his style in every one of the many political offices he was to hold.

Roosevelt in this session teamed up with Democratic Governor Cleveland again in the field which was to be a lifelong interest for him, and was to have a great effect on his style as President—civil service reform. He had become interested in civil service reform even before he went to Albany; and after his first election in 1881 he became vice president of the New York Civil Service Reform Association. There had been no action in this area by any state or by the national administration. But in 1883, after a nationwide campaign by the National Civil Service Reform League, Congress finally passed the Pendleton Law providing for competitive examinations in the civil service, and for the creation of a Civil Service Commission. Roosevelt, knowing full well how distasteful the abolition or curtailment of the spoils system was to all political leaders, undertook nevertheless to pass legislation in New York similar to the Pendleton Law. When a bill to this effect had been introduced, Governor Cleveland informed Roosevelt and through him the "Roosevelt Republicans" that they would get the votes of all the Cleveland Democrats in pushing civil service reform down the throats of the regular politicians of both parties and their henchmen in the Assembly. It took some vigorous action and vitriolic debate (especially by Roosevelt), but the bill was passed. Nothing could have been less pleasing to either the Democratic or Republican bosses; but Roosevelt had showed that he was willing to cooperate even with Democrats to get a practical result. He would be doing this as President —even working with a Democratic congressman (Ben Tillman) whom he detested, and with whom he had not spoken for years.

Two other votes showed great courage in the face of threats of political retribution. One was against an appropriation for a private institution called the Catholic Protectory, on the ground that no state funds should ever be appropriated for any religious sect. He had already stated his opposition to a bill to provide money for a Protestant inebriate institution. The other vote was against a bill enlarging the liability of the press for libel, referred to generally as a bill for gagging the press. He made a fervent plea for liberty of the press, even though "We have all of us at times suffered from the liberty of the press, but we have to take the good and the bad." (There was to come a time when he was unable to take the "bad," and instigated a libel prosecution himself.)

Showing a style of action which was to become familiar during his presidency, he introduced a resolution directing the Attorney General to bring an action to dissolve the Manhattan Railway Company. He argued in the Judiciary Committee: "There is a strong and growing feeling of indignation among the people at the action of these great corporations. . . . If it becomes evident that these great public robbers cannot be reached by law, then among the people at large the temptation to take action that is outside the law becomes very strong. For the sake of protecting honest capital, we ought to punish, if we legally can, the deeds of the dishonest wealthy for fear that some day an uprising might come that will overwhelm innocent and guilty alike." He was not going to be able to use better or more thoughtful language against "malefactors of great wealth" even from what he was to call the "bully pulpit" of the White House.

The young minority leader of the Assembly next took to excoriating, in the most extravagant and unbridled terms, the entire Democratic Party—not only its members in the Assembly, not only those in the State of New York, but all Democrats throughout the nation. He did not limit his target to the Democratic Party of 1883, but attacked the Democratic Party throughout all its history.

Because of Roosevelt's feelings of self-righteousness and even of superiority over his colleagues, members of both parties verbally smacked him down in some instances. The press began to pillory him both by ridicule and by condemnation. One paper expressed very mildly the sentiment of an almost unanimous and more virulent press: "There is a growing suspicion that Mr. Roosevelt keeps a pulpit concealed on his person." This feeling of self-righteousness—which his biographer Putnam so well characterizes as "his often monotonous saintliness"[9]—was to last, along with an intense passion to do something drastic at once to curb whatever he thought was evil without first taking time out to think about it. Roosevelt must have felt the sting of the censure and the ridicule; but nothing he said publicly revealed it. After he became President, however, he did write to his son about this 1883 session: "I came an awful cropper, and had to pick myself up after learning by bitter experience the lesson that I was not all important and that I had to take account of many different elements in life." He did not always remember this lesson; but his realization that he had to work with "many different elements" governed his style of successfully coaxing much of his legislation out of Congress.

The legislative elections of 1883 returned a Republican majority in both houses of the legislature. Roosevelt immediately after his re-election declared himself a candidate for the office of Speaker of the Assembly,[10] and was supported by many newspapers throughout the state; but the old-time Republican leaders whose proposed "deals" with Tammany Hall had been thwarted by Roosevelt in the previous sessions were solidly against him. He decided that he had to campaign strenuously for the position—not only for its honor and dignity, but because it would give him the power to carry out his chief project in the next session, civic reform in the government of New York City. The spirit of political reform seemed to be in the air in both parties. The two bosses of the New York Republican Party, Platt and Conkling, had resigned from the United States Senate in a patronage squabble with President Arthur; and the new Republican state boss, Warner Miller, was a more liberal person, who believed in reforming the machinery of his party. Governor Cleveland, engaged as he was in a bitter struggle with John Kelly, the boss of Tammany Hall, had declared his independence of the Tammany machine and could obviously be relied upon by Roosevelt to cooperate in the effort to reform both political machines.

In his campaign for the speakership, Roosevelt showed the same style of relentless determination and energy which was to characterize his struggles for reform during his presidency. He avoided any pretense that the "office should seek the man." He not only wrote letters to all the newly elected members of the Assembly, each one of whom would have one vote for Speaker, but proceeded to visit them personally before the session opened. This meant travelling around the whole upper part of the state. That is just what he did, tracking down all the assemblymen he thought necessary, in their homes or offices or wherever he could find them.

But Miller, the new boss, did not take very kindly to the aspirations of the young man who had risen so fast, and whose chief boast seemed to be that no political leader could control him. Roosevelt definitely was not the type a newly designated state boss would seek out to place in the Speaker's chair. Miller had his own candidate, one Titus Sheard from upstate. When the party caucus for the naming of the Speaker assembled in Albany, there were not only Miller and the other Republican bosses throwing their strength around—all opposed to Roosevelt; there were also many lobbyists of big corporations in the state who had had their fill of this bellicose reformer. In this struggle, Roosevelt got his unpleasant first taste of brutal political in-fighting. He had practically clinched the designation insofar as the members themselves were concerned; and they alone had the legal voting power. But when his victory seemed fairly certain, the political leaders began to use all the local and state pressure they could exert upon some of the Roosevelt supporters, actually forcing them to desert him. Roosevelt struggled to hold them. There is no doubt that if the members of the Assembly had all been allowed to exercise their free choice, Roosevelt would have won. But the defections of his own men maneuvered by political and other pressures were too many. Sheard was elected. Roosevelt had learned a good lesson from this struggle. The organized machine had a latent power which could reach to great distances when it was aroused. He would have to be more wary the next time he tried to fight with it.[11]

The new Speaker felt obliged to appoint Roosevelt chairman of the Committee on Cities; but he packed the committee with members who had little or no sympathy with Roosevelt's views. He even tried to force his own henchman onto the committee as its clerk, until Roosevelt threatened a public fight on the issue.

Roosevelt began the year by further antagonizing the political leaders of New York City with the introduction of two bills. One bill gave the Mayor of the city the power to appoint and remove heads of city departments without the approval of the Board of Aldermen. The aldermen were very minor elected officials; practically all were political hacks subservient to political leaders. Their power to veto appointments or removals by the Mayor was sufficient to thwart any attempt by any reform Mayor to provide good government.

The other bill must have revived fond memories of young Roosevelt's first campaign efforts in the saloons along Sixth Avenue. It provided a great increase in the license fees of saloons. Of course, nearly all the local city political leaders of both parties were closely allied with the saloon interests, and it was at this alliance that the bill was primarily aimed.

Shortly after the organization of the legislature, each house appointed a committee to investigate the municipal departments in New York City. Roosevelt became chairman of the Assembly committee. Investigating committees like this one had frequently been named in the past as a sop to public opinion; but they had been uniformly unproductive. The political leaders had always been able to sidetrack the activities of an investigating committee once it began to get close to discovering the unsavory truth. An attempt was made in 1884 to sabotage Roosevelt's investigation even before it began, by trying to join together the committee of the Senate and the committee of the Assembly into one large legislative committee. Roosevelt, quick to realize that this would frustrate his work by the addition of more recalcitrant members, strenuously objected; and he again prevailed.

He took charge of the investigation himself, and soon began to draw blood. The corruption he succeeded in uncovering attracted the attention of the whole country, and, of course, increased the reputation and stature of the chairman. The next few months were to show the depth of Roosevelt's determination, love of action, energy and zeal for reform—a style which was to dominate his presidency. The hearings of his investigating committee were held in New York City on Fridays, Saturdays and Mondays, so that the members could be back in Albany for their legislative duties on the other days of the week. The political leaders of both parties began to create delays and diversions—a process which was easy because both the Senate committee and a grand jury in New York County were ostensibly conducting simultaneous investigations—though without much enthusiasm. Witnesses would often give the excuse that they had been subpoenaed by a rival investigator, and had to absent themselves in obedience to the subpoena. Books of account and incriminating documents seemed to have disappeared all over the city. But Roosevelt kept at it doggedly. From New York on Monday night, he would dash up to Albany to carry on his onerous duties as chairman of the Assembly Committee on Cities, and to push his own bills, particularly his bill to abolish the veto power of the Board of Aldermen.

He kept shuttling between Albany and New York twice a week until the 13th of February. On that day, grim personal tragedy struck—twice. In the morning, he received a telegram that his expected child—the later famous Alice Roosevelt Longworth—had been born the night before. He planned to remain in Albany for that one day to see his aldermanic bill passed, when a second telegram arrived to announce a sudden turn for the worse in his wife. He rushed out to get the first train to New York. When he arrived he learned that his wife was dying. To add to his shock and grief, his mother also lay dying downstairs in the room where his revered father had died six years earlier. Later that night his mother died; the next day his wife succumbed.

Roosevelt, according to friends, spent the next few days—at the church services with two coffins in the aisle, where the political and social élite of New York were present, at the cemetery, at home—all in a constant daze. "He does not know what he does or says," one wrote.

The Assembly had adjourned in his honor; there were speeches by his followers and also by his opponents. All seemed to be affected by this double tragedy; and all were anxious to show the respect and esteem which the bereaved husband and son had earned, in spite of his eccentricities, arrogance and self-righteousness. Three days after the double funeral, Roosevelt had recovered sufficiently to be back at his Assembly desk. He even made a speech that day on his aldermanic bill, which was passed. Then he rushed down to New York to take up his committee hearings. He was back at work in earnest, saying: "I have never believed it did any good to flinch or yield for any blow, nor does it lighten the blow to cease from working."

Far from trying "to cease from working," he began a period of a few months which were perhaps the most continuously active ones in his whole life. The committee looked into many offices of the city government; it looked into the vile conditions and the graft in city jails; it looked into the connections between crime and politicians, and between the police and criminals; it looked under almost every rug and it uncovered a mass of sordid evidence wherever it looked.

The committee report was due March 14. Its counsel prepared a draft report which he gave the committee on March 13, the day before it was due to be presented to the Assembly. Roosevelt and his colleagues found the draft inadequate; and Roosevelt single-handedly began at once to write another complete, fresh report—writing all night long with a relay of stenographers, sending it down to the printer page by page. He continued to write on the final deadline day while he was sitting at his Assembly desk during the session, interrupting his writing every once in a while to make some comments on bills which were being considered. Finally, the report was finished; and it was submitted right on the deadline, together with nine bills which had been drafted under his supervision. These bills became known as the "Roosevelt Reform Bills."

Now began some real in-fighting by the opponents all over again, operating under the watchful eye of the New York City political boss sitting right in the Assembly chamber. All kinds of complicated parliamentary devices were used to produce delay in acting on the bills. The debate became personal and acrimonious. Roosevelt grew more and more peremptory and arrogant, demanding that all other bills be laid aside in favor of these nine. Of course, his personal tragedy, the strain of constant work and little sleep for weeks, a complete absence of sleep the night before while he was writing the brand-new report—all these might well excuse some of his behavior. He complained about the epithet "arrogant" being applied to him, and told a reporter: "I am not arrogant. I am simply in dead earnest." He would often get the two mixed together in later life. In time the sympathy of many of the members of the Assembly shifted toward him in spite of the efforts of the machine bosses and of Speaker Sheard's bizarre parliamentary rulings—or perhaps because of them. Indeed, even Sheard eventually phoned Roosevelt an apology of sorts, and promised to help advance the bills on the calendar himself.

At the end, every one of his nine bills was passed. It all was due to the personal drive and energy of the young man of twenty-five who, in view of his bereavement, could have just quit work for the session without obloquy. Instead, he had wrestled successfully with every hurdle which the legislative process could present, manipulated as they were by experienced, sophisticated, ingenious and unprincipled politicians who abhorred reform—especially the kind of reform embodied in these bills.

The directness, the boldness, the lack of equivocation, the leadership he exercised among his committee members were all in the style he was to follow as President. The experience of this one year with legislators and with outside political pressures—to say nothing of the preceding two years—helped to train him for his forthcoming Presidential battles with the Congress and with the same outside political pressures which were to hit with even greater force. He got to know at first hand about municipal administration and maladministration, the corruption of political machines, the power of political bosses, and their unscrupulous, devious, and often vicious methods of using it. And he learned enough about the Police Department of the city—its graft, its favoritism in appointments and promotions, its political connections and controls, and all the sordid details of gambling, prostitution and other forms of vice—to prepare him for those he was later to meet as police commissioner of New York City.

The most important result of this third year in the Assembly was Roosevelt's own mellowing into a more realistic and more practical reformer. He was impressive, forceful, and relentless against criminal activity; he would never try to appease wrongdoing, or temporize with people who opposed his efforts by under-handed dealing. This caused resentment, but there was no more of the ridicule or derisive laughter of his second year. He was still the educated, cultured gentleman, but he had given up much of his "dude" manners and his supercilious *hauteur.* He put it like this in a conversation many years later with his friend and co-worker, Jacob Riis: "I looked the ground over and made up my mind that there were several *other* excellent people there [in the Assembly] with honest opinions of the right even though they differed from me. . . . We did not agree in all things, but we did in some, and those we pulled at together. This was my first lesson in real politics. It is just this: If you are cast on a desert inland with only a screwdriver, a hatchet, and a chisel to make a boat with, why, go make the best one you can. It would be better if you had a saw, but you haven't. So with men."[12]

It was a great lesson in politics, which nearly every successful President has had to learn at some time or other in his career. He had learned it in the infancy of his political life.

Roosevelt's attitude toward labor, however, did not change. He opposed a bill setting a twelve-hour limit on the working hours of streetcar employees. He argued that to do this was to fly in the face of the law of supply and demand, and that to pass the bill because it remedied a cruel situation of over-long hours of labor was as inadvisable as to try to repeal the law of gravity because its operation caused pain. He also argued against the bill because it would tie labor to the protection of the state; and to offer labor that kind of paternalism was both un-American and "insulting." He even talked about the bill spreading socialism and communism, that it was un-American for streetcar conductors to propose such a law—it was a form of coddling.

He had opposed a bill raising the pay of the New York City firemen to $1200 a year, and had fought against the creation of pensions for teachers in the public schools of New York City. With his usual style of self-righteousness, he repeat-edly sermonized that every man should stand on his own bottom—apparently forgetting that *his* own bottom was an inheritance from his father.

Roosevelt's early reactionary attitude toward organized labor had been shown also on several prior occasions: his supporting a supposed anti-riot bill which was really an anti-strike bill; his refusal to vote for the abolition of contract convict labor in the state, saying it was "maudlin sympathy for convicts." He had even opposed the resolution for a referendum on the Convict Labor Bill in 1883 in a speech stating that the criminal preyed on society like a wolf and should be killed or imprisoned like the wolf. The referendum was passed, and he urged voters to vote against it. They voted for it. In his inflexible style, Roosevelt still opposed it in the 1884 Assembly. In his speech against the bill the future leader of the great progressive movement in the United States and its Presidential candidate of 1912 admitted, or rather boasted, that he did not pretend to have the particular interests of working men at heart but would "mete an equal measure of justice to every citizen of this State no matter what his occupation or nationality."

He was then, and for many years to come, obsessed with the idea, as he wrote in a magazine article the next year, that labor's chief trouble was the professional "labor agitators," who were "always promising to procure by legislation the advantages which can only come to working men . . . by their individual or united energy, intelligence and forethought." Roosevelt even opposed and helped finally to defeat a bill which provided a minimum wage to minicipal laborers in New York City, Brooklyn and Buffalo of $2.00 per day or 25 cents per hour. This feat called forth great praise from the press of New York City; the *Times* lauded him for opposing "the spirit of demagogism" of those who favored the bill. In the year following his departure from the Assembly, he described the bill as "one of the several scores of preposterous measures that annually make their appearance purely for the purposes of buncombe." He added that the bill was "of no consequence whatever to the genuine laboring man," but was of interest only to those "professional labor agitators."[13]

Roosevelt kept his distance during this period from labor organizations. He knew that they watched legislators' votes carefully. He said, however, that they cared little about a man's honesty or other virtues but only whether he voted for the "demagogic measures brought forward in the interests of the laboring classes for which an honest and intelligent man could not vote." Legislation to regulate the wages and hours of adult male workers was the particular object of his scorn; but where the health and safety of women and children in factories were involved, his philanthropic impulses rather than any progressive change in his labor policy made him willing to help the otherwise helpless individuals by state action. He saw no inconsistency between this humanitarian interest in safety measures for women and children and his opposition to almost anything to improve the lot of workers as a whole.

Obviously he had not begun to grasp the extent of the fundamental changes in the conditions of the working man which the Industrial Revolution had brought about. Nor did he understand even the rudiments of the functions or necessity of legitimate labor unions. He had also failed to appreciate the possible role of government in creating a greater social justice in a world of social and economic inequality. He had, it is true, begun to realize that the concentration of economic power in gigantic corporations was an evil which had to be strictly regulated for the public good; and much of his later political life as Governor and President was to be devoted to this end. But until the years of his presidency, he was to fail to see fully the direct effect of this overwhelming economic power on what Franklin Roosevelt was later to call those "at the bottom of the economic pyramid," or to understand even then what government should do about it.

There are reasons to explain all his early attitudes toward labor in the eighties, though perhaps not to justify them. There were not many in public office in 1882–84 who grasped the significance of what was happening in American economic and social life. Especially was this true of the wealthy citizens in Roosevelt's own social class—even those whom he would not later include in "the wealthy criminal class." Of course, they all knew about the poverty of many people, especially of the recent immigrants; but obviously the only way to help these unfortunates was through private charity. Roosevelt's father had been very active in such charities, and that was the limit to which his generation thought they should go. The idea that government—and particularly the national government—should do something about it was revolting; it was socialistic or even communistic; and it was un-American for anyone even to suggest it, especially the victims of the system. The purpose of government in those days, as Theodore strongly believed, was to maintain law and order with strict impartiality among competing groups—not to reform social evils. The real cure for poverty lay within each individual. In theory they were all equal under the law. Failure to rise out of economic misery was due to some fault of the individual. Some people did make their own way to a better life; why couldn't they all? Today it is easy to ridicule this attitude, but those with the background and education of Theodore in the 1880's felt that ours was not "an unjustly ordered system of life," and that "an ounce of performance on labor's part was worth a ton of legislative promises to change in some mysterious manner that life system."[14]

The bad effects of the Industrial Revolution appeared much later in the United States than they did in England and in the industrial countries of western Europe. This was due in large part to geography. In England and in Europe when the dire effects came from the substitution of machines for human hands in the manufacture of goods, there was little or nothing that the workers could do, except for a few who escaped to America. In America, particularly along the Eastern seaboard where the same process of industrialization was taking place, the displaced worker could at the beginning always head toward the ever-expanding West, where he could get free land from the government, suitable for farming. In fact for two hundred years, the moving Western frontier had been the refuge for those of all occupations who sought a better life than they could find on the Eastern coast. In the eighties, unfortunately, the last Western frontier was being reached; nearly all the good land was gone by 1890; the old refuge was no longer there. At the same time, immigration was adding millions of people to the already overcrowded East. In the first year of Roosevelt's service in the legislature (1882), for example, 800,000 foreigners arrived, mostly unskilled, unable to speak English, and illiterate even in their own tongue. In the next ten years over 5 million more immigrants arrived. Furthermore, the tide was changing from the North European countries which Roosevelt admired to the other parts of Europe—central, southern and eastern—toward the natives of which he had less than friendly feelings. It was not long before the new group of immigrants constituted the overwhelming majority. These men, many of whom had been peasant farmers, could not have gone west even if there had been good land left; all their financial resources had gone into the cost of coming steerage class to America. So they just remained in the East to provide a steady and hungry supply of workers, willing to work for any wages, any hours and under any conditions of labor. Unfortunately, a number of these new immigrants were extremists, and even anarchists; and they presented a problem to the decent trade unions of America as well as to employers and the devotees of law and order.

It apparently never occurred to Roosevelt or those who shared his views that when hundreds of thousands of mature adults were willing to leave their machines and risk starvation in a strike, there must be some grave underlying reasons which called at least for investigation by the state. After a strike had been extinguished by the policemen, little or nothing was done by the state except to prepare to meet the next strike in the same way. This was considered during Roosevelt's legislative days as the ordained method for government to cope with strikes. He expressed that point of view himself during his three years in Albany—and indeed for several years afterward. There was to be one exception during these years, as we shall see, in the sweatshop industries in tenement houses; but that exception was primarily a matter of public health rather than of necessary social or labor legislation. It was to take Roosevelt a good number of years in public life to learn that the last thing most industrialists wanted between themselves and their employees or between themselves and their consumers was "fairness and impartiality." They wanted only to take advantage of the great superior power that capital then had over labor, and that monopoly then had over consumers; and they wanted government only to protect them from the natural resentment and resistance their attitude would cause.

Much later, in 1913, he wrote in his *Autobiography* that "one partial reason —not an excuse or justification for [my] slowness in grasping the importance of action along the lines of government control of corporations and government interference on behalf of labor . . . to secure a more genuine social and industrial justice" was the "parlor reformer," and "the corrupt and unattractive nature of so many of the men who championed popular reforms." He wrote that his own legislation efforts were devoted "to keep the just middle," which "was not always easy . . . when on one side there were corrupt and unscrupulous reactionaries."[15] This was quite obvious post facto self-delusion. He was opposed to labor because his party, his own social class, his friends and all rugged individualists were. He was against them because he still believed in laissez-faire and had not yet grasped the full social impact of the industrialization of the United States, and the vast discrepancy in the bargaining power between the workers and the capitalists. To his great credit, it must be said here that as he became more mature and realistic his style toward labor and consumer problems changed completely.

Roosevelt and the labor movement both grew to a more important and more effective stature simultaneously during the two last decades of the nineteenth century. During these twenty years, there were in New York State 6,460 strikes —about 25 per cent of all the strikes in the United States.[16] The depressions of 1882, 1893 and 1897 each caused a greatly increased amount of unemployment, and the highest percentage was in New York.

In New York, Samuel Gompers, an immigrant Englishman, was making his living in the late 1860's by manufacturing cigars in a tenement house. He was also busy building up a union. His belief was that unions should devote themselves to economic matters rather than political; and that they should drop all aspects and elements of radicalism, which were alienating public support. By 1881, he and other leaders had created a national federation of craft unions which had as its goals simple economic objectives, such as shorter hours, higher wages and better working conditions. By 1886, this loose federation became the more highly organized American Federation of Labor, which took over and amalgamated the American labor movement under Gompers's leadership.

At the same time, there was developing in American industry the principle of laissez-faire expounded largely in Herbert Spencer's *Social Statics* (1865), and using as a basis a quotation of Thomas Paine, "That government is best which governs least." Its philosophy was clear and simple: that the state should exercise no functions between management and labor, except to keep the peace between them—by force if necessary—and to protect them both from foreign competition by means of high tariffs. Such matters as fixing maximum hours and minimum wages, compelling better working conditions, and welfare legislation in general had no place in the role of government. It was this philosophy which permeated American thought generally during the later years of the Industrial Revolution, which had picked up increasing pace after the Civil War.

The one notable exception to Assemblyman Roosevelt's attitude toward labor and social legislation came when Samuel Gompers managed to get him interested in a pending bill to abolish the manufacture of cigars in tenement houses in New York City. Roosevelt, having been appointed as one of a legislative committee of three to look into the merits of the bill, made several personal visits to cigar-makers' homes in the tenement districts. Before he made his first visit, he was inclined to oppose the bill. He later explained this in terms of the economic philosophy of the day: "The respectable people I knew were against it; and it was contrary to the principles of political economy of the *laissez-faire* kind; the business men who spoke to us about it shook their heads and said that it was designed to prevent a man doing as he wished and as he had a right to do with what was his own."[17]

When he made some visits, however, what he saw was horrible, and deeply affected him. Cigar-making was carried on by men, women and children living, cooking, eating, sleeping in the same one-room apartment (no bathroom), all surrounded by cigars and piles of tobacco. He was appalled, and became indignant; and he pitched in to help pass the bill. His concern, however, was based primarily not on the economic plight of the poor workers as much as on the danger to the public health, the possibility of the spread of disease, and the unwholesome atmosphere in which American children would grow into American citizens. Roosevelt spoke in favor of the bill at the hearing on it before Governor Cleveland, acting, as he put it, "as spokesman for the battered, undersized foreigners who represented the union and the workers." Cleveland, at first inclined to a veto, was persuaded to sign it.

The manufacturers took the law to the courts. Their lawyer was one of the most distinguished in the country, former Attorney General and Secretary of State of the United States, William M. Evarts. When the case reached the Court of Appeals it was declared unconstitutional on the highly technical ground that the title to the bill did not adequately express its purpose. The distinguished counsel had argued this point: "The citizens of New York, jealous of interference with their homes, reading the title of the bill, would be deceived, misled, and thrown off guard."[18]

The legislature thereupon in 1884 passed a new bill in a slightly modified form which remedied the technical defect in the title. Roosevelt again supported it, conceding, however, that it was a dangerous breach of prevailing doctrines of political economy, and "in a certain sense a socialistic one." But he warned that unless we "modify the principles or doctrines on which we manage our system of government," the cigar-makers and their children would never be fit for American citizenship. The bill was worthy of becoming law as a "hygienic measure alone."[19]

The cigar-makers' journal took due note of Roosevelt's statement at the Governor's hearing on the bill to the effect that his own district was not influenced by any trade unions, and that he personally was opposed to most trade union measures, but that this bill was an exception. The publication of the union referred to him quite coolly if not sarcastically as the "Hon. Theodore Roosevelt representative of Fifth Avenue, the aristocratic district of New York [who] advocated its passage on sanitary, moral, and economic grounds."[20]

When the bill again reached the Court of Appeals, there appeared the same distinguished counsel for the manufacturers. His argument at the Bench speaks eloquently of the social conscience of the period. It was based on these theses: that tobacco was a disinfectant and a prophylatic; that the bill had been conceived by socialism and communism; and that home manufacture was in fact well suited to the "proper culture of growing girls." The New York Court of Appeals decided that the bill was unconstitutional as violating freedom of contract and the due process clause. The court's reasoning and language in rejecting the claim that this was a proper exercise of the police power of the state were as callous as Mr.

Evarts's arguments: "It cannot be perceived how the cigar maker is to be improved in his health or his morals by forcing him from *his home and its hallowed associations* and beneficient influences to ply his trade elsewhere." (Emphasis added)

This decision, and especially the language of the opinion, made a deep impression on Roosevelt. About twenty-eight years later, he wrote in his *Autobiography:* "It was this case which first waked me to a dim and partial understanding of the fact that the courts were not necessarily the best judges of what should be done to better social and industrial conditions." He particularly resented the use of the words, "home and its hallowed associations," as being a mockery in view of the revolting conditions which he had seen with his own eyes. "Of course, it took more than one experience such as this tenement cigar case to shake me out of the attitude in which I was brought up, for the people with whom I was most intimate were apt to praise the courts for just such decisions as this, and to speak of them as bulwarks against disorder and barriers against demogogic legislation. . . . But as a result of numerous such decisions, I grew to realize that all Abraham Lincoln had said about the Dred Scott decision could be said with equal truth and justice about the numerous decisions which in our own day were erected as bars across the path of social reform, and which brought to naught so much of the effort to secure justice and fair dealings for working men and working women, and for plain citizens generally." He later wrote that the decision postponed "anything like effective reformation of tenement house conditions . . . for fifteen or twenty years, and during that time men, women and children were guaranteed their 'liberty' to fester in sodden misery."[21]

Roosevelt's early attitude toward labor while in the legislature was soon hardened to the point of brutality by his consecration to the political style of "law and order." On May 4, 1886, while he was ranching out west, a crowd of legitimate strikers unfortunately augmented by some uninvited socialists and anarchists were protesting in Haymarket Square in Chicago against police violence during the strike, as well as against the anti-strike activities of management. About 180 policemen were summoned to break up the protest. Someone (never identified) threw a bomb into the group of policemen; eight were killed and sixty-seven wounded. Eight well-known anarchists who were in the crowded square were arrested and placed on trial. The trial was conducted in the midst of widespread public indignation and demands for revenge. Though there was no evidence that any one of the eight had thrown the bomb, they were all convicted. Seven were given a sentence of death, and one a sentence of life imprisonment. Roosevelt, at his ranch in Dakota, read about the incident in his newspaper. He wrote his sister an oft-quoted and revealing letter immediately after the incident: "My men are hard-working labouring men who work longer hours for no greater wages than many of the strikers. . . . I believe that nothing would give them greater pleasure than a chance with their rifles at one of the mobs . . . I wish I had them with me and a fair show at ten times our number of rioters; my men shoot well and fear very little."

As the 1884 Albany session came to an end, Roosevelt's interest began to turn to national political affairs, particularly to the Republican National Convention which was to take place in Chicago in July of that year. The delegates to that convention were to be selected at the New York Republican State Convention in April. Roosevelt was a delegate to the state convention from his district. It had been rumored that he was against the nomination of either Blaine or Arthur, who were the choices respectively of two groups of the Republican political leaders of the state, and that he was in favor of the nomination of George F. Edmunds of Vermont. So far had Roosevelt progressed politically by now, that in spite of this rumored opposition to the choices of the political leaders of the state, he was chosen by the state convention to head the four delegates-at-large sent to the national convention from New York State. The United States Senators from New York, Warner Miller and Thomas C. Platt, were for Blaine. Miller, Roosevelt still believed, had kept him from the Speakership to which he had aspired in early 1884. Some writers claim that it was his personal hostility to Miller and his desire for revenge which motivated his advocacy of Edmunds and his opposition to Blaine. At any rate, when he was elected a delegate-at-large, he showed a good deal of his blunt, independent political style; he went over to shake his fist in Miller's face and said: "There damn you, we beat you for last winter" (when Roosevelt had been defeated for the Speakership).[22]

At the Republican National Convention in Chicago, Roosevelt and his friend, Henry Cabot Lodge of Massachusetts, did their best in their hopeless mission to nominate Edmunds. It was typical of Roosevelt's style in later political life that the opposition to Blaine and his advocacy of Edmunds gradually became a righteous—almost a religious—cause to which he devoted every ounce of his energy.[23] Blaine, however, was nominated on the fourth ballot. An obscure Republican congressman from Ohio named William McKinley went over to Roosevelt and asked him to make it unanimous for Blaine, as was quite usual in such circumstances; but Roosevelt refused.

The action of the convention was to bring young Roosevelt to the hour of decision as to his political future and the course he should follow. Up to now he had been a remarkably successful young idealist in politics. He had been a lion throughout his three years in the legislature; there had been no trace of the cunning or scheming of the fox. By forthright, almost blatant, refusal to recognize or cater to the political bosses in either party, and by courageous blocking of their collusive schemes, he had built a national reputation. Now his idealistic antagonism to Blaine, in which he had been joined by many high-minded civic leaders, had ended in defeat at the hands of the political leaders of his Republican Party, the party to which he always preached and practiced loyalty.

After Blaine was nominated Roosevelt, in a rage, left the convention—and Chicago. It was obvious that there would be a revolt against Blaine by many prominent Republicans. Roosevelt's momentous decision was whether he should continue to be the idealistic young man in politics and join the large number of civic-minded leaders in the revolt, or whether he should become the practical politician, the loyal Republican, the man of realistic discernment who could pick his way up the political ladder. The leaders in the revolt were all famous and respected men, most of whom had watched Roosevelt's courageous battles in Albany with admiration and public acclaim and some of whom were personal friends: Charles Francis Adams, Jr., President Eliot of Harvard University, William Lloyd Garrison, Carl Schurz, Henry Ward Beecher, Thomas Nast, George W. Curtis, I. Henry Harper of *Harper's Weekly,* George H. Putnam, Henry Holt, Dean Van Amringe of Columbia University. These people were, like Roosevelt, opposed to Blaine largely because of his unsavory financial record as Speaker of the House of Representatives; they all thought of Roosevelt as an idealist and a reformer like themselves. But although they all publicly and vigorously repudiated Blaine, Roosevelt remained silent out on his ranch in Dakota.

He broke silence only after he had first come east for a conference with Henry Cabot Lodge. Then on July 19, 1884, in an interview with the Boston *Herald*, he announced his decision: he was going to remain loyal to his party.

The interview contained a few significant examples of his future style as the party's national leader: "A man cannot act both without and within the party; he can do either, but he cannot possibly do both. . . . I did my best and got beaten; and I propose to stand by the result. . . . Whatever good I have been able to accomplish in public life has been accomplished through the Republican party; I have acted with it in the past, and wish to act with it in the future. I went as a regular delegate to the Chicago convention, and I intend to abide by the outcome of that convention. I am going back in a day or two to my western ranches, as I do not expect to take any part in the campaign this fall."[24]

The attack upon him which followed was speedy and virulent. The Boston *Transcript* called him a "back-sliding reformer who in attempting to fly off on the winds of his ambition has met with a terrible fall." The bolters from the party who refused to support Blaine became known as "Mugwumps," a term of derision that became fixed in Roosevelt's vocabulary. With his style of self-hypnosis and self-righteousness, he was soon able to reach the conclusion that the only right-eous people in politics were those who campaigned for Blaine; and that Cleveland, the Democratic nominee, was the corrupt one of the two candidates. Instead of sitting it out in his Western refuge as he said he would, he returned east for active campaigning for Blaine and, of course, for the Republican Party and all its virtues. "It might be right to bolt," the future bolter from the Republican Party who would cause its defeat in 1912 said in a speech to the Young Men's Republican Club in New York City in 1884, "but you must be certain that the time is right, that you are acting to reform, not to destroy the Republican party. . . . I am thankful that I am still, where by inheritance and education I feel I belong, with the Republican party."

Blaine's defeat was so complete and widespread that even Congressman Cabot Lodge lost in his district in Massachusetts.

The next two years—1885 and 1886—were devoted by Roosevelt to matters nonpolitical: ranching, hunting and writing. He did not return to the Assembly; nor did he ever explain why.

In late 1886 he returned to politics—and to a personal political disaster. He became the Republican candidate for Mayor of New York City in a three-cornered race with Hewitt, the Democratic candidate, and Henry George, the Independent. Roosevelt, in his usual style toward philosophies he could not appreciate, called George "an utterly cheap reformer." Quite understandably, he devotes only one sentence in his *Autobiography* to this campaign.

Roosevelt's campaign speeches were not very impressive.[25] He repeated often that the Republican Party and he stood for "law and order," and for "radical municipal reform"; that "we stand against George on account of his theories, and against Hewitt on account of the practices of his followers [Tammany Hall]." He repeated his theory as of that date about labor: that labor's problems could be cured only by a "capacity for steady, individual self-help, which is the glory of every true American." Labor was overwhelmingly for George. It regarded Roosevelt as a capitalist with inherited wealth who was not only opposed to labor's aims but was even ignorant of what the aims were. The labor press practically ignored both him and his candidacy; whenever they did notice him, they attacked him.

The contest from the very beginning was between only Hewitt and George. Probably the only reason he accepted the nomination in this hopeless race was his desire to remain in the good graces of the political leaders. Having apparently made up his mind to return to politics, he was taking the standard realistic route to advancement.

Hewitt was elected; Roosevelt ran third.

His humiliating defeat was primarily due to the widespread fear felt by many conservative Republicans of "socialism" coming to power under George. They switched their votes, which customarily would have gone to the Republican candidate, to Hewitt as the only way to stop George. One important political truth his defeat did make him appreciate was that the labor vote could no longer be dismissed as nonexistent—or even not important. On the other hand, labor also learned from this election a powerful lesson—that it had great clout at the ballot box, and that it would have to use it to achieve its goals. The advocates of the status quo viewed the large labor vote of that year with alarm; the lessons of the mayoralty election of 1886 were not soon to be forgotten.

Roosevelt had now gone through three substantial political defeats in fairly rapid succession: his defeat for the Speakership in 1884; his defeat at the Republican National Convention in 1884; and his ignominious defeat for Mayor in 1886. His political future did not seem as bright as it had three years earlier. He took to writing again; but, while he enjoyed writing, it was pale and dull as compared with politicking. His interest in politics soon brought him back east from his ranches, this time into the Presidential campaign between Cleveland and Benjamin Harrison in 1888.

He campaigned strenuously for Harrison; eulogized once more the virtues of the Republican Party; condemned all "so-called Independents" and Mugwumps; and called for a high tariff policy of protection. He stressed that it was "a disgrace to us as a nation that we should have no warships worthy of the name, and that our rich sea-bound cities should be at the mercy of any piratical descent from a hostile power. We are actually at the mercy of a tenth-rate country like Chile." He argued that the surplus in the Treasury should be used to "prepare a navy capable of upholding the honor of the Nation."

He pointed out to the Republican campaign strategists that they should not let the opponents pick the battleground of the campaign; that it need not make its fight solely on the question of a protective tariff—which that year was the issue the Democrats had picked. "I do not think it wise to make our fight purely on one issue *and that the issue of our opponents' choosing.*" (Emphasis added) It was the same style of campaigning that Franklin was later to use almost without exception.

Harrison was elected President. Roosevelt after the election made a speech at the Federal Club dinner in New York City to celebrate the victory, again to condemn the Mugwumps and "the so-called Independents," and to belittle the fact that Cleveland had received more popular votes than Harrison. Then he offered some advice—unsolicited—to the new administration. It showed how little Roosevelt had advanced at this stage in his social thinking about human beings and human rights.

"Personally, I wish the Congress would revise our laws about immigration. Paupers and assisted immigrants of all kinds should be kept out; so should every variety of anarchists. And if anarchists do come, they should be caught as speedily as possible, that the first effort to put their principles into practice should result in their being shot down. . . . We must soon try to prevent too many laborers coming here and underselling our own workmen in the labor market; a good round head tax on each immigrant, together with a rigid examination into his character would work well." This only four years after the Statue of Liberty in New York Harbor had been dedicated and decorated with the immortal lines of Emma Lazarus:

> Give me your tired, your poor,
> Your huddled masses yearning
>   to be free . . .
> I lift my lamp beside the
>   golden door.

Roosevelt wanted a political job in 1889, and he paid no heed to the adage that "The office should seek the man." He was ambitious, and he was anxious to get back into the mainstream of American politics. It was always his style whenever he wanted something to go after it with unabashed zeal, foxlike cunning and impatience. Blaine, the former object of his condemnation, had been made Secretary of State. Roosevelt, through his friend Lodge, got Blaine to tell Harrison about his urge to get into the federal government in some capacity. Roosevelt was actually hoping that Blaine might appoint him Assistant Secretary of State; but Blaine had apparently had enough of this "brilliant and aggressive young man" and of his political style. Blaine pointed out in a letter to Mrs. Lodge that in the State Department "matters are constantly occurring which require the most thoughtful concentration and the most stubborn inaction. Do *you* think that Mr. T.R.'s temperament would give guarantee of that course?"[26]

President Harrison himself had similar doubts; but under pressure from Lodge he offered a job which recognized Roosevelt's past interest in civil service reform, a place on the four-man Civil Service Commission. Roosevelt promptly accepted. The President was in time to regret his offer—as so many politicians would who gave Roosevelt political power; but it would then be too late to do anything about it.

Roosevelt took office on May 13, 1889. He was only thirty-one years old; the Civil Service Law itself was only six years old. It had been passed at the behest of a few earnest advocates, but all the active politicians had really been against its enactment. The average voter knew little about it and cared even less. In the one month which elapsed since Harrison had been inaugurated, the new Republican administration began to tear apart the civil service merit system. It started in the Post Office Department, which was headed by John Wanamaker, a good merchant and a generous campaign contributor to Republican candidates, but not much of a believer in the merit system of civil service. Thirty thousand fourth-class postmasters were shortly fired by him and his subordinates, and replaced by deserving Republicans. The other departments of the administration did as well proportionately for the stalwart and needy Republican officeseekers. This was typical of what had been going on in Washington during the six years the Civil Service Law had been on the books. Its enforcement had been so weak that practical politicians did business as usual. The general feeling in most of official Washington, as well as among a great part of the citizenry, was that the whole thing was the work of a lot of "fool reformers."

Roosevelt, full of energy from the past six years of ranching and hunting out west, was thus given a golden opportunity to put into practice his style of action, zealotry, courage and independence. He lost no time. He went to work on the theory, as he wrote Lodge, that: "When my duty is to enforce the law, that law is surely going to be enforced without fear or favor." After six weeks he wrote optimistically that he had strengthened the administration by showing that there was no longer "any humbug" about the Civil Service Law. But for his efforts he got little thanks and even less support from the President. Roosevelt complained to Lodge that the President "has never given me one ounce of real backing. He won't even see us, or consider any method for improving the service." Harrison, after his presidency was over, expressed a different view of their relationship. He said that he and Roosevelt had cooperated harmoniously to improve the civil service, but he added: "The only trouble I ever had with him was that he wanted to put an end to all evil in the world between sunrise and sunset." This is a remarkably true appraisal of Roosevelt's general style, and of his dedication in every political job he took. Indeed, as civil service commissioner a new righteous cause had been instilled in him. Promoting this cause was one of many pronounced successes in his style of propagandism. He awakened a public interest in and approval of civil service reform—mostly with the roar of a lion, as he attacked men of power in the government who sought to continue to tear down the merit system in favor of the spoils system. Mr. Wanamaker, the Postmaster General, was among his first targets. Wanamaker believed, according to one of Roosevelt's biographers,[27] that one of his own great services rendered to Harrison was to prevent him "from making the irreparable blunder of accepting the drastic program of civil service reformers, most persuasive of whom was young Theodore Roosevelt."

Roosevelt soon uncovered corruption on the part of some postal officials in Baltimore, and boldly recommended that thirty-five of Wanamaker's recent appointees in that city be dismissed. When nothing happened, he took his evidence to the House Civil Service Committee (which as a result of the mid-term elections of 1890 was then Democratic). There he was, of course, cordially received. The Democratic majority of the committee, in its report in June 1892, upheld Roosevelt. Only a man of fierce political courage and independence, consumed by a desire to do his job well and to get ahead, would thus turn to the Democrats he so often excoriated for help against the complaisant inaction of his own political party and its President. But he had turned to Democrats before, and he would do it again as President. It was part of his style at times when his own party would not adequately support him. The report which the committee of the House filed had some effect on the national election of that year, in which Harrison was defeated and Cleveland returned to the White House.

After Cleveland's election, Roosevelt got Carl Schurz—one of the old Mugwumps whom he had verbally castigated in the Blaine incident—to intercede with Cleveland, whom he had so brutally attacked in the 1888 campaign, to retain him in the civil service office. Cleveland not only reappointed him but gave him substantial cooperation and support, which his Republican predecessor had so long and so completely withheld. Roosevelt remained in the commission until May 8, 1895.

In his *Autobiography* he minced no words about the atmosphere and general feeling in Washington concerning the commission: "The first effort of myself and my colleagues was to secure the general enforcement of the law. In this, we succeeded after a number of lively fights. But of course in these fights we were obliged to strike a large number of politicians, some of them in Congress. . . . We soon found ourselves engaged in a series of contests with prominent Senators and Congressmen. . . . Sometimes they had committees appointed to investigate us . . . sometimes they tried to cut off the appropriation for the Commission."[28]

Roosevelt spoke of his style in meeting the action of those congressmen who voted to cut off the appropriations. It was a foxlike, simple tactic, which showed he was learning to be a practical politician. He adopted, in his own language, the "simple expedient of not holding examinations in their districts. . . . This always brought frantic appeals from their constituents, and we would explain that unfortunately the appropriations had been cut . . . the constituents then turned their attention to the Congressman, and the result was that in the long run, we obtained sufficient money to enable us to do our work."

Roosevelt, during his six years as a civil service commissioner, had doubled the number of the classified positions (subject to examination) and exposed prior corruption in the system. But his main achievement was the result of his style of arousing public enthusiasm and support behind him—a quality of style which was to dominate his presidency. A veritable revolution had been incited by him in public thinking about the civil service. The old extreme doctrine of "To the victor belongs the spoils" had been punctured by his energy and determination to a point where it never was fully revived. Roosevelt had been able to inspire and arouse a vigilant public moral sense about the merit system, as he would about many others in the future.

In 1895 the new Fusion Mayor of New York City, William M. Strong, asked Roosevelt to become the president of the New York City Police Commission. He accepted. On May 5, 1895, he became a member of the board and, pursuant to the Mayor's wishes, was elected its president. It was a bi-partisan board of two Republicans and two Democrats.

If Roosevelt's life as civil service commissioner had been beset by hostile politicians, political pressures and constant bitter bickering and controversy, it was a bed of roses compared to his new career as police commissioner. The benign neglect shown by his predecessors in the enforcement of the Civil Service Law was as nothing compared to the complacency of the police commissioners in New York City before Strong's reform administration. In the police force itself every new appointment had to have some political backing; every promotion had its price, and the idea of promotion on the basis of merit was regarded as naïve (a captaincy, for example, was reputed to be worth $10,000 in cash). Every desk job was paid for; nearly every police officer assumed that it was natural to take money for winking at law violation.

Roosevelt was no ignoramus about what was going on in the New York City Police Department. Back in 1884, as an assemblyman and the chairman of the committee investigating the departments of the city, he got an earful of stories of the incompetence and graft. His report to the legislature in 1884 had called for a single commissioner—instead of the board of four—to be appointed solely on the merit system. But now, eleven years later, there was still the board of four, no civil service worthy of the name, and an undiminished amount of graft and hearty cooperation between the police and criminals. It was not only Tammany Hall which was to blame for this infection. The Republican city machine was a partner—though naturally not an equal one. Lincoln Steffens, then a reporter, included also among the guilty collaborators with the police "many business men in local business; gas, transportation, banks, and the great financiers."

Roosevelt had no illusions about what he was up against in his new position.

As he wrote to his sister: "I must make up my mind to much criticism and disappointment; conditions make it absolutely impossible to do what is expected of me." His foresight was correct on all counts; but the experience was going to add much to his stature, and would play its part in augmenting his aggressive, independent style as President.

No greater opportunity had been afforded him before this to display so lavishly his love of perpetual motion, his boundless energy, his incorruptibility by political or any other influence, his zeal for reform, his flamboyance and flair for personal publicity, his love of dramatic action tantamount to a kind of adolescent exhibitionism, his uncompromising stubbornness, his belligerence and his absolute love of power. All were to be parts of his later Presidential style. He dominated the board just as he had dominated the Civil Service Commission, although legally each member had the same power; indeed, he acted at many times as if he were the sole commissioner. He was not only dominating, he was domineering; he had the spotlight on himself and wanted to keep it there, and he did not treat the other three commissioners with much tact. With one he had a serious and almost continuous altercation in public until he persuaded Strong, after almost two years, to fire him for incompetency or worse.

From the very start he got most of the publicity from the reporters who covered police headquarters. They included Steffens, Arthur Brisbane and Joseph B. Bishop, his later worshipping biographer. A continuous fanfare of publicity followed him. Even his prominent large teeth began to get their first wide notoriety.

He would make it a practice to prowl the streets late at night, dressed in the formal evening clothes which he had worn at some social event earlier in the evening but covered by an opera cape, with a large hat pulled down over his face so that he could not be recognized—often accompanied, at his own request, by a reporter. Policemen asleep on duty, or getting some liquid refreshment at the back door of a saloon, or engaged in conversation with some undesirable character, would find themselves called up for hearing the next day and disciplined. In warm weather he discarded his vest but would appear in his office with a wide black silk sash instead, with long tassels. These incidents and his spectacular clothes were always publicized, and the citizens were delighted to learn that at last they had a real policeman—perhaps a little strange—but with zeal for reform. This zeal about reform and other matters he would always have, and many times to excess. One biographer spoke of his often "killing mosquitoes as if they were lions."

His weapons for creating a better Police Department were the same as he had used and would use (with few exceptions) all of his political life: full publicity of all events in the department, strict adherence to law, and complete disregard of politicians. Disciplinary trials of policemen, which formerly had been conducted in secrecy, were now carried on in public so that everyone would know the results of breach of duty. Neither political influence nor payment of money was any longer able to get a man appointed or promoted; appointments and promotions were made on the basis of merit as shown by written examinations.

Perhaps it was his style as police commissioner which first gave him a reputation of adolescence and immaturity. Bishop wrote of him, as of that time, in the *Evening Post,* that "he has what is essentially a boy's mind. What he thinks he says at once. It is his distinguishing characteristic."

His initial popularity began to fall precipitately when he made it clear that he was going to enforce the very unpopular law requiring saloons to close on Sunday. Roosevelt was no prohibitionist. He had said so very emphatically while in the Assembly in 1884. He believed that liquor could not be controlled by law. But he was determined as police commissioner to enforce compliance with *every* law—even this law about Sunday closing of saloons. The law had been on the books for a long time, but no one before him had ever really tried to enforce it. The front doors of saloons were always closed on Sunday, and that fact satisfied most of the church people. But the rear doors of saloons owned by those who were willing to cooperate with the police were always available. The problem, as Roosevelt saw it, was the evil that followed in the wake of such an open-and-closed door policy. Once this type of corruption was tolerated, it led quite naturally and inevitably to corruption in other fields of crime more serious, such as gambling and prostitution. This, rather than sympathy with the law itself, was the impelling motive for his crusade—for a crusade it soon became—against the open back door of the saloon on Sunday.

He announced within two months after taking office, in his usual direct manner, that he was about to close every saloon in New York on Sundays. His statement to the press about this on June 20, 1895, was unequivocal and blunt as his statements always were and always would be:

"I do not deal with public sentiment. I deal with the law. How I might act as a legislator or what kind of legislation I should advise has no bearing on my conduct as an executive officer charged with administering the law. I am going to see if we cannot break the license forthwith of any saloon-keeper who sells on Sunday. This applies just as much to the biggest hotel as to the smallest grog shop. . . . Woe be to the policeman who exposes himself to the taint of corruption."[29]

Roosevelt later boasted, "I have for once absolutely enforced the law in New York." This was an exaggeration, as many of his boasts were and would be. But he did succeed in rebuffing all attempts at intimidation, and all threats from politicians and newspapers. He did enforce the law partially, and did diminish the extent of bribery from saloonkeepers.

The political leaders, particularly Platt, unable to persuade or threaten Roosevelt into relaxing his crusade against the saloons, conceived the plan of using two of the other commissioners on the board to block in any way they could *all* the activities of Roosevelt in *all* fields. This led to open quarrels and constant fighting and bickering among the commissioners at public meetings of the board. The citizenry, including even the reformers who had been supporting Roosevelt, became irritated and disgusted by the public brawling. The bellicose president of the board was roundly criticized even in friendly newspapers.

The opponents of Sunday closing of saloons next turned to a clever expedient which did much to defeat and even to humiliate Roosevelt. They revived obsolete blue laws and brought cases before magistrates to enforce them. Included were forgotten ordinances against Sunday sales in soda fountains, florists, delicatessen stores and even shoe shining by bootblacks. The reform Mayor himself became weary of the complaints which ensued. And Boss Platt grew even more enraged.

Roosevelt scrupulously refrained from an open break with Platt. He proclaimed himself—nay, insisted that he always was—a loyal and enthusiastic Republican. But so far as enforcing the law was concerned, he never yielded either to Platt's importunities or to his threats.

In an article for *Forum Magazine* dated September 1895, he expressed his political philosophy about the general enforcement of all law, no matter how unpopular any particular law might be. It also expressed his style as a party leader, even when President:

"The implication is that for the sake of the Republican party of which I am a very earnest member, I should violate my oath of office, and connive at law-breaking. To this, I can only answer that I am too good a Republican to be willing to believe that the honest enforcement of law by a Republican can redown to the discredit of the party to which he belongs. . . . *I am not an impractical theorist, I am a practical politician. But I do not believe that practical politics and foul politics are necessarily synonomous terms.*" (Emphasis added)

To add to his troubles, Roosevelt found that as police commissioner he had antagonized labor by continuing to adhere to his style of pugnacious remarks about striking "mobs," and also by furnishing police protection to strikebreakers during legitimate strikes. In 1895 the *Evening Post* quoted him as saying: "We shall guard as zealously the rights of the striker as those of the employer, but when riot is menaced, it is different. The mob takes its own chance. Order must be kept at whatever cost. If it comes to shooting, we shall shoot to hit. No blank cartridges or firing over the head of anybody." To Roosevelt, as it had been in the Assembly, a "labor riot" was too often synonymous with a "strike."

Roosevelt wrote his sister that "organized labor is the chief support of William Jennings Bryan in the big cities; and his utterances are as criminal as they are silly. All the ugly forces that seethe beneath the social crust are behind him." His special scorn was reserved for liberal Governor John P. Altgeld of Illinois, who had pardoned some of the anarchist defendants in the Haymarket tragedy, and who had protested against the action of President Cleveland in sending federal troops into Illinois in the Pullman strike. Roosevelt went so far as to refuse personally to meet Altgeld, saying, incredibly, that he might have to face him "sword to sword upon the field of battle."

He was to be continually torn between his fear of the great corporations and their immense power and his fear of organized labor and the restless impoverished farmers. He liked to think of himself as the neutral between management and labor as well as between industry and consumer; and that attitude was to dominate his style of labor relations and consumer protection until the beginning of his presidency when, as we shall see, it began to change for the better. As police commissioner, he began to soften just a little in his attitude toward unions, but not on the priority of maintaining law and order in strikes.

It was at this time that Roosevelt gained an intimate glimpse of the ghastly conditions in the slums of the city. He had read Jacob A. Riis's *How the Other Half Lives,* published in 1890, and had been deeply impressed by it. Now as police commissioner (and, ex-officio, a member of the health board) he had many opportunities to look at life in the tenements at close hand. He would make frequent visits to the cheap tenement neighborhoods. What he saw there made a profound impact upon his social thinking. After he left the White House, he wrote of these visits: "My experience taught me that not a few of the worst tenement houses were owned by wealthy individuals who hired the best and most expensive lawyers to persuade the courts that it was 'unconstitutional' to insist on the betterment of conditions. . . . They made it evident that they valued the constitution not as a help to righteousness, but as a means for thwarting movements against unrighteousness."[30] This was a great step forward for a man who had so often in the past spoken contemptuously of social reformers, and so piously about the sanctity of our courts and judges.

After his two years with the police, Roosevelt, in spite of the failures and the frustrations, did leave behind a substantial record of accomplishment. Never had there been a more effective enforcement of the law in general. Many internal reforms in the Police Department were made, in addition to those enumerated; incompetent and corrupt policemen were dismissed in unprecedented numbers. Promotions based solely on heroism in the force were frequent; Roosevelt took particular pride in recognizing physical courage of the men. But far above the specific reforms was the reputation for independence and political courage he created in the city and beyond, and his record of absolute loyalty and support for the honest members of the police force which endeared him to his men. These characteristics were an inspiration for deserving policemen which they would remember long after he had left. His relations with human beings always followed the same style.

While he was still police commissioner, there came the Presidential campaign of 1896 between Bryan and McKinley. The police commissioner apparently regarded Bryan and "free silver" as even more dangerous than open saloons on Sunday or labor riots. He fairly leaped into the campaign on the side of hard money and Republicanism. Mark Hanna, the Republican National Chairman, frightened at the growing popular appeal of Bryan, asked Roosevelt to speak at many of the places where Bryan had already spoken. This is just what Roosevelt was most eager to do—always ready for verbal combat as well as physical. He also campaigned by writing magazine and newspaper articles. Some of the language he used in his articles and speeches during the campaign was extraordinary even for his fiery tongue and rampaging campaign style. The Democratic-Populist candidate was a "windy demagogue," whose objective was "a government of the mob," leading to a "red welter of lawlessness as fantastic and as vicious as the dream of a European communist."

He paid his respects to the obvious labor support for Bryan by claiming that Bryan did not have the support of the legitimate workers at all, but only of "the professional laboring man of the type that labors as little as possible, and continually strives to delude such workingmen as are ignorant and foolish enough to be misled into some movement which cannot but end in disaster."

With respect to preliminary labor injunctions, which in the last two years had become a growing menace to legitimate strikes, Roosevelt did not back down from his position that such an injunction issued in the Pullman strike was not only proper but actually prevented national anarchy. "The men who object to what they style 'government by injunction' really want anarchy by providing that the law shall only protect the lawless and frown scornfully on the law-abiding." He added that what they really wanted was a "debased judiciary and an executive pledge not to interfere with violent mobs."

He campaigned extensively in Illinois, Altgeld's state, putting the Governor in the same category as "Debs and other inciters to riot and mob violence, who, if he had his way, would plunge this country into terrible civic disturbance." Indeed Altgeld was painted by him as much "more dangerous . . . much slyer and more intelligent than Bryan," and "would connive at wholesale murder."

He came gallantly and vociferously to the support of the United States Supreme Court as "an independent and upright judiciary" against Democratic attacks for having declared the income tax law unconstitutional. As President, he would come to have quite a different attitude toward the Supreme Court—and also toward an income tax law. All those who supported Bryan were apparently only the "shiftless, and vicious, and the honest but hopelessly ignorant and puzzleheaded voters." This kind of rhetoric was repeated over and over again in speech after speech, and in article after article. Roosevelt's style of oratory never changed—and never failed deeply to move vast crowds of people.

It is remarkable, in the light of this violent defense of labor injunctions, that when he became President on his own in 1904, the labor injunction was to be one of the chief bones of contention between him and the conservative Republican Congress—with Roosevelt on the side of abolishing the injunction! This was not the only drastic switch in Roosevelt's style as to labor matters—or as to the judiciary itself.

But labor and silver were not the only issues in the campaign. Roosevelt did not neglect the others.[31] In a magazine article written a year before the election, Roosevelt prophesied with great confidence what the issues would be in 1896.[32] And he stated his own views on each. There was to be the tariff of 1894, which had been passed in the Cleveland administration, for example; and Roosevelt condemned it as providing protection only for certain interests rather than for the general welfare. "Never before did United States Senators appear so openly as the guardians of, and attorneys for, those peculiar aggregates of capital which are commonly styled 'trusts.' " We shall see the failure of Roosevelt, as President, to do anything substantial about the tariff—chiefly because of the opposition of those same "guardians of capital."

There was to be the issue of America's foreign policy.[33] Roosevelt's later style in this field as Assistant Secretary of the Navy and as President during his first term was all set by now (1895).

"We should build a first-class fighting navy," he wrote, "a navy not of mere swift destroyers, but of powerful battleships. We should annex Hawaii immediately. It was a crime against the United States, it was a crime against white civilization, not to annex it two years and a half ago. The delay did damage that is perhaps irreparable; for it meant that at the critical period of the island's growth the influx of population consisted, not of white Americans, but of low-caste laborers drawn from the yellow races. We should build the Isthmian Canal, and it should be built either by the United States Government or under its protection. We should inform Great Britain, with equal firmness and courtesy, that the Monroe Doctrine is very much alive, and that the United States cannot tolerate the aggrandizement of a European power on American soil."

Roosevelt also had some very advanced ideas in 1896 about the proper role of the Vice President in the American government, which he discussed in another magazine article. "He [the Vice President] should always be a man who would be consulted by the President on every great party question. It would be very well if he were given a seat in the Cabinet. It might be well, if, in addition to his vote in the Senate in the event of a tie, he should be given a vote on ordinary occasions and perhaps sometimes a voice in the debates." These radical ideas were all abandoned when Roosevelt became President and had the power to put some of them in effect.

When he himself became Vice President, he grew so disgusted with the office that he paid no attention to it during the six months of his tenure. On June 11, 1903, speaking about the office of Vice President after his experience of a year and a half as President, he said that it was "an office which, by the way, I should particularly like to see abolished."

For those who complained about the striking down of the law on income tax by the Supreme Court, he had additional words: "This represents a species of atavism—that is, of recurrence to the ways of thought of remote barbarian ancestors. Savages do not like an independent and upright judiciary. They want the judge to decide their way, and, if he does not, they want to behead him. The Populists experience much the same emotions when they realize that the judiciary stands between them and plunder."[34] And again, "The worst foe of the poor man is the labor leader, whether philanthropist or politician, who tries to teach him that he is a victim of conspiracy and injustice when in reality he is merely working out his fate with blood and sweat as the immense majority of men who are worthy of the name always have done and always will have to do. . . . It is both foolish and wicked to teach the average man who is not well off that some wrong and injustice have been done him and that he should hope for redress elsewhere than in his own industry, honesty and intelligence."[35] This style too was to change during his presidency.

Roosevelt's speeches before and during his presidency were not models of very good speech-writing. He depended more on violent gestures with fist or with fingers, on his gleaming white teeth which he constantly displayed in a grin wherever possible, on the thrust or quick motion of his body—and on the extremism of his epithets and name-calling. His speeches in form and development do not follow logical processes. They are nearly all over-long, and full of repetitions of thought and language. They must have been very enjoyable to listen to with all their colorful name-calling and denunciation, and with his razzle-dazzle personality and the violent gesturing of which many photographs remain. In those days before talking movies and radio, people enjoyed lengthy, effusive oratory. Woodrow Wilson was the first Presidential orator of the twentieth century to speak with brevity, preciseness, logic, and brilliance—and to enthrall rather than dazzle his audiences. But to read Roosevelt's speeches in cold print, they are rather boring and seem to be even more demagogic than they must have sounded.

Franklin Roosevelt, as President, was unable to make any of the characteristic gestures and body movements of Theodore; he had to hold onto the lecturn with at least one hand in order to maintain his balance. Nor could he bounce around the platform as Theodore did. His most effective gesture was one of the most difficult to get across to an audience—an upward shake of the head accompanied only by a broad smile or grim facial expression. I have seen it made hundreds of times, and it never failed to register. Instead of name-calling, Franklin relied more on dignified though often virulent language. The two styles of oratory—both extremely effective—were at opposite ends of the pole.

It was with a sense of relief that, after his Herculean and vitriolic campaigning, Roosevelt was able to resign from his problems as police commissioner in April 1897, and to begin his next political experience—this time on the national scene again—as Assistant Secretary of the Navy. The newly elected President, William McKinley, just inaugurated a month earlier, had obviously heard, or read, all about Roosevelt and his style as a civil service commissioner in Washington and as a police commissioner in New York City. Based on what he knew, McKinley was not too anxious to appoint Roosevelt to anything in his administration. But he was subjected to great pressure from Senator Lodge. That McKinley knew his man very well is evident from his remark at this time to Lodge: "I hope he has no preconceived notion which he would wish to drive through the moment he got in." His "hope" was to be quickly dispelled. In addition to the pressure from Senator Lodge, the President was also subjected to pressure from

William Howard Taft, John Hay, and the big boss himself, Mark Hanna. Tom Platt, at Roosevelt's specific and unabashed request, had after some hesitation joined these other prominent Republicans in recommending Roosevelt for the job. Platt did this with very mixed political feelings. He deeply disliked Roosevelt as a man, and did not trust him as a politician. But he was very anxious to get him out of the political life of New York City and New York State. Platt had come to the conclusion that getting him a job in Washington was the best way to do it, on the theory, as he later put it, that Roosevelt "would do less harm to the [Republican] organization as Assistant Secretary of the Navy than in any other office that could be named." This was to turn out to be one of his less solid political conclusions.

Platt's support in this instance was based on more than the mere desire to get rid of Roosevelt, however. In early 1896 Platt and Joseph H. Choate, who had been Roosevelt's friend and supporter since his earliest days in politics, became rival candidates for election by the New York legislature as the next United States Senator from that state. Roosevelt had let it be known that he would be neutral in that dispute. But he eventually joined those who were supporting Platt. This switch was, of course, because in return he wanted Platt to use his influence with McKinley for the Navy position. It shows Roosevelt's evolving political style: where he wanted something important, either a political position or legislation from Congress, he was willing to compromise, and even to make his peace with the very politicians he was constantly opposing and often denouncing.

There were a number of reasons for Theodore Roosevelt's anxiety for the Navy job. He had always been interested in foreign policy and particularly in armed naval preparedness. He was one of the group of determined imperialists and expansionists of that time—inspired largely by Admiral Mahan and led by Senator Lodge—who kept agitating for a powerful Navy and for an expanded role for the United States in world affairs. Roosevelt knew that the Assistant Secretary of the Navy would not be the one to make the final decisions in either of these fields. But he also realized that the position would provide a means of access to, and an opportunity for the persuasion of, those who would make the decisions. So did all his friends who were busy expounding the imperialist philosophy; and they wanted to get one of their own into this position on whom they could rely. Also he was glad to get away from the restrictions of bi-partisan boards, and back to a place of unrestrained leadership where he was always at his best.

Roosevelt was fortunate in that his immediate superior, Secretary of the Navy John D. Long, was willing to delegate very substantial authority to his Assistant Secretary, and also that Long was out of Washington frequently, leaving Roosevelt as the Acting Secretary. This gave him an opportunity to use his own style of action, energy, directness and independence—a very different style from Long's. It also gave him his opportunity to exercise constant insistence on a large two-ocean Navy, with a sufficient number of big battleships, as he strove for the expansion of the United States into a world power. Above all, it developed his blatant jingoism, a true belief in the virtues of war, weapons and military conquest —always, of course, in a "righteous war."

It was not long after he arrived in the Navy office that Roosevelt started to urge immediate help for Cuba by the invasion of the island—then in revolt against Spain—in the name of humanity, to save the Cubans from the horrors of persecution by the Spanish rulers. Soon he was again arguing for the annexation of Hawaii, and then the Philippines. Japan had to be watched carefully, he was insisting, because of Hawaii and the Philippines, and also because she was building a Navy which might soon surpass ours. Germany was even more dangerous, for she was showing a tendency "to stretch out for colonial possessions which may at any moment cause a conflict with us." "The Monroe Doctrine," he warned, "had more to fear from Germany than from Great Britain."

Early in his political career, and long before he became Assistant Secretary of the Navy, he had shown a passion for war, just as in his boyhood he had shown a passion for building up his own body. Both of these urges had their common origin partially in the physical weakness and sickness which had afflicted him in boyhood. When in 1886, for example, war seemed to be imminent with Mexico, he had wanted to organize his Western ranch hands into a cavalry battalion. In the same year he had made a Fourth of July speech saying that he wanted "to see the day when not a foot of American soil will be held by any European Power." By 1894 he was already demanding that the United States seize and annex the Philippines, and build a canal through Nicaragua. He had reached a high point of jingoism in 1895 when President Cleveland formally asserted that the Monroe Doctrine gave the United States the right to insist upon a peaceful settlement of the Venezuela-British Guiana boundary dispute. Roosevelt told a reporter that Cleveland, in his emphatic, almost belligerent, handling of the crisis, was right. If war should come, he had said in a burst of unbelievable bluster, "American cities may possibly be bombarded, but no ransom will be paid for them. Moreover, a great many of our friends seem to forget that we will settle the Venezuela question in Canada. Canada would surely be conquered, and once wrested from England it would never be restored." He had written Lodge on December 27, 1895: "This country needs a war, but the bankers, brokers and Anglo-maniacs generally seem to favor peace at any price."

Small wonder that McKinley had some qualms in 1897 about putting Roosevelt in the Navy.

Roosevelt's *Autobiography* points out that when in 1882 he published his first book, *The History of the Naval War of 1812,* "the Navy had reached its nadir, and we were then utterly incompetent to fight Spain or any other power that had a navy at all. . . . After the Civil War, our strongest and most capable men had thrown their whole energy into business, into money-making, and into the development and, above all, the exploitation and exhaustion at the most rapid rate possible of our natural resources—mines, forests, soils and rivers."[36] These men, "reinforced by the mollycoddle vote and by many others soft physically and morally," and by pacifists, some of whom were "wise and high-minded," some with "no imagination and no foresight," and some "who form the lunatic fringe in all reform movements"—all these "put a stop to any serious effort to keep the nation in a condition of reasonable military preparedness."[37]

Theodore Roosevelt, in his eagerness for the Navy post, had promised McKinley and Hanna that he would stop his jingoistic utterances; and he even had asked Lodge to explain to Secretary Long that he would be a loyal subordinate, doing whatever Long told him to do. He did not wait very long after his appointment to break both promises. Long was not as enthusiastic as his Assistant Secretary was about building up the Navy. Roosevelt was able to restrain himself on this matter only for a few months—up to June 2, 1897. On that day, in an address to the War College, Rooseveltian rhetoric took the place of the restraint he had promised. He spoke of "the most valuable of all qualities, the soldierly virtues. Peace is a goddess only when she comes with sword girt on thigh. The ship of state can be steered safely only when it is always possible to bring her against any foe with her leashed thunder gathering for the leap. . . . No triumph of peace is quite so great as the supreme triumph of war." He called, of course, for a strong Navy, but not one merely for defense; he hinted that we had to intervene in Cuba right away to protect its inhabitants from the tyranny and concentration camps of Spain, and that unless we did, we might as well forget the Monroe Doctrine. A few more speeches of equal belligerence followed; and, at last, Long took forceful steps to make Roosevelt promise once again to reform.

But these were heady and exciting times, due in great measure to the yellow journalism of Hearst and Pulitzer who also were urging war with Spain over Cuba. Roosevelt was motivated by two different impulses. One was to build a strong Navy; the other was his passion for warfare. He was not always sure which was uppermost in his mind at any one time. He was urging help for the wretched Cubans, but he also said that it would be a good experience for the Navy. He did add in the *Autobiography* that our own direct interests were great because of the Cuban tobacco and sugar, and especially because of Cuba's relation to the projected Isthmian Canal.

Roosevelt was convinced when he took office that war with Spain would come. Cuba had been subjected to "unspeakable horror, degradation and misery" during its revolution, which had been dragging on for years. He was able to do a great deal to prepare for the war. For example, he was instrumental in getting Dewey put in command of the Asiatic Fleet, "the fleet where it was most essential to have a man who would act without referring things back to the home authorities." In order to do this he had to get Dewey advanced over "an officer senior to him of the respectable common-place type who was being pushed by certain politicians who had influence with the navy department and with the President." Dewey got the command. Roosevelt also made some administrative changes and periodic personal inspection of naval installations and ships.

Roosevelt boasted that, "whenever I was left as acting secretary, I did everything in my power to put us in readiness," because, as he put it, "I suppose the United States will always be unready for war." His repeated efforts for a big Navy were very much like the later efforts of Franklin, but Franklin seemed to have a little more success than Theodore. The major difference in the two situations is that Franklin and his superior, Josephus Daniels, had great affection and respect for each other. This close personal relationship did not exist between Long and Theodore.

In January 1898, the battleship *Maine* was sent to Havana, ostensibly to protect Americans in Cuba. Within a few weeks, on February 15, it was blown up. Without waiting to hear any facts about the explosion, Theodore Roosevelt, following his usual style of acting in haste and reflecting at leisure, immediately said: "It was an act of dirty treachery by the Spaniards."

McKinley, however, struggled for peace, in spite of the renewed and invigorated fervor of the jingoes—a course which prompted Roosevelt to remark that "the President has no more backbone than a chocolate eclair." Ten days after the sinking of the *Maine,* Secretary Long took the afternoon off. Roosevelt, now Acting Secretary, almost immediately sent his famous telegram to Admiral George Dewey, then at Hong Kong with the Asiatic squadron. The telegram ordered him, if war was declared, to proceed at once to the Philippines. Roosevelt did this in spite of Long's prior specific admonition *not* to take "any step affecting the policy of the Administration without consulting the President or me." Long was, of course, outraged by this insubordination, but for some reason he did not fire Roosevelt or even countermand the order. In fact, the order proved to be largely responsible for Dewey's easy success in Manila Bay, because he was able to get there fast, fully prepared with supplies and ammunition accumulated at his station at Hong Kong. Roosevelt's impulsive act was in line with his style of always trying to be prepared *in advance;* he had for the same reasons also ordered the Atlantic Fleet to take certain stations off Cuba which would faciliate attacks by them if and when war were declared.

War did come. Shortly thereafter, on May 6, 1898, Roosevelt resigned from his office, personally to join the war for which he had been arguing for almost a year.

He had concluded then, and he reaffirmed his conclusion in his *Autobiography*, that the "war was both just and necessary." He added that "there are few humane and honorable men who disagree." This last observation is not true, and his first is subject to many questions; but both are examples of his style of complete self-delusion when he thought he was right, and of his conviction that his own conclusions were always better and more widespread among the people than those of anyone else. He seldom, if ever, felt any doubt about his own opinions.

Roosevelt's own estimate of his usefulness in the Navy Department, made in a letter to Lodge shortly after his resignation, was neither modest nor inaccurate: "When I was Acting Secretary, I did not hesitate to take responsibilities . . . I have continually meddled with what was not my business because I was willing to jeopardize my position in a way that a naval officer could not."

Very early in Roosevelt's verbal campaign to rescue Cuba and drive the Spaniards out, he had indicated in many letters that if war came, he was going to take a personal part in it *"at the front."* There is no doubt that part of this determination was due to his admiration and passion for what he called the "soldierly virtues." But, in addition, he explained in a letter dated March 29, 1898, some other reasons just as weighty to him: "I have consistently preached what our opponents are pleased to call jingo doctrines for a good many years. . . . I cannot afford to disregard the fact that my power for good . . . would be gone if I did not try to live up to the doctrines I have tried to preach. . . . It would be a good deal more important from the standpoint of the nation as a whole that men like myself should go to war than . . . let others carry on the war that we have urged."[38]

He tried time and again to enlist in the New York State militia and in other military outfits without success; but his chance came when Congress authorized the raising of three national volunteer cavalry regiments. The Secretary of War offered Roosevelt the command of one of them; but, uncharacteristically for one who was as self-assured and as self-confident as he was, he suggested that his Army friend Colonel Leonard Wood head the regiment, and that he would become second in command. This was done; and thus was created the First United States Volunteer Cavalry Regiment. But because it was recruited in good part from Western ranchmen it was soon nicknamed the "Rough Riders," and was to become famous for many years—and politically very useful to Roosevelt.

Many people, including the then President of the United States, the Secretary of the Navy and Senator Cabot Lodge, urged him not to leave his post in

Washington, but to no avail. Some of the Cabinet wives, according to Chauncey M. Depew, remonstrated with him on the ground that he had six children,[39] one only a few months old, and that he had no right to leave the burden to his wife. His answer was: "I have done as much as anyone to bring on this war . . . and now that the war is declared, I have no right to ask others to do the fighting and stay at home myself."

The story of Roosevelt and the Rough Riders, which was to grow into a political legend, borders at times on the ridiculous. It is not relevant to this book, except as it shows his style of action and great courage and, above all, the leadership he could exercise and the inspiration he could instill in his fellow men.

Roosevelt has written in great detail about his regiment, about equipping them, training them and getting them to Cuba, about their fights in the jungles —and, finally, the famous charge. During the time before his regiment got to Cuba he showed an adolescent fear that the war might be over before he could get into it. He also expressed his dismay at the confusion, inefficiency and lack of preparation in the Army which he found when he got to Cuba. During the famous charge up Kettle Hill (not San Juan Hill, as popularly believed), Roosevelt showed reckless courage, dashing around at the head of his regiment (for he was now a Colonel) with a handkerchief tied to his hat to distinguish him. The fighting action on the hill lasted only one day. But the casualty list in his regiment was long; and, at times, only good luck saved it from complete annihilation. Richard Harding Davis was on the spot as an experienced and hardened reporter; and he wrote that it was remarkable that any member of the regiment survived. Roosevelt's personal courage and his selfless devotion to the needs of his men between battles brought him their undying affection. They also brought him nationwide fame and commendation.

Although he had disclaimed any idea that going to war was a pleasure for him, he certainly proceeded with great zest, determination and impatience to get into the thick of it. He called the charge up the heights near Santiago his "crowded hour." The sickly child, now grown into a tough fighting man, must have been in his mind as he wrote twenty years later: "San Juan was the great day of my life."[40] This was quite a statement, since it included in its sweep at least two separate days of taking the oath as President of the United States.

He was even proud of the heavy casualties in his regiment, for they showed that it had been in the most dangerous fighting. Roosevelt's style had never been, nor ever would be, crimped by modesty; and none of it hampered his own account of his fighting record. "I do not want to be vain," he wrote to Lodge, "but I do not think anyone could have handled this regiment quite as I have." He boasted more formally, but to the same effect, in a book he wrote, *The Rough Riders.* In the White House he would later confide to his military aide, "I know now that I would have turned from my wife's deathbed to have answered that call." That statement, even allowing for his usual exaggeration, says a great deal about Roosevelt's style of action when sufficiently aroused.

In September 1898 Roosevelt and his Rough Riders—or those who were left of them—came home to Montauk, Long Island. In a farewell speech to his troops Roosevelt showed that, though still something of an adolescent in his zeal for fighting, he was growing in maturity as a human being:

"I am proud of this regiment . . . it is primarily an American regiment and it is American because it is composed of all the races which have made America their country by adoption and those who have claimed it as their country by inheritance." He made no distinction—as he used to—about the immigrants of Anglo-Saxon–Norse origin and those who had come from southern and eastern Europe. And he ended with a tribute to the black soldiers who had fought their way up the hill with his own regiment.

He would always try to look after and care for politically any one of his Rough Riders, some of whom were quite literally "rough," and all of whom he considered his protégés. At times, it was not easy. For example, in writing to the former second trumpeter of the Rough Riders in answer to his request for a job in Washington two days after Roosevelt became Vice President, he wound up his letter with a grim sense of humor: "Personally, I have great confidence in you, but of course, there would have to be much explanation in connection with that man you shot."[41]

Theodore was now basking in—and enjoying—the sunshine of public acclaim for his heroism in Cuba. He would soon have to look for a job, for being unemployed was something he had never relished, and never would. He was convinced that his future lay in politics, and it was to politics that he now again turned. After all, he had held continuous public office since 1890, and was a seasoned politician. It is not really strange, in hindsight, that Roosevelt had never served out his full term either as civil service commissioner or police commissioner or as Assistant Secretary of the Navy, or even that he had not run for re-election to the New York Assembly after his three successful consecutive years as a member. It was his restless, roving spirit that drove him to new challenges.

His next political experience—perhaps the most fruitful of all—came in an office which he did not have to seek. This time the office really sought him; and the call came through the efforts of the old political leader with whom he had had so many differences in the past, Thomas C. Platt, now again United States Senator from New York. He was once more in 1898 the undisputed Republican political boss throughout the State of New York.

The kind of complete bossism which Platt maintained over the legislature and the Republican officeholders was a phenomenon which disappeared completely in New York State by the time Alfred E. Smith first became Governor. There remained, of course, local county bosses of great power in their own domains; but the all-pervasive statewide power which Platt wielded has not resided in any one man—Republican or Democrat—in New York State for at least the last fifty years. Roosevelt has recorded that "at that time [1898] boss rule was at its very zenith." He attributed it to people's fear of Bryanism, including such rabid doctrines as free silver, and to the anxiety of businessmen, wage-workers, and the professional classes generally which caused them to turn to whoever opposed Bryan. With special eagerness, he said, did they turn to the Republican Party. He asserted that this worked only to the advantage of Republican bosses, who were "already in fairly close alliance with the privileged interests. . . . The alliance between the two kinds of privilege, political and financial, was closely cemented."[43] It is important to Roosevelt's style that he believed, as he said, "As so often happens, the excesses and threats of an unwise and extreme radicalism had resulted in immensely strengthening the position of the beneficiaries of reaction."[44] He was later, as President, in the same style to urge the Congress with respect to many pieces of legislation designed to regulate "financial privilege" and the "beneficiaries of reaction" that regulation was the only effective way to remove the threat or possibility of "an unwise and extreme radicalism."

Roosevelt stated flatly that: "In New York State, United States Senator Platt was the absolute boss of the Republican party. The control by Mr. Platt and his lieutenants over the organization was well-nigh complete. Big business was back of him; yet at the time, this, the most important element in his strength, was only imperfectly understood. It was not until I was elected governor that I, myself, came to understand it." This understanding about "big business" being in back of Platt was to influence his style in Albany, as his later understanding of the business interests in back of Senators Aldrich and Hanna and Allison and Spooner and Orville Platt (of Connecticut) was to influence his style in Washington.

Fortunately again for Roosevelt, Boss Tom Platt himself in 1898 had a serious problem on his hands. The incumbent Republican Governor of New York, Frank S. Black, was under a dark cloud because of extravagance and corruption in the administration of the Erie Canal system in the state. His re-election as Governor, should he be renominated, seemed very doubtful if not impossible. Platt began to look for another candidate whose chances of election would be brighter. Many Republican politicians suggested the new national military hero of San Juan Hill, believing he could surely be elected. Some Republican newspapers throughout the state had already "nominated" Roosevelt even before his motley crew of Rough Rider survivors had landed. Besides, had not Roosevelt, ever since 1882, acquired and maintained a great reputation as a reformer? And would this not serve to balance out the scandals of the Black governorship? But Platt had had a taste of young Roosevelt while he was in the Assembly, and even more recently while he was the police commissioner of New York City—and the taste had been a little sour, and was still a little sour! He was afraid that as Governor, Roosevelt might well turn out to be, as Platt put it, "a bull in a china shop."

Prominent Republicans like Chauncey M. Depew and Senator Lodge argued with Platt that the only way to save the governorship from an expected landslide Republican defeat was to name a man who could answer embarrassing questions about the Erie Canal scandals by pointing to his own long fighting record as a reformer. Roosevelt was just such a man. Roosevelt while in Cuba had commented on the New York newspapers' boom for him by saying that his popularity was only temporary and, besides, that he was more interested in "national than state politics." Nevertheless, he took extraordinary care to let his friends and political supporters back home know that the crown of the governorship would not have to be offered to him more than once—that he would of course "pay heed to the voice of the people." However, it was not "the voice of the people" but only the hand of Tom Platt which could make him the Republican nominee. And the hand of Platt would be withheld unless he could receive some assurance from the colonel of reasonable political cooperation. So Roosevelt called personally upon Platt at the Fifth Avenue Hotel in New York City on September 17, and they had a serious conference. Platt in his biography, a dozen years later, wrote, "We buried past differences," and Roosevelt agreed "to consult with me and other party leaders about appointments and legislation in case he were elected." By his later conduct, Roosevelt seems to corroborate what Platt wrote about their meeting.

The campaign for Governor would today be condemned as "corny," but at the end, at least, it was politically very skillful. Just as Franklin D. Roosevelt was later to do in all his campaigns, and as Theodore had advised Harrison to do (see page 24 above), Theodore decided to pick his own battleground in this campaign rather than let the opponents pick one. Obviously, the Democrats would want to talk about the scandals of the Erie Canal; therefore, Roosevelt barely mentioned the Erie Canal. Instead, he picked Tammany Hall, and especially its then arrogant and autocratic leader, Richard Croker. Roosevelt was very fortunate in that, late in the campaign, it became known that Croker had arbitrarily refused a nomination to a worthy judge who had served on the State Supreme Court Bench for twenty-eight years, only because the judge had refused to appoint one of Croker's henchmen—a hack—as clerk of the court. Croker's arbitrary action made headlines; it also gave Roosevelt his chance to campaign against Croker, whose many misdeeds were being publicized, rather than against his Democratic opponent, Van Wyck. His object was to make the people understand that it was Croker and not the nominal candidate who was his real opponent. There is no doubt that Roosevelt had learned a lot about political style.

Apart from Croker, the chief subjects he discussed were patriotism, good government, national issues of all kinds and, of course, the cavalry charge Roosevelt had led up "San Juan Hill." He began his campaign tour of the state accompanied by seven former Rough Riders in full military regalia. It seems a little hard to believe today, in this more sophisticated period, but at each station stop a Rough Rider bugler would appear on the rear platform of his train, and, to the great applause of the audience, blow the traditional tune for a cavalry charge. Roosevelt, as the sound of the bugle died down, would appear, and would make some opening remark as relevant to the gubernatorial issues as this one at Fort Henry, a small upstate village: "You have heard the trumpet that sounded to bring you here. I have heard it tear the tropic dawn [sic] when it summoned us to fight at Santiago." The campaign tour became one continuous Fourth of July celebration. Maybe this type of campaign was adopted as a clever expedient not only to divert attention from the Canal scandals, but more importantly to conceal the fact that Roosevelt really had no program which he could talk about. He had had very little time even to think about one.

His opening speech, on October 3, 1898, was entitled: "The Duties of a Great Nation." Instead of outlining some state problems or programs, the speech was more suitable for a campaign for national office. After some generalities and platitudes about good government in both the nation and the state, he depicted the role that the United States should play in world affairs: "There comes a time in the life of a nation, as in the life of an individual when it must face great responsibilities whether it will or not. We have now reached that time. . . . We can see by the fate of China how idle is the hope of courting safety by leading a life of fossilized isolation."

This was to be the keystone of his position in foreign affairs all during his presidency. He was very specific in 1898 about what this responsibility entailed: "Greatness means strife for nation and man alike. . . . Greatness is the fruit of toil and sacrifice and high courage. . . . Events have shown that war is always a possibility even for us. The surest way to avert war, if it can be averted, is to be prepared to do well if forced to go to war; otherwise, other powers will have just contempt for us . . . and do things . . . which they would carefully refrain from doing if they were sure we were ready to resent them. . . . We want to build up our navy."

His attitude toward labor had softened a little, probably as a result of his mayoralty campaign. He recognized that working men have "special interests" which should be helped, although "the help that will most surely avail the man who works is self-help. But the history of the trades-unions has shown that very much can also be done by that form of self-help where many join together to help one another."[45] On October 27 he promised that all remedial labor laws would be "carried out to the letter." Referring to his Rough Riders, he said he had treated rich and poor, Northerners and Southerners, all with an equal justice. If elected, he would treat management and labor similarly. Boss Platt was watching all this campaigning with more than mild interest and concern. In Platt's autobiography of 1910, he described it:

"Roosevelt made a dramatic campaign. He fairly pranced around the state. He called a spade a spade, a crook a crook. The Rough Rider romped home on election day with over 17,000 plurality. I had always maintained that no man besides Roosevelt could have accomplished that feat in 1898."

While the crowds delighted to come to his rallies and share in the carnival spirit, the political leaders of the state, in spite of Platt's later enthusiasm, were not too happy about the way the campaign was going. Roosevelt remarked glumly one day, not recognizing the irrelevancy, that "New York cares very little for the war." He was being criticized for all his imperialistic talk, for his almost exclusive discussion of national issues, as well as for ignoring the Canal scandals of the previous Republican governorship. Rumors were skillfully started by the opposition that Roosevelt never actually charged up San Juan Hill at all.

He was desperately anxious to win this, his first large-scale personal campaign. So, abandoning all dignity, he started a tremendous lobby to get the Medal of Honor which he thought he had earned in Cuba. His old friend Lodge did his best, even making a personal appeal to the President; but the Army, remembering Roosevelt's attacks on it of incompetence while he was in Cuba, refused to heed Lodge's plea of the medal's "tremendous importance to the election in New York." Ironically, it was Croker who came to Roosevelt's rescue from probable defeat by his handling of the renomination of the judge. Roosevelt won by the very slim majority of only 17,794 votes—hardly the "romp" which Platt called it. It was not exactly a landslide, but he had learned during the campaign that he possessed that great ability which cannot be acquired but must be born in a man—the ability to sway masses of people.

He was now started on his final preparation for the presidency, in the Executive Chamber of the State Capitol in Albany—just as Franklin Roosevelt would also do, and Wilson in Trenton.

What kind of Governor did Theodore Roosevelt make? Roosevelt had his own appraisal just as he had had about the way he handled the Rough Riders. It was equally modest: "I think I have been the best Governor within my time, better than either Cleveland or Tilden." Many impartial observers and historians might think this estimate a trifle high. The more important question for us is how much did the experience in Albany help him after he reached the White House, and how did it affect his style as President? The answers to these questions are unqualifiedly positive. Much of his later style in dealing with political bosses, with regulation of huge corporations and trusts, with labor, with taxes and with opposition to reform legislation of all kinds was shown at Albany. One thing is certain: since the days of his service on the third floor of the Capitol building (where the Assembly Chamber is located) he had developed into a more practical politician, a more flexible, temporizing, compromising realist as he began his service on the second floor (where lies the Executive Chamber). Somewhere on the famous marble staircase between the two floors in the Capitol building he had lost a great deal of his truculence, his impatience with the less-privileged, his hostility to politicians, his contempt for labor leaders, his insistence on perfection —even a little of his self-righteousness. At least he had learned to stretch his conception of righteousness. He even said later that one "must have a due regard for opportunism in the choice of the time and method of exercising righteousness and attacking evil—just exactly as I did when I was Governor." In addition, he had developed or rather had augmented an energy and a zest for action, a capacity for growth, a love of sustained work and a flamboyant style which was to amaze all those who touched him.

Nothing showed his new style as a political leader better than his relations after election with Boss Platt. Roosevelt knew full well what Platt's power was in Albany. As Governor-elect, Roosevelt wrote: "Senator Platt is to all intents and purposes a majority of the Legislature." Yet, if the results of the confrontations between the two were tallied during the two years of the governorship, Roosevelt would seem to have done better with Platt than Platt did with Roosevelt. This was accomplished without any open break between the two men—a style of dealing with political leaders which he would use in Washington, and a fact which speaks eloquently of Roosevelt's growth.

The way he expressed it in his *Autobiography* is even more characteristic: "My desire was to achieve results, and not merely to issue manifestoes of virtue . . . at that time, the public conscience was still dormant as regards many species of political and business misconduct, as to which during the next decade it became sensitive." (Roosevelt was himself going to have a substantial role in awakening that social conscience during the next decade while he was President.) "I had to work," he continued, "with the tools at hand and take into account the feeling of the people. . . . My aim was persistently to refuse to be put in a position where what I did would seem to be a mere faction struggle against Senator Platt. . . . In each case, I did my best to persuade Mr. Platt not to oppose me. It was only after I had exhausted all the resources of my patience that I would finally, if he still proved obstinate, tell him that I intended to make the fight anyhow."

Roosevelt generally saw Platt in New York on Saturdays, for Platt was in Washington and Roosevelt in Albany during the rest of the week. "I always insisted on going openly. . . . Solemn reformers of the tomfool variety . . . were much exercised over my 'breakfasting with Platt,' " but "breakfasts with Platt always meant that I was going to do something he did not like, and that I was trying courteously and frankly to reconcile him to it." Roosevelt summed it up, perhaps again too optimistically if not too modestly: "In every instance, I substantially carried my point, altho' in some cases not in exactly the way in which I had originally hoped."

It seems a little impossible to visualize Assemblyman Roosevelt, or Civil Service Commissioner Roosevelt, or Police Commissioner Roosevelt, doing any of these things with Platt—much less writing about them as he did. In addition to his growth in political practicality, there was an increased self-confidence. He was sure that the people as a whole, who knew him as a crusading reformer and an anti-machine Republican, would understand his relations with Platt, and be certain that he was not betraying the cause of good government in these breakfast meetings.

Of course, their wills had to clash; and the first conflict came even before the inauguration. It was the matter of appointing a man to run the Canal honestly and efficiently. The Canal was under the Superintendent of Public Works; and Roosevelt thought "it was by far the most important office under me." Platt had offered the place to one Francis J. Hendricks, who had accepted. Platt put the matter to the Governor-elect as a *fait accompli*. Roosevelt liked and respected Hendricks, and later appointed him to a different important office; but since Hendricks lived in a city along the line of the Canal, he did not think it wise to appoint him. "Moreover," Roosevelt wrote, "what was far more important, it was necessary to have it understood at the very outset that the administration was my administration and was no one else's but mine. So I told the Senator politely that I was sorry, but that I could not appoint his man. This produced an explosion. . . . Although I was very polite, I was very firm, and Mr. Platt and his friends finally abandoned their position."

Roosevelt's memory in 1913 when the *Autobiography* was written was again a little faulty as to these events of 1898; or else he was concealing some facts which would have proved that he was even a better politician than he described himself to be. What Roosevelt actually did after the first "explosion" by Platt was to offer a constructive compromise—something novel in his style, but which would remain a fixed part of it in future. He made a list of four acceptable names, let Platt select one of them, and everybody was satisfied.[46] He was now even a practical enough politician to give Platt a rather free choice on most minor offices. He realized that this courtesy would help him get his program of legislation through, which was his chief interest nearly always as Governor and as President. He did keep a few of the minor jobs for some personal friends and, of course, for some needy former Rough Riders.

It was in the field of legislation that the two men clashed most frequently and incisively. This was quite natural. Platt was not only in successful businesses himself, but was a close ally of all big business. He looked with confidence to big business for big contributions, which he would use to elect legislators who would naturally be thereafter beholden to him. Big business in turn expected protection from Platt against hostile legislation, and assistance from him for favorable legislation. Big business was equally generous with Democratic bosses—so it could rest easy no matter which party prevailed. In fact both parties, in an emergency, would work together to protect their benefactors.

Roosevelt knew all about these sordid political arrangements from his Assembly days, and he knew what tough opposition he would have to meet in passing legislation to which big business was not likely to show affection. Only a man of iron determination, dedication and energy—and above all, one who was able to mass public opinion behind him—would have attempted it. He did not jump into the fray immediately. Indeed his Inaugural Address and his first Annual Message to the legislature of January 2, 1899, were fairly innocuous—even Platt could not find in them any real danger to his own policies or to his big business patrons.

The Inaugural, after stressing the importance of "common sense, honesty and courage" in government administration, showed the style and dedication as a party leader which he was to continue through his presidency: "It is only through the party system that free governments are now successfully carried on. . . . The usefulness of a party is strictly limited by its usefulness to the State and, in the long run, he serves his party best who most helps to make it instantly responsive to every need of the people."[47] This was naturally the style of a middle-of-the-roader who would himself define what was "responsive" in accordance with his own social views.

In the first Annual Message he first put in his invariable plug for a strong imperialistic and non-isolated America, which, he added, has just "carried to a brilliant triumph one of the most *righteous wars* of modern times" (emphasis added; it was the Spanish-American War). Then before discussing specific matters, he made a bow to the prevalent economic doctrine of the trickle-down theory of prosperity; that if the top of the economic pyramid was prosperous, it would trickle down to the workers and farmers at the bottom, the theory which Franklin Roosevelt would later so vehemently repudiate. He devoted more space to labor issues and labor legislation than to any other subject, thus demonstrating the fact that the Governor now realized that labor in New York State was a problem which had to be met; it could no longer be dismissed either with the pious reasoning of self-help or the denunciation of labor leaders or agitators. The message served as an inspiration to labor in its struggles to better conditions, and it was so hailed by most of the wage earners of the state.

Although he did not forsake his old view that "each man's salvation rests mainly with himself," and that "no amount of legislation or organization can supply the lack of individual initiative, energy, honesty, thrift and industry," he did add some of his newer views about unions and even about direct help from the state: He stressed the need for enforcing the existing New York legislation about hours of work for women and children, industrial safety and sanitation, and hours of work for males on street railways; and he recommended the creation of a Board of Factory Inspectors to have the responsibility for such enforcement, and also an additional number of factory inspectors. He condemned "sweatshops" and deplored the difficulty of enforcing the legislation which had been already passed in New York "prohibiting the use of dwellings for the purpose of manufacture." He recommended that a permit or license be issued for all buildings used for manufacture, and that the enforcement of the eight-hour per day law for state employees with the prevailing rate of wage be lodged with some state agency. And he emphasized the importance of the Board of Mediation and Arbitration in settling labor disputes and preventing strikes and lockouts.

Certainly there was nothing radical about any of his message, although its philosophy was in advance of, and negated many of, his convictions as an assemblyman. Not for several months after inauguration did Roosevelt do anything to disturb Platt's complacency; but when he did, it created a substantial disturbance.

The feathers began to fly when Roosevelt started to put his full weight behind a bill, introduced by a Democratic senator, John Ford, to tax—for the first time in the state's history—the value of all franchises which the street railway, gas, electric and water companies had received in the State of New York. Roosevelt added his own recommendation of a specific tax on the earnings resulting from the franchise. His old friend and adviser Elihu Root, who was counsel and lobbyist for a gas company, made remonstrances, but the Governor brushed them aside politely. He sought to explain his views in a letter to Platt, who was alarmed and outraged, and who had objected strenuously: "Ought there not be some arrangement by which, if the franchises prove very valuable, a portion of the gross earnings should be paid to the public treasury?"

"I have no sympathy whatsoever with the demagoguery against corporations when these corporations render public service," Roosevelt explained to a state senator, "but where by act of the legislature and through taking possession of a part of the public domain the corporation gets advantages, it should be taxed for them in some intelligent way."[48] All this seems rather impeccable—even conservative—reasoning today; but it was quite revolutionary in 1899, indeed practically unheard of. Roosevelt later called this fight to tax franchises "the case of most importance in which I clashed with Senator Platt . . . and was the first step I ever took toward bringing big corporations under effective governmental control." His presidency was to be one such "step" after another.

In addition to Platt, all the big business lobbies were galvanized into action. At the same time, however, the small landholders, farmers and householders who saw that their own taxes would be decreased if utilities could be taxed, began a counter-lobby in the legislature, which made the outcome seem gloomy to Platt and his business colleagues. Roosevelt lost no time in appealing to this self-interest of the people to rally them behind the cause—as he was later to do time and again in his own effective style.

He describes the legislative struggle which followed: "I had made up my mind that if I could get a show in the Legislature, the bill would pass, because the people had become interested and the representatives would scarcely dare to vote the wrong way. Accordingly, on April 27, 1899, I sent a special message to the Assembly, certifying that the emergency demanded the immediate passage of the bill. The machine leaders were bitterly angry; and the Speaker actually tore up the message without reading it to the Assembly. That night they were busy trying to arrange some device for the defeat of the bill—which was not difficult, as the session was about to close. At seven the next morning I was informed of what had occurred. At eight I was in the Capitol at the Executive Chamber, and sent in another special message, which opened as follows: 'I learn that the emergency message which I sent last evening to the Assembly on behalf of the franchise tax bill has not been read. I therefore send hereby another message on the subject. I need not impress upon the Assembly the need of passing this bill at once.' I sent this message to the Assembly, by my secretary, William J. Youngs, with an intimation that if this were not promptly read I should come up in person and read it. Then, as so often happens, the opposition collapsed and the bill went through both houses with a rush."[49]

The *Autobiography,* however, neglected again to mention two important additional facts in the struggle. First, he stated, "After I was elected governor, I had my attention directed to the franchise tax matter." He does not give any credit at all to Senator Ford (a Democrat) for actually having drafted and introduced the bill. And second, Roosevelt omits the fact that on March 27 he had recommended the creation of a legislative commission to study the whole tax structure, including franchise taxes, and to report to the next session—a step which was immediately condemned and denounced by Senator Ford as a shrewd device to avoid a showdown with Platt in 1899. While Roosevelt at the time denied this vehemently, he did say that "the Ford bill was badly drawn and was so crude a measure as to provoke a revolt or else be inoperative." He does not explain in the *Autobiography* or any place else why he reversed himself within a short time about his proposed legislative committee as the close of the legislature drew near, and threw all of the power of the Executive Chamber and the aggressive personality of its occupant into the fight to pass the Ford Bill. He finally succeeded in passing it, in spite of Platt, the utilities, the lobbyists—and all.

There ensued a very interesting and telling exchange of letters between the Governor and Platt in which this excerpted statement is important:

"It seems to me that our attitude should be one of correcting the evils, and thereby show that, whereas the Populists, Socialists, and others really do not correct the evils at all, or else only do so at the expense of producing others in aggravated form, on the contrary we Republicans hold the just balance and set ourselves as resolutely against improper corporate influence on the one hand as against demagogy and mob rule on the other. I think it is in the long run the only wise attitude. . . ."[50]

This statement about the "just balance" was the foundation of Roosevelt's later style as President until the last two years. He would think of the proper function of government as maintaining a just balance between management and labor, between producer and consumer, and between the extremists at both ends. It was the underlying concept of what he was to call the "Square Deal"— impartiality and fairness to both sides of legitimate antagonisms. Toward the end, and, more pronouncedly, during his years as leader of the progressive movement after his presidency, he realized that government's role in order to attain social justice had to become more active than that of a mere umpire. When the legislature adjourned, Roosevelt with thirty days within which to sign or veto the bill showed the great skill he had acquired as a political in-fighter. The bill was actually objectionable, because it put the power of "taxation in the hands of the local county boards, and as railways sometimes passed through several different counties, this was inadvisable."[51] The opposition urged him to veto the bill on that ground; but he knew that if he did, he would have great difficulty getting a new bill passed. Roosevelt did not mention another and more compelling reason for finding it "inadvisable" to give the local counties the power: that in New York City, Tammany Hall would have this great power over Republican business. Instead of vetoing the bill therefore, he called a special session of the legislature. He then told Platt and the other protestors that if the special session passed a new bill vesting the taxing power in the state where it belonged, he would sign it and veto the Ford Bill; otherwise, he would sign the Ford Bill in spite of its imperfections. This was an ingenious maneuver; and after much protest, many threats and attempts by opponents to get further amendment, it succeeded. A new bill was drafted, passed and signed.

The new law was condemned by the *New York Times* as the "robber baron science of taxation ruthlessly applied," and by the Brooklyn *Eagle* as "communistic" and "an invasion of Bryan's vocabulary, or an infringement of geographical rights of use and sale in Bryan's territory."

But Roosevelt's style *vis-à-vis* corporate financial power was now set—and would never be abandoned. This milestone law was an example and precedent of progress in reaching for economic justice. It definitely set Roosevelt apart from the leaders of his own party, and also from the then governing philosophy of his party—the philosophy of laissez-faire in corporate financial power.

Roosevelt's handling of the franchise tax was not the only controversial matter in his term as Governor. Labor legislation and union activities provided plenty of controversy with lobbyists for employer organizations who sought to block his program. There was conflict on this subject even within Roosevelt's own mind. His attitude toward labor and labor unions began to take on a more realistic coloration; but he continued to be obsessed by the fear of strikes and violence like those of the Haymarket riots and the Pullman and Homestead episodes.

As the first session got under way, the trade unions of the city, the Consumer League of New York and other civic organizations began to bring pressure on the legislature to outlaw labor in tenement sweatshops. Roosevelt enthusiastically joined them. His objective was clearly expressed: ". . . That the uneconomic, unwholesome, and un-American sweatshop system shall disappear from our industrial life." Legislation in 1899, as Roosevelt had requested, provided additional inspectors, made it mandatory to obtain a special license for tenements in which manufacturing was conducted, required appropriate labelling of tenement-made goods, and extended the power of factory inspectors. It was the first really effective bit of legislation against the sweatshops in New York State.[52]

The difficulty became one of enforcement. Roosevelt made several inquiring trips to the tenement districts. He was the first Governor of New York ever to make such inspection trips. He also met with labor union officials to draw up better civil service examinations for inspectors. While Roosevelt realized the difficulty of adequate control of the evil, he followed his usual style of trying as hard as possible. "We cannot be excused," he told the legislature, "if we fail to cut out this ulcer; and our failure will be terribly avenged, for by its presence it inevitably poisons the whole body politic and social."[53]

He finally decided that the best way to attack the sweatshop problem was to set up a new tenement house commission, representative of many groups, to draw up legislation to help "those who are least able to protect themselves and whom we should specially guard . . . from the rapacity of those who would prey upon them." He pressed hard for this commission, and finally got it in 1900. To it he appointed men who had the experience and ability and the courage to create something new. And out of it finally came the much-heralded and renowned Tenement House Law of 1901, which outlawed further construction of the "old-law" tenements in New York City and Buffalo, and set up new standards of light, air and sanitation. If he had done nothing else as Governor, this great accomplishment in the improvement of tenement house living would have earned him a respectable place in gubernatorial history.

But where strikes were concerned, Roosevelt had not as yet mellowed much from his earlier days; and his good labor record as Governor was spoiled by his style in strikes. The prevailing prosperity during the period of Roosevelt's governorship, as the nation moved out of the Depression of the mid-nineties, caused a great increase in the membership of unions—and a new batch of strikes. In 1899 and 1900, more strikes in New York and in the nation were successful than in any previous period in American history.

There were several examples of his continuing trigger-happy style when strikes occurred. Roosevelt used police to club down a strike on the Metropolitan Street Railway Company which had been called to protest the absence of enforcement of the ten-hour-a-day law. In a strike in which about 7,000 men were engaged on the docks of Buffalo, there was no violence of any kind, but the stoppage was causing wheat to pile up in the harbor. Roosevelt wrote: "When trouble was anticipated just now in Buffalo, I at once sent Major General Roe out there and got the whole brigade of National Militia in the neighborhood in shape to be used immediately. The labor men came up to protest. I told them instantly that I should entertain no protest; that the militia would not be called out unless the local authorities stated that they needed them; but that the minute this condition was found to exist, they would be called out, and that I should not consider for a moment the protest that this was 'intimidating the labor men,' because it would not intimidate anyone unless he was anxious to commit lawlessness and that in that case it would be my especial care to see that he was intimidated."[54]

Strikes by laborers on the Croton Dam in Westchester County had been called on several occasions to protest working conditions, shamefully low pay, and extortion by employers on food, shelter and transportation; but the sheriff and deputies had always been able to break them. In 1900 a new and larger strike was called. Here again, there was no actual disturbance; but the leaders of the strike warned that the very presence of troops would result in ending the calm and would probably produce bloodshed. The sheriff of Westchester County finally called for assistance by troops. Roosevelt jumped to respond by rushing up from New York City 1300 infantry and cavalry troops with full equipment. They set up camp under the name of "Camp Roosevelt." In fact, however, there was no rioting and little violence until the troops came. In a short time, one of the troops was killed by a bullet from a source never identified. Roosevelt's condolence message to the soldier's family spoke eloquently of his attitude on strikes in 1900. He said the dead soldier was on a "roll of honor side by side with the names of those who died in open battle with their country's foes." The strikebreakers at Croton were protected by the troops. Large gatherings of strikers were forbidden. The ringleaders of the strike were arrested. Finally when in spite of all this the strikers refused to go back to work, a new crew was installed and the strike was over.

Roosevelt in both years pressed for employers' liability legislation in "dangerous occupations," emphasizing, however, that though "liability of employers to employees is now recognized in the laws of most of the great industrial communities of the world . . . employers ought not to be burdened to such an extent as to endanger ordinary business transactions."[55] He did not get this law for which labor was particularly anxious passed, but he did get several others—enough to say truthfully that he had fulfilled his campaign promises to labor.

Instinctively he felt that something had to be done about economic inequalities. This new T.R. put his thoughts in a letter to a lieutenant of Platt:

As for my impulsiveness and my alliance with labor agitators, social philosophers, taxation reformers and the like, I will also go over all these questions with you when we meet. I want to be perfectly sane in all of these matters, but I do have a good deal of fellow feeling for our less fortunate brother, and I am a good deal puzzled over some of the inequalities in life, as life now exists. . . . I would a great deal rather have no change than a change that would put a premium upon idleness and folly. All I want to do is cautiously feel my way to see if we cannot make the general conditions of life a little easier and a little better.[56]

Above all, his style as Governor was to discuss matters with labor leaders as equals, and to remain on friendly terms with them. He could not yet divest himself, however, of his almost automatic reaction in the case of strikes, even peaceful strikes. He could not yet realize that to an embittered group of workers laboring under inhuman conditions and starvation wages, the very awareness of troops watching them was a provocation to violence rather than a deterrent. As he left the governorship, he was disappointed that labor still was not in his political camp in spite of his determined efforts to help them.

Another element of style which Roosevelt developed as Governor, and would continue as President, was his reliance for advice on intellectuals and experts. Platt objected to these associates as "visionary reformers." But Roosevelt felt the need and saw the benefit of expert advice—just as much as Franklin Roosevelt would later. He wrote to the president of Cornell University: "I have come to the conclusion that I have mighty little originality of my own. What I do is to try to get ideas from men whom I regard as experts along certain lines and then try to work out those ideas."

Following this program, Roosevelt formulated that part of his second Annual Message as Governor which dealt with trusts in collaboration with Arthur T. Hadley, the president of Yale, and with two college professors, as well as Elihu Root and James B. Dill, who had drafted the New Jersey statute on holding companies. The proposed message had been shown to Platt and to Odell, then the Republican State Chairman. Odell asked Roosevelt to modify the trust sections for it might drive industry out of the state; he also asked for modification of some other portions. Platt was also opposed to parts of the message. Roosevelt compromised a little, but stood firm on the corporation section.

It does not require an expert in literary style to see that the trust part of the message was a collaboration with others. Indeed it is so different from the stilted style of the rest of the message and the style in general of Roosevelt's writings and speeches during this period that it has all the earmarks of having been entirely ghost-written. During his presidency, Roosevelt's style was going to be forceful on this most vital issue.

Roosevelt did not succeed in having any of his recommendations on monopolies and trusts enacted while Governor. But he had put the whole subject intelligently, succinctly and clearly into the public forum, had crystallized his own thinking on the subject and pointed the way to important reforms he would achieve in this field later as President. Needless to say, these unprecedented views emanating from the Executive Chamber were anathema to Platt and to big business. Platt was beginning to realize that his job now was to get Roosevelt out of that Executive Chamber—in fact out of the state. It was not going to be easy; but Platt (much to Roosevelt's *ultimate* benefit) would find a way.

One of the other big clashes with Platt arose also in connection with big business. It involved the appointment of the Superintendent of Insurance, whose position "made him a factor of immense importance in the big business circles of New York."[57] Roosevelt, when he came to the Executive Chamber, found in the superintendent's office a "veteran politician and one of Mr. Platt's right-hand men," Louis Payn. Payn's term was to expire in 1900; and before the legislature met in January 1900, Roosevelt announced that he was not going to reappoint him. His chief reason was Payn's alleged close relations with various men of high finance in Wall Street, leading to some surreptitious moneymaking for himself. But Roosevelt, in order to get the old superintendent out, first had to get his successor confirmed by a Senate, which unfortunately the Republican machine, with the assistance of Tammany, could control with an overwhelming majority. Until confirmation took place, Payn, under the law, would remain in office. Platt insisted on the reappointment of Payn, and the deadlock continued between Platt and the Governor until shortly before the end of the session. Here again, the "pretended reformers," as Roosevelt called them, were giving the political boss comfort and assistance by "loudly insisting that I must make an open fight on United States Senator Platt himself and on the Republican Organization." Wilson and Franklin Roosevelt were to suffer in this same way from extremist reformers who always wanted a fight for perfection rather than acceptance of what was possible in substantial reform; but they would seldom be as vocal about it as Theodore. Theodore Roosevelt knew that such a personal or factional fight with Platt would be hopeless. By now, he was no longer a political amateur—as were the "pretended reformers"—and he offered to compromise again by suggesting to Platt "two or three organization men whom he would be willing to appoint," just as he had done with respect to the selection of a Superintendent of Public

Works the year before. Platt still insisted on Payn—or nobody. Roosevelt offered to appoint another man, this time a really close personal friend of Platt. Again Platt refused, threatening a fight which he predicted would destroy Roosevelt and possibly the Republican Party as well. Roosevelt persisted in not naming Payn. Finally, at the very last minute, Platt gave in.

Historians have all recognized this dilemma of Roosevelt *vis-à-vis* Platt. It constituted what Professor Binkley has called "a game of wits between two semipros. . . . As governor, instead of committing political suicide, he did enough tightrope walking to learn not to lose his balance."[58] In an article which Roosevelt published during his governorship (*Century,* June 1900), he explained the flexibility of his style in dealing with Platt as well as with the giants of industry: "Sometimes it is a sign of the highest statesmanship to temporize." This was quite an advance from his intransigent days. Telling a friend how he had succeeded in handling Platt, he coined a phrase which would thereafter always be associated with him: "I was entirely good humored and cool in my dealings with Platt . . . I have always been fond of the West African proverb: 'Speak softly and carry a big stick, you will go far.' "

Another incident in connection with the insurance business was to set Roosevelt's style for the rest of his political life in his attitude toward mere bigness in business as an evil in itself. A bill was pending in the legislature during the 1900 session to limit the aggregate volume of insurance which any New York company could undertake. Roosevelt, predisposed to favor this type of legislation, was giving it very careful study. He finally decided that the many real evils which existed in the business of writing insurance "could not be eradicated by limiting or suppressing a company's ability to protect an additional number of lives with insurance." On the other hand, he was busy gathering data for a large program of corrective legislation regulating the insurance companies. This had nothing to do with size alone, and he expected to recommend it in his next term as Governor —for which, however, he was never to run. This question of corporate size as an evil per se was regarded by him in the same way after he became President.

One of the greatest and most lasting accomplishments of Roosevelt as President was to come in the field of conservation. This too did not spring up in the White House overnight. Like so many other of his later Presidential policies, conservation had become a fixed part of his style as Governor. In his first Annual Message, he discussed the forests of the state, saying that the forest reserve as it then existed "would forever be a monument to those who first founded it," urging the acquisition "of additional land with emphasis on the essential need both for the land then in the reserve and for future acquisitions of land to preserve . . . and protect it, not only against the depredations of man, but against the most serious of all enemies to forests—fire." In his second Annual Message[59] he spent even more space on the question of protection of fish, game and forests from man and from fire. Other conservation recommendations were made: lumbering must be permitted only on the basis of scientific management of the forests; the state should not permit factories which use bird skins or bird feathers to be made into ornaments or wearing apparel; game protection must be expanded and enforced. He also recommended something that we now take for granted, but which might possibly never have happened—that the beautiful and dramatic Palisades of the Hudson River should be preserved for all time in their natural state; and that New York and New Jersey should each appoint a commission to meet in joint session and lay plans for the preservation of the twelve miles of Palisades.

Roosevelt had neither the desire nor the intention to leave Albany after his first term. He wanted to be re-elected, and to finish many things which he had started. He could look back upon a record of substantial accomplishment which must have increased his desire for a second term. In addition to the measures already discussed, he had sponsored bills to limit many of the existing corporate privileges and practices; he had signed a state statute prohibiting combinations in restraint of trade. Although he had failed to secure legislation for compulsory publicity of corporate activities and records, he had signed bills which regulated the corporate use of "other peoples' money," such as the investment policies of savings banks; and he had signed a bill which opened corporate stock books for inspection by stockholders and creditors. He had obtained a new Civil Service Law. Although he did not get an employer's liability law or state control of employment agencies, as he had tried, he had secured additional labor legislation to make effective the eight-hour day and prevailing wage scales in state government work; enforcement of the law regulating hours of labor on street railways; stricter protection against industrial hazards of injury; reduction of hours of drug clerks; the first state hospital for incipient tuberculosis; and some bills to help farmers and consumers, such as prevention of adulteration of food products.

The State of New York under his leadership had definitely moved away from laissez-faire. By 1900, Roosevelt, at the age of forty-two, with a long experience of politics and public office—an experience often marked by inconsistencies and reversals of opinion but always showing a steady growth—was now ready for the development of the fundamental principles of the Square Deal.

In his *Autobiography* he explained his triumphs over Platt in terms of his ability to appeal to the people directly for approval of his policies when he found them floundering against the solid walls of the machine—an ability and style which he was to use time and again as President:

". . . I made up my mind that the only way I could beat the bosses whenever the need to do so arose (and unless there was such need I did not wish to try) was, not by attempting to manipulate the machinery, and not by trusting merely to the professional reformers, but by making my appeal as directly and as emphatically as I knew how to the mass of voters themselves, to the people, to the men who if waked up would be able to impose their will on their representatives. . . .

"In theory," he continued, "the Executive has nothing to do with legislation. In practice, as things now are, the Executive is or ought to be peculiarly representative of the people as a whole. As often as not the action of the Executive offers the only means by which the people can get the legislation they demand and ought to have. . . ."[60]

As early as January 1900, during the impasse between the Governor and Platt over the reappointment of Louis Payn as Superintendent of Insurance, Platt had suggested to Roosevelt the Vice-Presidential nomination on the ticket to be named at the Republican National Convention later that year. Roosevelt did not recognize that what Platt really wanted was again to get rid of him in New York, and to put him in as innocuous a place as possible—and, at the time, no appropriate position seemed less dangerous to political bosses or to the economic status quo than that of Vice President. Roosevelt told Platt flatly that he did not want to be Vice President. But his legislative program as well as his firm independence during his first term as Governor had been quite enough for Platt. He seemed to be unable to control this Governor in the style to which he had been accustomed.

The last thing he wanted was two more years of the same. When finally the reasons for Platt's eagerness dawned on Roosevelt, he wrote Lodge:

... The big-monied men with whom he [Platt] is in close touch and whose campaign contributions have certainly been no inconsiderable factor in his strength, have been pressing him very strongly to get me put in the Vice-Presidency, so as to get me out of the State. It was the big insurance companies, possessing enormous wealth, that gave Payn his formidable strength, and they to a man want me out. The great corporations affected by the franchise tax have also been at the Senator. In fact, all the big-monied interests that make campaign contributions of large size and feel that they should have favors in return, are extremely anxious to get me out of the State.[61]

The more clearly he recognized Platt's real motives, the more stubbornly he resisted, and the greater became his determination to run for a second term as Governor. He told the press that he would rather return to private life than become McKinley's running mate. He even went to Washington to repeat his resolve personally to McKinley himself and to the Republican national boss, Mark Hanna. But Platt persisted. Roosevelt was pressured on all sides. The Western states were making a bona fide move to draft him for Vice President; he was even threatened by Platt that he would not be renominated by the New York Republican Party as Governor. He was told that if he refused to run, the Western voters who idolized him, and who were loudly demanding him, would probably turn to Bryan (which to Roosevelt was indeed a horrendous prospect); acceptance was put up to him as a matter of party duty. McKinley and Hanna, who had been less than enthusiastic about him on the ticket—in fact they made an initial effort to keep him off—finally announced that they were willing to accept him. Eventually he succumbed.

Once the nomination was made (in one of the few instances in our history of a bona fide draft), Roosevelt in his characteristic style left all reservations behind and plunged into action. And what action! He campaigned as no Vice-Presidential candidate before him had ever campaigned. He felt he was chosen to lead a kind of holy war. The "cause" in 1900, as it had been in 1896, was Republicanism and all that it involved: the gold standard, the high tariff of protection, big business, imperialism and expansion in world affairs. The "cause" was, above all, opposition to Bryan and the Populists. Roosevelt campaigned as if he were in a crusade, because he really believed that he was. President McKinley, on the other hand, retired during the campaign to his home in Canton, Ohio, and from his front porch delivered an occasional speech of generalities and platitudes. Roosevelt therefore had a free hand—or took it—in defining the issues on which the Republican Party would go to the polls. He lost no time in doing this. Abandoning the Rough Rider antics of his gubernatorial campaign, he adopted and presented as his criterion of administration for the next four years his own struggles and accomplishments as Governor. He visited twenty-four states on trips which totalled 21,000 miles. He had long ago completely forgotten any physical disabilities, and undertook the gruelling pace of the campaign saying to Hanna: "I feel as strong as a bull moose."

There was much general moralization in his speeches about the duties and responsibilities of America, and the crowds fairly ate it up. They flocked to see him, his energetic forceful gestures, to listen to his strong language, his shrill fervor, his blatant patriotism, his violent denunciation of Bryan, the Populists, Altgeld, isolationists, and all those who "insulted the Flag" by opposing expansion and fulfillment of the American destiny. He now fully recognized his ability to move vast masses of humanity with his sermons on good Americanism, and he took advantage of it, revelling in the enthusiastic roars of approval from his audiences across the nation.

Even while Roosevelt was Governor he had felt called upon from time to time publicly to discuss foreign affairs far beyond his jurisdiction. He had then expressed the views which would become the basis of his style as President. In February 1899, for example, he delivered an address at the Lincoln Club dinner (to which he gave the title: "America's Part of the World's Work"). In it he pointed out that the war had brought us new duties in the West and East Indies. "We cannot," he said, "with honor shirk these duties." He explained what these duties were—showing not only the expansionist style he was later to use, but also his racial sense of white superiority:

"It is the idlest of chatter to speak of savages as being fit for self-government . . . and it usually covers another motive—it means that people are afraid to undertake a great task, and cover up their fear by using some term which will give it the guise of philanthropy. If we refrain from doing our part of the world's work . . . it will have to be done by some stronger race, because we will have shown ourselves weaklings. . . . It is infinitely better for the whole world that Russia should have taken Turkestan, that France should have taken Algiers, and that England should have taken India. . . . And the same reasoning applies to our own dealings with the Philippines. . . . They must be made to realize . . . that we are the masters."[62]

In October of 1899 in Cincinnati, he paid his respects to what he called "The Copperheads of 1900"—those Americans who were anti-imperialist and anti-expansionist and who, he said, gave moral support to Aguinaldo, who was then leading an insurrection against the U.S. in the Philippines. He condemned Aguinaldo's "apologists" in the United States as the natural successors and imitators of the Copperheads of the Civil War. He said the "anti-expansion" movement was synonymous with "anti-American and anti-patriotic movement." "We are no more imperialists," Roosevelt insisted, "than Sam Houston who annexed Texas, or the pioneers who founded Marietta, Ohio."

In campaign speech after speech, he hammered home the contentions that free silver would bring ruin and chaos to the industrialist, the farmer and the worker in equal share; that legislation to control the trusts or giant corporations should be advanced with caution, without "indiscriminate denunciation of corporations generally"; that the first step to correct the abuses inherent in large aggregations of financial power was "to find out the facts; and for this purpose publicity as to capitalization, profits, and all else of importance to the public is the most useful measure." He added to the necessity of publicity the use of the taxing power and regulation and close supervision—in summary, everything he had done or tried to do in the State of New York. No one who listened to or read his campaign speeches of 1900 should have been surprised by his actions when he succeeded to the presidency.

In foreign affairs, his themes were bitter and denunciatory toward all aspects of Bryanism: We must expand and take our place among the world powers; he went so far as to equate the Louisiana Purchase by Jefferson—the statesman he disliked so thoroughly—to the conquest of the Philippines; he ridiculed the naïve protestations of Bryan about "the consent of the governed" in the Philippines; he defended imperialism and expansion as the duty of America.

Not until the day of his death did Roosevelt give up his style of extremism in campaign speaking. In 1900, he carried it so far that even Mark Hanna took occasion to reason with him and suggest that he modify his violent style a bit. As an example: "It is a terrible and most lamentable truth that our soldiers who are now facing death in the Philippines are forced to recognize in the Bryanistic Democracy their most dangerous foe. . . . No Tagal general, not Aguinaldo himself, can do as much to prolong the fighting, can do as much to increase the bloodshed of American and Filipino alike, as had been done by the Kansas City Democratic Convention."[63]

In all his campaign speeches of 1900 ran the recurrent theme that the United States had at last come out of its isolation and was becoming a world power of greatness—and the resolve to "march forward, to fresh triumph . . . to do the work which Providence allots us . . . to win honor and renown as has never had vouchsafed to the nations of mankind."

The extremist rhetoric which Roosevelt used almost smothered the one important constructive proposal he made during the campaign in domestic matters, the one which was to play so large a part in forming his style as President— regulation of corporate big business. In spite of its vagueness, it did much to counteract the unfavorable reaction of many independent voters to the blatant deference which McKinley had displayed to the huge corporate interests, and to attract younger and more progressive men to the Republican Party.

Mr. Pringle in his Pulitzer prize-winning biography of Roosevelt (p. 159) points out an ironic coincidence in the newspapers following Inauguration Day, March 4, 1901. The front pages told about the great enthusiasm aroused by the newly elected Vice President, and that everyone's spoken or unspoken question was whether he would be the nominee for President four years hence. On the inside page of the newspapers of that day, there appeared an announcement of the formation by J. P. Morgan of the United States Steel Corporation. It would be only a matter of months before the papers would be filled with the news of the battle between the young man on the front page and the venerable founder of the young corporation on the inside page.

While Roosevelt was Vice President, he had little or nothing to do. Practically all of the letters he wrote in that period were dated in Oyster Bay. This lack of action for one who has been called "pure act" naturally increased his aversion for the office. It also gave him time to think about the future election of 1904 when McKinley would have served a full two terms.

On September 14, 1901, a bullet relieved Roosevelt of the position he did not want and had fought so hard to avoid—and catapulted him into the White House as President of the United States.

In addition to his vast political experience, Roosevelt brought with him a very clear and definite conception of the presidency. It was very different from McKinley's, his predecessor, and from Taft's, his successor. Nothing is as determinative of a President's style as his conception of the presidency, for most of the important things he does in office depend on that conception.

In his *Autobiography*,[64] Roosevelt explains at great length his concept, and the difference between it and that of many other "high-minded Presidents."

"The most important factor in getting the right spirit in my administration was my insistence upon the theory that the executive power was limited only by the specific restrictions and prohibitions appearing in the constitution or imposed by Congress under its constitutional powers. . . .

"I declined to adopt the view that what was imperatively necessary for the nation could not be done by the President unless he could find some specific authorization to do it." This view he called the Buchanan-Taft doctrine.

"My belief was that it was not only his [the President's] right, but his duty to do anything that the needs of the nation demanded unless such action was forbidden by the Constitution or by the laws." This view he called the Lincoln-Jackson doctrine.

The difference between the two doctrines is what separates the "weak" President from the "strong" one.

"Under this interpretation of executive power," he continued, "I did and caused to be done many things not previously done by the President and the heads of the departments. I did not usurp power but I did greatly broaden the use of executive power. . . . I acted . . . whenever and in whatever manner was necessary, unless prevented by direct constitutional or legislative prohibition."

On the occasion of the anthracite coal strike discussed later, when a congressman, learning of Roosevelt's daring plan to seize the mines, objected on the ground that the Constitution forbids the taking of private property for public use without due process of law, Roosevelt fairly shrieked at him: "The Constitution was made for the people and not the people for the Constitution."

His theory has often been referred to as the "stewardship" theory; the phrase was his own:

"Occasionally," he said, "great national crises arise which call for immediate and vigorous executive action, and . . . in such cases it is the duty of the President to act upon the theory that he is the steward of the people, and . . . that he has the legal right to do whatever the needs of the people demand, unless the Constitution or the laws explicitly forbid him to do it."

In the field of foreign affairs particularly, he would bypass Congress without hesitation unless it was legally impossible to do so. In 1906 when he was seriously considering intervention during a Cuban insurrection he told Taft that he would "not dream" of asking Congress for authority to do so. In fact, he did *not* ask for the authority; but he *did* intervene. He felt that making foreign policy was the President's job—an attitude which all modern strong Presidents take—pointing out that a legislative body was "not well fitted for the shaping of foreign policy." The foreign policy of his two administrations was definitely all his own.

Theodore Roosevelt held the same theory of Presidential powers as Wilson and Franklin Roosevelt after him, and as Jackson and Lincoln (and Hamilton) before him, namely, that all the executive power vested in the federal government by the Constitution belongs to the President—subject only to the checks expressly given by the Constitution to Congress. As he proceeded to run the government more and more by executive order, Congress, which for thirty-five years had dominated the presidency in both foreign and domestic matters, became alarmed. It expressed its concern by a formal resolution. The resolution requested the President to file copies with Congress of his executive orders, together with a citation of the particular statutes under which he issued them. This resolution, which clearly implied that a Presidential executive order had to have a statute authorizing it, was in itself an interpretation of the executive power in direct variance with Roosevelt's. Needless to say, it was ignored by the President.[65]

For five months after taking his oath of office, Roosevelt did nothing startling —which in itself was an aberration of his style. But Wall Street still felt uneasy, worrying whether the unexpected calm in the White House was merely the kind which usually precedes a storm. Roosevelt had himself said he was going to follow McKinley's policies; and the editorials of the conservative newspapers seemed to be whistling to keep up their courage as they praised Roosevelt's apparent sympathy with McKinley's policies. They also cited his strict loyalty to a party which still embraced all the principles of McKinley, a loyalty which they said was so strong as to preclude any individual radical judgments. If there was to be any substantial change, Wall Street naturally expected to be consulted, or at the very least informed about it, in advance; for that is what McKinley and his post-Civil War predecessors nearly always had done.

Nothing showed more dramatically the role of Wall Street in White House affairs than the fact that while the new President was drafting his comparatively innocuous first Annual Message to Congress of December 3, 1901, J. P. Morgan sent two of his partners to Washington, George W. Perkins and Robert Bacon, to look figuratively over his shoulder while he wrote—with the objective of persuading him to speak softly and to forget about the big stick. Some other men helped also: A. J. Cassatt, the president of the Pennsylvania Railroad, Senator Mark Hanna and Senator Nelson Aldrich (both conservative Republicans) and the Secretary of War Elihu Root. The message had more of their style than of Roosevelt's, especially where big business and trusts were concerned. It berated all attempts at hasty, broadside attacks on corporations. It stressed the necessity of calm study and of restrained action. But it did recognize that there were some evils which had to be corrected, one of the chief being "over-capitalization." "There is widespread conviction, in the minds of the American people," he wrote, ". . . that combination and concentration should be, not prohibited, but supervised and within reasonable limits controlled; and in my judgment this conviction is right." He reverted to the theories of his gubernatorial message of 1900 in asserting that the first essential was to get all the facts—by publicity. But he ominously added: "What further remedies are needed in the way of government regulation, or taxation, can only be determined after publicity has been obtained." Very significantly, he pointed out the inability of the several states to regulate these huge corporations, and expressed confidence that a constitutional law regulating them by the national government could be framed.

There was no mention of the possible use of the Sherman Antitrust Act in connection with any trusts. It was quite a bombshell therefore when the Attorney General suddenly on February 18, 1902—two months later—announced that he had been directed by the President to proceed under the Sherman Antitrust Law to break up the Northern Securities Company. The complacent world of the big industrialists and financiers had not the slightest intimation or expectation of this extreme kind of action.

The attack of President Roosevelt upon the Northern Securities Company certainly justified Mark Hanna's gloomy foreboding, as McKinley died, that "anything could happen now that that damn cowboy" was President.

Morgan was not a man who was accustomed to White House hostility, or even to White House independence; nor was he ever too shy to express his resentment. Twice he came down to Washington personally to suggest to the President of the United States that any alleged illegality in the formation of the Northern Securities Company would be "fixed up" by a conference between the Attorney General and the Morgan lawyers. This suggestion was turned down by Roosevelt calmly and quietly; and Morgan then came to the point which interested him even more deeply than the Northern Securities Case. What was the President going to do about Morgan's other interests, particularly his new United States Steel Corporation? Was he going to attack them too? Roosevelt apparently adopted the same "cool" style he had used in Albany with Tom Platt. "Certainly not," he answered, "unless we find out that in any case they have done something we regard as wrong."

It is not easy even today when certain aspects of this situation still exist to grasp the extent of the grip combinations of economic power had upon the economy of the republic in 1901, and the power which their concentration of wealth had over the processes of government.

Following the Spanish-American War, and largely because of it and the expansion of territory which ensued, farm income rose; employment grew; and above all, industrial production rose at a startling rate. In fact, American industry for the first time began seriously to compete with the industry of the rest of the world. Within the two years of 1898–1900 the United States had become an empire whose geography stretched halfway around the globe. The expansion had its effect on American industrial growth. Even more important was the form of organization big business was adopting under benign laissez-faire government since the end of the Civil War. "Trusts" as early as the eighties had become a common word in the American language; and the term in its normal usage by the people was always one of opprobrium. To the consumers of the nation, trusts were organized to raise prices without restraint. To the workers of the nation, they were organized to reduce wages. To the small businessmen of the nation, they were organized to wipe out all competition. Nearly every citizen, except a comparative handful at the top, felt substantially and continuously the evil effects of the operations of trusts.

Roosevelt saw all this very clearly. The rapid growth of these combinations in restraint of trade which the Sherman Act of 1890 was supposed to stop was frightening. By 1902 all the railroads of the country—which had the power to make or break shippers (including the shippers of farm products) by manipulation of freight rates—had been combined into only five or six groups of management. The men in control were well known: Vanderbilt, Gould, Morgan, Hill and Harriman. The story was essentially the same in industrial consolidation. Within three years after the Spanish-American War, there had been set up the copper trust, the tobacco trust and the steel trust. The Thirteenth Census of the United States reported that by 1909, 44 per cent of all of the manufactured goods in the United States was being produced by only 1 per cent of all the industrial firms. The trusts even began expanding overseas into international cartels.

But dangerous and obnoxious as this transportation and industrial concentration was, an even greater peril lay in the burgeoning financial control by the giants of Wall Street over all industry and transportation. Three or four great Eastern investment banking houses closely associated with some of the largest commercial banks and insurance companies in New York City were in charge of a pool of capital which controlled and regulated the credit resources of the United States to a degree at least as great as the Federal Reserve System does today. They were the ones who usually originated and generated the formation of the new trusts, and who made sure that they alone controlled the boards of directors and the management of the new corporations. The result was a money trust whose tentacles reached from Wall Street into every part of the United States and created a power which in some respects was greater than the power of the government itself. That this should alarm the ordinary citizenry was not surprising; but it even alarmed the conservative and generally complacent Congress into setting up an investigative joint congressional commission in 1898 to look into these trusts and the extent of their dangerous concentration.

It found many evils but did very little to remedy them: the gradual abolition of competition either by swallowing up competitors or eliminating them; grossly watered capitalization; and stupendous fees and commissions for promoters paid from the proceeds of the sale to innocent investors of this watered stock. Indicative of the huge profits of these trusts was the disclosure by this commission that the annual dividends of the Standard Oil Company for the past decade was 40 per cent per year. The wealth—and consequent power—of those at the top was swollen each year by the absence of any graduated income or death taxes. In 1900, there were about a dozen men at the peak of this vast pyramid; and among them there stood out one dominant gigantic personality—John Pierpont Morgan. The Pujo Committee reported later, and the facts seem to be beyond dispute, that Morgan had the power almost single-handedly to create or prevent national panics, depressions and various types of financial disaster. He was appropriately known on the Street as "Jupiter." At least twice Theodore Roosevelt would have to turn to him to assist the White House stave off catastrophe after the President had tried alone, and had failed.

At the same time, the differentiation between classes of citizenry in America which had given rise to violence in the last two decades of the nineteenth century, but which had been temporarily subdued in the national unity which attended the Spanish-American War, arose again and became exacerbated. Organized labor, with its rapid growth of membership and power, had become concentrated in the American Federation of Labor. Its membership in 1897 was about 25,000; by 1900, it was doubled; by 1904, it was 1,676,000. As it grew it increased its strike activities, in many of which there were violence and death. Immigration was producing overcrowded cities at an alarming rate. During the decade and a half after 1900, more than 13 million immigrants arrived—with racial, religious and cultural characteristics taken from their places of origin—no longer from northern and western Europe but from Italy, Poland, Russia and Austria-Hungary. At the bottom of the economic pyramid in the America of the Roosevelt administrations were the disenfranchised and "second-class" Negro citizens, the poorly paid unskilled American laborers, and the illiterate and impoverished immigrants—all living either in rural slums or in the squalor of city tenements.

The tensions of antagonism between growing industry and growing labor, between the city and the farm, between the "natives" and the new immigrants provided part of the milieu in which Theodore Roosevelt took on the duties and responsibilities of the presidency. It was, of course, a far cry from the conditions of 1933 which Franklin D. Roosevelt was to face on his first Inaugural Day; but it had dangers of its own which Theodore could see and measure, and which he had the courage, activism and political wisdom to try to meet. The style of every President is necessarily related to the conditions of society which he has to face. Theodore Roosevelt was no exception.

Roosevelt, through his Attorney General Philander Knox, sprang his anti-trust action with the same style of secrecy and surprise as Franklin Roosevelt was to use in his Supreme Court plan in 1937. Not even Elihu Root or Lodge or Mark Hanna had heard of it in advance. Nor had the big senatorial four been told. But there was this vital difference: Franklin's plan depended for success upon action by Congress; Theodore's plan was purely executive. He apparently had concluded that an independent assertion of executive power would best serve to show that *he* was the President, and that he intended to act as a President within his own broad conception of the presidency. The only way open to him to meet the entrenched capitalist monopoly was by the statute which, ironically, had been passed by an equally conservative Republican Congress (with not much expectation that it would be actively used) ten years earlier. Roosevelt must be credited as the first President to see how great a threat to American economic life was posed by monopolies. It is doubtful that he failed to see also the powerful and favorable political effect this bold executive action would have upon the great mass of American citizens. It was clear notice to the world that the McKinley style of partnership between the White House and the powerful men of big business was now at an end. In a reference on August 14, 1904, for example, to the Northern Securities Case, Roosevelt in a letter explained why he considered it so important: "The Northern Securities case is one of the great achievements of my administration. I look back upon it with great pride, for through it, we emphasized in signal fashion . . . the fact that the most powerful men in this country were held to accountability before the law."[66]

Roosevelt built his Presidential career on his willingness and ability to fight the alliance—which he was convinced was an unholy one—between Big Business and Big Bosses. The action indicated a style of government by executive action which Roosevelt would use whenever he could. This landmark antitrust proceeding resulted in complete victory for the government in the United States Supreme Court, which affirmed the order of the lower court dissolving the trust. The national popular elation at the mere announcement that the Northern Securities Case was to be filed, and the even greater enthusiasm and satisfaction which greeted the action of the Supreme Court, testified to Roosevelt's ability to judge the temper of the people. Politically it was a ten-strike!

This successful antitrust proceeding was followed by another one—equally successful—against the meat trust in the corporate person of Swift & Company. During the remainder of his two terms, the Attorney Generals of the Roosevelt administrations started dissolution proceedings, obviously with his approval if not at his instigation, against forty-four of the largest industrial combinations in the country, including the Standard Oil Company, the American Tobacco Company and the DuPont Corporation. The decisions in these cases put at rest the original legal contentions of the trusts that regulation of corporations was the responsibility of the several states, and not of the national government.

Theodore Roosevelt deserves the nickname which was applied to him of "trust buster." But his real interest in trusts and his objective in handling them was not in "busting" but in regulating them. Busting a trust meant dissolving it into the component parts which had joined together in forming the trust, or compelling the combination to divest itself of one or more parts which it had acquired by purchase or merger or exchange of stock. It would restore competition by recreating competitive units. Regulating them was a different concept. The combination would remain intact, but the government would supervise the issue and sale of its securities, examine and publicize its records, impose restrictions on repressive practices such as rebates and preferential treatment of some customers, assure adequate taxation of its assets and incomes, protect minority stockholders from the majority, impose fairness in the election of directors, and so on.

Roosevelt thought—and often repeated publicly—that the development of large corporations was inevitable in the modern industrial era, and even beneficial; and that the process could not, and should not, be stopped, but that it should at all steps be carefully controlled. He repeated this philosophy clearly in his second Annual Message of December 1902: "Our aim is not to do away with corporations; on the contrary, these big aggregations are an inevitable development of modern industrialism, and the effort to destroy them would be futile unless accomplished in ways that would work the utmost mischief to the entire body politic. We are not attacking the corporations, but endeavoring to do away with any evil in them."[67]

He was politically wise enough to know, however, that middle-class and working Americans would hail his frontal attacks on the very existence of trusts; and he continued them. His success in "busting" trusts did not unduly deter his efforts to get regulation. The mild proposals for regulation contained in his first Annual Message were completely ignored by the Senate leadership. But Roosevelt, in his usual style, took his case to the people immediately: "I achieved results only by appealing over the heads of the Senate and House leaders to the people, who were the masters of both of us."[68]

Roosevelt's decision to use the Sherman Law was—per se—typical of his style. For it was purely executive action; and he always preferred executive action, in which he did not have to make any request of Congress. When Roosevelt became President in 1901, both houses of Congress had safe Republican majorities—nearly all of the members of which were conservative. The influence and power of the lower House had nearly all shifted to the Senate. The controlling group in Congress during the McKinley administration consisted of members of the Senate, and their leaders were Nelson W. Aldrich of Rhode Island, John C. Spooner of Wisconsin, Orville H. Platt of Connecticut and William B. Allison of Iowa. They were the "powerful four" of the Congress. Aldrich was their leader, and he was known as the "Boss of the Senate." The title was an apt one. There were other very powerful figures in the Senate—Mark Hanna of Ohio (who was also the chairman of the Republican National Committee), Matthew Quay of Pennsylvania, Henry Cabot Lodge of Massachusetts, Tom Platt of New York, Joseph B. Foraker of Ohio. They all had one identical characteristic: a conservative economic and social viewpoint, dominated by allegiance to the interests of big business.

The House of Representatives until 1903 acknowledged quite frankly the leadership of the big four. In 1903, however, Joseph G. Cannon, a rough and able politician, became Speaker; he was determined to regain for the House the power and prestige it used to have. He succeeded; and he soon became a veritable czar of the lower house. Legislation was passed by it only with his approval. Even the powerful four of the Senate became careful to consult him. Until 1910 he ruled the actions of the House as few Speakers ever have. He, too, was deeply conservative, and believed thoroughly in the status quo.

The Democratic Party, which might have been expected to provide some opposition to the conservative majority, was without effective leadership; and it lacked any kind of cohesion. The only possible challenge to the views of Congress lay in the very young man in the White House. This solid wall of congressional conservatism and devotion to the status quo should be borne in mind in assaying the efficacy of Roosevelt's onslaught upon it with his progressive recommendations. It was really worse than a Democratic majority in Congress would have been. For he had to be careful not to attack or divide his own party, and at the same time persuade it to go along with many reforms with which it did not agree. Roosevelt's style *vis-à-vis* Congress proved to be more successful than the line-up of economic and social views among its members would lead anyone to expect.

He had already learned as Governor that the most important way to translate programs and ideas into action was through the legislative mill. Unless he could take action by executive order, the "mill" therefore received his major time and attention while it was in session. But he had also learned that to enact a program his own party had to be used as the chief instrument. He would try now and again successfully to do it against his own party's wishes; but this was more difficult. The surer way was not an open fight with the bosses of the party, nor an open fight to reform the party (as 1912 would again prove). It was to recognize, without catering to, the political congressional bosses, to arouse and marshal public opinion behind him, and to use adroit maneuvers against them in their own game. Roosevelt seemed to have a kind of genius in his style of coaxing or threatening from an unwilling Congress—especially from the Senate where opposing special interests were most powerful—bills which he wanted and which the Congress did not.

The Presidents who came before him and after Lincoln generally regarded the legislative field as outside their own domain. The founding fathers, in their view, had set up a Congress to deal with legislation, and legislation should be left to the Congress. True, the Chief Executive had a check. Roosevelt was the first President in forty years to realize that to be a "strong" President, he had to become an integral part of legislation and of the legislative process at nearly every stage. Only in this way would he be able to accomplish anything substantial in the way of reform. Congress on the other hand was perfectly satisfied—nay, enchanted—with the status quo, and wanted no change.

"In theory," Roosevelt wrote: "The executive has nothing to do with legislation. In practice, as things now are, the executive is or ought to be peculiarly representative of the people as a whole. As often as not the action of the executive offers the only means by which the people can get the legislation they demand and ought to have."[69] Reform, action, progress—all required the loud firm voice of a President, the only "steward" that the American people had. And there was much more required than a loud voice; there had to be leadership, tenacity, boldness of the lion and at the same time the caution and cunning of a fox, popular personal appeal, strategic and tactical flexibility, knowledge and experience with the legislative process, willingness to cooperate and to compromise as well as to fight with congressional leaders, the power of persuasion—as well as intimidation —of congressmen, the ability to use pure threats and to "work with the devil" to get what he wanted, the energy to arouse public opinion—yes, even flattery, cajolery, horse trading and the political use of minor patronage. They were all necessary qualities for a successful operator in the White House; and they were displayed in abundance in the style of Theodore Roosevelt—sometimes one, sometimes many, sometimes all together.

Two later twentieth-century Presidents expanded the role—Wilson and Franklin Roosevelt—to the point where the White House would send up proposed bills for enactment and carefully watch every detail of them as they came up for discussion. Professor Clinton Rossiter points out that each of these modern strong Presidents came to the presidency fresh "from a successful term as the governor of a progressive state," where each had been successful in leading the legislature; and "that each came [to the White House] at a time when the state of the Union demanded that new laws be placed on the books; none was strangled by wearing the old school tie of either house of Congress."[70] The revolution in the relations between the President and Congress was fostered by each of these men—and their success with legislation is one of the most important criteria the American people use in measuring the success of their Presidents.

Theodore, unlike Franklin Roosevelt, did not come to power at a time of deep national economic misery which provided a massive popular wave of demand for revolutionary measures. Nor did he have, as Franklin would have, a Congress so frightened by a calamitous depression that it was ready to give the President any legislation, any power, that he asked for if only the President would take the responsibility.

The progressive movement in America was just beginning in 1900. Theodore Roosevelt, as much as any other man, was able to dramatize it and start it to swell until it finally became the crusade of 1912. The growth of the progressive movement was itself an enormous influence on the conservative Congress, and helped Roosevelt get his reform legislation. But he had to be cautious with Congress— sometimes almost timid—and to practice always the art of the possible rather than of the desirable, in a manner which Franklin was not obliged to follow in 1933. Theodore knew he could do nothing without the congressional leaders, that he had to work with them—and he did. His greatest skill was in knowing how to work with them and, at the same time, bring pressure against them, sometimes amounting even to intimidation. His most potent weapon against Congress was his ability to create a strong public opinion to support him. And in arousing it, he would not hesitate to use all the tricks he knew: for example, in order to get more battleships he would speak publicly about the grave possibility of an early war with Japan—although his private letters of the same period show that he did not believe war could come in the near future. He would, as another example, publicly use the threat of proposing tariff revision in order to get some other pieces of legislation, although his private letters clearly show that he did not think revision at all desirable or even possible, and that he personally did not want it. This failure to obtain any general tariff revision during his entire presidency can be mentioned as one of his major failures in public service. His success with the Hepburn Act (discussed later) showed how powerful his political strategy could be, how it could combine the lion and the fox, and what a great operator he was in the way he used everything he had learned about political maneuvering to get the legislation he was after.

While he always proclaimed that he believed in the essentiality of great power for the Chief Executive, he had also been educated in the actualities of political realism by a profound reading of American political history, and by the rough and tumble of political participation for more than twenty years. He recognized and respected the political responsibilities to their own constituencies of those with whom he worked, especially congressmen. In his horse trading with them he never forgot their own political problems; they in turn recognized this fact and it helped Roosevelt in his bartering with them. In formal meetings he was just as careful to be courteous as he was careful to respect senatorial courtesy in making political appointments. Behind the scenes, however, he would use all the weapons a strong President has. He was willing to trade on his popularity even though he knew that he might thereby possibly reduce his popularity. He once wrote a newspaper editor of his "contemptuous amusement over the [current] discussion about his popularity or waning popularity or absence of popularity." "I am not a college freshman," he wrote, "and therefore I am not concerned about my popularity save in exactly so far as it is an instrument which will help me to achieve any purposes."[71]

Roosevelt's relations with "Uncle Joe" Cannon began long before Cannon succeeded Thomas B. Reed as Speaker of the House. Cannon was chairman of the House Appropriations Committee when Roosevelt was civil service commissioner, wanting "more clerks, more money and [seeming] rather annoyed and not a little surprised that his modest requests should not be instantly granted. . . . In the Navy Department he was always asking for more, for no matter how large the navy was, it would never have been quite large enough for him. . . . In those early days there were some lively passages between the youthful Civil Service Commissioner and the young Assistant Secretary of the Navy, breezy, impetuous in the attitude of his own inerrancy, and the older, more deliberate and experienced chairman, having no private ends to serve but always with his eye on the balance sheet."[72]

But those who predicted that the door to the White House, always open to Cannon during the McKinley administration, would be closed to him during Roosevelt's were wrong. In spite of their dissimilarity of views, which widened until there was a complete break during the last year of the second administration, there was great intimacy between them, for they were joined by a mutual abiding faith in the Republican Party.

After "Uncle Joe" became Speaker, he conferred two or three times a week with the President when Congress was in session—and sometimes daily. He did not particularly like Roosevelt personally; and he cared even less for his progressive policies. Yet they got along together almost to the very end. Roosevelt always respected Cannon's political judgment, especially on the feasibility of passing legislation, or of making a reasonable legislative compromise. He frequently sought Cannon's advice—and did not hesitate to ask him, frankly on a personal basis, for his help. Cannon later stated: "At times I had the impression that Roosevelt was using me as a means of either meeting opposition to one of his theories by arguing the question, and at other times [sic] of clarifying his own views by thrashing out the subject from every point of view. . . .

". . . I think Mr. Roosevelt talked over with me virtually every serious recommendation to Congress before he made it, and he requested me to sound out the leaders in the House, for he did not want to recommend legislation simply to write messages. He wanted results, and he wanted to know how to secure results with the least friction. He was a good sportsman and *accepted what he could get* so long as the legislation conformed even in part to his recommendation. (Emphasis added)

"It was at times difficult to deal with Mr. Roosevelt because he did annoying things. I recall two incidents that were decidedly embarrassing."[73] One was when he called in two newspaper correspondents and told them that he held in his hand exact copies of telegrams sent by John D. Rockefeller to senators opposing "any anti-trust legislation" (see page 82). After the bill was passed, "an investigation demonstrated that the Rockefeller telegrams originated in the brain of the President."

"An episode no less sensational occurred in February 1906."[74] The President on that occasion apparently leaked a letter which he had written to the Speaker, marked "personal and confidential," but which authorized him to show it to the chairmen of the Committees on Appropriations, Naval Affairs, and "such other Republicans as you think advisable." The letter, says Cannon, "gave an indefinite presentation of possible trouble with the Japanese, and urged increased appropriations for the defenses of the Pacific coast and at Pearl Harbor, and a larger authorization for the navy."[75] However, the committees, not agreeing with the President, did not report an increase. Whereupon Representative Hobson of Alabama—a Democrat and an enthusiastic advocate of a large Navy—produced a copy of the "confidential" letter from the President to the Speaker, and showed it to several Democrats, one of whom happened to be in the confidence of the Speaker. The two letters were compared and found to be identical except for the omission of the first sentence which authorized the Speaker to show the letter to the aforementioned heads of certain committees and other Republicans. Uncle Joe wrote, "Mr. Hobson was embarrassed, but he frankly apologized to the Speaker for the use he made of the letter and said he had been tricked."[76] Mr. Roosevelt—generally violently opposed to all Democrats—was willing to use them whenever it was helpful to him, and especially when he was at odds with his own party leaders.

He understood the use of congressional power as thoroughly as he did executive power. He knew who wielded power in Congress, and what made these men of power "tick." And he succeeded in finding a style of relationship with them —polite but not cordial—which until the last year of his tenure produced substantial agreement on many pieces of legislation. Roosevelt's style *vis-à-vis* Congress constituted a realistic approach to legislation; it was to consult in advance many of the congressional leaders in addition to the Speaker, in order to see what he could reasonably expect. He frankly said so in many letters, for example:

"Take the tariff speech . . . it not merely presented my carefully thought-out views, but those of men as diverse in feeling as Hanna, Spooner, Aldrich and Allison. In financial matters, I do not want to find that I am asking for something which the leaders of the party in Congress violently oppose; unless, of course, absolutely necessary. . . . I should not like to commit myself to details, for instance, until I found how far the next speaker of the House, Joe Cannon, would go with me."[77] And again, to his friend, Bishop, ". . . but of course in all my utterances I have to bear in mind not only what I believe, but what I can get the heads of the party in the House and Senate to adopt."[78]

This does not mean that once he found the leaders against him, he just gave up. If that had been the case, he would have accomplished little indeed—and would not be counted among the great or near-great Presidents. In bringing pressure to bear for passage of legislation, he did not hesitate, if necessary, to appeal even to the House of Morgan. For example, he wrote George W. Perkins, a partner, on December 26, 1902, in connection with the Department of Commerce bill: "Will you not at once try to get whatever influence you can bear on Henderson on its behalf."

He was particularly quick to feel the sensitivity of Congress about its own prerogatives in foreign affairs. That kind of sensitivity has always existed in Congress, and has been greatly magnified by the actions of American Presidents since 1960. Roosevelt was careful not to allow it to reach a boiling point. During the height of the activity in Panama and other parts of the world, which he was carrying on without consulting Congress, "Uncle Joe" Cannon came to see him. When he left, Roosevelt dictated a letter to his Secretary of State of which this is an extract:

"Uncle Joe Cannon was in this afternoon and was very nice indeed, but evidently slightly nervous that the prerogatives in Congress in foreign affairs should be overlooked by us. I told him I would ask you to keep in close touch with Congressman Hitt and consult with him on any point where there would be a chance of Congress feeling that it had power of action . . . Congress is evidently prepared to be a little sensitive on the subject, and we might as well forestall possible criticism."[79]

Roosevelt kept a watchful eye on the progress on the Hill of all legislation he wanted. He would communicate about pending bills directly with all of the powerful leaders—often in forceful terms—and he sought their advice and, more often, their help on legislation. He frequently asked for suggestions in the actual drafting of legislation as well as his proposed messages to Congress. This was definitely a part of his style, and the Morison compilation of his letters is full of examples.[80] It not only gave him practical help; it also flattered the leaders and served to soften any later or earlier blows which he had used.

All of these qualities of legislative leadership he displayed in his fight for corporate control of the huge corporations, the recommendation for which the Congress of 1901 had so contemptuously rejected. He made his "appeal over the heads of the Senate and House leaders," for the legislation all through the year of 1902. The theme of his appeal was to remain the same for the balance of his tenure: "We do not wish to destroy corporations, but we do wish to make them subserve the public good." He found that all around the country, wherever and whenever he spoke on the subject, the people approved. Heartened and encouraged by this approval, he renewed his recommendations for control in his second Annual Message, but with much more vigor. In language similar to the later words of Franklin Roosevelt, he said:

"This country cannot afford to sit supine on the plea that under our peculiar system of government we are helpless in the presence of new conditions. . . . The power of the Congress to regulate interstate commerce is an absolute and unqualified grant . . . I believe that monopolies, unjust discrimination which prevent or cripple competition, fraudulent over-capitalization, and other evils in trust organizations and practices . . . can be prevented under the power of Congress to regulate commerce among the several states."

With masterful understatement, he made clear the threat he could exert without asking Congress, by executive action under the Sherman Law. "The Congress," he said, "has not heretofore made any appropriation for the better enforcement of the anti-trust law as it now stands. . . . Much more could be done if the Congress would make a special appropriation for this purpose." Of course the Northern Securities Company Case had not yet been decided at the time of this message. The opinion in that case in 1904, however, definitely put an end to any doubts about the constitutional correctness of Roosevelt's position.

He repeated his recommendation of the first Annual Message for the creation of a new Cabinet post, to be known as the Secretary of Commerce and Industries, to deal with questions "affecting labor and capital . . . and the steady tendency toward the employment of capital in huge corporations. . . . The creation of such a department would in itself be an advance toward dealing with and exercising supervision over the whole subject of the great corporations doing an interstate business."

This was Roosevelt's ultimate program. But consistent with his style of willingness to compromise for what was possible, he settled for legislation giving him his new Cabinet post of Secretary of Commerce and Labor, a Bureau of Corporations in the new Department with power to inspect and partially publish corporate activities and earnings, his bill to forbid rebates to big shippers, and his bill to increase the Attorney General's power to expedite antitrust actions. By no means did this legislation signify the solution of the trust problem. But it did establish precedents showing that executive power could be made available to cope with the ever-growing expansion and complexity of corporate organization and power. Theodore Roosevelt was the first President to demand that the authority of the national government be exercised to lessen economic inequalities and to insist "that we must abandon definitely the laissez-faire theory of political economy and fearlessly champion a system of increased government control." This was the core of the thinking behind the later New Deal, the Fair Deal, the New Frontier and the Great Society. Roosevelt showed the way and paved the road which Wilson and Franklin Roosevelt and Truman would follow in moving the control of American enterprise from Wall Street to Washington and in restoring the influence of the elected representatives of the people over the industrial and financial activities of monopolies. Wall Street was at last brought under some limited measure of control by Theodore Roosevelt. It would succeed from time to time in the twentieth century in slipping away from Washington; but those executives who were willing and able to exercise strong Presidential power could re-establish control—as in the years following March 4, 1933—and always without curbing private initiative or abolishing the private profit system of free enterprise. Theodore Roosevelt laid the modest tentative beginnings of what the New Deal was later to prove massively: that political democracy could be used to modify and improve the economic system.

Roosevelt was a strong executive but one who as an administrator wanted results more than neatness and order in style. He was as completely unorthodox in administration as he was in so many other facets of his presidency. We have seen him in many administrative posts—very minor as compared with the White House—in which he showed his impatience with all the red tape, obstruction and slow motion of an orthodox bureaucracy. He yearned to be the sole boss and the sole occupant of the center of the stage; and he showed those predelictions to his board colleagues—whom he considered frustrating to his own energy, skill and indefatigable motion. He wanted to make all the decisions himself. All of this style he transferred to the White House. He ignored the usual chain of command, and just as he frequently bypassed the State Department in foreign affairs, he frequently ignored his Cabinet heads in domestic affairs by consulting or corresponding directly with officials way down in the departmental hierarchies. He ran the Army himself; he ran the building of the Panama Canal himself—in spite of Taft's nominal jurisdiction as Secretary of War over both; and, of course, he ran the Navy himself. When Congress refused to give him certain powers in the building of the Canal—such as concentrating all authority in the hands of one man, Goethals—he did it by executive order in spite of Taft's reservations about the legality of this course, and in spite of many public protests. The famous voyage of the American Navy around the world was secretly arranged in all its details by him—in consultation with the naval officer who was to command the expedition.

Roosevelt would reach for his information on which to base policy decisions wherever he could get it, and would not rely only on his departments to furnish it. Indeed, on occasions, he would even ask some newspaper men to check on the operations of one of his departments out in the field. Just as he had once said, when campaigning for Blaine for President in 1884, in answer to some of his critics: "It is altogether contrary to my character to occupy a neutral position in so important and exciting a struggle," he might have later remarked with equal truth that it was altogether contrary to his character to occupy a passive role as administrator, as so many of his predecessors had done.

He was often criticized for dealing with some of the more notorious Republican senators and other obnoxious Republican political leaders. He defended this policy in a letter to his friend and biographer, George Haven Putnam of New York, dated November 15, 1904, right after his election of that year, saying he would continue to do this for the next four years:

"I have dealt with [Senator] Quay and with all similar men . . . because, not being a fool, and having certain policies for the welfare of the Republic at heart, I realized that I could succeed in these policies only by working with the men of prominence in the Republican party."

However, he was realistic enough to know to whom he owed his election in 1904. He added in the same letter:

It is a peculiar gratification to me to have owed my election not to the politicians primarily, although of course I have done my best to get on with them; not to the financiers, although I have staunchly upheld the rights of property; but above all to Abraham Lincoln's "plain people"; to the folk who work hard on farm, in shop, or on the railroads, or who own little stores, little businesses which they manage themselves.

But the gentle folk, the people whom you and I meet at the houses of our friends and at our clubs; the people who went to Harvard as we did, or to other colleges more or less like Harvard, these people have contained many of those who have been most bitter in their opposition to me, and their support on the whole has been much more lukewarm than the support of those whom I have called the plain people. . . .[81]

A great deal of information as to his style as President is furnished by himself in his letters. It has been estimated that during his public career he wrote no fewer than 150,000. Copies of these have been preserved, along with those received by him from all sorts of people—politicians, statesmen, heads of state, literary personalities, Prime Ministers, artists, historians, signifying the vast spread of his interests and reading. Much of his hates, his loves, his admiration, his contempts, and his resentments appear in these private letters time and again with a repetition often boring. He seldom minced words, and when writing to people he trusted, he never withheld candid judgments—often taking the precaution to advise his correspondent not to leave the letters around where other people might read them.

Theodore Roosevelt was the first President to recognize the value to himself and to the American people of the press as a means of communication with his constituents all over the United States. Until he became President in 1901, the White House newspaper correspondents had to get their White House stories by standing outside the front door and buttonholing important visitors as they entered or left conferences with the President. The reporters shivered in the cold or roasted in the Washington heat as they waited. The President, with his keen eye and flamboyant interest in spreading the news—his news—via the working press, and also with his interest in reporters as human beings, ordered a small anteroom set aside inside the White House for their exclusive use. Later during his administration, when the Executive Office west wing was added, he made certain that it included an appropriately equipped press room. Thus was the close President-reporter relationship initiated and continued. He was the first to begin to take full advantage of the benefits of publicity through personal contacts with the working press; and as usual he was most effective whenever he could make a personal contact with anyone.

Oliver Gramling, historian of the Associated Press, wrote that "Washington's emergence as the news center of America was one of the notable journalistic phenomena in the first decade of the twentieth century," and he gives as one of the major causes "the vigorous news personality of Theodore Roosevelt who seemed able to dramatize himself or a platform plank with equal ease."[82] According to Mark Sullivan, "Roosevelt's fighting was so much a part of the life of the period, was so tied up to the newspapers, so geared into popular literature, and even to the pulpit . . . as to constitute for the average man, not merely the high spectacle of the Presidency in the ordinary sense, but almost the whole of the passing show, the public's principal interest."[83] Sullivan also quotes a critic of the President: "Roosevelt has the knack of doing things, and doing them noisily, clamorously; while he is in the neighborhood, the public can no more look the other way than the small boy can turn his head away from a circus parade followed by a steam calliope."[84]

He was a prolific letter-to-the-editor writer, either praising or condemning articles he had read; and he would frequently explain his own public policies in detail in those letters. It was his good fortune that the years of his presidency coincided with the development of mass circulation of newspapers and popular magazines; and the man in the "bully pulpit" took full advantage of both. Because he was always on a verbal warpath, it was said that the newspapers kept headlines permanently set with the words: "Roosevelt Flays," followed by a blank space to be filled in with the appropriate name as soon as the Presidential diatribe was delivered.

Roosevelt was the first President to go out of his way to talk frequently with the working newspaper men, give them good stories to print when other news became scarce in the capital and generally to seek their goodwill. It all paid off; no previous President had ever received as much personal coverage as he did. After developing close contacts with the reporters, he used the mass communication which they could provide to bolster his political leadership through public opinion. He knew, and he repeatedly said, that before asking for public support, the public would have to be an *informed* public. It was only the press and his own public speeches which could supply the information; there was no television or radio.

He would meet reporters by casual appointments with them, or would send for one or two by name, or send out word for all who were interested in a certain subject to come into his office at an appointed time. There had not yet been instituted any pattern of formal press conferences on fixed days and hours, which Woodrow Wilson later started. Professor Elmer E. Cromwell described what he calls the only consistent pattern of Theodore in meeting the press as: "the audience granted while the President was being shaved in the late afternoon. Often five or six reporters would meet with him then, drawn both by the opportunity to question the Chief Executive and the skill of the barber, who managed to work in spite of the fact that his client would frequently spring from his chair to emphasize a point or stride up and down the room expanding on a subject for minutes at a time."[85] His bullish ebullience and what James MacGregor Burns has called his "frightening vigor" were not cowed even by the deadly razor.

He knew all the tricks of journalism—and he used them. He would often himself leak facts to the reporters. On at least one occasion the leaked "fact" was intentionally false: the "news" that John D. Rockefeller had sent telegrams to some senators in opposition to Roosevelt's pending rate legislation (see page 82). He would on occasions cunningly use a leak to convey a threat, as when he leaked an intention (which he really did not have) to call a special session of Congress to pass his rate bill. He made frequent use of the trial balloon, which has now become a very popular device of the White House.

The present tradition that all reporters are entitled to be treated on an equal basis had not yet developed; so Roosevelt was able—as his successors were not —to pick the reporters he wanted to see. He acted as his own press agent, often handing out news himself at the White House, and insisting that any White House news issued by anyone else must always be submitted to him for approval. There was no formal press secretary at the time.

He was also the first President to use Presidential trips as a primary source of publicity for himself and as a method of educating the people by speeches about his policies, and of creating a favorable public opinion behind his next move or his last move with Congress. It was one of his ways of advertising his policies as well as himself.

One of Roosevelt's greatest skills in public relations was his ability to dramatize a situation by action rather than to rely on a lecture about his objective. Sending the American fleet around the world was his most dramatic use of this skill. It showed the American people the value of a powerful Navy; and it also showed the Japanese people that we were physically prepared to face them in any rivalries in the Far East. It was more persuasive than any number of speeches or laws. So was his method of announcing so suddenly his new antitrust policy in 1902 by selecting a recent, well-advertised and very unpopular merger like the Northern Securities Company as an object of attack.

In all, Theodore has been adjudged one of the great White House experts in public relations. As a part of that style, he could coin new phrases which "caught on," became popular, and, in turn, accentuated his own popularity and leadership. The list (including some covered elsewhere in this chapter) was a long one: "Speak softly and carry a big stick," "strenuous life," "muckrakers," "malefactors of great wealth," "lunatic fringe," "square deal," "Goo-Goos," and (after he had left the White House and sought to get back in) "My hat is in the ring."

Within the first year of the new administration which had ushered in "trust busting," there came another severe test of leadership—this time in the field of labor and in the form of a nationwide strike. In this crisis Roosevelt showed anew not only his style of decisive action and bold creation of new precedents but also how far he had progressed from the trigger-happy law and order days of quickly sending troops to strike areas. In this new national strike, he again made plans to send troops, but not in order to quell any violence by the strikers or to protect strikebreakers. The purpose of sending the troops under his plans was unprecedented in previous American labor history.

On May 12, 1902, the entire anthracite coal industry came to a standstill as a strike was called by John Mitchell, the president of the United Mine Workers and one of the great labor leaders in our history. Not only were wages too low; hours in the mines were too long; and the dangerous work was too often destructive of life, limb and health. In 1901, there had been 441 fatal accidents and innumerable injuries. There were, of course, no workmen's compensation laws. But there was the usual extortion of workers in the company stores, and the unbelievably squalid conditions in the housing rented at high prices to the miners.

The operators of the mines had refused to make a new contract with the union, had refused even to recognize the union or to treat with it on an industry-wide basis. The coal trust which controlled the mines was particularly powerful because it also controlled the transportation of the coal; more than 70 per cent of the anthracite coal mines were owned by six railroad corporations. Big unionism is the only logical answer to this kind of big concentration of management; but this truism was not yet generally the opinion of the majority of Americans in 1900.

As the strike continued through the spring and summer, coal became scarce and prices rose drastically. By October the shortage of coal was causing physical distress; schools were closing down for lack of heat; the coming of winter threatened sheer disaster throughout the Northern part of the nation. The coal trust, by refusing to transport bituminous coal in its railroad coal cars, removed the one and only possible alternative to anthracite coal. By August, Roosevelt had already been contemplating another antitrust action; but he was advised by his Attorney General that he could not succeed. By September exaggerated newspaper reports of violence in the mining region had begun to appear. The operators continued their arrogant refusal even to negotiate with the union.

Roosevelt finally decided to intervene; but not in his old style. Instead, on October 1, he politely asked the leaders of both sides to meet with him in Washington in the Blair House. We have grown accustomed to this style of Presidential personal intervention in nationwide strikes as almost routine procedure. In fact under the Railway Labor Law and the Taft-Hartley Act, intervention by the President is now mandatory. In 1902, it was unprecedented. But the intervention was clearly an exemplification of Roosevelt's style as the "steward of the people."

When they all met in Blair House, Roosevelt asked both sides to agree, in the interest of the health and welfare of the nation and as a matter of patriotism, to binding arbitration. Mitchell, on behalf of the workers, agreed immediately, asked the President to name the arbitrators, and promised to abide by their decision if the operators would also agree. The operators' spokesman, however, the president of the Philadelphia and Reading Coal and Iron Company, George F. Baer, arrogantly and irately refused at once. Instead, he lectured the President of the United States about wasting everybody's time "negotiating with the fomentors of anarchy," when all that was necessary was for troops to be sent to keep order. Baer was the author of two famous statements during this strike, each of which proved helpful to the strikers at the bar of public opinion. First, that "mining was a business . . . not a religious, sentimental or academic proposition," and second, that "the rights and interests of the laboring man will be protected and cared for —not by the labor agitators but by the Christian men to whom God in his infinite wisdom has given the control of the property interests of this country."

Roosevelt described part of the meeting as follows:

"The representatives of the miners included as their head and spokesman John Mitchell, who kept his temper admirably and showed to much advantage. The representatives of the operators, on the contrary, came down in a most insolent frame of mind, refused to talk of arbitration or other accommodation of any kind, and used language that was insulting to the miners and offensive to me.

They were curiously ignorant of the popular temper; and when they went away from the interview they, with much pride, gave their own account of it to the papers, exulting in the fact that they had 'turned down' both the miners and the President.

"I refused to accept the rebuff, however, and continued the effort to get an agreement between the operators and the miners. I was anxious to get this agreement, *because it would prevent the necessity of taking the extremely drastic action I meditated. . . .*"[86] (Emphasis added)

What a different style from that of Assemblyman, or even Governor, Theodore Roosevelt! By lifting the phone he could at the request of the Governor of Pennsylvania (who was very willing to make the request) have followed Cleveland's example in sending troops during the Pullman strike of 1894—an act which at the time he had so highly praised. Coal would probably have been produced and sold more cheaply in time for the 1902 congressional elections, which were greatly worrying Hanna and Lodge because of the probable reaction of the resentful voters. He did not lift the phone; he stood firm, although by his own description he was at "his wit's end" as to just what he could do to help get coal for the nation.

The episode in Blair House was quite an education for him. He saw in the person of Mitchell what a responsible labor leader was: dignified, firm, respectful, willing to cooperate but not to surrender, ready to listen to reason but keenly alive to the needs of his members. Not quite the "labor agitator" Roosevelt used to castigate! Even more important, he saw what a powerful, respected industrialist could be like: arrogant, arbitrary, disrespectful even to the President, inhuman, interested solely in dollars and even arrogating to himself the role of a deity in handling other human beings.

Roosevelt wrote Hanna that he felt "downhearted" over the result of the meeting between the miners and operators, but added ominously: "I feel most strongly that the attitude of the operators is one which accentuates the need of the government having some power of supervision and regulation over such corporations."[87]

The Governor of Pennsylvania, however, did do just what President Roosevelt had refused to do. Shortly after the failure of the White House meeting, he called out the entire militia of the state. The operators confidently expected that, under this protection, enough of the miners would return to work to produce coal. They were sorely disappointed; the overwhelming majority of the workers remained on strike.

Roosevelt finally determined upon a plan which showed his enlightenment in the field of labor and social justice, and also proved what Henry James had said of him: "He is pure act." He decided to send federal troops into the anthracite coal region (after arranging secretly for the Governor of the state to ask for them), not, however, to intimidate the strikers or encourage them to return to work, but to seize the mines physically and to have the Army run them as if they were in a receivership. He told only two of his Cabinet—Root and Knox—about his plan. He then himself carefully picked the commanding officer to lead the troops; and he energetically laid down all the meticulous details of his plan of action, to take effect when he gave the signal. He would give that signal only if he could not peaceably make the operators come to realize "their own folly." This did not prove necessary as an agreement was reached. "I was greatly relieved at the result, for more than one reason. Of course, first and foremost, my concern was to avert a frightful calamity to the United States. In the next place I was anxious to save the great coal operators and all of the class of big propertied men, of which they are members, from the dreadful punishment which their own folly would have brought on them if I had not acted; and one of the exasperating things was that they were so blinded that they could not see that I was trying to save them not only for their sakes, but for the sake of the country, the excesses which would have been indulged in at their expense if they had longer persisted in their conduct."[88]

This statement about the settlement, like many other statements in his *Autobiography,* written in 1913 when recollection might possibly have become dim (but probably more selective and self-serving), is a little disingenuous—also a frequent characteristic of his style as President. The strike was settled under circumstances many of which Roosevelt does not mention. It is easy to understand why he should gloss over the details of the negotiations which led to the settlement; they show once again the immense power of J. P. Morgan over all phases of American industrial life. The facts are that Elihu Root, the Secretary of War, at the suggestion of the President, went up to New York in his personal, unofficial capacity as a private citizen to talk to Mr. Morgan about the strike. Root told Morgan about Roosevelt's idea for an independent arbitration board, and asked for Morgan's help. Morgan saw the dangers of continued privation and misery throughout most of the nation without coal, and must also have learned about the "drastic action" Roosevelt was planning to take if the strike continued. He sent for the arrogant George Baer, who obediently and quite meekly came up to New York. Two days later, Morgan came down to Washington bringing with him the approval of the operators—with some conditions only as to the membership of the arbitration board to be appointed. These conditions were ironed out, again with Morgan's help; and the strike was over. Morgan had done practically overnight what the President of the United States had tried unsuccessfully to do for months. But this was the first time in American labor history since the Civil War that the federal government had intervened in a labor dispute without automatically helping management. It was in essence a statement by the federal government that labor also had some rights which it could not ignore. This was the essence of the "Square Deal" as the phrase was used during his presidency—giving both sides to a legitimate peaceful controversy equal and fair treatment to protect the rights of both. It was a new style for Roosevelt, and a landmark in the development of his social consciousness. Thus within the first twelve months of his presidency, Roosevelt had for a second time amply justified Mark Hanna's prediction that "anything could happen."

Nothing gave Roosevelt greater room to display his style of executive activism than foreign affairs. Nothing fascinated him more or gave him greater satisfaction. In general, Roosevelt's style in domestic affairs was much more restrained than in foreign affairs. In domestic affairs, while he was intent on fitting individual rights and freedoms into the new industrialism, he was always anxious not to subvert the social and economic institutions of his day. It was to be a gradual, not a precipitate process of reform. In foreign affairs, however, he was aware that a gradual process of evolution would not be sufficient to give America the place he wanted her to have in world affairs. Here, power was all-important; ethical conduct might even be looked upon as weakness. So he acted quickly, independently of Congress, and forcefully—and sometimes with ignoble methods (which, of course, he always self-righteously justified).

As the American national leader in world affairs, he was far out in advance of the mass of his countrymen; but his countrymen followed behind him with pride, enthusiasm and a growing patriotism. He saw clearly the new world struggle for power as the speed of transportation and communication increased, and as American industrialism spilled over into foreign trade to compete with the exploding industrialism of the great empires based in Europe. He had little patience with Americans who failed to appreciate, as he did, the swirl of mighty forces in all parts of the globe and their effect on the United States.

His style in foreign affairs would vary from case to case. At times it was one of a soft voice and of great restraint; at times it was the big stick and an aggressiveness often tantamount to jingoism. Sometimes it was a combination of both. But in no case was it one of retreat, or avoidance of any crisis which might affect the national interests of the United States. In some instances, it was actively to intervene in situations where those interests might in future be furthered—even though the United States had no immediate concern in them. Roosevelt's style of dealing with the major powers of the world would also change from time to time as world events occurred, as different foreign alliances were formed and re-formed and, above all, as the interests of the United States were affected by any change or imminent prospect of change.

In a confidential letter to our new Ambassador to Russia on the eve of his departure for his post, written on February 6, 1905, while the outcome of the Russo-Japanese War still looked uncertain, he laid bare his thinking as of that date (already changed in emphasis, as we shall soon see) about our relationships with the world and the style of foreign affairs we should follow:

I greatly admire the Russian people; but I think the Russian government represents all that is worst, most insincere and unscrupulous and most reactionary, and undoubtedly our people who live in Japan are better treated by the Japanese and have more sympathy with them than is the case with those who live in Russia. I like the Japanese; but of course, I hold myself in readiness to see them get puffed up with pride if they are victorious, and turn against us, or the Germans, or anyone else. However, I do not believe that any alliance with, or implicit trust in, any foreign power will ever save this country from trouble. We must rely upon our own fighting power in the first place, and upon our being just and fair in our dealings with other nations in the second place. . . . Our Navy is excellent. We will have no trouble with Japan, or with Germany, or with anyone else if we can keep our Navy relatively in as good condition as it is now. And if we continue to show that we are honestly desirous to deal honorably and fairly by all nations . . . while yet being ready to defend our own rights if the necessity arises. . . . England's interest is exactly ours as regards this Oriental complication, and is likely to remain so. . . . Moreover at present, the Germans seem inclined to act with us . . . [it is] my belief that the two countries will be able to work together as regards our policy in the Far East. . . . If peace should come now, Japan ought to have a protectorate over Korea (which has shown its utter inability to stand by itself) and ought to succeed to Russia's rights in and around Port Arthur, while I hope to see Manchuria restored to China. . . . I do not believe that Japan has the slightest intention of making an alliance with Russia . . . [but] if the Russians beat her, and she finds that England and America separately or together will give her no help, she may conclude that she has to make what terms she could with Russia.[89]

Much of this letter showed a prophetic vision of the next decade; some of it, such as the recommendation of a Japanese protectorate over Korea, was to lead to far-distant difficulties.

The Alaskan boundary dispute between the United States and Canada (1902–03) provided an example of the style of both the soft word and the big stick. While he consented softly to the English proposal for a commission of six (three to be appointed by each side) to consider the matter and make recommendations to settle the dispute, he announced belligerently at the same time in an interview with an English newspaper correspondent that if gold were discovered in the disputed region (as it later was): "I shall send up engineers to run our line *as we assert it* and I shall send troops to guard and *hold it.*" (Emphasis added) He actually did order Root, the Secretary of War, to move some additional troops "quietly and unostentatiously" into Alaska to be ready. He also let it be known that he would instruct the American members whom he had appointed to the proposed international commission "in no case to yield any of our claims." Nor would he even submit the matter to binding arbitration, as he was so often to urge other nations to do with their disputes. His threat of armed force to "hold the line" was probably the deciding factor leading to an amicable determination wholly satisfactory to Roosevelt.

Even more far-reaching was the big stick diplomacy (1902–03) in Venezuela. This arose out of the failure of Venezuela to meet her obligations to citizens of Germany and Great Britain who had concessions in Venezuela, and to her refusal to pay her debts to the nationals of those countries who had lent her money. The revolutionary President of Venezuela, Cipriano Castro, was later described by Roosevelt as an "unspeakably villainous little monkey." Germany and Great Britain, acting together, imposed a blockade of the Venezuelan coastline. Roosevelt was not fond of either Great Britain or the British at that time. In 1904, he wrote: "The average Englishman is not a being whom I find congenial or with whom I care to associate. I wish him well, but I wish him well at a good distance from me. If we quit building our fleet, England's friendship would immediately cool."[90] However, this style toward England would soon change. He felt even more hostile to Germany—and considered her even then actually dangerous to the United States and its interests. He thought it a possibility, to be vigilantly watched, that Germany and England might form a hostile combination against the United States. With this attitude, Secretary of State Hay was in complete accord. In fairness to the President, it should be pointed out that these were the prevailing views of his countrymen at the time.

The Monroe Doctrine as it was written, and as it was generally understood in 1902, did not specifically condemn coercive action in, for example, collecting just debts; it was specifically directed only to a European country seeking to occupy new territory in the Western Hemisphere permanently. Even Roosevelt, in discussing the Monroe Doctrine in his first Annual Message, had said: "We do not guarantee any [American] State against punishment if it misconducts itself, provided that punishment does not take the form of the acquisition of territory by any non-American power." The German Ambassador to the United States had informed Secretary Hay that Germany would have to take some kind of action by force in Venezuela, because Castro had arbitrarily rejected her offer to have The Hague Tribunal arbitrate her claims. Hay quoted the above excerpt from Roosevelt's message, and raised no objections. The blockade was followed by British and German seizure of Venezuelan gunboats and by bombardment of some harbors. Roosevelt, learning in advance of the British and German proposed armed tactics, selected defensive positions off Venezuela and ordered mobilization of the fleet in the Caribbean under Admiral Dewey. Germany then suggested that the three powers create some kind of joint syndicate which would take possession of the finances of Venezuela—by force if necessary. Roosevelt's reply, after some reflection, was that the American people construed the Monroe Doctrine as including control, and that collection of debts in the proposed manner could be an exercise of control. Germany and Venezuela did finally agree to arbitrate at The Hague. The facts about Roosevelt's role toward the end of the controversy are not clear even at this date. Later, during World War I (in 1915), when public opinion was quite inflamed against Germany, he claimed that Germany backed down and agreed to arbitration only because of an ultimatum delivered by him to the German Ambassador that unless Germany did agree, he would order Dewey and the American fleet to Venezuela.[91] Pringle maintains that, in the light of the formal documents, this version is "romantic to the point of absurdity."[92] Whatever is the correct version, there is no doubt as to the big stick; the only doubt concerns the soft voice.

The same kind of situation soon arose in Santo Domingo, with Germany, Italy and Spain trying to collect debts for their nationals. In addition, violence broke out on the island, Americans were fired upon and some American property was destroyed. This called for action. The dictator of Santo Domingo asked Roosevelt to assume a protectorate over the island. After taking the first step he wrote his son: "Sooner or later it seems to me inevitable that the United States should assume an attitude of protection and regulation in regard to all these little states in the neighborhood of the Caribbean."[93]

On May 20, 1904, as a result of his problems in the Caribbean, the President enunciated the famous Roosevelt Corollary to the Monroe Doctrine. This was first contained in a letter he wrote to Root, who read it at a Cuban anniversary dinner in New York. Later it was formally incorporated in his Annual Message in December 1904 in practically identical language, except that it specifically mentioned action by the United States as "an international police power." It was a bold statement of future policy by the United States toward the debt-ridden, unstable governments of Latin America:

"If a nation [in a neighboring country] shows that it knows how to act with reasonable efficiency and decency in social and political matters, if it keeps order and pays its obligations, then it need fear no interference from the United States," he wrote. But "Chronic wrongdoing, or an impotence which results in a general loosening of the ties of civilized society, may in America as elsewhere, ultimately require intervention by some civilized nation; and in the Western Hemisphere the adherence of the United States to the Monroe Doctrine may force the United States, however reluctantly, in flagrant cases of such wrong-doing or impotence, to the exercise of *an international police power.*" (Emphasis added)[94]

This Roosevelt Corollary, in effect, assumed for the United States an international police power in the Western Hemisphere. Its extent was soon revealed by further Rooseveltian actions. In January 1905, the United States practically compelled Santo Domingo to sign an agreement under which the United States sent an American down to the island as collector of Dominican customs and as director of its national finance. This new agreement was promptly submitted to the Senate for ratification. The Senate turned it down by the votes of a combination of the Democratic minority and some anti-imperialistic Republicans. Undaunted by this senatorial rebuff, which disgusted but did not dismay him, Roosevelt proceeded to do the same thing by executive agreement alone. It was his style, and it worked. The terms of the treaty were put into effect by the President; two years *later* the Senate formally did ratify it. Roosevelt expressed himself quite frankly on several occasions about the treaty-making powers of the

Senate—especially whenever it turned him down.

In the Santo Domingo matter, for example, he wrote: "The Senate is wholly incompetent to take such a part. After infinite thought and worry and labor, I negotiated a treaty with Santo Domingo which would secure a really satisfactory settlement from every viewpoint. The result is that by a very narrow margin, we find ourselves without the necessary two-thirds vote. The Senate ought to feel that its action on the treaty-making power should be much like that of the President's veto; it should be rarely used."

John Hay, the Secretary of State, who had always carried out without question the Presidential directives, died in July 1905. Roosevelt moved his old friend and adviser, Elihu Root, from his post as Secretary of War to that of Secretary of State. With considerably more caution, greater respect for constitutional law, and greater personal influence on the President, Root probably prevented many more similar incursions into Caribbean affairs which Roosevelt wanted to make without Congress.

Roosevelt's style of action in the Caribbean was certainly extra-constitutional. All sensitivity of diplomatic negotiations was bludgeoned out by the big stick. While his policy did help the material well-being of Santo Dominicans and did modernize the Monroe Doctrine, it also signified the start of "Dollar Diplomacy" in Latin America. It created long-lasting resentment throughout the continent which was to continue until the Good Neighbor policy changed American relations with the countries of the Caribbean and Central and South America.

Not even the Venezuelan and Santo Dominican affairs—in fact no other act by Roosevelt—showed so well how far his style of independent executive action would go in foreign affairs as did that of the Panama Canal. He seemed to regard the Caribbean as an American sea, in which America had to keep peace and stability. This was emphasized more and more as he realized how important it was to the United States to get the Canal built and placed under its exclusive jurisdiction. The Panama Canal also illustrates his overwhelming passion to make the United States a great world power, his style of expansionism and imperialism, his impetuous impatience if not actual contempt for weaker nations of the world (especially those in Central and South America), his insistence on acting without the concurrence or sometimes without even the knowledge of Congress, his style of self-delusion and his usual dogmatic certitude about the righteousness and correctness of his conduct at all times, and his propensity to justify his outrageously arbitrary acts by later writings and explanations which did not pay too much attention to the evidence.

Roosevelt's world of 1901 was one of striving by the United States, Germany, France and Japan for commercial aggrandizement all over the globe, in competition with Great Britain's dominating position. These were the "civilized nations" of the world; most of the rest were looked down upon by him as inferior, and some as "semi-barbarous peoples." In such a world, armed might was an essential; and with armed might the civilized nations, he believed, owed an international police duty toward the inferior nations, "which must be performed for the sake of the welfare of mankind." America's new empire after the Spanish-American War had to be protected; dominance in the Caribbean was an obvious necessity; vigilance in the Pacific was essential.

Of course all this had led to the necessity for a larger Navy—a project close to Roosevelt's heart from the early days long before the Spanish-American War. In his very first message to Congress, he discussed proposals to strengthen the

Navy at greater length than any other subject, including even the regulation of corporations. During all his tenure, he constantly kept hammering at the Congress to take action on the Navy with the result that, when he left the presidency, the Navy was easily twice as strong as when he assumed it.

And a canal connecting the two oceans had to be built so that a great American Navy could go from one ocean to the other with ease. Even as Governor of New York, Roosevelt had volunteered some unsolicited and unwelcome advice to Hay, who was also the Secretary of State during McKinley's presidency, about how such a canal should be built irrespective of existing treaties. Under the Clayton-Bulwer Treaty of 1850 between the United States and Great Britain, the canal was originally to have been built as a joint enterprise of the two nations. Roosevelt's unsolicited advice was to ignore this treaty and to build it alone—even if Great Britain did not concur. "A nation has the right to abrogate a treaty," he wrote, in a novel conception of international law, "for what she regards as a sufficient cause." He also added that the canal should be "wholly under the control of the United States alike in peace and war"; otherwise it would in time vitiate the Monroe Doctrine.

A new treaty which did provide for construction and control by the United States and reserved to it the right to fortify the canal was signed with Britain before Roosevelt became President. He mentioned it in his first Annual Message of December 3, 1901. He sent it to the Senate on the same day for ratification; and the Senate did ratify it thirteen days later. Then followed a drama of intrigue, bribery, conspiracy, intimidation, double-crossing, fomenting of revolution and arbitrary use of brute power which resulted in a harvest of long-lasting ill-will toward the United States. It also put a permanent stigma on Roosevelt's own official reputation. But it did get the canal. And it got the canal "wholly under the control of the United States alike in peace and war," just as he had advocated years before he became President. The story of this accomplishment by the big stick still in some of its details holds substantial mystery; and it is too complicated to relate here even partially, except as it showed Roosevelt's style.

After De Lesseps's project to build a canal across what is now Panama collapsed in 1887, attention was directed to an alternative route across Nicaragua. De Lesseps's company receivers then entered the picture under the name of the New Panama Canal Company—the identity of whose stockholders was not revealed at the time and has never been made known since. A highly placed and distinguished Republican lawyer of New York City, William Nelson Cromwell, was engaged by the new company to press its claim to the Panama site, and to obtain payment for the site from the United States if it intended to use it. The lawyer's immediate objective, if the New Panama Canal Company was to have any standing, was to see that the United States did decide upon Panama rather than Nicaragua as the place for the canal. One of the first steps—a very important one—in this highly complicated endeavor was to make a campaign contribution to the McKinley-Roosevelt ticket of 1900 in the sum of $60,000. The agent for the new company was a Frenchman named Philippe Jean Bunau-Varilla—a man of great ability, imagination and resourcefulness, and no scruples. What each of this team (Cromwell and Bunau-Varilla) did in finally arranging all the political, financial and diplomatic moves leading to the ultimate adoption of the Panama site is still not wholly clear. But so far as the Republican Party was involved, as, for example, in omitting from its platform of 1900 a preference for the site in Nicaragua, and obtaining the support of Mark Hanna for the Panama site, Cromwell deserves all the credit. Nature lent a helping hand during the Senate debate by staging a violent volcanic eruption in Nicaragua. The Senate, on June 28, 1902, voted for the Panama site.

Now it was Roosevelt's turn. The Panama site belonged to Colombia. There was no independent nation of Panama at the time; Panama was just a part of Colombia, separated from the capital by many miles of almost impenetrable forest. To Roosevelt's surprise and chagrin, the "inferior" state of Colombia was not so easy to handle. Hay on January 22, 1903, negotiated and signed a treaty with the Colombian minister in Washington, Tomás Herrán, known as the Hay-Herrán Treaty. Under the treaty the New Panama Canal Company was to have received from the United States $40 million, and Colombia $10 million plus an annual subsidy of $250,000 per year; but complete sovereignty of a three-mile zone across the Isthmus was to be given to the United States in perpetuity. This was, of course, derogatory to the sovereignty of Colombia; and the then dictator of Colombia, José Manuel Marroquin, together with the Colombian Senate and the support of the people of Colombia, repudiated the treaty on August 12, 1903.

Roosevelt and Hay were both outraged at this repudiation. Roosevelt did not speak—or even think—"softly" in this matter. He wrote Hay: "Those contemptible little creatures in Bogota ought to understand how much they are jeopardizing things and imperiling their own future." Later, he wrote: "We may have to give a lesson to those jack-rabbits." In spite of some open threats that the United States might again turn to Nicaragua, Colombia stood her ground. Roosevelt's reaction to the formal act of repudiation by the Senate of Colombia was: "The Colombians are entitled to precisely the amount of sympathy we extend to inefficient bandits." There is little doubt that in addition to resisting incursions upon her sovereignty, Colombia was looking for more money. But the additional money she sought was not to come from the United States; it was to come out of the $40 million windfall which Cromwell had helped the new Panama Canal Company get.

To save any part of this money for mysterious stockholders, Roosevelt now entered upon a tactic which could have caused considerable American and Latin American bloodshed, and which certainly violated every fundamental of international law.

Cromwell and Bunau-Varilla began taking some very direct action themselves. They started to foment a revolution in Panama to secede from Colombia. The plan was for Panama, once it became an independent nation, to agree with the United States on the construction of the canal. Roosevelt virtuously refused to join in any attempt like this. This would be "underhanded means," he stated. At the same time he privately wrote that he would "be delighted if Panama were an independent state." He prepared for trouble with Colombia by sending some Army officers (in civilian dress) to examine the coasts and find points of vantage in the event of any conflict in the Gulf of Mexico or the Caribbean Sea.

At the same time, he began to prepare more direct plans. Three days after Colombia formally rejected the treaty, Roosevelt received a very welcome memorandum written by Professor John Bassett Moore of Columbia University, a recognized authority on international law. Roosevelt was getting ready to act on it, because it fitted so well with his views, his aims, and his general style of using the big stick with "backward nations."

Moore's memorandum (which seems to have disappeared for a long time after this) referred to an old United States treaty in 1846 with Colombia (then, and until 1862, known as New Granada) which contained this clause: "the right of way or transit across the Isthmus of Panama shall be free and open to the Government and citizens of the United States," and the provisions of the clause were made applicable to "any modes of communication that now exist, or that may hereafter be constructed." Professor Moore then calmly set at rest any possible doubts as to whether this provision would cover the building of a canal *and* the surrender of so much sovereignty by blandly making a suggestion which he knew would appeal to the President: "Once on the ground and duly installed, this Government would find no difficulty in meeting questions as they arose. The position of the United States is altogether different from that of private capitalists who, unless expressly exempted, are altogether subject to the local jurisdiction. The United States is not subject to such disabilities, and can take care of the future." This suggestion pays greater tribute to Moore's practicality than to his expertise in international law; but it was pure Roosevelt where "inferior" countries were involved. Roosevelt then wrote Hay that if "we have a color of right to start in and build a canal, my off-hand judgment would favor such proceeding." He was always ready to act on a color of right in the case of weaker nations, no matter how diffuse the color might be. His "off-hand judgment" very rapidly developed into a coldly reasoned policy; and by September 1903, he was getting ready to act without further negotiations with Colombia. When Hanna cautioned that patience was necessary, and expressed confidence that Colombia would come around, Roosevelt answered that he doubted that "the only virtue we need is patience." "I feel," he added, "we are certainly justified in morals, and therefore justified in law, in interfering summarily and saying that the canal is to be built and that they must not stop it."

A successful revolution by Panama made it unnecessary for Roosevelt to use the Moore suggestion. If the revolution had not come or had failed, it is fairly clear that Roosevelt would have acted in accordance with it. He had actually drafted a paragraph in October 1903 to be included in his forthcoming Annual Message to Congress recommending this course, or substituting the site in Nicaragua; but he expressly stated his preference for going ahead with the site in Panama "without further parley with Colombia," a course which he described as "the one demanded by the interests of this nation." This was really the "big stick."

Whenever he was ready to use the big stick he usually used big language in advance. He wrote Hay: "At present, I feel that there are two alternatives. (1) To take up Nicaragua, (2) in some shape or way to intervene when it becomes necessary so as to secure the Panama route without further dealing with the foolish and homicidal corruptionists in Bogota. I am not inclined to have any further dealings whatsoever with those Bogota people."

It cannot be shown that Roosevelt incited or even took any part in the "most just and proper revolution," as he described the Panamanian revolt against Colombia; but he certainly knew all along about the activities of Cromwell and Bunau-Varilla who *were* its instigators. During their efforts they both saw Hanna frequently—and they occasionally even saw Roosevelt personally. They shrewdly played on Roosevelt's political ambitions for election in 1904 by pointing out that only speed and boldness could avoid his "coming before the people [in 1904] without a solution of the canal problem." Roosevelt insisted later not only that no one in the government "had any part in preparing, inciting or encouraging the revolution," but also that "his understanding was and is that Cromwell had nothing to do with the revolutionary movement." So far as Cromwell is concerned, all the evidence is to the contrary.

The revolution did occur, with all the drama (and bribery) of nearly all Central American revolutions; and it was successful. Part of the success was due to United States Marines, who landed from warships which Roosevelt had dispatched to Panamanian waters to prevent violence and "maintain free and uninterrupted transit" as provided in the old treaty. On November 6, 1903, Panama became a free and independent nation. Within an hour and a half it was recognized by the United States. A treaty about the Canal negotiated by its first minister to the United States, the indefatigable and resourceful Bunau-Varilla, was signed eleven days later. The treaty gave the United States perpetual control of a ten-mile strip across the Isthmus, authorized the United States to fortify it, and to safeguard the independence of Panama. Panama got $10 million and an annual payment of $250,000 to begin nine years later; the New Panama Canal Company got its $40 million; Colombia got nothing.

Again with his exaggerated sense of self-righteousness, Roosevelt wrote to a critic of his actions against Colombia in the matter of the Canal: "My feeling is that, if anything, I did not go far enough."[95] This unshakable confidence in the correctness of *all* his actions had none of the style of Franklin, who frankly admitted that he could not make a hit every time he came to bat. Theodore was proud of what he had done—so proud that he became indiscreet about it. In an address three years after he left the White House, he boasted: "I took [sic] the canal zone and let Congress debate, and while the debate goes on, the canal does also."

The aftermath of "taking" the Canal Zone is interesting, though not strictly relevant to this book since most of it occurred after Roosevelt left the White House. Colombia felt cheated and outraged; and she continued to press her claim for justice. When Wilson became President, he signed a treaty giving Colombia an official apology for what the United States had done to her—and $25 million. Roosevelt's old hatred of Wilson now reached a boiling point. He said, "The payment can only be justified upon the ground that this nation has played the part of a thief, or of a receiver of stolen goods." He rallied his friends in the Senate to oppose ratification of Wilson's treaty. World War I, however, stopped further action and debate; and in 1919 Roosevelt died.

Harding's administration in 1921 had different fish to fry in Colombia, and needed Colombia's oil to do so. The guiding genius of this new international attitude was Senator Albert B. Fall, who in time would go to prison in the Teapot Dome oil scandal of the Harding administration. Senator Lodge, Roosevelt's closest friend, now spoke on behalf of Wilson's treaty—mentioning all the valuable oil concessions in Colombia which were then going to the British, and pointing out that $25 million would mean fairer treatment for American oil men in the granting of these concessions. The indemnity, he said, "carried no admission of wrong-doing of any kind, but was simply a question of the amount to be paid in consideration of the recognition by Colombia of the independence of Panama."

The controversy about the whole of the Panama Canal negotiations and the disposition of the $40 million which the New Panama Canal Company received from the United States has remained alive to date. There is no doubt that Roosevelt's objective throughout this sordid episode was to promote the interests of the

United States—and that the objective was fully achieved. But a little less activism, a little more patience, deliberation and restraint—and, it must be added, less anxiety about the future political effects in 1904—would have left Roosevelt's reputation in this "most important action [he] took in foreign affairs" considerably brighter.

Roosevelt's ruthless style in "taking" the Panama Canal and his style in the Caribbean generally are closely related to each other. From the beginning, he saw that both the Canal and the Caribbean had much to do with the defense of the United States. Either a canal or a two-ocean Navy was necessary. During the Spanish-American War it had taken the battleship *Oregon* sixty-eight days, running at full speed, to reach one coast of the United States from the other coast —a distance of 13,000 miles—around South America. Obviously, it was imperative that the American Navy be able to get to the Pacific quickly. And also unless the United States took the responsibility of maintaining order in the Caribbean, it would not take too long for the Monroe Doctrine to be reduced to a piece of paper, and the Canal itself might be endangered. For the same reason of national defense, continued expansion by the United States was necessary in the Pacific —as Admiral Mahan had written. As a devotee of imperialism, Roosevelt felt that the nation also had to become a "member of the ruling class." The world was divided into the rulers and the ruled. America must be one of the rulers, if she was to compete with her world rivals.

It was in building the Panama Canal that Roosevelt initiated the style of using a government corporation—the Panama Railroad Company—with its greater flexibility and efficiency, and its ability to make quick decisions on the spot without referring questions back to Washington. The style has been followed since 1904 by both Democratic and Republican Presidents in creating from time to time nearly a hundred government non-profit corporate semi-public agencies.

Roosevelt used the same activism and the same cunning in pressing for his legislation for control of corporations. Business was opposing with all its usual vigor his program for a Bureau of Corporations in the proposed Department of Commerce and Labor. Roosevelt made no attempt to disguise his objectives in setting up this bureau. His candor petrified big business, since he described one of the bureau's proposed functions as to "investigate the operations and conduct of all interstate corporations." The organized lobby in opposition to the proposed bureau was a powerful one, and very well financed. Roosevelt knew that he had to meet that lobby head-on; and his style in doing so went at times to great lengths, even for him. He did not hesitate to use pure falsification. One day, for example, he called in the newspaper men, cautioned them first against revealing the source of what he was about to tell them, and then said that telegrams had been received by several senators from John D. Rockefeller, urging that they vote against the legislation.[96] This was not true; and Roosevelt knew that it was not true. But it raised the public clamor and support that he wanted. Partly as a result of the false story, the legislation was passed in spite of the powerful lobby. It was true that a few telegrams urging defeat of the bill had been sent by John D. Archbold, an officer of Standard Oil Company who might perhaps be considered an agent of Rockefeller. But Roosevelt knew enough about public opinion to realize that the name Archbold was not big enough or sufficiently known to inflame the public mind. So he deliberately, cunningly and unscrupulously substituted the name which was then synonymous with all the evil aspects of industrial monopoly. It was again the use of ignoble means for noble objectives.

Roosevelt was also politically shrewd enough—and enough of a fox—to put a discreet lid on the investigating activities of the bureau provided for in the law until the nomination and election of 1904 were over. He wanted to get all the support he could from corporations in 1904; and he was not going to raise too hostile a finger until his next four-years tenure was assured. This kind of chicanery was a part of his political style whenever it became essential; indeed, to him it was only political realism. Although it did not conform with his many political sermons on uprightness and candor in government, it was one of the factors which made him a Presidential giant.

Political realism also made him dodge during his first term some very perplexing national problems left behind by McKinley. These included tariff reform and currency reform. Roosevelt was well aware in 1902 of the great split in his own party about tariff revision, and therefore, as the national party leader, he had to be careful about the course to follow. He explained on August 12 of that year in a letter to his friend, Nicholas Murray Butler, president of Columbia University, "Now as to the tariff, there is no question there is dynamite in it. There is a wide-spread feeling that it should be altered, but there is equally wide-spread feeling as to what the alterations should be. . . . My hope is that the Democrats will take some extreme position. . . . I hope that when the test comes . . . [the people] will find themselves obligated to choose, not between one policy and all other possible policies, but between two given policies." A hand-written postscript shows the style of a great political leader and operator: "I do not wish to split my own party wide open on the tariff question, *unless some good is to come.*" (Emphasis added) He took the same view toward any radical currency reform, and the panic of 1907 was partly the result of his political opportunism.

As early as July 1902, Roosevelt's correspondence begins to mention his renomination in 1904, and to discuss the best way of bringing it about.[97] His actions generally during his first term—as in the matter of tariff and currency reform—were motivated by his burning political ambition and determination to get elected in 1904 on his own. He carried his caution on the tariff in that election year of 1904 to great extremes for a man of his general style of independence and courage. He wanted no fight which could possibly affect his nomination. As he wrote to a congressman: "What I personally feel is one thing. What I am willing to express for quotation as to the action of the Convention is another thing, for I am not willing to say anything which may seem to conflict with the action the Convention may take. . . ."[98]

Most of his minor appointments in 1904 were political—also aimed at the nomination and election later in that year. After making an appointment of a man whom he had once vitriolically denounced, he described part of his style as a political leader: "In politics, we have to do a great many things we ought not to do." He sought the favor of all the veterans of the Civil War by granting a pension to all over sixty-two years, irrespective of physical impairment—not by getting legislation to that effect but by issuing an executive order.

Roosevelt did his best in spite of his often-expressed views of the superiority of whites over blacks to overcome the "lily white Republicanism" of the South. His style was to seek out qualified Negroes in the deep South for important appointments. He continued this humanitarianism with shrewd political finesse as a deft way of getting Negro votes. For example, he announced that he would appoint a Negro named Roulhac as United States Attorney for the Northern District of Alabama. He even kept William D. Crum, a prominent Republican

Negro leader, as Collector of Customs in Charleston, S.C., by successive interim appointments over the indignant protests of Charleston whites and in the face of the refusal of the Senate to confirm him because of these protests.[99]

The famous luncheon in the White House at which Roosevelt's guest was Booker T. Washington, the Negro leader and the head of Tuskegee Institute in Alabama, was not a social occasion but a purely political one. The furore from white Southerners was tremendous, and went to the ridiculous extreme of accusing Roosevelt of encouraging dangerous concepts of racial and social equality. This did not prevent him from continuing to seek Washington's wise and realistic advice on the appointment of Southern Negroes. His first letter as President was addressed to Mr. Washington on September 14, 1901, calling off his proposed Southern trip because of the death of McKinley and his own accession to the presidency. It added: "I must see you as soon as possible. I want to talk over the question of possible future appointments in the South exactly on the lines of our last conversation together." Answering a letter which congratulated Roosevelt on his luncheon with Washington, Roosevelt in his style of self-righteousness, or in this case more of self-delusion, wrote: "I would not lose my self-respect by fearing to have a man like Booker T. Washington to dinner if it cost me every political friend I have got." Morison, who compiled the letters, notes wryly in a footnote that Roosevelt "did not again invite a Negro to dine at the White House."[100]

His ideas about blacks in 1904 are shown in a letter dated June 8 to Booker T. Washington dealing with his efforts to prevent a "lily white" delegation from Louisiana to the forthcoming Republican National Convention. "The safety for the colored man in Louisiana is to have a white man's party which shall be responsible and honest in which the colored man shall have representation but in which he shall not be the dominant force—a party in which . . . he shall hold a percentage of the offices. . . ."[101]

In a private letter to his friend Owen Wister on April 27, 1906, he reviewed his attitude toward Negroes as of that date:

I certainly agree with you that as a race and in the mass, they are altogether inferior to the whites. . . . It also remains true that a great deal that is untrue is said against . . . [the Negroes] and that much more is untruthfully said in favor of the white men who live beside and upon him. . . . These white men of the South who say that the negro is unfit to cast a vote, and who by fraud or force prevent his voting, are equally clamorous in insisting that his votes must be counted as cast when it comes to comparing their own representation with the representation of the white men of the North . . . this talk about the negro having become worse since the Civil War is the veriest nonsense. He has on the whole become better. . . . All I have been doing is to ask, not that the average negro be allowed to vote . . . but that the occasional good, well-educated, intelligent and honest colored men and women be given the pitiful chance to have a little reward, a little respect, a little regard, if they can by earnest useful work succeed in winning it.

These are hardly like the words of Lyndon Johnson to Congress in 1965: "We shall overcome." But they are quite advanced for the age of Theodore Roosevelt.

His overwhelming ambition to get elected to a second term led him to do many things which he could not look back on with great pride. One of the most important steps he had to take to ensure his second term was to wipe out Senator Mark Hanna's competition for the Presidential nomination. The election of the Republican nominee in that year, whoever he was, seemed fairly well assured. The only doubt was about who would get the nomination. Hanna therefore presented the only danger to Roosevelt's continuance in the White House after 1904. Hanna had played the major role in making McKinley President; he embodied all of McKinley's political and economic conservatism. While he was not one of the senatorial reactionary die-hards, Roosevelt's own progressivism had already advanced to a point which presented a direct antithesis to Hanna's conservatism.

Roosevelt's great striving for a second term was not entirely due to his personal enjoyment of power, though unquestionably that entered largely into it. Both of the Roosevelts loved and wanted political power, great power, also for an additional reason—they realized that such power was the only way they could attain the liberal objectives they had in mind.

To get this power again in 1904 Theodore Roosevelt stretched his "righteousness" in other political moves to extreme limits. He sought the favor of powerful senators by appointing many of their friends and constituents to minor offices for which he knew they were wholly unqualified. So carefully did he use patronage during this period that for political reasons, he hesitated to approve even such a competent and staunch friend and supporter as Gifford Pinchot. Apparently after vaguely committing himself to someone else as Assistant Secretary of Agriculture, he learned from the Secretary that Pinchot was available for that office. He wrote Pinchot on July 16, 1904: "I did not suppose that you would care for the Assistant Secretaryship. . . . Do you care for it? Do you think your agricultural knowledge is sufficient for you to take it? I had already, to a certain extent, committed myself to Davidson's friends, and it may be that this commitment has gone too far to make it possible to reverse my action. *It may also be that the agricultural interests which are behind Davidson would not be satisfied with you. Do you think I could get them satisfied with you?*"[102] (Emphasis added)

Remarkably, Roosevelt had so thoroughly but temporarily softened his tone about the giant corporations that even J. P. Morgan and other financiers came to his support. The political operator in the White House had been courting these men for a year, even inviting J. P. Morgan to dine at the White House. For a while the Standard Oil Company was kept out in the cold; but before the election even Archbold, the very man who had signed those telegrams which Roosevelt had falsely attributed to Rockefeller, was finally invited. Roosevelt knew exactly where the campaign funds were coming from for the 1904 election.

The Bureau of Corporations for which Roosevelt had fought so hard, and which was supposed to be investigating the big corporations, had been in existence for nineteen months, and had done nothing substantial. Even more striking was the fact that he had personally handpicked to be the new Republican National Chairman and the manager of his campaign of 1904 the very man who—as the head of the new Department of Commerce and Labor—was supposed to be making sure that the bureau did do something, George Cortelyou. Cortelyou's job now, as chairman, became one of ingratiating himself into the crowd of "malefactors of great wealth" and getting campaign contributions from them. His statutory duties of investigating these generous contributors to the campaign were forgotten by him—and also by his chief, the candidate.

Even the third Annual Message to Congress in December 1903 was framed so as not to divert the expected big campaign contributors from repeating their generous performances of 1900 and 1896 which had redounded to the great benefit of McKinley and the Republican Party. That message was a soft voice indeed, and had not the slightest display or even hint of a big stick—or of any stick at all. His discussion of the Bureau of Corporations reads almost like an apology for it in his repeated insistence that the legislation creating it was enacted "on sane and conservative lines," that "we were not attacking corporations, but endeavoring to provide for doing away with any evil in them; that we drew the line against misconduct, not against wealth; gladly recognizing the great good done by the capitalist. . . ."[103]

No Lorelei ever sang a sweeter song than this one, designed to lure campaign contributions into the proper channels. The harmony of the song was a little jarred a few months later by an event which Roosevelt could not possibly postpone until after election. The Supreme Court of the United States on March 24, 1904, decided that Roosevelt had acted constitutionally in directing the prosecution of the Northern Securities Company under the antitrust laws. This decision added millions of enthusiastic common people to the Roosevelt ranks, but apparently did not stem the flow of corporate campaign contributions.

In those days, political managers were not hampered by laws either limiting the amounts of contributions or providing for publicity about the contributors and the extent of their political generosity; above all there was no prohibition on corporations from contributing corporate funds. It was routine for all records of political contributions to be destroyed right after election. The reader must bear in mind that the mores of political gifts had not even begun to crystallize in 1904. Although one might have expected Theodore Roosevelt to have done so, it was Woodrow Wilson in 1912 who first forbade his campaign directors to accept corporation contributions (see pages 154–155). The issue is now, in 1975, reaching a new crescendo.

It was not until a year after Roosevelt's election in 1904 that some of the ugly facts about the campaign contributions began to appear. The New York Life Insurance Company, the Mutual Insurance Company and the Equitable Assurance Company had given about $50,000 each of corporate money. E. H. Harriman had contributed the same amount, and had collected an additional $200,000. Later, in 1912, an old guard Senate—opposing in that year Roosevelt and his Bull Moose party—became suddenly virtuous, and began to investigate the campaign contributions of eight years ago, 1904. It found that of the total of $2,195,000 given to the Roosevelt campaign chest, 72½ per cent had come from large corporations. Morgan testified that he had given $150,000 in cash. Cortelyou as a witness had developed an almost completely blank memory—not even recalling which bank was the depository of the campaign funds. The records, he said, had all of course been destroyed. Bliss, the treasurer of the campaign, was beyond the subpoena of the Senate—he was dead. The Standard Oil Company, Archbold did testify, had contributed $125,000 in cash. This cash had been the subject of such ugly rumors during the 1904 campaign that Roosevelt had ordered that the money be returned—but it never was. There is no doubt that Roosevelt knew in general what was going on; but he did nothing to stop it unless a particular contribution began to cause public scandal. There always has been something pitiful about the gullibility of big industrialists and financiers who through the years—and even now—have believed that money could inevitably buy favors from public officials. No more eloquent proof exists than the contributions, both as published and as concealed, to the Republican Presidential campaign chest in 1972. No matter how often this confidence has been proven to be ill-founded, big businessmen never seem to learn; perhaps this is the result of those instances where their confidence was proven justified. In 1904, however, it was to be disproved. As one example: only a short time after Election Day in 1904, the Bureau of Corporations awoke from its long sleep and began a thorough investigation of the oil industry.

When the Democratic candidate in 1904, Alton B. Parker of New York, began late in the campaign to attack Roosevelt for accepting these corporate gifts, he made the mistake of going beyond the facts which could be proved—which were bad enough. Instead of relying on the facts themselves, he went further and openly said that the contributions were "blackmail," given in return for the continued silence and inactivity of the Bureau of Corporations. This gave Roosevelt the chance to become indignant, and to engage vociferously in his style of self-righteous indignation. In his first words in answer to the growing resentment about corporate largesse in the Republican campaign, he made the remarkable statement that the fact "that contributions have been made is not the question at issue"; and he added: "The assertion that there had been made any pledge or promise by me, or that there has been any understanding as to future immunities or benefits in recognition of any contributions from any source is a wicked falsehood." (The same defense was to be made by Republican leaders in 1972.) Needless to say, no proof was available of any such explicit understandings. Roosevelt's strong disclaimer to the charge struck a responsive chord in the American people, and helped his remarkable victory. It was a victory larger in the percentage of popular vote (56.4%) than any prior election in American history.

Although Roosevelt had successfully rebutted the charges of accepting corporate campaign contributions in exchange for promises of preferential treatment, and even of immunity from prosecution, he must have felt the charges deeply. He must have realized that accepting such contributions, especially in secret, would always give the appearance of a guilty quid pro quo even though in fact there was none. He had not only the style and the great ability to mold public opinion but also to recognize it and to follow it, when he believed such opinion was either correct or absolutely unchangeable. In this instance, almost immediately after his victory he hastened to suggest reform. In his Annual Message of December 6, 1904, only a month after the election he recommended "the enactment of a law directed against bribery and corruption in Federal elections." He went further and asked for a law to require the "publication . . . of the expenditures for nominations and elections of all candidates . . . also of all contributions received and expenditures made by political committees."[104] This recommendation was ignored by the Congress.

In his Annual Message of December 5, 1905, to the new Congress, he went even further, showing his concern about what had happened during his victorious campaign of 1904. He repeated verbatim what he had written in his last message, and recommended the prohibition of all campaign contributions by corporations in federal elections. He also suggested the same course to all the states, and he included expenditures for lobbying for legislation in Congress or in the legislatures of the states.[105]

In the next Annual Message, December 3, 1907, Roosevelt went far ahead of his time—and recommended what he called "a very radical measure," viz. that "Congress should provide an appropriation for the proper and legitimate expenses of each of the great national parties . . . and the stipulation that no party receiving campaign funds from the Treasury should accept more than a fixed amount from any individual donor." This novel idea was just beginning in 1973 to get some support from reform groups. But in 1907 it got nowhere!

In the election of 1904 the old combination of Populists and Democrats dissolved; and many of both who had supported Bryan twice returned to the Republican fold. What Roosevelt was doing in anticipation of the convention of

1904 was building his own following, as all strong Presidents have done. He was creating a coalition which cut across the borders of the regular party and would ensure his nomination: progressive Republicans and independents, labor leaders, farm leaders, Southern Negroes and the old reformers (whom he had so often condemned). It was almost entirely a personal victory; he himself had supervised practically every detail of the convention, the platform and the campaign.

It was, however, a lackluster—even a boring—campaign, except for the one tempest about campaign contributions. It was waged between a conservative judge, Alton B. Parker, and a Roosevelt who seemed to be almost equally conservative. In the campaign of 1904, no one could foresee the 1908 Roosevelt or, even less, the 1912 Roosevelt. But Roosevelt wanted above all else to win, and his campaign style of 1904 showed it. His conservatism reached a climax of a sort on election night, when he made a statement, evidently rehearsed and thought about for some time. It was the worst political blunder of his life—one he was to regret deeply in the future. Affirming the two-term tradition (even though his first term was not a full one), he announced: "Under no circumstances will I be a candidate for or accept another nomination." It was to take him eight years to break this pledge, the last four of which were years of great frustration. In his *Autobiography,* however, he denied that his 1912 nomination was a breach of his pledge, explaining that the two-term tradition meant only two consecutive terms. He went so far as to say that the consecutive two-term tradition was a "good custom," but that "It would be very unwise to have it definitely hardened into a constitutional prohibition."

During the campaign Roosevelt popularized a phrase he had coined, which has survived, and which is still used often in making comparisons with later Presidents' descriptions of their programs. In referring to his negotiations and conduct during the anthracite coal strike, he said it was simply giving both labor and capital a "Square Deal." Students of semantics have enjoyed comparing that phrase with the subsequent phrases of the "New Freedom" of Wilson, the "New Deal" of Franklin Roosevelt and the "Fair Deal" of Truman—giving all kinds of fanciful ideas about how one phrase led to the other.

But the "Square Deal" was no more a systematic and well-defined program than was the later "New Deal." It was a vague middle way which showed his aversion to radicalism and his fear of mob rule as strongly as his refusal to accept reaction or even laissez-faire and the status quo. By favoring labor in one instance and capital in another he was maintaining—or trying to—an equilibrium, uneasy as it was, much like his "balance of power" in world affairs. It was just as middle-ground in 1905 as the "New Deal" was one-sided in 1935.[106] However, during the years after his departure from the White House, when he began to consider seriously trying to get back into the presidency, Roosevelt used the phrase with a different—and much more progressive—twist.

He is reported to have said on the night before his inauguration in 1905: "Tomorrow, I shall come into office in my own right. Then watch out for me." The Congress needed no such admonition. It was "watching out" for his every move. It was still controlled by old guard Republicans with an even larger majority; and it had little taste for cooperation with the popular President, in spite of his remarkable election victory. To the lame-duck Congress which assembled in December 1904, he sent his Annual Message—as bold and forthright as his triumph at the polls a month earlier warranted. As he had cautiously played down his progressivism during the year before the election, he set about immediately making up for lost time.

What he asked for in his Annual Message of 1904—after election—was legislation empowering the Interstate Commerce Commission not only "to denounce a particular rate imposed by railroads as unreasonable" (a power which it already had), but also to decide and put in effect "what shall be a reasonable rate to take its place—a rate to take effect immediately and to remain in effect until it is reversed by the court of review." He went even further than this unprecedented recommendation, calling for government "in increasing degree [to] supervise and regulate the workings of all railways engaged in interstate commerce" as the "only alternative to an increase of the present evils on the one hand, or a still more radical policy on the other." The "more radical policy" had been demanded by some farm organizations and by the old Populists, and even by the more conservative middle classes and by the Southern and Western state legislatures; it was a policy calling for government ownership of the railroads as the only effective way to stop railroad abuses.

Joe Cannon and the Senate leaders knew as well as Roosevelt did that his rate proposals had wide support throughout the country which tariff revision did not have—especially among farmers and small manufacturers. Cannon was willing to compromise on this issue; Roosevelt nearly always was ready to compromise. In return for not pressing tariff revision (which the great operator, Roosevelt, never really expected to do), Cannon let Roosevelt's railroad program pass the House. It did not, however, fare so well in the Senate; but committee hearings on it were set for after adjournment. Roosevelt then followed his style of appealing to the people directly, and now more authoritatively, for he was President in his own right. He had no microphone as his later successors were to have; but he had enough energy and enthusiasm to make his appeal in person, going from city to city in many sections of the country. The fight to get the bill through the Senate was to take eighteen months of strenuous effort, courageous fighting and shrewd back-door manipulation by Roosevelt. It called for both the lion and the fox. In this struggle with the old guard led by Senator Aldrich, Roosevelt showed all the characteristics of his style in dealing with congressional opposition.

On January 30, 1905, his first appeal for popular support for rate legislation was made with characteristic courage before an audience which he knew had little or no sympathy with his views—the Union League Club of Philadelphia. There, a month before his inauguration, he laid down some of the basic tenets of his Square Deal.

"Neither this people nor any other free people will permanently tolerate the rise of the vast power conferred by vast wealth, and especially by wealth in its corporate form, without lodging somewhere in the government the still higher power of seeing that this power in addition to being used in the interest of the individual or individuals possessing it, is also used for and not against the interests of the people as a whole."

He kept up his public campaign, travelling in the spring of 1905 through the Middle West and Southwest on his way to a reunion of the Rough Riders. He had plenty of time; Congress was not to meet until December 1905. He warned publicly—brandishing his big stick—that he might fight for tariff revision. In the fall, he carried his campaign into the South; and while he spoke there principally about railroad regulation, he did not neglect irrelevancies which could help him. He rallied popular support for himself (and his bill) by praising the old Confederate courage and fighting ability during the Civil War. He knew also how to inspire favorable publicity to help his fight. It was no mere coincidence that many magazine articles soon appeared, discussing the iniquitous railroads and their minions in the United States Senate—all written by close friends of the President.

His opponents, on the other hand, were trying to frighten the American people into believing that the bill was the beginning of the end of private property, calling bogus conventions of paper organizations to pass bogus resolutions, spreading garbled news dispatches by spurious telegrams, making threats to small newspapers through their advertisers, and spreading false propaganda among farmers. These tactics were wholly unsuccessful because they were so obviously contrived. Public opinion, for many years inflamed by railroad abuses, fell in line behind the constant pounding of the President.

In his Annual Message in December 1905 he again showed his style of balancing the characteristics of the fox and the lion. He repeatedly abjured the use of radical or hasty action; in the matter of fixing rates, he urged "moderation, caution and self-restraint." He did not (as Franklin later would do) consider it his "premise to indicate the exact terms of the law which should be enacted," but merely to call to the attention of Congress "certain existing conditions with which it is desirable to deal." Railroad books should be open to the same inspection by the government as those of national banks; he was making these recommendations not "in any spirit of hostility to the railroads"; "on the whole our railroads have done well and not ill, but the railroad men who wish to do well should not be exposed to competition with those who have no such desire." The bill would be a defense for the railroads against "irrational clamor" and against "dishonest competitors"; under the "new conditions of industrialism which *the law-makers of old* could not foresee and . . . provide against; the evils have become so serious and menacing as to demand entirely new remedies." (Emphasis added)

The similarity of these words to the later arguments by Franklin Roosevelt on the need for new remedies for new conditions not foreseeable by the founding fathers, and on how necessary it is to reform, if we would preserve, the private property system, is obvious. Theodore Roosevelt was fighting the same contention over the railroads as Franklin would later have to fight over agricultural relief, minimum wages and a host of other problems: that the respective states are the ones to regulate these matters, and not the federal government.

Theodore's message—as expected—fell on deaf ears on the right; but it also was surprisingly rejected by the left as not adequate. Roosevelt could now play the lion as well as the fox; he pulled no punches in his determined fight for rate regulation. The Attorney General became very active—suspiciously suddenly—in proceeding against some railroads for illegal rebates. Three of them were indicted in December 1905. Then as the rate fight went on, the biggest corporation of them all, the Standard Oil Company, was subjected to more scrutiny by the formerly somnolent Bureau of Corporations. The bureau reported to the President, and the President forwarded the report to the Congress, that the company had made enormous profits through secret rate favoritism.

Liberal senators like LaFollette, for example, felt that the Hepburn rate-fixing bill embodying Roosevelt's ideas would be entirely ineffective unless it included the power of the commission to evaluate properties of the railroads in order intelligently to fix fair rates. He expressed his views to the President, who replied in a vein which always dominated his thinking about legislation: "But you can't get any such bill through this Congress. I want to get something through." Roosevelt was proved right. When LaFollette presented his views to the Senate, only six Republican senators voted with him. But Roosevelt, concentrating always on the "art of the possible," kept on plugging for the bill as drafted—even over the opposition to the bill of his closest political friend, Senator Lodge.

Senator Aldrich now entered the fray as leader of the opposition; his new strategy was to amend the bill by providing such broad judicial review as to emasculate the power of the commission. Aldrich failed in this but then adopted an even more skillful but unscrupulous tactic; he turned the floor leadership of the bill to a man who was a racist, intemperate demagogue from South Carolina's back country, "Pitchfork Ben" Tillman. Roosevelt, decrying the "antics" of Aldrich, decided nevertheless to "walk with the devil"; he joined the forces of Tillman though he had refused for months previously even to speak to him. But, even with the support of LaFollette, they could not get enough votes; so Roosevelt, always flexible, returned to his original position. Finally he rallied all but three votes when the bill on May 18, 1906, was passed. All the senators agreed —even Tillman himself—that without Roosevelt's leadership, skill and fast footwork there would have been no Hepburn Act. His style of threatening, of retreating, of compromising for what was possible, of perseverance, of flexibility in cooperating with members of the opposition party whom he personally hated, and, above all, of rallying public opinion had made the old guard senatorial leaders vote for vital legislation to which they were actually deeply opposed. The bill as passed not only permitted the Interstate Commerce Commission to set aside a rate schedule and substitute reasonable rates; it did something even more extraordinary—it opened up the books of the railroads to commission scrutiny, and it fixed uniform accounting methods. The chief compromise by Roosevelt came in the nature of the judicial review.

It was indeed a milestone in the development of federal government control over private industry. And the message of 1905 was a landmark in Roosevelt's social and progressive progress. It was sent to Congress just as the bitter fight over the Hepburn Act was reaching a high tempo. As Professor Mowry has said so well of this 1905 message:

"Three of the most cherished powers of private business had been the right to set its own prices for services, the right to maintain its books and records in secrecy, and the right to negotiate with labor without interference by a third party. The President's 1905 message challenged the exclusiveness of all these rights and proposed their severe limitation."[107]

The passage of the Hepburn Act in 1906 was one of the events which made 1905 and 1906 the most important years of Roosevelt's presidency and the zenith of his political career. There were many other events during these two years in both domestic and foreign affairs. They all had one common characteristic— controversy. Some of it was useful to the country and to Roosevelt; some of it was senseless and useless to both. But controversy was the chief diet of his political life. He enjoyed it; he invited it; if it did not come naturally, he sought it out and embraced it. His relish for it was a part of his political make-up, like his love of power and action, and his ready assumption of responsibility.

When he felt the time was right, he took on the fifteen-year-old fight which Dr. Harvey Wiley of the Department of Agriculture had been waging with the support of several civic groups for a federal law requiring accurate and descriptive labeling of foods, beverages and drugs in interstate commerce. Twice the bill had succeeded in the House but with no success either time in the Senate. In the Senate the members who were interested financially in the food and drug business, or who acted as the spokesmen of such business, made allies with their colleagues from the South who never wavered in their defense of states' rights. Their combined forces presented a stone wall of opposition to all such legislation as a federal pure food and drug bill. During his first term, Roosevelt, with his eye on re-election in 1904 and anxious to avoid too many antagonisms, gave the bills no support. But after election, having had many discussions with Wiley, he recommended a law "to regulate interstate commerce in misbranded and adulterated foods, drinks and drugs." This was another landmark in reform, and in the growth of the power of the federal government in matters which had generally been left to the respective states. It was also the signal for a bitter fight, undertaken even while Roosevelt was already in the struggle for railroad rate regulation. Senator Aldrich on the Senate floor repeated the battle cry of all conservatives and of all spokesmen for big business whenever some curb on the powers and freedom of business was suggested: that the bill imperiled "the liberty of all the people of the United States." In February 1906, however, without explaining then or later the reasons for his sudden shift, Aldrich permitted the pure food and drug bill to be reported out of committee onto the floor of the Senate. It was passed by the Senate with only four states' rights Democrats voting against it. But the bill encountered rough sledding in the House.

Shortly before this, Upton Sinclair had published *The Jungle,* which described the unspeakably filthy and unsanitary conditions in the slaughterhouses owned by the meat packers. Roosevelt, an omnivorous reader, read the book and was as revolted as every other reader. He directed the Secretary of Agriculture to investigate; and he personally appointed the two persons in the Department of Agriculture to lead the investigation. Senator Albert J. Beveridge of Indiana, who had been aware of the slaughterhouse conditions for a long time, now introduced a bill in the Senate—without any overt support from the President but certainly with his full knowledge and acquiescence—providing for *federal* meat inspection in the slaughterhouses. The bill passed the Senate, but when it came over to the House, the chairman of the Committee on Agriculture kept it locked up in committee. He was a New York gentleman-farmer, James Wadsworth, on whom the meat packers confidently relied to protect their business interests. When the Hepburn Act finally became law, Roosevelt had the time to get into the fight—and did so with his usual style of vigor, cunning, ruthlessness and political courage.

Just as he had used the threat of tariff revision in order to beat Republican senators into line for the Hepburn Act, he now began to use the threat of publicity to get the Beveridge bill passed. And he was not very subtle in his style of threat. He had already received the report of his investigators; and he wrote Wadsworth that the facts uncovered by the report were "hideous." "I was at first so indignant," he told the congressman, "that I resolved to send in the full report to Congress." But he would not do this if Wadsworth would get behind the Beveridge bill. "I should not want to make the report public," he said in a very transparent threat, "with the idea of damaging the packers. I should do it only if it were necessary to secure the remedy."

The threat did not work, at first. Thereupon, he got more pugnacious and even less subtle; but at the same time, with an operator's instinct, he carefully withheld his "knockout" punch. Instead, he sent Congress a special message urging passage of the legislation, to which he annexed only the first part of the report, which was labelled "Preliminary." The new threat was quite clear: he would publish the fuller, more devastating parts of the report, if the committee chairman continued the blockage. The publication of the preliminary report, however, with all the disgusting details, began to have a disastrous effect on the sale of meat, especially to markets abroad. Now in order to restore their sales of canned meat, the packers decided that the government stamp of inspection would be not only helpful but absolutely essential. Of course, the packers did not want real inspection or enforcement; they wanted only enough inspection to reduce the sales resistance. Roosevelt, however, continued to insist upon drastic standards and upon genuine inspection and enforcement. As usual, there came compromise. Inspection, it was agreed, would stop as soon as a plant failed to conform to the standards; in this way, there would be no stamp of inspection at all for any below-standard plants. This would in practice bar any substantial sales of the product. The stamp itself became an essential mark of respectability. With this fight over in the House, the original pure food and drug bill requiring the accurate labelling of foods, beverages and drugs in interstate commerce was also released from the House committee and passed.

Looking back on April 18, 1907—with pardonable pride—to his record of fighting monopoly and seeking to regulate big business, Roosevelt in a letter to Senator Thomas M. Patterson explained why he was now such a steady target of abuse by those who had been affected by his past actions. Some excerpts show his style of virile, caustic, undiplomatic language, as well as his determination not to change his style of action against these corporations:

The trouble with Harriman and his associates is that they have found themselves absolutely powerless to control any action by the national government. There is no form of mendacity or bribery or corruption that they will not resort to in the effort to take vengeance. The Harriman-Standard Oil combination and the other owners of predatory wealth hate me far more than they do those who make a profession of denouncing them, for they have learned that while I do not attack them in words as reckless as those often used against them, I do try to make my words bear fruit in deeds. *They have never before been obliged really to reckon with the federal government.* They have never before seen practical legislation such as the rate bill, the beef inspection bill and the like become laws. They have never before had to face the probability of adverse action by the courts and the possibility of being put in stripes. Such being the case, and inasmuch as they have no moral scruples of any kind whatsoever, it is not to be wondered at that they should be willing to go to any length in the effort to reverse the movement against them.[108] (Emphasis added)

This thought is very similar to Franklin's later explanation of big business hatred toward him, namely, its loss of control over the White House. Striking also is the similarity of the following letter dated April 16, 1907, to Senator Lodge, to Franklin's remarks in 1936 about the antipathy to him of members of the exclusive millionaire clubs, as well as the kind of rumors they used to spread about him: "I saw some friends who had been to New York recently; they say that New York's view of me—the view of the clubs, of high finance and of the 'educated intelligencia'—is one of hatred, terror, but above all, horror. They now think that I have become partially insane through excessive drinking." Neither of the Roosevelts seemed to lose much sleep over this kind of self-interested hatred and vindictiveness. Franklin would go so far as to declaim during the 1936 campaign, "I welcome their hatred."

While Theodore was fighting the battles for domestic reform in 1905–06, world affairs again began to demand attention. In foreign affairs, as in domestic, Roosevelt would always take the center of the stage—and never leave it. A relative once described this style: "When Theodore attends a wedding he wants to be the bride, and when he attends a funeral he wants to be the corpse. . . ." His conception of the presidency as one of strong, flexible and active leadership led him to a style in foreign affairs even more striking than in domestic matters. He realized, as have most subsequent Presidents, that unforeseen events involving the national interests of the United States require all these qualities in a President for quick and decisive action. His style became one of personal, and very often secret, diplomacy, carried on at times without even the knowledge of his Secretary of State. He did have his own trusted group of friends with whom he would sometimes confidentially consult. This small circle included three foreign diplomats whose discretion he trusted and whose judgment he wanted. They were Ambassadors Jean Jusserand of France, Cecil Spring-Rice of Great Britain, and Speck von Sternburg of Germany. In turn, they and many American Ambassadors abroad often consulted directly with him instead of going through the regular channels of the State Department. For example, it was several weeks before the State Department learned that the Japanese had approached Roosevelt to act as mediator in the Russo-Japanese War.

It was his conviction—substantially ahead of his time—that whatever of importance happened anywhere in the world was important to the national interests of the United States. And he was determined that the United States, as a world power, should play its part in all those events and in the decisions which grew out of them. He had had the same convictions when he was in the Navy Department. There and in his early presidency he urged constantly that the American military and naval power be increased so that the United States could play its role, if necessary, by force. As he gained experience and maturity in the presidency, however, he decided that, while strength and power and force were always essential for the United States and always had to be kept up to the armed might of the other nations, there was a great deal more that was necessary. Now instead of war he would seek to maintain a balance of power in the world, and would aim at international cooperation to promote stability in all the important geographical areas, to settle international disputes by arbitration, and to avoid wars. Roosevelt, as President, gradually became a very different and wiser kind of world statesman from the man who in 1898 had exalted the virtues—if not the necessities—of war, and had urged the power to wage an offensive war as the only means of holding world respect. He still believed in the essentiality of strength —including, always, an ever-increasing Navy. He still believed that isolationism for the United States would be forever impossible, and that to maintain a balance of power a strong Navy had to be able to back up any move that the President would make. The Navy had to play an integral part in American foreign policy. But this was no longer based *solely* on American material interests, as formerly. It now became also a matter of maintaining world prestige in order to provide world leadership in prevention of war both in Europe and in Asia, in the Atlantic and the Pacific. It was a much broader horizon, and a much more ambitious program.

In his Inaugural Address of March 1905, Roosevelt admitted that the United States could not proceed in world affairs on its own, but had to rely upon other friendly nations in the world, and on negotiation instead of the immediate use of force. Not that he would ever hesitate to make the display of power; but he recognized that that alone was no longer sufficient. In that inaugural speech, he laid down what might well pass for the rudiments of a Good Neighbor policy:

"Toward all other nations, large and small, our attitude must be one of cordial and sincere friendship. We must show not only in our words, but in our deeds, that we are earnestly desirous of securing their good will by acting toward them in a spirit of just and generous recognition of all their rights." But certainly not by any unilateral disarmament. "Justice and generosity in a nation . . . count most when shown not by the weak, but by the strong."

He had come to realize that if he was to lead America into the position of a world power, he would have to use the same style of playing the power game as the other world powers were using—Britain, Germany, Russia and Japan.

In spite of this broader concept, he remained to the end an imperialistic expansionist. In fact expansion and colonies were essential aids to a strong Navy —and a strong America. And as long as the world rivals struggled for empire, the United States had to keep up with them. His was not the idealist's approach to world affairs but a tough-minded and realistic one. He accepted as facts of twentieth-century international life the rivalry among the great powers of the world and that soft appeals for peace and humanity would never resolve their conflicts of interest. It was in the self-interest of America to lead the way and use her influence to promote stability in all parts of the world. He still believed in colonialism almost as an obligation of the superior races (mostly the white) to train the backward peoples for self-government.

The first test of his new theory of balance of power came in the Far East. He was the first President to realize how much the national interests of the United States could be affected by what was happening in that part of the world. He also realized how closely connected the events in the Far East were with the European rivalries, how pregnant any conflicts in Asia were with possibilities of reverbera- tions in Europe, which in themselves could also entangle the United States. Japan was emerging as a strong nation. At the same time Japan, Germany, Great Britain, Russia and France were strenuously competing with each other for trade, including trade with the newly awakening giant, China. Our own exports in 1904 to Japan and China had already surpassed our South American exports.

Instead of his old admiration for Russia as she conquered the "inferior sav- ages" of Turkestan and the eastern parts of Siberia, and even as she advanced into Manchuria to bring them all the blessings of civilization, Roosevelt now began to take a much less favorable view of Russian aggressiveness and arrogance in the Far East—and her absolutist and despotic monarchy. On the other hand, his old fear of Japan as our potential future enemy was diminishing. He used to fear Japan's designs on Hawaii and the Philippines; now he began to look upon her as the natural and effective counterbalance to Russia in the Far East.

In his desire to maintain a balance of power and stability in eastern Asia, Roosevelt used his style of personal action and super-executive authority in a way which made all his earlier stretchings of constitutional executive power seem slight by comparison. England and Japan in 1902, for example, had entered into an alliance. Roosevelt, in addition to his new attitude toward Japan, had become convinced that America's interests were fairly identical with British interests in that part of the world; and accordingly, he would have been pleased to join as a formal party this Anglo-Japanese agreement.

Theodore Roosevelt was a strong, moving and often violent leader of the American people, but one who also realized that he could not get too far ahead of public opinion. In 1901, as Vice President, he answered Captain Mahan, who had written him about Mahan's new book *The Problem of Asia and Its Effect upon International Policies:* "I feel that the United States and England should ... work together in China and that their cooperation in China ... is of the utmost importance for the future of Asia and therefore of the world. But . . . while something can be done by public men in leading the people, they cannot lead them much further than public opinion has prepared the way."[109]

An open peacetime participation in such an entangling alliance as the pact between Great Britain and Japan was too much even for the self-confident Roosevelt to hazard. Instead, he resorted to secret diplomacy. Without informing Congress or the American people, he had his special representative in London, Senator Lodge, and his special representative in Tokyo, Secretary of War Taft, make an unofficial gentleman's agreement for the United States to act, in the event of a crisis in the Far East, as if it *were* a formal party to the Anglo-Japanese treaty. This commitment, which flouted the treaty-making powers of the Senate, was kept secret from the American people for twenty years; even then it became public only through the private research of an historian. Unfortunately, this kind of conduct by a President acting alone in foreign affairs as though he were accountable to no one became more frequent in the administrations of Woodrow Wilson and Franklin Roosevelt, and especially of Lyndon Johnson and Richard Nixon. Of course, Theodore Roosevelt—like the others—was convinced that what he was doing was always in the best interests of the people for whom he was the steward.

The "Open Door" policy for trade with, and in, China announced by Secretary Hay in 1899 to the great commercial powers in Europe—England, Russia, France and Germany—had been accepted and followed. By the summer of 1903, however, Roosevelt became apprehensive about the adherence to the Open Door policy by Russia. Hay had made several protests to the Russian Ambassador with no success. Japan was also watching with suspicion the Russian advance in China and in Korea.

Because of Russia's aggression in Manchuria and in Korea, her obvious ambition to establish control of continental Asia (including India), and her refusal to pay heed to Japan's repeated admonitions to moderate her aggressive policy in Korea, where Japan was herself determined to maintain her own sphere of influence, conflict between the two became inevitable. Britain, the United States and Japan had a common interest in Manchuria, based on their extensive trade there. It was commercial interest which held these three together, and it was this unity of interest which encouraged little Japan to strike at the huge Russian bear.

The first blow fell on Russia on February 8, 1904, in typical Japanese fashion by a Pearl Harbor-like attack on the Russian fleet. The attack was almost as disastrous to the Russian fleet as the one at Pearl Harbor was to the United States' Pacific fleet. The Russo-Japanese war—without any declaration of war—was on. There is no doubt where Roosevelt's final sympathy was in this conflict. His first reaction was the wishful thought that the belligerents would fight each other to exhaustion, and that peace would come on terms "which will not mean the creation of either a yellow peril or a Slav peril."[110] But later, as Japan began to achieve a series of spectacular victories, he hailed the Japanese as "playing our game." He even thought for a while of going to the aid of Japan with our fleet if it should become necessary to block the aggression by Russia.

His style of carrying a big stick and speaking softly is exemplified in a confidential letter to the Secretary of State during the Russo-Japanese war on July 19, 1904:

"I am not feeling any too kindly toward Russia, and I want you to think well what we should do in case they seize an American ship. My own inclination is to notify them immediately that we will not stand it. Of course, I would put our statement in polite language, but very firmly, and I should do it with the intention of having our squadron bottle up the Vladivostok fleet, in case they attempted to cut up rough."[111]

On the same day, he sent another confidential letter to the Acting Chief of the Bureau of Navigation of the Navy: "In strict confidence I would like your Board to be considering what we should do in case it becomes necessary for our Asiatic Squadron to bottle up the Vladivostok Russian squadron. I do not antici-pate the slightest trouble, but in view of Russia's attitude toward neutral vessels carrying what she is pleased to call contraband, I want to be prepared for emergencies."[112]

But Japan needed no armed help. By the spring of 1905, the Japanese were the victorious masters of Korea and also of part of Manchuria. Japan under her treaty with Britain now asked and obtained recognition of her preferred status in Korea. She then asked the same recognition from the United States. Again Roosevelt, in his style of personal diplomacy, authorized Taft to agree to this status by the so-called Taft-KATSURA agreement, in return for which Japan gave up any designs on the Philippines.

Roosevelt decided that if he were to succeed in keeping some balance of power in the Far East, it would be best if the existing war were ended. He thereupon adopted a style in foreign affairs unique in American history up to that point. To both warring nations, he secretly proposed mediation by himself. At first, both refused; but Roosevelt kept the proposal open. Japan, victorious but fairly well exhausted, was the first to accede; and in 1905 she began some secret conferences with Roosevelt to that end, about which Roosevelt did not notify the State Department. Russia still resisted, intent on having one last big naval showdown with Japan. The showdown soon came; and the Russian fleet was annihilated. Japan still wanted Roosevelt to mediate.

Roosevelt continued with a long series of maneuvers and negotiations toward mediation. With his growing self-confidence and self-reliance, he again did not inform his Cabinet or Congress, or the State Department—or, of course, the people of the United States—about these efforts he was making all on his own.

He took on the enormous political risk of mediation with his usual style of readiness to shoulder responsibility. Success would mean the end of the war, and worldwide personal glory and acclaim for Roosevelt—which he would cherish. Failure would mean not only personal humiliation for the President, but a loss in the national interests of the United States in the Far East. To undertake mediation here—nay, to reach out for it as he did—showed a political courage as well as a love of action and ready assumption of national and world leadership. Of course, there was in him always a zest for personal glory and a deep concern for his own place in history. But it also shows wisdom in maintaining a balance of power in that part of the world. An unchallenged control and domination by either Russia or Japan in the Far East or in the Pacific Ocean could be dangerous to the United States.

He finally succeeded in getting the belligerents to meet in a peace conference at Portsmouth, New Hampshire. The parties were originally very far apart in their demands; but they acceded to the many suggestions which Roosevelt made from time to time as mediator. The treaty of peace was signed on September 5, 1905. It was all due to Roosevelt's efforts, and it fulfilled his wish to keep the Open Door policy alive in China and to establish a balance of power in East Asia which he hoped would promote his underlying motivation—safeguarding American interests in the Pacific.

But some seeds of future conflict were also planted by his mediation. One of them was the result of Roosevelt's success in persuading Japan to withdraw her demand for a huge indemnity; this created a great and lasting resentment among the Japanese which continued until 1945. Another was the "go-ahead" signal acquiesced in by Roosevelt for the Japanese to take a free hand in Korea in exchange for the Japanese promise not to interfere in the Philippines.

The United States presidency was beginning for the first time, in the person of Theodore Roosevelt, to show signs of becoming the office of a world leader.

Roosevelt in his next dealings with Japan showed how much his style had gained in maturity in foreign relations since his days as Assistant Secretary of the Navy and his repeated calls for war against Spain. The problem arose over Japanese immigration to California. The effects of Japanese immigrants residing and working in California began to be felt in the California labor market quite substantially by 1900—and were publicly referred to in that year by the Governor of California as the "Japanese menace." In 1906 the school board of San Francisco went so far as to pass an ordinance which put all Oriental children—Japanese, Korean and Chinese—in segregated schools. Japan lodged a formal protest. She also began discrimination against American business. Roosevelt assured Japan that the United States did not have the "slightest sympathy with the outrageous agitation against the Japanese." In his Annual Message of 1906 he lectured California on the subject of good manners, and called the action of the school board a "wicked absurdity." Without constitutional authority he interceded with the California legislature and Governor, and invited the Mayor and school board to the White House to confer with him. He persuaded them to repeal the ordinance. He even threatened the California legislature that he would use force if necessary to ensure the rights of Japanese-Americans. Finally, a gentleman's agreement was worked out by him with the Japanese Ambassador in Washington. Under this arrangement Japan would stop giving passports to laborers ("coolies") and would recognize the right of the United States to pass legislation to exclude Japanese immigrants who held passports originally issued to travel in any country other than the United States. The immediate crisis was thus temporarily averted by his bold personal actions; but the problem was far from solved, and the Japanese people far from mollified.

In a letter[113] to Senator Hale, he recognized the anomalous position into which one state could put the President and the national government: "Our federal form of government, with all its advantages, has very great disadvantages when we come to carrying out a foreign policy." His chief concern of course was that all the work at Portsmouth would be wiped out if Japan, which he saw as the first defense against Russia, were to be sufficiently aroused by the actions of one state.

During this period of high tension, many people and newspapers in both the United States and Japan talked openly and recklessly about war. In 1907 Roosevelt was worried about the possibility, and expressed pessimism about Japanese-American relationships. It is possible that this expression was only a feint, a sly move to get a reluctant Congress moving on his demands for more battleships. Evidence to substantiate this lies in the fact that he was already planning in 1907

—again secretly—to send the American fleet around the world, including a visit to Yokahama, hardly a move to take if he really was afraid of a Japanese attack. At any rate in November 1908, the Root-Takahira agreement was signed, which seemed to settle disputes so far as written documents can. And Roosevelt did get two more battleships. Unfortunately, the balance of power in the Far East for which he had labored so hard did not last very long.

Roosevelt's diplomatic handling of the various crises with Japan in 1907 was completely different in style from the way the Roosevelt of 1898 probably would have sought to handle them. So was his new enthusiasm for arbitration rather than war as a way of settling disputes between nations. Secretary of State Hay had, before 1905, signed arbitration agreements with nine countries by which arbitration could be instituted by executive agreement without consent of the Senate. The Senate protested; and Root, now Secretary of State, after abandoning the old treaties entered into twenty-four others which did require approval of two-thirds of the Senate before arbitration could actually begin. Roosevelt also instructed his delegates to the Second Hague Conference (discussed later) to work for model arbitration treaties, and for something akin to a permanent international court. Both endeavors failed. Roosevelt was deeply disappointed by the attitude of the Senate toward arbitration agreements. He tried, but failed, to get what he called "any feasible scheme which will tend to minimize the chances of war occurring without previous efforts to secure mediation or arbitration." The arbitration agreements proposed by Roosevelt would exclude any matter involving the "honor, independence, and vital interests" of the signers, and Roosevelt would of course be the arbiter of what these vague exceptions would include.

Roosevelt's newly acquired hatred of war did not diminish, however, the intensity of his style of contempt toward what he called the backward or "barbarous" nations, which he continued to believe should be kept in discipline by the nations he called "civilized." For example, there were the "backward nation and people" of China—where he was determined to maintain American commercial interests without regard to the feelings, resentments and new-found pride of the Chinese people. As a result, the Chinese in 1905 started a boycott against all American-made goods. There was plenty of justification for the boycott. The Chinese Exclusion Treaty of 1883 had come up for renewal in 1904. In his message to Congress of December 1904, Roosevelt expressed officially what he had always thought and said privately: "We should not admit masses of men whose standards of living and whose personal customs and habits are such that they tend to lower the level of the American wage-earner."[114] He meant, of course, Chinese "coolies"; and he was reflecting the attitude of Americans generally and Californians specifically. His own views were, however, a little more enlightened than those of many Americans. He did favor granting citizenship to intellectual or otherwise qualified Chinese. In 1904, the all-important election year, Roosevelt was ready to bow to politics again, even to the extreme views of Californians. True to his style of watching his own political career in all matters, he announced that he would sign the pending Chinese Exclusion Bill—and he did.

Roosevelt's reaction to the boycott of 1905 was typical of his style toward "backward people." On November 15, as the boycott led to violence and insults toward Americans, he concentrated a strong naval force off the Chinese coast. An expeditionary force of 15,000 men was prepared. China backed down; tranquility and the Open Door policy remained in effect—on paper. But the anti-

American feeling on the part of the young Chinese was intensified, and would express itself in the future. Instead of accepting the new nationalism of China, Roosevelt kept to his style of treating her as a colonial toward whom the only policy should be force.

The world cruise of the American fleet was another example of Roosevelt's insistence on a world position for the United States, and the acceptance of that position by the other powerful nations. It had many aspects of his style. It was foxlike in arousing enthusiasm in Congress and in the American public for bigger naval appropriations. It was lion-like in displaying American naval power to the Japanese, in order to still for a while the bellicose spirit of the younger Japanese naval officers.

The style of action and independence behind the journey is also very illustrative. Of course, in spite of the obvious dangers of the expedition, he did not consult Congress in advance about it. This enraged the chairman of the naval affairs committee, who threatened to withhold money for the fleet's necessary supplies. Roosevelt blandly replied that there was enough money left to get it halfway around the world, and if Congress wanted to keep it there instead of bringing it home, that would be their responsibility. As a result of this soft reply and the big stick behind it, the money was provided.

Roosevelt's unprecedented personal intervention in the war between Russia and Japan made a great impression on the American citizenry in many different ways. One was the arousal of the outraged indignation of all American isolationists; and also of those millions of Americans who completely rejected the idea of any danger of war in the world, and who were confident that if such a war did occur any place in Europe or Asia, it could never possibly involve the United States.

Ignoring the clear voices of protest, Roosevelt proceeded in the same style to intervene in another foreign dispute—this time on the other side of the globe. A crisis in French Morocco was building up at the same time as the crisis in the Far East. There were elements in it which made it more dangerous to the peace of Europe than did the Japanese-Russian dispute. The immediate issue was the Open Door in Morocco; but the basic issue lay in the commercial and territorial rivalries of Germany, France and Great Britain in North Africa. In 1904, France and Great Britain had blithely agreed that the French should be pre-eminent in Morocco, and that they should, in turn, recognize the pre-eminence of Britain in Egypt. There were other secret treaties between them of which neither the Kaiser nor Roosevelt had knowledge. France and England had agreed, for example, that Morocco should be ultimately split into two parts—one for France and one for Spain. Italy was to be given a free hand in Tripoli in return for her acquiescence in this partition of Morocco.

Germany was late as compared with France and England in seeking commercial advantages in Morocco; but she made up in truculence for what she had lost in time. The Kaiser in 1905 dramatically docked his ship in Morocco, came ashore, and announced that Morocco "was an independent nation where all foreign powers were entitled to equal rights—including commercial and trading rights." With tension growing in Europe, as it had ever since the end of the Franco-Prussian War, the Kaiser appealed to Roosevelt to help "keep Morocco open to all nations on an equal basis." Roosevelt was a little gun-shy with all the protests of Congress and of many millions of Americans about the Russo-Japanese intervention ringing in his politically sensitive ears. However, as rumors of early war increased, he again courageously decided to do something to avert the conflict which he saw coming, and which might possibly involve the United States. He did finally arrange for both France and Germany to attend an international conference which the Sultan of Morocco had called at Algeciras. When a deadlock occurred at the conference, Roosevelt interceded once more; and he worked out a compromise which all sides accepted.

He certainly had led America a long way down the road into the center of world affairs. It was not that he was creating a transformation in the ideology of the American people against "entangling alliances." He was exercising bold leadership in specific instances as they arose, one by one, and as they threatened the interests of the United States. As Professor Warren puts it, "he was . . . drawing the nation through the back door as it were, ever closer to the center of the world stage."[115] While America would vehemently pull back again into her shell after World War I, Theodore Roosevelt had had the vision to see that the interests and security of the United States were often involved in events thousands of miles from its shores.

The contrast between the two Roosevelts in offering or accepting the role of mediator in the face of American isolationism is striking. Theodore seemed to grab at each opportunity in spite of the clamor at home against any foreign intervention. Franklin, on the other hand, on the eve of the outbreak of World War II did offer his services in the role of an intermediary (i.e., one to carry messages back and forth between the nations), but was meticulously careful to impress upon the press conference called to announce his offer that it was definitely *not* one of mediation.

Theodore Roosevelt's successful peace settlements in the Far East and in the Mediterranean won him the Nobel Peace Prize for 1906. He deserved it. He had been instrumental in avoiding wars in 1905–06 in either of which all the great powers of Europe and Japan could have become participants.

He followed it up by his active participation in the Second Hague Peace Conference. He had suggested such a conference in 1904, but it had to be deferred because of the Russo-Japanese war. It was finally called by the Czar of Russia in 1907. There Roosevelt tried to have established a World Court; a multilateral agreement to limit armaments and the size of battleships; and a further extension of the idea of international arbitration.

The old jingoism and yearning for the glories of the battlefield had gone; his cry was now for peace, for the reduction of naval armaments and for international arbitration!

The Algeciras affair, along with the joint action of Britain and the United States *vis-à-vis* Russian aggressiveness in China, marked another great change in the Roosevelt style—one which was to have its influence during the rest of the century, with the exception of a short period during Wilson's prewar days. All of Roosevelt's anti-British feeling of 1895 had disappeared, as he (abetted by Hay, Taft and Root) realized more and more not only the great protective capacity of the British naval might, but also the identity of the ultimate interests of the two countries. His expression of growing friendship with Britain and his confidence in her reliability abound in his private letters and communications. In 1905, he observed, for example, that "in keeping ready for a possible war, I never take into account war with England. I treat it as out of the question."

In his dealings with foreign nations Roosevelt relied, wherever he could, on personal communication. For example, he frequently conferred with Speck von

Sternburg of Germany and Cecil Spring-Rice of Great Britain directly instead of relying on the channels of the State Department.

Roosevelt's great accomplishment in foreign affairs was the fact that he was able to show the American people—sometimes over their own protest—that American resources, influence and power entailed a responsibility to participate in the affairs of the rest of the world—and in any part of the world. At a time when foreign relations were a minor consideration with the American people, he was determined that America should take her place among the leading nations of the world, and he succeeded in leading her, in a few short years, to such position.

Even while he was imperiously taking part in Far Eastern and European controversies, he was having plenty of controversies at home.

One of the worst—a controversy which was not finally settled until a half-century after his death—grew out of a riot in Brownsville, Texas. The details are important because they illustrate Roosevelt's tendency to make quick horseback decisions, his dogmatic, unshakable conviction that what he did was always right, his exaggerated zest for speedy action, his political cunning—at times quite unscrupulous—his dogged stubbornness and refusal to concede error . . . and probably a trace of the early racism which he never completely abandoned.

On the night of August 14, 1906, a group of soldiers who were members of three Negro companies stationed at Fort Brown nearby were accused of taking part in a raid on the town. This was denied; but there *was* a raid by then-unidentified people. In the shooting which occurred during the disturbance a white bartender was killed and a white policeman wounded. Not one of the Negro soldiers was ever identified as being present, or ever admitted responsibility or participation. No proof was ever presented, and no one was accorded a trial or even a court-martial. The commanding officer concluded, however, that his troops were at fault at least for engaging in a "conspiracy of silence" by refusing to divulge the names of the men who were guilty. In all probability there was no such conspiracy—because none of the troops was present at the raid or knew who the raiders were.

Roosevelt, however, arbitrarily ordered all the members (167) of the three companies—six of whom were wearing the Medal of Honor earned in battles with the Indians, Spaniards and Filipinos, and some of whom were ready for retirement on pensions—discharged "without honor" and without the right ever to enlist again. The dishonorable discharge meant complete destitution for many of the men. They not only lost their jobs; they also lost all pension rights and became ineligible for residence in old soldiers' homes. Even if there had been three or four guilty soldiers—which was denied—to punish this severely three whole companies or 167 men because no one would come forth (assuming anyone knew) and point out the "culprits" among his comrades was carrying guilt by association to outrageous extremes.

Roosevelt signed this order on November 5, 1906; but in his worst style of political opportunism and low cunning, if not actual deceit, he did not release the order until after the congressional elections were held on the following day, November 6. Obviously his sense of outrage at the alleged killing by the Negro soldiers was not great enough for him to be willing to sacrifice or endanger the Negro vote, which he knew would turn against his party the next day because of his action if it had become publicized. The vote of the Northern Negroes in

Theodore Roosevelt's day had always been Republican. The Washington *Post* pointed out that if the order had been released when it should have been and if only one-half of the Negroes who voted that day in Cincinnati had switched, Roosevelt's own son-in-law, Representative Nicholas Longworth, would have gone down to certain defeat.[116]

A storm of criticism broke out, as soon as the news was published, from practically all Negroes, millions of shocked and outraged white citizens, and the press. A shift in Negro voting thereafter was not the only political result of Roosevelt's action in the Brownsville matter. The course he followed brought about a bitter conflict between the President and Congress (except, of course, the anti-Negro congressmen from the South); it hastened the widening split which was beginning to develop between these two branches of the government. Senator Foraker of Ohio was ambitious to become the nominee of the Republican Party in 1908. The drastic action by Roosevelt over Brownsville gave Foraker the issue he thought he needed to further his ambition. He instituted a private inquiry, and then charged publicly that this was "An American Dreyfus Case." For two years he kept up his campaign for justice for the discharged Negroes. As Foraker called for a congressional investigation of the entire incident, Roosevelt again in a style of self-righteousness, stubbornness and self-delusion sent a harsh message to Congress containing many obvious misstatements of known facts. Foraker continued to accuse and to probe, and on the floor of the Senate he presented facts tending to show that the shooting had been done by a posse of white vigilantes who (along with most other Brownsville white residents) resented the presence of the three Negro companies of troops. (Senator Foraker accused the white vigilantes of starting the riot and then blaming it on the soldiers.)

This personal fight between Roosevelt and Foraker made many headlines. It became the subject of bitter personal charges and countercharges at—of all places—the annual Gridiron Club dinner in 1907. Roosevelt, not being able to take the jibes and jokes of the reporters about the Brownsville affair, had the bad taste to include in his speech (usually expected to be funny) a serious defense of his action, as well as a savage attack on the Ohio senator, who was present. Anyone who has ever attended a Gridiron dinner would know how out of place—even preposterous—this kind of conduct was. The senator answered in kind, to heavy applause from the sophisticated audience. Thereupon the President completely lost his head as well as his sense of humor and of decency, arose in a blaze of anger and shouted, "The only reason I didn't have them hung was that I couldn't find out which one did the shooting." He then abruptly stalked out of the dinner.[117] Roosevelt insisted to his dying day that the color of the soldiers had nothing to do with his decision. And he went to extremes in trying to mitigate the storm of protest (or to salve his own conscience) by making several Negro appointments, creating a Negro battalion of artillery, threatening a railroad unless it provided facilities for Negroes, denouncing lynching, and asking in his Annual Message of 1906 (one month after the discharge of the troops) for more facilities for education for Negroes—but never a word of apology or even regret.

Roosevelt did back down a little as a result of Foraker's presentation; he retreated from his position that none of the discharged soldiers could ever reenlist. He permitted the Secretary of War to reinstate those of whose innocence the Secretary was convinced. But this insignificant admission of error did him more harm than good. When Roosevelt left office in 1909, Brownsville was still a lively topic; and many more investigations were conducted by the Army thereafter.

The affair of Brownsville is not mentioned once in the *Autobiography*. The *Autobiography*, as indicated in many places in this chapter, was not exactly an unbiased account of his life. Most of the embarrassing episodes seem to have vanished from recollection. Most autobiographies or memoirs of former Presidents and high governmental officials are weighted in the writer's favor, but few are so utterly self-righteous and virtuous as his—and that too was consistent with his general style.

Roosevelt never succeeded in wiping out this blot on his otherwise reasonably fair record as to Negroes, at least when measured by the mores of his era. Nor did the controversy about the Brownsville affair ever end until recently—in the only honorable way it could.

To call Roosevelt's style in the Brownsville case a matter of self-righteousness may be a little euphemistic; perhaps it is more accurate to speak of it as his easy manner of self-delusion whenever troubled by misgivings. In the 1915 trial of the libel suit which the notorious New York Republican boss, William Barnes, Jr., had brought against him, the following cross-examination took place:

Q. How did you know that substantial justice was done?
A. (Roosevelt, the witness) Because I did it, because I was doing my best.
Q. You mean to say that when you do a thing, thereby substantial justice is done?
A. I do. When I do a thing—I do it so as to do substantial justice. I mean just that.[118]

The "substantial justice" handed out at Brownsville in 1906 was not rectified, at least as far as it could be, until sixty-six years later. On September 28, 1972, the Department of Defense suddenly announced without detail or adequate explanation that as a result of "administrative review," the records of the men had been cleared.[119] Stating that the mass punishment of 1906 was the only case of mass punishment in its history, and that it was a "gross injustice," the Army of the United States ordered that all the discharges be changed to "honorable." The next day, a better explanation was made public by the *New York Times*.[120] On March 18, 1971, Representative August Hawkins, a black Democrat of California, made a speech in Congress asserting that the discharged men were innocent. His revival of the case was caused by his recent reading of a book by John D. Weaver, published in 1971, entitled *The Brownsville Raid: The Story of America's Black Dreyfus Affair*. Mr. Weaver told the *New York Times* that his own interest in the case had been inspired by a "chance remark" made to him by his eighty-five-year-old mother. She was telling him of her visit to Brownsville at a time "when those soldiers were kicked out of the Army." Since Weaver's father had long been a Washington court reporter who had often covered federal court proceedings, he asked his mother whether his father had taken down the testimony at the trial of the soldiers. She answered: "Oh, there was no trial." When she insisted on this shocking statement, Weaver, in disbelief, "decided to look into it." From a "look," there developed a four-year minute study of all the available records of the case, all the so-called investigations which had been conducted by the Army, and all the inquiries which had been instigated by Senator Foraker. He "found there was no shred of evidence implicating . . . [the soldiers] in the raid at all. It apparently was some vigilante types who were sore at the black troops stationed there . . . A couple of people just accidentally got in the way of the bullets."

After reading the book, Congressman Hawkins introduced a bill in 1971 to exonerate the soldiers; and in response to a Pentagon inquiry turned over all his own information about the affair. The sudden 1972 action of the Army in clearing the men did not even mention Mr. Weaver's book or Congressman Hawkins's bill. Recalling President Roosevelt's deceitful delay in releasing the news of the dishonorable discharge until after Election Day in 1906 in a transparent effort to avoid losing some of the black vote, Hawkins drew a political parallel with the action of President Nixon in September 1972 shortly before the Presidential election of that year, announcing through the Army this decision to clear the names of the black soldiers. He said: "It seems strange that many years later another Republican President releases this decision just before the election. The black vote may have something to do with it."

It was generally assumed in 1972 when the Army took this action that all the discharged had died. However, two turned up. One was Dorsie W. Willis, who was living in Minneapolis where he had been compelled to earn his living by acting as a porter and bootblack in an office building ever since his dishonorable discharge. The story is told by the Minneapolis *Star* of February 12, 1973. A major-general was dispatched by the Army to Minneapolis to present Willis with a proper certificate of honorable service. Mr. Willis is reported by the newspaper to have said, "The dishonorable discharge kept me from getting a first-class job. They admit that they made a mistake but who's going to make up for it? They figured we were all dead, but I saw it in the papers. I told them one of us wasn't dead anyway." After the presentation by the major-general, the old soldier said about the alleged "comspiracy of silence": "None of us said anything because we had nothing to say. It was a frame-up straight through. They checked our rifles and they hadn't been fired. And we was infantry. We never had any horses to ride." The second veteran was Edward Warfield, eighty-two, now living in Los Angeles, as reported (with photograph) in the Minneapolis *Tribune* of April 20, 1973.

The most senseless of all Roosevelt's many controversies were those which he frequently waged with reformers. This is all the more bewildering because Roosevelt's eminence in history is largely due to the fact that in domestic matters a good part of his presidency was devoted to fighting for reform, insisting that reforms in economic and social matters could be successfully accomplished by political techniques. He himself turned out to be the greatest reformer in the White House since Lincoln. He seemed at times to be blind to the fact that in most of his fights for reform, he had been helped to victory by these very reformers whom he would so often condemn.

Roosevelt frequently castigated liberals and reformers who were in advance of him in his early days, or who fought for objectives which he espoused in later days. They were all derisively termed "Mugwumps," "muckrakers," or "goo-goos." (The term "muckrakers," which he invented and made popular, was based on a character in *Pilgrim's Progress* who was interested only in evil and filthy things.) In fact the "muckrakers' " writings in respectable magazines, books and newspapers had helped him time and again in his fights with Congress by forming a strong public opinion behind him. His attacks on them have puzzled historians, and have baffled explanation.

It may be that this style was the result of his perpetual fear of the militant left, who were constantly calling for more and more reforms. While he saw clearly that many abuses called for reform, and even while he adopted one reform plank after another from past Democratic platforms and from Populism and Bryanism, he was always obsessed by the fear that the reformers' control of the government (which he sometimes referred to as "mob rule") might become extreme and prove even worse than business control. By 1912, however, he would be ready to embrace almost the entire reform program; but he was not President then, and would not be President ever again. His own explanation is summed up in a letter he wrote to Upton Sinclair in February 1906. The exposures by Sinclair's book, *The Jungle,* had led to Roosevelt's crusade, as we have seen, for passage of the pure food bill and to his enthusiastic support of the meat inspection bill. He wrote Sinclair: "A quarter of a century's hard work over what I may call politico-sociological problems has made me distrust men of hysterical temperament." But, he added, "all this has nothing to do with the fact that the specific evils you point out shall, if their existence be proved, and if I have power, be eradicated."[121]

When the meat inspection bill and pure food bill became law, Roosevelt wrote a glowing letter of praise to Senator Beveridge, who had sponsored them. But to Upton Sinclair or Samuel H. Adams, who had written articles in *Colliers* about the patent medicine fakes, or to the other reformers who had worked so hard in support of the legislation—not a word.

Throughout his career he used the same style, and there were many examples. He was combative to opposition even when the opponents were basically sympathetic to him and to his aims; their fault, in his mind, lay in the fact that, because of "their hysterical temperament," they pressed too hard for their aims and always demanded perfection in the reforms they urged. He never seemed to realize that in order to obtain reform it is necessary to have zealots and even extremists who dramatize the evils, who plow the path for the doer, and who make it possible ultimately to get respectable compromises.

Senator Robert M. LaFollette, a reformer, a progressive and one who could fight against President Roosevelt as well as with him for good causes, wrote in his own *Autobiography:* "This contemner of 'reforms' made reform respectable in the United States, and this rebuker of 'muckrakers' has been the chief agent in making the history of 'muckraking' in the United States a national one, conceded to be useful."

Roosevelt's style of controversy reached the zenith of futility and the nadir of Presidential dignity in his denunciation of "nature fakirs." A reverend, William J. Long, had written an article attributing human characteristics to some wild animals; and the great naturalist John Burroughs had severely attacked Long for it in the *Atlantic Monthly.* Other qualified scientists did the same. President Roosevelt just could not resist the temptation to get into this fight, which had of course nothing to do with the presidency, the nation or with any politicians or politics—in fact, it did not legitimately affect him or his office in any way. In early 1907, he held an interview which was printed under the caption: "Roosevelt on the Nature Fakirs." He later wrote Burroughs concerning this interview that he was "unable to contain myself," admitting that "as President, I ought not to do this. . . . I felt that I had to permit myself some diversion." Long replied by ridiculing Roosevelt's professed love of nature and of animals and by excoriating Roosevelt's many hunting trips on which he had killed an estimated total of 1,000 animals. Roosevelt, in the mind of the general public, came off second best—not only as a wanton killer but as an undignified President. But his style never permitted him to apologize publicly or indeed to admit error in public. So, he kept up his diatribe against the "nature fakirs." The episode shows his impetuousness and his eagerness to get into the middle of any controversy. He did admit to a friend privately that it was "bad judgment," and that it showed that "a President ought not to go into anything outside of his work as President." He added, however, that that "is rather a hard proposition to live up to."

Roosevelt indeed found it not only "hard," but impossible. Whether it was simplified spelling, nature fakirs, a falling birth rate, marriage and divorce, football or a score of other extraneous controversies, he had to be in there. It did not bother him when he lost an argument; instead of admitting defeat, he would burst forth on something else. This boundless energy, this razzle-dazzle personality, bluntness, and pugnacity all helped his popularity, for the American people of his time apparently loved that style. It seemed almost that Roosevelt enjoyed being criticized and even ridiculed during these irrelevant and bizarre ventures. His people chuckled, and their newspapers had a field day for cartoons. They listened in amazement—but in admiration—as he burst forth in his most bellicose and over-strenuous style, often exercising very extreme language. It would always provide dinner and cracker-barrel conversation about "Teddy." It was so human, in fact so much like their own neighbors! The tactics which helped to make him so popular in his day would probably not come through so favorably with the more politically sophisticated American public of today. But through it all, Roosevelt had what he called a "corking" time.

From the very beginning of his presidency—in his first Annual Message of 1901—Roosevelt showed his deep dedication to the cause of conservation. He submerged all his usual partisanship when dealing with this subject. Often he pursued his course against the opposition of the most powerful political leaders of his own party, and sometimes against the united opposition of both parties. The bold style he employed in conserving national resources for the use of future generations was unusual—almost unique—because it was not hampered by his great loyalty to his beloved party, which had expressed no respect for any of the principles of conservation.

While still a small boy, Theodore began to take an interest in natural history. "I remember distinctly," he wrote in his *Autobiography,* "the first day that I started on my career as zoologist. I was walking up Broadway and I passed the market to which I used sometimes to be sent before breakfast to get strawberries, I suddenly saw a dead seal laid out on a slab of wood. That seal filled me with every possible feeling of romance and adventure . . . I measured it . . . and, at once began to write a natural history of my own, on the strength of that seal."[122] As he matured, his love of the outdoors grew more and more pronounced. It is best described in Albert Bushnell Hart's Introduction to Roosevelt's *Winning of the West* (p. ix): ". . . from boyhood to the end of his life, he was a western spirit and natural backwoodsman. It was no accident that took him into Dakota [in 1884] any more than it was an accident that sent him to Africa [in 1909]. He loved the open air and big spaces and the society of wild animals. He loved mountains and mountain-lions and days of hardships, and a night camp under a tree."

While he was ranching in the West, he saw the forests at first hand, and also the desert lands which could be reclaimed by the use of water. At that time his was a purely physical enjoyment of nature, and there is not much trace of his future concern with its preservation. Words like these describing his experience in ranching out west came naturally from his pen: "We knew toil and hardship and hunger and thirst; we saw men die violent deaths as they worked among the horses and cattle; but we felt the best of hardy life in our veins and ours was the glory of work and the joy of living."[123]

With this background, it was an easy task for Gifford Pinchot, the undisputed leader of the conservationist movement in the United States at that time, to convert Roosevelt to the ardent conservationist he became. They had known each other casually, but became intimate friends and collaborators in 1899 while Roosevelt was Governor.

We have seen his interest as Governor in the forests and streams of the state —and in their preservation. As soon as the new President returned to Washington in 1901 from his predecessor's funeral, Pinchot and Frederick H. Newell, the father of the Reclamation Service, conferred with Roosevelt at the White House and outlined their ambitions. Pinchot recalled: "The new President knew what we were talking about. We left, two very happy men, authorized to draft for the message [of 1901] what we thought it ought to say on our twin subjects. It was a Heaven-sent chance."

This was a subject which, he saw from the start, called for national action; the states could help in their own areas, and indeed at the end most of them were persuaded by him to do so. But the massive objectives he enunciated and pursued could be reached successfully only by the central government. In forestry management, in preserving and using actual resources, and in building the great storage dams for reclamation of arid lands, the projects were all too big for any one state; and besides, nearly all the benefits of conservation projects naturally spread beyond state borders. For seven years, he steadily sought to convince the Congress to take the many actions which the individual states could not take even if they had been willing.

He got his first success when Congress, on his personal plea to Joe Cannon in 1902, passed the Newlands Act which created a national reclamation service. Its function was to construct, with money derived from land sales, reservoirs and irrigation works, so that vast arid, waste lands could be made fertile. So hard and relentless was Roosevelt's style as an administrator in pushing the work of reclamation under this law that when he left the presidency, thirty vast irrigation projects were completed or in progress.

Aided and guided by his friend Gifford Pinchot, he next turned his attention to the forests of the nation, which had been subjected to spoliation, depletion and exploitation by lumber interests for over a century. He created a really effective Forest Service by transferring jurisdiction over the forest reserves from the inefficient Land Office in the Department of Interior to a new bureau in the Department of Agriculture. At the head of it, he named Pinchot.

Roosevelt next concerned himself with river sites suitable for the development of water power as well as irrigation and recreation. The utility companies, ever since the discovery that electricity could be created from falling water, had, with the help of their many representatives in Congress, been grabbing the best of the sites by very cheap and long leases for private development of power. Even Muscle Shoals—later to become the heart of the TVA under Franklin Roosevelt —was saved from the private utilities only by a veto of legislation in 1903 by Theodore Roosevelt. Time and again he had to use all his energy, resources and political skill to block similar raids by utilities, and congressional giveaways. He followed the same course in the conservation of coal lands and other mineral lands, which formerly had been transferred from government ownership to private hands at ridiculously low prices.

By 1907, the conservative Congress and the lumber and mining interests which controlled it combined to fight with renewed vigor most of Roosevelt's conservation measures. In no other field did Roosevelt show a more efficient style of in-fighting, political courage and cunning in getting results.

One example will show how much of the lion and the fox he could combine to fight all his opponents, and to defeat them. Senator C. W. Fulton of Oregon, a Republican, thought that all these new forestry notions were useless and impractical schemes of "dreamers and theorists." He therefore introduced in the short session of 1907 an amendment to the Agriculture Appropriations Bill, which outlawed the creation of any *new* forest reserves in the states of Oregon, Washington, Idaho, Montana, Colorado or Wyoming. Nothing could have pleased the lumber interests more. The amendment was readily passed—without even a roll call. Roosevelt was now faced with the dilemma of having either to veto the whole bill, which would leave the entire Department of Agriculture (including the Forest Service) without any funds, or of signing it and thus barring himself from creating any new forest reserves in those six heavily forested states. The anti-conservationists in Congress and their clients in the timber industries were now certain that they had the President completely "boxed in."

But they underestimated both the guile and the political courage of their President. He had ten days to sign or veto the bill. During those ten days, Pinchot suggested, and at Roosevelt's request prepared, Presidential proclamations setting aside—as an executive function—twenty-one *new* forest reserves, consisting of 16 million acres all in the six states covered by Senator Fulton's amendment. Roosevelt first signed all the proclamations. After that he signed the Agriculture Appropriations Bill. By this device he got his funds—and also his forests. The blast of indignation and protest which followed these "midnight" proclamations, mingled with the fury of balked expectations and foiled greed, caused only glee and satisfaction to the President, as he later duly recorded in his *Autobiography*.

Roosevelt's love of nature and devotion to its conservation then led him into fights—which he won—to preserve the nation's natural scenery in the Grand Canyon, Niagara Falls, and scores of other areas. Also he created five of the present great national parks. He was able to get legislation in 1906 under which he created sixteen of the great national monuments, such as the Muir Woods in California for example. And he created, by executive orders, fifty-one national wild life refuges.

With his usual style of energy, having determined that the individual states had to take action also within their respective jurisdictions, he called a White House Conference of Governors to convince them. It was the first Governors' Conference ever held; but it included many who were not Governors: the Cabinet, the Supreme Court Justices, Bryan, Andrew Carnegie, and many scientists. It was an example of his style of doing spectacular and dramatic things to advertise skillfully great causes in government. The conference issued its historic Declaration of Governors, which was a landmark, enumerating principles of conservation which have been followed in subsequent years by all progressive state governments: natural resources belong to the people in perpetuity; they are all interdependent; each state should create its own conservation commission to preserve them for the people, and to cooperate with each other and with the federal government to that end.

Similarly Roosevelt created another innovative commission to study inland waterways, river development and use, including their use in the manufacture of electricity. Congress ignored its findings because, as Roosevelt caustically stated in his last Annual Message in 1908, Congress was under the domination of the electric utility companies. But the principles which the commission enunciated and which Roosevelt included in his message still survive, and indeed form the fundamental philosophy of TVA: "that every stream is a unit from its source to its mouth, and all its uses are interdependent."

While controversy still goes on about the statesmanship and quality of Roosevelt's "stewardship" in many fields, there is practical unanimity about the style and results of his activities in the field of conservation. Dr. Charles Van Hise, an expert and great activist in the field, wrote two years after Roosevelt left the White House: "What he did to forward this [conservation] movement . . . will place him not only as one of the greatest statesmen of this nation but one of the greatest statesmen of any nation at any time." When one considers that this was accomplished over the opposition of tremendous and powerful private interests, of a conservative Congress which dragged its feet, and of practically all the powerful Republican politicians, it becomes clear what can be done by a great operator in the White House.

Roosevelt's escalated progressivism had been made painfully obvious to all conservatives in his 1905 Annual Message. In the one of 1906 it went further and deeper—especially with respect to corporations. He again recommended legislation as he had in 1905 outlawing political contributions by corporations, and urging the use of federal power rather than the power of individual states to exercise a "far more complete control than at present over the great corporations" engaged in interstate business, including publicity of corporate accounts, government inspection of corporate books, and valuation of railroad properties by government in order to fix fair rates. The effort he recommended should not be to prevent combinations of capital, but to control them in order to prevent injury to the public. He also requested limitation of preliminary injunctions in labor disputes; he condemned lynching, and denounced the practice of dispensing different kinds of justice for black and white; and he put forward a law to improve the education of Negroes, saying, "The white man if he is wise will decline to allow the negroes in a mass to grow to manhood and womanhood without education." He showed even more pronouncedly his new style toward labor, repeating his recommendation for a law limiting the hours of labor of railroad workers; he suggested now the gradual reduction of hours of labor down to an eight-hour day. He again urged the abolition of child labor in the District of Columbia, and a federal investigation of child labor in all the states with publication of the findings. He urged mediation and fact-finding in labor disputes by state and federal agencies, with publicity given to the findings, as a means of preventing actual strikes.

The message was particularly radical for those days when it came to the subject of taxation. Roosevelt asked for a graduated inheritance tax by the federal government, "and if possible for a graduated income tax," with the understanding that if there was no way under the Constitution, "there will be no alternative to a constitutional amendment." He recommended that even marriage and divorce be subjects of federal rather than state action, going out of his way to condemn the falling birth rate.

It was hardly a message to inspire the confidence of big business or trusts. It started rumors of an incipient stock market break—which did come three months after the message, on March 14, 1907. The break was immediately attributed by some industrialists to the very rigorous investigation of Harriman's Union Pacific Railroad then being conducted by the Interstate Commerce Commission. On March 15, instead of easing the investigation of the Union Pacific under these attacks, Roosevelt directed an investigation by the commission of the *entire* railroad industry. By summer, the stock market break was developing gradually into the panic of 1907. The President did not cool things much in a speech he made on August 20, accusing "certain malefactors of great wealth" of bringing about the panic to make him reverse his regulatory policies. In October, there began a run on some banks whose funds had been used by speculators to corner the copper market. Thousands of depositors withdrew their money. Many banks closed. Bank credit became almost nonexistent. Even the great Trust Company of America seemed doomed. All the makings of a bad economic disaster were at hand, when J. P. Morgan deposited enough private money to keep the Trust Company of America open. Other Wall Street money also went into other banks to save them. And the Secretary of the Treasury, while Roosevelt was rushing back from a hunt in Louisiana, put $25 million of government funds in New York banks. The situation was saved. But bad flaws in our money system had become apparent, which were not cured until the days of Woodrow Wilson. Roosevelt congratulated his Secretary of the Treasury, and added, "I congratulate also those conservative and substantial business men who in the crisis have acted with such wisdom and public spirit." Here again, Morgan had shown his all-pervasive power; he had come to the aid of the badly frightened President who was not too familiar with the intricacies of high finance and economics.

The money shortage was also affecting the brokerage houses of Wall Street. Moore & Schley, a prestigious firm of brokers, was in danger because it held a large block of stock of Tennessee Iron & Coal Co., a small but aggressive competitor of the United States Steel Corporation. A loan to Moore & Schley would have done the trick; but Morgan, Gary and Frick of the United States Steel Company saw a chance to make a handsome profit by buying out their financially distressed competitor. Gary, realizing the antitrust implications and knowing Roosevelt's repugnance to any violation of the Sherman Law, was shrewd enough to make the deal contingent on approval by the President—who actually had no legal power to approve. A breakfast meeting with Roosevelt and Root at the White House was arranged quickly for the next day. Gary and Frick blandly told the President that morning that if he would approve, they would buy the Tennessee company at a price somewhat in excess of its true value, "and prevent further failures of important business concerns." But they pointed out that it had to be done before the stock market opened at 10:00 A.M. They told the President, as he later wrote to his Attorney General, "that as a mere business transaction, they do not care to buy the stock." Roosevelt added in his letter that "I felt it no public duty of mine to interpose any objection."

This decision, so quickly made on the spur of the moment, was to hound Roosevelt and his party politically through the next five years, and Roosevelt personally for the rest of his life. In essence it was a promise of immunity, which was exactly what he had stated he would never give when pressed a few months earlier by Harriman and the railroad industry to stop his campaign against the Harriman railroads. Of course, he had been misled by the shrewd and unscrupulous stock manipulators, Gary and Frick; and he was also alarmed at what the result might be of a refusal on his part. It was perhaps the only instance of importance where fear brought about a change in his style of dealing with "malefactors of great wealth"—fortunately only temporarily. While this incident has been painted by some commentators as proof of Roosevelt's "babes-in-the-wood" lack of expertise and experience in financial matters, it also can be considered an example of his continuing change in philosophy on the Sherman Antitrust Act. He was becoming more and more convinced that the remedy for overconsolidation was not fragmentation but regulation. He had reached the point of belief that practically all large businesses were interstate in their activities, and that therefore they should all be subject to government regulation, though not necessarily broken up into smaller units.

There can be no doubt that his impulsive, "horseback" action at breakfast contributed to the growth of the steel monopoly. A perfect example of Roosevelt's style of self-delusion and self-righteousness was the fact that when Taft in 1911 started an antitrust litigation against the United States Steel Company, based in part on this acquisition which the President had approved in such a rush, Roosevelt came to a final break with his friend, protégé and handpicked successor.

In each succeeding Annual Message Roosevelt not only repeated the progressive recommendations of the prior messages which had not been passed; he made substantial additions to his program to achieve a Square Deal and a greater social justice. In his next Annual Message, December 1907, for example, he went further even than the year before, stating that the most vital and immediate need of regulation of business was with the railroads. "There should be either a national incorporation act or a law licensing railway companies to engage in interstate commerce upon certain conditions," and the Interstate Commerce Commission should have "power to pass upon the future issues of railroad securities" and "to make a physical valuation of any railroad" for that purpose.

He repeated all his prior recommendations, nearly all of which are now the law of the land. Their presence on our statute books, though they did not pass during his own administration, owes a great deal to Theodore Roosevelt's continued and unabated fighting for them, pushing them, appealing to the people for them, using all the force and prestige he could bring to bear upon a conservative, resisting Congress.

The style of Roosevelt's messages to Congress was repetitive, sermonizing and boring. The startling vigor of his speeches in his method of delivery is missing in the printed pages. They are all over-long, and cover too much minutiae. Their language could seldom create enthusiasm.

Congress paid slight attention to his 35,000-word December 1907 Annual Message. The following month, he sent a special message—probably the most radical of all. In it he said that the recent decision of the Supreme Court invalidating the Employers Liability Act (because it applied also to intra-state railroads) and "the gravely significant attitude toward the [interstate commerce and antitrust] laws render it desirable that there should be additional legislation as regards certain of the relations between labor and capital, and between the great corporations and the public."

The special message suggested immediate amendment of the Employers Liability Act so that it would apply only to interstate railroads; it then repeated the gist of the 1907 Annual Message and all his recent previous messages; but he added some new and unheard-of proposals: legislation, for example, to regulate stock market "gambling." Recalling the panic of last year, he denied that his administration had brought it on, blaming it on "speculative folly," "predatory wealth," and "rottenness" in some businessmen of "great wealth" who consistently had fought all his attempts at reform. He did not hesitate—as Franklin Roosevelt would, except in rare instances—to name names, blaming as examples the officers of the Standard Oil Company and the Santa Fe Railroad. He recommended close supervision by a federal official of all bond and stock issues. He did not forget to include a denunciation of certain federal courts for some of their recent decisions.

During the last two years of his second term—1907 and 1908—Roosevelt moved out miles in advance of his party. He began taking on his 1912 coloration swiftly and enthusiastically as, piece by piece, he recommended an expanded program of what in 1907–08 was a startling advance in social welfare. The core of his program was essentially the same as the core of the later New Deal and subsequent Democratic programs, namely, the extension of federal authority and its exercise solely for the benefit of the great mass of Americans in all areas where the states individually could not adequately operate. Whether Roosevelt led this advance because he revelled in the use of power and more power which he would have as Chief Executive of these new federal functions, as some historians have urged, or whether it was because he saw clearly that the challenge of changing times and changing financial, industrial, and commercial conditions and operations could be met only by federal action—there can be no doubt that his style and leadership began the program and prepared the way for the later leadership and style of Wilson and Franklin Roosevelt in expanding federal power. It was probably a combination of all these which moved the innate urge in Roosevelt for action and leadership. Although he continually sought to depreciate Bryan and the earlier Populists, and steadfastly refused to give them any credit, it is clear that they saw earlier than he what the Industrial Revolution had already done, and what it would do if allowed to go on without spreading its benefits more widely and equitably among the American people. He unabashedly took from their programs plank after plank—and blandly put them forward as his own. Toward the end of 1908 there was only a small difference between him and Bryan.

Although he had begun his presidency and startled his party by his style of antitrust prosecutions, beginning with the Northern Securities Case and continuing through forty-three more prosecutions emanating from the Attorney General's office, he gradually came to conclude that "trust busting" would not by itself completely meet the new problems of centralized business. And so his style became a search for adequate methods (as he said in his December 1907 message) by which "the public at large can protect itself from certain evil effects of this business centralization." He cited, as examples of what he meant by beneficent regulation, the pure food law and meat inspection laws which business had opposed as "ruining a great American industry," but which had "worked unmixed and immediate good."

His special message of January 1908 bristled with bitter and denunciatory phrases, such as "representatives of predatory wealth . . . accumulated on a giant scale by all forms of iniquity, ranging from the oppression of wage workers to unfair and unwholesome methods of crushing out competition, and to defrauding the public by stock jobbing and the manipulation of securities"; and references to the "apologists of successful dishonesty," attacks on judges who "truckle to the mob" or "issue injunctions" or fail "to stop the abuses of the criminal rich" —words which make some of the most vitriolic of Franklin Roosevelt's later denunciations of the "money-changers in the temple" and the "selfish interests of special privilege" seem mild by comparison. This message marked the final breaking point with his own party in Congress, and with all conservative forces in the land.

His relationship with the old guard had been deteriorating since 1907; so had his influence with the congressional Republican leaders. This is normal as a President reaches the end of his term, and his legal powers—including, of course, his power of patronage and disciplining—come closer to an end. But in this case, the process was accelerated and exacerbated by his strong recommendations for reform which the congressional leaders did not favor, and by his public condemnation of those whom he blamed for the opposition.

It also marked breaks with his old friends Joseph H. Choate and Nicholas Murray Butler. One fighting sentence in this message may have been the trigger to Choate's retort, "I don't believe it," and to the exchange of letters which ended his friendship with Butler. The sentence was: "I do not for a moment believe that the actions of this administration have brought on business distress; it is due to the speculative folly and flagrant dishonesty of a few men of great wealth."

Dr. Butler wrote:

Of all your real friends perhaps I, alone, am fond enough of you to tell you what a painful impression has been made on the public mind by your special message sent to Congress on Friday of last week. I am besought on every hand to know whether I, as a friend whom you trust and who has no ulterior end to serve, cannot in some way bring you to see what damage has been done both to your own reputation and to the Presidency itself by the message. You may imagine that the task is anything but a grateful one. . . .

My honest opinion is that so far as the message has had any purely political effect, it is to bring Mr. Bryan measurably nearer the White House than he has ever been before.

President Roosevelt coldly and aggressively responded:

My luke-warm friends [have been] upset . . . [my] real supporters have hailed it as they have no other speech or action of mine for a long time. To me, your regret is incomprehensible. To me, it seems that I have the right to the fullest and heartiest support of every good man whose eyes are not blinded by unhappy surroundings, and who has in him a single trace of the fervor for righteousness and decency without which goodness tends to be an empty sham. If your soul does not rise up against corruption in politics and in business, why, then, naturally you are not in sympathy with me.[124]

Looking back to his style in the days as assemblyman, as Governor, and as McKinley's successor, this dramatic advance into the liberal world—though foreshadowed since his election in 1904—was startling. Just a short time before —January 1, 1908—he sent his Attorney General (Charles Bonaparte) a letter of many pages of congratulation on a speech which Bonaparte had made on Roosevelt's theme of a "square deal for the rich and poor alike." The letter, as with so many of his letters, reads exactly like an impassioned political speech. In it, he emphasizes the feeling that "law-defying corporations of immense wealth have until within the last half dozen years treated themselves and have expected others to treat them, as being beyond and above all check from law." He stressed the opposition which had come from big business, "who find their tools in a portion of the public press . . . their agents in some men in public life . . . in some men in the pulpit, and most melancholy of all, in a few men on the bench."[125]

The message and the letter show how keenly Roosevelt felt the opposition to his proposals which had come from his own party. That opposition had only increased his determination for reform and had added to his vindictiveness toward those who were blaming the panic of 1907 on his proposed reform activity. There is quite a similarity between Theodore Roosevelt's invigorated style for reform during the last two years of his presidency as a result of the attacks and opposition of big business, and the "Second New Deal" of Franklin Roosevelt in 1935 which came, at least in part, as a result of the attacks upon him of the American Liberty League, the American Manufacturers' Association and other right-wing groups (see page 340). Both men had the style of meeting growing attacks with renewed determination—and bitterness.

There was great similarity also between the two Roosevelts in their attitude toward selection of judges.

Theodore Roosevelt remembered very thoroughly the kind of judges he encountered when he was in the New York Assembly, those who—to his great disgust—twice struck down legislation to banish cigar-making in the squalid tenements of New York City. He then ascribed their reactionary social outlook to the wealthy, privileged group from which they came. After Roosevelt became President he delineated very clearly, when the first vacancy occurred on the Supreme Court, what his own style would be in appointing justices of that Court. It would not depend on the group from which the judge sprang. In a letter to Senator Lodge dated July 10, 1902, he explained why he expected to appoint Oliver Wendell Holmes to that vacancy. In general, Theodore Roosevelt's letters are much more revealing of his immediate thinking and of his long-time planning than Franklin Roosevelt's were to be. His philosophy on the judiciary, which was to control his general style of appointment, is laid out in the following excerpts from this letter:

I want to go over the reasons why I am in his favor. He possesses high character and high reputation both of which should . . . attach to any man who is to go upon the highest court of the entire civilized world. . . . The labor decisions which have been criticized by some of the big railroad men and and other members of large corporations constitute to my mind a strong point in Judge Holmes' favor.[126] The ablest lawyers and greatest judges are men whose past has naturally brought them into close relationship with the wealthiest and most powerful clients, and I am glad when I can find a judge who has been able to preserve his aloofness of mind so as to keep his broad humanity of feeling and his sympathy for the class from which he has not drawn his clients. . . . Our Supreme Court should show . . . their entire sympathy with all proper efforts to secure the most favorable possible consideration for the men who most need that consideration. Finally, Judge Holmes' whole mental attitude . . . is such that I should naturally expect him to be in favor of those principles in which I so earnestly believe.

In the higher sense, in the proper sense . . . [a man] is not fitted for the position unless he is a party man, a constructive statesman, constantly keeping in mind his adherence to the principles and policies under which this nation has been built up and in accordance with which it must go on; *and keeping in mind also his relations with his fellow-statesmen, who in other branches of government are strong in co-operation with him to advance the ends of government.*

Now I should like to know that Judge Holmes was in entire sympathy with our views, that is with your views and mine . . . before I would feel justified in appointing him.[127] (Emphasis added)

While Franklin outlined no formula as specific as this for selecting Supreme Court justices, he did show in his speeches and messages during his 1937 battle with Congress over the reorganization of the Court that he too wanted justices with "principles," "policies" and "views" akin to his own. Also, like Theodore, he wanted justices more willing to cooperate with the other two branches of government, or as Franklin would express it, work with the other branches as "a three-horse team."

In 1908, Theodore Roosevelt experienced a small part of what Franklin was to encounter in 1935 and 1936: the Supreme Court handed down a decision adverse to Roosevelt and his policies. It declared unconstitutional the Employers Liability Act of 1906 for which Roosevelt had worked so hard. During the same year the United States Court of Appeals for the Seventh Circuit reversed Judge Landis's fine of $29 million imposed on the Standard Oil Company for taking rebates. These two events strengthened Theodore's belief that one of the great obstacles to social and industrial justice was the attitude of courts dominated by justices who had grown up and had been appointed years before social and economic changes demanded new approaches for their solution. The same was to be true in 1936 of Franklin. And both of them used the same style to meet these reversals—bold attack!

Most of Roosevelt's inability to transform all his fighting spirit and progressive faith into more legislation in 1907–08 was due to his colossal mistake in announcing right after his election in 1904 that he would not be a candidate in 1908. For a man otherwise so successful and clever as a political operator to have unnecessarily made himself a lame-duck President so early in the term seems incredible. He would be only fifty years old in 1908; he loved his job and its power; he welcomed its burdens and responsibilities; and he looked forward to a role as private citizen with extreme distaste. Even within a strict two-term tradition, he need not have announced his renunciation of power until at the earliest the spring of 1908. To have done so in 1904 was completely contrary to his style of using every device to hold onto power and control.

During the session of Congress beginning in December 1907, Roosevelt sent up twenty messages asking for legislation. They were all rejected—except only a new modified employees liability bill, two battleships instead of the four he had asked for, and a very limited currency expansion bill.

The President's power in Congress was as low or lower in 1908 than Franklin Roosevelt's was to be in late 1937 and in 1938. Franklin's power and control over Congress was gradually revived, and even multiplied, as the foreign situation worsened and Hitler began his triumphant march in Europe. As in 1933, when the crisis deepened into possible disaster, a frightened Congress became more ready to shift responsibility to the President. Theodore had no such impetus given to his waning leadership. Whatever power he could have derived from Congress's concern about the possibility of another term for himself as President, he had thrown away. There is little doubt that, had he been willing, he could have been nominated in 1908 in spite of his 1904 disavowal—and elected. In fact, he had to take forceful steps during the Republican Convention of 1908 to prevent a genuine stampede for his own renomination. Nothing bears stronger testimony to Roosevelt's iron will than his stubborn refusal—just because of his ill-advised statement of 1904—to yield to the tremendous pressure being exerted on him to run again.

At the same time, his love of power and his intense satisfaction in political manipulation, which had been his style for so many years, made it impossible for him to resist the temptation of indulging in one last hurrah, one last display of power politics. He decided to pick his successor himself—a pyrotechnical display of his power-oriented style.

It was a test of the efficacy and strength of Roosevelt as the head of his party. But this style of forcing candidates onto a party is not necessarily good either for the party, the party head or the successor. It certainly was not for the Republican Party, Roosevelt or Taft in 1908.

But Roosevelt had made his choice, and true to his style he set about to force it on his party with all the energy, courage and ruthless cunning which he could command. It did not bother him that in his biography of Thomas Hart Benton, written long ago, he had criticized Andrew Jackson for doing the same thing.[128] For example, he quite shamelessly used patronage to build up Taft.

The only possible rival to Taft in 1908 was the militant Republican Governor of New York, Charles Evans Hughes. Roosevelt at one time had showed some preference for Hughes as his successor; but Hughes in a display of independence had rejected Roosevelt's help. In 1908, Hughes yielded to those urging him to take some action to get the nomination; and he announced that he would expound his national views at a meeting of the New York Republican Club on January 31, 1908. The meeting and the forthcoming speech by Hughes were widely advertised. Roosevelt was waiting for his chance to strike at Hughes's candidacy, and he did so with all the sly cunning of the fox. He had been working on his vitriolic special message to the Congress, which he knew would grab all the headlines. Hughes's speech was released to the press so as, hopefully, to cover the front pages on February 1. Roosevelt, with the publicity value of his own fighting message in mind, sent it up to Congress—not by coincidence—on January 31, so that the press stories would appear on February 1. The headlines the next day were devoted exclusively to Roosevelt, and Hughes was relegated to the back pages. Professor Harbaugh reports Roosevelt saying blandly to the press the next day, "If Hughes is going to play the game, he must learn the tricks."[129]

Although Roosevelt kept giving advice (mostly unsolicited) and encouragement to Taft after the nomination, he refrained from speech-making—not because he would not have loved making campaign speeches again, but because he was shrewd enough to see that this would cut down Taft's own stature. But to expect him to refrain from doing anything public during the campaign was too much. He had to break out in print—and what he said showed how strong his loyalty still was to the Republican Party which had so rebuffed him in Congress, though he differed so violently with the politicians who led the party and with the corporations which backed them.

Nothing is stronger evidence of the low state of his influence with the Republican political leaders in 1908 than his failure—in spite of extraordinary efforts—to put into the Republican platform an anti-injunction plank in labor disputes along the lines he had recommended in at least five previous messages to Congress. The National Association of Manufacturers was too powerful for him now; and it succeeded through Aldrich in framing a plank which actually approved the judicial practice of issuing injunctions in labor disputes without notice. On the other hand, the Democratic National Convention, through the efforts of Samuel Gompers, adopted a plank which sought practically to outlaw all labor injunctions.

In October, during the campaign, Gompers made the public charge that the Republican Party by its platform had thrown down and discarded labor; he urged all working men to vote for Bryan, the Democratic candidate. Roosevelt thereupon fell back on his style of self-delusion. He released a long bitter letter criticizing Gompers and stating that the Democratic plank was extreme and went further than his own past declarations on the subject. This was a patently untrue characterization, and Roosevelt must have realized it. He asserted that the Republican platform was a good, moderate middle course. He knew better; he knew the bitter truth that the National Association of Manufacturers had had their way with the Republican leaders, and had prevented Roosevelt from having his own plank inserted.

Taft was elected; but it was as much a Roosevelt triumph as Taft's. The Republican majority of the popular vote dropped by one-half from that of 1904; its majority in the Congress also fell; but it did still retain control.

Roosevelt was now, in fact, a "lame-duck" President; but his style for the last three months of his presidency remained the same. The same lion's roar, the same pressure for reform, the same belligerency with Congress, the same love of, and participation in, controversy—above all, the same zest for action.

His eighth and last Annual Message to Congress in December 1908 following the election of Taft had none of the earmarks of a message by a "lame-duck" executive. It was a clear, bold call for future action. While it was excessively wordy and preachy, as were all his Annual Messages, he was summarizing his latest political and economic philosophy.

Like the others, it covered a myriad of topics; some were new, but most of them had been discussed in previous messages. Action was proposed in all of the fields covered and for every issue of the day—except only the tariff. It repudiated anew all the old laissez-faire notions of liberty of contract which kept workers at starvation wages and long hours, and which permitted each man to do with his own exactly what he wanted to do. "What may have been an infringement of liberty half a century ago," he said, "may be the necessary safeguard of liberty today." It was a courageous call for centralized action in Washington as the only way of meeting most of the pressing problems which the states acting individually could not meet. It was all to be called in 1912 the "New Nationalism," but for Roosevelt it was clearly not "new." He had pointed out several times as President that the opponents of real regulation always sought refuge in the doctrine of states' rights, "knowing full well how futile state regulation would be." Roosevelt started the great shift on "states' rights" between the two major parties. While his views were rejected by his own party, the Democratic Party of his day began to sympathize with them and gradually to adopt them. The Republican Party by the middle of the century had become the party relying on states' rights to thwart centralized control; and the Democratic Party, long the champion of states' rights, would become in Congress the champion of the centralized state—excepting only its Southern members, who would continue to worship states' rights whenever civil rights for blacks became the issue.

The message in some of its very minor passages resulted in major controversies between the President and Congress of a bitterness unprecedented since the days of Andrew Jackson. Roosevelt sought, for example, to increase the functions of the United States Secret Service; Congress sought to limit them. Roosevelt in his most reckless style then charged in a special message that Congress wanted to limit the powers of the Secret Service chiefly because "the Congressmen did not themselves want to be investigated." A new low was then struck in the executive-legislative relationship. Congress first tabled that part of the Annual Message dealing with the Secret Service and all of the special message on the same subject. Then Congress formally rejected his entire special message on the ground that it lacked due respect.

Speaker Cannon wrote subsequently, "In the last years of his administration President Roosevelt became involved in a quarrel with the House of Representatives, and in my judgment he was to blame."[130] The President took offense because the Committee on Appropriations in 1908 sought to limit the activity of the Secret Service, which had grown tremendously without warrant of law.

For the first time since Mr. Cannon had become Speaker he was not consulted about President Roosevelt's last Annual Message. He "was as much surprised as anyone when it was found that this Message contained an assault upon Congress, and especially upon the House of Representatives, because of the amendment limiting the activities of the Secret Service. The President's Message as it was read from the desk created a sensation. All the recommendations made in the Message were forgotten in the indignation produced by the criticism of the legislative department of the Government. It caused a storm on both sides of the Chamber, and members were ready and eager at once to pass a vote of censure and return the Message to the President with the announcement that the House of Representatives would not receive a message of that character from the President."[131] The Speaker counselled the leaders against taking this action. However, two days after the message had been received, Representative James Breck Perkins of New York—a warm personal friend of the President's and chairman of the Committee on Foreign Affairs—rose to a question of privilege and offered a resolution calling attention to the offensive language. Cannon says: "The resolution was adopted unanimously. I at once appointed as the members of the Committee, Mr. Perkins, as Chairman,"[132] three Republican friends of the President, the Democratic minority leader of the House and the chairman of the Democratic caucus. They reported unanimously in less than a week, requesting the President to furnish the House with any information which would justify the language used in the message.

Cannon continues: "President Roosevelt still had it in his power to make peace with the House. But he declined to do so. He was stubborn. While quick to demand an apology from others, it was his weakness never to be able to admit a wrong or retract a false accusation." The committee was to report on December 17. "Just at 12 o'clock on that day, after I had taken the Chair and called the House to order, the President's Secretary called up the Speaker's Room by telephone and delivered a message from the President to the Speaker" peremptorily commanding the Speaker to come to the White House at once. The Speaker's secretary explained that the Speaker had taken the chair, that the House had been called to order, and that the Special Committee was ready to report. He in turn was told that the President desired the Speaker to leave the chair and that he desired to see him *before* the report of the Special Committee was taken up in the House. At that moment (when the Speaker's secretary delivered the President's message), Mr. Perkins was on his feet demanding recognition to present his report. "That report was of the highest privilege. I held the gavel in the air for a moment as my Secretary delivered the President's telephone message, which was probably the only one of its kind ever sent by a President to the Speaker of the House. . . . I simply brought down the gavel and recognized Mr. Perkins. Then I told my Secretary . . . to say that the Speaker would be pleased to call upon the President as soon as the report of the Committee was disposed of."[133]

Of course the President could have talked with the Speaker during the preceding week, or even earlier that morning, but he chose to test the Speaker's loyalty to him or to his duty. The Speaker reports that he "had no hesitancy in making the choice."[134] The President was in an "ugly mood" when the Speaker went to the White House directly after the adoption of the report of the Special Committee. Among other imprecations, "he rather satirically expressed regret that in his [next] message he would be compelled to present evidence that would implicate men very close to the Speaker, in fact the Speaker's own Secretary. In language more forcible than polite, I told the President that I had not the slightest desire to interfere with his Constitutional prerogative to send any kind of a message which he desired. . . . I added if he thought the Speaker could be intimidated by the threat to implicate his friends and his own Secretary . . . he had yet really to get acquainted with the Speaker of the House. . . .

"I had no idea what the President meant by this veiled threat implicating my Secretary, and I did not wait to inquire. . . . When I returned to the Capitol I called my Secretary into the private office and told him what the President had said."[135]

Cannon had already received intimations from newspaper friends that the President planned to use in his next message an article Busbey had written five years earlier while a Washington correspondent before he became secretary to the Speaker.

The message came in on January 4, after the Christmas holidays, and "it was more offensive than the one to which the House had taken exception. . . ." The President "intimated that Busbey [the secretary] had inspired the whole fight against the Secret Service. The President gave a long extract from a newspaper article published in 1903. . . . I had never seen this article before, had never discussed the matter with Mr. Busbey, did not know that he wrote any criticism of the Secret Service, and did not know what his views were. . . ." Sometime after the controversy Cannon asked Busbey who had really inspired the article. "He promptly replied, 'Roosevelt.' . . .

"The use of that old newspaper article by President Roosevelt was the weakest move I ever knew him to make."

Cannon continues the story:

"The House adopted the report by an almost unanimous vote. For the first time since the administration of Andrew Jackson the House of Representatives refused to accept a message from the President. . . . People must not take too seriously the reports that President Roosevelt and I became personal enemies and political opponents because of that one clash. I hope I am incapable of such petty meanness."[136]

Roosevelt at the end began to lose all sense of discretion. He ordered the Attorney General to indict the *New York World* and another newspaper for printing charges that the $40 million paid to the New Panama Canal Company had really gone to some American businessmen, including Roosevelt's brother-in-law, Douglas Robinson. The libel suit, fortunately for the doctrine of free speech, was dismissed in the courts.

The Roosevelt who left the White House on March 4, 1909, was quite a different person from the one who had occupied it even as late as 1906. In the 1906 congressional elections he had campaigned strictly as a Republican, supporting all his party's candidates whether they were progressives or conservatives. But the results of the 1906 election had greatly impressed him. The Republican majority was reduced; organized labor was successfully mobilizing against his party; the Socialist Party vote was on the increase—and had been since 1900. The spirit of change—a shift to the left—was definitely in the air. There was no doubt that the American people wanted the great reform movement to go on. Roosevelt, who had played the major part in starting this movement, was quick to realize, as a good politician, the changing tempo in the public mind. When he did so, his own ideas became more flexible, and they also shifted to the left. As the shift occurred, his attitude toward the financiers and their spokesmen and defenders in Congress became more determined. In 1908, he blasted the "ruling clique" in the Congress with which he had dealt amicably for years. He became more benevolent to those whom he used to consider radical or even revolutionary, like Bryan, LaFollette—and even some of the socialist leaders.

This helps to explain his greatly increased demands for more reform legislation during his last two years in office. With each of his reforms, he seemed able further to awaken the American people to the crying need for even *more* reform. That was one of his greatest contributions to American life, and a contribution which persisted for many years after his death. Indeed, practically every reform which was to be made during the Taft and Wilson administrations—and even a few of those in the New Deal—was included in his 1907 and 1908 messages to Congress and in his speeches of those years. These speeches also contained all the essentials of the historic radical speech to come in 1910 at Osawatomie and to reappear in the "New Nationalism," or Bull Moose program, of 1912. His policies of 1907–08 also split the Republican Party in Congress between a dominant and increasingly stubborn conservative majority and a small minority of progressives like Borah, LaFollette, Beveridge and Dolliver.

The post-Presidential activities of Roosevelt are a great, absorbing saga in themselves; but they do not belong in this volume because he was no longer President. He has been rated here on the basis only of his White House performance, as have the other Presidents in this volume. His accomplishments after he left the White House—and his many failures—are irrelevant to his standing as a President, even though they had substantial influence on the subsequent political history and thought of the United States.

Roosevelt's great achievements during his presidency were those of enlightened conservatism. He was already able to perceive the mighty problems—social and economic—being created by all the cultural, financial and demographic forces let loose upon American life by the Industrial Revolution. Others including many of the big industrialists and the Republican leaders in Congress may have seen them also, but they did little or nothing about them—willing to wait for their gradual resolution in the natural processes of a growing civilization. Roosevelt saw the human cost involved in this waiting; and he determined that the cost was not only too high, but too dangerous in failing to divert the victims of this new industrialism away from the paths and panaceas of radicalism. He knew that something had to be done about it; and that only government—the federal government—was in a position to do it. He created a viable government response; and as far as he could, he literally forced it down the throats of those who believed, as he once had, that all the government should do was furnish protection to ensure law and order. Roosevelt made reform not only possible but popular. Wilson and Franklin Roosevelt, who saw the truth with an even stronger sense of social justice, were to carry on the program of reform in the direction dimly recognized by Theodore Roosevelt toward a more active welfare state. Some of Theodore's advances were contradictions of a few of his most cherished earlier conservative prejudices. He hated for nearly all his political life everything about

Bryan and the Populist movement, but he finally adopted nearly all their tenets. Some observers, for example Mencken, contend that these compromises were carried out for his own strategic purposes and were "yielding to ideas which were intrinsically at odds with his congenital prejudices."[137] I believe rather that they were indications of his own political and humanitarian growth. Of course he was always a practical political leader interested in his own political career, and well acquainted with the ways of acquiring and using political high office. He realized and admitted that these ways were not always in accord with the high principles which he continually professed and frequently disregarded. No successful politician could have abided by those principles unwaveringly and without interruption. His success with Congress had to be accompanied by a relaxation of his principles, accompanied by a style of negotiation, adjustments, compromises and courageous action.

Although Roosevelt had been hailed in 1901 as a "madman" by Mark Hanna, the spokesman of the old guard (and big business), his administration—in spite of all contemporaneous commentators—was essentially one of conservatism. No one wanted more strongly than he to preserve the essence of American democratic institutions. What he sought, in spite of a radical style and continuous sound and fury, was to reform them—in order to preserve them.

James Bryce, who was the Ambassador from Great Britain in many of Roosevelt's years in office, and who had written extensively about the American government in his *American Commonwealth,* wrote the President a letter on March 6, 1909, two days after he had left the White House. The following excerpt pinpoints the essence of Roosevelt's great accomplishments and his place in American history. It is especially significant because in Bryce's *American Commonwealth* (written in 1888) he had expressed a rather low opinion of all Roosevelt's predecessors for a century, except Lincoln. In fact, one of the chapters in the book is entitled "Why Great Men Are Not Chosen Presidents":

Now that you may have a little time to read letters, I want to tell you what has been much in my mind in reflecting on your seven years of office. You seem to me to have done more for the advancement of good causes, more to stir the soul of the nation and rouse it to a sense of its incomparable opportunities and high mission, for the whole world as well as for this Continent, than any one of your predecessors for a century save Abraham Lincoln himself. The results will endure; some of them will be even greater, I venture to think, than we can yet see. The bringing about of peace between Russia and Japan, the construction of the Canal, the setting on foot of the conservation of resources movement, all fall into their places along with and cohere with this appeal to the Nation's heart and its larger thoughts for the future which you have made.[138]

In a confidential letter sent to his old friend Lodge on June 1, 1908 (to be used by Lodge only if necessary to stop a threatened third-term stampede for Roosevelt at the Republican National Convention of that year), Roosevelt reminisced proudly about his conception of executive power and his stewardship theory. It was the basic foundation of his style:

While President, I have *been* President emphatically; I have used every ounce of power there was in the office and I have not cared a rap for the criticisms of those who spoke of my "usurpation of power"; for I believe that the talk was all nonsense and that there was no usurpation. I believe that the efficiency of this government depends upon possessing a strong central executive, and wherever I could establish a precedent for strength in the executive, as I did for instance, as regards external affairs in the case of sending the fleet around the world, taking Panama, settling affairs of Santo Domingo and Cuba; or as I did in internal affairs in settling the anthracite coal strike . . . or as I have done in bringing the big corporations to book—I was establishing a precedent of value. *I believe in a strong executive; I believe in power.*[139] (Emphasis added)

The fact is that in both foreign and domestic matters, Roosevelt extended executive authority to the furthest limit permitted in peacetime by the Constitution—if not further. Strength in the Chief Executive was, in his view, a national asset per se and not a danger. "A strong people need never fear a strong man," he once said. He felt that it was his positive duty to resist any attempts by Congress to limit the Presidential power—and he did.

2

WOODROW WILSON

(1856–1924)

President, March 4, 1913, to March 4, 1921

"Gentlemen; a toast: I give you the Governor of the State of New Jersey, Woodrow Wilson—a liar and an ingrate."

The occasion was a small private dinner given six months after the inauguration of Governor Wilson, by the man who proposed the toast, James R. Nugent, the politically powerful chairman of the Democratic State Committee of New Jersey. He and an even more powerful New Jersey Democratic leader—a former formidable United States Senator, James Smith, Jr.—had in routine but ruthless political fashion forced the nomination upon the Democratic Convention of New Jersey in September 1910 of a strange candidate for Governor. Their man had been a college professor for twelve years and a university president for eight. Neither of these political bosses had ever met him personally before the nomination. True, he had become a renowned scholar, writer, and lecturer on American political and governmental subjects; but he had never held any political public office and was a complete novice in practical or party politics.

The nominee they forced on the reluctant delegates at the New Jersey State Convention in September 1910 was, to the surprise of many battle-wise politicians, elected in November.

Smith and Nugent now fully expected to run the state through this amateur Governor and theoretical scholar with substantial attention to the political and financial benefit of themselves, their friends, and the large corporate interests of New Jersey, who had in the past contributed so generously to the Democratic (as well as Republican) campaign chests. Smith, particularly, saw this electoral victory as a stepping stone by which he could return immediately to the United States Senate. But from the day after Wilson's election, both political bosses, all their close friends and most of their corporate allies got a jolt to their great expectations nearly every day.

The toast offered by Nugent—"a liar and an ingrate"—was an expletive based on the disappointment, chagrin, outrage and resentment with which these corrupt politicians now realized that they had picked and forced upon their party the wrong man.

At the next table to Nugent's small party there happened to be a group of officers of the New Jersey National Guard who were stationed at a camp nearby. Nugent sent some wine over to the officers' table, and asked them to join him and his guests in a toast. As the host spat out his unexpected words, there was silence. Nobody drank, except the host. His guests and the officers put their glasses down on the table—some first poured the wine on the floor—and together they left the room and Nugent, alone with his bottle.[1]

A few days later, Nugent was deposed by a formal vote as state chairman; and a supporter of Wilson was elected in his place. One year after the little dinner ended so abruptly, Woodrow Wilson was nominated by the Democratic National Convention in Baltimore for the presidency of the United States.

Wilson, as we shall see in some detail, deserved neither epithet—"liar" nor "ingrate." What had happened to the short and abortive political relationship between him and the New Jersey Democratic bosses on this occasion is not only an interesting story in itself, but a very important indication of Wilson's future style as Governor and as President in dealing with machine politicians.

Wilson later described the disagreement in New Jersey in his own clear, dry style in speaking of the fracas between them: "They did not believe that I meant what I said; and I did believe that they meant what they said."[2] In other words, they did not believe him when he told them that, if elected Governor, he had no intention of breaking up the party machine and substituting one of his own; that he would consult with the party leaders (as well as with other people) on political appointments and on proposed legislation, but that his would always have to be the final decision on both. He, in turn, *did* believe them when they said that that was satisfactory to them, and was all that they expected, including the fact that they had no intention of trying to send back to the United States Senate its former member, James Smith, Jr., now the Big Democratic Boss of the State of New Jersey.

The New Jersey bosses had offered Wilson the gubernatorial nomination in New Jersey in 1910 for the same reason that the New York bosses had offered the gubernatorial nomination a dozen years earlier in New York to Theodore Roosevelt. They wanted to win. And their selection in each case appeared to them to be the most likely, if not the only one who could win.

In 1910 it seemed to be much less risky for the New Jersey bosses to make such an offer. They were dealing with a schoolmaster, supposedly naïve and unsophisticated in the ways of practical political men. In 1898, the New York bosses had been dealing with an experienced, courageous and independent officeholder, with vast political experience in legislative and administrative office, who had on several occasions defied and defeated more than one political boss. But, in fact, the bosses in New Jersey later fared much worse in the choice of Woodrow Wilson than the New York bosses did with Theodore Roosevelt. We have seen (Chapter One) that Roosevelt, after election, conducted his legislative and administrative governorship independently, opposing the views of the bosses on important legislation and on appointments to high office; that he made it his style to "get along" privately with them as well as he could—with Platt and Odell and the others—without an open public break. In fact it was one of the accomplishments of which he was proud, and about which he later often boasted. Wilson was made of different stuff. He not only resisted the New Jersey political bosses in important legislation, patronage and administration, but far from trying to avoid a public fight with them, he seemed to relish it—the more public, the better.

When Theodore Roosevelt began developing his political style, he was a young man of twenty-two standing on the lowest rung of the ladder of elective state politics. His style developed and changed over the years through the numerous public offices he held until and even after he reached the presidency. By the time he was elected Governor he was only forty years old, and had already occupied four previous important offices, one in state government, one in the City of New York government, and two in the federal government. He had also made a campaign as the candidate of his party for the mayoralty of the City of New York. When Franklin D. Roosevelt began to develop his political style on almost as low a step of the ladder he was only twenty-eight years old. By the time he was elected Governor, he was only forty-six years old and was entering into his third political office of importance, having already run in a nationwide campaign for Vice President of the United States. Wilson, on the other hand, started on the second rung from the *top* of the elective political ladder, with no previous political office in his life, and with no chance gradually to develop a political style; he was already a man of fifty-four, and not in robust health. These differences in personal political history were all to be important in the matter of the Presidential style of each of the three men in later years.

Wilson's road to the governorship-presidency was an unothodox, if not a unique one. His life is a paradox in its admixture of professionalism and amateurism. Although his brief two years of governorship provided Wilson with more than the usual hard political experience in dealing with all kinds of political forces: voters, delegates, legislators, professional politicians and outside backers, promoters and opponents (good and evil), certainly no one ever reached a prominent State House in the United States who in a literal sense was more of an amateur politician. The political knowledge which later served him best and which most influenced his style as President was the knowledge he had gained from a lifetime study of government and political science—American and British —and a meticulous study of the ways, wiles and methods of successful statesmen.

In the youth and early surroundings of Woodrow Wilson there was even less to suggest the possibility of a political career (especially one leading to the top) than there was in the early life and background of either of the Roosevelts. While there was no log cabin in Wilson's life either, and no real physical privation, there was also none of the affluence and patrician atmosphere, no Harvard gold coast or wide European travels, no landed estates or independent fortune which provided the leisure and independence for political life.

Much of Wilson's later style can be traced to his father, a staunch man of books, and particularly of The Book. His forbears had come from Scotland to County Down in Ireland, thence to America. Wilson's mother, of the Woodrow family, too was descended from a long line of pure Scots men of letters—ministers, educators, editors.

In later life Woodrow Wilson would himself comment on the two strains of his blood which met at Staunton, Virginia, where he was born December 28, 1856. There were the Woodrows, pure Scots and scholarly, but (as he told Joseph Tumulty in the White House) "canny, tenacious, cold and perhaps a little exclusive." Then there was the "Irish in me, quick, generous, impulsive, passionate, anxious to help and to sympathize with those in distress, and like the Irishman at the Donnybrook Fair, always willing to raise (sinking into an adopted Irish brogue) me shillalah and to hit any head which stand firrninst me." And he added: "I tell you that when these two fellows get to quarreling among themselves, it is hard to act as an umpire between them."[3]

In later life these traits led to different styles in political action. Some contemporaries saw more of the Irish than the Scots, and vice versa; perhaps that is one reason why they seemed to see different people while looking at the same man.

Woodrow Wilson (who was christened Thomas Woodrow Wilson and who through college always signed his name Thomas W. Wilson) was born while his father Thomas was pastor of the First Presbyterian Church of Staunton. Called from one pulpit or seminary to another at short intervals, the family had to move frequently. Their posts were all in the South, one section of the country in which the later President was to boast that nothing had to be explained to him. When the Civil War broke out, the family was in Augusta, Georgia, where the father was the pastor of the First Presbyterian Church. The Reverend Dr. Thomas Wilson kept slaves at the time; and he sided enthusiastically with the South and with the Southern wing of the Presbyterian Church in its split during the war.

Though the war itself spared Augusta and the Wilsons, the ravages visited on other cities of the South, the miseries and degradations and humiliations of the Reconstruction period left their marks on little "Tommie" (which had become his nickname). Much of the sympathy that would provide the inspiration, compassion and love of humanity was ground into him as he watched the wrecked lives and homes of those who had been so profoundly damaged during the aftermath of the war in Augusta and in other cities of the South.

Theodore Roosevelt's father, satisfied with his son's mind, impressed upon Teddy (two years younger than Tommie) the necessity of improving his body. We have seen the effects of this on Roosevelt's style. Tommie's body, while not physically strong, was not nearly as weak as Theodore's; but Tommie's father concentrated upon his boy's mind, his spirit, his religion, his understanding—and above all his speech. The pastor and his entire family spent much time together: daily prayers with everyone on his knees, singing hymns at dusk on the Sabbath, long reading out loud of fiction classics by the father with the whole family lying around listening with fascination. The pastor was teacher to Tommie, and also playmate and confessor. He spent much time, patience and perseverance on his son's speech and use of words. President Wilson's literary style did not come solely from his own vast reading; it all began with his father.

Dr. Wilson had an obsession about the use of the precise word to express a precise thought. Even in ordinary conversation with his son he would stop and search for just the right word, *le mot juste;* when he found it, the doctor would show his pride and the son his admiration. The father drilled the same habit into his son. The talk at the dinner table was of a high order, and even though young Tommie could not read with ease, he could take part in the good conversation. To make such conversation explicit, the dinner table was often cluttered by reference books brought in by the father to make some point clear and, above all, precise.

The preacher set aside Sunday afternoons for serious tutoring of his son, giving of his wisdom and the knowledge which he had himself acquired through life—in literature, science, and, of course, theology. On Mondays the two would go to the practical schools of life in and around Augusta—the mills, cotton gins, factories, furnaces making power, machines making ammunition for the Confederacy. The boy was then examined closely about the things he had seen and what he had been told about them. If he said he understood, the father was not satisfied. Tommie was told to put it in writing. The writing was then literally dissected by the old pastor. What did that sentence mean? What did he mean by that word? When Tommie explained, his father would often say: "Well, if that's what you meant, you did not say it precisely; try again and if you don't say it precisely we'll have another try at it. Look this word up in the dictionary; see if you can find a more precise one." Above all the father literally made the boy think on his feet —and express exactly what he was thinking. The father and son even played the game of trying to improve upon the precision of language of Charles Lamb and Daniel Webster.

The generations since 1912 who have marvelled at the cold exactness, the scholarly word, the all-expressive phrase of President Woodrow Wilson's style can look to this father-son relationship for their foundation. It was no mere coincidence that his father both in the pulpit and in other speeches expressed contempt and disdain for florid oratory and "high-falutin' " rhetoric. Neither characteristic ever appears in Woodrow Wilson's style. Indeed, very early in life in his association with other boys at the various schools, he learned that his *métier* would never be participation in physical activities but an ability to sway his companions by the use of words—in literary societies, public debating, elocution. As President too, one of the bases of his style of leadership and mastery of men would be the use of words.

And it was of course to his father that he owed the deep religious faith in a Scots Presbyterian life which remained with him always. We shall see how much Wilson's conviction—implanted in him early in life—that a divine Providence controlled the actions of righteous men and would always guide man to the right if only he would allow himself to be guided, would have to do with his Presidential style when he had to assume responsibility at the same time to such a God and to the American people.

Life as a boy included moving with his father from pulpit to pulpit, from city to city. In 1870 the preacher became a professor of theology in Columbia, South Carolina. Perhaps it was here that the boy's first real hatred of the works of war was born. Columbia had been reduced to smoldering ruins by General Sherman only five years earlier and was still two-thirds demolished; the State of South Carolina was still completely in the hands of carpetbaggers and the untutored riffraff of Reconstruction days. At the age of seventeen he became an active member of the church and in his Calvinist faith from that day on he prayed on his knees at his bedside every night. The pronounced immediate effect of this allegiance and direct moral responsibility to a Divine Power was an improvement in the young Woodrow's studies and a renewed devotion to wide reading of books. His reading soon took him into the realm of politics—or, as he preferred to call it, statesmanship. The story is told that in his late teens his cousin found him reading in the library under the portrait of a man she did not recognize. Woodrow told her: "That is the greatest statesman who ever lived, Gladstone, and when I grow to be a man I mean to be a great statesman too."[4] It was natural in that period of decline in the presidency for the young man to look for heroes in Great Britain, whence his grandparents had come to America.

There followed a year of the then primitive, rigorous life at the struggling Presbyterian Davidson College in Charlotte. But poor diet, little heat, lack of decent living facilities and exercise caused illness which made him leave because of serious nervous indigestion. He returned home for a year and a half to the same atmosphere which had done so much for his mental and spiritual development. Then came a call to another pastorate in Wilmington, North Carolina.

As he grew out of his teens, he was beginning to develop some of his great understanding for relations between people while he watched the rawest forms of politics and economics in the Reconstruction of the South, and also some of his later driving force for service.

In 1875, at the age of nineteen, he started for Princeton, then known as the College of New Jersey. As the son of a Presbyterian minister he was entitled to free tuition.[5]

Scholastically, Wilson was not adequately prepared for Princeton, and his first year's grades showed it. But as his perception of his own future became clearer, he devoted more time and energy to his studies, and his class standing improved. He was helped, as later in the White House, by shorthand which he had learned in a correspondence course. As he improved, his self-confidence grew. For his four years average he rated above 90 per cent, but was only number 41 of the 42 who did. His average had been pulled down by his weakness in mathematics and science. In his own specialties, which he selected as far as the curriculum permitted, and in all the reading and writing which he did in his free time, he excelled. In fact he soon became known at Princeton as a speaker, debater and writer on matters of government.

His father's coaching in oratory continued to come from afar—by letters. "Study manner, dearest Tommie, as much as matter," one letter cautioned; "Sentences ought to resemble bullets—that is, be compact and rapid, and prepared to make clean holes." The young man followed this advice closely, and his later writings showed the result. He drove himself to learn all that he possibly could about government, its theory and its history, and about the lives, careers and styles of the statesmen of the past and present. His preacher ancestors had concentrated on principles and religious and moral doctrine. Wilson realized early at Princeton that great principles of humanity as distinguished from theology depend on great men, capable of exercising the leadership on which all human progress eventually rests.

He was attracted particularly to the lives and speeches of British statesmen, masters of the spontaneous type of oratory required in the give-and-take of the British parliamentary system rather than the formal fixed speeches of the current type of American oratory. In fact he organized a Liberal Debating Club which operated on the British parliamentary system where great issues were debated as in the House of Commons; questions were asked and if the "Prime Minister" could not defend his policies to the satisfaction of the club, he and his government were turned out. Naturally, young Wilson was acting "Prime Minister" a good part of the time. To add to his absorption with government, statesmen, and oratory, he happened upon the bound volumes of the *Gentlemens Magazine of London,* at that time running a continuous series of articles entitled "Men and Manner in Parliament," in which the debates in the Houses of Parliament were published. If anything was needed to confirm his youthful decision upon a public career it was the *Gentlemens Magazine,* aided by his experience in the Liberal Debating Club.

The stars to which young Wilson could look up and dream about reaching formed an inspiring galaxy—Disraeli, Gladstone, John Bright and scores of others. Wilson himself stated to one of his biographers, William Bayard Hale, that "no one circumstance did more to make public life the purpose of his existence, nor more to determine the first cast of his political ideas" than these articles about the British statesmen.[6] His purpose in Princeton became clear and single: to prepare himself for public life.

Theodore Roosevelt had made up his mind at an early age that he was going to become a member of the "ruling classes." Being a young man of direct action, he went about it in the most direct way—by joining a local Republican Club. Wilson's determination to enter public life was fixed at a slightly earlier age but his method was quite different. Nothing probably would have repelled him more than the thought of joining such a club. He turned to developing his mind—and then his reputation—as a political thinker, writer and speaker. This difference in approach became significant in creating the difference in their respective political styles.

What Wilson did at Princeton toward his objective was as much his own way of work, independent of the college routine of instruction, as was Theodore's work at Harvard toward building up his body by and for the strenuous life. And he went about it as methodically as Theodore did. In addition to his studies of the different kinds of successful and unsuccessful attempts at government in history and of the lives of political leaders, he turned to specific writing and extemporaneous speaking—leaning back on his early rigorous paternal training in preciseness of expression and in debating and thinking "on his feet." He became indifferent to studies or subjects not related to government and public leadership. He joined the American Whig Society, one of the two debating clubs at Princeton, and quickly became its acknowledged leader. To get additional practice in elocution, he would often go down alone to the woods and declaim from a volume of Burke or Chatham. During vacations he spent hours on week-days making speeches to the empty pews of his father's church in Wilmington.

Wilson coveted prizes in speaking and debating. Some he got; some which he hoped to get, he did not. When this happened he was depressed and needed consolation from friends—and above all from his father. One of the big prizes he and his friends thought he would surely win and which undoubtedly through his undergraduate days he had dreamed of winning was that for the annual debate between the two societies. The story of what happened would ordinarily be too trivial for this chapter except for its great significance as an element of his style even as President. Wilson of course was one of the three representatives of his society for the coming debate and was by now considered the star. The debate was to be extemporaneous; the subject was picked by a committee and turned out to be "Free-Trade versus Protection." The sides were picked by lot drawn from a hat, and young Wilson drew the slip in favor of "Protection." He promptly tore it up, declaring he would not debate, that he was a convinced free-trader and that nothing could ever make him advance arguments with which he really did not agree. This was indeed going to be an unorthodox statesman.

His writings at Princeton brought him as much campus fame as his speeches and debates. Two of his articles appeared in the *Nassau Literary Magazine*. It is no accident that they were both on European statesmen. One, on Bismarck, was published in his sophomore year. The other in his senior year won a prize; it was on Pitt.

The startling differences between the public leaders in Britain and those in the United States which must have impressed itself on Wilson from the very beginning was something that occupied his mind, as we shall see, for many years. Apart from the brilliance of mind and tongue of the foreign statesmen as contrasted with the mediocrity of members of our own Congress in Wilson's day, there was the realization that an open parliamentary government—where leadership had to be maintained in daily question-and-answer periods before the whole world—was so much more democratic than the government in Congress by closed committees.

In his senior year at Princeton, 1879, when he was only twenty-three (the age at which Theodore was first elected to the Assembly), his thoughts were crystallized in an article entitled "Cabinet Government in the United States." It was accepted by the *International Review,* a prestigious magazine of which, ironically, one of the editors was the future Senator Henry Cabot Lodge.

So much more time has been spent discussing the college and home work of Wilson than of the Roosevelts because it was there—and in later academic life —that he was to acquire the political skill and style which the Roosevelts acquired in practical political experience and public office. It began to show first in this article, which contained political wisdom and practical insight far beyond Wilson's years or experience. It showed congressional government as it actually was practiced rather than as described in the ordinary books on civics. He argued that frank and open debate was the essence of a popular representative body; but that "Congress is a deliberative body in which there is little real deliberation; a legislature which legislates with no real discussion of its business. Our government is practically carried on by irresponsible committees. There could be no more despotic authority wielded under the forms of free government than our national Congress now exercises. . . . Congress should legislate as if in the presence of the whole country, in open and free debate." He was brutally frank about the lack of real leaders in Congress, attributing the vacuum to the committee system. One remedy he suggested was giving Cabinet officers a seat in Congress and participation in debates to ensure a strong Cabinet, a strong Congress and the fixation of public interest.

Here was the beginning of his style as President (from which he never deviated), of insistence upon open, frank discussion and decision on public affairs. Here too was the beginning of his style of executive responsibility and leadership. "There is no one in Congress," he wrote at this early age, "to speak for the nation. Congress is a conglomeration of inharmonious elements; a collection of men representing each his neighborhood, each his local interest; an alarmingly large proportion of its legislation is 'special'; all of it is at best only a limping compromise between the conflicting interests of the innumerable localities represented."

This was fifty years before Presidents Franklin D. Roosevelt and Harry S. Truman would more succinctly point out that the only representative or lobbyist of all the people was the President of the United States.

It was an article which—as he graduated from Princeton—began to get him notice off the campus, and even outside the state.

His family now hoped that he would add another to the long line of Woodrows and Wilsons who had filled the pulpit. But he had found other causes which he could love and for which he could fight just as hard. However, the way of the statesman was not well defined as a profession; there were no universities especially directed toward a career in statesmanship as there were in law, medicine, and engineering with, say, a nomination for public office instead of a degree.

One thing is clear about his travel up to the governorship and from there to the presidency. The nomination was not a reward for the services of a party hack as in the case of Harding, or the services of a great general as in the case of Eisenhower, or even for continued excellence and statesmanship in the ascending scales of public responsibility and public office as in the case of the two Roosevelts. The nomination ultimately came to him as a result of voluminous writings of scholarship which, as George Creel has said, "shot light through the confusions of government."[7]

But how should he proceed now that he had finished at Princeton? The nearest approach seemed to be the law, which he hated in its technicalities and disliked in its commercial applications, but which he thought of as a "branch of political science." So as a good Southern gentleman he entered Thomas Jefferson's University of Virginia in Charlottesville in 1879. For one who felt that the precepts of the law fed to him were "as monotonous as hash," and who forced himself to swallow "the vast mass of its technicalities with as good grace and as straight a face as an offended palate will allow," he did pretty well at law school—while it lasted. Here too, as in Princeton, it did not take him long to become a leader among the students. And also as at Princeton he was known and liked; frequently he met with the pleasure-bent set, as well as with the more somber and studious set. He seemed to be equally at home with both, although his gaiety, wit, charm and clownish antics were severely restricted to small private groups of friends and never used in public. That was to be his style also in the White House. He had a good enough tenor voice to join the chapel choir and glee club and just about enough physical stamina to play a little baseball or to row in boat races.

But he let nothing interfere with his reading on favorite topics (which had little direct connection with the practice of law) or with his writing, writing, writing.

The *University Magazine* accepted two articles during his first year. Again, they were about statesmen—British statesmen: John Bright and Gladstone. He delivered an oration on Bright and was already so well known as an orator within his first six months at the Charlottesville law school that there were numerous requests for admission from non-university men and women, and the hall, contrary to ordinary custom, was opened to the general public.

In the university at Virginia, as at Princeton, there were two literary and debating societies. He immediately joined one, where he won the annual prize for oratory.

But the constant reading, debating and writing, added to the lessons in law which he had to study if he wanted to pass, were too much for his frail body— so subject to indigestion. In the early winter of his second year, he also suffered from catarrh and dyspepsia and such a bad cold that he had to give up and go home. He continued to study law at home in Wilmington by himself for a year and a half. The monotony was broken only by ceaseless reading in his favorite subjects, to which he had now added an interest in the classics, and by repeated orations to the empty pews of his father's church during the week.

In 1882 he took his bar exams and passed with high grades. He tried the practice of law in Atlanta with a partner. Neither of them could attract clients; after a year or so they gave up. At the age of twenty-seven he was still dependent on his father for a living. After much family discussion he decided that he needed some profession to supply a moderate income and adequate leisure with which to pursue his long-standing ambition. "What better can I be, therefore," he wrote a friend, "than a professor, a lecturer upon subjects whose study delights me?" So in 1883, he enrolled at Johns Hopkins University to study politics, constitutional history, public finance and international law. His father's savings paid for his first year; he won a scholarship for the second.

Two years later, he finished and published his first book—an instant success —*Congressional Government. A Study of Government by Committee.* He had worked on it practically all during his two years at Johns Hopkins. It won great praise from competent reviewers and was accepted by the university as a thesis for a doctor's degree.

Congressional Government deserved its great success. It pointed out that the presidency had fallen from its lofty pedestal of dignity and heights of power not because of lack of constitutional authority but "because the power of Congress has become predominant." Congress had accomplished this by a steady and increasing usurpation, by trying to manage things beyond its legitimate jurisdiction, and by arbitrary control of the purse and over the power of appointments by the President. It was a statement of congressional government as it was in practice rather than intended in Article I of the Constitution. His future political antagonist, Theodore Roosevelt, was to put a temporary halt to this kind of government. Wilson took up the style in 1912 which completely reversed the relative positions of the two supposedly co-equal branches of government.

Congressional Government was immediately recognized as a work of importance, but its prestige grew over the years slowly but surely. In 1892 it won the John Marshall Prize at Johns Hopkins; James Bryce in his *American Commonwealth* acknowledged his debt to it and quoted from it; it was translated into several foreign languages, and has been reprinted thirty times in the United States, the last time in 1956. Because of the fame of his book he received several offers to teach. The one he accepted was at Bryn Mawr, the new Quaker college for women which was to open the following year.

He had been engaged to Ellen Axson for two years. Marriage had been impossible because of his impecuniousness but the proceeds of the book and this, his first steady job (at $1500 a year), enabled them to get married in June 1885. The couple went to live at Bryn Mawr (which then had two buildings and forty-two students). He soon developed a great distaste for teaching at Bryn Mawr but stuck at it for three years. He tried for a job in Washington in the federal government but was offered nothing suitable. In 1888 he transferred to the faculty of Wesleyan College, where he made a brilliant reputation as a lecturer. Two years later as a result of strenuous efforts by old Princeton friends, he was offered a professorship at Princeton in jurisprudence and political economy. As a Princeton professor he spent most of his efforts lecturing on politics.

In 1900, when the United States was being propelled into the maelstrom of the outside world—in both the Atlantic and Pacific—by the force of the Spanish-American War, and later even more violently by the force of Theodore Roosevelt, Wilson showed quite clearly—twelve years before he was elected—what he thought the President's role had to be in foreign affairs and the style he was to follow when the role would fall to him.

In 1900 he said: "When foreign affairs play a prominent part in the politics and policy of a nation, its Executive must of necessity be its guide: must utter every initial judgment, take every first step of action, supply the information upon which it is to act, suggest and in large measure control its conduct."

Good as his writing was, however, his speaking showed him at his best. He described his own satisfaction with his command of the spoken word, realizing frankly that it had brought him his greatest success at college and law school. He said of oratory, "It sets my mind—all my faculties—aglow . . . I feel a sort of transformation—and it's hard to go to sleep afterward." He felt an "absolute joy in facing and conquering a hostile audience . . . to thawing out a cold one." This was the characteristic which had made his ancestors great preachers of The Book; it was what made him the master and leader of men when he spoke of the great causes in politics.

His classes trebled in size during his twelve years of professorship at Princeton. He was voted the most popular professor each year. At the 150th celebration of the founding of the College of New Jersey (when it became known as Princeton University), he was chosen to be the orator of the day. His oration on that occasion brought him national acclaim.

Wilson wrote several historical works during his years as a Princeton professor, climaxed by the most extensive of his books, *A History of the American People.* It was written for the general lay public, and the public bought it by the thousands. It was published by *Harpers Weekly,* whose president George Harvey had sought Wilson out. Harvey was later to play an important role in starting Wilson on the hard road of practical politics that would lead to the White House. Because of this background Professor Clinton Rossiter has written: "Woodrow Wilson was the best prepared President intellectually and morally ever to come to the White House."[8]

He began to be heard now in different parts of the United States discussing current public questions before all kinds of audiences. By reason of the forthrightness of his views and his style of grace and wit on the public platform he was gradually becoming one of the acknowledged leaders of national public opinion.

In 1902 the president of Princeton, Francis L. Patton, resigned and recommended to the trustees as his successor the university's foremost orator and favorite professor—Woodrow Wilson. He was unanimously elected. There seemed to be no real discussion of the successorship. It was taken almost for granted, although he had had as little executive experience as he had practical political experience when eight years later he was nominated Governor of New Jersey.

The flood of congratulations began to come in from all over the country. They ranged from the commonplace to the eloquent. Many bespoke the emotion or the prophecy of the old Scots Presbyterian minister, the father to whom Woodrow Wilson owed so much not only of his education, training, indoctrination, but also of the steel and leadership which had come down through the generations. The elder Wilson was now on his deathbed in his son's home. He called in his three granddaughters and said to them with the confidence born of eighty-one years' experience: "Never forget what I tell you. Your father is the greatest man I have ever known . . . *This is just the beginning of a very great career."* Only the year before, the preacher had told an old family servant who still remembered the president of Princeton as "Tommie" that some day his Tommie would be a candidate for the presidency of the United States, and made the servant promise that he would vote for him as the preacher's proxy.[9]

Princeton prospered greatly during the first years of Wilson's presidency. It prospered materially because of increased generosity on the part of alumni. Wilson's fame as a speaker also brought great prestige. He raised the education standards both for admission and for continuation. Within a year or so he initiated a preceptor system of conferences between students and younger teachers, intended to serve to make students think rather than to be lectured. But at the same time, Princeton was developing into more and more of a place for the sons of rich men to spend a pleasant four years. One of the characteristics of the university was its eating clubs. There was room for only about one-half of the number of upper classmen who could become members. This meant that for two years the lower classmen would spend much of their time and energy trying to make sure that they would be elected when they became upper classmen. This was all contrary to Wilson's notions of a university as a training ground for citizenship and leadership in a democratic society. He determined to abolish the clubs, and started a relentless and bitter struggle. He wished to change them into quadrangles for all students who might participate in social and intellectual companionship, into small colleges with a substantial amount of self-government. The plan was not to abolish the clubs but absorb them into the larger scale of activities. As the full import of the quarrel, and especially its effect on the eating clubs, became apparent, the discussion became a bitter dispute and a violent feud in which all Princeton seemed to take a part. Finally, after long debates, Wilson ended up in humiliating defeat. It is important here only as it shows how great were the fighting abilities of Woodrow Wilson and how personal his fights could become, even breaking up old friendships.

This defeat was merely a curtain raiser to the acerbating, acrimonious issue of the location of a graduate college which was in the elementary stage of contemplation. Before scholastic plans had matured, the issue centered upon its location. Professor Andrew F. West obtained a pledge of $500,000, with another half million in prospect, for the graduate college which contemplated its location on a site remote from the university center. Dean West's plan would have created a school segregated from the main college, which would have marked its exclusiveness, aggrandized by a sumptuous building.

This to Wilson was untenable. He desired close proximity to the college, making it an integral part, supplied with highly competent graduate instructors, proper laboratories, an adequate library and other pertinences requisite for advanced study. As William Bayard Hale put it: "The fact of the matter is, he didn't want a hundred nice young gentlemen to come to Princeton and live apart pursuing the higher culture. The notion violated the ideal of democracy, deliberately set about to create a scholarly aristocracy, introduced a further element of disintegration—when what Princeton needed was integration. His own thought was aflame with the picture of a great democratic society of students in which under-graduates and post-graduates should meet and mingle, the contagion of education flying like sparks struck out by the dash of mind on mind, beginners discovering that scholars were vital men . . . while specialists were constantly reminded of the common underlying body of truth and so prevented from growing isolated, unsympathetic and idiosyncranized."[10]

The struggle which ensued was between the advocates of the continuances of a system attuned to autocracy against that of a democracy where social status would play no part. This is well summarized in one sentence of Wilson's Pittsburgh address to alumni on April 17, 1910: "The universities would make men forget their common origins, forget their universal sympathies, and join a class —and no class ever can serve America." Another sentence is prophetic and even now in the process of realization: "I know that the colleges of this country must be reconstructed from top to bottom, and I know that America is going to demand it."[11] The fight was a bitter one, fought in the manner that was to characterize his future style. James Kerney observed: "His arrogant methods alienated many who might have otherwise helped with the reform at Princeton. But it was both his weakness and his strength to take a worthy cause and divert it into a personal quarrel."[12]

The battle was put to an end on May 18 by the bequest of $3 million in the trusteeship of John M. Raymond of Salem, Massachusetts, and Andrew West of Princeton. The university architect was put to work on a scheme of magnificent proportions.

Wilson had lost the fight—only to fight on and on in greater arenas. For the dispute had come to the notice of the people of the United States and they understood its intent; and politicians, ears to the ground, took notice. On September 15 at the Democratic Party New Jersey State Convention, he was nominated for the governorship. A week later, he resigned as president of Princeton and soon thereafter found himself on the way to the presidency of a greater and more democratic constituency.

He had not sought the gubernatorial nomination. Why, then, was he nominated?

The great national swing to reform was not unknown to the leaders of the Democratic Party in New Jersey. They therefore realized the popular appeal that the Princeton leader of the fight against privilege and for democratic principles would bring in heading the New Jersey party ticket. By his speeches, made in almost every area of the United States, and by his widely read erudite writings, he was already a national figure of sizable stature and already mentioned as a potential Presidential candidate.

The bosses wanted a candidate who could win. They fancied that they could take care of his ideals later. There were others, however, who were promoting Wilson's candidacy—chief among them Colonel George Harvey, the editor of *Harper's Weekly* and friend of William C. Whitney, Thomas F. Ryan, and J. P. Morgan, as well as of the Democratic bosses of New Jersey. They admired his eloquence, his leadership and his conservatism. Wilson was a self-proclaimed conservative, opposed to William Jennings Bryan and Bryanism. He was a conservative who advocated "views which would hold liberal and reforming programs to conservative and strictly constitutional lines of action, to the discrediting of rash and revolutionary proposals. . . ."[13] The chagrin of these gentlemen—though not expressed as vulgarly as Nugent's—became equally virulent when, as Governor and as President, Wilson's liberal and reforming programs, although within the bounds of the Constitution, maintained the fighting stand for reform that he had exercised as president of Princeton. That style was never abandoned.

A strange anomaly emerged at the convention. Wilson was opposed by liberal members of the party because, as the candidate of the bosses and of big business, they expected him to be under their control. Joseph P. Tumulty described the unnatural alignment thus: "All the old guard moving with Prussian precision to the nomination of the man who was to destroy for a time the machine rule in New Jersey and inaugurate a new national era in political liberalism while all the liberal elements of the state, including fine old Judge Westcott of Camden and young men like myself were sullen, helpless. Every progressive Democrat in the Convention was opposed to the nomination of the Princetonian, and every standpatter and Old Guardsman was in favor of Woodrow Wilson. . . . Behind the lines, in the 'offing' was the Insurgent Group, young men like Mark Sullivan and John Treacy—stout defenders of the liberal wing in the Convention, feeling sullen, beaten and hopelessly impotent against the mass attack of the machine force."[14]

The informality of Wilson's acceptance speech matched his informal attire. He had come to the convention hall from a game of golf—not a sport then indulged in by the masses. But the speech was one—simple, precise and forthright —attuned to the masses. It was highlighted by the following passage:

"As you know, I did not seek this nomination. It has come to me absolutely unsolicited, with the consequence that I shall enter upon the duties of the office of governor, if elected, with absolutely no pledges of any kind to prevent me from serving the people of the State with singleness of purpose. Not only have no pledges of any kind been given, but none have been proposed or desired.

"The future is not for parties playing politics, but for measures conceived in the largest spirit, pushed by parties whose leaders are statesmen, not demagogues, who love, not their offices but their duty and their opportunities for service."[15] The members of the convention, led by the enthusiasm of the astonished liberals, cried: "Go on, go on" when he paused. Tumulty reports: "Men all about me cried in a frenzy: 'Thank God, at last, a leader has come!' "[16]

A leader *had* come whose style of speech would continue to sway people by its simplicity, preciseness, directness and lucidity.

Every vestige of privilege was embedded in New Jersey, which had long been known as the "Mother of Trusts." The ex-president of Princeton, at first a bit timid in this new area of public speaking, quickly gained confidence and campaigned vigorously for all the reforms which he was to press upon an unwilling legislature when he became Governor. People listened, took heart, and elected him. The needed reforms which he made clear to them will be described as he fought for them as Governor. The style of the campaign demonstrated Wilson's later style as President. Tumulty wrote: "Since the founders of the Republic expounded free institutions to the first electorates of this country there had probably been no political campaign which went so directly to the roots of free representative government and how to get it as that campaign which Woodrow Wilson conducted in New Jersey in the autumn of 1910."[17]

During the campaign Wilson's opponents prepared a well-conceived trap into which a man of lesser character with more political experience would have stumbled.

The progressive leader in the Republican Party in Hudson County—a well-regarded liberal, George L. Record—stirred the public by a letter challenging Wilson either to debate the issues in various parts of the state or to answer nineteen questions with reference to the control of the "old guard" Democratic Party.

Wilson was silent for several days, keeping everyone on tenterhooks. When he spoke the campaign collapsed. Mr. Wilson's election was assured. Mr. Tumulty reported: "One day while we were seated in the tonneau of the automobile discussing the Record challenge, Mr. Wilson pointed his finger at Jim Nugent and said, very significantly: 'I intend to reply to Mr. Record, but I am sure that it will hurt the feelings of this fine fellow.'

"A few days later, without consulting anyone, Mr. Wilson replied to Record's challenge. It was a definite, clean-cut, unequivocal repudiation of the Old Guard's control of the Democratic party, and a convincing answer to every question that had been put to him. It rang true. Old-line Republicans after reading this conclusive reply, shook their heads and said, regretfully, 'Damn Record; the campaign's over.' "

One of Record's questions was: "Do you admit that the boss system exists as I described it? If so, how do you propose to abolish it?"

Mr. Wilson said, "Of course I admit it. Its existence is notorious. I have made it my business for many years to observe and understand that system and I hate it as much as I understand it. . . . I would propose to abolish it by the reforms suggested in the Democratic platform, by the election to office of men who will refuse to submit to it, and who will lend their energies to break it up, and by pitiless publicity."[18]

The Democratic bosses were not bothered. Like the ostrich with its head in the sand they told themselves, "This is a great campaign play." Even while Senator James Smith listened to the final speech of the campaign, he pulled Tumulty by the coat and, in a voice just above a whisper and with tears in his eyes, said: "That is a great man, Mr. Tumulty. He is destined for great things."[19] He was unmindful of the personal import of Wilson's words.

Senator Smith had left the Senate under a cloud due to the investigation of the Sugar Trust. He had not entered the preferential primary race—the first held in the State of New Jersey. Therefore, it was to be expected that the Lower House of the legislature (control of which had been won by the Democrats) would have elected the winner of the preferential primary, James E. Martime. Smith demanded that he be elected by the House with the support of Wilson. He considered the preferential primary "a joke."

No word came from Wilson. Wilson, as was to be his style as President, listened to everyone and kept his own counsel. Liberals wondered whether the use of the preferential primary for the first time in the selection of a United States Senator was to be ignored; politicians wondered whether Wilson would refuse to support the man who had led the forces which had nominated Wilson at Trenton. He did.

When he had made up his mind, he visited Senator Smith at his home in Newark. It was a gentlemanly meeting; Smith refused to withdraw. "Mr. Wilson . . . could not permit his sympathy as an individual to interfere with his duty as he conceived it, as an official pledged by all his public utterances to support progressive principles, among which was the preferential primary system, and committed to a course of *active leadership* [emphasis added] in matters which concerned the state at large, in which category the selection of a United States Senator certainly fell."[20] Following this meeting Wilson made a formal announcement; the contest between the Boss and the novice political leader was in the open; and the campaign for the votes of the legislators was begun and won, inspiring Boss Nugent's toast: "I give you the Governor of the State of New Jersey, Woodrow Wilson—a liar and an ingrate." One newspaper headline read: "The Cloistered Professor Vanquishes the Big Boss!"

It has been said that Wilson was willing to compromise a principle. One of his essays had presaged his willingness to compromise. He had written: "Politics is a war of causes, a joust of principles."[21] He had opposed bossism before his nomination as Governor; he accepted the support of the bosses in order to obtain the nomination; indeed, he would never have been nominated if it were not for the support of the bosses. He made the most of that expediency. When he ceased to make reasonable compromises, his power of accomplishment ceased—notably in his fight for the League of Nations. Wilson was elected by an overwhelming majority—with a single exception, the largest ever given a candidate for Governor of New Jersey. The nomination was due to the bosses. The magnitude of the victory was due to the people. It was Wilson's victory over the bosses that gave him the power to force reform legislation upon reluctant legislators, to win the attention of the progressives of the nation and thus to become the President of the United States.

The door of the Governor's office was kept open so that members of the legislature—both Democrats and Republicans—could have easy access to him at any time. This was symbolic of his belief that there should be no separation between the legislative and executive branches of government, that—as in the British parliamentary system which he had studied, written about and admired

—there should be a leader of legislative action and that the Governor was that leader.

On the day before he took office, he called a meeting of several of the strongest leaders of the legislature, including the Republican progressive George L. Record and several newspaper editors. He outlined his program—the reforms pledged in the platform—direct primaries, a corrupt practice act, laws regulating public utilities, and an employers' liability act. This was no conservative program; progressive ideas were sweeping the country. As he had campaigned he had learned, and as he had grown in political prominence he had met progressive leaders from other parts of the country who furthered his education, and changed some of his preconceived ideas.

They all agreed on the legislation, though—with the exception of Record—it was an agreement of expediency, not of conviction. Enemies of Wilson stormed and fumed about the "secret meeting." Wilson countered with the statement that "There was absolutely nothing secret about the conference. . . . It was simply a continuation of the policy I have followed ever since my election of consulting everyone who was interested in the reforms which concern the whole state. . . . Mr. Record is well known to be one of the best-informed men in this state with regard to the details involved in most of the reforms proposed. He is particularly versed in legislation elsewhere, as well as in New Jersey, with regard to ballot reform and corrupt practises, as well as with regard to the regulation of primaries. He generously consented to put his unusual store of information at the service of the conference, which was non-partisan in its purpose and meant in the public interest."[22]

Would that he had maintained the objectives of non-partisanship when he selected the committee to accompany him to the Paris Peace Conference.

The amateur politician had pulled a ten-strike! Its publicity, its novelty awakened the interest of the public, the fight was big news and the supporting battle ranks were forming. He had given substance to the answer to a self-examination he had made after his nomination, when he had wondered: "Am I equal to this big work when I failed in a much smaller one?" Then, reassuring himself, he said: "Yes, I believe I am, for now I shall be speaking to the American people, not to an academic group rooted in tradition and fearful of progress."[23] He had established a custom, followed by Franklin Roosevelt, of talking to people of all parties and not only to Democrats, emphasizing the non-partisanship of his appeals for support of reform legislation.

He never lost faith in the people—not even after the Senate defeat of the treaty following World War I. Even then he said, "In spite of all that has happened, I have not lost one iota of my faith in the people.

"They may act too quickly or too slowly, but you can depend upon them ultimately; you can depend upon their search for the truth and for what is right, and that is more than you can say about some of the so-called intellectuals who are actuated by prejudice and are sometimes more selfish than the masses."[24]

His ability to appeal to the electorate and make them understand the issues was his mainstay in battling intransigent members of the legislature controlled by the bosses. The legislators, many unwillingly, had defeated ex-Senator Smith's demand to be elected Senator because of the pressure of the people of the State of New Jersey, led by Woodrow Wilson. They did not expect to continue this obeisance; most of them were boss-controlled; they and the bosses had been controlled for years by the powerful corporations of New Jersey. They had no intention of paying further heed to the "Presbyterian Priest."

The "Presbyterian Priest," as Boss Smith labeled him, had difficulty finding sponsors to introduce his legislation, but he succeeded. The Primary Elections Bill was introduced by an assemblyman from Monmouth County who gave it his name—the Geran Bill. Boss Nugent easily arranged a coalition with the Republicans, whose powerful control was also at stake. They controlled the Senate and to proceed through them would have been the easiest course. But Nugent wanted greater satisfaction; he wanted his Democrats to defeat Wilson in the Lower House which they controlled. Therefore he called a conference on the bill.

The Governor amazed everyone by politely asking to be invited. How could they refuse? So he went. His intervention was challenged as unconstitutional. From the Legislative Manual he read a clause which directed the Governor of New Jersey to communicate with the legislature at such times as he might deem necessary, and to recommend such measures as he might deem expedient and he was there for that purpose. He spoke for three and a half hours. He knew the Constitution and it was to be his style henceforth to assert his rights of legislative leadership. The conference, called to defeat the Geran Bill, voted to make it a party measure. The Republican opposition grew faint and petered out. Their greatest debacle was a public hearing of the Senate elections committee, where the opposition to the bill failed to appear and the proponents devastated the opposition stand. James Smith, Jr.'s, private secretary sent word to his boss that open opposition to the Geran Bill was useless.

Nugent then tried other wiles. He visited the Governor and lost his temper. There followed the famous repartee: "I know you think you've got the votes," he exclaimed. "I don't know how you got them."

"What do you mean?" queried the Governor sharply.

"It's the talk of the State House that you got them by patronage."

"Good afternoon, Mr. Nugent," said Governor Wilson, pointing to the door.

"You're no gentleman," shouted the discomfited boss.

"You're no judge," replied Mr. Wilson, his finger continuing to indicate the exit.[25] (This preceded the toast incident.)

Instead of impeding any Presidential aspirations which Wilson had, this incident enhanced his reputation. The Governor of the State of New Jersey had fired the chairman of the Democratic State Committee from his office! Wilson wrote: "It was a most unpleasant incident, which I did not at all enjoy; but apparently it did a lot of good. It has been spoken of with glee all over the country, and editorials written about it. . . . They commend me to the rank and file, and particularly to the politicians themselves, I believe, but they do not leave me pleased with myself. I feel debased to the level of the men whom I feel obliged to snub. But it all comes in the day's work."[26]

The Geran Bill passed the Assembly with one-third more votes than was needed and the Republicans in the Senate joined the Democrats in passing it unanimously.

The Geran Bill—or the Primary Elections Bill—did away with conventions, easily controlled by bosses; every candidate for office from that of Constable to Governor was to be nominated directly by ballot of the people; all party officers, committeemen, delegates to national conventions and the like were to be elected by popular ballot; and the primary elections at which all this was to be done were to be conducted by the state under strict laws, the election officers being chosen from citizens who had passed special civil service examinations. The respective party platforms were to be written by the party's candidates for the legislature, meeting together with the state committee—the men who, if elected, were themselves to carry out the platform promises.[27]

Thus were the direct powers of government restored to the people. It was an unthinkably audacious undertaking in conception and notable in execution—a part of Wilson's future style. Also to be followed in the future was the style of invading enemy territory which he described in a letter on March 5:

... I have begun my speechmaking (this time at various dinners of boards of trade, which affords me a convenient platform) and am pouring shot into the enemy in a way which I hope reaches the heart of his defenses. Tomorrow I meet all the Democratic members of the Assembly in conference and shall have my first shot at them direct. Besides that, I shall draw various individuals into my office and have talks with them. . . . Somehow . . . I keep my *stubborn* optimism. I cannot manage to think ill of my fellow men as a whole, though some of them are extraordinary scoundrels. Fortunately, in this strange game most of the scoundrels are cowards also. The right, boldly done, intimidates them. . . .[28] (Emphasis added)

One of the most potent forces in Wilson's public career was his absolute faith in his own objectives and in himself. Over and over again he fought for what was, in his mind, right, with the firm belief that right would prevail. This was the keystone of his character.

The 1911 election for the Assembly was held under the Geran Law; although Smith and Nugent tried to discredit Wilson by doing everything possible to return a Republican legislature, Democratic majorities exceeded the 1910 Assembly majorities. Wilson was about to speak to a large audience in Indianapolis when he received word of the passage of the bill. The toastmaster read the telegram to the audience, and "the crowd stood up and shouted for Wilson." Needless to say, "the scholar in politics" had greatly augmented his prestige. The State of New Jersey, in one session of the legislature, had become a progressive state.

Ray Stannard Baker ably said, "He was able to give the impression of being a strong progressive, without frightening his more conservative following with extreme or revolutionary proposals. He kept the confidence of both groups; he gave them a sense of being a leader who knew not only exactly where he was going and why, but how he was going. He clearly placed himself."[29]

Wilson himself made an interesting analysis:

Radical—one who goes too far.
Conservative—one who does not go far enough.
Reactionary—one who does not go at all.
Hence we have invented the term, label,
Progressive, to mean one who (a) recognizes new facts and adjusts law to them, and who (b) attempts to think ahead, constructively. Progress must build, build tissue, must be cohesive, must have a plan at its heart.[30]

The passage of the Geran Bill oiled the way for other reforms: the passage of the Corrupt Practices Bill, the Osborne-Egan Act regulating public utilities, improvements in school legislation, requirements for inspection of food storage and of factories, and in regulating hours and conditions of labor for women and children. However, Wilson was forced to compromise in order to secure a measure for the compensation of disabled workmen; compromise was a novelty to him but it would not remain so.

He met resistance in his fight for municipal reform—long a matter of his concern, particularly in areas controlled by Smith and Nugent and other entrenched interests—and had to accept an emasculated bill. He failed in his great ambition to revise the state constitution along parliamentary lines—an overambitious objective—and he failed to convince the Republican Senate to approve a federal constitutional amendment authorizing income taxes; he did win unanimous approval in the Democratic-controlled Assembly. He had achieved the passage of every piece of legislation promised in the platform of the Democratic Convention, and wrote with justified pride an accurate assessment to his friend, Mary Allen Peck: "The result was as complete a victory as has ever been won, I venture to say, in the history of the country.—I came to the office—when opinion was rife on all these matters . . . and by merely standing fast, and by never losing sight of the business for an hour, but keeping up all sorts of (legitimate) pressure *all the time,* kept the mighty forces from being diverted or blocked at any point. The strain has been immense, but the reward is great . . . I am greatly and deeply happy that I should have been of just the kind of service I wished to those who elected and trusted me."[31]

It was well that he had accomplished so much in his first year because, as he loomed larger and larger as a possible candidate for the presidency, the Republican members of the legislature and the boss-influenced Democratic members were in no mood to cooperate with him. In fact their obdurate hostility was increased in proportion to his ever-growing national popularity—his invitations to speak in every section of the country and the tumultuous reception to those speeches. Walworth reports that "By the end of the session the implacable streak in his nature was asserting itself and he was attributing personal maliciousness to politicians who differed with him because of loyalty to the opposing party."[32] This trait grew with the years and handicapped his last big fight with the Congress of the United States.

There was one fly in the ointment of his legislative accomplishments and he met it with stubborn fearlessness, a trait which was reflected in his past and would continue into the future. The Democratic platform had contained the promise to eliminate dangerous railroad grade crossings. The legislation was passed, but the railroads resisted the Governor's signature and presented cogent arguments against its provisions; the bill was badly drawn, and Wilson considered it unfair to the railroads. It was a popular measure, not only in New Jersey but throughout the nation. The timing was particularly significant because it was shortly before the Baltimore Convention and it was feared that his veto would have adverse repercussions, as he certainly would be charged with being influenced by the New Jersey railroad interests. Fully cognizant of this, Wilson vetoed the bill. The following is an excerpt from his courageous veto message: "I know the seriousness and great consequence of the question affected by this important measure. There is a demand, well grounded and imperative, throughout the state that some practicable legislation should be adopted whereby the grade crossings of railways . . . should as rapidly as possible be abolished. But there is certainly not a demand in New Jersey for legislation which is unjust and impracticable. . . . I do not believe that the people of the state are in such haste as to be willing to work a gross injustice, either to the railroads or to private owners of property, or to the several communities affected."[33]

The Washington *Post* as early as April 21, 1911, summarized Wilson and the nation's interest in him: "Republicans as well as Democrats are frankly admitting the ability with which Governor Wilson is administering the affairs of New Jersey. Those who looked on him as a dilettante in politics have been amazed by his grasp of public questions and his businesslike method of handling them. The chief asset of this scholarly statesman seems, after all, to be his fund of hard, common sense. He is proving himself as able in practice as he was illuminative in theory. It is not surprising that the country is watching Governor Wilson with interest, and that he is being viewed as a national rather than purely local figure."

He was being viewed also by powerful members of what today is termed the "Establishment," who were fearful of the "radical" ideas of progressives like Bryan, LaFollette, Theodore Roosevelt—a late convert but vehemently progressive. Both the Republican and Democratic parties were split into two diverse groups, the conservatives and the progressives. Led by the initiative of Colonel George Harvey, the banking and money interests (including J. P. Morgan, Thomas Fortune Ryan, and William F. Whitney) and the political bosses decided that they could stem the tide of the "radicals" by securing the nomination of Woodrow Wilson. The wily George Harvey had proposed Woodrow Wilson for President of the United States at a dinner at the Lotos Club in New York City as early as February 3, 1906. He had become interested in Wilson when he, as well as Morgan, attended Wilson's inauguration in 1902 as president of Princeton. They were impressed by the leadership qualities of his speech; and they considered him to be a conservative!

In that same year this enigmatic man had also made his mark on the minds of men searching for advance instead of a status quo. As Professor Wilson, he addressed the Contemporary Club in Indianapolis on April 25 on "What It Means to Be An American." It was a "lively, amusing and eloquent" speech. On May 5 an open letter appeared in the Indianapolis *News,* headed: "A Suggestion to Democrats: A Man Like Woodrow Wilson Wanted for Leader." The letter suggested:

It seems to me that this would be a good time for the Democrats to break entirely away from the older men, and to take one wholly unidentified with past quarrels. . . . The type of man that I have in mind is represented by Prof. Woodrow Wilson, of Princeton University, who lectured in this city a few days ago. . . .

Of course, I understand that a suggestion like this will be deemed strange and fanciful by many people who have come to take a distressingly practical view of our politics. But if there ever was a time when an infusion of imagination and idealism was needed in our politics it is in these days of railroad mergers, shipping trusts, beef trusts and steel combinations. We need to get back to the old ideals, and in order to get back to them we must enlist under a man before whose eyes they gleam with undimmed brightness.[34]

Newspapers throughout the nation responded in like manner.

Harvey, Morgan and the others had probably been comforted when two years earlier, on November 29, 1904, Wilson speaking at the dinner of the Society of Virginia at the Waldorf Astoria in New York called for the rejuvenation of the Democratic Party which, he declared, was under the domination of unsafe leaders, meaning Bryan. He would "read them out of the party," and "It is now high time . . . [that those] who wish for reform without loss of stability should join with it to reassert the principles and return to the practices of the historic party which has always stood for thoughtful moderation in affairs and a careful use of the powers of the federal government in the interest of the whole people. . . ."[35]

The fact is that Wilson was not inconsistent, but each faction read its own interpretation into his words and would continue to do so. He had always believed that reforms were necessary. His first book, *Congressional Government,* pointed to necessary reforms. He was trying to reform Princeton. He was a Jeffersonian. He "would hold liberal and reforming programs to conservative and strictly constitutional lines of action." However, as the progressive movement developed, his horizons widened.

Individuals such as Colonel Edward Mandell House of Texas, interested in politics, became intrigued by this man whose personal magnetism stirred public comment all over the nation, and sought to meet him. Having met him, these men were more profoundly stirred and sought to promote him as the Democratic candidate. On November 24, 1911, through Colonel Harvey, House met Wilson. They instantly found a compatibility, a unison of viewpoint and trust, a basis for mutual respect—personal and mental—that was to last until Wilson returned from the Paris Peace Conference, broken in health and embittered by mistrust that even extended to his attachment to the Colonel. Speaking in Pennsylvania, where Vance McCormick and A. Mitchell Palmer had been advancing his candidacy, he met and won the support of William B. Wilson, leader of the miners' union, who was later to be his Secretary of Labor. Pennsylvania was the first state to declare for Woodrow. Old friends—Walter Hines Page, later Ambassador to Great Britain, Cleveland H. Dodge, Robert Bridges and others—selected a young Princetonian, William F. McCombs, a lawyer practicing in New York, to manage a campaign to gain national organization support and national publicity. *Harper's Weekly* carried Wilson's name at its masthead as a candidate for the presidency. His candidacy mushroomed through the nation as Wilson Clubs were established in almost every state. Simultaneously the old guard of the Democratic Party became alarmed. He was, of course, opposed in the primaries by the Smith forces in his own state but won nearly all of its delegates, and the New Jersey delegation played an important part in the Democratic National Convention that met in Baltimore on June 25. In the Ohio primaries, he split the delegation with the favorite son, Governor Harmon, and in the Wisconsin primaries he swept the state, thereby emphasizing his progressive support.

Everything was running smoothly until Wilson's frankness and naïveté ruptured the friendship with Colonel Harvey and his conservative adherents, and his indiscretion in writing "the cocked hat" letter threatened the loss of progressive support.

Joseph Tumulty described the Harvey incident thus:

"Everything was serenely moving in the Wilson camp when like a thunderclap out of a clear sky broke the story of the disagreement between Colonel Harvey, Marse Henry Watterson [a key Kentucky supporter] and the Governor of New Jersey. I recall my conversation with Governor Wilson on the day following the Harvey-Watterson conference at a New York Club . . . which for a few weeks threatened to destroy all the lines of support that had been built up throughout the past months of diligent work and organization.

"The Governor and I were seated in a trolley car on our way from the State Capitol to the railroad station in Trenton when he informed me, in the most casual way and without seeming to understand the possible damage he had done his own cause, of what followed the conference the previous day. It was like this: the conference had ended and they were leaving the room when Colonel Harvey put his hand on Woodrow Wilson's shoulder and said: 'Governor, I want to ask you a frank question, and I want you to give me a frank answer. In your opinion is the support of *Harper's Weekly* helping or hurting you?' In telling me of it, Woodrow Wilson said: 'I was most embarrassed, and replied: "Colonel, I wish you had not asked me that question." "Well, what is the answer?" Colonel Harvey insisted pleasantly. *"Why, Colonel, some of my friends tell me it is not helping me in the West."* (Emphasis added) Colonel Harvey said: "I was afraid you might feel that way about it, and we shall have to soft-pedal a bit." ' Mr. Wilson was so serenely unconscious that any offense had been taken that when informed by me a little later that his name had disappeared from the head of the editorial column of *Harper's Weekly* he did not connect this with the interview."

After realizing what he had done, Wilson wrote a letter revealing his insensitivity to personal relations—not a purposeful insensitivity but a lack of awareness. Wilson's letter was as follows:

(Personal)   University Club
                                                    Fifth Avenue & Fifty Fourth Street
                                                    December 21, 1911

My Dear Colonel:

Every day I am confirmed in the judgement that my mind is a one-track road and can run only one train of thought at a time! A long time after that interview with you and Marse Henry at the Manhattan Club it came over me that when (at the close of the interview) you asked me that question about the *Weekly* I answered it simply as a matter of fact and of business, and said never a word of my sincere gratitude to you for all your generous support, or of my hope that it might be continued. Forgive me, and forget my manners.

                                                    Faithfully, yours,
                                                    Woodrow Wilson[36]

After receiving Colonel Harvey's reply which—though pleasantly worded—revealed that he was hurt by what Wilson had said, Wilson (on January 11, 1912) wrote a longer apologetic and appreciative letter.

On January 20 the following notice was published in *Harper's Weekly:*

The name of Woodrow Wilson as our candidate for President was taken down from the head of these columns in response to a statement made directly to us by Governor Wilson, to the effect that our support was affecting his candidacy injuriously.

The only course left open to us, in simple fairness to Mr. Wilson, no less than in consideration of our own self-respect, was to cease to advocate his nomination.

We make this explanation with great reluctance and the deepest regret. But we cannot escape the conclusion that the very considerable number of our readers who have cooperated earnestly and loyally in advancing a movement which was inaugurated solely in the hope of rendering a high public service was clearly entitled to this information.[37]

Harvey turned his support to Wilson's chief rival, Champ Clark of Missouri. The old cry of Wilson's "ingratitude" spread through the country, weakening his support wherever it was heard. Colonel Watterson made a written statement saying that Wilson was "rather a school master than a statesman," and that "Governor Wilson is not a man who makes common cause with his political associates or is deeply sensible of his political obligations; because it is but true and fair to say that, except for Colonel Harvey, he would not be in the running at all."[38]

Contributions were down to a trickle. The "bandwagon" crowd turned away to Clark, Underwood and Harmon. Campaign headquarters were wreathed in gloom. Suddenly, however, the liberals in the Democratic Party, spurred by newspaper stories inspired by a publicity agent, rallied greater strength to Wilson. The inspired report was that the real cause of the break was Wilson's refusal to accept the support of Wall Street interests.

The liberals, in their turn, had been confronted by a Wilson "bête noire." His supporters were looking forward with confidence to the Jackson Day dinner to be held January 8, 1912, where Mr. Wilson was expected to outshine the other candidates in oratory and appeal. Suddenly, two days before the dinner a letter appeared in the press written from Princeton, New Jersey, on April 29, 1907, to Mr. Adrian Joline, a Princeton alumnus and well-known New York lawyer at the time of the split in the Democratic Party over Mr. Bryan's silver plank. Mr. Joline had become a bitter opponent of Governor Wilson. The letter read:

My dear Mr. Joline:

Thank you very much for sending me your address at Parsons, Kan., before the board of directors of the Missouri, Kansas and Texas Railway Company. I have read it with relish and entire agreement. Would that we could do something at once dignified and effective, *to knock Mr. Bryan once for all into a cocked hat!* (Emphasis added)

Cordially and sincerely yours
Woodrow Wilson

Everyone was in a tizzy except Josephus Daniels of Raleigh, North Carolina, a friend of both Bryan (who was staying with him at the time) and Wilson. Wilson's reaction was expressed in a letter written the day before the dinner, closing in typically expressed calm belief in the will of Providence: "I believe very profoundly in an overruling Providence, and do not fear that any real plans can be thrown off the track. It may not be intended that I shall be President, but that would not break my heart—and I am content to await the event,—doing what I honorably can, in the meantime, to discomfit my enemies!"[39]

He was urged to make a statement and started to draft one which contained this sentence expressive of his past and future style: "The Joline letter merely illustrates my habit,—I hope not a bad habit, however impolite—of speaking bluntly the opinions I entertain."[40] Before he had completed the statement which he never published, Josephus Daniels came in. Everyone, knowing that Bryan had been at his home, shot questions at him.

"Wilson smiled one of his inimitable smiles of inquiry and asked, 'What did you say to him?'

"The answer was:

"I said, 'Bryan, you must give these college presidents time to catch up with us.' "[41]

On the afternoon of the dinner, Wilson spoke before the National Press Club: "Even if a man has written letters it ought not to embarrass him if they are published. Even if a man changes his mind it ought not to embarrass him."[42]

There was more to plague him that day. The Nugent gang were grabbing the New Jersey places at the dinner and to be booed by members of his own state would make a bad impression; the Hearst people were demanding recognition. Wilson refused to have dinner with him—even to meet him. He told his friends, "I want the Democratic presidential nomination and I am going to do everything I can, legitimately, to get it, but if I am to grovel at Hearst's feet, I will never have it!"[43] The "Presbyterian Priest" kept his Scots calm.

An overflow banquet was arranged at another hotel to take care of Wilson's Jersey friends. He made a speech there before the main dinner speech. Then he went on to the Raleigh Hotel to find the greatest gathering of the kind ever held up to that time. Everyone of importance in the party was there. Baker reports that "Colonel George Harvey, whose 'break' with Wilson was then being hotly discussed in the press, did not come up to greet his former friend. Just in front of the speakers' table sat the little group of Wilson's New Jersey enemies headed by Boss Nugent. They refrained from joining in the applause when Wilson appeared; when they attempted, a little later during Wilson's address, to express their disapproval, a cry of 'Shame' went up from the group around them."[44]

All eyes were on Bryan. How would he greet Wilson? He greeted him with the same cordiality as he greeted Clark—Wilson's principal opponent—and with Bryan's hand on Wilson's shoulder they talked for a few minutes. Wilson spoke after the other candidates had spoken and just before the last speaker, William Jennings Bryan.

There was no dramatic, grandiloquent oratory. He paid tribute to Bryan's character and devotion. He spoke of the problems facing the nation—simply and directly: "Now, what has been the matter? The matter has been that the government of this country was privately controlled and that the business of this country was privately controlled; that we did not have genuine representative government and that the people of this country did not have the control of their own affairs.

"What do we stand here for tonight and what shall we stand for as long as we live? We stand for setting the government of this country free and the business of this country free."[45]

At the close of the speech, Wilson, turning to Bryan with "a really Chesterfieldian gesture," said: "Let us apologize to each other that we ever suspected or antagonized one another; let us join hands once more all around the circle of community counsel and of interest which will show us at the last to have been indeed the friends of our country and the friends of mankind."[46] The character of the man showed through the grace of these words; they brought a roar of appreciative applause.

Bryan told a friend after the dinner, "It was the greatest speech in American political history." Applause throughout the press of the nation and among the people of the nation followed. Even the bosses were won. Roger Sullivan, Illinois boss who was to play a major role at the convention when it seemed deadlocked, greeted Wilson in a friendly way and said: "That was a great speech, Governor. I cannot say to you just what the Illinois delegation will do, but you may rely upon it, I will be there when you need me."[47]

It was Roger Sullivan who, when informed that William F. McCombs, manager of the Wilson campaign, had phoned the Governor that the case was hopeless and thereby won Wilson's permission to release the 354 delegates who had voted for him, rushed over to McCombs and said to him, "Damn you, don't you do that. Sit steady in the boat."[48] This, in spite of the fact that his delegation was largely pledged to Clark.

Wilson's apparently perfunctory interest in the convention proceedings contrasted with the decisiveness and sagacity of his decisions. McCombs bent his energies to win the conservative East and, in particular, the support of Tammany Hall. Wilson listened to McCombs, listened to Tumulty, listened to William G. McAdoo who, active in direction of the campaign, clashed daily with the sick and irritable McCombs. When he was faced *inevitably* with making a decision, it was made decisively in favor of righteousness and the progressives. There were several notable instances.

First was Wilson's telegram supporting Bryan's position on the selection of a temporary chairman of the Baltimore Convention. The Eastern conservatives expected to choose Alton B. Parker, "the representative *par excellence* of the extreme conservative wing of the party."[49] Bryan, attempting to head off the Parker choice, telegraphed each of the candidates asking them to help him oppose the choice, and asking them to wire a reply. As Ray Stannard Baker describes the scene, "McCombs was panic striken. He was angling for New York and wanted nothing done that would further alienate Boss Murphy. Parker, himself a New Yorker, was Murphy's own pet candidate.

"Before Bryan's message was sent out, the Baltimore *Sun* had wired Wilson, asking his views regarding the selection of Parker. Wilson responded immediately, writing his reply in pencil, on a bit of paper:

" 'My friends in Baltimore, who are on the ground, will know how to act in the interest of the people's cause in everything that affects the organization of the convention. They are certain not to forget their standards as they have already shown. It is not necessary that I should remind them of those standards from Sea Girt; and I have neither the right nor the desire to direct the organization of a convention of which I am not even a member.—Woodrow Wilson' "[50]

A noble hands-off stand! McCombs was delighted.

"Later, on the same day, Wilson received Bryan's message—McCombs was newly alarmed. He called Wilson on the telephone, urging him to be cautious, and suggested a reply which beautifully straddled the issue."[51]

Mrs. Wilson and Joe Tumulty pointed out that Bryan was not asking Wilson to interfere in the work of the convention, he was asking him where he stood. Wilson, sitting on the edge of his bed, wrote his reply to Bryan:

You are quite right. . . . The Baltimore convention is to be a convention of progressives —of men who are progressive on principle and by conviction. It must, if it is not to be put in a wrong light before the country, express its convictions in its organization and in its choice of the men who are to speak for it. You are to be a member of the convention and are entirely within your rights in doing everything within your power to bring that result about. No one will doubt where my sympathies lie, and you will, I am sure, find my friends in the convention acting upon clear conviction and always in the interest of the people's cause. I am happy in the confidence that they need no suggestion from me.[52]

Clark straddled the issue, asking for harmony; the other candidates, with the exception of Governor Burke of North Dakota, supported Parker. Bryan's action and Wilson's firm position helped unite the progressives on a definite issue, though the vote itself was lost when the convention elected Parker by a slight margin. Bryan's respect for Wilson was increased, and the enthusiasm of the progressives for Wilson bounded. McCombs was unhappy to the point of tears; this marked the beginning of a break in the Wilson-McCombs relationship. The wedge was deepened by Wilson's support of Ollie James of Kentucky, a close friend of Bryan's, a progressive and a Clark man, for permanent chairman. When Bryan, in a telephone conversation with Wilson, pointed to the fact that Mr. James was a Clark man, the Governor replied, "It does not matter. He is our kind of fellow and I am sure my friends can rely upon him to treat our cause well." It was a strategic move of great importance—impressive to the progressives and to other members of the convention, for Ollie James had been for years a popular figure in the Democratic Party.

It was becoming more and more clear that Wilson had decided to cast his lot with the progressives and his reputation as a conservative was disappearing.

This did not make Mr. McCombs happy; nor did a heated discussion held over the telephone between Wilson and McCombs. Tumulty reports that after the balloting started, "The candidate himself seemed to take only a perfunctory interest. . . . He never allowed a single ballot or the changes those ballots reflected to ruffle or disturb him. Never before was the equable disposition of the man better manifested than during those trying days. Only once did he show evidences of irritation. It was from receipt of word from Baltimore—that his manager, Mr. McCombs, was indulging in patronage deals to secure blocks of delegates. Upon considering this news he immediately issued a public statement, saying that no one was authorized to make any offer of a Cabinet pact for him and that those who had done so were acting without authority from him."[53]

The heated telephone conversation began with protests by McCombs, answered by the Governor: "I am sorry, McCombs, but my statement must stand as I have issued it. There must be no conditions whatever attached to the nomination."[54] That was the end of the conversation. However, Wilson then told Tumulty that McCombs had asked him to promise that, if nominated, he would not appoint William Jennings Bryan as Secretary of State; according to McCombs, many delegate votes from the Eastern states depended upon such a promise. Said Wilson, "I will not bargain for this office. It would be foolish for me at this time to decide upon a Cabinet officer, and it would be outrageous to eliminate anybody from consideration now, particularly Mr. Bryan, who has rendered such fine service to the party in all seasons."[55]

Forgotten was Mr. Wilson's former distaste for Mr. Bryan; the Governor was capable throughout his career of changing like to dislike, as well as dislike to like. He did the former more frequently, as we shall see.

The progressives developed strength in the convention by the clear-cut victory they won on Bryan's bold initiative in fighting on the floor of the convention the unit rule by which a state had to vote solidly for the candidate who had the majority of its delegates' votes. A young man from Ohio, Newton D. Baker, a Wilson supporter, bound under the unit rule to vote for Harmon, came to prominence by arousing the convention to a high pitch of enthusiasm.

Though victorious, Bryan, that old convention pro, was uneasy. He sensed that "the representatives of Morgan, Belmont, and Ryan were at work."[56] Therefore, to head them off, he astounded the convention the following day by offering a bold, audacious resolution:

"Resolved . . . as proof of our fidelity to the people, we hereby declare ourselves opposed to the nomination of any candidate for President who is the representative of or under obligation to J. Pierpont Morgan, Thomas F. Ryan, August Belmont, or any other member of the privilege-hunting and favour-seeking class.

"Be it further resolved, that we demand the withdrawal from this convention of any delegate or delegates constituting or representing the above-named interests."[57]

When the violent reactions of the proponents and opponents were quelled, the Great Commoner stated: ". . . this is an extraordinary resolution, but extraordinary conditions need extraordinary remedies. . . ."[58]

Bowing to the argument that the convention had no right to expel delegates chosen by sovereign states, he withdrew his demand that the delegates be made to leave, but refused to withdraw the rest of it. The resolution carried by a vote of 883 to 201½ because delegates were loath to place themselves in favor of a candidate who was in "the privilege-hunting and favour-seeking class." Boss Murphy leaned over to Belmont and said: "August, listen and hear yourself vote yourself out of the convention."

Nominations and balloting followed. The climax of despair came when the New York delegation switched its vote from the ultra-conservative Harmon to Champ Clark. But drama followed drama. "Alfalfa Bill" Murray, a delegate from Oklahoma, rose to inquire: "Is this convention going to surrender its leadership to the Tammany Tiger?"[59] The avalanche that was expected to follow Tammany Hall's switch to Clark died aborning. By Friday night the convention was dead-locked; Wilson's vote stood at 354, and all attempts to pick up additional votes failed. McCombs asked the Governor to release his votes in favor of Underwood. Wilson, characteristically righteously, replied, "No, that would not be fair. I ought not to try to influence my friends in behalf of another candidate. They have been mighty loyal and kind to me. Please say to them how greatly I appreciate their generous support and that they are now free to support any candidate they choose."[60] He proceeded to draft a message of congratulations to Champ Clark, whose nomination was anticipated. It was at this time that Roger Sullivan, William McAdoo, Albert Sidney Burleson of Texas and others stopped McCombs from releasing the Wilson delegates.

"The crisis came on the fourteenth ballot. When Nebraska was called, Senator Hitchcock asked that the delegation be polled. Bryan rose in his place and demanded recognition. An expectant convention went quiet.

" 'The Presiding Officer: For what purpose does the gentleman from Nebraska rise?'

" 'Mr. Bryan, of Nebraska: To explain my vote' . . .

" 'As long as Mr. Ryan's agent—as long as New York's ninety votes are recorded for Mr. Clark, I withhold my vote from him and cast it—'

"Pandemonium broke loose.

" 'I cast my vote for Nebraska's second choice, Woodrow Wilson.' "[61]

Although Wilson gained only a few votes on this ballot the convention was in an uproar; Clark was furious but his vote had reached its peak and from that time Wilson began to pick up votes slowly but steadily. Public opinion and newspaper support egged on the delegates.

"When the newspaper correspondents, rushing up from their tents at Sea Girt informed the Governor—"You've passed him, you've passed him"—requested a statement, Wilson remarked: 'You might say that Governor Wilson received the news that Champ Clark had dropped to second place in a riot of silence.' "[62] Their expectant jaws must have dropped!

On the seventh day, on the forty-third ballot, Roger Sullivan delivered 58 Illinois votes for Wilson. Virginia and West Virginia followed. Wilson was nominated on the forty-sixth ballot!

Franklin Roosevelt took joy whenever a brass band blared forth the strains of "Hail to the Chief"—the louder the better! Not so Woodrow Wilson, the scholar sensitive to his privacy and that of his family. Roosevelt was laughing and joking, enjoying every second when the waiting mob of people and the hoards of newspaper men rushed into the Executive Mansion at Albany as McAdoo switched the California vote and clinched his nomination. Not so Woodrow Wilson; the brass band waiting for the final word of his nomination overwhelmed him—accompanied as it was by crowds of people trampling over his lawn into his home, invading his privacy—with depression. His life had changed and would continue to change. This realization tempered his success. He had written to his wife years before, "Success does not flush or elate me, except for the moment."

Nevertheless he took pleasure in the less boisterous expressions of congratulations: telegrams and letters from the people of the United States, editorials and news columns in the papers, the warmth of letters from friends such as Colonel House, Walter H. Page, Cleveland Dodge. He awaited eagerly House's return from Europe where he had gone for reasons of health. The newspaper men came in droves from every part of the country, each looking for a story that they could dramatize and—as is their custom—they seized upon the slightest morsel and made the most of it.

A good example is the headline of one of the New York papers: "Wilson Feels Like a Frog." Wilson had said when asked about all the mail he was receiving that, in trying to reply, he felt somewhat like the frog that fell into the well. "Everytime he jumped up one foot he fell back two."[63] This would have amused Roosevelt; Wilson was not amused.

Amidst all of the hubbub Wilson found time to compose a message to the country which he gave to the newspaper men at noon. It was a reassurance to "honest and enlightened businessmen" and a promise of government "released from all selfish and private influences, devoted to justice and progress."[64] This was to be the keystone of his style.

While on vacation in Bermuda following his nomination an audacious photographer violated Wilson's privacy, and he lashed forth: "You are no gentleman." (Again that phrase!) "If you want a good thrashing, keep that up." They did not "keep that up."

From the day of his nomination onward he disliked the third estate en masse. In spite of this he continued to meet with them and even inaugurated regular press conferences when he became President. He did, however, have many individual friends among the press and enjoyed the company of those whom he could trust.

He gave a frank talk shortly after the convention to the newsmen who had been in attendance at Sea Girt during the convention. Joseph Tumulty gave the dinner in order that the candidate could meet the newspaper men in "the most intimate way and obtain from him what he pleased to call the inside of his mind."[65] The Governor made a speech which not only revealed his views of the presidency but laid bare the great problems that would confront the next administration and that he, in fact, would tackle in noteworthy manner. Tumulty says, "In referring to Theodore Roosevelt, he said that he had done a great service in rousing the country from its lethargy—but beyond that he had failed, for he had not, during his administration attacked two of the major problems: the tariff and the currency, which he, Wilson, considered to be the heart and center of the whole movement for lasting and permanent reform in America."[66]

An excerpt from this speech clearly points the way to the reason for Wilson's often slow approach to action on important matters and to his style of operation:

"As a candidate for the Presidency I do not want to promise Heaven unless I can bring you to it. I can only see a little distance up the road. I cannot tell you what is around the corner. The successful leader ought not to keep too far in advance of the mass he is seeking to lead, for he will soon lose contact with them. . . . We cannot arbitrarily turn right about face and pull one policy up by the roots and cast it aside, while we plant another in virgin soil. A great industrial system has been built up in this country under the fosterage of the Government, behind a wall of unproductive taxes. Changes must be brought about, first here, then there, and then there again. We must move step to step with as much prudence as resolution. In other words, we are called upon to perform a delicate operation, and in performing a delicate operation it is necessary for the surgeon who uses the knife to know where the foundation of vitality is, so that in cutting out the excrescences he shall not interfere with the vital issues."[67]

It has been my experience that political headquarters always seethe with conflicts—ideological and tactical—personal jealousies, and the confusion caused by the haste with which the organization is thrown together plus the clash of personalities involved. These conditions were not only true of the Wilson campaign organization but true to an exacerbated degree. It fell to Colonel House, upon his return from Europe, to fathom the rights and wrongs of McCombs and his feuds with McAdoo and others; to decide matters of policy upon which there had been and was great division; and to recommend to the Governor the ongoing organization of the committee, and matters of sensitive political strategy.

Colonel House, having heard only McCombs's side, was inclined toward him, but Wilson asked him not to make up his mind until he had learned the ins and outs of it by personal contact at headquarters. The Colonel's diary reports: "I afterwards learned the wisdom of this advice, for I had not been in New York more than two weeks before I knew that there was another side. Later I found that it was almost wholly McCombs' fault and that McAdoo was scarcely to blame at all. McCombs was jealous, was dictatorial—he was not well enough to attend the campaign himself, and could not sit by and allow McAdoo to carry on the work and get a certain amount of newspaper publicity. This latter was particularly galling to McCombs."[68]

As we have seen, McCombs's political judgment differed from that of progressive leaders, and Wilson's nomination would have suffered if his advice had been followed. At the time when House was attempting to straighten the situation, the Governor was faced with another political contretemps involving Tammany Hall in which McCombs was again trying to influence Wilson in favor of supporting the Hall's desires. Wilson refused to approve the renomination of Governor Dix, which Murphy demanded. There was always the possibility that Tammany would "knife" Wilson's Presidential vote if he remained obdurate, and he was remaining obdurate.

It was at this time that Colonel House started keeping a diary. On September 25 he wrote: "The New York situation is acute, and it is necessary for some definite policy to be decided upon. The break between Murphy and National Headquarters is becoming wider each day, and the newspapers are printing numerous false interviews which make it yet wider. I am anxious to hold the party together, so that every available means may be used for the common good. My dislike of Tammany and its leaders is perhaps stronger than that of Governor Wilson; yet, having had more political experience, I am always ready to work with the best material at hand. My idea is to have them decide upon some unobjectionable Tammany man for Governor of New York who would not bring discredit on the party. . . ."[69]

Avoiding an open break, Murphy astutely refrained from taking any part in the direction of the gubernatorial convention and let the word get about that

Governor Dix need not be renominated. Governor Dix was not renominated. Wilson ostensibly had won; however, one of Tammany's "boys" was nominated in this "hands-off convention," later elected and still later impeached. House had saved Wilson from what would have been a costly political break with Tammany in terms of the Presidential vote; the wily Murphy had been bested in his show of power but not in power itself. McCombs was retained as chairman of the National Committee but he was given a strong executive committee which came to be called the "veranda cabinet" and upon which Wilson relied.

It is said that in 1912, Theodore Roosevelt, by splitting the Republican Party and by alienating many of its members, put Wilson in the White House. Wilson recognized that Roosevelt, not Taft, was his principal opponent, and singled him out, to the crowd's delight, in his acceptance speech: "There is no indispensable man." Years later that phrase was to be used again and again—not effectively this time—against another Roosevelt, Franklin D. The acceptance speech was one of Wilson's few speeches prepared for reading. At one point he stopped altogether and said, "I wish I did not have to read this."[70] He thoroughly disliked reading a speech and seldom did. He would prepare carefully, make notes by hand or on his little typewriter; fully conversant with his material, he would almost always speak without notes or reading copy. Speaking directly to his audience with "fire-like sincerity and conviction," he convinced men of his ability to lead. He had a veritable genius for making direct contact with his audience. But he felt impeded by the confinement of reading a speech. Before his trip west in the campaign for nomination he was urged to prepare his addresses in advance. "But," he said, "it is not my way. I cannot make speeches to a stenographer."[71]

He had other definite ideas. He emphatically did not believe in "barnstorming." It was with considerable difficulty that McAdoo persuaded him to make some speeches at important points throughout the country. He thought it unbecoming the dignity of a Presidential candidate to indulge in "rear platform oratory." After a vacation in Bermuda, he succumbed to the pressure of his campaign managers and did both. There is an occasion of note which describes Wilson's integrity, his determination and his innate political sagacity, as well as the unorthodoxy of many of his actions when angered. George M. Palmer, chairman of the New York State Democratic Committee, desired the Governor to speak in Syracuse, New York, arguing that although New York's vote was considered safely in the Democratic column Wilson's speech would help carry two or three upstate congressional districts which would otherwise be doubtful. The Governor objected as he had learned that Boss Murphy would be there and, in addition to his dislike of Murphy, he felt that the Republicans would make good campaign use of their meeting. "He was emphatic in saying that he did not want to be brought into contact with Tammany in this way; and that he did not want any identification with it or what it stood for." McAdoo asked the Governor if he could make an engagement for him, provided he got assurances that Wilson would not have to meet Murphy, and Wilson replied that he could. As McAdoo describes it: "Palmer said that if the Governor would accept the invitation, he would be spared any embarrassment of that kind. . . .

"When we got to the clubhouse . . . Palmer led the way into a public dining room, and headed for a large round table. No sooner had I got inside the room than I saw Murphy seated at this table . . . I was astonished at seeing Murphy there, and my astonishment was not diminished when Governor Wilson was placed in the seat next to Murphy. I sat on the Governor's left.

"The Governor did not recognize Murphy until he had sat down beside him. It was a tense and disagreeable moment. Governor Wilson returned Murphy's greeting with a stiff nod and sat a moment without saying a word, then he rose abruptly and left the table. I followed him. . . . We did without luncheon and walked around outside until the time approached for the Governor to speak."[72]

The insistence of his managers also prevailed upon him to tour the country as people wanted to see in person this unusual politician—an ex-professor, author and college president. Wilson explained the public's curiosity and his first feeling of ease with this new experience: "When I first began campaigning the people seemed to regard me as some remote academic person. They came not to see me, of course, but many of them wanted to see what manner of man I was, what sort of human animal, what freak of nature I might be."[73]

"I remember distinctly when the first feeling came over me that I had arrived in politics. It was when an old fellow back East a few weeks ago slapped me on the back and shouted: 'Doc, you're all right; give it to 'em!' "[74]

He had arrived, he had adapted his erudite style to that of the masses; but a letdown in dignity was never to his liking. His interest was in bringing the issues to the people in simple, clear terms that they could understand. Perhaps this style emphasized its value to Franklin Roosevelt. I use the word "emphasize" because I think that it was also the style that was natural to FDR.

Wilson painted his objectives in broad strokes and did not particularize about the details. He spoke of tariff, trust and monetary reforms, of immigration, and of giving the country back to the people instead of perpetuating privileges. It is certain that, if pressed, he could not have specified his methods of attacking these problems; and it is certain that detailed plans would have called attention to actual or fancied blemishes, and would not have served a practical politician, which Wilson had become.

His campaign statement on the greatest domestic achievement of his future administration, banking and currency reform, is a good example of his frankness and his unwillingness to grasp at solutions: "I do not know enough about this subject to be dogmatic about it; I know only enough to be sure what the partnership in it should be and that the control exercised over any system we may set up should be, as far as possible, a control emanating not from a single special class, but from the general body and authority of the nation itself."[75]

The ranks of Wilson supporters were greatly strengthened by the enthusiastic conversion of Samuel Gompers, head of the American Federation of Labor, who was to remain his staunch friend and supporter throughout his presidency. Gompers later wrote, "Woodrow Wilson was not my choice for the presidential candidate for the Democratic party. . . . Certain of his earlier academic writings indicated that he did not understand labour problems. . . . [Having gone to see him at Trenton during the 1912 campaign] I felt my prejudices disappearing before the sincerity and the obvious humanitarianism of the man."[76] It is here interesting to note that Wilson's first important speech of the campaign was made on Labor Day at Buffalo to workmen. It demanded the breakup of the "old partnership between money and power which now block us at every turn."[77]

This book is being written as the vast scandal of corporations' gifts made to the Nixon 1972 campaign is reaching greater and greater proportions; it is significant that in the year 1912, Woodrow Wilson, urging Henry Morgenthau to take the chairmanship of the Finance Committee, said, "I shall insist that no contributions whatever be even indirectly accepted from any corporation. I want especial attention paid to small contributors. *And I want great care exercised over the way the money is spent.*"[78] (Emphasis added) In 1973, Senate Watergate hearings showing lavish illegal expenditures of 1972 campaign funds were on daily television and the subject of conversation in every house of the land, lending special significance to Wilson's instructions of 1912.

Wilson's health had never been robust and was greatly taxed by the necessities of the campaign; he had to limit the amount of travel and of speaking. He was, at this time, subject to severe headaches, neuritis, and to his old complaint of "ill-behaved digestion." The sight of one eye had been defective for some years. Campaigning against the untiring, vigorous, omnipresent Theodore Roosevelt, who had overcome all of his physical disability, was a great strain on Wilson, who had strengthened his mind but not his body. Realizing his limitations he disciplined himself to limit his physical exertions not only in the Presidential campaign, but even as President (until, with great stubbornness and against all advice, he embarked on the trip to sell the League of Nations to the United States).

The climax of the campaign was the Madison Square Garden speech in New York City on October 31, five days before election. The cheers of the audience could not be silenced for an hour and four minutes! It was an audience certain of victory and certain of victory for a man who gave promise of fulfilling their progressive ideals.

The *New York Times* reported: "Governor Wilson of New Jersey, who has spent many years of his life in studious paths and has been referred to by his opponents as a cold and bookish professor, last night turned a regular old-fashioned political meeting of 16,000 persons . . . into a wild, raving, cheering, yelling, roaring, stamping mob of enthusiasts that needed no songs and no hymns and no encouragement to keep it at a high pitch."[79]

Ever-sensitive to people he understood, in his opening paragraph Wilson said: "Fellow citizens, no man could fail to be deeply moved by a demonstration such as we have witnessed tonight. And yet I am the more thrilled by it because I realize that it is the demonstration for a cause and not for a man. All over the country, from one ocean to another, men are becoming more aware that in less than a week the common people of America will come into their own again."[80]

Typical of Wilson was the way in which he spent election night before the returns were received. He dined in the intimacy of his own immediate family and after dinner Mrs. Wilson read aloud from Browning's poetry. Here was a man about to be the sinecure of the eyes of the world, not merely of the United States, calmly awaiting the verdict of the voters without an intimate friend or a member of his staff or of his active supporters or campaign advisers present. It is indicative of his personal relationship with individuals outside his family. Letters between them were warm and affectionate; personal contacts were restrained. There were, to be sure, occasions where he could relax with family and intimate friends for he was a wonderful mimic, had great wit and humor; but at crucial moments he wanted to be alone with his family and relax in professorial style.

News of his victory came at 10:00 P.M., fittingly accompanied by marching bands of Princeton students chanting:

> Tune every heart and every voice,
> Bid every care withdraw;
> Let all with one accord rejoice,
> In praise of Old Nassau.

The victory was augmented by the fact that, under Wilson's leadership, the Democrats had carried both houses of Congress, the House being Democratic by 147 members, the Senate by 6 members. In addition it was a progressive victory because the combined vote of Wilson and Roosevelt was 10 million, compared with 3 million for the conservative Taft.

Wilson's short statement made the following day contained the significant words, "the time has come now to do a lot of thinking."[81]

Indeed, he spoke these words from the heart, for he had to fill in the details of his broad statements and he had to do one of the tasks most difficult for any executive—find men equipped to fill Cabinet and other executive positions. There was also the question of foreign affairs, an area in which he had no expertise and which was brought to his attention even while he vacationed directly after the election.

Refreshed from four weeks in Bermuda where he had been free to embroider his objectives with some substantive thinking, he flushed with anger when confronted with the down-to-earth demand inspired by the old bosses and financial interests that he resign his governorship, not waiting until he assumed the presidency on March 4. With white heat he stated that his work as Governor was not completed. He intended to fight for the antitrust legislation that he had promised and would, therefore, not resign the governorship until the legislature which convened January 1913 acted. "At his request a series of seven regulatory bills to curb the abuses of the great corporations in the state were drafted. They were aimed particularly at price-fixing and the restraint of trade and applied the doctrine that Wilson had long advocated. 'Guilt is personal.' Directors of corporations violating the law would be liable to fine and imprisonment."[82]

Wilson never had and never would give up a fight. The "Seven Sisters" acts were passed and he signed the bills (which—done in haste and imperfectly drawn —were later repealed) on February 19. He did not resign until March 1, three days before he took the oath as President. His Scots-Irish stubbornness and determination would not permit him to do so any earlier—for in so doing he would have allowed the old bosses to return to power ahead of time.

Even after he became President he returned to New Jersey to press for parts of his legislative program that he had not achieved and to endorse candidates whom he considered progressive and not boss-ridden. He was not successful in obtaining any of his legislation, not even jury reform which he most ardently desired. Arthur Link points out: "Overshadowed by more spectacular events in Washington, this denouement of Wilson's career in New Jersey has been largely forgotten. And yet it, particularly the jury reform controversy, clearly revealed some of the weaknesses of his leadership—his greater concern for getting things done than for the nature of the achievement itself, and his inability to work with men whom he disliked and distrusted."[83]

This was emphatically true from time to time, but it cannot be used as a generalized criticism. More pertinent is Link's later statement that: "He discovered, as all other Presidents before and since have discovered, even strong Presidents like the Roosevelts, that a President of the United States usually has to recognize local and state party organizations and then try to use them for constructive national purposes. Thus, instead of continuing to fight with the rising Hague organization, he soon came to terms with it and in fact helped it secure its hold on Hudson County. He even made peace with the Smith-Nugent organization in Essex County."[84]

Broad strokes of Presidential policy had now to be given definition. In order to do this Wilson had a lot to learn. He conferred with Carter Glass of Virginia, head of the subcommittee on banking of the House of Representatives, who was quoted in the *New York Times* of December 27, 1912, as saying, "The President-elect has more ideas about currency reform and expresses them more incisively than any man I know of."[85] He discussed legislation with leading congressmen and senators and men of ideas like Louis D. Brandeis who had, during his campaign, advised him on the problems of trusts; and he consulted Colonel Goethals on problems of the Panama Canal and the Canal Zone. He began the custom of talking over governmental policies with Colonel House and depended almost entirely upon him for suggestions and advice in selection of Cabinet members. He was in close touch with Bryan.

On the day after election McCombs had arrived with a "slate" for Cabinet appointments, expecting Wilson to reward the faithful, including McCombs. Wilson gave him an icy stare and publicly stated that "No announcement [of any appointment] will have the least authority which is not made over my signature." Within a few days he also said that he would call a special session of Congress not later than April 15 for immediate consideration of the tariff and other problems. So it was essential that all of these matters be given immediate attention.

In choosing a Cabinet, a task which he found "wholly hateful," he was limited by the availability of men experienced in government because the Democratic Party had been out of power for sixteen years, and those who shared his philosophy were not numerous; his own knowledge and writings about the possible functions of a Cabinet raised the question in his mind—now that he was actually faced with appointing one—"What *is* the Cabinet?"

"Are we to have a purely administrative cabinet, and individual choice of policy by the President; or are we to have responsible party government, parties being made responsible not only for the choice they make of Presidents, but also for the character and motives of the men they bring forward to give him counsel . . . ? Either system would be constitutional under the existing provisions of our fundamental law; the former literally constitutional, the latter within the permissions of the Constitution . . . the historical method of appointment . . . has unquestionably regarded the cabinet as a party council."[86]

What kind of counsel would Bryan give? Wilson owed his nomination to Bryan. He had acquired great admiration and affection for him. They shared many objectives, but he had doubts about his political wisdom and judgment. Bryan had both great assets and great liabilities. He could marshal party strength in the country and in the Congress for the reforms they both advocated, but he had no executive experience and gave no promise of having any. Wilson could not offer Bryan, who for sixteen years had been the idol of the liberal wing of the Democratic Party, anything less than Secretary of State and Bryan had no experience whatsoever in foreign affairs. He was a reformer, not a statesman.

Wilson discussed the Bryan problem again and again with Colonel House, who could see no way out except an Ambassadorship to England or Russia—and that Bryan would not take. Finally on December 21 the post of Secretary of State was offered and tentatively accepted. But the future Secretary informed the Governor that Mrs. Bryan and he would not serve intoxicating liquors at their table. This steadfast adherence later gave rise to much newspaper and cartoon hilarity. Wilson, however, said that they could serve what they pleased. Thus one important State Department problem was solved. He attempted to help Wilson solve other appointment problems, all of which were rejected, for the "deserving" were an undistinguished group. This foretold the tenor of Bryan's State Department appointees when he took office. By the end of 1914 Wilson was conducting important foreign affairs without Bryan's knowledge.

During his years in office Bryan was both a thorn and an asset. He resigned as Secretary of State in 1915, protesting what he regarded as President Wilson's unnecessarily provocative notes to Germany on submarine warfare. A recent *New York Times* article said: "Just before the break, Wilson sent his Secretary of the Treasury to try to persuade Bryan to remain. McAdoo warned the Great Commoner that his public career would end if he resigned and went public. 'I believe you are right,' Bryan said. 'I think this will destroy me, but whether it does or not, I must do my duty according to my conscience.' William Jennings Bryan is the most dramatic example of those who campaigned actively against a policy of his former team."[87]

This recollection became noteworthy during the Watergate hearings of the Nixon administration when the loyalty of the "Nixon Team" became the great factor in the whole history of the Watergate actions and the ensuing "cover-up."

There were two other appointees for whom no search and no counsel was necessary—McAdoo and Josephus Daniels, for whom Wilson had respect and affection; it was merely a question of which posts they should be asked to take. The final decision was the Treasury for McAdoo, for which he was eminently fitted, and the Navy for Daniels—a pacifist who had to be prodded into building up the Navy. He was, however, a tower of strength in influencing members of Congress to support Wilson's reforms, for they had respect and affection for him. Throughout the Wilson years, he was a loyal supporter of the President.

There was no problem in selecting a Secretary of Agriculture—not a politician, but a friend of Colonel House—David F. Houston, chancellor of Washington University in St. Louis, a renowned economist, a scholar and educator. Not a progressive, he often found his conservative views amenable to change and made sizable contributions to the Wilson program. Opposed to direct federal assistance to underprivileged groups, he opposed until 1916 a measure to establish a long-term federal rural credit system. After the outbreak of World War I, he successfully resisted the demands of Southern farmers for federal support of cotton prices. You would have thought him completely out of step with Wilson; but, like Wilson, Houston often yielded in face of necessity and in confrontation with the facts of a changing social structure. Of great importance was the fact that Wilson trusted Houston and gave him almost complete control over agricultural policies.

The untrained politician was firm in his determination to get "one thorough going politician" in his Cabinet who could effectively steer his reform legislation through Congress. In appointing Albert S. Burleson as Postmaster General he had an eight-term congressman from Texas who had great influence with Congress. He had been a supporter of Wilson even before that other Texan—Colonel House. Wilson's great fear was that Burleson was too much embedded in old organization and old-style politics, and therefore he hesitated. When he finally made his decision, Burleson said to Wilson: "I will be loyal to your administration and sympathetic with your policies. When I reach the point where I cannot give you my undivided loyalty, I will always tell you my candid views. I can't know what is in your mind, but I can tell you what is in mine." "Burleson," Wilson replied, "that is just the kind of man I want."[88] There came a time when Wilson did not want that frankness from members of his Cabinet, and many of his

Cabinet members were to become restive because they were not sufficiently consulted. Not Burleson! He was as good as his promise; he spoke his mind, accepted the President's decisions without argument and remained in the Cabinet until the end of the second administration. One incident indicates both Burleson's loyalty and Wilson's style of allowing his Cabinet officers to carry some of his trial balloons on advanced issues without getting into the fray himself if they did not promise success.

On April 4, 1913, the President said to Burleson, "For a long time I have thought that the government ought to own the telegraph lines of the country and combine the telephone with the post office. How have you been thinking in this matter?"[89] Burleson (not Wilson), in his first annual report, submitted to Congress December 1913, came out in support of governmental ownership of all telephone and telegraph facilities.[90] Conservative criticism was so strong and chances of congressional action so slim that Wilson stayed in the background, merely giving a bit of halfhearted support.

Those who today recall Justice James Clark McReynolds think of him as the chief target of Franklin D. Roosevelt's unsuccessful attack on the Supreme Court, that one of the "Nine Old Men" who wrote more opinions finding New Deal acts of Congress unconstitutional than any other Supreme Court Justice. An amazing fact is that when Woodrow Wilson made him Attorney General he had established a reputation as a trust buster—in the language of 1913, a liberal. A Democrat from Kentucky, he had been Theodore Roosevelt's Assistant Attorney General trying antitrust cases from 1903 to 1907, had then practiced antitrust law in New York City and, until Wilson nominated him as a Justice of the Supreme Court in 1914, tried antitrust cases as Wilson's Attorney General from 1913 to 1914. It was McReynolds who had prosecuted the tobacco and anthracite coal trusts during Theodore Roosevelt's presidency. No wonder that the President-elect considered him an able and progressive lawyer.

Wilson was also eager to find a qualified progressive to fill the post of Secretary of the Interior, for he attached great importance to conservation and wished to find someone who would resist the great lumber, oil, and water power interests which were seeking to seize control of government lands in the West. Finally, four days before the inauguration, Colonel House persuaded Franklin K. Lane, then chairman of the Interstate Commerce Commission, to become Secretary of the Interior. Lane did not meet the President until he went to the White House to be sworn in. "Mr. President," he introduced himself, "I am your Secretary of the Interior."[91]

Lane was the center of several hard Cabinet fights over conservation policies which he publicly, and in Congress, advocated between 1913 and 1920. He helped devise programs for the development of Alaska, to open the public domain to fruitful exploitation, and to facilitate the harnessing of the enormous hydroelectric resources of the American continent. Again, Wilson let his Secretary of the Interior wage the fight, coming in when the battle among proponents was at its peak to effect a compromise between them. Then Wilson took firm control.

Lane influenced the demise of frank and extensive discussion of domestic and foreign problems at Cabinet meetings, for he was constitutionally unable to keep his mouth shut in public and "leaks" to reporters came from him.

Lacking any suitable prospect for Secretary of War, Wilson took Tumulty's advice that there should be a Cabinet minister from New Jersey and his suggestion that Lindley M. Garrison, then vice-chancellor of the state, be named. He was a lawyer of repute and when summoned by Wilson said that he knew nothing about the Army or about politics. House had not been consulted and was amazed. His diary states: "The thing that impresses me most is the casual way in which the President-elect is making up his cabinet. I can see no end of trouble for him in the future unless he proceeds with more care."[92] And trouble there was aplenty —particularly with Garrison, who resigned in January 1916 after a bitter quarrel with the President over differences on the preparedness program.

William C. Redfield, a manufacturer, a former congressman, a believer in low tariff and—impressive to Wilson—a facile speaker, was named Secretary of Commerce. William B. Wilson, former Secretary-Treasurer of the United Mine Workers, who had been instrumental in influencing the Pennsylvania delegation to come out for Wilson, was named Secretary of Labor, a post newly created by Congress. His background was Scots-Irish, he had been a coal miner, a member of Congress and was a man of common sense.

With the exception of Bryan, no Cabinet member had a national reputation. Frank Cobb pointed out in the *World* on March 4, 1913, "Whether strong or weak in its various elements, this is no cabinet of political trade or barter. It was fashioned by no political boss. It was fashioned to placate neither sordid political interests nor sordid financial interests. Every member stands on his own merits, as Woodrow Wilson sees these merits."[93]

That was true, but it was also true that Woodrow Wilson would dominate the members of his Cabinet as he had dominated the New Jersey legislature and as he had tried to dominate the faculty at Princeton. "Those," as President Truman used to say, "who [couldn't] stand the heat [would have] to get out of the kitchen."

Wilson was intimate and confidential with only a few, and that within limits. He was, to all appearances, a cold man, a self-sufficient man; warmth, however, was expressed in his letters and that with profusion. He evidently contained the warmth within him and could pour it forth in the written word. In the month before inauguration, overwhelmed by isolation and loneliness, he wrote his friend and classmate Cleveland Dodge: "I shall not forget Friday evening. It refreshed and strengthened and delighted me in every way and my talks with you cleared both my head and my heart."[94]

And to Mary A. Hulbert: "And what a comfort it is to think of all the old, established things, particularly of the old friendships which can never alter or fail. They are so deliciously familiar, so dear to the taste and habits of our hearts. As the pressure of life increases, as the rush and hurly-burly grow more and more bewildering, old friends are not swallowed up and lost in the confusion; they stand out more distinct and lovely than ever; they are the solace of our souls. I think I should lose heart if it were not for them."[95]

McCombs, to his bitter disappointment, was denied a Cabinet post. Wilson told House on February 21, 1913, that "he never got anywhere with McCombs; that he was weak and vain; that he had no suggestion of value to make. He said it was becoming unbearable; that he had made a mistake while President of Princeton, in trying to reconcile that kind of people, and that he did not expect to make that kind of mistake again."[96] He was offered a position in exile— Ambassador to France; but McCombs wanted to be where he had power, so he refused. There was nothing to do but keep him on as chairman of the Democratic Committee.

Wilson's strong desire to have his chief adviser on projected reforms, Louis

D. Brandeis, as Attorney General, then as Solicitor General and finally as Secretary of Commerce, met with strenuous opposition from House, from Cleveland Dodge, from the press and from a host of wealthy Bostonians. He battled them all until March 1, 1913, and then gave in announcing Redfield as Secretary of Commerce. But the old fighter won and the nation won in the final tilt when he later appointed Brandeis to the Supreme Court.

Appointments had to be made, but Wilson's mind was more intrigued with the preparation of the public for the reforms that he would initiate upon taking office. Therefore, he made four fighting pre-inaugural addresses, "to rally the American people to moral dedication, in preparation for the coming battles to destroy overweening privilege and to liberate the nation's economic energies." Link says, "he spoke eloquently of simple things—of service, the public good, and the splendid opportunities ahead. When he had finished, no man could doubt that he stood on the threshold of the presidency fired with determination to govern wisely and well."[97]

He pulled no punches, and the conservative press followed in kind; the progressives heartily applauded each speech and this typical excerpt explains the reason: "Men have got to stand up now and be counted, and put their names down on this side or on that. . . . I want to appeal to you, gentlemen, to conceive of yourselves as trustees of those interests of the nation with *which your personal interests have nothing to do.*"[98] (Emphasis added)

Wall Street was worried, very worried. To calm such tycoons as Henry C. Frick, Henry P. Davidson, Otto Kahn and others, House, with Wilson's consent, conferred with them to assure them "that while he was a progressive, at the same time there would be no measure enacted into law, over his signature, which was in the least demogogic." The tycoons, House observed, were "like a lot of children whose fears must be quieted."

Wilson's high ideals took a mighty plunge when those of his choice to fill ambassadorial posts refused because they could not afford to live on $17,500 salaries and, at the same time, maintain pretentious homes and entertain in royal fashion. Walter Page, who became Ambassador to the Court of St. James, was the only one of those originally asked who accepted and he encountered financial difficulties which Wilson solved in a manner that would be unacceptable today.

Turned down by former President Charles W. Eliot of Harvard; by John R. Mott, a leader of the international W.M.C.A.; by Professor Paul S. Reinch, a Far Eastern authority at the University of Wisconsin; by his old Princeton friend, mathematics professor Dean Henry B. Fine; and by others, Wilson succumbed and gave ambassadorships to those he had previously characterized as "the merely rich, who were clamoring for them."

Bryan, who had many scruples, had none in respect to making political appointments throughout the State Department and his appointment of ministers was no exception. He frankly stated: "I am especially anxious to get something for Arkansas. We have not done anything for that state so far and it is one of our most reliable states."[99] "My own disposition, as you know, is to use prominent Democrats, not only as a reward for what they have been, but because distinction puts them in a position to do something in the future."[100]

Bryan had a second purpose in making a clean sweep of the foreign service, one with which the President agreed. He believed that members of the foreign service were members of a "snobbish professional elite fast developing into an aristocracy." As Wilson expressed it: "We find that those who have been occupying the legations and embassies have been habituated to a point of view which is very different, indeed, from the point of view of the present administration. They have had the material interests of individuals in the United States very much more in mind than the moral and public considerations which it seems to us ought to control."[101] Many of Wilson's own appointments were good, but Bryan's appointments gave free rein to the politicians and Wilson did not interfere— except when Bryan tried to break down the merit system for appointment by examination and promotion for merit of the consular service established by Theodore Roosevelt. Then he firmly insisted not only upon appointing consuls from the civil service list but also—as had Roosevelt and Taft—upon appointing secretaries in the diplomatic corps on a merit basis. Bryan's appointment of James M. Sullivan as Minister of the Dominican Republic became an embarrassing scandal.

Wilson, the day after inauguration, broke all precedents by giving a statement to the press: "The President regrets that he is obliged to decline to see applicants for office in person, except when he himself invites the interview. . . . It is his intention to deal with appointments through the heads of the several executive departments." It was Wilson's style to save his energy for important considerations and actions and to delegate responsibility to those who were to administer governmental affairs.

He did, however, depart from his rigid New Jersey stand against political patronage and went so far as to give each Cabinet member a list of Wilsonian progressives prepared by McCombs and the National Committee. Selection from the list was left to the members of the Cabinet, who were prodded by Colonel House and the Secretary to the President, Joseph P. Tumulty. "It was the only workable method, but he often did not know what his subordinates were doing; and as time passed he tended to care less and less."[102]

It was Postmaster General Burleson who brought the President dramatically face to face with the hard facts of the patronage necessities of the Democratic Party rank and file. Believing that he had to make certain that the best men were chosen, Wilson demanded to see the entire list of proposed appointments of postmasters throughout the country. "Burleson did not argue. He got together the documents relating to several score appointments that must be made immediately. Some of the candidates were represented by hundreds of letters, recommendations, petitions, protests. It took two stout messengers to carry them over to the White House. When Burleson himself appeared a little later, they were heaped upon the President's desk in formidable piles."[103] Wilson said: "Now, Burleson, I want to say to you that my administration is going to be a progressive administration. I am not going to advise with reactionary or standpat senators or representatives in making these appointments. I am going to appoint forward-looking men and I am going to satisfy myself that they are honest and capable."[104]

Burleson explained the dependence of members of Congress on their home vote, and the President's opportunity to convert reactionary Democratic stalwarts through small bits of patronage to his progressive viewpoint. After a two-hour session of plain talk, Burleson left Wilson obdurate and hostile, faced by the fact that Burleson had to make 56,000 appointments. A week passed before Wilson sent again for Burleson. As soon as he appeared, the President said: "Well, Burleson, let's consider these cases."[105] The welcome on the Hill which he was soon to seek became the easier for this lesson in practical politics.

Wilson was not carrying water on both shoulders; he was trying to stimulate support among his adherents and to bring some understanding to his opponents. Today his four pre-Presidential speeches would be classified as a "Madison Avenue" method of putting across the "New Freedom" for which he had campaigned.

It is a strange phenomenon that Wilson's lack of personal warmth to individuals in public life contrasted with the warmth he could evoke in crowds, and that warmth emanated directly from him to his audience—usually by his manner of speaking with them instead of to them. There was, however, a dramatic example of another kind at his inauguration. After taking the oath of office he turned to the crowd and noticed that the police had cleared a large area in front of the inaugural stand. "Let the people come forward," he commanded. There was a roar of approval as they rushed close to the inaugural platform. Only after they had done so did he commence his address, one of the shortest in history. Wilson's style in speaking—in addition to being precise and simple—was brief.

The peroration is well remembered.

"This is not a day of triumph; it is a day of dedication. Here muster, not the forces of party, but the forces of humanity. Men's hearts wait upon us; men's lives hang in the balance; men's hopes call upon us to say what we will do. Who shall live up to the great trust? Who dares fail to try? I summon all honest men, all patriotic, forward-looking men, to my side. God helping me, I will not fail them, if they will but counsel and sustain me."[106]

That the speech was well received can be measured by the words of his implacable enemy, Theodore Roosevelt. "In his appeal *to* the nation, President Wilson speaks *for* the nation. He interprets the vision of the nation. He addresses not a sleeping but an awakened conscience."[107]

The first Cabinet meeting, full of promise, was held at eleven o'clock on Thursday, March 6, and the Cabinet continued to meet on Tuesdays and Fridays until November, when the Friday meeting was discontinued; instead, Wilson would meet individually with its members. All the President's years of study of the functions of the Cabinet fell into discard when he came face to face with the problems of his own personality and those of the Cabinet members, and with the practicality of working in harness with individuals of varied backgrounds and duties without common objectives to bind them. Each had his own functional areas, and Wilson considered that their advice on policies which did not concern their own department was, with some notable exceptions, out of their province.

Josephus Daniels has described Wilson's method in these Cabinet meetings: "As President Wilson took his seat at the head of the table, he looked the moderator, fitting into place and power. His plan from the first was to present some matter or matters about which he desired what he was fond of calling 'common counsel,' and after he had received the reaction of Cabinet members, his practice was to call on each member to present any question that concerned departmental policies, for debate and exchange of views. At one Cabinet meeting he would begin with the Secretary of State, and at the next the Secretary of Labor would be called on first. . . . He never took a vote, pursuing a course, as he often said, more like a Quaker meeting, in which after full discussion the President would say, 'It seems to me the sense of the meeting is so and so,' and the policy thus ascertained would be the program of the administration."[108]

This "common counsel" deteriorated as disagreements and quarrels inevitably developed and as Wilson discovered that Franklin K. Lane leaked details to the press. In early September 1913, during one of the Mexican crises, Wilson ceased, except on rare occasions, to discuss important matters. Garrison termed the meetings "an interesting waste of time."[109] Colonel House's appraisal was: "As far as I can gather, he confers with none of them excepting in matters concerning their particular departments. Not one of them has been able to tell me a single thing regarding what the President has in mind for Mexico, or about anything else not connected with their own departments. I can readily see how embarrassing this is to them, and how it hurts their self esteem."[110]

As the European crisis developed, Wilson's secretiveness increased. House wrote: "[He] never seems to want to discuss things with anyone, excepting me. Even the Cabinet bore him with their importunities, and he often complains of them."[111] And again, during one of the many crises with Germany: "His immediate entourage, from the Secretary of State down, are having an unhappy time just now. He is consulting none of them and they are as ignorant of his intention as the man in the street."[112]

By letter and by personal contact, Wilson conferred with the individual members of his Cabinet, and thus developed his method of administering the executive branch. One cannot improve upon Arthur Link's description of his manner of operation: "Wilson's method of running the executive branch was to give virtually complete freedom to his Cabinet members in all routine matters and in the formulation of many important policies, so long as those policies did not conflict with his broad objectives or imperil the administration's standing in Congress and the country. For example, he approved when McAdoo launched the Treasury upon bold financial measures; followed Houston in opposing a bill for the establishment of a federal rural credits system; allowed several Cabinet members to institute segregation and defended them when their action provoked the impassioned opposition of northern humanitarians; and supported Garrison in a Philippine policy that partially repudiated Democratic platform pledges. Only in important foreign policies, in issues involving his leadership of Congress, and in the disposition of the patronage did he take a personal interest. . . . He rarely overruled a Cabinet member, and when he did the matter was so serious that the member's resignation had to follow [as in the case of Bryan and Garrison]."[113]

This style was confined to issues with which he had no background knowledge —or, as in the case of the segregation of blacks in the Post Office and Treasury Departments, where he (in spite of campaign oratory to woo the Negro vote) agreed with his Southern-oriented Cabinet that segregation was in the interest of the Negro. However, where the issues were of his own making, as in tariff, monetary and antitrust revision, his leadership was personal, strong and aggressive; he dealt directly with members of Congress and appealed directly to the people of the United States by speeches and by statements to the press. His object was "to destroy the wall between the executive and legislative branches in the formulation and adoption of his legislative programs. He accomplished this feat, not accidentally, but because he willed to be a strong leader and used his opportunities wisely; and historians . . . will probably rate his expansion and perfection of the powers of the presidency as his most lasting contribution."[114]

In taking account of the general breadth of Wilson's style of leadership at the beginning of his administration, it is necessary also to stress its accompanying narrowness. His conception of reforms was confined in 1913 to matters which he construed to be beyond the sole prerogatives of the states. At that time he considered women's suffrage, child labor laws, and other proposed legislation to alleviate the disadvantages of individuals the sole province of state governments. The mission of the New Freedom was to restore competition in the business world, not to uplift depressed groups by ambitious projects of federal intervention, not to abolish the sale of hard liquor, not to furnish credit to farmers or to enact laws for the betterment of the laborer.

Just as today there are rank conservatives and liberals of varying degrees in both the Republican and Democratic parties, so in 1913, in addition to conservative members of the Democratic Party, there was a sharp division between liberal and "advanced reform" supporters of Woodrow Wilson. By the end of 1913 there were many indications that the reformers were preparing for battle to break down Wilson's New Freedom dogmas.

Before that time, however, Wilson had successfully established his relations with Congress by bold leadership, resourcefulness and determination. In the very first months he pushed for tariff reform promised in the Democratic platform and in his campaign speeches. Although the Democratic-controlled Congress was for reduction of the high protective tariff which had existed with little change since 1846 in *principle,* each section of the country had its special industry for which its representatives wanted continued protection. For example, congressmen from Massachusetts announced that they would vote against removing the duties on shoes; senators from Colorado wanted to protect sugar rates; senators from North Carolina refused to see the cotton textile industry "unduly threatened by low tariff duties." Even before he took office, Wilson, on December 31, 1912, conferred in Trenton with Representative Oscar W. Underwood of Alabama, chairman of the House Ways and Means Committee, which would have charge of tariff legislation. Wilson was on solid ground for he had studied and written articles about tariff revision for many years. President Theodore Roosevelt's courage had failed him; he knew that revision was needed but he also knew the heated attitude of the individual members of Congress and he "stayed out of the kitchen." Taft —usually phlegmatic—waged action which resulted in the Payne-Aldrich Tariff Bill. Wilson had scornfully declared, "The wrong settlement of a great public question is no settlement at all."

So Underwood and his committee went to work and were ready with a bill on March 17, 1913. On that day the President called Congress into special session for April 7, 1913. Wilson's jaw set as he studied the bill. "[It] revealed a genuine determination to accomplish drastic reductions in rates on manufactured products. But the Committee—in response to pressure—had reversed its earlier action and voted to impose duties on all farm products, to retain protection for leather boots and shoes and sugar, and to impose a 15 per cent duty on raw wool."[115]

The old schoolmaster called Underwood to the White House and insisted that the bill be rewritten to provide for free food, sugar, leather and wool. He offered one bait, one small compromise on sugar duty, upon the stipulation that the Louisiana representatives, the chief sugar spokesmen, agree to support the entire tariff bill. Furthermore, he told Underwood that if the Congress passed the proposed bill, he would veto it. The bill was revised.

Wilson appeared in person before a joint session of Congress on the day after it convened to speak for the revised bill. It was an unprecedented appearance. No President had addressed the Congress in person in 113 years—not since Jefferson had discontinued the practice because of his belief in "separation of the powers." So critical were members of Congress when the announcement was made that

Vice President Marshall hesitated to request a unanimous consent and "declared it a question of high privilege on which unanimous consent was not required."[116]

Tension relaxed with the opening sentences:

"Gentlemen of the Congress:

"I am very glad indeed to have this opportunity to address the two houses directly and to verify for myself the impression that the President of the United States is a person, not a mere department of the government hailing Congress from some isolated island of jealous power, sending messages, not speaking naturally and with his own voice—that he is a human being trying to cooperate with other human beings in a common service. After this pleasant experience I shall feel quite normal in all our dealings with one another."[117]

The address lasted only ten minutes and the gracious closing words, "I sincerely thank you for your courtesy," were climaxed by a burst of applause. Wilson had accomplished two objectives: he had established contact with Congress which laid a basis for leadership, and he had exhibited the leadership required for the passage of his tariff legislation.

As they were driving home, Mrs. Wilson remarked that it was the kind of thing Theodore Roosevelt would have liked to do, "if only he had thought of it." Wilson laughed and said: "Yes, I think I put one over on Teddy."

The *New York Times* editorial of April 9, 1913, said: "The wonder is that in seven years Theodore Roosevelt never thought of this way of stamping his *personality upon his age.*"[118] (Emphasis added)

The next day he again broke precedent by appearing in the President's room of the Senate for a conference with the Finance Committee which would have charge of the new tariff bill. Upon leaving he remarked to the newspaper correspondents who crowded around him: "It is something that I hope the senators will permit me to do very often. The net result of our conference is that I am sure we will have no difficulty in keeping together on the tariff."[119] The press and the public responded, for here was innovation, here was leadership! There was criticism of course, great criticism. Former Speaker Uncle Joe Cannon expressed his vividly:

"President Wilson is engaged in smashing precedents. Someone has said that a precedent embodies a principle, and the human race has been living under precedents since the days of Moses. Some of them have led to the ways of error, but the Devil was the first smasher of precedents and the Devil has been busy through several thousands of years trying to smash good precedents. I would not intimate that the Devil could get into the White House grounds with a strict Presbyterian on guard, but some of the precedents he is smashing had good origin and have lived in good repute through a hundred years. They are Democratic too. He has delivered his messages from the throne of the Speaker of the House. In that he has smashed a precedent of a hundred years and followed one of the thousand years of autocratic government before the days of Washington and Jefferson."[120]

During the debate in the House the President was attacked for his "domination"; but the bill passed the House on May 8—in just one month—by a majority of 281 to 139. It took four months of hard debate in the then more conservative Senate.

Wilson's style of dealing with individual senators is well illustrated by this letter which he wrote to Senator H. F. Ashurst on April 24, 1913: "I have just learned . . . of your constituents who urged you to oppose the Democratic policy with regard to the tariff. May I now express my warm admiration of the course you have taken? It is not only in the highest degree manly, but it is most wise and public spirited."[121]

When the bill reached the Senate the lobbyists came forth in swarms, particularly the powerful sugar lobby. Wilson was alarmed, for on the success of his congressional leadership on the tariff would rest the success of his leadership on other legislation to follow. He had to succeed, and to succeed, he had to attack. Therefore, without consulting any members of his Cabinet, he wrote and issued a public statement which he gave to the press on May 26:

Washington has seldom seen so numerous, so industrious, or so insidious a lobby. . . . There is every evidence that money without limit is being spent to sustain this lobby and to create an appearance of a pressure of opinion antagonistic to some of the chief items of the Tariff bill.

It is of serious interest to the country that the people at large should have no lobby and be voiceless in these matters, while great bodies of astute men seek to create an artificial opinion and to overcome the interests of the public for their private profit.—Only public opinion can check and destroy it.[122]

Four days later, keeping in constant touch with each and every influential senator, never ceasing to press his advantage, he wrote Senator Robinson of Arkansas: "May I not give myself the pleasure of saying that I am proud to belong to a party consisting of such men as yourself, who can meet as you have met the suggestions of those who would have you prefer the interests of a locality to the interests of the nation and party."[123]

Telegrams and letters of praise poured in from the West and South; the East was not as enthusiastic. The President was successful in focusing the attention of the nation upon the senators in Washington. A kleig light was upon them and therefore it was difficult for any Democrat or any insurgent Republican to escape notice. Each man knew that his vote would be watched. This was matchless political strategy. Wilson would send the letters, telegrams, press statements on to the senators from whose states they came. It was a constant barrage, always accompanied by pleasant letters of transmittal from the President. He would make frequent trips to the Senate to confer with individual or groups of senators, and he received many at the White House. He courted all Democrats and all progressives whether Republican or Democrat. The bill passed the Senate 44 to 37—*with certain concessions*—on September 9, 1913, and was signed (after the Senate and House had ironed out their differences) on October 3. Wilson's little speech at the ceremony was touching:

"I have had the accomplishment of something like this at heart ever since I was a boy, and I know men standing around me who can say the same thing, who have been waiting to see things done which it was necessary to do in order that there might be justice in the United States."[124]

The words "with certain concessions" have been italicized to emphasize a style which he would continue until the fight for the League of Nations. As one historian put it, the new law "was by no means a free-trade measure, but it reduced duties on over nine hundred articles, especially on necessities, such as food and clothing, and it placed raw wool, iron ore, steel rails, and rough lumber on the free list. The sugar rates were reduced a fourth, and that commodity was to be placed on the free list from May, 1916."[125]

The European war followed within a year of the passage of the Underwood

Bill, bringing abnormal conditions which interfered with international trade. Therefore, one can only say that in the short time that it operated without artificial hindrance, it worked to the nation's advantage. It must be noted that free trade was not the underlying objective of the legislation. Its main purpose was to destroy special privileges and advantages that Republican protectionist policy had conferred upon American producers and to give relief to the little men in such basic areas as food and clothing. A by-product was a "rider" to the bill drawn by Representative Cordell Hull of Tennessee, later Secretary of State in Franklin D. Roosevelt's administration: the first income tax levy under the Sixteenth Amendment, which had been ratified two months previously.[126] It was small and intended only to offset an anticipated decrease in customs receipts, but it had greater impact upon future American history than did the Tariff Act itself, and has been called the most important feature of the Underwood Act. Of immediate importance was the establishment of Wilson's firm leadership of his party and of Congress. In the words of the editor of *The Nation* (London), "It raised him at a single stage from the man of promise to the man of achievement."[127]

The "man of achievement" gave the American people his finest example of responsible leadership in action in formulating and promoting the Federal Reserve Act in which all previous tradition was broken and a new policy of federal money control begun. This policy, differing in detail from administration to administration and from days of economic placidity to days of economic crisis, is today an uncontroverted function of our government. It may, therefore, be difficult to comprehend the asperity of the banking community to the very idea when it first saw light of day during the campaign. At that time it was merely an idea launched in the most general terms, for Wilson had not yet gone beyond general objectives in his own thinking; there was no agreement among Democratic leaders as to what kind of banking and currency system should be established and many of them were in a panic at the radical proposals of Bryan and the progressives. Two things were clear: that some monetary reform was imperative and that there was general disagreement about the method.

As early as 1897 Wilson had stressed the equal importance of currency reform and tariff reform. His public addresses, writings and his lectures at Princeton from that time show that he was giving thought to currency reform. However, he had merely the intention and a well-informed background knowledge, no preconceived plan to control the "money monopoly" as he had in regard to tariff reform.

There was in existence the plan put forward by Senator Nelson W. Aldrich —the Republican from Rhode Island—which provided for the establishment of one great central bank, controlled by member banks in various sections of the country. It was favored by the banking community which wanted a change, but one they could control. It was definitely not favored by Bryan, the Bryan Democrats or the progressives. The Progressive Party platform of 1912 denounced the Aldrich plan and said: "The issue of currency is fundamentally a government function. . . . The control should be lodged with the government and should be protected from domination or manipulation by Wall Street or any special interests."[128] There was so much opposition to the Aldrich plan that it was not even incorporated into the Republican platform.

During the campaign, pressed both by Bryan and by the bankers, Wilson gave broad but indicative replies to each. According to Bryan, Wilson wrote, ". . . no mere bankers' plan will meet requirements, no matter how honestly conceived. . . ." To the bankers, Wilson said he thought "the Aldrich bill was probably about

60 or 70 percent correct but that the remainder of it would have to be altered."[129]

While he was vigorous in his criticism of the credit monopoly, with fairness he pointed out that ". . . I do not suspect that any man has deliberately planned the system. I am not so uninstructed and misinformed as to suppose that there is a deliberate and malevolent combination somewhere to dominate the government of the United States. I merely say that, by certain processes, now well known, and perhaps natural in themselves, there has come about an extraordinary and very sinister concentration in the control of business in the country."[130]

This was the framework of thought within which the President-elect met on December 26, 1912, at Princeton with Representative Carter Glass of Virginia, who was to be the chairman of the House Banking Committee in the next Congress, and with the committee's expert adviser, H. Parker Willis. There was also Wilson's determination to secure constructive and practical legislation without delay. As in Princeton and when Governor of New Jersey, his style was action; and when members of his Cabinet later advised him to delay introduction of the Federal Reserve Bill until tariff legislation was passed—lest both pieces of legislation fail because of combined opposition—Wilson paid them no heed.

Although ill and in bed with a severe cold, Wilson conferred with Glass and Willis for over two hours on the memorandum of proposed legislation that they had brought with them. Glass reported: "Toward the end, Mr. Wilson announced it as his judgment that we were 'far on the right track' but offered quite a few suggestions, the most notable being one that resulted in the establishment of an altruistic Federal Reserve Board at Washington to supervise the proposed system. We had committed this function to the Comptroller of the Currency, already tsaristic head of the national banking system of the country. Mr. Wilson laughingly said he was for 'a plenty of centralization, but not for too much.' Therefore, he asked that a separate central board provision be drafted, to be used or not as might subsequently be determined 'as a capstone' to the system which had been outlined to him."[131]

Furthermore, significantly, Glass reported that Wilson "evinced the keenest understanding of what was being proposed and gave unmistakable evidence of his own grasp of the problem by suggesting alterations and additions which afterward withstood the test of fierce controversy."[132] He also wrote that he did not either "in this first interview at Princeton nor at any other . . . exhibit familiarity with banking technique. Very likely he knew little about it. But there was never a moment when he did not know what he wanted done or know what he would not permit to be done in this currency proceeding."[133]

It is interesting and impressive that through all the pulling and hauling between the various factions concerned, the "altruistic Federal Reserve Board at Washington" emerged intact in the final legislation; the provision of the Aldrich plan for a great central bank, owned by private banking institutions and controlled by them, did not. There was great doubt that any monetary reform could be passed by Congress because of the wide divergence of views between the conservative banking groups, the "radical" views of Bryan and of Senator Owen, chairman of the Finance Committee of the Senate, the opinions of Secretary of the Treasury McAdoo and of Carter Glass, and those reported by Colonel House after conversations with Paul M. Warburg, an able Eastern banker and other people in the large banking firms. (Parker Willis wrote that Colonel House, eager to play a part in the discussion and to help his friend the President, tiptoed silently about, "apparently vested with very large powers of a vague sort."[134]) Colonel

House did not confine his "tiptoeing" to the bankers; he went wherever trouble was brewing, even bearding the lions of liberal opposition Bryan and of Samuel Untermyer, who in 1912 had been counsel to the Investigating Committee which had exposed the evils of the "money trust."

McAdoo also collected the opinions of bankers, economists and political leaders to present to the President with his comments attached. The task of composing equitable and effective legislation that could be passed was formidable and had to be tackled in the extreme heat of a Washington summer at a time when there was no such thing as air conditioning and short tempers were further shortened. No wonder members of the Cabinet counseled the President to wait until the tariff legislation had been enacted; to wait until disagreements within the party could be reconciled; to wait until the provision of the bill could satisfy both the progressives and the banking interests of the West who were more amenable than those of the East.

Meanwhile McAdoo prepared his own compromise bill designed to meet objections of both the Bryan and the conservative groups.

Owen, too, had drafted a bill—not a compromise bill, but one reflecting his and Bryan's view. Wilson was now face to face with the central issues: Should control of the new system lie with the banks or with the government; should the new system consist of twenty autonomous regional banks with a national board of supervision and control or of one central bank; how should currency be issued? After listening to every viewpoint—as was his custom—he turned to Louis D. Brandeis, in whose judgment he had confidence. Brandeis agreed that "power to issue currency should be vested exclusively in government officials, even when the currency is issued against commercial paper," and that the board should be distinctly a government body and "the function of the bankers should be limited strictly to an advisory council."[135]

Before disagreement became a public issue it was necessary to bring the sponsors of the three bills together and to reach an agreement—difficult as that would be—in private. Therefore, on June 18 Wilson summoned McAdoo, Glass and Owen to a conference at the White House. It was a tense, stormy session in which Wilson, having made up his mind, was adamant. He was convinced that the government, not private interests, must be supreme. Wilson, once he had made up his mind, was always adamant.

Glass, convinced that the President was wrong, headed a delegation of bankers to the White House to convince the President of this. Instead, Glass was himself convinced by the President's discussion with the bankers. The table was turned when the President asked the bankers quietly:

"Will one of you gentlemen tell me in what civilized country of the earth there are important government boards of control on which private interests are represented?"

There was painful silence for the longest single moment I ever spent, and before it was broken, Mr. Wilson further inquired:

"Which of you gentlemen thinks the railroads should select members of the Interstate Commerce Commission?"

There could be no convincing reply to either question, so the discussion turned to other points of the currency bill; and, notwithstanding a desperate effort was made in the Senate to give the banks minority representation on the reserve board, the proposition did not prevail.[136]

Glass, entirely convinced, graciously said, "Mr. Wilson knew more about these matters than I did,"[137] and vigorously defended the change in his bill. There had been and continued to be mutual respect and affection between the two men.

The President also supported the Bryanites in their contention that Federal Reserve notes should be "obligations of the United States." This and other amendments were incorporated into the bill upon Wilson's insistence. Bryan now came to the support of the amended Glass Bill. The next hurdle—a considerable one—was to win the support of the recalcitrant members of the Committee on Banking and Currency. Always forthright at this time, Wilson invited them to the White House.

As Glass described the scene, "The President made an impressive presentation of the main provisions of the bill, set forth the need of prompt action, and urged united support. He supplied 'a large part of the essential quality' of tact," which Glass observed he himself lacked, and he added, "A good spirit prevailed, only one member exhibiting the least sign of ill temper."[138]

To appreciate the attention to detail and the zest with which Wilson proceeded at a time when he had both the tariff bill and Mexican problems with which to contend, one must read Wilson's own words:

Not an hour can I let it out of my mind. Everybody must be seen; every right means be used to direct the thought and purpose of those who are to deal with it and of those who, outside of Washington, are to criticize it and form public opinion about it. It is not like the tariff, about which opinion has been definitely forming long years through. There are almost as many judgements as there are men. To form a single plan and a single intention about it seems at times a task so various and so elusive that it is hard to keep one's heart from failing. *Fortunately my heart has formed no habit of failing. The last thing I ever think of doing is giving up.* [139] (Emphasis added)

On June 23 he made a characteristically short address to the Congress, stressing the fact that it was necessary to supply new and freer means of credit to meet the requirements of business expansion. His closing paragraph was pregnant with his philosophy of government: "I have come to you as the head of the government and the responsible leader of the party in power, to urge action now, while there is time to serve the country deliberately and as we should, in a clear air of common counsel."[140]

The Glass Bill was signed almost six months later—on December 23, 1913 —after stiff and bitter opposition by the radicals of the Democratic Party in the House of Representatives (in spite of Bryan's endorsement) and by the conservatives in the Senate. The country was with the President. He wore down the opposition by keeping the Congress in session and by personal bombardment of its members, meeting with them himself, sending Bryan, McAdoo, House, and others to speak with them. The appellation "Dictator in the White House" that was to be flung at Franklin Roosevelt had its precedent in these days. It did not daunt Roosevelt but it irritated Wilson.

His former friend George Harvey, in an article in the *North American Review* for November, did not dampen his praise with bitterness. He wrote: "No President of the United States has demonstrated greater capacity for true leadership. None barring Lincoln, was confronted at the outset by a larger number of perplexing problems. None has met his difficulties with more sagacity or resolved them more skillfully. Recognition of that fact is as universal and ungrudging as it is gratifying." There could be no greater tribute than this from an erstwhile friend no longer eager to praise. Arthur Link points to the fact that the creation of the Federal Reserve System was the crowning achievement of the first Wilson administration. The system was not created to prevent industrial depression or banish poverty. The framers of the act hoped merely that it would provide the country with an absolutely sound yet elastic currency, establish machinery for mobilizing the entire banking reserves of the country in times of financial stringency, prevent the concentration of reserves and credit in New York City, and, finally, preserve private enterprise in banking on the local level while at the same time imposing a degree of public regulation.[141] The bill, engineered by a President able to deal competently with people of differing objectives and ideals, provided for twelve Federal Reserve banks, privately controlled, regulated and supervised in the public interest by the "capstone" of the Federal Reserve Board, consisting of five public members appointed by the President and two ex-officio members, the Secretary of the Treasury and the Comptroller of the Currency.

As soon as the Federal Reserve Act was signed it became public knowledge that the President had been seeking the advice and recommendations of the Democratic leaders upon antitrust legislation; that he was determined to carry out his campaign pledge to destroy monopoly and restore free competition. It was no longer sufficient to rely merely upon enforcement of the Sherman Act. Campaigning for the nomination in February 1912, he had well expressed the business horizon and his objectives: ". . . nobody can fail to see that modern business is going to be done by corporations. The old time of individual competition is probably gone by. . . . We will do business henceforth when we do it on a great scale, by means of confrontations. But what we are afraid of, as we have said in the Sherman Act, is such use of corporations as will be in restraint of trade; that is, such use as will establish monopoly."[142]

Wall Street thought that they could outsmart the President by an over-clever and obvious maneuver. J. P. Morgan, Jr., made a noble public statement: "An apparent change in public sentiment in regard to directorships seems now to warrant us in seeking to resign from some of these connections.

"Indeed it may be, in view of the change in sentiment upon this subject, that we shall be in a better position to serve such properties and their security holders if we are not directors."[143]

George F. Baker and other Wall Street giants followed the leader. Was it a capitulation? Scarcely. The House of Morgan had surrendered only thirty of its sixty-three directorships in thirty-nine corporations, and "the withdrawals were so arranged as to leave the bankers with one member on most of the boards with which they had been affiliated."[144]

Wilson seemed to accept the announcement as sincere, stating in his message to Congress of January 20, 1914, ". . . at last the masters of business on the great scale have begun to yield their preference and purpose, perhaps their judgement also, in honorable surrender." Nevertheless, he implacably proceeded to recommend the program of legislation already prepared:

1. Laws to prohibit interlocking directorates.

2. Laws giving more power to the Interstate Commerce Commission to "superintend and regulate the financial operations" of railroads.

3. Laws clarifying the existing antitrust acts. "Nothing hampers business like uncertainty."

4. A law creating a federal trade commission to advise, guide, and inform business.

5. ". . . penalties and punishments should not fall upon business itself, to its confusion and interruption, but upon individuals who use the instrumentalities

of business to do things which public policy and sound business practice condemn." Here he expressed his long-held conviction that the guilty individual must be reached.[145]

Wilson was at the zenith of his influence. Two pieces of legislation were passed. The third passed the House by a vote of 325 to 12, received the approval of the Committee on Interstate Commerce in the Senate, but had to be dropped by the President because it was deemed unwise to press for it during the unsettled conditions of the investment market at the outbreak of the European war. The Federal Trade Commission of five members was created with large powers of investigation; the Clayton Antitrust Act was passed (October 14, 1914), clarifying the Sherman Law, prohibiting interlocking directorates and providing that labor organizations should not "be held or construed to be illegal combinations in restraint of trade" (a rider, with which Wilson was not entirely happy, added by liberals and friends of labor). It was difficult for the President to release pressure for passage of the Rayburn bill, which gave the Interstate Commerce Commission the power to pass on stocks and bonds of railroads and other common carriers. It was a measure at the core of his program; it was near passage; and it was not in the nature of the man to bow to opposition.

Opposition, however, had been reaching a fever point. The *New York Times* mirrored it, saying, "The country is mighty tired of the Democratic policies toward business, so tired of them that nothing but the meddling of the Progressives can prevent a Republican victory in the Congressional elections this fall."[146]

Was he pressing his reforms too quickly and would he meet resistance that would parallel his experience at Princeton? These questions were never answered because the Archduke Franz Ferdinand and his wife were assassinated at Sarajevo and the man who had said shortly before going to Washington, "It would be the irony of fate if my administration had to deal chiefly with foreign affairs,"[147] was plunged into foreign affairs.

Even before the catastrophe of World War I, Wilson and his administration had faced one crisis after another—in Mexico, in the Caribbean, in Panama, in the Far East—with naïveté, with lack of background, with a New Freedom foreign policy based upon the belief that "moral force controlled the relations of powers, that reason should prevail over ignorance and passion in the formation of public opinion, and that men and nations everywhere were automatically progressing toward an orderly and righteous international society."[148]

Unfortunately the State Department lacked a strong bureaucracy capable of forming and guiding foreign policy; this was aggravated by Bryan's dismissal or demotion of key staff members to make way for political appointees. However, even had the State Department been properly staffed, it would not have greatly benefitted Wilson as he believed that the President alone must make and control foreign policy, governed only by public opinion and by what he considered to be the right thing to do. Furthermore, he preferred to work through individuals of his own choosing in whom he had confidence. This was his style.

The "right thing to do" insofar as the Far East was concerned had its variations as expediency demanded. In China, Wilson and Bryan's missionary spirit prevailed to China's financial detriment. At the very beginning of the new administration American bankers raised the question of their continued participation in a consortium established by contract with the Chinese government in 1909 of British, French, German bankers to build a network of railroads in central and southern China and to furnish funds to stabilize Chinese finances. The consortium was later joined by Russian, Japanese and—in 1911, at the instance of President Taft's Secretary of State—by a syndicate of American bankers headed by J. P. Morgan and Co.

Without consulting the other foreign governments concerned and without giving prior notice to them, the President on March 18, 1913—*fourteen days after his inauguration*—repudiated American participation in the consortium, stating: "The conditions of the loan seem to us to touch very nearly the administrative independence of China itself, and this administration does not feel that it ought, even by implication, to be a party to those conditions. . . ."[149] One may indulge in cynicism; the bankers were eager to get out of an unprofitable venture and withdrew the following day. Whether Wilson was right, as judged by Senator LaFollette, the progressives and a great part of the American public, or whether he was wrong, his manner of action demonstrated his unfortunate propensity to form and act at times upon judgments hastily made. The progressive attitude was expressed by Senator LaFollette in praise of the rejection of the "Dollar Diplomacy" of Taft: "Humanity is to be placed higher than Property in our international affairs. Patriotism is to be placed higher than Property in our international affairs. Patriotism is to be given precedence over Profits. National honor is to count for more than trust aggrandizement."[150]

Upon resigning on March 19 from the State Department, Assistant Secretary of State Huntington Wilson (who had been asked to continue in office for a few weeks) gave vent to a complaint that was to continue throughout Wilson's administration: "I had no reason to suppose that the officials on duty in the Department of State would learn first from the newspapers of a declaration of policy, which, I think, shows on its face the inadequacy of consideration given to the facts and theories involved. . . . I had no reason to suppose that the fate of negotiations which had *so long had the studious attention of the Foreign Officers of six great powers* would be abruptly determined with such quite unnecessary haste and in so unusual a manner."[151] (Emphasis added) Officials in the State Department have been bypassed in many administrations but seldom with such flagrancy and speed. This is an excellent example of the President's confidence in his own judgment and in his unquestioning belief that when he made a decision it was right.

He was faced with a more delicate situation with Japan—one that entailed the possibility of war. Almost as he stepped into the White House the Japanese Ambassador called upon the President (March 5) to express the concern of his government over legislation pending in California prohibiting Japanese ownership of land. A delicate constitutional question became the cornerstone of Wilson's action, one that has never been decided and one that he made no attempt to have adjudicated. Could California be allowed to pass legislation which might involve the entire nation in war? Wilson tried by all methods of persuasion to have the legislation softened, but it was not; to have it vetoed by the Governor, but he was unsuccessful; he also tried to smooth the ruffled feelings of the Japanese, which was successful only to the extent that war was avoided. Japan remained resentful.

At his very doorstep as he entered the White House was the vexing question of the recognition of the government of Victoriano Huerta who had, in early February, overthrown and arranged for the murder of the Mexican reformer, Francisco I. Madero. President Taft had delayed recognition of Heurta's de facto government because the "State Department planned to use recognition of Huerta's *de facto* government as a bargaining weapon in obtaining favorable settlement of certain outstanding disputes with Mexico."[152] This was obviously in pursuit of Taft's Dollar Diplomacy, so repugnant to Wilson.

Recognition of a de facto government was a policy set forth by Thomas Jefferson, previously adhered to with the exception of President Buchanan (also in the case of Mexico), who refused "to recognize any government in Mexico until it was 'obeyed over a large majority of the country, and by the people, and was likely to continue.' "[153] Following traditional practice, the European powers and Japan had extended recognition. They, too, had financial interests and further ambitions in Mexico. Of primary importance to American businessmen, who immediately put pressure upon the President to recognize Huerta, was the protection of their investment of about $1 billion (a tidy sum in those days) in property and railroad investments.

These were the early days in which important matters were still discussed with the Cabinet. On March 11, the President arrived at the Cabinet meeting with a typewritten copy of a statement which he issued on March 12, in spite of the fact that some members of the Cabinet thought it was hasty and that it was not necessary to raise the issue at that time. The fact that the President read the statement and led the discussion—rather than Bryan—is noteworthy. Secretary Houston pointed out: "This interested me at this time, particularly because it clearly indicated that the President was going to be his own Secretary of State."[154]

The statement dealt not directly with Mexico but with all of the nations south of the United States. Its crux was that cooperation was "possible only when supported at every turn by the orderly processes of just government based upon law, not upon arbitrary or irregular force."[155]

The ramifications of the Mexican situation are so great there will be no attempt to describe the details here, but merely to highlight them in relation to the President's style in dealing with them.

He saw the same privilege-seeking powerful bankers and capitalists arrayed against him in the foreign field as at home, and he was no more disposed to desert his ideals of democracy and morality on foreign soil than he was domestically. At the very beginning of his administration he pursued with boldness and speed the legislation he had promised; with equal boldness and speed he sought to thwart the ambition of big business to take over in weak foreign countries. Because he believed Huerta to be susceptible to their influence and to be unmindful of the dire needs of the majority of the Mexican people, he opposed him with the same overtones of vendetta as he had opposed Dean West at Princeton and with which he would fight Senator Lodge in the battle for the League of Nations. His powers of reasoning were blinded by the personalities involved; there was no modicum of compromise. He sought his information through irregular channels with no expertise in foreign affairs or even in the language of the country. He sent as his special agent to ascertain conditions and report directly to him William Bayard Hale, "a brilliant journalist who was temperamentally . . . unfitted for such a task."[156] He also sent an old friend of Mr. Bryan's, W. H. Sawtelle. The two observers had no official position, no knowledge of the country, and their reports only added more confusion to a situation already befuddled. His desire to rapidly democratize Mexico is analogous to the post-World War II desire to bring democracy speedily to countries that lacked the fundamental background of political and economic know-how and education. He said, ". . . my passion is for the submerged eighty-five per cent of the people of that Republic who are now struggling toward liberty."[157]

He kept in office for five months Henry Lane Wilson, the United States

Ambassador to Mexico, a holdover from the Taft administration who was imbued with Taft's Dollar Diplomacy and in whom he had absolutely no confidence, mainly because he intensely disliked to make changes in personnel—a characteristic that clung to him all through his administration. Franklin Roosevelt, too, had this trait and would maneuver around many an official rather than discharge him.

After Ambassador Wilson was recalled, the President decided to send a personal representative to Mexico to set forth his views for a satisfactory settlement. This was to be his method in dealing with the European powers before and during World War I. Even then he was setting forth his conditions and exhibiting his didactic propensities. The statement that he gave John Lind, who had been a member of Congress and Governor of the State of Minnesota, and who spoke Swedish not Spanish, contained only four points, a forerunner of the Fourteen-Point proposals to come at the end of World War I. He proposed:

(a) An immediate cessation of fighting throughout Mexico—a definite armistice solemnly entered into and scrupulously observed;

(b) Security given for an early and free election in which all will agree to take part;

(c) The consent of General Huerta to bind himself not to be a candidate for election as President of the Republic at this election; and

(d) the agreement of all parties to abide by the results of the election and cooperate in the most loyal way in organizing and supporting the new administration.[158]

Lind, like House in Europe, carried with him a letter of credentials, one that held the highest authority. This leaked to the press, of course, and the Senate, jealous of *its* role in foreign relations, became duly exercised. An inquiry was demanded. Wilson sacrificed his belief that the President alone had the power to make foreign policy to the exigencies of the moment, for he was in the midst of the battle for his domestic program and did not want to jeopardize his tariff and currency legislation. A true politician, he decided to lay the whole situation before the Congress and the people, and did so on August 27. He was enthusiastically received, demonstrating his undiminished popularity. Two significant parts of the speech have bearing upon the influence of the past and upon his future words and stance.

His brother wrote to him: "One thing that you said made me think of our dear father—'We can afford to exercise the self-restraint of a really great nation, which realizes its own strength and scorns to misuse it.' . . . He used to tell me . . . that it often required far greater courage to keep out of a fight than to engage in a test of physical strength."[159] The sentence quoted by his brother was Wilson's answer to those, including his Assistant Secretary of the Navy Franklin D. Roosevelt, who were demanding that we declare war upon Mexico; it also gave the country a foreshadow of the more noted "Too proud to fight" address in Philadelphia, on May 10, 1915, and his efforts to keep out of World War I.

Reporting that Huerta had flatly rejected his proposals, the President announced that we would now pursue a policy of "watchful waiting," would urge American citizens to leave Mexico, and would "follow the best practice of nations in the matter of neutrality by forbidding the exportation of arms or munitions of war of any kind" to either side in the civil war that was growing in intensity.[160]

The question of arms embargo was soon to become a matter of substance in the far larger problems of the European war.

In Mexico, the "constitutional" forces of Venustiano Carranza, Governor of the State of Coahuila, were preparing a counterrevolution. Wilson, although recommending the embargo which Congress passed, favored Carranza at that time. When Great Britain, declaring that it would not support Huerta against the United States, sent the British commissioner Sir William Tyrell to confer with the President to ascertain his Mexican policy, Tyrell was startled by the reply— no plan at all but a graphic example of the "Presbyterian Priest's" schoolmaster approach with which the British would have to deal in the future. Wilson said: "I am going to teach the South American republics to elect good men!"

"Yes," replied Sir William, "but, Mr. President, I shall have to explain this to Englishmen, who, as you know, lack imagination. They cannot see what is the difference between Huerta, Carranza and Villa."[161] (Villa was the third, and would prove to be the most trying, aspirant for Mexican domination.)

Wilson's altruistic policies were given wide support in England as well as in America, where there were also critical voices who asked, "What legal or moral right has a President of the United States to say who shall or shall not be President of Mexico?" Huerta was beginning to show signs of cooperation. It was short-lived. On October 10, he arrested and imprisoned 110 members of the Chamber of Deputies, composed mainly of followers of the murdered Madero. The President and Secretary Bryan drew a long document at the end of October concluding, ". . . the President feels it is his duty to bring to the attention of those governments which have recognized General Huerta the grave consequences which have followed the adoption of that course, and, in the name of the people of the western hemisphere, whose lands have been dedicated to free and constitutional government, *ask them to withdraw that recognition* [emphasis added] which has exerted so baneful an influence to the end that the people of Mexico may the more quickly put an end to arbitrary power and re-establish a government deriving its just powers from the consent of the governed."[162]

Thus did Wilson draft his first appeal to the other nations of the world in the puritanical belief that he could influence them for the betterment of the world. But the note only serves to show Wilson's intent, for the counselor of the State Department persuaded him not to send it. At the same time a note was prepared to send to Mexico City to accompany the message to the powers. It added a new concept to the Monroe Doctrine and began:

This Government having, in the announcement and maintenance of the Monroe Doctrine, shown its willingness to protect the people of this hemisphere from encroachment at the hands of European powers . . . is now prepared to assert with equal emphasis its unwillingness to have an American Republic exploited by the commercial interests of our own or any other country through a government resting upon force. If the influence at work in Mexico were entirely domestic this Government would be willing to trust the people to protect themselves against any ambitious leader who might arise. But since such a leader relies for his strength, not upon the sympathy of his own people, this Government . . . would be derelict in its duty if *by silence or inaction* it seemed to sympathize with such an interference of the rights and welfare of Mexico. . . .[163] (Emphasis added)

Counselor John Bassett Moore persuaded Wilson not to send this note also, writing that "nothing short of the clearest proof would at this juncture justify us in attributing to other governments, by means of a direct diplomatic communication, motives the imputation of which they would necessarily repel and resent."[164]

Both notes show a growing belligerence in Wilson's approach to foreign powers, a belligerence which would have caused an explosion if their transmittal had not been stopped. Mere chance interfered, as Bryan had given both communications to the counselor of the State Department, Moore, merely to polish. The two advocates of "moral diplomacy"—Wilson and Bryan—had, however, exhibited something of Wilson's future style.

It is true that Wilson came to the presidency with no practical experience in foreign affairs and without consideration of the problems with which he would be faced. However, he was not completely ignorant of the basic facts, for he had taught international law, modern history and comparative systems of government since 1885. As a scholar of history he had delivered a lecture at Columbia University in 1907 in which this excerpt well describes the attitude with which he assumed and administered the presidency:

". . . Our President can never again be the mere domestic figure he has been throughout so large a part of our history. The nation has risen to the first rank in power and resources. . . . Our President must always, henceforth, be one of the great powers of the world, whether he act greatly and wisely or not. . . . We have but begun to see the presidential office in this light; but it is the light which will more and more beat upon it, and more and more determine its character and its effect upon the politics of the nation."[165]

As a result of Tyrell's visit to the President, England curbed her pro-Huerta oil-conscious Ambassador to Mexico and, although not withdrawing recognition of Huerta, made it clear that he would receive no further British support. Other powers not eager to offend America during the European crisis had followed Britain's lead; therefore, Wilson achieved diplomatic isolation of the dictator without his "big stick" approach.

Not satisfied with this diplomatic victory, Wilson went headlong from one disastrous episode into another, first deciding to support Carranza's revolution, then ordering the Navy to seize Vera Cruz after a slapstick comedy episode which centered upon a demanded twenty-one-gun salute to the American flag. He sent his trusted but incompetent confidential agent, William Bayard Hale, to propose to Carranza the joint cooperation of the United States and the Constitutionists in the war against Huerta, in the belief that he could control Carranza. "Carranza . . . made it abundantly plain that the Constitutionalists did not want the advice and support of the United States and would oppose the entry of American troops into Mexico by force, if that was necessary. They wanted from the American government only one thing—recognition of their belligerent status, with the accompanying privilege of buying arms and ammunition."[166] Furthermore, when American troops landed at Vera Cruz, Carranza condemned the seizure as wanton aggression against the Mexican people.

Congress, the American public and the entire world were confused and upset by events set off by the President who had such a passion for peace. *The Economist* (London) commented: "If war is to be made on points of punctilio raised by admirals and generals, and if the United States is to set the example for this return to mediaeval conditions it will be a bad day for civilization."[167]

Stated concisely, Wilson triumphed when Huerta abdicated, but it was an empty triumph because Carranza would brook no advice and certainly no control. The situation worsened when General Pancho Villa, one of Carranza's chief allies, defected, plunging Mexico into civil war for another three years. Wilson dropped the obdurate Carranza and favored the obstreperous Villa, who had made known his willingness to follow Wilson's advice.

Meanwhile, on February 3, in an effort to aid Carranza, Wilson had lifted the arms embargo. In August 1914, John Lind was dismissed as adviser because he was too friendly to Carranza. Paul Fuller, a Wall Street lawyer who was familiar with Latin American affairs, was sent with secret instructions from Wilson on confidential missions to Villa's headquarters and to Mexico to propose the calling of a convention representing the revolutionary armies and the subsequent creation of a new provisional government. Envoy followed envoy, support of Villa changed to recognition of Carranza, the European war continued, Lansing had succeeded Bryan as Secretary of State and all of Wilson's noble intentions were embroiled in chaos. Finally, after severe provocation from Villa, whose raids into Texas were terrifying American citizens, the Punitive Expedition under the command of Brigadier General John J. Pershing was sent into Mexico in pursuit of Villa on March 15, 1916, with explicit instructions to commit no acts of aggression against Carranza. The seesaw of events continued. Carranza was alarmed at the size of the force in Mexican territory in pursuit of his enemy, Villa, and he at once began a diplomatic campaign to compel the expedition's retirement. After military skirmishes, ever-recurring threats of actual war and repeated commission meetings, the President ordered the return of Pershing's command to Texas on January 27, 1917. A constitutional government had been established in January, Carranza was elected President on March 11, 1917, and the United States extended de jure recognition on March 13, 1917. It had been a long struggle between two stubborn men, both seeking the independence of the Mexican people. As Arthur Link has said: "The tragedy was that Wilson had in large measure made this opportunity possible, yet had interfered in the wrong way so often that he embittered Mexican-American relations for many years to come . . . he, almost alone, stood off Europe during the days of the Huertista tyranny, withstood the powerful forces in the United States that sought the undoing of the Revolution, and refused to go to war."[168] This was in 1916, at a time when the Republican Party was stirring the people of the country to war and when his resistance to the war with Mexico might have kept him from being re-elected.

At the core of Wilson's campaign for democracy in Mexico, in Latin America, in the Caribbean and in his European crusade were the words he spoke in Philadelphia on July 4, 1914: "If I did not believe that the moral judgment would be the last judgment, the final judgment, in the minds of men as well as at the tribunal of God, I could not believe in popular government. But I do believe these things, and, therefore, I earnestly believe in the democracy not only of America but of every awakened people that wishes and intends to govern and control its own affairs."[169]

Wilson referred many times to his "one-track mind." It was, indeed, one-track on each one of the many domestic and foreign problems that faced him, but he had to run one problem simultaneously on each of many tracks from the day he took office. Sometimes they converged. For instance, Joseph Tumulty, who had been urging the President to take strong action in Mexico, quoted Wilson as saying to him at the end of June 1916: "Tumulty, some day the people of America will know why I hesitated to intervene in Mexico. I cannot tell them now for we are at peace with the great power whose poisonous propaganda is responsible for the present terrible conditions of affairs in Mexico. German propagandists are there now, formenting strife and trouble between our countries. Germany is anxious to have us at war with Mexico, so that our minds and our energies will be taken off the great war across the seas. It begins to look as if war with Germany is inevitable. If it should come—I pray God it may not—I do not wish America's energies and forces divided, for we will need every ounce of reserve we have to lick Germany."[170]

That Wilson was farsighted and "hard-nosed" as well as idealistic is proven in this case by the publication of the famous Zimmermann note, written at Berlin on January 16, 1917, to German Minister von Eckhardt in Mexico City. "On the first of February we intend to begin submarine warfare unrestricted. In spite of this it is our intention to keep neutral with the United States of America. If this attempt is not successful, we propose an alliance with Mexico on the following basis: That we shall make war together and together make peace. We shall give general financial support and it is understood that Mexico is to reconquer the lost territory in New Mexico, Texas and Arizona. . . . You are instructed to inform the President of Mexico of the above in the greatest confidence as soon as it is certain that there will be an outbreak of war with the United States. . . ."[171]

A conflict of the great powers in Europe had been brewing since 1906, but as with the years the war threat accelerated and the arms race increased, the people of the United States looked upon themselves as bystanders. Forgetting that the British had waged war on their colonies during the American Revolution and upon the States in 1812 by crossing the vast Atlantic Ocean with the primitive ships of those days, America still felt protected although transportation, transoceanic trade and means of warfare had been revolutionized in the hundred years that had elapsed. However, Theodore Roosevelt, as President, had foreseen the coming danger, had thrust himself into world affairs to mediate disputes of European and Asian nations (see pages 95–101) and had been instrumental in creating The Hague International Peace Tribunal, for he believed that the United States was now a world power and could not remain isolated.

Wilson's pacifist Secretary of State Bryan had been urging a peace plan since 1905, providing "not for arbitration, but for simple agreement that the signatories would submit their disputes to permanent commissions for investigation for a period of six months or one year. During this interval of investigation and 'cooling off' neither party would resort to war or increase its armaments. . . . The signatories were free to accept or reject the commission's findings, even to go to war, after the investigation and the cooling off period had ended."[172] The purpose of the Bryan plan was "to provide a time for passion to subside, for reason to regain its throne."[173]

With Presidential and Cabinet endorsement, the plan was submitted to the Senate Foreign Relations Committee on April 23, 1913. The senators' only alteration was that the Secretary omit the provision forbidding signatories to increase their armaments during the period in which the dispute was being investigated. Thirty nations, including Great Britain, France and Italy, negotiated such treaties during the following year. In an address to the entire diplomatic corps assembled at the State Department on April 24, Bryan said: ". . . No nation shall go beyond us in its advocacy of peace or in its work for peace." This sentence voiced the policy Woodrow Wilson would follow with many vicissitudes and discouragements until the United States was no longer "too proud to fight" and Bryan resigned as Secretary.

Colonel House "was convinced that a European war must necessarily attain such proportions that every part of the world would be touched, and that it was both the duty and the interest of the United States to do all in its power to avert it."[174] He wrote in his diary on January 22, 1913, "It would be my endeavor to bring about a better understanding between England and Germany; that if England were less intolerant of Germany's aspirations for expansion, good feeling could be brought about between them."[175] Even before Wilson's inauguration, the Colonel was planning to implant himself in European diplomatic channels. On May 9, 1913, he confided to his diary that he had suggested to the German Ambassador, Count von Bernstoff, "that it would be a great thing if there was a sympathetic understanding between England, Germany, Japan and the United States. Together I thought they would be able to wield an influence for good throughout the world. . . ."[176]

On July 3, 1913, not yet having said a word to the President about his self-imposed mission, Colonel House had lunch with the British Foreign Secretary Sir Edward Grey, Lord Crewe, and the American Ambassador to the Court of St. James Walter H. Page, in London. His diary reports: "We discussed the feeling between Germany and England. Sir Edward remarked that the great cause of antagonism between nations was the distrust each felt for the other's motives. Before leaving this subject I told him of my luncheon with Count von Bernstoff, German Ambassador at Washington, and that I had been surprised to hear him say he believed that good feeling would soon come between England and Germany. My purpose in repeating this was to plant the seeds of peace."[177]

As time went on House's mind became more fertile, more imaginative, more ingenious, more audacious. On December 2, 1913, his diary records that he told Sir William Tyrell, Lord Grey's secretary, who was in Washington to discuss the Mexican situation with the President, ". . . the next thing I wished to do was to bring about an understanding between France, Germany, England and the United States regarding a reduction of armaments, both military and naval. I said it was an ambitious undertaking, but so well-worth while that I intended to try it. He thought it one of the most far-reaching and beneficent things that could be done. He thought if we continued as at present, ruin would eventually follow, and in the meanwhile it would prevent us from solving the vexatious industrial problems we are all facing. He considered I had 'a good sporting chance of success.'

"I asked him to suggest my procedure, and we discussed that at length. He thought I should go to Germany and see the Kaiser first, and afterward the Ministers of Foreign Affairs and Finance. He said I would find them responsive to the idea, but that the Minister of Marine, von Terpitz, was a reactionary and largely responsible for the present German policy.

"He did not think it necessary for me to take any credentials. He advised having our Ambassador in Germany whisper to the Kaiser that I was 'the power behind the throne' in the United States. That if this were done, I would have to warn our Ambassador to tell official Berlin I did not care for 'fuss and feathers,' otherwise I would have red carpets laid for me all over Berlin.

"He thought I should proceed quietly and secretly, but, should also secure an audience with the Kaiser and say to him, among other things, that England and America 'had buried the hatchet' and there was a strong feeling that Germany should come into this good feeling and evidence their good intention by agreeing to stop building an extravagant navy and to curtail militarism generally.

"Sir William assured me that England would cooperate with Germany cordially, and had been ready to do so for a long while. He saw no cause for difference between them. With England, United States, France and Germany [agreed] we both thought the balance of the world would follow in line and a great change come about. He said the Kaiser was a spectacular individual and partook more of French qualities than he did of German. He likened him to [Theodore] Roosevelt.

"Sir William promised to give me all the memoranda passed between Great Britain and Germany upon this question of disarmament, in order that I might see how entirely right Great Britain had been in her position."

These are Colonel House's words. What weight can be placed upon them could only be learned if one had Sir William Tyrell's verification. At any rate, House evidently decided that it was time to discuss his grandiloquent project with the President. After all, his diary's first entry upon this matter was dated January 22, 1913, and it was now December 1913. The first mention of any consultation with Wilson on the matter follows this entry of December 3 in which it is said: "Ten days later, House discussed the plan with President Wilson and received his approval."[178]

Wilson, with his confidence in his great and good friend, his preoccupation with domestic and Mexican matters and his lack of background in foreign affairs, seems to have been carried along by House's delusions. The casual manner in which House reported his first conversation with the President on his proposed "Great Adventure" reflects the apparent casualness with which Wilson agreed to it. On December 13, 1913, in a letter to Ambassador Page in London, House wrote: "I spoke with the President about the matter and he seemed pleased with the suggestion; in fact, I might say, he was enthusiastic . . . he made a suggestion that he get the Appropriation Committee to incorporate a clause, permitting him to eliminate certain parts of the battleship budget in the event that other nations declared for a naval holiday. . . ."[179]

In March 1913, Mr. Winston Churchill, the First Lord of the Admiralty, had first used the words "naval holiday" when he proposed "that Germany and Great Britain should cease building first-class battleships for one year, thus giving the two nations a breathing space, during which time they might discuss their future plans in the hope of reaching a permanent agreement. . . . In Germany, however, the 'naval holiday' became a term of derision. The official answer was that Germany had a definite naval law and that the Government could not entertain any suggestion of departure from it. Great Britain then answered that, for every keel Germany laid down, the Admiralty would lay down two. The outcome, therefore, of this attempt at friendship was that the two nations had been placed farther apart than ever."[180]

It was against this background that private citizen House, this "personal friend of the President," this "power behind the throne," went undauntedly to Europe in May 1914 with Ambassador Page's encouragement. He sailed on a German ship, the *Imperator,* directly to Germany. He did have a private interview with the Kaiser on June 1, 1914. Full of confidence that he had been successful although he had received no promises, he went on to Paris, where there was a Cabinet crisis; with nothing accomplished he left for London. While in Paris he wrote the President: "I am glad to tell you that I have been as successful as anticipated . . . I am eager to get to London to see what can be done there. I have a feeling that the soil will be much more fallow."[181]

Wilson's interest, which had been less than mild, quickened and he wrote House with characteristic warmth: "Your letter from Paris, written just after coming from Berlin, gives me a thrill of deep pleasure. You have, I hope and believe begun a great thing and I rejoice with all my heart."[182]

In none of Wilson's letters to Colonel House was there a word of advice, comment or criticism. There is no record of Wilson having discussed House's letters or his mission with any of his advisers at the State Department or with party leaders, Cabinet members or members of Congress. Nor did the President have any knowledge of the details of his friend's proposals until he received an oral report at the end of August; for Colonel House, instead of going directly to Washington, went to his home on the north shore of Massachusetts. House then presented them as a missed solution of the problems of the world that might have averted the war which was by then a *fait accompli.*

This is the first demonstration of the working of that strange and unclear relationship which was to becloud American foreign policy. On Wilson's part it seemed to have been a relationship of faith and trust until the bitterness at the end. It was one of those "necessary friendships" which throughout Wilson's life so often influenced and sometimes warped his judgment. It was most confusing as time went on to European statesmen who assumed that House spoke at Wilson's direction.

House had reached London on June 9, and found himself in the midst of London's social season, going to dinner party after dinner party during the next three weeks, having occasional discussions with the Foreign Secretary, with his assistant Sir William Tyrell, breakfast with Chancellor of the Exchequer Lloyd George, and so on. While waiting for Ambassador Grey to give him some definite word that he might pass on to the Kaiser, the Archduke Franz Ferdinand, heir apparent to the Hungarian throne, was murdered by a Serb nationalist in Sarajevo. The British were more stirred by their Irish crisis and by feminist agitation, and the American Ambassador to Germany, James W. Gerard, ended his letter of July 7, 1914, "Berlin is as quiet as the grave,"[183] not meant ominously.

England was so unconscious of impending disaster that on July 3 House heard from Tyrell that Grey wanted him to let the Kaiser know of the peaceable sentiments of the British in order that further negotiations might follow. The Colonel wrote that very day to the President ending, "So you see things are moving in the right direction,"[184] and on July 7 he wrote a long letter to the Kaiser including the following paragraphs:

". . . I received every reasonable assurance of Your Majesty's cordial approval of the President's purpose and I left Germany happy in the belief that Your Majesty's great influence would be thrown in behalf of peace and the broadening of the world's commerce. . . .

"While this communication is, as Your Majesty knows, quite unofficial yet it is written in sympathy with the well known views of the President, and, I am given to understand, with the hope from His Britannic Majesty's Government that it may bring a response from Your Majesty, which may permit another step forward."[185]

The sad "response" came while Colonel House was on the high seas, having sailed confidently on July 21. On July 23, Austria, with the full support of Germany, sent to Serbia an ultimatum designed to provoke war. When the imminence of war became clear to the American people, financial circles panicked. The Secretary of the Treasury was called on the telephone by J. P. Morgan at 9:30 on Friday morning, July 31. McAdoo relates: "He said that in view of the demoralized condition of the market the Governors of the New York Stock Market would meet at ten o'clock to consider the question of closing the Exchange." Requested to give his advice, McAdoo hesitated and then said, "If you really want my judgment, it is to close the Exchange."[186] It was done that day. Anticipating runs on the New York banks on Monday, August 3, which might result in a panic, the Clearing House Committee requested McAdoo to come to New York on the evening of the 2nd. It was a grave situation and the committee recommended that emergency currency be issued immediately to the limit that the law permitted. Under the Aldrich-Vreeland Act, emergency currency could only be issued to national banks and then only under certain conditions. There was for that purpose already $50 million of emergency currency at the Sub-Treasury in New York.

Upon McAdoo's recommendation Congress passed an amendment to the Aldrich-Vreeland Act within twenty-four hours, under which, at the discretion of the Secretary of the Treasury, any state bank or trust company that had signified its intention of joining the Federal Reserve System might obtain emergency currency by depositing satisfactory collateral. Within the next three months the Treasury issued about $370 million of emergency currency to banks throughout the country. On November 16, 1914, the Federal Reserve Bank went into operation and the emergency legislation was no longer required. It was fortunate for the country that the Federal Reserve legislation had been passed, for it proved essential to the economy during the financial crises of the war years.

Germany declared war against Russia on August 2 and upon France on August 3; Great Britain declared war against Germany on August 4, 1914, the day that the Aldrich-Vreeland Act was amended.

Wilson met the situation with courage, firmness and confidence which was translated to the nation. On the morning of August 3, the day that brought the fateful news that Germany had declared war on France, the President clearly and firmly expressed his view to the newspaper correspondents who had gathered in the Executive Office—an unusually silent and expectant group. He also showed that he had fully grasped the problems facing the people of the United States: "Gentlemen . . . I want to say this . . . in the present state of affairs . . . you should be extremely careful not to add in any way to the excitement. . . .

"So far as we are concerned, there is no cause for excitement. There is great inconvenience for the time being in the money market, and in our exchanges and, temporarily, in the handling of our crops, but America is absolutely prepared to meet the financial situation and to straighten everything out without any material difficulty.

"I want to have the pride of feeling that America, if nobody else, has her self-possession and stands ready with calmness of thought and steadiness of purpose to help the rest of the world. And we can do it and reap a great permanent glory out of doing it, provided we all cooperate to see that nobody loses his head."[187]

Wilson, though thoroughly shaken, had not lost his head. Just as England, absorbed in her home difficulties, had not realized that the shooting of the Archduke and his wife would put fire to seething Europe, so Wilson—absorbed in his domestic New Freedom ambitions, lulled by the glowing reports from House of the likelihood of an understanding between England and Germany, and steeped in grief by the fact that his beloved wife at this moment lay dying—was stunned by the "incredible European tragedy."[188]

True to his style, his first act was to reassure the American people, to give them leadership, and then through the medium of the newspapers to issue a proclamation of neutrality. Joseph Tumulty wrote: "I recall the day he prepared his neutrality proclamation. At the end of one of the most strenuous days of his life in Washington, he left the Executive Offices where he was engaged in meeting and conferring with Senators and Congressmen, and I found him comfortably seated under an elm tree, serenely engaged with pad and pencil in preparing his neutrality proclamation. . . ."[189] Later, after a long Cabinet meeting, he went to the second floor of the White House where Mrs. Wilson lay dying and there, sitting by her bedside, wrote out in shorthand his brief message offering "good offices to the nations of Europe."[190] Of all the replies there was not one acceptance.

This offer of "good offices" is an example of Wilson's constant determination to do what he thought was right, in spite of obstacles or opposition. He had directed Bryan on the evening of July 28 to cable Ambassador Page in London: "Is there in your opinion any likelihood that good offices of the United States under Article 3 of the Hague Convention would be acceptable or serve any high purpose in the present crisis?"[191]

Page approached Sir Edward Grey several times, but it was plain that Grey did not want any suggestions at that time from America.[192] On August 3 (the day before Wilson sent his cable to the nations of Europe), the President had received a cable from Ambassador Page which read: "My very definite opinion is that there is not the slightest chance of any result if our good offices be offered at any continental capital. This is confirmed by the judgment of the British Foreign Office. We may have a chance after the war has reached a breathing space."[193]

However, there was a bit of encouragement in a long letter which Page wrote to the President on August 9: ". . . Be ready, for you will be called on to compose this huge quarrel. I thank Heaven for many things—first the Atlantic Ocean; second, that you refrained from war in Mexico; third, that we kept our treaty—the canal tolls victory, I mean . . ."[194]

Page was referring to the bitter fight which Wilson had waged to right a wrong enacted in the last months of the Taft administration. The Panama Canal, started in 1904, was to be opened for traffic in 1914 to the ships of all nations. However, under the provisions of the Panama Canal Act, American coastwise vessels were allowed free passage because, it was argued, the Canal having been constructed by the American people, with American capital, it was right to exempt American coastwise ships from payment of tolls. American ships in foreign trade were to be required to pay the same tolls as those of other nations.

The British, sensitive to anything that concerned the sea trade of the world, immediately protested that this provision was in conflict with the Hay-Pauncefote Treaty, ratified in 1901, which guaranteed equality of treatment for the ships of all nations. This was a moral issue which appealed to Wilson. He did not tackle it for a year because the Democratic Party's platform had approved of the act that Taft had signed (and he himself had spoken thoughtlessly in support of it in one speech during the stress of the campaign); the Republican platform had been silent, but the Roosevelt progressives were even more vigorous than the Democrats in their approval of exemption. Wilson bided his time as a good politician and leader of legislation should, because action to repeal the act would have created a furor which he could ill afford while fighting for his important pieces of legislation.

He was probably confirmed in the decision to delay by the discussion in the Cabinet meeting of April 15, in which he said he regarded the exemption as wrong "both economically and morally," and was in favor of repeal. Bryan defended exemption as he suspected that the transcontinental railroads were selfishly for repeal.

On June 19 Bryan cabled Page, who had been pressing for action: "The President is not prepared to take up the toll question at present and does not think it wise to enter upon a discussion of it while the tariff law is pending. You will be informed when he feels at liberty to make any communications on the subject to the British government."[195]

Grey understood, and the British refrained from exerting more pressure; but Page expressed his sentiments vehemently: ". . . The English government and the English people without regard to party—I hear it and feel it everywhere—are of one mind about this: they think we have acted dishonorably. . . . We made a bargain, they say, and we have repudiated it."[196]

When the President was ready to make the fight on what he regarded as a mistaken economic policy and a plain violation of the 1901 treaty with Great Britain concerning the Canal, he was aware that the groundwork with Congress would require considerable doing. He called a conference of the Foreign Relations Committee of the Senate to meet with him on the evening of January 26, 1914, at the White House, including Republicans as well as Democrats. Great hostility was evidenced at the conference by the members of the President's own party. There was also a "fighting minority" in the House.

Wilson's dexterity in handling the members of Congress is well illustrated as he proceeded on March 5 to lay his case clearly and ably before a joint session, "ending with a cryptic reference to the Mexican difficulty: 'I ask this of you in support of the foreign policy of the administration. I shall not know how to deal with other matters of even greater delicacy and nearer consequence if you do not grant it to me in ungrudging measure.' "[197]

He had already, a month earlier, made a long statement detailing his arguments for the information of the public, well aware that the Congress would be sensitive to public opinion.

There are several interesting examples of congressional response—even from Senator Lodge, to whom the President wrote on February 19: "May I not express my sincere appreciation of your generous action yesterday in replying as you did to the criticism of Senator Bristow? I feel honored by your confidence and your generous comprehension of my motives."

Senator Thornton of Louisiana declared, in a letter to the President of February 21, that, while remaining convinced of the country's right to favor its vessels, ". . . if in your judgment it would be for the advantage of the United States as a Nation to repeal the exemption clause of the Act, I would feel justified in being guided by your judgment." Wilson replied on the 27th, "I cannot tell you how deeply gratified I am by the generous attitude of the Senators towards me who realize that the chief responsibility for foreign relations rests upon the Executive and that the present situation is a delicate and trying one."[198]

Powerful newspapers came to his support. He saw members of Congress, had Burleson use his influence, and appealed to certain editors upon whose support he felt he could count: "As to the Canal tolls . . . I would greatly appreciate . . . any personal as well as editorial influence you could exercise with any member of the House or Senate from Maryland who may be in doubt as to support of this profoundly important matter."[199]

Interest was so great by March 5 that every seat in the gallery of the House was filled. But the fight continued, breaking the ranks of both Republicans and Democrats. Speaker Clark and Majority Leader Underwood refused to vote for repeal. The repeal was carried in the House by a vote of 247 to 162, a great victory; and in the Senate, where the battle was bitterly fought, by 50 to 35. It was signed by the President on June 15.

Postmaster General Burleson sat all of the last day at the telephone calling up members of the House urging the acceptance of the President's recommendation. (Although not specifically mentioned in regard to any one particular piece of legislation, it has been said that President Wilson was more adept in the use of patronage in effecting legislation than either of the Roosevelts.)

Arthur Link's evaluation of Wilson's victory is well put: "The significance of the President's personal victory in the tolls fight was not lost upon the country or the rest of the world; it was a clear vindication of the principle of honor and decent dealing among nations, and it came about in spite of all that purveyors of prejudice and local patriots could do."[200]

Wilson himself considered the passage of the bill, because it represented what he regarded as a clear decision upon a moral issue, as of the highest importance. He said to his brother-in-law, Dr. Axson: "If everything else in connection with this administration is forgotten, the action in regard to Panama will be remembered because it is a long forward step in putting the relationships of nations and the dealings of one nation with another on a par with the dealings of honorable men, one with another."[201]

There is no better example of Wilson's sense of morality in government or of his congressional leadership.

On August 6, Mrs. Wilson died and her body was taken to Rome, Georgia, for burial. Returning on the train to Washington, Wilson requested Admiral Grayson, their physician, to allow him to be quiet—"to think." There were a multitude of solutions required for problems raised in connection with the war; there were also vexatious, purely domestic, problems which could not be brushed aside. Upon one matter there was no controversy in his mind—that he must keep himself free from prejudice and remain, in thought as well as word, strictly neutral and impartial. This he stressed in his personal appeal "for impartiality of thought as well as of action" on August 18. The fact that Wilson was not yet ready to determine—in fact had not determined—who was responsible for the war is emphasized by these excerpts from his appeal: "We must be impartial in thought"; we must not "passionately take sides"; we must preserve the "fine force of undisturbed judgment"; it is easy "to excite passion and difficult to allay it." He later went so far as to forbid Army and Navy officers publicly to discuss the issues of the war, and appealed to motion picture audiences to refrain from demonstrating in any way in favor of either side.[202]

The war was creating serious imbalances in the domestic economy. Cotton was a glut on the market because there were no ships to carry it to the European markets which had been their chief source of trade. There was also a large wheat crop and considerable amounts were piled up awaiting shipping. Only 2 per cent of the world's shipping was under American registry; one-half was under the

British flag. The nations at war recalled most of their vessels, which were needed at home. German and Austrian ships were interned, either at home or in foreign ports. Most of the British ships were being used for military and naval purposes.

Wilson acted quickly by calling the Democratic congressional leaders to the White House as early as July 31, 1914, describing the shipping situation, and asking them "to provide ships to carry our commerce to all ports of the world." As a result a new Ship Registry Bill was drafted, introduced in the House on August 3 and unanimously adopted the same day. The Senate added several important amendments, but then receded under strong pressure from the President and approved the House version on August 17 by a vote of 40 to 20. It repealed the existing government requirement that foreign-built ships must be no more than five years old at the time they were admitted to registry, and it authorized the President to suspend certain regulations regarding the crew and the inspection of ships in the foreign trade of the United States. The act had little impact (only 104 vessels) because of British and French objection to the purchase of the German ships by Americans. The British government let it be known that it would not hesitate to capture any former German ship purchased by Americans and flying the American flag. Wilson was astounded. "Surely," he said, ". . . the British Government is in danger of taking a very unjustifiable and high handed action."[203]

This was the first of many difficulties with the British over shipping. After the *Dacia* incident the question of ship transfer ceased because private capital had found the venture too risky. The *Dacia* was purchased by an American mining engineer from the Hamburg American Line, transferred to American registry January 4, 1915, and loaded with 11,000 bales of cotton in Texas. Bound for Rotterdam, it was seized as it entered the British Channel by the French at Britain's suggestion, escorted to Brest, handed to the French Prize Court, put under French flag, renamed *Yser*—and later sunk by a German submarine.

Realizing that the Ship Registry Bill would not fully cover the need, even before its final passage, the Secretary of the Treasury called a conference on foreign exchange and shipping on August 14 stressing the need for an American Merchant Marine. The conference, instead of finding ways and means of providing private capital for the then profitable shipping industry, "passed the buck" to Congress, adopting a resolution urging Congress do something to ameliorate the situation but offering no suggestions. Private capital has always been the solution of the businessmen of this country, but private capital does not venture forth when times are uncertain. As the cotton crop piled up on the wharves, the President wrote: "America cannot properly be saved by any man who for a moment measures his interest against her advantage."[204] He immediately exerted leadership by urging a more effective program for the government to provide ships to carry cotton and other products, and to prevent cotton from being declared a contraband which would destroy German and other markets. (After much negotiation cotton was declared non-contraband by Britain on October 25.) He also vigorously supported a plan for a "cotton loan fund" to enable Southern producers to hold their surplus until conditions improved. This plan was superbly engineered by McAdoo, who secured the cooperation of bankers in raising a fund of $135 million. (However, on August 20, 1915, the British reversed their earlier decision and cotton was made contraband, adding woe to the cotton producers, the economy of the South and the administration.)

In August 1914 the President strongly endorsed a shipping bill that McAdoo had drawn, remarking when he first read it that "the government ownership of merchant ships, no matter how desperate the need of them might be, would arouse the hostility of every reactionary in the United States," and that "the bill would be opposed by all the powerfully entrenched interests. They would call it 'socialistic' he said." McAdoo goes on to say that as Wilson handed back the draft of the bill, he said, "with a smile, 'We'll have to fight for it, won't we?'

" 'We certainly shall,' McAdoo replied.

" 'Well, then, let's fight,' he said.

"We did. We fought for it, and as I look back over the prolonged battle, I recall it as a fantastic nightmare of partisanship and politics."[205]

They fought for eighteen months. However, the act passed in May 1916 creating a United States Shipping Board was not the original bill but one which was drafted to meet the objections of the senators who had helped defeat the original Ship Purchase Bill. It met their objections by preventing the Shipping Board from purchasing any ships under belligerent registry.

During the lengthy debate on the original bill these fears, warnings and protests were expressed by American opponents and by our future Allies. "A fleet of government owned merchant ships on the high seas means a daily tinderbox for war."[206]

Jusserand, the French Ambassador, delivered a sharply worded verbal warning against the purchase of German ships to the White House on August 27, 1914. The Joint Neutrality Board, in an opinion rendered for Counselor of the State Department Lansing on September 16, 1914, vindicated Jusserand's argument by declaring that the purchase of German vessels by the United States would be an even graver infraction of neutrality than the Ship Registry Act of August 18 which itself violated traditional law.[207]

The British were constantly adding to the contraband list, thus depriving American citizens of what they considered their rights of trade. American economy suffered and great pressure was put upon the President. Thus in September 1914 the President, through the State Department, requested that the British honor the terms of the Declaration of London drawn up by the representatives of the maritime powers at the London Conference of 1909. Its provisions forbade placing food and raw materials on the list of contraband. However, the Declaration had not been ratified by the British Parliament and therefore, although it had been ratified by our Congress, the British refused to adhere to it. The sometimes acrimonious notes were turned away with soft but firm answers by the British, who tried their best to keep on good terms with the Americans. Ambassador Page, personally not as neutral in feeling as the President, had difficulty suppressing his own thoughts in presenting the American claims. The controversy continued with Wilson's persistence until German submarine warfare made it academic.

The Republicans' attack on the Ship Purchase Bill is best demonstrated by Senator Root's letter of February 4, 1915: "The great fundamental vice in the bill is that it is a measure of *state socialism* (emphasis added) which, if established, will inevitably destroy individual liberty. It is wholly unRepublican, unAmerican, and destructive of the principles upon which free government has been built up and maintained."[208]

Root and Lodge, as well as other Republicans and many Democrats, charged that the administration intended to purchase German ships lying in American harbors, that the Allied governments would not recognize the legality of such a transfer, and that violent conflict was bound to ensue when the shipping board sent the former German ships to sea and Allied cruisers captured or sank them.

This is significant of Wilson's developing style of increased, unreasoning obstinacy in adhering to the letter of his demands for legislation, refusing to recognize the arguments of opposition even within his own party. Link writes: "At any time during this early stage of the debate the President could have allayed such fears and perhaps assured adoption of the Ship Purchase bill if he had only done what Root and Lodge were challenging him and the democrats to do, accept an amendment offered by the latter forbidding the shipping board to purchase any ships owned by belligerents. By accepting such an amendment, Wilson also could have quieted the extraordinary fear then current in England that he meant to challenge the British maritime system with his fleet of former German vessels."[209] The President, however, could give no such assurance, as it was his and McAdoo's intention to purchase ships of the belligerents because it was the only way they could obtain them quickly. Furthermore, to Wilson the struggle typified the struggle between democracy and special privilege, "between himself and those sinister spokesmen of reaction, Root and Lodge."

The bitterness of the fight festered Lodge's dislike of Wilson until it resulted in a fierce hatred that never abated. He wrote Theodore Roosevelt: "I never expected to hate anyone in politics with the hatred which I feel towards Wilson. . . ."[210]

On September 7, 1916, the President signed the bill creating the United States Shipping Board which became one of the most important pieces of legislation of the Wilson era, albeit far different from the controversial legislation to which he had so long clung. Historians date the birth of the American Merchant Marine from the passage of the act.

The economic plight of the South—which depended on cotton for a living—cannot be overemphasized. Its trade with Europe depended upon ships to transport the cotton. Under pressure of world demand the production of cotton had increased by about 10,900,000 bales between 1897 and 1913. In 1913 the average price was 13½ cents a pound; by the middle of August 1914 the price had fallen to 6 cents and the cost of production was 9½ cents.[211] Wilson's attitude toward assistance to those engaged in the growing and sale of cotton was confined to his narrow viewpoint that the business of government was to protect the little man by regulating business but not by giving him financial aid in times of stress.

The National Farmers' Union had an answer to Senator Morris Sheppard of Texas who lamented: "Ruin [is] now running riot in the South. May God in his infinite wisdom point us some path to safety."[212] On September 18, 1914, it put forth a simple plan that offered a comprehensive solution: "Let Congress first reinforce the market by offering to buy three or four million bales of cotton at twelve cents a pound; then let Congress give definite relief by imposing a tax of ten cents a pound on all cotton produced in 1915 in excess of one half the crop of 1914."[213] The plan of price support and a form of pursuasion leading toward acreage reduction was hailed by leaders in all parts of the South. It was not until the days of Franklin Roosevelt's New Deal that—in another crisis—the concept achieved realization. Woodrow Wilson would not countenance it. His Secretary of Agriculture, David F. Houston, warned that the federal government would not yield to this unprecedented demand for special privileges and an unconstitutional regulation of agriculture. His words are so expressive of his attitude and that of Wilson: "It is not a question of sympathy—the cotton growers have the sympathy of the whole world in their distress, but a question of sound business and good government."[214]

In these days when the South is considered the conservative section of the country, it is interesting to note Arthur Link's observation: "We can better understand the cotton controversy when we view it in light of the political situation prevailing in 1913 and 1914. That controversy was no isolated episode; on the contrary it was a revealing phase of a long struggle between a *relatively conservative administration* (emphasis added) and a powerful pressure group, the so-called agrarian radicals, who, along with the advanced progressive groups, were seeking to extend the authority of the federal government into many new areas."[215]

It was not, however, only the agrarian groups in the South who were concerned, for the day after Houston's rebuke to the Farmers' Union, a conference of Southern governors, senators and congressmen meeting in Washington demanded immediate action along the lines of the Farmers' Plan.

Wilson, receiving a delegation of North Carolineans at the White House on October 7, used the worn conservative cliché that "the cotton crisis had to be met not with the heart, but with the head," and "within the limitations of economic law and safe finance."[216] Franklin Roosevelt thought in terms of the individual, Wilson in terms of principle. Before Congress adjourned on October 24, the President obtained a bill for which he had applied heavy pressure; it provided only for federal inspection and licensing of agricultural warehouses in order to facilitate borrowing by farmers against warehouse receipts. That was within his concept of regulation of business.

It was then that McAdoo upon Colonel House's advice launched his cotton loan fund plan providing new credit to the farmers. But this was a total failure because it was so cumbersome that only seven loans, totalling $28,000, were made before it was forced out of business in February 1915.[217]

Cotton went through many vicissitudes. Its trade increased when Britain removed it from the contraband list; decreased when Britain put it on the contraband list; and finally—because the South was becoming violently anti-British—the British Foreign Office promised to maintain the price of cotton at 10 cents a pound and cotton brokers in England made large purchases.

The cotton crisis of 1914–15 left deep scars and a residue of intense anti-British sentiment upon the South, and led to resistance to military and naval expansion at a time when Wilson needed Southern votes.

Wilson's awareness of his dependence upon a friendly Congress which would follow his leadership increased in October 1914 as the November congressional elections approached. At stake were both his domestic program and foreign policy leadership. He realized that there was a relationship between the two. He told Secretary Daniels: "Every reform we have won will be lost if we go into this war. We have been making a fight on special privilege. We have got new tariff and currency and trust legislation. We don't know yet how they will work. They are not thoroughly set."[218]

The President felt that he "could not undertake any kind of political canvas for he must remain in Washington to devote [his] whole thought and attention . . . to the duties of the hour."[219] But political action he did take. He waged a campaign at his Washington desk, writing letters of endorsement to Democrats whose re-election was in jeopardy; writing long letters designed for publication to Congressman Doremus, chairman of the Democratic Congressional Campaign Committee (on September 4) and to Congressman Underwood (October 17), appealing to the people on the party's record and the need of their support until the "scheme of peace and honor and disinterested service . . . be brought to its full realization."[220] In addition to stressing legislation then under consideration, he launched boldly into new domestic objectives: the development of the water power of the country and the conservation of our natural resources. With the optimism of a professional campaigner he asserted that the "questions which plagued business" had been "thoughtfully settled," and "the apparent antagonism between government and business cleared away and brought to an end."

His new style as a politician was, in view of his past, startling. He had come to realize that political bosses who could control congressional votes were important. Therefore he cultivated them by supporting the candidates of their choice. In New York, for example, the anti-Tammany faction, backed by McAdoo and other friends of the President, had presented Franklin D. Roosevelt and John Hennessy as their candidates in the primaries for United States Senator and Governor. Although he had been at sword's point with Tammany since the beginning of his career, and although the organization had nearly defeated him two years before at the Baltimore Convention, Wilson now wrote letters cordially endorsing its candidates Governor Glynn and Ambassador James W. Gerard. Both were successful in the primaries, and Wilson, showing his party loyalty, had made peace with Tammany.

When, in September, he made a gesture of reconciliation by appointing a New Jersey organization congressman to the bench, his arch-enemy Boss Nugent came to the President's support. On October 12, 1914, Wilson wrote to Congressman Henry T. Barney: ". . . You call my attention to the fact that some gentlemen connected with the recently organized Wilson-Bryan League are urging Democrats in Illinois to vote for the Progressive candidate for the Senate of the United States rather than for the nominee of the Democratic primaries. You ask me if I approve of this. Certainly I do not. *I have held myself very strictly to the principle that as a party man* (emphasis added) I am bound by the free choice of the people at the polls. I have always stood by the result of the primaries; I always shall do so; and I think it is the duty of every Democrat to do so who cares for the success and sincerity of his party."

This was no sudden turn to expediency. Wilson had found that his success with the session of Congress just closing had been largely due to the support of regular Democratic Party members. This realization is best illustrated by his confession to Burleson: "What you told me about the old standpatters is true. They at least will stand by the party and the administration. I can rely on them better than I can on some of my own crowd."[221] And to Tumulty he said: "My head is with the progressives in the Democratic party, but my heart, because of the way they stood by me, is with the so-called Old Guard in the Senate. They stand without hitching."[222]

He courted the old-line Democrats, even Champ Clark who had been his chief opponent at the Baltimore Convention. Just as he could turn away from old friends, he could turn toward old enemies. He wrote Clark on October 19, 1914: "Just one final word of friendship and congratulations upon the closing of the session. I want to say how sincere a pleasure it has been to me to be associated with men like yourself devoted to the interests of the country through the action of the Democratic Party. . . ."

At this point it is interesting to review Wilson's construction of neutrality because its definition became more concrete and thus clarified the rights of private interests to trade with the powers at war as the election approached. Except for the timing of the President's decisions, there is no evidence that directly connected them with the election.

In his neutrality proclamation of August 4, he drew a clean distinction between specific unneutral acts, which the proclamation forbade, and the general practice of selling war supplies, which it permitted. The government was to be absolutely neutral; private businesses *at their own risk* were permitted to make loans and to trade with England, France and Germany. The enactment of the Ship Registry Act was consonant with that philosophy. But the President changed his mind about bank loans in answer to an inquiry to the State Department from J. P. Morgan as to what the attitude of the government would be in regard to making loans to belligerents. He himself composed the reply on August 15: "There is no reason why loans should not be made to the governments of neutral nations, but in the judgment of this government, loans by American bankers to any foreign nation which is at war are inconsistent with the spirit of neutrality."[223]

A totally different answer was later given to those engaged in trade. On October 15, a new circular of the State Department was issued, making it clear that American citizens were under no duty not to furnish contraband goods to belligerents and that the government had no obligation or authority to interfere with their sale and transportation.[224] That the President approved this policy is evidenced by his note of October 13 to Mr. Bryan. "Mr. Lansing was kind enough to submit the enclosed to me. I return it with the assurance that I think it is desirable that such a statement should be issued, and this statement seems to be excellent."

The inconsistencies between Wilson's attitude toward bank loans to belligerents and trade in contraband (including munitions) is clearly explained by the economic situation of this country. We were still a debtor nation with large balances against us in London and therefore there was a pressing need for us to sell our goods; there was no economic necessity of making loans.

It is probably not mere coincidence that the hotly contested bill increasing taxes was passed two days later (October 17) and that the congressional elections were less than three weeks away. Wilson was a congressional leader with a well-developed knowledge of the jugular vein of the people and their representatives.

Decisions changed with kaleidoscopic speed. By the end of October—even before the election—the government was forced to alter its lending policy because France and England no longer had funds with which to purchase our materials. Lansing prepared a memo at Wilson's request which altered his position from "the true spirit of neutrality" to one based on "strict legality," and a credit of $10 million was extended to the French government by the National City Bank. This was the first of many large financial commitments made by American banks to the Allied countries. The election results were satisfactory, although not overwhelmingly so. The Democrats maintained control of both houses of Congress.

The President had engaged in politics, not altogether congenial to him, but the election enabled him to meet with not undue opposition in the next Congress much of the new legislation made necessary by the war.

There is no doubt that Wilson's purpose to maintain strict neutrality was modified because the economic life of the country depended upon the munitions traffic, which increased during 1914, 1915 and 1916 and influenced a desire for Allied victory. Great Britain had successfully prevented our ships from carrying supplies to Germany and neutral countries in her vicinity, although we had entered protest after protest. Therefore Germany instituted her successful submarine warfare against ships bound for England, causing American fatalities and financial loss. This created greater public sympathy for the Allies and eventually led to America's entry into World War I.

In his second Annual Address to Congress on December 8, 1914, Wilson spoke with realism: "While we have worked at our tasks of peace the circumstances of the whole age have been altered by the war." But his realism did not encompass a limited but vocal demand for preparedness led by Representative Gardner and Senator Lodge, who had introduced resolutions for a special investigation of the national defenses on December 7 and 8, 1914. The President was definitely opposed—so much so that he called Gardner to the White House on December 7 to ask him to abandon the project. And when Gardner ignored this appeal, Wilson—with a display of anger—hinted that some lobby was responsible for the preparedness agitation. This was an occasion when George Creel's description—"What was always most impressive—was his remarkable control over as hot a temper as ever burned within a human being"[225]—did not apply. Answering those who were urging large measures of preparedness, Wilson's speech contained these words: ". . . We are at peace with all the world. No one who speaks counsel based on fact or drawn from a just and candid interpretation of realities can say that there is reason to fear that from any quarter our independence or the integrity of our territory is threatened. . . . We are the champions of peace and of concord . . ."

America would rely for her defense not upon a Standing Army, nor yet upon a Reserve Army, but "upon a citizenry trained and accustomed to arms. . . . More than this carries with it a reversal of the whole history and character of our polity. More than this, proposed at this time, permit me to say, would mean merely that we had lost our self-possession, that we had been thrown off our balance by a war *with which we have nothing to do, whose causes cannot touch us,* whose very existence affords us opportunities of friendship, and disinterested service which should make us ashamed of any thought of hostility or fearful preparation for trouble. . . . (Emphasis added) But I turn away from the subject. It is not new. There is no need to discuss it. . . ."[226]

The outpouring of approval—evinced in hundreds of letters—left no doubt that the mass of American people, with the exception of groups of German Americans and of anti-British Irish, believed as he did. Link says, "Only a public demand of the most gigantic proportions could have persuaded Democratic leaders in Congress that it was necessary to defy the resolute man in the White House."[227] Such was the power of his leadership at that time. As a result, Congress voted the Navy approximately the same amount as it had received the previous year and the Army was awarded merely a moderate increase in manpower.

Wilson had not, however, buried his head in the sand. He was not without a plan and in his address to Congress he followed up the sentence quoted on page 194, "We are the champions of peace and of concord," with these significant words:

"And we should be very jealous of this distinction which we have sought to earn. Just now we should be particularly jealous of it, because it is our dearest present hope that this character and reputation may presently, in God's providence, bring us an opportunity such as has seldom been vouchsafed any nation, the opportunity to counsel and obtain peace in the world and reconciliation and a healing settlement of many a matter that has cooled and interrupted the friendship of nations. This is the time above all others when we should wish and resolve to keep our strength by self-possession, our influence by preserving our ancient principles of action."[228]

This and other parts of the speech were interrupted by applause and the President received a standing ovation of approval.

Colonel House left for Europe on January 31, 1915, on his second peace mission. Wilson no doubt was alluding to this possibility in his address, for House had been prodding the President to take a positive policy in foreign affairs, and also to build up our Army and Navy. House believed—as both Roosevelts believed—that "it was of vital importance that the moral influence of America should be based upon an adequate material force, especially a strong army and navy. There was even the possibility that if the nation were placed on a war footing as rapidly as possible, the United States would be in a position to insist that the belligerents stop fighting, by a threat of entering the war against the side that refused reasonable terms. And with Europe on the road to exhaustion, the combined economic and military strength of America would permit her to decide what were reasonable terms. . . . In any event it seemed the part of wisdom to prepare a force sufficient to support the diplomatic demands we might be compelled to make upon the belligerents, should either side disregard our rights as neutral"[229]—which, of course, they did.

It is evident that House had not been persuasive with his preparedness arguments, but his proposal for a renewed effort to place the United States in the role of peacemaker was in line with the President's evangelical thinking. It is true that the country was not in a mood for preparedness, but Wilson, not foreseeing the necessity for it, made no effort to convince the people. Indeed, he led them away from it. Speaking to the representatives of the Associated Press in New York on April 9, 1915, he said: "The basis of neutrality, gentlemen, is not indifference; it is not self-interest. The basis of neutrality is sympathy for mankind. It is fairness, it is good will. . . . It is impartiality of spirit and judgment." And, indicating his hope of the ultimate purpose of America's neutrality, he said: "We are the mediating nation of the world."[230]

The immediate crisis which sent House to Europe was caused by the British action in seizing American vessels bound for the neutral ports of Sweden, Holland and Italy, escorting them to British Prize Courts in Great Britain or Gibraltar, and holding them and their copper cargo for months without a hearing. There was also the *Dacia* incident (referred to on page 188). Ambassador Page in London had fortunately won the respect and affection of the British, and negotiations were always facilitated by the cordiality of the relations he maintained with the Foreign Office. However, he did not always present American protests as strongly as desired. House says, "Both Wilson and the State Department were convinced that the avoidance of future trouble could best be secured by letting the British understand clearly . . . that we regarded British Admiralty policy as infringing on our neutral rights and material interest."[231]

The main purpose of the trip had been under discussion for several months. Colonel House had had frequent conferences with the German and British Ambassadors in Washington concerning the possibility of American mediation. Greatly encouraged by these talks—and not discouraged by the lack of interest of the German government reported by Ambassador Gerard, or the discouraging communications from the British Foreign Secretary—Wilson sent House to Europe to explore the possibilities, thus giving free rein to the theory that hope springs eternal in the human breast.

Excerpts from House's diary of January 12, 1915, present an interesting account of the casualness with which Wilson treated the Colonel's mission, the paucity of the directions (if any) that he gave him, and the professorial manner in which he relaxed when one would have thought his mind would have been concentrated upon the details of the mission: ". . . We had exactly twelve minutes' conversation before dinner, and during those twelve minutes it was decided that I should go to Europe on January 30. . . . There were no visitors for dinner. After dinner the President read from A. G. Gardiner's sketches of prominent men until half-past eight when Senator LaFollette came. When he left, the President resumed reading. I was surprised that he preferred to do this rather than discuss the matters of importance we had between us. He evidently had confidence in my doing the work I came to Washington for, without his help. . . ."[232]

As a matter of fact Wilson was not so nonchalant as it would seem, although it is strange that he did not have detailed discussions with House that evening. Secretary Bryan had been suggesting mediation proposals to foreign emissaries in Washington and American Ambassadors in the European capitals since September 1914. He had been signally unsuccessful. Colonel House, at the same time, with Wilson's knowledge and approval had been meeting and corresponding with the same people on a more realistic basis with slightly more encouragement from them.

In choosing House over Bryan, Wilson demonstrated his confidence in House's ability and discretion, and his distrust of Bryan's. He was fearful that Bryan "in the present state of passion on the other side of the water" would only exasperate the belligerents and hence prevent any real progress.[233]

As Franklin Roosevelt would frequently do, Wilson circled around Bryan instead of offending him with the truth and thereby causing greater hurt. Colonel House wrote: "The President said that he, Mr. Bryan, did not know that he, the President, was working for peace wholly through me, and he was afraid to mention this fact for fear it would offend him. He said Mr. Bryan might accept it gracefully, but not being certain, he hesitated to tell him. . . . The President had a feeling that I could do more to initiate peace unofficially than anyone could do in an official capacity, for the reason I could talk and be talked to without it being binding upon anyone."[234]

In the same diary entry House recorded Wilson as saying: "Bryan was simply obsessed with the idea of mediation. He would permit Bryan to resign before he would let him undertake such a delicate mission, for which he was unfitted."[235]

It was House who had to break the news to Bryan. (This is a trait not uncommon in other Presidents. President Roosevelt's counsel had to do the same when it was necessary to inform Vice President Wallace that there was opposition to his renomination in 1940. He also had to inform Secretary Morgenthau that

President Truman wished his resignation before the President left for Potsdam. The Secretary, an old friend, never forgave Judge Rosenman, not appreciating the fact that he was merely carrying a directive from the President. Mr. Wallace went straight to the President, who was constitutionally unable directly to give offense and the President modified his message.)[236] In this case: "The Secretary of State was visibly upset, saying that he planned to go to Europe himself; however, he added quickly, House was certainly the best choice if the mission were to be undertaken by a private individual."[237]

Colonel House did have an hour's talk with the President on January 24. He reports: "He asked me to tell Sir Edward Grey his entire mind, so that he would know what his intentions were about everything. . . . He said, 'Let him know that while you are abroad, I expect to act directly through you and *to eliminate all intermediaries.*' (Emphasis added) He approved all I had in mind to say to Sir Edward and to the Germans. He said: 'There is not much for us to talk over, for the reason we are both of the same mind and it is not necessary to go into details with you.' "[238]

House went first to London, where he suggested general disarmament and an international organization as a basis for the peace settlement; then to Paris and on to Berlin, where he proposed freedom of the seas, an end to British naval practices, and the German evacuation of Belgium.

While House was in England he had been discouraged by a letter of the German Under Secretary of Foreign Affairs Zimmermann urging him to come to Berlin and at the same time stating that House's suggestion of a German indemnity to Belgium was hardly feasible.[239] Grey and Herbert Asquith urged House to stay in England, arguing that there would be little purpose in a visit to Berlin unless the Germans consented beforehand to the essential points of the restoration of Belgium and postwar disarmament.[240]

It is indicative of Wilson's drive and determination, his belief in the possibility of House's mission and wavering faith in the British that he replied forcefully to the Colonel, who had transmitted to him the British advice: "Your dispatch of the 17th received. It will, of course, occur to you that you cannot go too far in allowing the English Government to determine when it is best to go to Germany because they naturally desire to await some time when they have the advantage because of events in the field or elsewhere. If the impression were to be created in Berlin that you were to come only when the British Government thought it the opportune time for you to come, you might be regarded when you reached there as their spokesman rather than as mine. Do you think you can frankly state this dilemma to Grey? He will doubtless realize how very important it is to learn Germany's mind at the earliest possible moment. No one can be sure what a single day may develop, either in events or in opinion. *The whole atmosphere may change at any moment.*"[241] (Emphasis added) This was no expression of "implicit confidence in your judgment"; it was a well-couched command.

The emphasis is placed on the sentence, "The whole atmosphere may change at any moment," because it did indeed change in a way not anticipated by Wilson or by House. On May 7 the British liner *Lusitania* was sunk by a German submarine, drowning 1,198 people, 128 of whom were American citizens.

House had returned to London in late April. After the sinking of the *Lusitania* he realized that his mission had been a failure and that the United States would soon be drawn into the war. On the night that the news reached London, Ambassador and Mrs. Page were having a dinner in honor of Colonel and Mrs. House;

it was too late to call it off. "That President Wilson would act with the utmost energy Colonel House took for granted. This act, he evidently believed, left the United States no option. 'We shall be at war with Germany within a month,' he declared."[242] Yet he tarried in London for a month working to discover a plan by which Germany might be induced to give up her submarine warfare if England would lift the embargo on foodstuffs.

America was outraged; but at the same time the vast majority of the American people wanted the President to protest, yet not to lead them into war. The President made no move for three days. He pursued his usual routine, playing golf, taking a drive, going to church so as to demonstrate the calmness that he wished the American people to maintain. He saw no public officials; he asked for no advice. Then on Monday evening, May 10, he spoke his famous words to 4,000 newly naturalized citizens in Convention Hall in Philadelphia: "The example of America must be a special example not merely of peace because it will not fight, but of peace because peace is the healing and elevating influence of the world and strife is not. *There is such a thing as a man too proud to fight.* (Emphasis added) There is such a thing as a nation being so right that it does not need to convince others by force that it is right."[243]

As President Truman was later accused by Sam Rayburn of "shooting from the hip," so could President Wilson have been characterized. He explained to a friend: "I have a bad habit of thinking out loud. That thought occurred to me while I was speaking . . ."[244] And a short time later he told reporters: "I was expressing a personal attitude, that was all . . . I did not regard that as a proper occasion to give any intimation of policy on any special matter."[245]

The speech raised a furor both of praise and condemnation. To some he was a saintly leader; to others a coward. The words lived on.

The President, in a three-hour session of the Cabinet on the morning of May 11, 1915, reviewed the recent incidents that had followed the German war zone declaration of February 4 which had read: ". . . Within this war zone neutral vessels are exposed to danger since, in view of the misuse of the neutral flags . . . and of the hazards of naval warfare, neutral vessels cannot always be prevented from suffering from the attacks intended for enemy ships. . . ."[246] To this, after great consideration, the President had addressed notes to *both* the German and the British nations. To the Imperial German Government he had sent a warning that "they would be held to *strict accountability* [emphasis added] for such acts of their naval authorities and [this government would] take any steps it might be necessary to take to safeguard American lives and property and to secure to American citizens the full enjoyment of their acknowledged rights on the high seas. . . ." The note was persuasive; not belligerent as some had advised.

To London the State Department had sent a note vigorously protesting the way in which British ship captains, acting under authority of an Admiralty order of January 13, 1915, had been hoisting the American flag as a *ruse de guerre* when they thought they were in danger. It had emphasized that it would be a "serious and constant menace to the lives and vessels of American citizens" if U-boat commanders could not reliably distinguish between American and British ships, and that part of the responsibility for the loss of American vessels would fall upon the British government if British masters did not stop misusing the American flag.

There was, of course, dual responsibility which the American people realized when it was so clearly laid before them by Wilson's calm, considered action, which was his style of dealing with war crises.

Then came the sinking of the British *Falaba*, which resulted in the death of one American, and of two American ships—the *Cushing* attacked by a German aircraft in the North Sea on April 29, and the *Gulflight* torpedoed in the Irish Sea on May 1. The climax, of course, was the sinking without notice of the *Lusitania* (a British passenger ship with little contraband cargo) with the loss of so many American lives. All of these were unarmed ships.

The President, after this review, read the note he had prepared which virtually demanded that the Imperial German Government abandon submarine warfare altogether against unarmed merchantmen. Under pressure from Bryan, Wilson agreed to issue a statement suggesting arbitration of the dispute; but under stronger pressure from Lansing, Garrison, Burleson and Tumulty, he recalled the statement, which had already been cabled to Berlin. Bryan pleaded for compromise even more strongly than before. Wilson stood firm, however, and Bryan resigned on June 9 rather than sign the second note, in which the President appealed to the Imperial Government to renew its allegiance to "the rights of humanity which every Government honors itself in respecting." The German reply was for the second time evasive and unsatisfactory, and for a third time Wilson addressed the German government. He was both conciliatory and peremptory. He admitted that it might be possible for submarine warfare to be conducted within the rules of visit and search, and he invited the German government to join him in achieving freedom of the seas. But he ended with the warning that a repetition of ruthless sinkings would be regarded by the United States as "deliberately unfriendly"; in other words, would lead to diplomatic rupture and possible war.[247]

Published in the press on May 14, the first *Lusitania* note evoked warmer and more overwhelming praise than anything the President had said or done since issuing his appeal for neutrality in August 1914. *The Times* (London) wrote: "Nothing less than the conscience of humanity makes itself audible in his [Wilson's] measured and incisive sentences."[248] He was still calm, persistent upon the avoidance of war, reflective of popular sentiment and—in this instance—responsive to the voices of advice.

His idealism was tinged with realism, as this letter clearly shows:

Of course it goes without saying that I am deeply touched and rewarded above my desert by the extraordinary and generous support the whole country has given me in this German matter, but you will understand when I say that the very completeness and generous fullness of the trust for the time reposed in me increases my sense of overwhelming responsibility,—and of a sort of inevitable loneliness; and that for a man like myself, who by no means implicitly trusts his own judgments, the burden of affairs is added to, not subtracted from, by such confidence. *I know, moreover, that I may have to sacrifice it all any day, if my conscience leads one way and the popular verdict another.*[249] (Emphasis added)

What a revealing and prophetic letter!

The President received the unsatisfactory reply from Germany to the first *Lusitania* note on May 31. On June 1, he met with the Cabinet asking for full and free discussion, which was at times acrimonious. To smooth Bryan's feelings because of the hostility expressed to his remarks at the Cabinet meeting, Wilson asked Bryan, as well as Lansing, to prepare an outline of a note to Germany. "I feel that I very much need all the counsel I can get, and I shall, of course, chiefly value yours," he wrote to Bryan.[250] He, however, worked all day of June 3, 1915, and into the early morning of June 4, writing and rewriting the second *Lusitania* note. Then the members of the Cabinet and Counselor Lansing met at 10:00 P.M. to hear the President read the document, which concluded: "The Government of the United States, therefore, very earnestly renews the representations of its note of the thirteenth of May, and relies in these representations not only upon the general principles of international law hitherto recognized among nations but also upon the solemn covenants of the treaty of 1828 between the United States and [the] Kingdom [sic] of Prussia."[251] The President had firmly restated his original stand. He laid down his notes and turned to his advisers for their suggestions. It was a disorganized discussion with no clear direction. There was, of course, Bryan's point of view, which he had reiterated before and after the meeting, and which led to his resignation on June 9. His difference with Wilson was basic, for he was willing to submit the dispute with Germany to arbitration and to limit the rights of American citizens by warning them not to travel on merchant ships of the belligerent powers or on those carrying munitions. Wilson, while he was willing to give to Germany ample opportunity to alter the policy she proclaimed, was determined not to sacrifice nor even to debate any American rights. In all his notes he merely announced them.[252] This was a demonstration of his unwillingness to haggle over principle.

Although Wilson and Bryan differed over policies, although Wilson trusted Colonel House's discretion and opinions more than those of Bryan, and although the President frequently acted without consultation with him, there was a strong bond of affection between them. Neither Wilson nor Bryan ever doubted the sincerity of the other, or failed in personal admiration and respect. Bryan came to the White House to say "Good-bye." Each man congratulated the other on the purity of his motives and parted as they said to each other: "God bless you!" Wilson, however, was "greatly relieved now that Mr. Bryan had gone, since he had been a constant source of concern to him."[253]

Of equal concern was the choice of a successor for he believed that Lansing, who was the natural choice, "would not do, that he was not a big enough man, did not have enough imagination, and would not sufficiently combat or question his views, and that he was lacking in initiative."[254] Wilson desired a knowledgeable man of conviction, not a "yes" man (which he mistakenly believed Lansing to be). Lansing, after serving as Acting Secretary while the fruitless search was on, was appointed. When at the Peace Conference the Secretary proved the contrary to a "yes" man, the President was decidedly displeased. Secretary Lansing's account of his appointment is interesting because it portrays the reasons for Wilson's growing antagonism to his friend of long standing, Walter H. Page: "With his usual deliberativeness in such matters, Mr. Wilson delayed reaching a decision. Among other names he undoubtedly considered the Honorable Walter Hines Page, the American Ambassador to London—strongly urged I am informed—by Colonel E. M. House. The President and Mr. Page were old friends. There was a marked similarity between their methods of thought, their cultural developments, and, above all, their idealism. . . . However, Mr. Page's prejudice in favor of Great Britain had embarrassed the Administration and caused Mr. Wilson many anxious hours. In view of the President's fixed determination to preserve a strict neutral attitude toward all the belligerents that was the obstacle which stood between him and the vacant secretaryship."[255]

Upon House's advice Frank L. Polk, corporation counsel of New York City, replaced Lansing as Counselor of the State Department. House regarded the position as of first importance, for upon the tact (which Lansing lacked), the firmness, the legal ability of the counselor would largely depend the tone of official relations with the belligerents in these days of irritating crises.[256]

The crises developed rapidly. The response of German war activists to Wilson's second note is typified by the words Count Ernst von Reventlow wrote in the Berlin *Deutsche Tageszeitung:* "If President Wilson persists in his refusal to recognize the German declaration of a war zone, we are not able to conceive of an agreement or even a real understanding."[257] There were many, however, who found that Wilson's appeal to German moral sentiments and friendship for the United States was comforting if it did not mean the abandonment of the entire submarine campaign.

The British Ambassador to the United States summed up the American response. He wrote: "The prevailing sentiment is undoubtedly for peace, not perhaps peace at any price but peace at a very considerable price."[258] He was not speaking for Theodore Roosevelt, or his following—small but vociferous; but his remarks were particularly applicable to the ex-Secretary of State, who had set out on a peace campaign which appealed to the existing anti-war sentiment.

The German reply, which actually hedged the main issue, was termed totally unresponsive and unacceptable by editors throughout the United States. In brief, it stated that it would do everything within its power not to jeopardize the lives of American citizens but it could not understand why Americans had to travel on enemy passenger ships, and it would not object if four enemy liners ran up the American flag if not enough American and neutral passenger liners were available for the North Atlantic traffic.

American public opinion became increasingly anti-war as most were encouraged by the slight concession in this note and did not hearken to such editorials as: "Not one of our moderate demands is accorded even the courtesy of frank recognition; all are in effect denied; each and every one is either tacitly spurned or impudently ignored."[259] *Now* Wilson stiffened his attitude, using his own judgment rather than that of the war-fearing public.

At the bottom of the third and last note which Wilson wrote on the *Lusitania*, sent on July 21, 1915, the Kaiser pencilled: "In tone and bearing this is about the most impudent note which I have ever read since the Japanese note of August last! It ends with a direct threat!"[260] It was not impudent; it merely made a polite but definite threat of war, or of a rupture in diplomatic relations if any new incidents occurred. Two excerpts are indicative of the contents of the message: ". . . The rights of neutrals in time of war are based upon principle, not upon expediency, and the principles are immutable. It is the duty and obligation of belligerents to find a way to adapt the new circumstances to them. . . . Friendship itself prompts [the United States government] to say to the Imperial Government that repetition by the commanders of German naval vessels of acts in contravention of those rights must be regarded by the Government of the United States, when they affect American citizens, as deliberately unfriendly."[261]

The President again displayed a calmness to the situation by returning to his vacation home at Cornish, New Hampshire, where he played golf, took auto rides and courted Mrs. Galt. Wilson's boldness attained results. Germany buried her indignation in a note relayed by Ambassador Bernstorff to the State Department stating that Germany might be willing to submit the question of indemnity for the loss of American life on the *Lusitania* to arbitration. The President, sensitive to American opinion, decided to let the *Lusitania* negotiations rest for a while, for he did not think public opinion would permit arbitration "at present." In addition, Great Britain had renewed her interference with our sea trade and the time might be at hand when the President would have to honor the promises that he had made in his note to Germany of July 21, to stand forthrightly for the freedom of the seas as much against Britain as against Germany. Calmness at this time when he was performing an international juggling act was an asset to the nation and a notable tribute to his style, particularly since it required consummate self-control. His natural temperament was that of an activist, impatient and persistent, "driven as by demons to almost frenzied efforts to achieve immediate and ideal solutions."[262]

Not only had Britain resumed obstruction of our shipping trade, seizing ships and cargoes, but in late June 1915 the London Foreign Office handed Ambassador Page a memorandum on British blockade practices which revealed the continued British assumption of the right to control all American commerce with Europe.[263] Then on July 23, 1915, the Foreign Office finally delivered its formal reply to the American note of March 30, 1915, concerning the blockade of the Central Powers; it made no important concessions on the fundamental issues to the American point of view.[264]

One crisis followed another—with Great Britain and with Germany; they simmered along, patched up here, compromised there. They alarmed Americans and stimulated a debate over foreign policy and a demand for preparedness which Wilson was now ready to accept.

The demand for preparedness provoked a dispute between the President and the Secretary of War over the method of organization that led to the resignation of the inflexible Mr. Garrison in February 1916. Wilson had, in fact, decided that he no longer desired the service of the able, austere, competent but unimaginative Secretary who had, from the beginning, worked so closely with the professional Army men and followed their lead in matters of policy that many anti-militarists believed he was virtually a tool of the military class.

Garrison, never a favorite of Wilson, always an outsider in the Cabinet circle, had many of the President's own qualities, some of which were occasionally softened in the President but in Garrison never. He never compromised, insisted upon doing the "right" instead of the "political" thing. Unlike Wilson he was garrulous and "a great nuisance at Cabinet meetings because he not only talked so much, but tried to inject his opinions into every department. He tried Wilson's patience by continuing to argue a point long after the President and his associates had agreed upon the merits of a case."[265] "He broke with the President because Wilson did the necessary instead of the heroic thing in a time of crisis, that is, because he compromised on an issue that Garrison considered a simple question of right or wrong."[266] Wilson had decided that Garrison must go as early as June 1915; therefore his departure was illustrative of Wilson's style of procrastination while waiting for a culmination of events. Garrison's reason for his departure highlights Wilson's occasional—and usually dramatic—willingness to compromise. It illustrates also Wilson's recognition of the rights of the Congress. Joseph Tumulty wrote: "It was precisely because the President respected the constitutional prerogatives of the Congress, and Mr. Garrison did not, that the break came."[267] In a letter to Garrison Wilson expressed his position, to which he did not adhere in the League fight because he differentiated between treaty making and legislation, and so strongly held the opinion that it was the President's prerogative and not that of the Congress to determine foreign policy: "It would never be proper or possible for me to say to any Committee of the House of Representatives that so far as my participation in legislation was concerned that they would have to take my plan or none. . . ."[268]

The issue did not concern the Navy; it concerned the Army. The General Board of the Navy and the Army War College were prepared to answer the President's request of July 21, 1915, transmitted through the Secretaries of War and Navy to recommend programs adequate to supply the needs of security. Wilson had come reluctantly to the conclusion that there must be a preparedness program. Colonel House had been urging upon the President since the late fall of 1914 the need for an immediate naval and military program. When he returned from Europe in July 1913, he had argued in favor of preparation for war, convinced that the "evasions" of Germany would continue so long as she could count upon American unpreparedness. The strength of his conviction was not lessened by the news that Mr. Bryan planned a trip to Europe as Apostle of Peace, where, House feared, the impression of American pacifism would be intensified by the Commoner's speeches.[269] House's diary of July 10, 1915, comments: "The trouble with the President is that he does not move, at times, with sufficient celerity."[270]

The War College moved with celerity, for it had been preparing for this moment. It submitted a long-range program aimed at achieving naval equality with the British by 1925. The President on October 15 approved this plan which envisaged the construction, during the first five years at a cost of $500 million, of ten battleships, six battle cruisers, ten cruisers, fifty destroyers, one hundred submarines and lesser craft. Even the Navy League had not asked for more.[271]

The Army plan proposed not only substantial increases in the regular Army, but to substitute a national reserve force—a Continental Army of 400,000 men for the National Guard as the first line of defense. On November 4, 1915, the President presented the plan to the country and urged its adoption in an address at the Manhattan Club in New York City. The anticipated denunciation by the progressives, by labor and by farm organizations led by Bryan burst upon him. But unanticipated and most damaging was the strong denunciation by a large group of Democratic radical members of Congress, most of them Southerners and Westerners, led by the new House majority leader and farmer-lawyer from North Carolina. The anti-preparedness leaders were able to pack and control the House Military Affairs Committee. Therefore Wilson faced a very tough situation when he delivered his Annual Message to Congress in December 1915, stressing patriotism, preparedness and a new shipping bill. Then before going on his honeymoon with Mrs. Galt, in typical style he called the House and Senate leaders to the White House and asked for the opposition's aid. The honeymoon interfered with his usual style of continuous contact with congressmen while he was in the process of fighting for legislation. Therefore, the Democratic members either became apathetic or remained opposed to the defense program.

Link describes the situation:

"Preparedness advocates were most alarmed, however, by the situation of the Military Affairs Committee. The leaders of this body had never got on well with Secretary Garrison, whom they thought dictatorial and responsive only to the military point of view. Now the Committee were at positive loggerheads with Garrison over the most important feature of the administration's army plan, the Continental Army. The Army War College had emphatically asserted that because of constitutional limitations on federal control of the state forces, the

National Guard could never be legally subjected to the control of the President and War Department. Garrison reiterated this argument before the Committee, adding that any army plan that made the National Guard the core of the reserve force was not only futile but also dangerous, because it could provide no effective force at all. The Committee members, however, were adamantly opposed to the idea of a national reserve force . . . a large, effective reserve army, under the absolute control of the War Department, seemed to the rural Democrats on the Committee the very symbol of uncontrolled militarism. Southerners, moreover, feared that a President hostile to their racial system might enlist Negroes in the volunteer reserve force."[272]

Faced with general apathy and a bitter congressional fight upon his return from an ill-timed honeymoon, Wilson set out on a tour of the East and Middle West to convince the past source of his support—the people—of the necessity of defending the Western Hemisphere against hostile attack, of the need for military power, of the explosive and unpredictable European situation. His style when Congress opposed him had been to go to the people. This he did again and again.

Friendly crowds have often proven to be unfaithful barometers of public relations. Majority Leader Claude Kitchin observed, "I see no real change in the attitude of Members since the President's Western tour."[273] Garrison and the military spokesmen had thoroughly antagonized the committee. Recognizing that he faced a stalemate, the President bowed to the committee, abandoned the Continental Army, and accepted "federalization" of the National Guard. Garrison resigned, and the relationship between the committee and the executive department became normal. Wilson did not hoist the standard of defeat very frequently, but he did it graciously, appointing the liberal Newton D. Baker, who until a month before his appointment on March 7 had been opposed to preparedness. It was a wise move politically and it was to prove a wise choice, for Baker became not only an excellent Secretary of War but an agreeable member of the Cabinet.

Army legislation, however, hit another snag. After the Hay Bill passed the House, the French packet *Sussex* was torpedoed in the English Channel on March 24, 1916. The President announced on April 18 that if the Germans did not thereafter adhere to the rules of cruiser warfare in their submarine operations, the United States would sever diplomatic relations; on that same day the preparedness leaders in the Senate, using the *Sussex* as a pretext, passed the War College-Garrison program, establishing a National Volunteer Army of 261,000 men.

"Thus the issue between the moderates and the preparedness advocates was frankly raised in the ensuing struggle between the two houses for control of the major aspects of the military bill. *In this struggle Wilson displayed all his powers of leadership and mediation.* (Emphasis added) He quickly spotted weaknesses in the Hay bill to federalize the National Guard and obtained their correction. He threw his support behind Secretary Baker's suggestion for the creation of a Council of National Defense. And in the struggle between the House and Senate he offered a compromise, in which the House's demand for a smaller army and the Senate's plan for a larger number of regiments would be reconciled. When the conferees adjourned without agreement on May 5, Wilson entered the controversy again, pleading with the House members to meet the Senate halfway.

"Under steady Presidential pressure the legislative deadlock was finally broken, and on May 13 the conferees agreed on a bill embodying mutual concessions. . . . The Garrison plan for a large national reserve force was abandoned, but the National Guard was thoroughly integrated into the federal defense structure. . . . In addition, the War Department was allowed to establish a number of volunteer summer training camps patterned after the highly successful experimental camp at Plattsburgh, New York. Finally, the War Department was authorized to construct and operate a nitrate plant. . . . Later legislation provided for a Council of National Defense."[274]

There is no better example of Wilson's leadership of Congress or of the fulfillment of his statement to Congress at the special session of May 8, 1913, when he had told the members that he was a real person, "not a mere department of the Government, hailing Congress from some isolated island of jealous power" (see page 166). He entered the fray; he faced the congressional differences realistically and compromised where compromises were essential to his objectives; he won his objectives; and he emerged the leader of congressional action for preparedness.

It was a right-about change of policy, for he had advocated "strict neutrality" since the beginning of the war. He had been slow to recognize the advantages and necessity of preparedness; his noble stand had encouraged the wariness of the public of entanglement in the war; he had procrastinated; and when he had the courage to reverse his position, he had difficulty in overcoming the pacifist opposition to which he had given encouragement and leadership. It is true, as Franklin Roosevelt was to discover, that a President must lead public opinion and his leadership cannot successfully be too far in advance of it. Wilson had not only heeded the American desire for neutrality but had led it. It is quixotic that this prolonged battle for neutrality, in fact as well as in theory, was to become his greatest asset in the 1916 campaign for re-election. When the Governor of New York, Martin Glynn, made the keynote address at the Democratic Convention which renominated Wilson on June 14, 1916, as Link says, "he invoked historical parallels to prove that Wilson's diplomacy of note writing had good precedent in the American past. But this would be a dull recital, he averred; and he was about to pass over that portion of his address when the immense crowd were on their feet, shouting, 'No! No! Go on.' This was an unexpected development, but Glynn sensed the electrical quality of the situation and at once launched into his historical exposition. As he cited one case after another in which the United States had refused under provocation to go to war, the mighty throng would chant 'What did we do? What did we do?' and Glynn would roar back, 'We didn't go to war, we didn't go to war.' "[275] This led to the popular slogan, "He kept us out of war," which was the backbone of Wilson's re-election campaign. He himself never used this phrase, and it is said that he disapproved of it.

The country and the President had been reorienting themselves during the latter part of 1915 and early 1916 in domestic as well as foreign viewpoints. Much of this was due to the influence of the progressives and to Wilson's realization that he would need their support if he was to win re-election. It was not only this pragmatic view which moved him. He was a fast learner and had found that the common welfare required that he move out of his constricted view of constitutional powers and dependence upon states' rights. The change in his orientation is well shown in his speech to the Gridiron Club of December 9, 1916—after his re-election: "The day of cold thinking, of fine-spun constitutional argument, is gone, thank God. We do not now discuss so much what the Constitution of the United States is as what the constitution of human nature is, what the essential constitution of human society is, and we know in our hearts that *if we ever find a place or a time where the Constitution of the United States is contrary to the constitution of human nature and human society, we have got to change the Constitution of the United States.*"[276] (Emphasis added)

This speech was made about three weeks before he sent Louis D. Brandeis's name to the Senate in nomination for the Supreme Court of the United States. He had not observed the usual protocol of asking the approval of the nominee by Senators Lodge and Weeks of Massachusetts—Brandeis's home state—and was acting in face of the assured opposition of great wealth, to the consternation of Colonel House, who had disapproved Brandeis's appointment to the Cabinet in 1914. The appointment's reception by the progressives was well expressed by one of their leading members, Amos Pinchot: "It took courage and sense to make this appointment and I take off my chapeau to the President."[277] It was not only courage that was shown. The move was a signpost of Wilson's newer philosophy, for Brandeis was then the leader of sound liberal thinking in this country. And Senator LaFollette wrote: "In appointing Mr. Brandeis to the Supreme Bench President Wilson has rendered a great public service. . . . To take him after three years of identification with the struggle for social justice, knowing the powerful forces arrayed against him is proof indisputable that when the President sees the light he is not afraid to follow it."[278]

As is often the practice with a convert, Wilson had campaigned for the New Nationalism of the progressives with fervor, vigor and ardor. He espoused the federal rural credits bill, which would have passed in 1914 if Wilson had not said that he would veto it if Congress enacted it. He would have vetoed it in 1914 because it provided for financial support by the federal government through direct subsidies. Wilson at that time vehemently opposed direct intervention by the government for any special class. In 1916 he favored not only the Rural Credits Act, which he signed June 17, 1916, but also the Federal Workman's Compensation Act, which was passed in August; the Child Labor Law, which he signed "with real emotion" September 1916; the Adamson Act, which imposed an eight-hour day for railway workers beginning January 1, 1917; and the act establishing the Federal Tariff Commission, July 1916, which pleased business. Thus between June and September 1916 he had accomplished a veritable social revolution—under his leadership the Congress had passed the most progressive legislation in the history of the country up to that time.

For all these measures he had prodded congressmen, as was his style when he pressed for action; he paid them the courtesy of going to the President's room at the Capitol to meet with them, and he invited them to the White House for conferences. And for all of these antecedents of the New Deal—and the foundation upon which it developed—he received votes and praise from the progressive members of the Democratic, Republican and the remnants of the Progressive parties. Whether or not he embraced these measures at first because of political motives, expediency gave way to ardent advocacy because he came to think of them as the right thing to do. He was flexible when convinced.

As is the custom, the President of the United States wrote the platform of his party in consultation with its most influential members. The platform of 1916 contained "an open bid for Progressive support in the form of a plank approving an advanced program of social legislation, promised a neutral foreign policy, endorsed reasonable preparedness, commended the cause of woman suffrage to the states, and denounced groups that placed the interests of foreign countries above the interests of the United States. [Of particular interest] . . . the platform committed the party to support entrance by the United States into a postwar League of Nations pledged to enforce peace by collective security measures against aggressors."[279]

Link comments: "Wilson had already personally committed the country to this project in a significant address at Washington on May 27 before the League to Enforce Peace, a non-partisan organization, formed in 1915 to propagate the League plan. It is interesting that in preparing this address which alleged America's willingness to depart from its historic policy of isolation, Wilson consulted only Colonel House and Secretary Lansing. In spite of his failure to confer with Democratic Congressional leaders . . . the Democrats willingly accepted a plank embodying the far-reaching proposal. It was a significant commentary on Wilson's mastery over the Democratic leaders."[280]

Bryan became the hero of the convention when he urged the delegates to renominate Wilson and thanked God the country had a President who did not want war. Wilson was nominated by acclamation.

Charles Evans Hughes had resigned from the Supreme Court to become the Republican candidate. His was a lackluster campaign until he seized upon the issue of the Adamson Act, which imposed an eight-hour day for railway workers. It is necessary to briefly review the history of this act in order to understand the quick rally of business to Hughes and the avalanche of liberals to Wilson, well characterized by none other than the then ardent liberal Walter Lippmann: "I shall vote not for the Wilson who has uttered a few too many noble sentiments but for the Wilson who is evolving under experience and is remaking his philosophy in the light of it, for the Wilson who is temporarily at least creating, out of the reactionary, parochial fragments of the Democracy, the only party which at this moment is national in scope, liberal in purpose, and effective in action."[281]

In the early spring of 1916 the presidents of the four railroad brotherhoods presented demands for an eight-hour day, no reduction in wages, and time and a half for overtime. On June 15 the railroad managers rejected these demands, but they did offer to submit them to arbitration. The U.S. Board of Mediation failed to obtain an agreement and a general railroad strike was declared. On August 13 Wilson invited the union chiefs and the railroad managers to the White House, appealing for compromise in the national interest. When both sides refused to compromise, Wilson decided, in his familiar style of taking without hesitation the action he thought right, that the workers' demand for an eight-hour day was correct. But they must abandon their demand for punitive overtime pay, and a federal commission should be appointed to study the entire railroad labor problem.

The brotherhood chiefs accepted the President's proposal on August 18, but the managers rejected it immediately. Wilson summoned another group of railroad presidents who met in the East Room of the White House on August 21 in 100° of heat. When they refused Wilson's appeal that they accept his compromise in the name of humanity, he left the room saying with saintly hot temper: "I pray God to forgive you, I never can."

On August 27 the railroad union then issued orders for a nationwide strike on September 4. On August 28 Wilson went to the Capitol to confer with the Democratic leaders, and on the 29th he outlined to a joint session of Congress legislation to prevent a strike, legislation which endorsed the eight-hour day and provided for a commission to study the railroad problem. It was passed by both houses and signed by the President on September 3.

This was indeed forthright action in the country's interest and in the interest of the laboring man. It was not impelled by the votes of the laborer; it was impelled by Wilson's ire at the intransigence of the railroad presidents and the justice of the cause of the railroad laborer. Lippmann rightly described the Wilson who was "evolving under experience," and "remaking his philosophy in the light of it."

Hughes's ineptitudes do not concern this book except for his courtship of the German-American vote, and that concerns us only for Wilson's sharp and telling reply to the President of the American Truth Society, who tried to compel the President to state his views: "I would feel deeply mortified to have you or anybody like you vote for me. Since you have access to many disloyal Americans and I have not, I will ask you to convey this message to them."[282]

The Democratic Party in 1916 was a minority party. Wilson had won in 1912 largely because of the split in the Republican Party. He won in 1916 because of the new coalition of the Democratic Party and what in today's parlance are tagged by the inclusive term "liberals."

Meanwhile, since the fall of 1915 President Wilson had been urging House to take another trip to Europe. This time the objective was definite in Wilson's mind; House was to persuade the European powers that they should agree upon mediation, with Wilson as the mediator. His dream was to establish "a universal dominion of peace through law."[283] This "dream" was not based upon idealism or morality, but upon practicality. German-American relations were becoming more and more tense and might worsen to the point of a break in diplomatic relations and even to war—which Wilson was determined to attempt to prevent. Wilson's objective of a return to a status quo ante bellum had long been fixed in his mind for, from the beginning, he had believed that no one nation had caused the war, that each nation had its own ambitions and that these ambitions should be negated.

On September 3, 1915, House started to explore European reception. He wrote Sir Edward Grey: "Do you think the President could make peace proposals to the belligerents upon the broad basis of elimination of militarism and navalism and a return as nearly as possible to the status quo? Will you not advise me?"[284]

On October 13 House was told by the British Ambassador in Washington that Grey's impression was that neither side was ready to discuss peace, and that the great objective of the present war was security against future aggression. The note sent by Grey through his Ambassador asked the direct question: "How much are the United States prepared to do in this direction? Would the President propose that there should be a League of Nations binding themselves to side against any power which broke a treaty; which broke certain rules of warfare on sea or land . . . or which refused, in the case of dispute, to adopt some other method of settlement than that of war?"[285]

House's long reply, approved and edited by Wilson, repeated a phrase contained in his original letter of September 3: "It has occurred to me that the time may soon come when this Government should intervene between belligerents and demand that peace parleys begin upon the broad basis of the *elimination of militarism and navalism. . . .*"[286] (Emphasis added)

It was not until November 9 that House received Grey's reply to this in the form of a question. He asked what House meant by "elimination of militarism and navalism," and whether House agreed that the peace of the world could be secured only by the United States' joining a League of Nations and guaranteeing the peace settlement. In relaying Grey's message to the President, House begged him to come out forthrightly behind Grey's proposal. "This is the part I think you are destined to play in this world tragedy, and it is the noblest part that has ever come to a son of man. This country will follow you along such a path, no matter what the cost may be."[287] Wilson's natural egotism was inflated; the League of Nations became a definite concept to which he forever after clung tenaciously and pursued boldly and zealously in spite of the immediate obstacles which the foreign governments imposed and the later obstacles imposed by Congress. Grey had put teeth into Wilson's intentions by delineating them, but Grey had not espoused them; he was merely asking what Wilson had in mind. When House's letter, which he termed "the most important letter I ever wrote," reached Grey on November 8, 1915, the British Foreign Minister was in no mood to think or talk seriously about peace.

In spite of polite but perfunctory messages from Grey, Wilson insisted on December 15 that House go to London as soon as arrangements could be made. His determination drove him in spite of lack of encouragement. House arrived in London on January 6, 1916; he spent three days in Berlin from January 26 to 29, and six days in Paris where he made some very rash promises never discussed with the President. He became convinced that neither side was ready to begin serious peace discussions and wrote the President that: "Hell will break loose in England this spring and summer as never before," but he was certain Wilson could intervene before the summer was over.[288] Before returning to London on the 11th he wrote Wilson: ". . . a great opportunity is yours, my friend—the greatest, perhaps, that has ever come to any man. The way out seems clear to me and, when I can lay the facts before you, I believe it will be clear to you also. . . ."[289]

In London he had further talks with Grey and with members of the Cabinet, which Ambassador Page refused to attend, for "not one of them has any confidence in the strength of the President for action.

"Therefore . . . I told House that I couldn't go with him to any such conference and I wouldn't."[290]

As a matter of fact, House made promises in Paris and in London that went far beyond any authority he had and that were contrary to Wilson's stated position that the war end in a stalemate and a return to the "status quo ante bellum." Although House was presumptuous and carried away by the authority he had assumed and delusions he entertained, Wilson's style of unquestioning trust, his effusion in expressing his confidence in his friend without any limitation was instrumental in building up the delusion of House that he had *carte blanche* to proceed as he decided on the spur of the moment. Wilson had written the Colonel before he left for Europe: "You ask for instructions as to what attitude you are to take at the several capitals. I feel that you do not need any."[291] He went on to say: "I agree with you that we have nothing to do with local settlements

... territorial questions, indemnities, and the like, but are concerned only in the future peace of the world and the guarantees to be given for that. . . ."[292] Yet House made such territorial promises as that Alsace-Lorraine would be returned to France and the absurd suggestion that Germany be awarded Turkey in exchange. Wanting to curry favor with the United States, each nation nodded as if in agreement and spoke in vague terms to House for he was Wilson's personal envoy. As Link says, "House had heard what he wanted to hear in Paris and London. He had deluded himself into believing that the British and French wanted American mediation for a negotiated peace. It did not matter that this was not true, or that British and French leaders had said nothing to indicate that it was either true or possible. House was out of touch with reality by the time of his conversation in Paris and his return to London. He consequently not only misinformed and misled President Wilson but also encouraged him to base fundamental foreign policy on the assumption that American mediation was possible in the immediate future."[293]

It is true that Sir Edward Grey and the Colonel drew the now famous so-called House-Grey Agreement, and that upon his return to the United States President Wilson approved the agreement with the change of only one word—an agreement that went far beyond Wilson's proposal to act as a mediator and his desire that Europe return to a "status quo ante bellum." The memorandum of Sir Edward Grey which House submitted to Wilson on his return from England read:

Colonel House told me that President Wilson was ready, on hearing from France and England that the moment was opportune, to propose that a Conference should be summoned to put an end to the war. Should the Allies accept this proposal, and should Germany refuse it, the United States would probably enter the war against Germany.

Colonel House expressed the opinion that, if such a Conference met, it could secure peace on terms not unfavourable to the Allies; and, if it failed the United States would probably[294] leave the Conference as a belligerent on the side of the Allies, if Germany was unreasonable. Colonel House expressed an opinion decidedly favorable to the restoration of Belgium, the transfer of Alsace and Lorraine to France, and the acquisition by Russia of an outlet to the sea, though he thought that the loss of territory incurred by Germany in one place would have to be compensated to her by concessions to her in other places outside Europe. If the Allies delayed, accepting the offer of President Wilson, and if, later on, the course of the war was so unfavorable to them that the intervention of the United States would not be effective, the United States would probably disinterest themselves in Europe and look to their own protection in their own way.

I said I felt the statement, coming from the President of the United States, to be a matter of such importance that I must inform the Prime Minister and my colleagues; but that I could say nothing until it had received their consideration. The British Government could, under no circumstances accept or make any proposal except in consultation and agreement with the Allies. *I thought that the Cabinet would probably feel that the present situation would not justify them in approaching their Allies on this subject at the present moment;* but, as Colonel House had had an intimate conversation with M. Briand and Mr. Jules Cambon in Paris, I should think it right to tell M. Briand privately, through the French Ambassador in London, what Colonel House had said to us; and I should, of course, whenever there was an opportunity be ready to talk the matter over with M. Briand, if he desired it.[295] (Emphasis added)

> Foreign Office   Intd. E.G.
> 22 February

It is surprising that the President agreed with proposals that were at such wide variance with the position he had taken before Colonel House left for Europe, and even more surprising that he read the Grey memorandum with his eyes open to the escape clause which Grey had carefully inserted (section italicized). Such was his eagerness to act as mediator that he accepted the territorial changes agreed to and suggested by House with seeming nonchalance, and said to House: "It would be impossible to imagine a more difficult task than the one placed in your hands, but you have accomplished it in a way beyond my expectations."[296]

Wilson's eagerness to take world leadership, his exaggerated self-confidence and egotism seem to have led him to make complete American neutrality and a statement of the ambitions of the belligerents negotiable ideals, thereby creating a new style.

It is also remarkable that Wilson, in his eagerness, glossed over the fact that Grey labelled the statement "A Memorandum," not an agreement, and in no manner expressed his own or his government's present agreement with what "Colonel House told me."

The final dénouement came in late August when Sir Edward Grey, spurred by the success of the British offensive beginning July 1, 1916, and the failure of the German attack on the French fortress of Verdun, turned down House's repeated pleas for implementation of the "agreement" and said definitely that a peace conference could not yet be held. This excerpt from one of Grey's telegrams in answer to House's importunities is significant: London, May 12, 1916, "I have received your telegram. My opinion without consulting colleagues and Allies is of little value, and for me to consult them now as to a peace conference would, I think, at best lead to a reply that mediation or a conference was premature. . . ."[297]

While House was in London, Wilson impetuously—which was sometimes his style—espoused a proposal of Lansing's without thought to the consequent unfavorable effect it would have upon House's mission and upon Anglo-American relations. In abstract the idea was good, but not in the context of existing conditions. The proposal threatened to change the rules of wartime to the great advantage of the Central Powers. Briefly, Lansing had proposed and the President had agreed that "The administration would have to act quickly to revise its rules since it was manifestly unfair to insist that a submarine should stop and warn an armed merchantman when the latter had the capacity to destroy its foe without ado. . . . The safest and fairest solution would be to insist that merchantmen cease to carry guns large enough to sink a submarine, and to treat armed merchant ships as warships when they visited American ports."[298]

The President, his mind bent upon a solution to the submarine danger and to averting war with Germany, grasped this solution. Both Wilson and Lansing were confounded by the violent reaction of the British government, of Ambassador Page and of Colonel House, because they firmly believed that this "modus vivendi" was advantageous to the Allies. As Wilson later explained to Colonel House: "Germany is seeking to find an excuse to throw off all restraints in under-sea warfare. If she is permitted to assume that English steamers are armed she will have found the excuse. If the British will disarm their merchant ships she will be without excuse and the English will have made a capital stroke against her. We are amazed the English do not see this opportunity to gain a great advantage without losing anything."[299]

With the great Atlantic Ocean stretched between, Wilson had not the slightest conception of the inflammable tension that burned in the European capitals. Professional logic guided his reasoning, which was quickly brought into contact with reality by the brouhaha Lansing's suggestion raised in Great Britain. The furor was so intense, so disruptive to House's negotiations, so provocative to Page's already frayed patience with his country's attitude, that after conferring with the Cabinet on February 15, Wilson and Lansing decided they had made a mistake and Lansing retracted the proposal under a smoke screen of diplomatic jargon. It is interesting that Sir Edward Grey's memorandum was issued after the retreat.

Lansing's statement was so diplomatically subtle that it initiated a congressional revolt. Many members of Congress interpreted it to mean that the American government would defend the right of its citizens to travel on all armed merchantmen. Accordingly, a resolution was introduced in the House within two days requesting the President to warn all American citizens to refrain from travelling on armed merchant vessels; and in the Senate the following day a resolution was introduced asserting that the American government should not acquiesce in the German armed ship decree. Then a movement was organized to force the Foreign Relations Committee to report the bills introduced on January 5 at Bryan's request which would have prohibited the issuance of passports to Americans travelling on any belligerent ship, and American and neutral vessels from transporting American citizens as passengers while carrying contraband.

Such confusion reigned on Capitol Hill that Wilson resorted to his well-known style of inviting congressional leaders to the White House. Their questions were many and piercing; their disagreements equally so. No diplomatic language would satisfy them. Link describes the scene: "Then, according to one newspaper account, he 'stopped speaking English and talked United States.' The American Government, he said, would go to almost any lengths to defend the right of Americans to travel on defensively armed merchant ships. He would consider it his duty to hold Germany to strict account if a German war vessel should torpedo without warning an armed merchant vessel carrying American passengers. Indeed he would sever diplomatic relations if this occurred. Moreover, he would regard adoption of a resolution warning Americans against travelling on armed ships as a rank discourtesy.

"Senator Stone [chairman of the Senate Foreign Relations Committee] heretofore Wilson's most loyal and admiring supporter in the upper house, was not persuaded. . . . The American people did not want to go to war to vindicate the right of a few people to travel or work on armed vessels. There was nothing to do but warn Americans to stay off such ships. Growing excited, Stone banged his fist on the table and exclaimed, 'Mr. President, would you draw a shutter over my eyes and my intellect? You have no right to ask me to follow such a course. It may mean war for my country. I must follow my conscience in this matter.' "[300]

The President's words were carried to other congressional members. To add to the acrimonious situation, Germany repeated her intention to treat armed merchantmen as warships. Rumor piled upon rumor at the Capitol. One rumor has a following today among revisionists: "Wilson wants war." The revisionists base their belief upon the House-Grey Agreement, by which they claim Wilson was laying a foundation for American entry into the war on the Allied side. But this theory is out of tune with the very nature of the man, whose every action and policy was molded by his deep religious faith, by the steadfastness with which he held to his conviction—and surely there can be no doubt of his conviction from the beginning of the European war that the United States must remain neutral in spirit as well as in fact—and by his repeated efforts to act as mediator, as the savior of world peace, permanent peace. He was, to be sure, slowly and reluctantly beginning to realize that war might be inevitable; but he was not leading the people of the United States into war. He was not preparing them to think of the possibility of war as Franklin Roosevelt did before World War II.

However, much as he desired to avoid war, he would not relinquish his principles. It is largely for this reason that the revisionists believe he was courting war. And, in fact, his adherence to principle did contribute to the entry into the war although he was not maneuvering to bring us into it. Wilson spent all of his energies trying to be neutral, to preserve American rights, to become the mediator of this war and the savior of the world from future wars. Franklin Roosevelt faced facts; Wilson tried to neutralize facts.

The hysteria on the Hill was met by calmness at the White House. Wilson refused to be stampeded by Speaker Clark, who telephoned the White House on February 24 asking that the President see him, Representative Flood (chairman of the Foreign Affairs Committee of the House) and Claude Kitchin (House majority leader) as soon as possible. He saw no one. This situation, he knew, was not only the gravest challenge to his own leadership, but one of the gravest challenges to the President's conduct of foreign affairs in American history. On such an occasion he meditated in seclusion; he reviewed the position he would have to take to maintain leadership at home while not impairing his relations in Europe; and he carefully debated the means by which he could successfully demonstrate his conviction that in foreign affairs the President should lead and the Congress should follow. He would have to make known his position in no uncertain terms before he met Clark, Kitchin and Flood.

With the instinct of the politician, Wilson seized upon a long letter he received on the 25th from Senator Stone as the vehicle upon which to couch his answer to Congress and to the people of the United States. Stone's letter said in part: ". . . The situation in Congress is such as to excite a sense of deep concern in the minds of careful and thoughtful men. I have felt that it is due you to say this much. . . .

". . . Up to the last you should be left free to act diplomatically as you think for the best to settle the questions involved. I need hardly say that my wish is to help, not to hinder you."[301]

Wilson's reply was not meant for Stone's ears alone, for he gave both Stone's letter and his letter to the press. Nor was it meant only for the Congress and the American people. He required their support in order to demonstrate to Germany that he had their backing; and it was—if he achieved their backing—a warning to Germany that she could not trample upon America's rights. The salient parts are:

. . . You are right in assuming that I shall do everything in my power to keep the United States out of war. I think the country will feel no uneasiness about my course in that respect. . . .

. . . The course which the Central Powers have announced their intention of following in the future with regard to undersea warfare seems for the moment to threaten insuperable obstacles, but its apparent meaning is so manifestly inconsistent with explicit assurances recently given up by those powers with regard to their treatment of merchant vessels on the high seas that I must believe that explanations will presently ensue which will put a different aspect upon it. We have had no reason to question their good faith or their fidelity to their promises in the past and I feel for one confident that we shall have none in the future. . . .

For my own part, I cannot consent to any abridgment of the rights of American citizens in any respect. The honor and self-respect of the nation is involved. We covet peace, and shall preserve it at any cost but the loss of honor. To forbid our people to exercise their rights for fear we might be called upon to vindicate them would be a deep humiliation indeed. . . .

It is important to reflect that if in this instance we allowed expediency to take the place of principle, the door would inevitably be opened to still further concessions. Once accept a single abatement of right, and many other humiliations would certainly follow, and the whole fine fabric of international law might crumble under our hands piece by piece. What we are contending for in this matter is of the very essence of the things that have made America a sovereign nation. She cannot yield them without conceding her own impotency as a nation, and making virtual surrender of her independent position among the nations of the world. . . .[302]

After issuing copies of the correspondence to the press, Wilson invited the Speaker and a delegation from the House of Representatives to meet with him the following morning. He lost no time in pressing his case with the Congress. Speaker Clark informed the President "that the delegation had not come to argue but simply to inform the President about the formidable movement in the House for a resolution to warn Americans against traveling on armed ships."[303]

"Wilson replied quietly but emphatically, saying that he intended to 'see this thing through,' and that he could not help it if Congress would not support him. Congress and the people would give him united support if they wanted to avoid war. Any yielding to Germany now, particularly adoption of a warning resolution, would only encourage both belligerent alliances further to transgress American rights, and the whole fabric of international law would fall to pieces."[304] Upon leaving the White House, Clark told reporters that it was "very clear to all that the President stands on his letter to Senator Stone."[305] The letter to Stone, although it contained refutable inaccuracies, crumbled the opposition. Clark's account of the President's firm stand withered it. The McLemore and Gore resolutions, in the face of Wilson's strong stand supported by wide newspaper approval, could muster few votes and were tabled. It was a remarkable show of the force of Wilson's leadership.

At this very time Germany, encouraged by the certainty that the McLemore and Gore resolutions would pass by a large majority, was formulating plans to increase her submarine warfare to the point of total war against all shipping, belligerent and neutral. Hence the news of Wilson's letter to Stone came as a great shock—a realization that all-out submarine warfare would lead to war with America. Wilson had achieved his second goal, particularly after the resolutions died a decisive death. There was hesitation and disagreement in Germany among the proponents of all-out submarine warfare and a pause in its instrumentation.

In this country, Wilson's political position was strengthened by the fact that Republican members of the Congress formed the nucleus of the group that surrendered.

Two conflicting characteristics of Wilson's style are well illustrated here: his refusal to see the delegation from the House of Representatives while he deliberated in solitude, and his hastily drafted answer to Stone's letter. He would often procrastinate about a decision until he had mulled over it a considerable time; he would often act impetuously, without sufficient facts and consideration. Other characteristics are apparent—his skillful and bold leadership; his absolute faith in his own objectives, his belief that what he considered right was right and must prevail; his practice of maintaining close relations with Congress; and his concept of his duty as a leader of men.

There were marked changes in Wilson's and the American people's attitude toward the belligerents as the Germans abated their submarine warfare for several months; as the torpedoing of the *Sussex* brought the two nations to the brink of war (see page 224); as Great Britain's popularity waned because of the ruthless manner of her suppression of the Irish Rebellion of April 24, 1916; as the British and French seized and examined parcels in the American mails; and particularly as the British published on July 18, 1916, a blacklist of eighty-seven American firms with whom British subjects were forbidden to trade because they were suspected of trading with the Central Powers.

The pendulum of outrage swung to Great Britain. Wilson told reporters on July 24 that the "blacklist got on his nerves,"[306] and when things got on his nerves he sometimes bided his time; but in this case he did not. He had written Colonel House the previous day an explosive letter, indicative of his capacity to show the Irish in him when aroused:

I am, I must admit about at the end of my patience with Great Britain and the Allies. This black list business is the last straw. I have told Spring-Rice [the British Ambassador] so, and he sees very clearly. Both he and Jusserand [the French Ambassador] think it a stupid blunder. I am seriously considering asking Congress to authorize me to prohibit loans and restrict exportations to the Allies. It is becoming clear to me that there lies latent in this policy the wish to prevent our merchants getting a foothold in markets which Great Britain has hitherto controlled and all but dominated. Polk and I are compounding a very sharp note. I may feel obliged to make it as sharp and final as the one to Germany on the submarines. . . .[307]

The note that was sent on July 26, though drafted in the State Department, was rewritten by Wilson with all the asperity that his letter to House had indicated. Acting Secretary of State Polk smoothed out a few of the toughest phrases.

In writing to Colonel House on July 27, Wilson reported with a comment untypical of the master of the English language: ". . . It was evident to Polk when he last saw Spring-Rice that the British Government was not a little disturbed (and surprised, poor boobs!)."[308] There was not a word of reply, and on August 2 insult was added to injury by an Anglo-French prohibition of consignments of American tobacco to neutral ports for re-export to Germany. This brought representatives of the Southern farmers to Washington to demand that their representatives and senators obtain relief if the State Department did not act at once to have the order rescinded. The President, as was his style in times of crisis, went at once to the Capitol to confer with senatorial leaders. Wilson's courtesy in frequently going to the Capitol instead of summoning the leaders to the White House was an evident sign of his desire to work with the Congress, and was appreciated. He brought with him a joint resolution empowering the President to retaliate against nations denying shipping privileges to blacklisted firms; it was incorporated in the shipping bill then in committee conference.[309] Wilson acted with speed to counteract the action of his future Allies by having Lansing draft a resolution which was added as an amendment to the revenue bill—a means of obtaining action quickly for the bills were already in process. It empowered the President to prohibit the import of any or all products from any country that discriminated against the products of American soil or industry, or prevented them from going to other countries in contravention of international law. Another amendment offered by Senator Thomas authorized the President during a war in which the United States was not engaged to deny use of American ports to ships of nations that denied ordinary privileges to American vessels. It also empowered the President to use the armed forces to enforce its terms and imposed heavy penalties for violation; and empowered him to deny use of American mails and communications services to citizens of countries that interfered with American mails or communications.

Wilson, one can easily see, was neutral in condemning combatants of either side when they infringed upon the rights of the United States. After two wars with Germany, the fact that we had serious altercations with the Allies in World War I has been forgotten, except by historians. Our Ambassador to Great Britain, however, was only mindful of our relations with Great Britain, and had been for some time. A great friend of the President, one of the first to promote his presidency, the relationship with Page is a classic example of Wilson's style of discarding friendship when there was no longer a meeting of minds. Wilson was incapable of differing and still retaining friendship.

Page came to Washington in mid-August, as Wilson said, "for a vacation in which it is our hope that he may get back a little way at least to the American point of view about things."[310] Secretary of State Robert Lansing wrote: "I gained the impression from our conversations and I think Mr. Wilson did too, that Mr. Page had come to the United States to explain the attitude of the British people toward the United States and to plead their cause with the American government. He certainly sought to have us surrender many of the legal rights of the American citizen on the high seas instead of trying to persuade the British to cease their illegal interferences with those rights. . . . One of the chief results of Mr. Page's visit to the United States was to make the President more than ever irritated against the British. He considered that they had exerted improper influence on our Ambassador and had convinced the latter that Mr. Wilson, if he remained neutral, could not participate in the peace negotiations, a purpose which was very close to the President's heart and for which he was constantly planning. . . . [Page] was attempting to drive Mr. Wilson into open hostility to the Germans and open sympathy with the British. If he had read aright the character of the President, Mr. Page would have avoided taking such a course *because it was the one way of arousing Mr. Wilson's spirit of obstinacy.* (Emphasis added) It was folly to try it. . . . It was not his insistent demands in favor of the British but the gross misconduct of the Germans, which at last forced the President to break relations and to call on the United States to take up arms on the side of the Allies."[311]

Then Wilson used a practice that is well known to me, for President Franklin D. Roosevelt employed it to his associates' amusement and to the great annoyance of at least one victim. Roy Howard, editor of the Scripps-Howard newspapers, had an appointment with Governor Roosevelt at his Hyde Park home when Roosevelt was a Presidential candidate. Knowing that he was going to ask questions that the Governor either did not want to answer or on which he did not wish to be misquoted, he told his counsel that he wanted him in the room during the entire interview. Howard, not realizing that Rosenman was there under orders, later complained, and it was repeated: "That damn Jew wouldn't leave the room."

Wilson had Page to luncheon at the White House twice but he had other guests too and there was no opportunity for intimate discussion. It was not until September 22 that Page was able to have a private interview with the President at his summer home, "Shadow Long" in Long Branch, after having sent Wilson an urgent telegram when Congress had passed legislation retaliatory to England's

"Black List." He stayed the night. Each man had his say; neither convinced the other. "It was in this interview that Page had hoped to show Mr. Wilson the real merits of the situation, and persuade him to adopt the course to which the national honor and safety pointed; he talked long and eloquently, painting the whole European tragedy with that intensity and readiness of utterance and that moral conviction which had so moved all others . . . but Mr. Wilson was utterly cold, utterly unresponsive, interested only in ending the war. . . . Page came away with no vexation or anger, but with a real feeling for a much suffering and a much perplexed statesman. . . . The two men never met again."[312]

Wilson's mind was still centered upon ending the war, with no advantage gained by either side. During his campaign for re-election he refrained from pressing the issue because he felt that neither Germany nor Great Britain would seriously consider his intervention at a time when his own future was uncertain. His lack of success in the past did not daunt him. The timing was not right; he would have to await the election results.

"The conditions which prevailed in foreign affairs in the latter part of September and early part of October, 1916, had changed but little, if at all, at the time of the presidential election and they continued unchanged for the succeeding three weeks. During that period, however, the President reached the conclusion that the time had arrived when conditions were favorable for his making an attempt to bring the warring nations into a conference for the negotiation of peace. Ignoring Mr. Page's declaration that the British would oppose a neutral's taking part in such a conference, Mr. Wilson worked out a plan for approaching the belligerent governments with the great end in view of restoring peace."[313] Mr. Wilson's stubborn determination would brook no curb, especially from an Ambassador in whom he had lost confidence. (Page did resign, but Wilson never answered his letter of resignation. He asked House to take Page's place, but House refused. He had no one else and events began to move so rapidly that Lansing asked him to stay; although he truly desired to resign he recognized the urgency of staying at his post and did so.)

In addition to the other difficulties with Great Britain, the President was now being pressed by tremendous financial demands from them; by threats of increased submarine warfare by Germany; and by the growing alarm of the American public. It is scarcely surprising that he stated in the first draft of his peace note on November 25 that: "The position of neutral nations . . . has been rendered all but intolerable. Their commerce is interrupted, their industries are checked and diverted, the lives of their people are put in constant jeopardy, they are virtually forbidden the accustomed highways of the sea, their energies are drawn off into temporary and novel channels, they suffer at every turn. . . ."[314]

Wilson did not use hasty judgment in preparing this appeal. Among the Wilson papers is a bulky folder containing documentary material upon which he worked—magazine and newspaper articles, flimsies of dispatches, selections from the speeches of the leading foreign statesmen, and his own memoranda and notes. Link points out that "These papers were mostly concerned with the attitude of public opinion at home and abroad."[315] The diplomatic situation was well known to him.

In sharp contrast to the casual style in which he sent Colonel House off to

Europe on former peace missions, Wilson spent weeks preparing a proposed draft
—not a final paper—which he read aloud to Colonel House on the 27th, and
which he discussed with Secretary of State Lansing. His biographer, Ray Stannard Baker, writes: "No one with any knowledge of the crisis that then existed
can read this note in its original form before it had been whittled down by the
fears and sympathies of his advisors, without regarding it as one of the strongest
papers Wilson ever wrote. . . . What could have been more sensible than to ask
the fighters to stop for a moment, discuss what the war was all about, and define
what each wanted as the price of peace?"[316]

Whittled down it was! He had shown his usual style of stubborn determination
when House on November 14 and Lansing and Polk on the 15th had counselled
against writing a note to the belligerents demanding that the war cease.[317] His
mind was set upon sending a note, and a note he drafted with painstaking care.
Then his style changed. So eager was the President to have acceptance by the
warring powers that he dropped his stubborn determination and responded to the
arguments for deletions in his draft which House and Lansing thought would
bring offense to one side or the other. However, he refused the Colonel's suggestion that he add something "which would make the Allies believe he sympathized
with their viewpoint."[318] His advisers kept counselling delay.

The delay was costly to Wilson's plans. On December 12 the German government issued a call for a peace conference, thus euphemistically "pulling the rug
from under" Wilson. The reason? Apparently they now realized that it would
require a long struggle to maintain their present military supremacy and they
were being seriously affected by the British blockade and the fighting qualities of
the French armies. Berlin had decided it would be wise to sit around the peace
table while they were in a strong position. It was for that same reason that the
British refused to do so.

Robert Lansing's opinion was that Wilson "would have been justified in
immediately abandoning his plan of addressing the belligerents. Its success
seemed hopeless to the most optimistic in view of the atmosphere of hostility
which would be created in all the Allied countries by the arrogant proposals of
the Central Alliance, and by the suspicion with which the President's appeal
would certainly be received.

"However, Mr. Wilson was not to be turned from his purpose, though in the
circumstances he ought to have been. Having made up his mind as to what he
should do, nothing could swerve him from his purpose. This characteristic of Mr.
Wilson was a defect which he evinced on other occasions. It was an unfortunate
stubbornness of purpose which defied fact. He lacked the ability of rapid readjustment to changed conditions so necessary in the successful conduct of foreign
affairs."[319]

His biographer, however, states that: "It is forever the problem of the idealist,
however clearly he may see the ultimate truth, to act so that his action counts
in a bitterly practical and selfish world."[320]

Wilson went straight ahead. He read the note as edited to the Cabinet on
December 15. Secretary McAdoo and Houston expressed strong doubts as to the
wisdom of sending it. Houston suggested that "it would be resented and might
be regarded as an act of friendship toward Germany and possibly as a threat.
. . . The President said: 'It may be wise to send nothing, but I will send this note
or nothing.' "[321]

The note was dispatched on December 18. It was a powerful document in spite of the whittling. Wilson had reworked it several times and had, in fact, added strength. Although not phrased in the form of questions, two were implied and one stated. He called attention "to the fact that the objects which the statesmen of the belligerents on both sides have in mind in this war are virtually the same, as stated in general terms to their own people and to the world." This not only raised great indignation in each belligerent country, since each believed the generality that their objectives were noble and just; it also offended each of them to have their objectives classed with their opponents', which were obviously base. It should have provoked their statesmen to question their aims; it did not. Wilson, however, asked for a direct answer, for "such an avowal of their respective views as to the terms" upon which the war might be ended and the peace guaranteed "as would make it possible frankly to compare them." The Allies did not reply to the question at all, nor to the note until January 10, 1917; the Germans even later. Waiting, waiting, he wrote on January 3, 1917: "My heart aches that no way can be found out of the present wilderness of war."[322]

Certainly an answer was expected when Wilson stated that he was not offering mediation or proposing peace but hoped his request would lead to an interchange of views, and this in turn to a conference. He would "be happy himself to serve or even to take the initiative in its accomplishment." The prospective brides shied away from the persistent suitor. Each side believed that it would achieve ultimate victory in the war and obtain objectives which it would not openly state at this time.

The world, however, took notice with extravagant praise and with caustic criticism. Wilson took the criticism in stride, writing to Roy W. Howard on January 2, 1917: "Neither side in the war is pleased with anything I write unless it can be construed as favorable in feeling to them. . . ."[323]

Great praise came from members of the Congress. Champ Clark, Speaker of the House, wrote to the President that it was "the best of all your good performances, saying precisely what should be said." Senator Hitchcock of Nebraska introduced a resolution of endorsement; the Senate postponed consideration until January 2.

Coming so soon after the German attempt, both abroad and at home, some critics coupled the two and believed that Wilson was allied to the German "peace" move and was influenced by Germany. Lansing, realizing the various doubts raised as to the meaning of the note, tried to explain to the press who, in turn, misinterpreted his explanation. Headlines streamed throughout the nation with the news that ". . . the Government was contemplating abandoning its neutrality and was about to enter the war!"[324] The perpetrator of such an indiscretion was usually treated by Wilson to icy coldness; but in this case he couched his letter to Lansing conveying a reproof and an order to issue a corrective statement courteously. The second statement was made, but first impressions have a habit of surviving and the belief was widespread that America was near to war with Germany. The contending countries interpreted Lansing's statement according to their own lights. Officials in Berlin decided that mediation was more than ever to be avoided. The British Ambassador told Lansing that his first statement was "the only thing that saved the situation" so far as his government was concerned—that if it had not been issued the resentment in Great Britain toward the President "for his untimely attempt to inject himself into the peace movement of the Central Empires" would have known no bounds.[325]

Lansing's statement may have erased British resentment but it also enforced their determination not to state their peace terms; why go out on a limb if they could be certain of American support?

It must be said here that Lansing's negative attitude toward sending Wilson's communication to the warring powers on December 18, and his subsequent actions just described, completed Wilson's growing distrust and lack of confidence in his Secretary of State. "Lansing . . . was brilliant while executing routine business and often bungling while conducting important negotiations. . . . Unable to find a good replacement or to dismiss Lansing in the midst of various crises, Wilson thought that he had no recourse but to conduct all important negotiations himself."[326]

This distrust explains Wilson's growing style as a diplomatist which has stamped his historical record as egotistical, jealous of others and unwilling to delegate authority. As President of the United States he bore the responsibility and he assumed that responsibility because he would not delegate it to those in whom he had no trust. However, as time went on and the strain to his delicate constitution grew greater, his assumption of responsibility went to the extreme and he acted without consultation, without the advantage of gaining the viewpoints of others who could have sharpened his awareness even though he might not have accepted their opinions in every case. Traits intensify with age. Wilson's assumption of diplomatic responsibility and his distrust of others led to his criticized secretiveness in the dealings with foreign diplomats at the Peace Conference.

In pursuing his peace objectives he showed no impatience; he could not be rushed by Lansing's importunities to deal sharply with the Germans whose submarine warfare was an increasing menace or with the British detention of American shipping and censorship of mail. With unruffled calm, he wrote Lansing on the 27th in 1916: "I will be glad to discuss this and other kindred matters with you when we have seen just what the several belligerents are willing to do about discussing terms of peace."[327]

On that very same day he received the curt German reply to his request for peace terms, which according to the Official German Documents was calculated "to prevent any meddling on the part of President Wilson in peace negotiations."[328] The Imperial German Government would be ready to cooperate with the United States in the "sublime task" of preventing future wars only after the present conflict was ended between victorious Germany and her enemies.[329] The Allies also curtly refused the German peace note which was offered "without sincerity and without import."[330] Their unsatisfactory reply to President Wilson's note did not arrive until January 10.

The British Prime Minister, Lloyd George, who had now succeeded Sir Edward Grey, summed up the British position in a speech in London: ". . . War is better than peace at the Prussian price of domination over Europe. We made it clear in our reply to Germany; we made it clearer in our reply to the United States."[331] A few days later the President received additional terms from Germany via Ambassador Bernstorff and Colonel House that excited the impressionable Colonel, but upon Wilson's analysis proved worthless. House shifted his hopes upon the slightest encouragement from Great Britain but he also realistically faced the fact that we must prepare for a war certain to come. When, at the beginning of January, House brought up the question of preparedness, Wilson responded: "There will be no war. This country does not intend to become involved in this war. We are the only one of the great white nations that is free from war today, and it would be a crime against civilization for us to go in."[332] Wilson was beginning to wean himself from the Colonel's diplomatic apron strings.

The President of the United States did not give up; he never would. He was not adverse to preparedness but—as always—he considered the bulwark of his strength to rest in people. He believed in the judgment of the people of the warring nations just as he believed in that of his own people. Therefore he started at the beginning of January to draft, redraft and draft again on his little typewriter the famous "peace without victory" address delivered before a joint session of Congress on January 22, but spoken for the peoples of England, France, Russia, Germany, Austria-Hungary, etc. At his direction telegrams were sent in advance to our Ambassadors in each of the warring nations, giving the text so that it could be released to their press to appeal directly to the "silent mass of mankind everywhere who have as yet no place or opportunity to speak their real hearts out concerning the death and ruin they see to have come already upon the persons and the homes they hold most dear."[333]

Again he consulted with House and with Lansing. Again they protested certain statements which might give offense and Wilson heeded House's advice. Lansing objected to the phrase that formed the crux of Wilson's speech, "peace without victory"; in fact Lansing objected to the entire speech because it appealed to the peoples of Europe over their governments. Wilson went ahead. As he later wrote his friend Cleveland Dodge in the style imbued in him by his ecclesiastical forebears: ". . . I have an invincible confidence in the prevalence of the right if it is fearlessly set forth."[334]

Ambassador Page was alarmed when he received the advance copy of the speech. He cabled the President that any expression which seemed to the Allies to be an interference with the course of events at a time when they hoped to gain a marked military advantage would arouse such a storm of criticism that it would greatly weaken the President's influence. Lansing took the opportunity to urge again that Wilson "modify the phrase in some way," but his only reply was a brusque "I'll consider it," from which Lansing concluded that "he had no intention of striking out the words or of amending his language."[335] He did not.

The speech was attacked and applauded for its two central concepts—peace without victory and a League for Peace. Both had poignant future significance. The words to which Lansing and Page had so strenuously objected are contained in the following excerpt; passed over was its ominous warning.

". . . The statesmen of both of the groups of nations now arrayed against one another have said in terms that could not be misinterpreted, that it was no part of the purposes they had in mind to crush their antagonists. But the implications of these assurances may not be equally clear to all—may not be the same on both sides of the water. I think that it will be serviceable if I attempt to set forth what we understand them to be.

"They imply, first of all, that it must be a peace without victory. . . . Victory would mean peace forced upon the loser, a victor's terms imposed upon the vanquished. It would be accepted in humiliation, under duress, at an intolerable sacrifice, and would leave a sting, a resentment, a bitter memory upon which terms of peace would rest not permanently, but only upon quicksand."[336] These were prophetic words. The sting, the resentment, the bitter memory were to incite Hitler to World War II.

The first concept raised a great furor in Europe; the second, although widely acclaimed by the press, raised great furor in the United States Senate. Ever-careful of his relations with the Congress, Wilson sought always to cement his partnership with it. His words on this occasion are particularly noteworthy of his style, which was later to change: "I have sought this opportunity to address you because I thought that I owed it to you, as the counsel associated with me in the final determination of our international obligations, to disclose to you without reserve the thought and purpose that have been taking form in my mind in regard to the duty of our Government in the days to come when it will be necessary to lay afresh and upon a new plan the foundations of peace among the nations."[337]

Then came the part that was to stir a lasting battle with the members of Congress with whom he had sought so smoothly to associate his ideas: ". . . It is unconceivable that the peoples of the United States should play no part in that great enterprise. . . . They cannot in honor withhold the service to which they are now about to be challenged. They do not wish to withhold it. But they owe it to themselves and to those other nations of the world to state the conditions under which they will feel free to render it.

"That service is nothing less than this, to add their authority and their power to the authority and force of other nations to guarantee peace and justice throughout the world. Such a settlement cannot now be long postponed. It is right that before it comes this Government should frankly formulate the conditions upon which it would feel justified in asking our people to approve its formal and solemn adherence to a League for Peace. I am here to attempt to state those conditions. . . .

". . . If the peace presently to be made is to endure, it must be a peace made secure by the organized major force of mankind.

"The terms of the immediate peace agreed upon will determine whether it is a peace for which such a guarantee can be secured. The question upon which the whole future peace and policy of the world depends is this: Is the present war a struggle for a just and secure peace, or only for a new balance of power? If it be only a struggle for a new balance of power, who will guarantee, who can guarantee the stable equilibrium of the new arrangement? Only a tranquil Europe can be a stable Europe. There must be, not a balance of power, but a community of power, not organized rivalries, but an organized common peace. . . . Right must be based upon the *common strength,* not upon the individual strength, of the nations upon whose concert peace will depend. . . ." (Emphasis added)

These were words that brought forth a torrent of praise from liberals like Senator LaFollette, who called the speech "the greatest message of the Century,"[338] and torrents of criticism from Senators Reed, Borah and Lodge. Reed vowed that he would never consent to membership in a League of Nations.[339] Borah introduced a resolution reaffirming faith in the Monroe Doctrine and in Washington's and Jefferson's policy of non-participation in European politics.[340] Lodge, revising his previous support of the League idea, made the first of many speeches against it. Bryan, dedicated to peace, applauded Wilson's ideals, but enunciated the cornerstone of the Senate's future resistance to the League: he was against membership in any League of Nations which would be able to decide when the United States should go to war.[341]

The President's greatest faith was placed in the belief that the people of Europe would so strongly respond to his appeal for peace that their governments would be forced to accede to their outcry. It was the first time that an American President had tried to reach the people of Europe; and it was his determination and his faith in the power of the individual that inspired him to speak these words:

". . . I would fain believe that I am speaking for the silent mass of mankind everywhere who have as yet had no place or opportunity to speak their real hearts out concerning the death and ruin they see to have come already upon the persons and the homes they hold most dear."[342]

There were many encouraging responses in both the European and the American press. There were also many discouraging responses reflecting extreme hostility and suspicion of the President's motives. Official Europe waited for the President's next move. Ambassador Spring-Rice added a warning to his government: ". . . The awestruck comments of the press on his epoch-making speech are only an earnest of what may come. The President's great talents and imposing character fit him to play a great part. He feels it and he knows it. He is already a mysterious, a rather Olympian personage, and shrouded in darkness from which issue occasional thunderbolts. He sees nobody who could be remotely suspected of being his equal, should any such exist in point of intellect or character. You will see, therefore, that if he is human and if the Democratic party is human, the temptation to mediate is overwhelming."[343] It is an interesting judgment of the man.

Germany made the next move, not Wilson. She announced that beginning on February 1, German submarines would sink *all* ships without warning in a broad zone around Great Britain, France and Italy, and in the eastern Mediterranean. Neutral ships already in the war zones or on their way would be safe against ruthless attacks during a period of grace. One American passenger ship would be permitted to sail between New York and Falmouth, provided that the United States government guaranteed that it carried no contraband and that it was clearly marked with alternate red and white stripes and appropriate flags.[344]

The Germans were aware that the United States might enter the war, but they had no fear, for America had no trained army, insufficient transport and no will to fight. Furthermore Germany now had sufficient submarines to sink whatever ships America might have. This moment she had awaited. Moreover, "as is to be observed in the instructions governing the intensive U-boat warfare, we are always ready to do justice to the necessities of the United States as far as in any way possible. We beg the President, in spite of all, to take up and continue his efforts; and we declare ourselves perfectly ready to discontinue the intensive U-boat warfare as soon as we receive satisfactory assurance that the efforts of the President will lead to a peace which would be acceptable to us."[345] The communication specified vast territorial gains that Germany demanded. Wilson had spoken on January 22 to the people of Germany and the German commentators had been profuse in praise, but the Kaiser took no heed. The German people may have applauded Wilson's altruistic sentiments in the abstract but they followed their war leaders.

Lansing's diary of January 24, 1917, notes that: "For nearly three months there has been leaking through from Germany persistent reports . . . that the German shipyards are building submarines with feverish haste, and the supporters of unrestricted use of them are gaining strength."[346]

He had written the President on December 8 and again on December 21, 1916, regarding two recent submarine attacks, suggesting that his government must take some position. Wilson, absorbed in his peace plans, made no reply; his belief was that the Secretary was trying to lead him into war.

Lansing's description of Wilson's attitude at this time must be read and contrasted with a description of Wilson's earlier method of working. Together they demonstrate the change which was solidifying in him. "To my letter of December 8th, the President made no reply. Undoubtedly he hoped that the belligerent governments would respond to his appeal in a way that would make an answer unnecessary. He apparently did not wish to discuss a policy of action on an hypothesis so at variance with his hope and expectation. I believe that it is not going too far to say that he did not even wish to think about a state of affairs arising which would be so contrary to his desire and would almost certainly destroy his plans for personal mediation and world organization.

"My subsequent intercourse with the President . . . leads me to this conclusion. If facts were hostile to his intentions or seemed to stand in the way of his settled purpose, he was disposed to ignore entirely their existence, or to refuse to recognize them as controlling. . . . I am inclined to believe that one who informed him of unpleasant facts or possibilities, however certain they might be, was unconsciously credited by Mr. Wilson with being unsympathetic with the policy which he had decided to follow. He resented having his ideas bound down by the logic of events."[347]

Earlier, at the time of the torpedoing of the unarmed French ferry boat *Sussex* on March 24, 1916, there were many exchanges between the President and Secretary Lansing by letter, by memo and by conference regarding one sentence in the communication which finally read: "Unless the Imperial Government immediately declares that it abandons its present method of submarine warfare against passenger and freight-carrying vessels the Government of the United States can have no choice but to sever diplomatic relations with the German Empire."[348]

Lansing wrote in this connection: "The sentence concerning which the President and I had exchanged views went forward in substantially the language of my last letter. . . . It was in the nature of an ultimatum for which I had so earnestly pressed, though it lacked the force of the one contained in the note which I had originally drafted.

"I have gone thus minutely into the correspondence between President Wilson and myself concerning a single important sentence in the so-called 'Sussex Note' for two reasons. First, because it shows the manner in which the most important communications to the belligerent governments were drafted, the careful scrutiny given to every phrase and word, and the way in which collaboration entered into the preparation of an important note. The second reason is that our exchange of views in regard to the substance and language of this particular sentence refutes the all too common charge that the President was unreasonably stubborn and declined to consider suggestions or to listen to criticism of anything which he had written.

"In this particular case . . . Mr. Wilson at first rejected my suggestion of the note clinging to the expressions which he had first used, but, when I advanced new reasons for changing them and proposed a formula embodying my idea in language which closely followed his, he accepted the amendments. There were other portions of the same note, where he changed my expressions and where I modified his. In fact the drafts which we exchanged were pretty well cut to pieces, and the final one was much like a patch-work quilt there were so many parentheses, interlineations and deletions.

"Mr. Wilson suffered . . . from the unjustified popular impression that he resisted all advice and was impervious to reasoned counsel and logical argument.

... The impression is wrong. He was not wilfully obstinate or unreasonable."[349]

The paragraphs which follow are of interest, not because of the evolving change in the man but because of his attachment to language.

"Possibly the changes, which Mr. Wilson found the most difficult to make and which it was hardest to get him to make, related to particular words and phrases which he had written into a document. I do not say that he had pride of language. I am not positive that he had. But he did have a peculiar fondness for certain words which appealed to his sense of fitness and for certain phrases which he had coined. Some of these words were used in an unusual way, some appeared to me incongruous, some extravagant, and some quite out of place. Nevertheless, Mr. Wilson liked them, and they had much to do with the 'Wilsonian style' for they were repeated again and again in his writings and utterances.

"Recognizing that the changing of words or particular phrases used by the President was especially distasteful to him and that suggested changes of this sort he resisted and sometimes seemed to resent, I always endeavored, in offering modifications or amendments to anything which he had written, to preserve his language just as far as it was possible and still change the sense to conform to the thought I had in my mind. If the style of expression was varied but little, it was much easier to persuade the President to modify the thoughts expressed in a note or document."[350]

Wilson's mind was so set upon keeping out of war that his immediate response to Lansing upon the receipt of the German communications on the evening of January 31, 1917, was "that, if he believed it was for the good of the world for the United States to keep out of the war in the present circumstances, he would be willing to bear all the criticism and abuse which would surely follow our failure to break with Germany; that contempt was nothing unless it impaired future usefulness, and that nothing could induce him to break off relations unless he was convinced that, viewed from every angle, it was the wisest thing to do."[351] However, now deeply shocked by events, he worked in his own style; he instructed Lansing to prepare a *tentative* draft of a note breaking off diplomatic relations with Germany which would be a basis for future consideration. Colonel House was called by the State Department Counsel Mr. Polk, presumably to support Lansing's arguments; he arrived at the White House the next morning and did urge that relations should be broken. The Cabinet was to meet on Friday, February 2. It is significant of Wilson's style that he waited until February 2 before calling his Cabinet to meet with him. He usually delayed such action until he was nearing a decision himself.[352] According to Secretary Houston, the President asked as they sat down, "Shall I break off diplomatic relations with Germany?" He immediately followed this question with a somewhat startling statement: "He would say frankly that, if he felt that, in order to keep the white race or part of it strong to meet the yellow race—Japan, for instance, in alliance with Russia, dominating China—it was wise to do nothing, he would do nothing, and would submit to anything and any imputation of weakness or cowardice. This was a novel and unexpected angle."[353] He had spoken in the same terms to Lansing. This was certainly a surprising look into the future; Wilson was viewing the future peace of the world in terms of racist concepts.

At this time of crises, the President consulted the opinions of members of the Cabinet in a session that lasted two and a half hours, going so far as to ask: "What is the proposal? What is the concrete suggestion? What shall I propose? I must go to Congress. What shall I say?"[354] But he still clung tenaciously to "peace without victory," for he argued at one point that probably greater justice would be done if the conflict ended in a draw.

Directly after the Cabinet meeting he went to the Senate Office Building and conferred with the chairman of the Foreign Relations Committee. Stone called together all of the senators available. The Senate had adjourned; no Republicans could be found and only sixteen Democrats, mostly ardent champions of neutrality. When faced by the facts, all but two advised an immediate break in relations. This was evidently the deciding factor in Wilson's decision to move against his desire to give Germany yet another chance by redefining American policy, with a final warning that a German offense against American shipping would lead to a rupture in diplomatic relations.

He debated with himself in the seclusion of his room: What was right? What was wise? The next morning, February 3, he called a joint session of Congress at which he announced the break in relations.

He went that far and no further, for in his usual style, he tenaciously held to his pursuit of peace. The message contained no such condemnation of German barbarism as Lansing had advised, nor was it a stirring appeal to the American people to prepare for inevitable war. "We do not desire any conflict with the Imperial German Government. We are the sincere friends of the German people and earnestly desire to remain at peace with the Government that speaks for them. We shall not believe that they are hostile to us unless and until we are obliged to believe it."[355] There was no trace of belligerency in those words, nor in these: ". . . I refuse to believe that it is the intention of the German authorities to do in fact what they have warned us they feel at liberty to do. . . . Only actual overt acts on their part can make me believe it even now."[356]

There was no threat of war in the speech. The only positive action indicated was that if the "sobriety and prudent foresight of the German leaders proved unfounded he would return to Congress to ask that our seamen and our people [be protected] in the prosecution of their peaceful and legitimate errands on the high seas."[357]

The speech was heralded by all factions. The Milwaukee *Germania Herald* reflected pro-German sentiment, saying that the President would bring the country through the crisis with peace and honor as he had done in the past.[358] This was the hope of non-interventionists and of many senators when they adopted a resolution on February 7, approving the President's recommendation, by a vote of 78 to 5. That old belligerent Wilson-hater Senator Lodge, who voted for the resolution, wrote Teddy Roosevelt: "He may escape [war because of British success against the submarines]. I think it is not improbable. His one desire is to avoid war at any cost, simply because he is afraid. He can bully Congressmen, but he flinches in the presence of danger, physical and moral."[359]

New peace committees were formed all over the country. The Army was forbidden to make any unusual troop movements "which will excite apprehension or suggest anticipated trouble, and especially that no basis should be given for opinion abroad that we are mobilizing."[360]

However determined the President was that there should be peace, he was acutely aware of the possibility of war and acted with calmness to prepare—not flinching "in the presence of danger." He went to the offices of the Secretaries of War and of the Navy on February 5 and 8 to discuss these preparations;[361] he asked for reports on the condition of the nation's fighting forces on February 19.[362] He conferred frequently with members of Congress who were sponsoring Army and Navy bills; and he asked for special authority to commandeer shipyards and munition plants in the event of war or national emergency.[363] The War College was set to work on a conscription bill which was introduced in the Senate on February 10, 1917.[364]

At each session of the Cabinet from February 6 to February 23 the situation of our merchantmen was discussed. Ships were not sailing. Should nothing be done? Should shipowners be allowed to arm? Should the United States furnish arms and gun crews? Should naval vessels be sent to convoy our merchant vessels? (Franklin Roosevelt resisted heavy pressure to convoy our ships until July 25, 1941, a few months before Pearl Harbor.)[365] McAdoo was insistent that ships sail and therefore that they be armed and provided with trained gun crews without delay, and, of course, be convoyed. But the President "said that he could not act as suggested, without going to Congress. Action might precipitate war, and he did not wish to force the hand of Congress. It was its province to determine the matter of peace and war."[366] Members of the Cabinet presented many arguments. It is an interesting comment on Wilson style that Houston felt that the President "agreed with everything we said, but appeared to take an attitude of resistance to make us prove the case; and it was natural and wise that he should do so, seeing that the final responsibility was his and that it was a terrible thing to lead a great nation into such a war. I felt confident that he held the same views as we did."[367] Whether Wilson would have delayed action longer is moot; on February 25 he was handed the intercepted note signed by the German Foreign Minister Zimmermann offering in case of war to make an alliance with Mexico (see page 180).

On February 26, the President called the Congress in joint session and asked for authorization "to supply our merchant ships with defensive arms, should that become necessary, and with the means of using them, and to employ any other instrumentalities and methods that may be necessary and adequate to protect our ships and our people in their legitimate pursuits of the seas." With shrewdness and insight he said: "No doubt I already possess that authority without special warrant of law, by the plain implication of my constitutional duties and powers; but I prefer, in the present circumstances, not to act upon general implication. I wish to feel that the authority and the power of Congress are behind me in whatever it may be necessary for me to do. We are jointly servants of the people and must act together and in their spirit, so far as we can divine and interpret it." Once again he had stressed his belief in the partnership of the executive and legislative branches of the government.

Immediately after the address the Armed Shipping Bill was introduced in both houses of Congress; on March 1 it passed the House of Representatives by a vote of 403 to 13, but without the controversial request for broad authority to use "any other instrumentalities or methods" to protect American lives and commerce. In the Senate it was filibustered to death by the extreme non-interventionist Senators LaFollette and Borah. After "one of the bitterest parliamentary wrangles in the history of the country,"[368] a manifesto was signed by seventy-five senators, stating that they favored the Armed Shipping Bill but were prevented by a small minority—12 votes—from expressing their support of the measure.[369] The President bitterly declared that "a little group of willful men had rendered the great Government of the United States helpless and contemptible."

Wilson, however, was not helpless; he had stated in his address that undoubtedly he had the authority without legislative action to do the things which he requested Congress to sanction. Therefore, on March 9 the President decided that he would forthwith put guns and naval crews on merchant ships and called Congress into special session for April 16.[370] The work of arming ships was begun and the crews were ordered to fire on submarines that approached within striking distance.

Events moved so quickly that hindsight makes his intemperate statement one of his major political errors. It aroused a nationwide anger against the filibusters. Students of the University of Illinois hanged LaFollette in effigy on March 5. The legislators of Ohio, Washington, Arkansas and the Assembly of Idaho adopted resolutions on March 5 strongly denouncing the filibusters. Other states condemned the "willful" senators.[371] Newspapers attacked them vociferously. Many of these men had been Wilson supporters; Stone, chairman of the Foreign Relations Committee, was one of them. The abuse they took rankled and stayed with them, affecting their future attitude toward the President. By April 2 there was no longer need of the Shipping Act; therefore the Wilson order of March 9 was of very limited effectiveness. However, so bitter was the feeling on all sides that when the President rode to the Capitol for the inaugural ceremonies on March 5,[372] he was guarded more heavily than any President since the Civil War. Little note was taken of his speech, which was his last plea for peace while America was neutral. "This was nothing but another inaugural address, it was his denunciation of the 'willful men' that rang in all ears; it was the fateful crisis confronting the nation that stirred all hearts."

It crystallized public opinion; it helped to efface the impression that many people held of his indifference or cowardliness in the face of German action; it revealed the strong emotions of the man who had so frequently been pictured as lacking emotion. And of greatest importance, it emphasized his quality of leadership.

On March 18 Wilson was brought face to face with "the overt act." Three unarmed American vessels had been torpedoed and sunk by the Germans, two without warning. Wilson agonized over the action that was indicated. He was still doubtful, still seeking some way to avoid a declaration of war. Lansing, having argued that war was inevitable, left the President (on the 19th) without a definite impression as to what his decision would be. "I was hopeful that he would see the future as I saw it, but was by no means certain. I felt that he was resisting the irresistible logic of events and that he resented being compelled to abandon the neutral position which had been preserved with so much difficulty."[373]

Knowing "the President's deliberate way of dealing with every question, no matter how critical it might be and his preference for written statements which he could 'mull over,' " Lansing wrote him a long letter that evening setting forth the reasons for our immediate participation in the war.

The President had lunch alone with Mrs. Wilson; then he walked over to the Navy Department to talk to Secretary Daniels. Daniels wrote in his diary: "Wished everything possible done in addition to Armed Guards to protect American shipping, hoping this would meet the ends we have in view. He had been urged to call Congress and to declare war. He still hoped to avoid it and wished no cost and no effort spared to protect shipping."[374]

That afternoon he received Frank Cobb, editor of the *New York World,* an old friend. The conversation reported by Cobb was a virtual oral "mull over." After explaining that he had tried every way he knew to avoid war, Wilson said: "I think I know what war means. . . . What else can I do? Is there anything else I can do? . . . War would overturn the world we had known . . . so long as we remained out there was a preponderance of neutrality, but, if we joined with the Allies the world would be off the peace basis and onto a war basis.

"It would mean that we should lose our heads along with the rest and stop *weighing right and wrong* (emphasis added) . . . a declaration of war would mean *that Germany would be beaten and so badly beaten that there would be a dictated peace, a victorious peace.* (Emphasis added) It means an attempt to reconstruct a peace-time civilization with war standards, and at the end of the war there will be no bystanders with sufficient power to influence the terms. *There won't be any peace standards to work with. There will only be war standards.* (Emphasis added)

" . . . Such a basis was what the Allies thought they wanted, and that they would have their way in the very thing America had hoped and struggled against . . . so far as he knew he had considered every loophole of escape and as fast as they were discovered Germany deliberately blocked them with some new outrage. . . .

"If there is any alternative, for God's sake, let's take it."

Cobb couldn't see any and told him so.[375]

Wilson resisted "the irresistible logic of events" as he so clearly foresaw their outcome. He called his Cabinet to meet the following day.

There is no better description of Wilson's *outer* calmness when there were momentous decisions at hand than Lansing's: ". . . The President came in and passed to his place at the head of the table shaking hands with each member and smiling as genially and composedly as if nothing of importance was to be considered. Composure is a marked characteristic of the President. Nothing ruffles the calmness of his manner of address. It has a sobering effect on all who sit with him in council. Excitement would seem very much out of place at the Cabinet table with Woodrow Wilson presiding. . . . When at last every Cabinet officer had spoken and all had expressed the opinion that war was inevitable and that Congress ought to be called in extraordinary session as soon as possible, the President said in his cool, unemotional way: 'Well, gentlemen, I think that there is no doubt as to what your advice is. I thank you' . . .

"The ten councillors of the President had spoken as one, and he—well, no one could be sure that he would echo the same opinion and act accordingly."[376]

This was his style. It was again exemplified by the fact that he had no further consultation on the subject with any of them except Lansing and that only upon technicalities. When Colonel House asked him why he had not shown the Cabinet the address which he then prepared, he replied that, "if he had, every man in it would have had some suggestion to make and it would have been picked to pieces if he had heeded their criticism. He had preferred to keep it to himself and take the responsibility."[377]

Wilson requested on March 21 that the Congress meet in special session on April 2 "to receive a communication concerning grave matters of national policy which should be taken immediately into consideration."[378] While his inner debate continued he nevertheless gave orders to the Secretaries of War and the Navy to increase their strength; Rear Admiral William S. Sims was sent incognito to England to establish confidential liaison "until the Congress has acted" with the British Admirality and to work out some plan of cooperation. "As yet," the President said, "sufficient attention has not been given, it seems to me, by the authorities on the other side of the water to the routes to be followed or to a plan by which the safest possible approach may be made to the British ports. As few ports as possible should be used, for one thing, and every possible precaution thought out. Can we not set this afoot at once and save all the time possible?"[379] His orderly mind was preparing for what was probably inevitable.

It is not the province of this book to analyze why he made the decision to declare war. Historians have expressed a gamut of deductions. It is, however, of significant interest to read those words which characterize the man and form the make-up of his style. It is notable that in 1911 he had written: ". . . there are times in the history of nations when they must take up the crude instruments of bloodshed in order to vindicate spiritual conceptions . . . liberty is a spiritual conception, and when men take up arms to set other men free, there is something sacred and holy in warfare."[380]

Added interest is gained by the encouragement given this deep-rooted spiritualism by Lloyd George's beguiling personal message sent through Ambassador Page to the President on February 10: "We want him to come into the war not so much for help with the war as for help with the peace. My reason is not mainly the military nor naval nor economic nor financial pressure that the American Government and people might exert in their own way against Germany; grateful as this would be I have a far loftier reason. American participation is necessary for the complete expression of the moral judgment of the world on the most important subject ever presented to the civilized nations. For America's sake, for our own sake, for the sake of free government, and for the sake of democracy, military despotism must now be ended forever. *The President's presence at the peace conference is necessary for the proper organization of the world which must follow peace. I mean that he must be there in person.*"[381] (Emphasis added)

His determination to be in a position to set the world in order, his belief that God would guide him to do right and give him the power to get others to do right, his naïveté in thinking that he alone could stem the territorial ambitions of experienced European diplomats probably brought him to the conclusion that "as head of a nation participating in the war the President of the United States would have a seat at the Peace Table, but that if he remained the representative of a neutral country he could best only 'call through a crack in the door.' "[382] Furthermore, the Allies at that time were in a precarious position, financially and strategically; it was now apparent that a German victory would mean a peace of domination and conquest in which Wilson's dream of creating a future of world amity would have no part.

Word came on March 15 that a liberal group had deposed the Czar, and promised to establish a constitutional government and carry on the war for democratic aims. Wilson decided on the 19th to recognize the provisional government of Russia. His was the first nation to do so, "to encourage the effort of this great democracy." The old order of things, said Wilson, has no chance of being re-established.[383] Such was his trust in mankind! His faith that a wave of democracy would sweep the autocratic governments of Europe was inflamed.[384]

"In his low measured tones and with that fine command of his emotions which Mr. Wilson always possessed,"[385] he addressed Congress solemnly gathered on April 2. The four previous days of stress in composing his mind and typing the words which would convey his decision to the world were not visible as he spoke:

". . . It is a war against all nations. American ships have been sunk, American lives taken. . . . The challenge is to all mankind. . . . Our motive will not be revenge or the victorious assertion of the physical might of the nation, but only vindication of right, of human right. . . .

"When I addressed the Congress on the twenty-sixth of February last I thought it would suffice to assist our neutral rights with aims, our right to use the seas against unlawful interference, the right to keep our people safe against unlawful violence. But armed neutrality, it now appears, is impracticable. . . . There is one choice we cannot make, we are incapable of making: we will not choose the path of submission and suffer the most sacred rights of our Nation and our people to be ignored or violated. . . .

"With a profound sense of the solemn and even tragical character of the step I am taking and of the grave responsibilities which it involves, but in unhesitating obedience to what I deem my constitutional duty, I advise that the Congress declare the recent course of the Imperial Government to be in fact nothing less than war against the government and people of the United States; that it formally accept the status of belligerent which has thus been thrust upon it; and that it take immediate steps not only to put the country in a more thorough state of defense but also to exert all its power and employ all its resources to bring the Government of the German Empire to terms and end the war."[386]

The simplicity, clarity, and cogency of these words brought tears to many eyes, "tears of emotions which had been stirred to their depths by the occasion and by the momentous declaration which had been uttered."[387]

Wilson then went on to describe the military and naval mobilization required, and concluded that ". . . in my opinion [the armed forces] *be chosen upon the principle of universal liability to service;* and the granting of adequate credits to the Government, sustained, I hope, *so far as they can equitably be sustained by the present generation, by well conceived taxation."* (Emphasis added)

He explained this unpleasant request: "I say sustained so far as may be equitable by taxation because it seems to me that it would be most unwise to base the credits which will now be necessary entirely on money borrowed. It is our duty I most respectfully urge, to protect our people so far as we may against the very serious hardships and evils which would be likely to arise out of the inflation which would be produced by vast loans."[388]

One can see how high his hopes were raised by the Russian Revolution of March 15, 1917. "Does not every American feel that assurance has been added to our hope for the future peace of the world by the wonderful and heartening things that have been happening within the last few weeks in Russia? . . . Here is a fit partner for a League of Honor."[389]

How often all of his aspirations were to be wounded in the future! And how consistently did he pursue them! They are summed up in the famous moving peroration:

"It is a distressing and oppressive duty, Gentlemen of the Congress, which I have performed in thus addressing you. There are, it may be months of fiery trial and sacrifice ahead of us. It is a fearful thing to lead this great peaceful people into war, into the most terrible and disastrous of all wars, civilization itself seems to be hanging in the balance. But the right is more precious than peace, and we shall fight for the things we have always carried nearest our hearts, for democracy, for the right of those who submit to authority to have a voice in their own governments, for the rights, and liberties of small nations, for a universal dominion of right by such a concert of free peoples as shall bring peace and safety to all nations, and make the world at last free. To such a task we can dedicate our lives and our fortunes, everything that we are and everything that we have, with the pride of those who know that the day has come when America is privileged to spend her blood and her might for the principles that gave her birth and happiness and the peace which she has treasured. God help her, she can do no other."[390]

Of all those who have written of this speech, the Secretary of State, who could criticize as well as praise Wilson, has described the scene and the style of the man so vividly that it would be foolhardy to try to paraphrase it. Lansing wrote: "As the sound of Mr. Wilson's voice ceased and he seated himself, there was for several seconds, which seemed like long minutes, a dead silence. It was the finest tribute ever paid to eloquence. Then spontaneously and as if with one voice the vast audience broke into a tumult of applause that was deafening. They clapped, they stamped, they cheered, they fairly yelled their approval and support. . . .

"Too much cannot be said of the impressive dignity with which President Wilson conducted himself. . . . His personality was dominant. His vibrant voice, modulated to the solemnity of the occasion and expressive of the grave support of his words, was firm and distinct. He had a great message to deliver and he delivered it greatly. The President's attractiveness of style, the finish of his diction and his persuasive power over his listeners were never better exemplified. His control of language and of his audience was a marvelous exhibition of his genius as an orator. One who heard that impressive address and saw the dignity and sternness of the speaker as he stood on the rostrum, recognized him as a leader of men than whom there was no greater within the boundaries of the United States."[391]

Nevertheless, Senator LaFollette, chewing gum and smiling sardonically, stood motionless with arms folded tight and high on his chest. But his past and future foe, Senator Lodge, shook Wilson's hand warmly, saying, "Mr. President, you have expressed in the loftiest manner possible the sentiment of the American people."[392] He spoke truly for the vast majority, but not for the German Americans or ardent peace-at-any-price group.

On Wednesday, April 4, the Senate passed the joint resolution by a vote of 86 to 6. Among the six, of course, were Senators LaFollette, Norris and Stone. The House passed the resolution by a vote of 373 to 50. The President signed the proclamation declaring a state of war with the Imperial German Government on Friday, April 6.

The President did not include Austria-Hungary in his message because the government of the Dual-Monarchy had "not actually engaged in warfare against citizens of the United States." This was on the face a sound and valid reason, but the truth is that there was a stronger reason—an endeavor to drive a wedge between it and the German government. It was felt that if an independent peace could be arranged with Vienna the war would quickly come to an end. This possibility was not visionary as information had been received that Austria was willing to listen to peace overtures. The attempt failed; on December 7, Congress declared a state of war with Austria-Hungary.

The failure of peace overtures was not the only reason. The President was as stubbornly determined to administer a complete defeat to Germany as he had previously been to maintain neutrality. "When the President turned from Peace to the War," wrote Colonel House, "he did it with the same resolute purpose that has always guided him."[393] When in November 1917 the "Supreme War Council" was set up, Colonel House and General Tasker H. Bliss were named by the President as American members. Wilson then realistically faced the expediency of United States participation in planning on all war fronts. This necessitated a declaration of war with Austria-Hungary and also of reconciling the declaration with his previous position, which he did with great skill in his annual address to Congress: ". . . The Government of Austria-Hungary is not acting upon its own initiative or in response to the wishes and feelings of its own peoples but as the instrument of another nation. . . ."[394]

His speech contained other words which heartened the Foreign Minister of Austria-Hungary, who compared them favorably with the Allies' contention that the members of their empire should have the right to govern themselves—a dismemberment position Wilson was to take when further efforts to obtain a separate peace were completely shattered by Emperor Karl's treaty which indicated the absorption of his empire by Germany. His words on December 4, 1917, were: "We owe it to ourselves to say that we do not wish in any way to impair or to arrange the Austria-Hungarian Empire. It is no affair of ours what they do with their own life, either industrially or politically. We do not propose or desire to dictate to them in any way. We only desire to see that their affairs are left in their own hands in all matters, great or small."[395] These words were sufficiently ambiguous for Wilson to use his gift of language to adapt them by precise definition six months later to fit his new position of self-determination by members of the empire.

It is of interest to note that during this period when new matters of foreign policy were arising upon which he had no preconceived positions, Wilson worked closely with Lansing; his decision of June 27 was based on Lansing's "Memorandum on Policy of the United States in Relation to the Nationalities Included in the Austro-Hungarian Empire," dated June 24, 1918.[396]

Wilson's capacity for popular leadership was ably demonstrated in his Proclamation of the Selective Draft Act, May 18, 1917, when he made each citizen feel that he was part of the fighting force: ". . . A nation needs all men, but it needs each man, not in the field that will most pleasure him, but in the endeavor that will best serve the common good. . . . The whole nation must be a team, in which each man shall play the part for which he is best fitted. . . . It is in no sense a conscription of the unwilling; it is, rather selection from a nation which has volunteered in mass."

The bill upon which the act was based had been drawn by the Secretary of War and submitted to Congress the day after the declaration of war. It provided that men of draft age should present themselves on registration day to local civil authorities, thus submitting their lives to their neighbors, not to an autocrat in Washington. This is no novelty to people of this generation, but it set a precedent then.

Secretary of War Baker's recommendation of Major John J. Pershing as commander for the first Army that had ever gone "from the New World to fight the Old" pleased the President. "Pershing had handled the policing expedition in Mexico with restraint and fidelity . . . he had shown himself an advocate of the principle of conscription. The President had read a letter from Pershing that interested him because of the light it threw on the man's loyalty to government policy."[397]

Pershing's account of his first and only meeting with the President until he came to France after the Armistice is instructive of Wilson's style of giving complete trust to an official in whom he had confidence, whose mission was technical and beyond Wilson's ken. It also indicates, much to Pershing's discomfort, the President's ability to compromise with his Allies during the war. "On the afternoon of May 24th, the Secretary of War and I called on President Wilson.

. . . After engaging in conversation with Mr. Baker for a few minutes on the subject of shipping, he turned to me and said, 'General, we are giving you some difficult tasks these days,' to which I replied, 'Perhaps so, Mr. President, but that is what we are trained to expect.' Mr. Wilson spoke of my recent expedition in Mexico and inquired about my acquaintance with France. I had naturally thought he would say something about the part our Army should play in the war in cooperation with the Allied armies, but he said nothing.

"Upon leaving, I said, 'Mr. President, I appreciate the honor you have conferred upon me by the assignment you have given me and realize the responsibilities [sic] it entails, but you can count upon the best that is in me.' His reply was, 'General, you were chosen entirely upon your record and I have every confidence that you will succeed; you shall have my full support.' . . . His manner was cordial and simple and I was impressed with his poise and his air of determination. His assurance of confidence in me was gratifying, but in the difficult situation that arose later regarding the manner of giving military aid to the Allies he was inclined to yield to the persistent importunities of the Allied representatives in Washington. In actual conduct of operations I was given entire freedom and in this respect was to enjoy an experience unique in history."[398]

Unlike President Franklin D. Roosevelt, who met in the White House Map Room (especially equipped at the beginning of the war) with the Chiefs of Staff every day that he was in Washington, Wilson took no part in shaping military plans. However, he often walked over to the War Department and talked with Baker, who described his effective way of working with the President: "He sorted things out in the order of importance. Things never got lost in his mind, but lay there until it was time to act . . . I deliberately thought a thing into its most compact form, and when he wanted details he asked for them."[399] Baker was cognizant that Wilson was irritated by the extravagant use of words and time in long discourses.

Wilson was adamantly opposed to a coalition Cabinet which was being urged upon him. He held tenaciously to the concept he expressed years before as a student of politics that coalition Cabinets—as exemplified in Great Britain—were inefficient. He regarded the proposal, which Franklin Roosevelt used so successfully, as "merely a partisan effort to embarrass the Administration." However, in positions below Cabinet rank, to military and civil appointments of first importance he sought highly qualified men without party consideration. Wilson recognized that business experts of the highest caliber were necessary in the organization of war industry, food distribution, and in war financing and so on. Wall Street came to Washington with Wilson's blessing and did a magnificent job—not without some disturbance to his equilibrium, as he pointedly and with a tinge of humor showed at a Gridiron dinner where these magnates were present: "My troubles with the war are slight compared with the difficulties of satisfying my distinguished dollar-a-year associates. Each thinks he ought to have all attention and is unhappy if any is given to others of his group. The result is that I am like an opera impressario, every member of whose troop wants to be recognized and applauded as the prima donna."[400]

The most striking feature of Wilson's war record is the way in which he acquired his vast authority over the American economy. Most of his emergency powers were delegated to him by laws of Congress. Confronted with the problem of raising and equipping an Army to fight overseas he asked for legislative authority for almost every unusual step.[401] That Wilson could be a realist in face of facts is demonstrated by his agreement with the Attorney General that several suits against monopolies should be postponed because their products were necessary for the supply of the armed forces. He also continued to battle with Congress with determination for what he deemed necessary and possible. He asked Herbert Hoover, who had done such a splendid job as head of Belgium relief, to chair a board to take charge of food production and distribution. Hoover pointed out that in Europe division of authority had bred friction, indecision and delay, and recommended a single executive who would use boards for advice and adjudication. To still the cries already current of a "food dictator," he proposed an "Administrator."

On May 19 the President, distinguishing between the normal activities of the Department of Agriculture and the wartime emergency needs, asked Congress for wartime legislation for the power to fix prices, inquire into stocks, costs and practices, prevent hoarding, requisition and license, and prohibit waste. The Congress did not desire to confer these powers to any individual even on a temporary basis. In June a bill was introduced in the House by the chairman of the Committee on Agriculture, providing for "a governmental control of necessaries . . . which shall be exercised and administered by the President"—a grant of power without precedent in American history, which was immediately assailed by legislators who feared dictatorship. Wilson insisted that the object was to free the control of speculators and profiteers, thus protecting the people against extortion. Only five representatives voted against it. The Senate, after a month's debate, passed a bill amended to provide for a food committee of three and for a joint Congressional Committee on the conduct of the war.

Pointing out that such "an espionage committee" had harassed Lincoln constantly, Wilson said that the bill was not only entirely foreign to the subject of the food bill, but infringed on the responsibility of the President. The amendments were removed when the bill went into conference; Wilson signed the Lever Act on August 10,[402] once more establishing his claim to congressional leadership.

In mobilizing the economy, resources and manpower of the country the President took assiduous pains to make it clear that the United States was in the war for its own reasons and not to fight the battles of England, France and Italy; therefore Wilson used the phrase "associated power." As soon as the United States declared war, each of the Allies sent delegations to Washington. The British sent the Balfour mission; the French General Joffre, the hero of the Battle of the Marne; the Italians a mission headed by the Prince of Udine. Although they received enthusiastic public welcome, the President sensed the public sentiments which were, indeed, his own and would not allow it to be thought that the United States was committed to fight for the glory of foreign empires. He did not delude himself into thinking that the Allied powers were fighting for the same objectives.

His talks with Arthur Balfour, the new British Foreign Secretary, are of particular significance to later controversies—both at the Peace Conference and in the fight for the League of Nations. "Private talks of the realities of peacemaking went on in the friendly atmosphere that House was adept at creating. The President saw no harm in informal discussion of war aims with Balfour. He himself lunched with the distinguished Briton with the Secretary of State present, but felt their talk was unsatisfactory. 'Lansing has a wooden mind,' he told House afterwards, 'and continually blocked what I was trying to convey.' He asked the Colonel to bring Balfour to a 'family dinner,' and *first to sound out their guest about secret treaties in which Britain and France were said to have won allies by promising territorial rewards at the peace table.* (Emphasis added) These agreements had been negotiated under the compulsion of necessity; and their spirit—distasteful to Sir Edward Grey and other British Liberals—was inconsistent with the war aims that the Allies professed in public and contradictory to Wilson's ideals of peacemaking. . . . The Colonel had told the President of the Treaty of London, under which Italy's ambition in the Adriatic region would be satisfied and had urged both Wilson and Balfour to refrain from discussion of war aims for fear that they might provoke controversies that would obscure the prime necessity—the defeat of German military power."[403] Nevertheless, House asked Balfour to have copies of certain secrets sent to the President and they were sent.[404] Colonel House's record clearly indicates that the existence of the secret treaties was discussed, but also that the President evidently did not make an issue of the topic.[405]

Again Wilson resorted to his style so well described by Lansing of brushing aside facts which ran contrary to his objectives, and continued to make it unmistakably clear in his public addresses that the American people would fight only for the kind of settlement that he had set forth. Just as Franklin Roosevelt had supreme confidence in his ability to influence Churchill and Stalin at final decisions, so Woodrow Wilson felt supreme confidence in his ability to influence world opinion as a means of gaining his ends at the Peace Conference. As he said in his address of December 4, 1917: ". . . No representative of any self-governed nation will dare disregard it by attempting any . . . covenants of selfishness and compromise. . . . The congress that concludes this war will feel the full strength of the tide that runs now in the hearts and conscience of free men everywhere."[406]

With less idealism and more realism he wrote to Colonel House on July 21, "England and France have not the same views with regard to peace that we have by any means. When the war is over we can force them to our way of thinking, because by that time they will, among other things, be financially in our hands. . . ."[407]

Perhaps he so successfully erased from his mind the unpleasant facts of the secret treaties that he was able to testify on August 19, 1919, to the Foreign Relations Committee that he had no knowledge of the secret treaties as a whole before he reached Paris: "The whole series of understandings were disclosed to me for the first time then." When queried as to his prior knowledge of specific secret treaties, he replied: "No, sir, I can confidently answer that 'No' in regard to myself."[408] Is it possible that he resorted to mendacity? Opinions differ.

It is true that his "one track mind" was centered only upon obtaining a just peace and a means of preventing future wars. That the President was conscious of the vast difference between his point of view and that of his European Allies is evidenced by his explanation to House of the reason that he sent his formal reply to the Pope's note to each of the belligerents suggesting a settlement of the war without consultation with his Allies. He wrote on September 2, 1917: "I felt morally certain that they would wish changes which I could not make. . . . The differences of opinion will be less embarrassing now than they would have been if I had invited them beforehand."[409] Wilson attempted the role of the fox.

On that same day he asked Colonel House to assemble a group of experts to plan a definite formulation of the American peace program. "I am beginning to think that we ought to go systematically to work to ascertain as fully and precisely as possible just what the several parties to this war on our side will be inclined to insist upon as part of the final peace arrangements. We ought to prepare our position either for or against them and begin to gather the influences we wish to employ, or at least ascertain what influences we could use; in brief, prepare our case with a full knowledge of the position of the litigants."[410] This group was organized with the approval of Lansing, who had great esteem for House—which was reciprocated. It was termed "The Inquiry" and was composed of men scholarly in their various fields. As a result Wilson often surprised his colleagues in Paris by his deep knowledge of the affairs of the Balkans, the bitter political struggle in Poland, or the delicate question of the Adriatic. If Wilson's theories seemed strange and impractical to the realists of Europe, at least they could find no fault with the accuracy of the facts.[411]

Late in October House was sent to London and Paris; while there—on November 7—the Bolsheviks seized the Kerensky Russian government for which Wilson had had so much hope. The Soviet appealed to the Allies to begin peace negotiations on a basis of no annexations and no indemnities. At the same time they revealed the secret treaties which the Czar had made with the Allies. Neither the Soviet appeal nor House's plea to the British and French leaders in Paris to announce liberal war aims as a means of keeping the Bolsheviks fighting were successful. House returned discouraged; the President decided that an authoritative statement of war aims would have to be made. This necessity was emphasized by the Christmas Day declaration of the Austrian Foreign Minister that the Central Powers desired no forcible annexations.

This is the background which led Wilson to formulate his Fourteen Points. In his scholarly style he asked Colonel House to have The Inquiry prepare data upon which he could draw. In all day and night sessions statistics were gathered, illustrative maps drawn; House brought the basic report to Wilson on January 4. The Inquiry collected opinions and facts in a convenient form for the consideration of the President, indicating the trend of opinion which seemed to be most clearly supported by the facts. President Wilson evaluated them in the light of what he believed to be practical idealism and clothed them in convincing phrase. The speech was great partly because of Wilson's genius for exposition, partly because it caught the shift of inarticulate opinion and expressed it with the authority of the President's high station.

An analysis of the Fourteen Points confirms the fact that Wilson knew about the secret treaties. He hoped to nullify them but he was very careful in selecting certain words that would not unduly excite the Allies he was courting in an effort to get their agreement to his most cherished objective, Point XIV: "A general association of nations must be formed under specific covenants for the purpose of affording mutual guarantees of political independence and territorial integrity to great and small states alike."[412]

Point I is an all-inclusive precept which caught the public imagination and approval. "Open covenants of peace, openly arrived at, after which there shall be no private international understandings of any kind but diplomacy shall proceed always frankly and in public view."[413]

It must be noted that Point XIV contains the word "must" as do Points V and VI. Point V reads: "A free, open-minded and absolutely impartial adjustment of all colonial claims, based upon a strict observance of the principle that in determining all such questions of sovereignty the interests of the populations concerned must have equal weight with the equitable claims of the government whose title is to be determined." This—at that time—was a forward position which was given scant recognition. Point VI: "Belgium . . . must be evacuated and restored. . . . " This was not controversial. The word "must" used in these three points is emphatic and indicates no room for compromise.

Points VIII, IX, X, XI, XII, and XIII, which dealt with specific territories that were involved in the secret treaties, were softened by the substitution of the word "should" for "must." According to Colonel House's diary, the President ". . . went into a discussion of where 'should' and where 'must' should be used, and he agreed that where there was no difference as to the justice of a question the word 'must' ought to be used, and where there was a controversy the word 'should' was correct. He went through the entire message and corrected it in this way. He wondered whether that point would be caught. I thought it was certain it would be."[414] The references to specific territories in Points VIII through XIII definitely prove that he had not erased the secret treaties from his mind at that time; they also mark the first softening of his adamant stand, slight though it was. Points II, III and IV were so controversial that there was neither a "should" nor a "must." Point II recommending "absolute freedom of the seas" was anathema to Great Britain; Point III recommending the removal of economic barriers was most unpopular in Congress; and there was not much promise of obtaining the reduction in armament which was called for by Point IV.

Point VI is of special interest to the world today for if it had been accepted by the Allies and adhered to by Wilson the entire future attitude of Russia toward non-Communist countries might not have continued to be tinged with the hostility and suspicion that increased with the years:

The evacuation of all Russian territory and such a settlement of all questions affecting Russia as will secure the best and freest cooperation of the other nations of the world in obtaining for her an unhampered and unembarrassed opportunity for the independent determination of her own political development and national policy and *assure her of a sincere welcome into the society of free nations* under institutions of her own choosing; and, more than a welcome, assistance also of every kind that she may need and may herself desire. *The treatment accorded Russia by her sister nations in the months to come will be the acid test of their good will, of their comprehension of her needs as distinguished from their own interests, and of their intelligent and unselfish sympathy.*[415] (Emphasis added)

This was a statesman's perceptive recommendation. In light of history Point VI highlights Wilson's keen sensitivity in diplomatic relations with other nations. In its immediacy it was a strong diplomatic plea which was directed to the Allies in order to keep Russia fighting on the Eastern front. It emphasizes his style of combining idealism with pragmatism. Unfortunately it was not successful. The Russian people did not want to fight; their leaders were more interested in propaganda and desired recognition of their government rather than idealistic words that did not echo their own. Discouraged, Wilson failed to follow his own words. On February 6 he wrote to John Sharp Williams: ". . . I do not know that I have ever had a more tiresome struggle with quicksand than I am having in trying to do the right thing in respect to our dealings with Russia."[416] These words express the plight of future Presidents.

His style in stating these objectives without arguing the merits of the points is brought forth in Colonel House's diary: "He was quite insistent that nothing be put in the message of an argumentative nature . . . because it would merely provoke controversy."[417]

It was not until the fall of 1918 that the Allies were persuaded and then only with the greatest difficulty to approve the Fourteen Points as the basis of the peace settlement. However, liberals in all the warring countries rallied to its moral position immediately and eventually inspired the revolt of the German people against continuance of the war. "It became for liberals all over the world something of a Magna Charta of international relations of the future,"[418] and thus has lived on.

The harsh treaty which the Germans imposed upon Russia on March 3, 1918, at Brest-Litovsk convinced Wilson that "peace without victory" was no longer possible.

The Allies, in the meantime, had decided that the Japanese should intervene in Siberia in order to organize non-Bolsheviks in Russia to continue the fight on the Eastern front and in order to protect the military supplies at Vladivostok. Under continued pressure from the French and British to approve this move, Wilson remained firm in his refusal to countenance a large *exclusively* Japanese Army in Siberia because "the Central Powers could and would make it appear that Japan was doing in the East exactly what Germany is doing in the West."[419] It is to be noted that the United States Government believed that intervention, unless definitely demanded by the Bolsheviks, would prove useless and perhaps disastrous.[420] The British, however, believed after the Brest-Litovsk Treaty that if the intervention were given an inter-Allied character, the Bolsheviks would not object. The pressure of the German transfer of troops from the Eastern to the Western front was affecting the chances of Allied victory. President Wilson, characteristically looking ahead, still feared that once Japanese forces were in Siberia, it would be difficult to persuade them to leave. Unfortunately for our future relations with the Soviet, at the end of July President Wilson reached an agreement with the Japanese which resulted in the landing at Vladivostok of a small American force and ultimately a Japanese Army of some size, "to render such protection and help as is possible to the Czecho-Slovaks against the armed Austrian and German prisoners who are attacking them, and to steady any efforts at self-government or self-defense in which the Russians themselves may be willing to accept assistance. . . ."[421] It is impossible to detail the history of this token American expedition here. It is necessary, however, to highlight the President's acumen in counselling against such an undertaking, and the error of his futile accommodation which resulted in long-lasting Soviet resentment against the United States. Unfortunately he did not employ his style of stubborn determination here.

In spite of the collapse of fighting on the Eastern front, the Allies mustered a triumphant counteroffensive in the summer of 1918. As their armies advanced the Europeans retreated from Wilson's idealistic war aims and were more and more inclined to impose crushing terms of peace upon Germany, including a punitive trade policy that would strangle her economy. The President, therefore, decided that the time had come to pledge the Allies to his principles and to the renunciation of imperialistic peace proposals. He used the address on September 27 opening the Campaign for the Fourth Liberty Loan as his vehicle.[422] He stressed that this war "has become a people's war and peoples of all sorts and races, of every degree of power and variety of fortune, are involved in its sweeping processes of change and settlement." Saying that "we can accept no outcome which does not squarely meet and settle them," he set out the issues:

"Shall the military power of any nation or group of nations be suffered to determine the fortunes of peoples over whom they have no right to rule except the right of force?

"Shall strong nations be free to wrong weak nations and make them subject to their purpose and interest?

"Shall peoples be ruled and dominated, even in their own internal affairs, by arbitrary and irresponsible force or by their own will and choice?

"Shall there be a common standard of right and privilege for all peoples and nations or shall the strong do as they will and the weak suffer without redress?

"Shall the assertion of right be haphazard and by casual alliance or shall there be a common concert to oblige the observance of common rights?

"No man, no group of men, chose these to be the issues of the struggle. They are the issues of it; and they must be settled . . . with a full and unequivocal acceptance of the principle that the interest of the weakest is as sacred as the interest of the strongest."

Then he reached the apex of his speech, which was to rouse the formidable opposition that attacked him for the remainder of his term in office.

"That indispensable instrumentality [of obtaining impartial justice] is a League of Nations formed under covenants that will be efficacious. Without such an instrumentality by which the peace of the world can be guaranteed, peace will rest in part upon the word of outlaws and only upon that word. . . . *And, as I see it, the constitution of the League of Nations and the clear definition of its objects must be part, is in a sense, the most essential part of the peace settlement itself.*" (Emphasis added)

On October 3, 1918, with her Army in retreat, Germany appealed to Wilson to take measures to end hostilities on the basis of the Fourteen Points. On October 8 Wilson replied that France and Belgium must be evacuated, that stringent guarantees must be given that fighting would not be resumed, and that the Fourteen Points be accepted without qualifications. The Germans responded with a request for a mixed commission to arrange for evacuation of their troops. Wilson flatly rejected this, stating that evacuation must be left to the Allied command. Finally, on October 20, the German Chancellor informed the President that his conditions would be accepted, that his government agreed to surrender on the basis of the Fourteen Points.

On October 23 the President communicated his correspondence with Germany to the Allies without comment or advice. It was now for the Allies, in conference at Paris and Versailles, to determine whether there should be an Armistice, and, if so, what its terms and whether they, like Germany, would accept the Fourteen Points as the basis of peace.

Meanwhile, on October 18, Colonel House at Wilson's request had sailed to represent the United States at the Supreme War Council, commissioned as "Special Representative of the Government of the United States of America," and carrying a letter appointing him the "personal representative" of the President. Characteristically Wilson sent him off saying, "I have not given you any instructions because I feel you know what to do."[423]

There was great difficulty both at home and with our Allies abroad over the terms of the Armistice. Great Britain objected to Point II concerning the Freedom of the Seas; the French and Italians—Clemenceau and Sonnino—were not at all in sympathy with the idea of a League of Nations.[424] In fact, there was disagreement upon many of the Fourteen Points, none of which had previously been submitted to the Allies for approval. Colonel House took the position that unless the Allies agreed upon the Fourteen Points, the United States would have to make a separate peace.[425] The President supported the Colonel's position by a cable sent on October 30: "I feel it my solemn duty to authorize you to say that I cannot consent to take part in the negotiations of a peace which does not include Freedom of the Seas, because we are pledged to fight not only Prussian militarism but militarism everywhere.

"Neither could I participate in a settlement which does not include a League of Nations because such a peace would result within a period of years in there being no guarantee except universal armaments, which would be disastrous. I hope I shall not be obliged to make this decision public."[426]

These were strong words cabled by a still determined President; House did not use them because all resistance except that of the British was withdrawn and an agreement was reached with them that the Freedom of the Seas would be defined at the Peace Conference. This was not done, evidently because of the faith that President Wilson put in the League of Nations.[427]

At home, Congress attempted to challenge the executive's conduct of foreign affairs by introducing a series of resolutions condemning negotiations with Germany and calling for unconditional surrender. Ex-President Theodore Roosevelt urged the Senate to repudiate the Fourteen Points and sent a public telegram to Republican leaders: "Let us dictate peace by hammering guns and not chat about peace to the accompaniment of the clicking typewriters."[428]

The Armistice was signed on November 11. Before that Wilson had abandoned his style of ignoring Roosevelt's attacks. Flustered by concerted efforts of the Republican leaders to discredit him with the public before the November elections, flabbergasted by the emergence of big business pouring big money into the old guard Republican Party with the thought of gaining control now that the war was ending, Wilson blundered. On the day after Roosevelt's telegram, October 25, he appealed to the voters to return a Democratic majority to Congress: ". . . the difficulties and the delicacies of our present task are of a sort that makes it imperatively necessary that the nation should give its undivided support to the Government under a unified leadership, and that a Republican Congress would divide that leadership." He seems to have overlooked the fact that many Republicans in Congress and many Republican citizens had supported his leadership during the war and also the reform legislation of his first administration. And there had been Democrats who had uniformly opposed him. It would have been more consistent with his political style practiced even as Governor of New Jersey if he had appealed for the election of those who shared his view regardless of party.

The Republicans captured both houses of Congress, giving Theodore Roosevelt the opportunity to say, on November 26, that "our allies and our enemies and Mr. Wilson himself should all understand that Mr. Wilson has no authority whatever to speak for the American people at this time. His leadership has been emphatically repudiated by them."[429] It would not have been possible for the European powers to have comprehended the fact that the elections of members of Congress depended to a large extent upon local issues and economic factors. Mr. Wilson had, by his appeal, not only alienated many Republicans but called worldwide attention to the congressional elections. Therefore the results lessened his prestige abroad and in the Congress, adding immeasurably to the difficulties he was to encounter at the Peace Conference and with the Congress.

With this blunder Wilson's congressional leadership and influence started its decline, although his self-confidence was not diminished and his stubborn determination grew. His idealism never wavered. His faith in his power as spokesman for the people was given a tremendous boost—although boost it needed not—by the ovation given him during his four-week tour of France, Italy and England on his arrival in Europe. "In Paris, the ride from the quay to his residence would have turned any man's head. The route was a solid mass of people waving flags, cheering wildly, weeping for joy. 'Le Grand Américain,' the press called him, '. . . le pur champion du droit et de la justice, le Christophe Colomb d'un nouveau monde.' Similar accolades were repeated wherever he went."[430]

He announced his decision to go to Paris on November 18, seven days after the signing of the Armistice. Secretary Lansing had told him frankly that he thought it unwise for him to attend the Peace Conference. "I pointed out that he held at present a dominant position in the world, which I was afraid he would lose if he went into conference with the foreign statesmen; that he could practically dictate terms of peace if he held aloof; that he would be criticized severely in this country for leaving at a time when Congress particularly needed guidance; and that he would be greatly embarrassed in domestic affairs from overseas."[431]

There were no airplanes capable of flying from Europe to America or ship-to-shore telephone communications, radio, or overseas telephone connections in 1918 by which Wilson could keep in touch with congressional leaders or other officials in the United States.

It is significant that the President made no comment to Lansing and turned the conversation into other channels. It did, however, affect the relations between the President and his Secretary of State who was a member of the Peace Commission which accompanied Wilson to Paris. Lansing's words are descriptive of the change not only in their relationship but in the shell-like quality Wilson was developing: "While this difference of opinion apparently in no way affected our cordial relations, I cannot but feel, in reviewing this period of our intercourse, that my open opposition to his attending the Conference was considered by the President to be unwarranted meddling with his personal affairs and was none of my business. It was, I believe, the beginning of his loss of confidence in my judgment and advice, which become increasingly marked during the Paris negotiations. . . . It had always been my practice as Secretary of State to speak to him with candor and to disagree with him whenever I thought he was reaching a wrong decision in regard to any matter pertaining to foreign affairs. There was a general belief that Mr. Wilson was not open minded and that he was quick to resent any opposition however well founded. I had not found him so during the years we had been associated. Except in a few instances he listened with consideration to arguments and apparently endeavored to value them correctly. If, however, the matter related even remotely to his personal conduct he seemed unwilling to debate the question. My conclusion is that he considered his going to the Peace Conference was his affair solely and that he viewed my objections as a direct criticism of him personally for thinking of going."[432]

Although Wilson's decision to go to Paris was announced on November 18, he had been considering it for some time. Lansing's description of Wilson's style of decisionmaking is again pertinent: "It was some days before the President announced that he would become the head of the American Commission. I believe that he did this with grave doubts in his own mind as to the wisdom of his decision, and I do not think that any new arguments were advanced during those days which materially affected his judgment.

"This delay in reaching a final determination as to a course of action was characteristic of Mr. Wilson. There is in his mentality a strange mixture of positiveness and indecision which is almost paradoxical. It is a peculiarity which it is hard to analyze and which has often been an embarrassment in the conduct of public affairs. Suddenness rather than promptness has always marked his decisions. Procrastination in announcing a policy or a programme makes cooperation difficult and not infrequently defeats the desired purpose. To put off a decision to the last moment is a trait of Mr. Wilson's character which has caused much anxiety to those who, dealing with matters of vital importance, realized that delay was perilous if not disastrous."[433]

In this case it is apparent that the President had made up his mind, not telling his Secretary of State. On November 14 he had cabled to House: "I assume also that I shall be selected to preside."[434] There were strong arguments to counterbalance Lansing's in favor of his going. No one had expounded the principle of the new international order with such eloquence and cogency. He was recognized as the prophet of liberal ideals throughout the world, and many believed that he ought to head the fight for those ideals in person at the conference. He believed that without his presence in Paris, the Allies would impose the kind of peace that could only breed future wars. The preoccupation with vindictive reparations and selfish territorial adjustments must be counteracted. He would be the voice speaking for humanity.

At the cabinet meeting on Tuesday, the 26th, the President told the Cabinet that leaders in certain European countries were urging him to attend the conference.[435] This is not borne out by the account in the *Intimate Papers of Colonel House* which reads: "The political chiefs of the Entente, however, did not accept with enthusiasm the idea of President Wilson sitting in with them as a peace delegate. Not without some embarrassment they let Colonel House see their feeling, and with equal embarrassment he transmitted his impression to the President. . . . The basic objection which they presented to House was that he ranked rather with a sovereign than with the Prime Ministers; they would gladly receive him with the honors due a sovereign, but it was not fitting that he himself sit in the Conference. . . . The French Prime Minister sent Lloyd George a telegram on November 15, a copy of which was sent to House who transmitted it to the President: 'A particularly serious question is to know whether the President intends to take part in the Conference. I ought not to hide from you that in my opinion this seems to be neither desirable nor possible. Since he is Chief of State he is consequently not on the same line as ourselves. To admit one Chief of State without admitting all seems to me an impossibility.' "[436]

Colonel House cabled the President on November 14: "If the Peace Congress assembles in France, Clemenceau will be presiding officer. If a neutral country had been chosen, you would have been asked to preside.

"Americans here whose opinions are of value are practically unanimous in the belief that it would be unwise for you to sit in the Peace Conference. They fear that it would involve a loss of dignity and your commanding position. . . ."[437]

That probably stiffened the President's resolute determination, for he cabled House on the 16th: "I infer that the French and British leaders desire to exclude me from the Conference for fear I might there lead the weaker nations against them . . . I play the same part in our Government as the Prime Ministers play in theirs. The fact that I am head of the State is of no practical importance. I object very strongly to the fact that dignity must prevent our obtaining the results we have set our hearts on. It is universally expected and generally desired that no one would wish me to sit by and try to steer from the outside . . . I hope you will be very shy of their advice and give me your own independent judgment after consideration."[438] House judicially replied: "My judgment is that you should . . . determine upon your arrival what share it is wise for you to take in the proceedings."[439] The President's eagerness was so great that he cabled House on the 19th: ". . . if the French Prime Minister is uneasy about the presidency of the Conference, I will be glad to propose that he preside."[440] Indicative of the opposition Wilson was to meet, Clemenceau told House that it would not do for the President to offer resolutions suggesting that he (Clemenceau) should preside at the meetings, for it went without saying that the head of the government where the conference was held should preside. By the time of Wilson's arrival in Paris, Clemenceau had told House that he entirely approved the President's sitting in the conference as a delegate. "It might be," House wrote in his diary, "that he believes it will pull Wilson down from his high pedestal."[441]

None of this was disclosed to the Cabinet, most of whom regarded Wilson's presence in Paris as not only desirable but absolutely essential. From Paris, General Tasker Bliss wrote to Secretary of War Baker, "I wish to God that the President could be here for a week. I hear in all quarters a longing for this. The people who want to get a rational solution out of this awful mess look to him alone. . . . In this dark storm of angry passion that has been let loose in all quarters I doubt if anyone but he can let in the light of reason."[442]

Whether Wilson blundered in going to Paris has been debated ever since. It is true that the very lack of modern means of communication between the two continents which should have kept him at home argued for his being in Paris. However, there is no question that he blundered gravely in selecting the members of his delegation—Lansing, in whom he had lost confidence; General Bliss, who was to prove an able aid; Colonel House, in whom he had placed an excess of confidence; and Henry White, a career diplomat who was only nominally a Republican and had no influence in Congress or with his party. Not only was this Wilson's second major blunder, but—true to his style of not desiring counsel when his mind was set—he never discussed his selection with his Cabinet or with any members of the Senate. A strong commission would have included an influential member of the Senate and an influential Republican, such as Taft, Elihu Root or Charles Evans Hughes. Lodge, who was chairman of the Foreign Relations Committee, would have been the natural choice except for his violent hostility to Wilson and Wilson's to him. There was no one on the Commission to Negotiate Peace who could influence the members of Congress; no one was left "in charge of the store" at home. Congress was neglected except for the appeal which ended Wilson's rather lengthy Annual Message delivered December 2, 1918: "May I not hope, Gentlemen of the Congress, that in the delicate tasks I shall have to perform on the other side of the sea, in my efforts truly and faithfully to interpret the principles and purposes of the country we love, I may have the encouragement and added strength of your united support? . . . I go to give the best that is in me to the common settlements which I must now assist in arriving at in Conference with the other working heads of the associated Governments. I shall count upon your friendly countenance and encouragement. . . ."[443]

Earlier in this address he seems to have conveniently obliterated from his mind the lack of enthusiasm that Clemenceau had so forcefully and so recently expressed as to his participation in the Peace Conference. He gave no hint of it to the Congress when he said: "The allied Governments have accepted the bases of peace which I outlined to the Congress on the eighth of January last, as the

Central Empires also have, and *very reasonably desire my personal counsel* in their interpretation and application, and it is highly desirable that I should give it in order that the sincere desire of our Government to contribute without selfish purpose of any kind to settlements that will be of common benefit to all the nations concerned may be made fully manifest."[444] (Emphasis added)

According to Houston's account: "When the President ended his appeal, many Republicans and some Democrats sat and looked sullen and as stolid as wooden men. The partisan spirit which had been so much in evidence since March, 1918, and which had been greatly stimulated during the Congressional campaign is much in evidence. It is menacing."[445] He wondered if the President sensed it while he was speaking. If he did, he erased it from his mind as he did other unpleasant facts which blocked his intentions.

Moreover the President's belief in his constitutional power to make foreign policy would impel him to ignore congressional displeasure. In his Blumenthal lectures as early as 1907 he had spoken of "One of the greatest of the President's powers . . . his control, which is very absolute, of the foreign relations of the nation. The initiative in foreign affairs, which the President possesses without any restriction whatever, is virtually the power to control them absolutely. The President cannot conclude a treaty with a foreign power without the consent of the Senate, but he may guide every step of diplomacy, and to guide diplomacy is to determine what treaties must be made, if the faith and prestige of the Government are to be maintained. He need disclose no step of negotiation until it is complete, and when in any critical matter it is completed the government is virtually committed. Whatever its inclination, the Senate may feel itself committed also."[446]

His driving force activated him to proceed in foreign affairs upon the basis of this belief, irrespective of and, indeed, heedless of political factors.

Wilson depended upon himself and not upon the commission members for negotiation; he depended upon the able experts he had brought along on the *George Washington* for factual material—men renowned in the fields of finance, history, economics, international law, colonial questions, map making, ethnic distinctions—all subjects to be discussed at the Peace Conference. "These groups were the President's real counselors and advisors and there was not a day throughout the Peace Conference that he did not call upon them and depend upon them," according to George Creel.[447] They were members of The Inquiry which Colonel House had organized. Colonel House, as always, was in the midst of negotiations, carrying on for and with the President. The contributions that these gentlemen made greatly assisted the President behind the scene but they carried no weight with members of the Congress.

From December 21 through January 6 Wilson visited the principal nations with which we were associated, being feted and making speeches of which the most dramatic was at the Free Trade Hall, Manchester, England, on December 30. In this speech his realism and vision were evident even while he was expressing his idealism:

". . . Therefore, it seems to me that, in the settlement that is just ahead of us, something more delicate and difficult than was ever attempted before is to be accomplished, a genuine concert of mind and purpose. . . . Men all over the world know that they have been embarrassed by national antagonisms and that the interest of each is the interest of all, and that men as men are the objects of government and international arrangements . . . *I am not hopeful that the individual items of the settlements which we are about to attempt will be altogether satisfactory*. (Emphasis added) One has but to apply his mind to any one of the questions of boundary and of altered sovereignty and of racial aspiration, to do something more than conjecture that there is no man and no body of men who know just how it ought to be settled. Yet, if we are to make unsatisfactory settlements, we must see to it that they are rendered more and more satisfactory by the subsequent adjustments which are made possible.

". . . We must provide a machinery of readjustment in order that we may have a machinery of good-will and of friendship. Friendship must have a machinery. . . ."[448]

Trouble in the Congress fed the jealous opposition which Wilson's popular acclaim in Europe had stirred in the European leaders. Several days before the President arrived in Paris, Senator Henry Cabot Lodge, chairman of the Foreign Relations Committee, demanded on the floor of Congress that heavy indemnities be imposed on Germany and the country be reduced to impotence. He advised the Allies that they need pay no attention to Wilson's theories about boundaries, for such matters were not his proper concern. And all plans for a League of Nations should be postponed until after a German peace settlement had been reached.[449] The battle had started.

As a consequence Lloyd George informed the British delegation at a secret meeting that the President was politically infirm at home, and—prophetically— that his pledges might not be honored. "His occasional threats to appeal to American public opinion, when he did not get his way at the Conference, conveyed no real menace. There was no assurance that his country would support him in a break with the Allies on any issue."[450] Incidentally, Lloyd George's description of Wilson is of great interest: "He was the most extraordinary compound I have ever encountered of the noble visionary, the implacable and unscrupulous partisan, the exalted idealist and the man of rather petty personal rancours."[451]

Secretary Lansing tried to block Wilson before the discussion of the organization of the League began. At a meeting with the American members of the commission assigned to draft a League covenant, the Secretary pressed for a resolution that would restore peace immediately, proclaim the general purpose of the League, and leave the details of the covenant for later consideration. Although this idea was categorically rejected by Wilson, Lansing the next day went over his superior's head to repeat his proposal at a session of the Council of Ten, leaders of the major powers, where the President could not oppose him without exhibiting to the world that the American delegation was divided.[452]

Wilson evidently considered it impolitic to dismiss Lansing during the peace negotiations. Of necessity displaying great control, he waited until February 1920, when he asked for Lansing's resignation, writing: "While we were still in Paris, I felt, and have felt increasingly ever since, that you accepted my guidance and direction on questions with regard to which I had to instruct you only with increasing reluctance. . . .

"I must say that it would relieve me of embarrassment, Mr. Secretary, the embarrassment of feeling your reluctance and divergence of judgment, if you would give your present office up and afford me an opportunity to select some one whose mind would more willingly go along with mine."[453]

Not even Colonel House could be relied upon to support the President's views. So eager was House to promote the establishment of the League that he willingly agreed to territorial claims and indemnities. Wilson, time after time, found himself resisting the concessions that the Colonel kept urging on him.

Before the conference was over Wilson had ceased to put his trust in the friend whose mind he had thought to be attuned to his every thought. Upon returning to Paris from a brief stay in the United States, Wilson found the press lavishly praising the Colonel's activities at the conference and intimating that progress had been made because he had not been hampered by the presence of the President. According to Mrs. Wilson, when the President learned of certain arrangements made during his absence, he was furious, storming that House had given away everything he had won before he left Paris. "He has compromised on every side, and so I have to start all over again and this time it will be harder, as he has given the impression that my delegates are not in sympathy with me."[454]

Jealousy may have played its part; however, it was high time that the President should realize the extent to which his implicit faith in House and the *carte blanche* he had entrusted to him had increasingly aggrandized his sense of power and his unauthorized agreements with foreign powers. Wilson had created his Frankenstein. As with older ties of friendship, Wilson eschewed restraint when the magic bonds were broken. When Wilson left Paris after the Peace Conference he never saw House again and never communicated with him. A simple entry in the Colonel's diary indicates his opinion that he was the puppeteer who pulled the diplomatic strings. After the first meeting of Clemenceau and Wilson, House wrote in his diary: "The President was perfect in the matter and manner of his conversation . . . neither said anything that was particularly misleading. They simply did not touch upon topics which would breed discussion. I saw to that in advance."[455]

On January 25, 1919, Wilson was accorded the privilege of opening the discussion on the League at the Second Plenary Session of the Peace Conference. It is to be noted that he again stressed realistically that it could not be made perfect at the outset, but the machinery must be created and perfected as experience demanded and as passions subsided: ". . . I may say without straining the point that we are not representatives of Governments, but representatives of people. It will not suffice to satisfy Governmental circles anywhere. It is necessary that we should satisfy the opinion of mankind. . . .

"It is a solemn obligation on our part, therefore, to make permanent arrangements that justice shall be rendered and peace maintained. This is the central object of our meeting. Settlements may be temporary, but the action of the nations in the interest of peace and justice must be permanent. We can set up permanent processes. We may not be able to set up permanent decisions. . . . In coming into this war the United States never for a moment thought that she was intervening in the politics of any part of the world. Her thought was that all the world had now become conscious that there was a single cause which turned upon the issues of this war. That was the cause of justice and liberty for men of every kind and place. Therefore the United States should feel that its part in this war had been played in vain if there ensued upon it merely a body of European settlements. It would feel that it could not take part in guaranteeing those European settlements unless that guarantee involved the continuous superintendence of the peace of the world by the associated nations of the world. . . ."[456]

Wilson "brushed under the rug" the unpleasant fact that Senator Lodge and other senators were waging a bitter battle against the League. He had supreme confidence that his leadership and the sentiments of the people of the United States would convince the Congress. His determination was that so well expressed in the 1960's by Martin Luther King—with the change of one word, "*I* will overcome." So he said: "You can imagine, Gentlemen, I dare say, the sentiments and the purpose with which representatives of the United States support this great project for a league of nations. We regard it as the keystone of the whole program which expressed our purposes and ideals in this war and which the associated nations have accepted as the basis of the settlement. If we returned to the United States without having made every effort in our power to realize this program, we should return to meet the merited scorn of our fellow citizens . . . and because this is the keystone of the whole fabric, we have pledged our every purpose to it, as we have to every item of the fabric. We would not dare abate a single part of the program which constitutes our instruction. We would not dare compromise upon any matter as the champion of this thing—this peace of the world, this attitude of justice, this principle that we are the masters of no people but are here to see that every people in the world shall choose its own masters and govern its own destinies, not as we wish, but as it wishes. . . ."[457]

On that same day it was decided that the Covenant containing the provision for the League of Nations should be included in the Peace Treaty. Neither Lloyd George nor Clemenceau cared greatly; Clemenceau was particularly indifferent because he had no confidence in the ultimate value of the League, his mind bent upon problems of security and reparations. However, Lord Robert Cecil who had charge of League of Nations questions for the British favored the League and worked with Colonel House upon the various drafts, which Wilson then synthesized with his own. It is very interesting in light of the Russian demand when the United Nations was formed in 1945 that in 1919 the British plan provided for separate representation for the British Dominions and India.[458] This was not done.

Without any opposition, the following resolutions were passed:

(1) It is essential to the maintenance of the world settlement, which the Associated Nations are now met to establish, that a League of Nations be created to promote international cooperation, to ensure the fulfillment of accepted international obligations, and to provide safeguards against war.

(2) This League should be created as an integral part of the general Treaty of Peace, and should be open to every civilized nation which can be relied on to promote its objects.

(3) The members of the League should periodically meet in international conference, and should have a permanent organization and secretariat to carry on the business of the League in the intervals between conferences.

The Conference therefore appoints a Committee representative of the Associated Governments to work out the details of the constitution and functions of the League.[459]

It was a great triumph for the President and further blinded him to actualities at home.

An interesting sidelight demonstrated the speed with which Wilson grasped ideas and led them into being. Approaching the dock to board the *George Washington* early on the morning of sailing from New York, Raymond Fosdick had asked a laborer how long he worked each day. The man replied: "Fourteen hours," and then, pointing to the *George Washington,* the workman continued: "Do you see that boat? There's a man aboard her that is going to Europe to change all that!"

When Fosdick brought the story to the President, with the recommendation that a bill of industrial rights be written into the peace treaty, Wilson replied that it frightened him to think how much the people expected, that it did not seem possible to take up such questions at the Peace Conference but that he hoped an international conference of labor would press for these things.[460]

Nevertheless, on December 16 he took up the idea with Colonel House of an international labor organization and asked him whether "something could be done and said at the Peace Conference which would bring the hours of labor throughout the world to a maximum of eight out of the twenty-four. He said it was entirely irrelevant to a Peace Conference, but wondered if it could be brought in." This idea he later developed so as to provide for the creation of an international labor organization under League auspices.[461] The International Labor Organization (ILO) was created, is based at Geneva, and is still functioning with United States participation.

Wilson's unweakened determination to obtain the objectives of the Fourteen Points caused him to resist French insistence that he tour the devastated regions. Sensing their desire to incite in him outrage at the German devastation of French territory and thus weaken his resistance to heavy reparations, he declared that if all France were a shell hole, he would not change his approach to the peace settlement. He did go, however, after Lloyd George informed the conference that he had been to the battlefields near Château-Thierry.[462]

The delay in starting peace talks irritated Wilson; the first meeting of the Supreme Council did not take place until January 12, a month after his arrival in Paris. Then it reminded him of an old ladies' sewing circle; twenty-two men talking and to no purpose. He had said while on the *George Washington:* "Twenty-five or thirty delegates in one room mulling and quarreling over the details of a treaty would be a criminal waste of time. . . ." He favored a small council, composed of the premiers of England, France and Italy and himself, to meet secretly and prepare tentative proposals for presentation to a general gathering of delegates in the public view. It was obvious to him that the first of his Fourteen Points—"open covenants openly arrived at"—could not be applied literally to all the proceedings at Paris.[463]

At the "old ladies sewing circle" meeting, it was decided to eliminate the military from the Supreme Council and transform it into a Council of Ten formed by the five major powers (which included Japan); they were to write the peace.

The style of the American scholar-prophet at these meetings puzzled the others. British secretaries thought him very tiresome and a "quaint bird" because of his passion for academic justice and his desire to get the "sense of the meeting." It seemed so hard to bring him to a decision on details on which European negotiators were accustomed to speak quickly and firmly. When Clemenceau asked his opinion, he reviewed arguments that had been made on both sides of the case. And when the Tiger canvassed the other members of the council and came back to the President with: "Well, what shall we do?" Wilson suggested referring the question to a committee of experts or asked whether anyone had prepared a resolution. If Clemenceau asked the President to express his own views, Wilson, writing in pencil and without revision, could phrase his thoughts with a clarity and conciseness that no colleague could match. They soon came to admire his control of his tongue, his utter frankness, his patient courtesy toward all shades of opinion, and his eagerness that decisions, when finally made, be carried out.[464]

His style of negotiation is also emphasized by Balfour's stated astonishment to see him "as good round a table as he was on paper." He was showing the qualities with which he had mastered in Washington—firmness, restraint, intelligence, eloquence.[465]

But this admiration did not prevent the Allies from pursuing their individual objectives. Although no one at Paris at any time urged the return of the German and Turkish colonies, Wilson was definitely opposed to their outright annexation by the various nations. The British colonial premiers insisted that the German colonies conquered by them must be annexed. The French strongly pressed their claim to Syria; the Japanese desired the German colonies in the Pacific north of the equator. Instead of annexation, the Council of Ten agreed that the colonies should be administered by the several countries under several different types of mandates to be supervised by the League of Nations. This was not until the President stated at the January 30 meeting of the council "that the time might come when he would be compelled against his own wishes to make a full public exposé of his views."[466] Thus he threatened to use his familiar style of going to the people.

But he neglected to keep in contact with the American people through the press. This was a third blunder. He alone among the leaders refused to meet with the press after one newsman had betrayed a confidence. He also kept silent about his strenuous efforts to obtain a freer dissemination of news by the council. Members of the Senate kept complaining that they were being kept in the dark.[467] The French and British took advantage of this situation to provide fuel for the President's political opponents at home. As early as January 1 such papers as L'Echo de Paris and the London Post were carrying editorials stating that the attitude of the Republican Senate majority "placed full power in the hands of the Allies," but that this power must be used wisely, as any open humiliation of Mr. Wilson might be resented.[468]

Ray Stannard Baker, attached to the American Peace Commission at the time, has given proof of the extent to which the campaign was organized and directed: "A secret document showing how the French press—a large part of which is notoriously controlled by the government—was being marshaled against the influence of the President and in support of French interests actually came into the possession of one of the American commissioners. It was in the form of official suggestions of policy of French newspapers and it contained three items: First they were advised to emphasize the opposition to Mr. Wilson in America, by giving all the news possible regarding the speeches of Republican Senators and other American critics. Second, to emphasize the disorder and anarchy in Russia, thereby stimulating the movement toward Allied military intervention. Third, to publish articles showing the ability of Germany to pay a large indemnity."[469]

The President, induced to regard private discussions as sacredly confidential, kept his pledge to the point of an absurd reticence. No American newspaper men could win a word from him with reference to any confidential matter until decisions were reached and duly announced.[470] Keeping this pledge was no hardship for Mr. Wilson; it fitted his style.

On February 14, 1919, the President, in the name of the commission constituted by the Peace Conference, presented the report on a plan for the League of Nations unanimously adopted by the representatives of the fourteen nations. This plan was the preliminary draft and was before the conference for consideration. Immediately after the presentation of this report, the President left Paris for the United States to be present during the closing days of the Congress in order to consider and sign or reject legislation enacted.

The Senate attack began immediately by Senator Poindexter on the 19th and Senator Reed on the 22nd. Instead of going immediately to Washington upon his arrival in the United States to confer with the Senate Foreign Relations Committee and report to the Congress, Wilson made his fourth blunder—a major one. On February 24 he delivered a fiery address to an audience of 8,000 Americans at Mechanics Hall in Boston where his ship had landed. It was impolitic to make the address and his intemperate language made the error more grievous. His fighting style was sustained. Condemning "narrow, selfish provincial purposes," he warned: "I have fighting blood in me and it is sometimes a delight to let it have scope, but if it is challenged on this occasion it will be an indulgence." Vaingloriously he declared: "Speaking with perfect frankness in the name of the people of the United States I have uttered as the objects of this great war ideals, and nothing but ideals, and *the war has been won by that inspiration.*" (Emphasis added) Asserting that peace could not be maintained for a single generation unless guaranteed by the united forces of the civilized world, he added: "Any man who thinks that America will take part in giving the world any such rebuff and disappointment as that does not know America. I invite him to test the sentiments of the Nation."

This was a direct challenge to Senator Lodge in whose home town he had chosen to issue it. The fact that a journalist wrote that the applause "leaped to thunder before the words were fairly out of his mouth" aggravated the situation; the senator had respected the President's request from Paris that the League Covenant not be discussed until it could be explained by Wilson to the members of Congress. Lodge felt rightly that Wilson had taken unfair advantage.[471]

Nevertheless Lodge attended the dinner on the 26th at the White House to which Wilson—at Colonel House's urging—had invited the members of congressional committees on foreign policy. Senators Borah and Fall had refused to come. For more than two hours the President talked with the thirty-four men, noting their honest anxieties, freely and frankly answering questions, pleading with them to accept the documents. He made no converts. Two days later—on the 28th—Lodge made his attack, starting his skillful method of offering amendment after amendment which kept the Senate debating until American participation in the League received its death knell. His eloquence dramatized an imaginary crusade by armed Americans in Europe's political jungles. Working on fears that had been aroused by the economic unrest that had resulted from demobilization and the reconversion of industry, he urged that the United States not be drawn "by any glittering delusions, through spurious devices of supra-national government, within the toils of international socialism and anarchy." He asked for "consideration, time and thought." Peace should come first, and disarmament. Declaring that his opinion of the commission that had drafted the Covenant was not one of "veneration," Lodge said: "I do not think their intellect or position in the world are so overpowering that we cannot suggest amendments to this league."[472]

Thirty-seven senators signed a resolution which made it clear that a League of Nations like that proposed could not win the approval of the two-thirds of the Senate required for ratification.

In 1890 Wilson had defined "Realpolitik": "A party likes to be led by very absolute opinions; it chills it to hear it admitted that there is some reason on the other side." In 1919 he reminded the Democratic leaders of the great purposes to which he had committed them.[473] He attended to domestic matters as rapidly as possible. Too rushed to confer with his aides individually, he told them that they must carry on without him for another three months.

Overtired, overwrought, he sailed for Paris on March 5. There he found that a full report of the Republican senators had been cabled to Europe; it was eagerly seized upon by those whom the President had to fight and added further complications to his task.

After almost four months of bitter wrangling which left Wilson physically and emotionally exhausted, the treaty was finished. On May 7 it was presented to the Germans. For almost two months they refused to sign the "dictat"; on June 28, in the Hall of Mirrors at Versailles, the signatures were affixed. Wilson sailed for home as disillusioned liberals in Europe and America expressed their dismay. John Maynard Keynes, technical adviser to the British delegation, resigned. It was Clemenceau, he asserted, who had triumphed at Paris. Wilson, that "blind and deaf Don Quixote" uttering pious platitudes, had been duped by the crafty European statesmen. Keynes expressed the views of many who regarded Wilson's surrender of the principles embodied in the Fourteen Points as compromises effected in order to obtain the League of Nations which he believed to be the panacea for all international problems.

Professor Sidney Warren points out that Wilson himself was largely responsible for the disenchantment. "The leader of a nation must have confidence in his capacity to influence events, but he must also be conscious of the limits of his power in a given situation."[474] Wilson's determination, his single track mind, his belief that he was right and that what was right would prevail led him to underestimate the operating force of power politics and to overestimate his ability to change the world. "Failing to recognize that insuperable difficulties might block him from achieving his objectives he proclaimed them with a certainty that raised false hopes. His lofty moral tone encouraged a widespread belief that Germany's defeat would be followed by a new universal order bringing peace to mankind. People everywhere came to see him as a modern St. George, and he suffered the fate of all heroes when their worshippers discover that they are mortal, that magic swords exist only in myths."[475]

Again Wilson brushed facts under the carpet. He told his delegation what he thought, that "though we did not keep [the British and French] from putting irrational things in the treaty, we got very serious modifications out of them. If we had written the treaty the way they wanted it, the Germans would have gone home the minute they read it. Well, the Lord be with us."[476] He cabled the American public that if the treaty were ratified, it would "furnish the charter for a new order of affairs in the world. . . . There is ground here for a deep satisfaction, universal reassurance and confident hope."[477] Perhaps he had persuaded himself; but the statement he made to his delegation would have had a ring of truth that would have been more persuasive with the American public who would have been sympathetic to the problems he had faced were they explained to them. The "Presbyterian Priest" was mortal and sometimes tripped—to his own detriment. The perfectionist was forced to compromise; he did not like the fact and would not publicly face it.

One of Wilson's gravest failures, and the one which was to have the most serious consequences in the years to come, was with respect to Russia. He not only agreed to exclude the Bolsheviks from the conference, despite the sixth of his Fourteen Points, but ordered American participation in the invasion of Russia. He agreed, however, only because his cogent arguments against the invasion met no response. He summed up his opposition by realistically stating, "In my opinion, trying to stop a revolutionary movement by troops in the field is like using a broom to hold back the ocean."[478]

Japan's threat to boycott the League forced him to recognize her economic control of Shantung—a control that none of the Western nations could have prevented without going to war with Japan. Many of the sacrifices Wilson made were like this one, unavoidable. His fifth error was not in making compromises but in not frankly explaining to the American people and the people of the world that he had had to compromise to win his objectives.

Those objectives to which Wilson gave birth have clung to many minds to this very day in spite of disappointing experience. On Monday, October 8, 1973, Senator J. William Fulbright at the Conference on Accomplishment of World Peace, held in Washington, spoke these words:

"Those of us who are called 'neo-isolationists' are, I believe, the opposite; internationalists in the classical sense of that term, in the sense in which it was brought into American usage by Woodrow Wilson and Franklin D. Roosevelt. We believe in international cooperation through international institutions. We would like to try to keep the peace through the United Nations, and we would like to try to assist the poor countries through such institutions as the World Bank. We do not think the United Nations is a failure; we think it has never been tried. . . .

". . . I concur, strongly in the efforts toward a 'structure of peace' but I am concerned with flimsiness of the structure. It is a makeshift and fragile, too dependent on agility and cleverness, too delicate to work for dull leaders or withstand incompetent ones. I remain, therefore, a Wilsonian, a seeker still of a world system of laws rather than of men, a believer still in the one great new idea of this century in the field of international relations, the idea of an international organization with permanent processes for the peaceful settlement of international disputes. . . . In the field of international affairs, I believe [that the inventive mind of man is sometimes capable of breaking through barriers of prejudice and ancient attitude and] such a breakthrough was achieved with the formation, first of Covenant of the League of Nations, then of the United Nations charter. The next breakthrough, urgently awaited, is to make the conception work."[479]

During the ocean voyage returning to Paris the President considered asking for revisions of the Covenant that would meet the views of critics in the United States. In order to do this he would have to ask for revisions that would make the League even less satisfactory to France as a guarantee of security. He met this head-on by calling Ray Stannard Baker on the very morning of his arrival at Paris, giving this directive: "I want you to say that we stand exactly where we stood on January 25 when the Peace Conference adopted the resolution making the Covenant an integral part of the general treaty of peace."[480] When House and Lord Cecil went to him on March 16 to urge amendment and clarification of certain articles of the Covenant, Wilson resisted—"with his usual stubbornness," the Colonel wrote in his diary. The President felt that any change at this time would be interpreted at home as yielding to the Senate and would damage the ratification of the Peace Treaty.[481]

Upon his return to Paris, at Colonel House's suggestion the meetings of the Council of Ten were discontinued in favor of the "Council of Four": Clemenceau,

Lloyd George, Orlando and the President. This made for speed and efficiency but also for such secrecy that it was impossible for the American delegation—even those whose work demanded exact knowledge—to keep track of the progress of negotiations. No American secretary was present, and the *procès verbal* drafted by Sir Maurice Hankey was not sent even to the American Peace Commissioners. Mr. Baker, who was the American contact of the American Commission with the press correspondents, wrote to House that, denied access to the *procès verbal,* he was compelled to gather information from his British friends.[482]

Lansing comments that disregard of Point I of Wilson's Fourteen Points calling for "opening covenants of peace, openly arrived at" was not surprising because he was "by nature and by inclination secretive. . . . In his conduct of the executive affairs of the Government at Washington he avoided as far as possible general conferences. . . . At Paris . . . he easily fell into the practice of seeing men separately and of keeping secret the knowledge acquired as well as the effect of this knowledge on his views and purposes. To him this was the normal and most satisfactory method of doing business."[483]

An instance of the strife that occurred at these meetings was reported to Colonel House by Lloyd George on March 28. Discussion of the Saar caused a flare-up, Mr. Wilson asserting that no one heard of the Saar until after the Armistice, and Clemenceau rejoining with an intimation that the President laid himself open to the charge of pro-Germanism and a hint that no French Prime Minister could sign a treaty which did not satisfy France's claim to the Saar. "Then if France does not get what she wishes," said the President, "she will refuse to act with us. In that event do you wish me to return home?" Clemenceau replied: "I do not wish you to go home, but I intend to do so myself," and he left the house. The final outcome was an agreement that a special administrative and political régime would be applied to the district so as not to interfere with French operation of the mines.[484]

Creel's contention that Wilson consulted with experts of the American delegation (see page 245) is borne out by Dr. Isaiah Bowman recalling that: "Three of us were asked to call at the President's house. . . . He remarked: 'Gentlemen, I am in trouble and I have sent for you to help me out. The matter is this: The French want the whole left bank of the Rhine. I told M. Clemenceau that I could not consent to such a solution of the problem. He became very much excited and then demanded ownership of the Saar Basin. I told him I could not agree to that either because it would mean giving 300,000 Germans to France. . . . I do not know whether I shall see Mr. Clemenceau again. I do not know whether he will return to the meeting this afternoon. In fact, I do not know whether the Peace Conference will continue. Mr. Clemenceau called me a pro-German and abruptly left the room.' "[485]

Although he had lost confidence in the members of his commission, Wilson —the trained scholar—sought the *specific* advice that he required from the scholars in his delegation. This practice also fitted his style as described by Secretary Lansing on page 228.

Discouraged, on April 7 he cabled the Navy Department asking at what date the *George Washington* could sail and at what date it could reach Brest. Whether this was a threat to the Allied commissioners or whether, in desperation, he seriously considered "throwing in the sponge" is variously interpreted. The fact is that beginning on April 8 compromise followed compromise—and it was not only Wilson who compromised. As to the Saar, Wilson suggested on April 9 to the council that no mandate of administration should be granted to France, but that the German sovereignty should be suspended for fifteen years, during which period an administrative commission under the League should have full rights in the Saar. A plebiscite should be taken at the end of the fifteen years to determine its ultimate sovereignty. Clemenceau agreed and the project was adopted by the council on April 10.

Wilson had the choice of forcing compromises such as that pertaining to the Saar or returning to the United States with no treaty and—of greater importance to him—no League of Nations. He sacrificed part of the Fourteen Points on the altar of the League, which he relied upon gradually to cure the many wrongs of the treaty. His conception lived on to be executed after World War II, which he had feared if an unjust peace was consummated at the close of World War I. He would not have been surprised by the imperfections of the United Nations, for his objective was to set up the machinery which time alone could perfect. The years between 1920 and 1945 could have witnessed the birth pains of the League which might have obviated many of those which mark the tortuous progress of the United Nations.

Wilson's acquiescence to the reparation demands of the Allies has been greatly criticized. Because of his habitual boredom with economic affairs, and because the United States' claims were limited to only a few ships, he left the settlement to Lloyd George and Clemenceau. However, he did with foresightedness caution the experts against fixing a sum that would destroy Germany completely, keep her from accepting their proposals, or sow the seeds of a war of revenge.

The President left Paris on June 28. Immediately after his return to Washington, on July 10, he presented the treaty to the Senate. On June 10, Senator Knox had served notice that the Covenant would have to be separated from the treaty. The bitter fight that ensued upon Wilson's return might have been obviated or lessened if he had consulted the Senate leaders before and during the peace negotiations. However, the scholar stood firm upon his interpretation of the Constitution, which was that the Senate was empowered to advise and consent, or refuse to consent, to treaties brought before it by the executive. "If they go beyond that, and undertake to change the treaty," he told newsmen in Paris, "then the executive can reject such action as exceeding the Senate's prerogative, and entering upon that of the executive."[486]

Professor Warren states: "To Wilson 'advise and consent' meant that the Senate role in the treaty making process began only *after* negotiations had been completed. Constitutionally he was correct, with ample precedent to support his view, but considering the extraordinary issue involved and the known views of the opposition, political wisdom would have dictated continuous consultation with Senate leaders while the treaty was being formulated. Wilson's studied indifference to the Senate, his failure to conduct a rigorous educational campaign on behalf of the League, is all the more remarkable in view of the many ominous signs of dissension prior to the Peace Conference."[487]

The congressional elections of 1920 were approaching; evidently Wilson had again conveniently forgotten the unpleasant experience of 1918 when the Republicans had so ably campaigned against him. Their forces were already marshalled. Again, convinced that the truth is mighty, firmly trusting the people to see the issues as he saw them, he relied upon them to make the right judgment even when confronted with many issues and confused by skillful politicians. He felt confident that he could successfully appeal to the people over the heads of senatorial opposition. His political acumen was blunted; he failed to consider the fact that two-thirds of the Senate would not be running for re-election and therefore would not be likely to heed the voice of the electorate even if it could be made vocal in support of the treaty.

When, on July 10, 1919, he addressed the Congress, more than two-thirds of the Senate and the people of the United States were favorably inclined to ratification of the treaty with the Covenant.[488] By his own stubborn determination to refuse all compromises, he forged his defeat. Perhaps this was one battle too many for the very tired but undiscourageable man. The spirit of his former attempts at rapport with Congress was changed; a new style of command was introduced. He "informed" the senators that a world settlement had been made and urged prompt and unqualified approval of the treaty. Dramatically, he asked: "Dare we reject [the League] and break the heart of the world?" And in an impromptu peroration he exclaimed: "The stage is set, the destiny disclosed. It has come about by no plan of our concerning but by the hand of God who led us into this way. We cannot turn back. We can only go forward, with lifted eyes and freshened spirit to follow the vision. It was of this that we dreamed at our birth; America shall in truth show the way. The light streams upon the path ahead, and nowhere else."[489]

Senator Borah saw no such vision; he and Senator Johnson led a small group of senators who constituted the "Battalion of Death" in implacable opposition. A substantial number of senators favored moderate amendments. America's entry into the League would have been assured if "the mild reservationists" and the outright supporters of the Covenant could have reached an agreement.

It was then that Wilson made his sixth and most fateful blunder: *he would not compromise.* For several weeks, he met almost daily with Republicans who were in various degrees favorable to the League. They assured him that if he accepted reservations the treaty would be ratified promptly; but if he remained obdurate, the Senate would obtain them anyway, after what would probably be a long and bitter fight. Wilson refused to yield, insisting that to attach reservations would require reconsideration of the treaty by the Allies and by Germany. He would consent only to reservations of an interpretive nature, provided they were not embodied in the treaty. He told McAdoo that he would not be adverse to the ratification of the treaty with the "mild" amendments, but that the opponents of the treaty had not advanced them in good faith and—with perception—he added that the moment there was any indication of willingness on his part to accept them, partisan opponents would immediately propose other and more objectionable reservations which would be impossible to consider.[490] The amendments of April 10 (see page 255) made at the Peace Conference had already been followed by these new demands.

Meanwhile Senator Lodge, astutely realizing that enthusiasm for the League would diminish with time and the pressure of special interest groups, decided to kill the Covenant by delay after delay, amendment after amendment. His first move was to read the 264-page treaty word for word to the members of the Senate Foreign Relations Committee; it took two weeks.

On August 19 Wilson met with the Senate committee at the White House. Addressing them at length, he said:

". . . Nothing, I am led to believe, stands in the way of the ratification of the Treaty except certain doubts with regard to the meaning and implication of certain articles of the Covenant of the League of Nations; and I must frankly say that I am unable to understand why such doubts should be entertained. You will recall that when I had the pleasure of a conference with your committee and with the Committee of the House of Representatives on Foreign Affairs at the White House in March last, the questions now most frequently asked about the League of Nations were all canvassed with a view to their immediate clarification. The Covenant of the League was then in its first draft and subject to revision. It was pointed out that no express recognition was given to the Monroe Doctrine; that it was not expressly provided that the League should have no authority to act or to express a judgment on matters of domestic policy; that the right to withdraw from the League was not expressly recognized; and that the constitutional right of Congress to determine all questions of peace and war was not sufficiently safeguarded. On my return to Paris, all these matters were taken up again by the Commission on the League of Nations, and every suggestion of the United States was accepted. . . . Nothing could have been made more clear to the Conference than the right of our Congress under our Constitution to exercise its independent judgment in all matters of peace and war. No attempt was made to question or limit that right. The United States will, indeed, undertake under Article X[491] to 'respect and preserve as against aggression the territorial integrity and existing political independence of all members of the League,' and that engagement constitutes a very grave and solemn moral obligation. But it is a moral, not a legal, obligation and leaves our Congress absolutely free to put its own interpretation upon it in all cases that call for action. It is binding in conscience only, not in law. . . ."[492]

This was a conception difficult for hard-headed Senator Borah to comprehend. Wilson complained at a Cabinet meeting a few days after the conference that Senator Harding—who became the next President of the United States—had a disruptively dull mind, and that it seemed impossible to get any explanation to lodge in it![493] These amendments to which the President had referred were written in the final draft of April 10[494] upon the advice of former President William Howard Taft and other Republican supporters of the League. It was Wilson's sole attempt to win the dissidents in Congress. But Republicans such as Lodge who at one time had advocated a League were intent upon winning the election of 1920; therefore it was necessary to discredit Wilson and Wilson's Treaty of Peace, including the League of Nations. Lodge's hatred of Wilson spurred his opposition.

Wilson's compromises in Paris stiffened his resolve to fight at home for his great achievement. When a reporter asked him on July 10 whether the Versailles Treaty could be ratified if the Senate added certain reservations, Wilson shot back, "I do not think hypothetical questions are concerned. *The Senate is going to ratify the treaty.*"[495] When Ambassador Jusserand urged the President to accept certain reservations, believing that they would satisfy the Senate, he replied: "Mr. Ambassador, I shall consent to nothing. The Senate must take its medicine."[496]

Was fatigue the answer to this change of style? It doubtlessly added to the acerbity with which he reverted to his old style in the fights at Princeton. But the underlying intensity of feeling reverted to his firmly held convictions concerning the President's control of foreign relations, his belief in party responsibility, his view of public opinion, and his own temperament.

As Nicholas Murray Butler commented: ". . . Wilson believed that the president was a virtual sovereign, responsible only to public opinion and not to Congress, in the conduct of external affairs. In ignoring the Senate in the appointment of the Peace Commission, in taking personal responsibility for writing the peace treaty, and in standing defiantly in its defense, he was, therefore, simply playing the constitutional role that he thought was proper for the chief executive. . . . Given Wilson's urge to dominate and his belief that the Republican leaders, particularly Senator Lodge, represented all the dark forces against which he was battling, it is difficult to imagine him sharing responsibility or dealing with his opponents on a give-and-take basis after his return from Paris.

". . . There was another reason that was more important than all the rest—Wilson's supreme confidence in his own creation and in the overwhelming support of the American people."[497]

This is what led him to leave Washington on September 3, 1919, for a month-long speaking tour of the Western states. To pleas from Dr. Grayson, Tumulty and Cabinet members that the strain would be too great, Wilson had but one response, "I promised our soldiers that it was a war to end wars; and if I do not do all in my power to put the treaty into effect, I will be a slacker and never able to look those boys in the eye. I must go. If the treaty is not ratified by the Senate, the war will have been fought in vain and the world will be thrown into chaos."[498] His foresight was correct; in the face of Dr. Grayson's warning that no doctor could be responsible for the outcome, his courage cannot be overestimated. Daily attacks of indigestion, headaches and neuritis in the shoulder would have kept a man less determined, less sensitive to his moral obligations, at home.

Within the next twenty-two days he travelled 8,000 miles, delivered thirty-four addresses, made dozens of rear platform talks. With characteristic vision he warned that if the Senate did not ratify the treaty with the Covenant unamended: "I can predict with absolute certainty that within another *generation* there will be another world war if the nations of the world do not concert the method by which to prevent it [and in that struggle] not a few hundred thousand fine men from America will have to die, but as many millions as are necessary to accomplish the final freedom of the world."[499]

On September 25 he delivered a well-reasoned and impassioned speech at Pueblo, Colorado. That night his vocal pleas to the people of the United States were forced to an end; he had terrific head pains and Dr. Grayson observed a curious drooping at the left side of the President's mouth, and a shattering of his nervous controls; the rest of the trip was cancelled. It was not, however, until four days after his return to Washington that he had a thrombosis—a clot of blood —that impaired the control of the brain over a side of the body already weakened by neuritis. His left arm and leg were helpless. The voice that had commanded the thought of millions was barely able to whisper.[500]

As a result neither the American public nor the Democratic members of Congress heard that voice which would have given them leadership. He had already lost his power to influence Congress; he could not now regain it through leadership of the public. This was to become sadly apparent in the 1920 Presidential election when Harding won by an overwhelming popular vote. By default Henry Cabot Lodge became the most vocal force in Congress. Under his direction, the Foreign Relations Committee drew up no less than forty-five amendments and four reservations to the treaty. The amendments were defeated, but the four reservations were expanded to thirteen, all of which were unacceptable to Wilson. The one on which the President was most adamant dealt with Article

X. It stated that the President would assume no obligation to preserve the territorial integrity or political independence of any other country or employ the armed forces for such an objective unless authorized by Congress. Wilson felt strongly that if the League Council recommended action against an aggressor, member states were morally obliged to go to the aid of the victim.[501]

On November 19, with voting but hours away, Senator Hitchcock rushed to the White House to tell Mrs. Wilson that unless the administration accepted the Lodge planks, the treaty would be beaten. Mrs. Wilson relates that she pleaded with her husband to accede, but he insisted that he had no moral right to consent to changes without expecting other nations to do the same. The country's honor was at stake. "Better a thousand times to go down fighting than to dip your colours to dishonorable compromise!" The handicapped President would not suffer a compromise with his ideals or his objectives. He dictated a note for Senator Hitchcock, his Senate leader: "In my opinion the resolution in that form does not provide for ratification but rather for nullification of the Treaty. . . . I trust that all true friends of the Treaty will refuse to support the Lodge resolution."[502]

To the bitter end, Wilson remained obdurate, advising Hitchcock and the Senate Democrats that the United States should enter the League wholeheartedly and unreservedly, accepting its responsibilities for world leadership, or it should not enter at all. Thus urged, the Democrats voted with the "bitter enders," defeating ratification on November 19 by a vote of 55 to 39. Had the Democrats disregarded the President's wishes the treaty would have been ratified by a vote of 81 to 13.[503] The President's health had improved to the extent that he was able to give leadership to Democrats who could defeat the amended treaty, but he was powerless to give constructive leadership for the adoption of the unamended treaty. He held to his conviction that it is the President who must make foreign policy and steadfastly disregarded the Senate's power to advise and consent.

Senator Jacob Javits has recently written that the reaction to Wilson's almost absolute authority over Congress came "when the President attempted to ride over senatorial sensibilities during the peace negotiations. His wartime powers had given Wilson a heady sense of executive prerogative and the League of Nations fell victim to the break between the President and Congress. The famous Lodge Reservations to the League Treaty were in reality reassertions of the Congressional authority to make war. If Wilson had been willing to negotiate with the United States Congress in the same spirit as he negotiated with the Allies it is probable that the United States would have become a member of the League of Nations. Whether that would have changed the disastrous course of events that led to the Second World War is an open question, but it is certainly worth considering. . . . The sense of his own moral rectitude, of the rightness of his own perceptions and of the evils of his enemies, prevented him from achieving the very objectives for which he strove. . . . The wartime willingness of Congress to surrender its constitutional responsibilities had blinded him to the fact that he would have to deal with very different responses when peace came."[504]

Wilson's hatred of Lodge played a great part in his stubborn rejection of the amendments. William Howard Taft wrote that Lodge and Wilson "exalt their personal prestige and the saving of their ugly faces above the welfare of the country and the world."[505] Lodge understood that Wilson's pride, his stubbornness, his self-righteousness would lead him into the trap he so cleverly set, for evidence suggests that Lodge intended to defeat the League and used the reservations to accomplish the purpose. In his own account of the League battle, Lodge wrote that he was convinced the President would prevent acceptance of the treaty with reservations if he possibly could. "I based this opinion on the knowledge which I had acquired as to Mr. Wilson's temperament, intentions and purposes . . . I made no mistake in my estimate of what President Wilson would do under certain conditions."[506]

He also wrote six years later that he "had very much at heart [the creation] of a situation where, if the acceptance of the treaty was defeated, the Democratic Party, and especially Mr. Wilson's friends, should be responsible for its defeat, and not the opponents of the treaty who were trying to pass it in a form safe for the United States."[507]

Wilson never accepted defeat. In his last public address, on Armistice Day, 1923, the ex-President declared: "I am not one of those that have the least anxiety about the triumph of the principles I have stood for. I have seen fools resist Providence before, and I have seen their destruction. That we shall prevail is as sure as God reigns."[508] It took time, the Second World War that Wilson had prophesied and Franklin D. Roosevelt's leadership, but Wilson's faith and his "higher realism" were rewarded.

His belief in himself and his powers of leadership remained with him to the end of his life, and is popularly termed his egotism. Despite his shattered health he still hoped that he might again be the leader of his party. After visiting the ex-President at his Washington home on S Street on October 23, less than four months before Wilson died, James Kerney wrote this account of the President's revealing words: "I am going to try and look at myself as though I did not exist, to just consider the whole thing in an impersonal way. From the messages I get I realize that I am everywhere regarded as the foremost leader of the liberal thought of the world, and the hopes and aspirations of that liberal thought should find some better place of expression than in the Senate. There is only one place, you know, where I could be sure of effectively asserting that leadership. Outside of the United States, the Senate does not amount to a darn. And inside the United States the Senate is most despised; they haven't had a thought down there in fifty years. You know and I know that I have a temper, and if I was to go to the Senate, I would get into a row with that old Lodge, who no longer counts for anything. The Senate would hardly provide the place for liberal leadership that the world is seeking so sadly. Think of the people of Poland and of Czechoslovakia and the other countries whose freedom we gave them—they know that they owe their very national existence to me, and they are looking to me to lead them. . . ."[509]

Ever intent upon his objectives, not even accepting physical defeat, this courageous half-paralyzed man even dared to think of himself as the Democratic nominee in 1924 who could bring salvation to the world. Call it egotism, but it was egotism inspired by noble motives. Franklin Roosevelt also thought that he could retain Stalin's confidence and create détente between Russia and the Allied nations after the war. Perhaps he could have, but he died without the opportunity. Wilson's opportunity had been at hand and his stubbornness prevented its realization. He never acknowledged his fault but pursued his ambition until his death.

William McAdoo has written that, "In Wilson there was a deeper impulse for accomplishment than I have ever seen in any other man. . . . His enemies have delighted in describing him as obstinate. Nothing is further from the truth. He was tenacious of purpose and nothing could deflect him from his objective once he made up his mind, after the most careful deliberation, as to the proper course of action. These are the essential characteristics of a great leader. Unless one has the conviction that his cause is right and is determined to achieve it, he cannot succeed."[510]

The definition of "obstinacy" and "tenacity of purpose" can be separated by but a hairline. One might read righteousness into "tenacity of purpose." If that is the inference, Wilson's style of tenacity was certainly actuated by righteousness which he believed to be guided by God Himself. "The way to success in this country," he said, "is to show that you are not afraid of anybody except God and His final verdict. If I did not believe that, I would not believe that people can govern themselves. If I did not believe that the moral judgment, the final judgment, is in the minds of men as well as the tribunal of God, I could not believe in popular government."[511]

The term "idealist" has been bound to Wilson in derision. He was an idealist whose vision transcended his times. He himself explained that: "The most expedient thing to do today is frequently not the best thing to do in the long run."[512] What was often termed "idealism" was actually a perception of the future, which seemed unrealistic at the time.

His perception of the future was not limited. While Lodge's committee was working to destroy the treaty of peace, Woodrow Wilson thought about consolidating and extending the New Freedom. This activist President went before Congress on August 8 to suggest that the Food Control Act be extended to years of peace and that its provisions against hoarding be applied to other essential commodities. So far ahead of his time was he in his interest in the consumer that he asked for licensing legislation that would "secure competitive selling and prevent unconscionable profits," and he favored the passage of laws to control the issue of securities. He advocated full publicity as a cure for profiteering and made a moral appeal to producers and merchants to deal fairly with the people.[513]

Labor strife was rampant in the nation. Threatened by a nationwide labor strike, the President, on August 25, addressed an appeal directly to the representatives of the railway shopmen making it plain that he was in no mood to throw off the responsibility for economic justice that the federal government had assumed during the war. The leaders of the union postponed their strike. In a Labor Day message the President announced that a conference should be called in which "authoritative representatives of labor and of those who direct labor will discuss fundamental means of bettering the whole relationship of capital and labor and putting the whole question of wages upon another footing."[514] The call for an industrial conference to take place on October 6 was issued on September 3.

When, on his Western trip, the President reached Seattle, a dramatic labor demonstration shocked him and caused him to answer it with equal drama. Representatives of the I.W.W. had prepared to call on Wilson to petition for release of political prisoners, but the city government announced that the radical leaders would not be allowed to "annoy" the President. The Presidential party drove through dense crowds of cheering citizens. Suddenly there were five long blocks of silence, sidewalks packed with overall-clad workers—their sleeves rolled up to show the brawny muscles of arms folded across their chests. Ex-soldiers wore overseas caps and others displayed hatbands reading "Release Political Prisoners." Not a sound, not a move, their eyes were turned away from the President. After the five blocks of silence, applause was resumed; the pale President acknowledged the cheers mechanically. The next morning, though it was Sunday, Wilson requested a delegation of labor leaders to make the call upon him that the timid government officials had forbidden. He was not forgetting the speech he had made a few days before: "Revolutions come from the long suppression of the human spirit. Revolutions come because men know that they have rights and that they are disregarded." It was a meeting filled with emotion; the leader of the labor delegation, unable to summon words, silently handed the petition to the President. Wilson took it with a hand that shook until he steadied it by gripping the lapel of his coat. In a voice that sounded strained he said that he would read their plea immediately, that he had been displeased by the decision of the local authorities to keep them away from him and deny their right of petition.[515] This personal style of human understanding and emotion is not demonstrated in the larger issues for which he fought.

Nor is his personal warmth exposed in dealings concerned with foreign or domestic matters. Little, in reading about his public style, does one conceive of a private style where the President could relax with family and intimate friends as the life of the party. He was an inimitable mimic. His humor and gaiety were a delight to his intimates all through his life. He was master of the can-can. He could make ludicrous faces. He could prance about in a feather boa, trailing a velvet curtain, uttering banalities in falsetto voice in imitation of a society lady greeting friends. He had an impersonation of "the drunken man" which became a family favorite along with a rendition of a pompous Englishman.[516] He would spend evenings reading aloud to friends and family, usually English classics and poetry. He would also frequently attend vaudeville shows, and especially enjoyed tap dancing. It refreshed him, he said, to consort with people who "took on no more at their hearts than they could kick off their heels."[517] He liked to start a phonograph record after dinner and show how a jig step was done.

His versatility is best succinctly described by William Bayard Hale: "It is a rare and interesting combination that this man presents. Perhaps nothing sums it up more vividly than this: he reads Greek and he writes shorthand."[518]

It is also a rare and interesting contrast that this man presented in his private associations with those stern, rigid, often cold associations with public officials. He seldom relaxed in their presence. The masses called Roosevelt "Teddy" and referred familiarly to the other Roosevelt as FDR, but they had no nicknames for Wilson—certainly not "Woody." Even at Princeton his enormous success as a teacher lay in lecturing to large classes rather than in communing with seminar groups.[519] So it was in appealing to masses of people rather than to individuals. An admiring newspaper man remarked that Wilson was the only speaker he ever heard who could get confidential with a crowd.

It was a gallant man who insisted upon performing his official duties to the very end. On Inauguration Day he had his final meeting with his Cabinet,[520] then put on his cutaway and gray trousers, took up his gloves and high hat, drank a stimulant to help overcome his pain, grasped the blackthorn stick without which he could not walk, and went to the Blue Room, where he exchanged courtesies with his successor. Helped into the automobile, he sat next to Warren G. Harding as they proceeded down Pennsylvania Avenue to the Capitol. In the President's room where he had conferred so often and so successfully with congressional leaders, he signed bills passed during the last hours of Congress and received a committee from the houses of Congress informing him that their session was over.

Without the drama that had marked his political career, he passed into private life, but not into oblivion. Asked at the last Cabinet meeting what he would do in retirement, he pointedly replied: "I am going to teach ex-Presidents how to behave."[521] Evidently Theodore Roosevelt's ill-tempered taunts still rankled. The scholar and master of the English language then added, "There will be one very difficult thing for me, however, to stand, and that is Mr. Harding's English."[522]

The Cabinet members, starting with Bainbridge Colby, the then Secretary of State, were preparing to express their sentiments. After Colby spoke, Secretary of the Treasury Houston was about to follow when he noticed that the President was struggling with emotion, so he refrained. The President's lips were trembling and tears rolled down his cheeks as he said brokenly, "Gentlemen, it is one of the handicaps of my physical condition that I cannot control myself as I have been accustomed to do. God bless you all."[523] Thus spoke the Scots Presbyterian whose whole philosophy of life and style had been self-control.

FRANKLIN D. ROOSEVELT

(1882–1945)

President, March 4, 1933, to April 12, 1945[1]

March 4, 1933, the day of the first inauguration of Franklin D. Roosevelt, was cold, cloudy and cheerless. It was as cheerless as the nation's economy; for by that day, the lowest depth of the Great Depression had been reached. This was the lowest point to which the United States economy had sunk in all its history.

The statistics which indicate what had happened to American business, agriculture, labor, finance and foreign trade are well known. They will not be repeated here: the mass of unemployed looking in vain for jobs, any kind of jobs; the ridiculous price which the farmer was able to get for his corn, wheat, milk and all the other products of his labor; the decline of industrial production; the unrealistic price of securities; the farm foreclosures, the loss of homes; the shanty towns made of tin and crates which had sprung up on the outskirts of most of our cities; the food kitchens and soup lines all over the United States; the aimless wanderings of young people, many of whom had just received their high school or college diplomas, drifting from place to place to find work, and finding none, continuing still to drift. And now on this Inaugural Day nearly every bank in the nation was closed—some by gubernatorial proclamation, some by bankruptcy resulting from their speculation with depositors' money, some out of commendable caution to preserve their assets.

All of these statistics were well known to Roosevelt. He had been Governor of the State of New York for the last four years; he had to know them; and he had done what he could in New York to relieve the suffering. As matters got worse, beginning in 1930 (and for farmers even earlier), the latest figures of disaster in the United States had been followed by him closely. He could tell you daily the new price of corn or wheat or any other staple; he kept count of the closed banks; he could give you almost daily the latest estimates of the growing army of unemployed—all matters of increasing concern and anxiety to him.

But far above all the cold statistics was the gnawing knowledge of what was happening inside the American people. For statistics by themselves were not his main worry; he was, as always, interested primarily in people. All his mature life he had thought in terms of men, women and children; and during his long tenure as President, people were his first concern. He always translated any information into terms of the miner, the worker, the farmer, the shopkeeper, even the banker —and their families. That was the chief reason for his ability to keep intimate rapport with the American people. When he talked with them on the radio, he was not thinking of numbers; he was thinking of them personally, and of each one of them who was listening. Each one who listened seemed to sense this, and most responded in kind.

Certainly, on March 4, 1933, Roosevelt needed no statistics to tell him the condition of America. He had just finished campaigning in nearly every state of the Union. He had seen hundreds of thousands of people in the streets of a hundred cities, and from the back platform of his campaign train in countless railroad stations, all crowding around to catch a quick glimpse of the man who was to determine their future. He had also made it his business to exchange frank, confidential opinions with powerful industrialists and financiers in many states. He had talked with farmers, small shopkeepers and workers almost daily since his nomination in July.

He had looked into the faces of these people and had read the Depression statistics in bold figures reflected in their eyes. In many he had seen actual hunger; in many more he had seen anxiety about the fact that their children were not receiving an education or even enough food and clothing. In all, he had seen fear, stark fear. In those who had jobs, there was the fear of losing them. In those who still held onto their homes or farms, there was the fear of foreclosure. In those who had no jobs, there was the fear of coming hunger for their families and themselves—there were 12 million of these. Assuming only that an average of four people depended on one job, 48 million people did not know, depending on the extent and safety of their savings, where their next meal or next month's meal or next year's meal was coming from.

These people had looked back at him, benumbed and bewildered by what was happening to them. They had followed all the traditional homely virtues; they had worked hard when they had jobs or farms; they had lived frugally, and had each week set aside some money to put in the bank for a "rainy day"; and, now, on this "rainiest" day of their lives, their banks were closed and their savings gone.

And, even in the faces of millionaire industrialists and financiers, he had seen all the same signs; worry, consternation at what was happening, helplessness—and, yes, the same fear. Fear of losing their fortunes, as so many of their friends already had; fear of losing their privileges and powers; and a consuming fear of whether a continuance of this misfortune would mean an end to the system of private property and free enterprise.

There had already been many ominous signs of unrest—the same kind which had preceded revolution so many times in history. People read of farmers who resisted foreclosures by chasing the sheriffs off their farms with pitchforks and rifles. They saw pictures of farmers dumping their milk voluntarily, and the milk of their neighbors by force, in order to try to get a better price for their products. They read about children coming to school without breakfast, and then going to bed hungry. There were even statements by some respectable Americans that it was no longer dishonorable to steal if your child was crying from hunger.

In February 1933, the head of the Farm Bureau had predicted to a Senate committee that unless something substantial was done for the farmers, there would be revolution in the rural areas in less than twelve months. Another had testified that if "lawfully constituted" leadership did not take action soon, "a new leadership perhaps unlawfully constituted" would act. William Green had testified that if a thirty-hour work week were not enacted, there would be a "general strike." The tragic fact was that no witnesses before the committee could offer any constructive program.

Whether armed revolution in 1933 was a real possibility or not, there is no doubt that the American system of free enterprise was in grave danger. There is also no doubt that the old faith that a democracy had the strength to meet any emergency was being badly shaken. The privileged few knew what had happened in countries abroad in this century when the great masses of humanity had faced similar conditions. Some of them were even perceptive enough in March of 1933 to see the beginnings of this in Germany. The leaders of industry and finance had all tried to impress the President-elect with their fears, with the necessity of doing something. But, as Roosevelt said in later years, few, if any of them, had any kind of solution; even fewer gave advice which might have diminished their own privileges and financial power.

It was a man whose soul had been deeply seared by watching so many hundreds of thousands of suffering Americans who pronounced with set jaw, bold tones and unmistakable determination the oath of office prescribed by the Constitution.

The oath was administered to Roosevelt by the Chief Justice of the United States, Charles Evans Hughes, with whom, only four years later, he was to engage in a fierce struggle to determine whether that Constitution was sufficiently flexible to relieve all this anguish and bring about a new kind of social justice.

Roosevelt stood, holding onto the arm of his eldest son, James, until the oath was completed, and then with the additional support of a cane turned and made his way a few steps to the lectern—for he could not walk without these props. There, leaning on the lectern for support, he could release his son's arm. He began his famous address.

His immediate audience on the platform and in the vast square before the Capitol was composed of people in high places in public life—Governors, congressmen, judges, political leaders—their families and friends, and a large number of prominent guests. But Roosevelt was not talking to them. He knew that on this day millions of stricken Americans were hanging on his every word, to try to learn what kind of man this was whom they had elected. What kind of a President was he going to be? What had been his past, and what did it indicate for the future? In the next few minutes they would get their answer as to the kind of President he was going to be, and what his conception was of the presidency and its powers.

Let us first take a quick glance at his past—for so much of the style of a President depends upon it. Upon that past also depends a President's conception of the nature of the presidency, and the philosophy which he brings with him to the White House—political, social and economic. This story of Roosevelt's past, as in the other chapters relating to the other "great" Presidents, is not intended to be biographical. Only those incidents and experiences which had a substantial effect on FDR's Presidential style and performance and on his views about the office will be included.

In this man's past there was no log cabin, no rising at dawn to milk the cows or to do the farm chores; he did not have to sell newspapers or walk many miles to school, nor work after school hours to help support his family. He had been born and brought up in the pleasant, rich, patrician life of an estate in Hyde Park in the Hudson River Valley. There was never any lack of funds to provide for all the things which were traditional for the members of his social standing. As a boy at home, there were private tutors; private governesses on the many trips with his parents abroad; summer vacations at Campobello Island, on the Bay of Fundy across the harbor from Eastport, Maine; education at Groton, one of the most exclusive private schools; four years at Harvard where he lived on the Gold

Coast, where his friends were also sons of rich men active in the gay social life at the turn of the century; Columbia Law School and admission to the New York Bar; and, finally, a position with the highly respected, conservative law firm of Carter, Ledyard & Milburn in New York City, which counted among its clients some of the richest men and largest corporations in the city. This was his early life and career.

In none of these activities did the young Franklin distinguish himself. At Groton and at Harvard, his scholastic averages were about C. He tried at both places to make athletic teams and failed. He did become president of the *Harvard Crimson,* the daily newspaper of the college, but it was a humdrum publication, certainly no crusader in the important causes of the day. He seemed to work at things just hard enough to get by, and no harder.

There was little in this pleasant, comfortable, sheltered life which could be said to train a man for any political job. Yet, there were some things which would stand him in good stead in the years of his presidency. For example, farming. At Hyde Park, his parents and he were always proud of the fact that their farm paid for itself. It was not exactly what we think of as "a dirt farm"; certainly it was not a "gentleman's farm" set up as a diversion. His was the fourth generation of his family who had deep roots in the soil.

This was a man who had learned to love farming and to talk farming. He spent many hours with the neighboring farmers; he spoke their language. Later, when as a political candidate for so many different offices, or as a state senator, Governor, or President, he visited farms in Dutchess County or in other parts of New York State or in other states—as he did whenever he could in days of drought, or days of plenty, or days of glut—he was no stranger to the farmers. And any of them would quickly recognize that Roosevelt knew about farming from actual experience, that he had it in his blood, that he understood the farmers' problems and was deeply concerned about their prosperity and security.

And the sea and ships. In his youth, long before there was any thought of politics, FDR developed a great love of the sea. At Campobello, he became an expert sailor, managing with great skill the tides and turbulent currents of Passamaquoddy. There are few sports that train a man to rigid discipline better than handling a boat in difficult waters in summer fogs. His love of the sea led him to learn as much as he could about it, and what it meant in the life of a nation. His favorite book at an early age was Mahan's *History of Sea Power.*

Early in his experience in the Navy Department, he was able to show his ability as a seaman and his knowledge of ships. Admiral Halsey, the renowned naval commander in the Pacific during World War II, has written of the time he was in command, as an ensign, of a destroyer which Roosevelt, as youthful Assistant Secretary of the Navy, had assigned to take him on an inspection trip of naval installations in Maine. When the inspection was over, Roosevelt volunteered to guide the destroyer personally through the narrow strait between Campobello Island and the mainland. Halsey had some serious doubts about the safety of his vessel. He describes the experience in *Admiral Halsey's Story:*[2]

"The fact that a white-flanneled yachtsman can sail a catboat out to a buoy and back is no guarantee that he can handle a high-speed destroyer in narrow waters. A destroyer's bow may point directly down the channel, yet she is not necessarily on a safe course. She pivots around a point near her bridge structure, which means that two-thirds of her length is aft of the pivot. As Mr. Roosevelt made his first turn, I saw him look aft and check the swing of our stern. My worries were over; he knew his business."

Twenty-five years later, Admiral Halsey was to learn that Roosevelt knew his business also as his Commander-in-Chief. Needless to say, this experience with the young ensign, along with similar experiences with Ensign Harold R. Stark (later Admiral Stark, Chief of Naval Operations in World War II) and other young naval officers, filled all the Navy officers with unaccustomed respect and admiration for their civilian assistant chief.

This love of the sea and his expertise with ships were what made Roosevelt so eager to accept the opportunity later in life of becoming Assistant Secretary of the Navy. Josephus Daniels, just nominated as Secretary of the Navy by the newly elected President, Woodrow Wilson, tells the story in 1932.

" 'How would you like to come with me as Assistant Secretary of the Navy?' I asked Franklin Roosevelt the day of Wilson's inauguration as we chanced to run into each other in the Willard Hotel. At that time, even before his quick answer, he may have reflected that another Roosevelt who had been a member of the New York Legislature [as Franklin then was] became Assistant Secretary of the Navy, and from that spring board, became Governor of New York and President of the United States. If that ambition was influencing his reply, he answered so quickly that there was no intimation of it.

" 'How would I like it?' he rejoiced with boyish enthusiasm. 'How would I like it? I'd rather have that place than any other position in public life. I'd just love it.' "[3]

This was a man who, ever since his youth, had been filled with unbounded self-assurance. The kind of life he had led in Hyde Park and in New York City before entering politics helped to give him that self-assurance which became one of his most prominent characteristics, and which always dominated his style as President. He was, with his mother's help, financially independent; he had social position; he could meet as an equal any of the great of his day. He was the handsome, healthy and fashionable sportsman, the popular society man of New York City, and the future squire of his beloved Hyde Park. He was secure, and he knew it. Indeed, people who knew him in those days have said that he was inclined to feel quite superior and sometimes offensively showed it; and that he would at times superciliously "look down his nose" at people.

I did not know him during those days, and cannot vouch for this or deny it. By 1928 when I first met him, however, this air of superiority and snobbishness had been knocked out of him by many cruel realities; but I have never met a man who had greater self-assurance and self-confidence.

Neither he nor his mother was interested in building a great fortune, especially during the speculative years of the early twentieth century. He had seen and socially mixed with many who had, and they did not impress him. This man never believed—as so many did in those days—that great wealth was synonymous either with great virtue or great ability. He grew up in the period of the formation of huge concentrations of wealth and economic power. The men who were later to come to hate him with a fervor almost unparalleled toward American Presidents were in control of the political life of the country as well as its financial life. Young Roosevelt watched this with growing distaste; and it was one of the phenomena of his early years which had impressed him deeply, and about which much was to be done.

Fortunately Roosevelt, instead of becoming a part of the corporate or estate practice of Carter, Ledyard & Milburn, was assigned mostly to defend small claims against its client, the American Express Company—often in the Municipal Court on the Lower East Side, the ghetto of New York. He used to tell me jokingly when he was Governor that he became known in his office as the "Attorney General of the Second District Municipal Court." This experience did not make him a great lawyer; but it did help to make him a great human being. Here, in the crowded, disorderly turmoil characteristic of these lower courts he met, and even in a literal sense "rubbed shoulders" with, the kind of people he had never before met, and had seldom ever seen. He told me he "loved it." It is not necessary to point out how much this experience was to help him in his political life.

His political debut had not been in the traditional frame. The Democratic leaders of Dutchess County saw in him not only a Roosevelt but a Roosevelt whose family had always been Democrats, and one who could help the local campaign chest. Roosevelt sensed this, of course. He jokingly reminisced later when he was President, in an extemporaneous speech, that one day when he was in Poughkeepsie, he was "kidnapped" by some of the local Democratic leaders and taken to a political picnic to be shown to the local Democrats, where he made his "first" speech, for which, the President added, "I have been apologizing ever since." The political leaders offered Roosevelt the nomination as New York State Senator. It was no great favor. The senatorial district was almost hopelessly Republican; no Democrat had been elected in it since 1856. His friend John Mack, one of the leading Democrats of Dutchess County, who was to make the nominating speech for Roosevelt in 1932, told him frankly that he would have only a 1 to 5 chance of winning. Roosevelt, having apparently made up his mind for a political career, was willing to take the desperate chance of success, perhaps feeling that in the event of failure he might be rewarded by some future nomination.

Of interest to us is that the campaign which he conducted in 1910 in the three counties of the senatorial district was his first lesson in campaigning, a lesson he never forgot, and which even affected his style as a campaigner and political leader as Governor and as President. In his acceptance speech in October, he said, "We are going to have a very strenuous month." They did. It was a large district, but he decided to visit personally every corner of it. So he hired one of the few automobiles then available, and drove up and down the dirt roads. He talked with farmers and villagers, discussing mostly problems which affected their pocketbooks—such as the new high tariff which a Republican Congress and a Republican President had just enacted—often referring to the particular problems of the village or town in which he was speaking, with occasional mention of the main themes of his public speeches: bossism and political corruption in both parties. He avoided national issues, and he appealed frankly to the rank and file of Republican voters, attacking only the Republican bosses. Nor did he neglect Democratic bosses, especially Murphy, of Tammany Hall.

He recognized that his victory in 1910 was the result primarily of these personal talks, rather than of any great theoretical principles. It was all very similar to his future campaign style, with one exception—he kept referring to his opponent by name. Further, he seldom overlooked a chance to ally himself with "Teddy"—stressing his relationship, and the resemblance of their political views. Roosevelt continued to do this in later years, even as late as his campaign for

Governor in 1928. I was with him in 1928, and in several crossroad extemporaneous speeches delivered from his campaign automobile, I heard him tell the same story—which went something like this:

"One of the newspaper men with me was standing at the edge of the crowd today back at the village of ————. He later told me an old farmer came up to him, and asked who that young man was up there talking.

" 'That's Franklin D. Roosevelt,' the reporter replied. 'He's running for Governor.'

"The farmer looked disappointed, even a little disgusted, and said, 'They told me Roosevelt was coming here today, but I thought it was going to be Teddy.' "

It was pretty corny, he admitted to me later, but he added: "The crowd loved it."

In answer to a question from a man in one of his meetings while running for senator, as to whether he supported Republican Governor Charles Evans Hughes's reform policies, which had been opposed by Roosevelt's Republican opponent, State Senator John F. Schlosser, he answered that he did, and he added: "I think he's one of the best Governors the state has ever had." Of course, this gave him the image of political independence which he was trying to create.

He had what was to become known as the usual "Roosevelt luck with weather." On Election Day, it rained; and the rain was hard enough to keep many Republican rural voters away. It is open to serious question whether he would have won in any year other than 1910. That was a year of a deep split in the Republican Party all over the nation, between the old guard and the progressives. It was also the year of a Democratic landslide throughout the United States. But in addition to the landslide, FDR's own style and intensity of campaigning had undoubtedly added to the size of his vote. In normally Republican states, many Democrats were elected in 1910 as Governors; especially interesting for us was the election in New Jersey of the president of Princeton University—Woodrow Wilson. In New York State, the landslide resulted in a Democratic Governor, a Democratic Assembly and a Democratic Senate. His own victory, he recognized, was the product of Republican rather than of Democratic votes. He never failed in later years to woo progressive congressional Republican leaders (like Hiram Johnson and George Norris) and, above all, the vast army of rank-and-file Republican voters.

This was a man who had shown in the first few days in his first elective position that he had the courage and independence to stand up to strong political bosses, and the perseverance to thwart them.

In Albany, this opportunity came to him quickly—an opportunity which was to give him a national reputation, and to call him to the attention of progressives around the country, including Woodrow Wilson. Anti-bossism in that progressive era, as in nearly every modern era, had become a popular theme. Roosevelt grabbed the opportunity to take a stand against political bosses when he joined twenty other young Democrats who had decided to oppose the rich and influential utilities magnate, William F. Sheehan, the candidate for the United States Senate of Boss Charles Murphy, leader of Tammany Hall. The group lined up behind a progressive candidate, Edward M. Shepard, a civic leader of great independence and good reputation. In those days, United States Senators in New York were not elected by the people of the state but chosen by the legislature.

Roosevelt had not himself originated this revolt against privilege, but he soon became its spokesman and leader. The myth was to grow up over the years—

never denied or even discouraged by Roosevelt—that he stood practically alone in 1911 against the juggernaut of Murphy and the other state bosses.

It was a long and bitter struggle, as the legislature deadlocked for two and a half months. In politics, nothing attracts favorable attention more than a fight on the "side of the angels"; and, as Roosevelt was to remark in 1940, he "loved a good fight." So, as the small band of fighters stood firm in 1910, the whole nation began to take notice. Over in New Jersey, at the same time, Governor Woodrow Wilson was engaged in a fight to prevent the legislature from electing Boss James Smith, Jr., as United States Senator from his state. Liberals and progressives everywhere yelled encouragement to the young senator.

Murphy finally realized that he could not get Sheehan elected, and proposed several alternative candidates, who were in turn rejected. Finally, after wrangling among the insurgents themselves, a compromise with Murphy was arranged in favor of Justice James A. O'Gorman, who was even more of a Tammany Hall man than Sheehan. It was clearly an anticlimax, if not an actual retreat. Roosevelt and several others wanted to continue the fight, but most of them, exhausted and harassed by political and other pressures, were anxious to quit. Nevertheless, Roosevelt did not hesitate to proclaim that the movement had been gloriously victorious. This twenty-eight-year-old neophyte, still "looking down his nose at people," still with a Harvard accent, still with a cutaway suit and pince-nez spectacles, had suddenly become a political hero in his own state and throughout the nation—a "progressive insurgent fighter" against political bossism.

This was Roosevelt's first personal contact with the strength of political bosses, their ruthlessness and ingenuity. Most important were the lessons it taught him about political intrigue, about political battling, about outside pressures exerted upon him and his group. But he learned also that political bossism could not be entirely evil, when it included as its protégés men like Alfred E. Smith and Robert F. Wagner, who were then Democratic leaders in the two houses of the legislature.

Many progressives were to remember Roosevelt for his courage in standing up against Murphy. But in later life, he would come to terms with the great political bosses of the nation. He had learned a great deal about them. He had come to realize the necessity of strong political leaders in any campaign—even though they had little interest in policy—for they had an unlimited interest in the strength and success of the party. And he began also to recognize the importance to any candidate, even for the presidency, of a strong political base in every precinct or district where it was possible to build one. Even while he was fighting with Tammany Hall, he was consulting the political leaders in his own district on matters of patronage.

He would be able, as Governor and as President, to deal with the big city political leaders not only in getting elected but in getting support for his legislation. It is a great tribute to his political shrewdness all through his political career that Roosevelt was able to use political bosses for his own objectives, and at the same time be the gallant champion against political bossism.

In Albany as a senator, he mingled with legislators from different kinds of constituencies and environments. He learned how to deal with those of different backgrounds, social and financial classes, and religious and ethnic characteristics. He learned about what makes a legislator "tick," and about the ways to influence his vote. As he developed in this new environment, his snobbishness grew faint, and then disappeared. He always would remember and respect what he had learned about the difference between the interests of a legislator whose first loyalty might be to residents of the district he represents and those of a Governor who had to think of the state as a whole. It was that same difference in loyalty with which he would often have to contend as a President who was the only representative of all the people of the United States.

He began to learn in Albany how to balance his principles and his methods with his own political ambitions, with the well-being of the people in his district, and with his relations with political leaders. He learned the force of selfish pressure groups, and what they could do to proposed legislation.

Roosevelt's legislative record in his first term can be characterized as mildly —not crusadingly—liberal. He was frankly progressive on such matters as direct primaries and public election of United States Senators. He was conscious of the fact that the constituents who had elected him were farmers, and that he had to maintain their support for the coming re-election when he could not again rely on a landslide. So, while clearly a progressive, he was not the kind of progressive who felt he could afford to alienate his voters. But by his second term in 1913, he had developed definite views in many fields to replace the vague generalities of his first campaign in 1910. He then came out for workmen's compensation; and he supported the remedial bills submitted by the Committee Investigating Factory Conditions, so that the New York State Federation of Labor endorsed his record.

Though he served less than three years in the legislature (his only legislative experience), it had proved to be a great educational experience—as many other statesmen have found it to be. He had started out in Albany as a strong, young lion; he wound up with some of the shrewdness and practicality of the fox.

In 1911, Roosevelt joined the long line of young progressives travelling to Trenton to talk with Wilson; and he soon became an ardent admirer and supporter. But there was little he could do. Murphy, who was opposed to Wilson, completely controlled the New York Democratic State Convention in 1912 by virtue of the unit rule, and he thus obtained control of all the ninety uninstructed delegates. He had even kept the rebellious Roosevelt's name from among the delegates.

The National Democratic Convention provided a bitter contest for the two-thirds vote necessary to nominate; but on the forty-sixth ballot, Wilson won—and without any help from the New York Tammany-controlled delegation. As the leader of the pro-Wilson forces upstate, Roosevelt got some of the credit for Wilson's surprising victory. On the day after the nomination, FDR was in New Jersey conferring with Wilson on how to carry New York State in the election to follow—again without Tammany support.

Roosevelt was re-elected senator in 1912; but in March 1913, he was on his way to Washington to take his oath as Assistant Secretary of the Navy, in the new administration of President Wilson. For seven and a half years, he got administrative and national political experience in the vast Department of the Navy. There he began to show some of the outstanding characteristics which were to mark his Presidential style.

The great political experience for Roosevelt in the Navy was getting to know the national scene, the national figures and international personalities of the day. He was quick to learn the political ways of Washington, and the intricate know-how of getting things done in that complicated city. It was from people, as always, that he learned new things, and he made it his business to meet and socialize in Washington with people of all kinds.

His was a difficult job of administration, with little or no experience to prepare him for it. He attacked the job with his usual zest, initiative and love of action; he used to say: "I get my fingers into everything—and there's no law against it."[4] This first role in public administration was a great success; and, what is equally important politically, it was *hailed* as a great success. It was one of the most effective bits of training for the bigger job which lay ahead.

He was to begin his style of experimentation. He used to say when he met insurmountable obstacles or immovable red tape, that "there was some other way to do it"—and he generally found it. Experimentation is a necessary corollary to action, and Roosevelt as President was to become an outstanding experimenter.

Roosevelt came to know organized labor the hard way, by actual contact and managerial necessity. He was in charge of the thousands of civilians working in the naval depots and navy yards located around the country. He learned how to deal with them and with their union leaders, how to obtain their cooperation, and, at the same time, how to handle the many pressures for economy in naval expenditures and for greater productivity and efficiency of naval workers. He was learning that labor leaders were, in their field, as able as he was in his. They were his equals, and he learned to treat them as such, not merely as recipients of a kind of managerial paternalism. They learned to respect him, just as twenty years later they learned to love him. He afterwards boasted that during his seven and a half years of keeping his employees hard at work to create the kind of Navy he wanted, there had not been a single strike.

He was around when Wilson, by his skillful leadership, was able to get drastic new legislation through Congress. He was also there when the President made his major mistake of neglecting the Republican Party and its leaders during the war and in the peace negotiations which followed. He was there when Wilson often isolated himself from the practical politicians of his own party. He learned both from Wilson's successes and his failures, and he showed later during his own presidency that he had learned thoroughly.

He was impatient with delay, and anxious to build up the Navy. His boss, Secretary Daniels, on the other hand was a pacifist and a procrastinator—so labelled by many naval officers and by Roosevelt himself.

It became obvious swiftly that Roosevelt was very much at home with the Navy and its officers. Daniels was not. As a result, naval officers frequently would take their problems to Roosevelt with a request that he take them to the Secretary, explain them, and get them signed. The enthusiastic young man of thirty-one was always willing to try. This became well known in the Department at the time, and was probably part of the "scuttlebutt" of the day in the high echelons of Navy officialdom.

For example, Ernest J. King, who was to become one of the Joint Chiefs of Staff in World War II, wrote about his recollections of the Assistant Secretary: "Naval administration lagged under Mr. Daniels, a well-known procrastinator. He had such difficulty in deciding which idea was better than another, that the Assistant Secretary of the Navy, Franklin D. Roosevelt, resorted to keeping crucial papers on his desk until Mr. Daniels was out of town, so as to sign them himself and get matters under way."[5] Like all "scuttlebutt," which always grows in the retelling, this was an exaggeration, especially in the use of the word "crucial." I have no doubt that Roosevelt, however, enjoyed this reputation in the Department, even though it did become magnified. There's no doubt, either, that to the extent that this reputation conformed with the facts, Daniels was well aware of it; but he never did anything to discipline his impatient young assistant.

Roosevelt owed, as he later was proud to admit, a great deal of his development as an administrator to Daniels. In spite of their vast personality and background differences, and in spite of the many public and private disagreements between them, they got along very well, although this was not always easy. Daniels, in contrast to his Quaker-like appearance, simplicity, modesty and ever-present warm smile, was stubborn and strong-willed; and he softened his pacifism only under extreme provocation. The older man, former editor of a small-town newspaper, a prohibitionist, a pacifist—a product of the farms of North Carolina —and the impatient patrician developed a close relationship. They had never met until the Baltimore Democratic Convention in 1912 which had nominated Wilson. But Daniels later described that meeting as one of "love at first sight," and tolerated much that Roosevelt did as Assistant Secretary with understanding and patience—all of which Roosevelt was long to remember and cherish. When, in 1920, the official relationship had to end so that Roosevelt could accept the nomination as Vice President, he wrote Daniels to thank him for what the Secretary had taught him "so wisely," and for having "kept my feet on the ground when I was about to sky rocket." He had learned much from Daniels, but particularly, he had learned patience and adaptability, both hallmarks of his future presidency.

The Navy which Roosevelt found in 1913, while greatly superior to the Navy of a generation before, was still quite puny compared with the British, or German, or even the French. The Assistant Secretary, from the first, was a big-Navy man, a battleship man—and closely in sympathy with the officials of the Navy League of the United States, which had long been urging that kind of Navy. Daniels, on the other hand, was more interested in improving the conditions of enlisted men in the Navy, such as getting better educational opportunities for them. And instead of urging a larger Navy, he kept proposing and arguing for international naval disarmament in the expressed hope that the day would come when large naval combat fleets would no longer be necessary.

Twenty years later, after Roosevelt had been President for only three months, and soon after the National Industrial Recovery Act became law (June 16, 1933), which, among other things, provided $3,300 million for public works, he immediately set aside $238 million for the Navy for the construction (conforming to the terms of the London Naval Treaty) of thirty-one vessels, including aircraft. In addition, the Naval Appropriations Act of 1933 provided for five more, and made appropriations for one cruiser (authorized in 1929). He later wrote that "this constituted a building program for 1933 of a size which had not been undertaken by this country since 1916. This was the beginning of a sustained program of my Administration to bring the United States Navy up to the treaty strength."[6]

But in 1914, the Assistant Secretary of the Navy could only talk, recommend, urge and push. All of this he did. When World War I began on August 1, 1914, Roosevelt was stimulated to additional efforts. He was shocked to find, hurrying back to Washington that day from a speaking engagement, that the Navy was just doing business as usual. He wrote his wife that "nobody seemed a bit excited about the European crisis," and that Daniels was chiefly concerned and "sad that his faith in human nature and civilization and similar idealistic nonsense was receiving such a rude shock." He added immodestly, but not uncharacteristically, that he "started in alone to get things ready and prepare plans for what ought to be done by the Navy."[7] He scoffed at Bryan's and Daniels's belief that because we were neutral, we "can go about our business as usual." In the same letter, he expressed the hope that "England ... with France and Russia [would] force peace at Berlin." Three days later, he wrote his wife again: "I am running the real work, although Josephus is here. He is bewildered by it all, very sweet but very sad."

It was not that Roosevelt was a warmonger. He simply realized that neutrality in a world at war was a fragile thing, that it was just sheer realism to prepare for any possibility of the war being brought to us. He realized even then that the United States could no longer live in isolation, dependent only on the sea (and the British Navy) to protect it. He was among the first in 1914 to become aware of this, just as he was in 1938.

Roosevelt had foreseen the coming of war more clearly and earlier than Daniels. He had stated to reporters when the war had come: "This will be the greatest war in the world's history." He also concluded, long before Daniels, that the United States would become involved in it. By October 1914, as the German Army crushed through Belgium in violation of treaty, and as the accounts of atrocities were reported, Americans began to get uneasy about their own defense. Roosevelt, sensing this, took to the stump, joining Theodore Roosevelt, General Leonard Wood, the Secretary of War, and many other prominent Americans in pointing out existing inadequacies and urging more realistic preparedness. All of this resulted in more national prominence for him. Daniels remained calm; but he must have spoken to Roosevelt about public expressions contrary to his own, for Roosevelt did become a little more cautious. For example, in his testimony before congressional committees, he made little of the split between them; but he did make it quite clear, by his more general statements, that his analysis of the Navy's readiness was much less optimistic than Daniels's. He even secretly supplied Congressman Gardiner, the leading advocate in Congress for a "big Navy," with data to prove Gardiner's contention that the Navy was unprepared.

He was determined to tell the truth about naval inadequacies as he knew them, and he did. He knew the possible consequences, as shown by a letter to his wife in October 1914: "The enclosed [statement which he had issued] is the truth, and even if it gets me into trouble, I am perfectly ready to stand by it. The country needs the truth about the Army and Navy instead of a lot of the soft mush about everlasting peace which so many statesmen are handing out to a gullible public."[8] One can already see the courage and self-confidence and political independence which he was acquiring. He was so conversant with every detail of naval management that merely by giving facts and technical data, he presented an irrefutable case for an enlarged Navy as soon as possible, and a strong naval reserve. This kind of knowledge and familiarity with everything about the Navy would be a characteristic of Roosevelt the President. His ability in the Navy to grasp facts and details quickly, and to remember them, was typical of his ability later to do the same for every department of the government while he was President.

It was not until the summer of 1915 that Wilson—noting all the sinkings by German submarines—changed his policy and began to advocate preparedness. Wilson asked for plans; Daniels turned to Roosevelt; Roosevelt leaped into action with enthusiasm. He was in Campobello at the time, recuperating from an appendix operation. On his return, it had been arranged for Daniels to take a vacation. Roosevelt wired Louis Howe, his assistant in the Navy Department, that he would then be Acting Secretary, and "that means that things will hum."[9]

Roosevelt at once tried to get Wilson to set up a Council of National Defense to supervise all industrial mobilization for war. However, just at that time (August 1915) there was a slight lull in the public outcry which had followed the

German submarine sinking of the *Arabic,* because of the subsequent apology by the German Ambassador. As Roosevelt wrote his wife on August 28, 1915, the President did not want "to rattle the sword" while Germany seemed anxious "to meet us more than half-way."[10] It was not until a year later that the council was authorized by Congress, while Roosevelt constantly chafed at the delay. By contrast, when Roosevelt became President and France, in May 1940, was being overrun, he immediately reconstituted the council under the same 1916 statute, which had not been repealed.

The extent of Roosevelt's grasp of naval details can be seen by reading the account of his testimony in the December 17, 1914, issue of the *New York Times.*[11] This was his first really important confrontation with a congressional committee, and he was pretty proud of his own performance. He wrote his mother: "The hearings are over—really great fun and not so much of a strain, as the members who tried to quiz me and put me in a hole did not know much about their subject and I was able not only to parry, but to come back at them with thrusts that went home. *Also was able to get in my own views without particular embarrassment to the Secretary.*" (Emphasis added)

Blocked from doing all he wanted in the Department, Roosevelt began in 1916 a campaign of speech-making to urge faster preparations for our entry into the war he saw as inevitable. It was the same problem he was to face years later in 1939–41, that of educating a peace-loving people, and making them aware of the danger they faced.

In the Presidential campaign of 1916, he wrote what he believed Wilson's campaign strategy should be—a strategy which he himself was to follow with such success in all his own later campaigns: Do not be defensive, but carry the campaign vigorously and offensively to the Republicans; do not let them pick the issues to be debated, they should be picked by Wilson; there is enough ammunition in those issues to last for months. And in the same letter of advice, there is a foretaste of Roosevelt's own style of experimentation as President: "Some of the domestic legislation is experimental" and may not work well in practice, but if they prove to be mistakes, they can be changed; "but there is enough legislation which has proved its wisdom."[12]

After the re-election of Wilson, Roosevelt diplomatically began to urge more drastic action upon the President. When on February 2, 1917, Germany proclaimed unlimited submarine attacks, Roosevelt was recalled to Washington from Santo Domingo. He found, in his own words, "the same thing—no diplomatic relations with Germany broken off, no excitement, no preparations, no orders to the Fleet at Guantanamo to return to their home yards on the East Coast."[13]

Roosevelt used to tell a story showing Wilson's state of mind in 1917, which he repeated in February 1939 in an informal, extemporaneous speech.[14] Impatient as FDR was in 1917 for action, he recalled, he went to see Wilson one day in March to obtain permission to bring the fleet up from Guantanamo and have it fitted up for war. This permission was denied; and in explanation, Wilson said: "I will tell you something I cannot tell the public. I do not want . . . the United States to do anything . . . by way of war preparations, that would allow the definitive historian in later days to say that the United States had committed an unfriendly act against the central powers."[15]

In the similar lonely travail through which Roosevelt was to pass in the summer and fall of 1941, seemingly trying to make up his mind about exactly what to do, he remembered both these statements by Wilson. One he followed;

one he did not. He, too, would refuse to go "faster than the great mass of our people would permit." However, he was not worried by any latter-day historian's definitive assessment of hostile preparations. Where he felt he had the power, he would make them. Furthermore, his idea of "attack" by a submarine was quite different from Wilson's. Roosevelt, as President, maintained that the very presence of an enemy submarine in American waters was an attack even before it fired a torpedo.

Roosevelt in February 1917 tried to persuade Wilson to take advantage of a loophole in an old forgotten statute, and lend (not give) to private merchant ships sufficient guns and crews to help them get past German submarines. Wilson refused to do this. Instead, on February 26, he asked Congress to pass a clear-cut statute authorizing it. But (as we have seen) a "little group of wilful men" filibustered, and the recommendation was never adopted. On March 12, to his Assistant Secretary of the Navy's delight, Wilson gave orders to place guns and crews on merchant ships without authorization by Congress.

Roosevelt had to go through much of this all over again when his turn came; however, he would not need any pressure or even suggestions from the Navy or anyone else to take any course short of war itself. He moved on his own, with vigor and defiance, although in late May 1941, he did pay some respect to "the future definitive historian" by saying as Nazi submarines continued to sink our ships: "The shooting has started (without any declaration of war) and history has recorded who fired the first shot."

When on April 6, 1917, America declared war on Germany, Roosevelt took on the colossal task of enlisting hundreds of thousands of sailors, and spending several billions of appropriations for the Navy. He went so fast in buying supplies that Wilson had to call him to the White House and tell him that he had practically cornered the market and would have to divide the supplies with the Army. Action he loved, and action he took.

Emory Land, a friend of Roosevelt's and an expert on naval construction (later to be named by Roosevelt as head of the Maritime Commission), referred to FDR, in an interview with Freidel, as a great "trial and error guy" because he was ready to try almost any new idea—even against the opposition of the experts in the Navy. Roosevelt's greatest personal success during the war was in his battle to have the North Sea mine barrage put down between Scotland and Norway. This was a new and startling idea; without him, it probably would never have been carried out. Its mission was to lock submarines out of the Atlantic and reduce the terrible toll being taken of merchant ships carrying the essentials of war. Roosevelt met with almost universal objection to the scheme from both American and British naval officers. But never was he to be more stubborn, aggressive and persistent. He appealed in person to Wilson on June 4, 1917, who approved the idea in general; but Roosevelt still could not get action. Exasperated, he sent Daniels what he described in a letter to Eleanor Roosevelt (dated October 29, 1917) as "a stinging memorandum,"[16] and sent a copy to the President. The memorandum was indeed "stinging" about the delay. He did not spare either the American or British Navy Departments. As a foretaste of what he was to do so frequently during the New Deal and World War II in bypassing the old, established departments and setting up new agencies with new administrators to carry out new ideas, he added: "If the suggested plan is carried out solely under the present organizations [American and British] its chance of success will . . . be seriously diminished. You need somebody with imagination and authority to make the try."[17] Here again was the "bold experimentation" which was to be Roosevelt's style as President. The next day the plan was approved—and it was very successful in operation.

It is quite remarkable how the Presidential traits of 1941–45 followed the traits of the Roosevelt of 1917–18. For example, in his speeches, he always distinguished between the German government and its people; he favored continued American armed strength even after the war had ended; he was constantly urging the "home front to back up the war front," although he had not yet reached the conception which he preached in World War II that they were actually the *same* front; he favored voluntary censorship rather than a compulsory one and he adhered to this in the face of some very serious breaches; he mocked those who believed in an easy victory by starving the Germans, or by waiting for some revolution; and he kept urging universal conscription of civilians for civilian work.

Roosevelt wanted to get into uniform; but Daniels, backed by Wilson, refused to let him resign. So, on July 9, 1918—with Daniels's permission and Wilson's approval—he went over to the war area in his capacity as a Navy Department administrator. On this trip, he met many of the wartime political leaders of the Allies.

Among his first activities in England was a series of conferences starting July 22 with Sir Eric Geddes, the First Lord of the Admiralty. They discussed, in particular, cooperation between the British and Americans in the production of war supplies to prevent duplication and to dovetail their efforts for future operations. In World War II, Roosevelt as President would make this a regular, routine operation by the Combined Chiefs of Staff in Washington. But it was something very new in 1918.

After the Armistice, FDR made a second trip to Europe—again as an administrator—this time to liquidate the American installations and equipment left behind by our returning Army and Navy. He demonstrated his urge for speedy action by obtaining President Wilson's permission to sell equipment directly rather than by the usual thirty-day advertisement for bids. He also got action from the slow-moving French, by threatening to take down certain naval installations and bring them home unless they made up their minds and acted quickly.

Some suggestion of his later policy of insisting upon "unconditional surrender" appeared when Roosevelt visited the Rhineland. He saw no American flag flying from one of Germany's former fortresses which he had known as a boy. When told that the reason for this was reluctance to humiliate the Germans, he retorted that the Germans must learn beyond doubt that they had been beaten; and he took the trouble to complain to General Pershing, who ordered the flag raised at once.

Roosevelt on his return from Europe (on the same ship as President Wilson) became a strong public advocate of the League of Nations and the Covenant. But he was not to be as doctrinaire and inflexible as Wilson, who demanded that the Senate approve the Covenant without change. Roosevelt was ready to compromise, to admit that some details might later have to be changed, that it was, after all, an experiment; and that the important thing was to recognize the principle and approve the general plan.

Before considering the next step in Roosevelt's political career—his nomination for the vice-presidency in 1920—we must take a look back at a political disaster which he brought upon himself in 1914, a year after he had become Assistant Secretary of the Navy. It again gave him, in brutal fashion, an insight into the massive strength of political organizations, which was to change his earlier attitude toward them considerably.

Roosevelt did not give up thinking about politics, especially New York State politics, even during his busy days in the Navy before the U.S. entered the war. He used the patronage at his disposal to place politicians in his debt, and saw to it that he got great publicity as he went on inspection trips to the Navy's yards and depots. Throughout Roosevelt's life from 1913 on, he seldom made political mistakes; but when he did make one, to quote Mayor La Guardia of New York City, "it was a beaut." The one he made in 1914 was not as disastrous as the two he was to make in 1937 and 1938; most people have forgotten all about it—much to Roosevelt's later relief.

I mention it here also as additional evidence of his self-assurance, which had grown entirely too quickly. He had in 1911 helped to stop Tammany Hall and its chief, Murphy, from electing their man a United States Senator. Why couldn't he defeat them again? He had learned some of the ways of political intrigue in that venture—but not enough. It was one thing—quite substantial, it is true—to win victory in a small body of men like the legislature, when you can keep in touch with everybody all the time, arguing, cajoling, promising, threatening. It was quite a different matter to tackle an entrenched, resourceful, aggressive political organization in a statewide primary election.

But full of energy and too much self-confidence, Roosevelt in March of 1914 began to try. He felt very strongly that a statewide election victory in New York was essential to his future career. There had been a continuing struggle with respect to New York patronage since the 1912 election between anti-Tammany forces in the Wilson administration, of whom McAdoo and House were the leaders backed by progressives upstate and reformers in New York City, and Tammany Hall led by Murphy backed by McCombs, the National Democratic Chairman. Roosevelt was allied with McAdoo, and was supported by the upstate progressives.

McAdoo, interested in building up an organization for himself as well as in defeating Tammany Hall, decided that a primary fight for both the governorship and the senatorial nomination in 1914 against Tammany was necessary, and could be successful. It is not quite clear exactly how Roosevelt got embroiled in this fight. Daniels believed that McAdoo persuaded Roosevelt that this was Roosevelt's great chance to run for the Senate and get a statewide office. Daniels himself advised him against it.

On August 13, 1914, he suddenly announced that he was a candidate for the Democratic nomination as United States Senator. He coupled this with a denunciation of Murphy so bitter that in self-defense Murphy had to put a candidate in to beat Roosevelt. The wily Murphy picked James Gerard, Wilson's Ambassador to Germany. Wilson remained silent.

The result was sheer slaughter. In much the same noble style that Roosevelt was to use as a candidate in 1940 and 1944, Gerard announced that he was too busy with his duties in Germany to campaign. He never came into New York; he never left Europe. In spite of strenuous campaigning by Roosevelt, in spite of his labor endorsement, in spite of his use of naval patronage against Tammany

Hall, he could not arouse any interest during these first weeks of world war. Without lifting a finger, the absentee Gerard won the nomination by almost 2 to 1. In New York City, Roosevelt got only 20 per cent of the vote. Even upstate, where Roosevelt looked expectantly for votes, he lost. Although he never forgot this debacle, I am sure he wanted everyone else to forget it. I heard him tell stories about every phase of his public life, but never heard him talk about this one. And none of those around him who knew about it ever brought up that distasteful subject.

As early as May 1919, the *New York Sun,* a conservative New York newspaper, advocated Roosevelt in an editorial, as a possible and formidable candidate to succeed Wilson. Roosevelt never took this seriously, and discouraged friends who wished to promote the idea. But he no doubt already had firmly in mind the White House possibility in the future—some day. He had the reputation of being a "progressive," and had carefully cultivated that affiliation; he had the name Roosevelt and an impressive administrative record. But he was enough of a political realist to see the popular tide turning quickly away from Wilson and the Democratic Party. He seized every opportunity he could, however, to advance his national reputation, and to become one of the spokesmen for "progressivism" by making fighting speeches for liberalism and condemning Republican conservatism.

Roosevelt's relations with Tammany Hall at this period changed kaleidoscopically. The truce between them had lasted since 1917. Now, for no good reason except perhaps to enhance further his reputation as an independent and as a fighter against political bossism, he made a bitter attack on the unit rule in the New York delegation—a rule which gave Tammany Hall complete control of the entire delegation. He must have known his attack would be repulsed in the delegation—and it was. However, the Convention Rules Committee invalidated the unit rule for New York.

At the Presidential Convention in 1920, McAdoo was the strongest contender —with Mitchell Palmer and James Cox trailing him. New York's favorite son was Al Smith. Roosevelt was chosen to second his nomination, again attracting national attention and acclaim by his short, forceful speech. New York voted for Smith for seven ballots; then seventy of them switched to Cox. Roosevelt, leading twenty others, switched to McAdoo. Cox was finally nominated, but not until the forty-fourth ballot.

In the meantime, there was a great deal of maneuvering by Roosevelt's friends in support of his nomination as Vice President. He knew it, and did nothing to stop it. Cox did finally pick Roosevelt as his running mate, although he had never personally met him. Roosevelt's national reputation and his name were the deciding factors. And, in one of the many changes of attitudes between Tammany and Roosevelt, Murphy gave his assent. Roosevelt was nominated on the first ballot by acclamation, after a seconding speech on his behalf by Al Smith.

It is not quite clear why Murphy did not try to block Roosevelt's nomination. Although he knew that the election of Harding and Coolidge was almost certain, he was giving Roosevelt a brilliant stage on which to show himself to the whole nation, and to buttress by personal appearances the national reputation he had acquired. Roosevelt showed a lot of courage in undertaking this hopeless battle, but he also revealed his shrewdness in realizing how much it could mean to him politically in the future. The lion and the fox were at work simultaneously—to the ultimate benefit of Roosevelt.

The young man's rise to such national stature in 1920—only ten years after his start in politics—was nothing short of spectacular.

The campaign of 1920 is relevant here only as it affected the style, prestige and manner of Roosevelt. He spent practically all his time campaigning, visiting hundreds of villages, towns and cities. He got to know nearly all the political leaders—national, state and local—in the United States and never lost touch with them. He learned how important they, and also the lower echelons of party workers, could be even in a national election. He met people of all kinds in all sections of the country. As President he got out of Washington periodically and visited as many as possible of the forty-eight states.

Roosevelt always appreciated the value of the experience he gained in his 1920 campaign. Twelve years later, as he was starting out on his first long campaign trip in 1932 as the head of the ticket, he wrote his old chief, Daniels: "I am dictating this just before leaving for the big trip to the coast, and I am glad that I had that 1920 experience; otherwise, I should be worried by the prospect" (September 12, 1932).

He made the League of Nations and progressiveness his chief campaign topics. But he soon found out that farmers cared little about the League or political theories; that they were more concerned with farm prices and the security of their farms; that laborers were thinking more about jobs, wages and the cost of living. He did hit responsive chords when he spoke of the liberalism of the Democratic Party and of its progressive policies; and as the campaign proceeded, he dwelt more and more on that theme. He descended once or twice to red-baiting, one of the political sports of that day. He was not always consistent. He played the role of a militant progressive, and didn't hesitate to call upon the name of Theodore Roosevelt as the great progressive—much like himself, was the suggestion. To counter the favorable impression this was making, the Republicans sent Theodore's son, young Theodore, Jr., out on the stump to shout that the candidate was only a "maverick" Roosevelt, and did not "have the brand of our family."

Speaking from early morning until midnight in so many states every day (twenty-six speeches in two days, for example, in the State of Washington), taking definite stands on the important issues all over the country—all this was something quite unusual, if not unprecedented, for a Vice-Presidential candidate. His opponent, Calvin Coolidge, emitted only a deep silence. But Roosevelt knew how much campaign activity was helping his national image.

Reminiscing about this campaign in an extemporaneous speech as President, on April 24, 1934, Roosevelt said: "The particular subject that we are here to talk about . . . goes back to my own life a great many years. I think it goes back, so far as I am concerned, to a privilege that I once had. It was the privilege of running for Vice President and being defeated. It is a privilege for this reason: during three months in the year 1920, I think I spent eighty-nine out of ninety-two days on a sleeping car. I went to forty-two states in the Union. I drove literally thousands of miles by automobile and I got to know the country as only a candidate for national office or a traveling salesman can get to know it."

He already had a definite conception of the role of the President as the leader of the nation and not as a tool of Congress. He even hinted at his later "quarantine" speech of 1937 by saying that membership in the League did not mean shooting from the hip at any nation threatening world peace, but that other measures would first be used such as "international ostracism." He added with great prescience that "every sane man knows that in case of another world-war, America would be drawn in anyway whether we were in the League or not." He even used the simile he was to repeat twenty years later in a more down-to-earth form in discussing lend-lease, when he said that the League was like a fire department, and that neighbors did not quietly sit on their porches when a house caught fire.

While Roosevelt did not really expect to win, he must have been jolted by the landslide. Even Al Smith, to whom Tammany devoted much more attention than to the national ticket, went down in New York in his try for re-election as Governor. But Roosevelt had patience. He could wait; he was only thirty-eight years of age.

During the long eight-year hiatus in his public life enforced because of his infantile paralysis, which followed the campaign of 1920, Roosevelt was to carry on a continuous correspondence with many of the prominent Democratic leaders whom he had met in the campaign—exchanging ideas with them on the state of the Union and of the Democratic Party. In spite of his illness, these leaders were all kept aware of his existence, his name, his influence and his interest in the organization and policies of the party. He did not entirely drop this practice during his governorship nor while he was President. As the head of a political party, this was his style.

Probably only a comparatively few of the people across the nation listening to the radio on March 4, 1933, had much knowledge or interest in all this past history of their new President. Roosevelt's past was not what they had voted for; in their despair and misery, they had turned to him for what they thought he could do for them *now*. But that past was what he had brought with him to Washington: his legislative experience, his administrative experience, his independence, his courage, his progressiveness, his political know-how, his vast knowledge of the United States and its peoples, its resources and its problems, above all, his warmth and interest in human beings.

One thing they all did know about his past. It had been a matter of newspaper comment, and photographs, radio announcements and nationwide publicity; and those who had seen him personally during the campaign knew it of their own knowledge: he was paralyzed from the waist down. His legs were useless. He stood upon steel braces reaching from a circle of leather-padded steel, on which his body rested, to the soles of his shoes. They locked at the knees at a flick of his hand when he wanted to lift himself up, and unlocked in the same way when he wanted to let himself down in a chair. He could not really walk, even with the braces; he propelled himself mostly by his hip movements, leaning on a cane and on someone's arm.

This disaster—infantile paralysis—had hit him at Campobello on August 10, 1921, at the age of thirty-nine, at a time when he was in perfect health, muscular, active and full of energetic movement. In two days, it had him on his back, unable to move—even to wiggle his big toe. A false diagnosis by a local doctor, and then by a specialist summering in Maine, resulted in a prescription of heavy massage which was not only excruciatingly painful but exactly the wrong treatment. Finally, after two weeks, the illness was properly diagnosed as poliomyelitis by another doctor. The massaging was stopped. Roosevelt came quickly out of his first few days of depression, and was soon making jokes about his affliction, expecting to get over it shortly. The rest of the family, more for his morale than their own, kept up an atmosphere of cheerfulness—including even his mother.

Then he was removed from Campobello on a stretcher to a hospital in New York City. He and his wife, Eleanor, had taken it for granted that he would soon be able to get back to work, but they got little encouragement. He did not leave the hospital until October 28. He went home and, though not improved and still having temperature and pain, started his exercises.

At this time, his mother began a long battle to persuade him to retire to Hyde Park, to the life of a gentleman of ease, amid the surroundings where he had his roots and which he loved so much. Besides, she was sure that the continuation of his politics and business would, no matter what the doctors said, kill him. Roosevelt and his wife resisted. Less than two weeks after his attack, lying in bed at Campobello struggling to be able to move his big toe, he became a member of a committee to raise funds for Vassar College. A few weeks later, he accepted a place on the executive committee of the Democratic State Committee. He became chairman of the drive for funds to build St. John's Cathedral in New York City. He kept his position as president of the Boys Scouts Foundation. He continued issuing political statements from his home, although it would be a long time before he could appear in person at political meetings. He was being mentioned in newspaper articles as a possible nominee for Governor or United States Senator in the fall of that year. While he was pleased by these comments, he did not take them seriously. Instead, he embarked on a program to persuade Alfred E. Smith to run again for Governor. Roosevelt not only wanted Smith; he was equally anxious to keep William Randolph Hearst from the nomination for Governor. This put Roosevelt back into New York State politics aggressively.

He resumed going down to his office several days a week at the Fidelity and Deposit Company which he had joined after the 1920 defeat. He formed a new law firm and to both activities he gave close attention. In a way, with no gadding about to clubs or social events, he was able to devote more attention to the problems at hand, and to confer more at home and in the office. He became calmer and more serene, and even more resolute than before. Though he could not stand without crutches, he never accepted completely and finally the idea of defeat in his efforts to regain normal legs. The self-control which he was compelled to develop was to help make it possible for him to live through the rigors of twelve of the most exacting and critical years of any presidency.

The Democratic victories in the elections of 1922 throughout the country encouraged Roosevelt to renewed efforts to oppose the isolationist foreign policy of President Harding, and the general isolationist sentiment of Americans. He was a major force in organizing and raising funds for the Woodrow Wilson Foundation. As early as 1923, he entered an essay contest—sponsored by Edward Bok—for the best plan to preserve world peace. He never submitted his essay because his wife had become one of the judges. It was, however, strikingly similar to what emerged years later in the Charter of the United Nations Organization. In fact, in 1944, he dictated and attached a memorandum to this essay, both of which are in the Franklin D. Roosevelt Library at Hyde Park, in which he proudly pointed out the similarities. But with a perfect sense of timing—later to be one of the chief characteristics of his style as President—he decried any efforts being made at the time by some writers for an international police force to guarantee peace. He realized the strength of isolationism in the United States. He wrote a friend: "We are going through such a period of national sensitivity that we must wait until people come back to a more normal perspective."

Roosevelt also played the role of businessman during these years with enthusiasm, but without much success. He speculated in dubious ventures. He would try one thing, then another, experimenting in making money much as he would more successfully later on in fields of government where he had more expertise. His activities in the business world make good reading for an investor on the advisability of avoiding highly speculative risks; but they are not important considerations for us—any more than his wild manner of playing poker, which I had many opportunities in Albany and Washington to watch with astonishment and some financial profit. Eleanor Roosevelt referred to her husband's business career euphemistically in an interview with Professor Freidel of Harvard: "In business, he was not experienced, and not always wise."[18]

His most intense political activity in this period was in support of Alfred E. Smith for the Democratic nomination for President, unsuccessfully in 1924 and successfully in 1928. Involved in this was the growing feud in America between the "Drys" and the "Wets." Roosevelt was very wary in those days of committing himself completely on the question of prohibition. He did not know how the majority of Americans felt, and took refuge in suggesting a national referendum to find out. He was not much of a lion on this question of prohibition until much later. He was trying to get the national debate away from "Rum and Romanism" onto the higher level of the many pressing economic and political issues.

However, the question of prohibition was splitting the Democratic Party. He straddled on prohibition for a long time; and advised Al Smith to straddle also. Smith did not follow this advice but boldly and publicly struck out at prohibition.

Roosevelt, in letters, statements and interviews, kept stressing the necessity of nominating a progressive Democrat in 1924 with the support of a united party. The two leading contenders were McAdoo, a "Dry" and a Klan candidate, and Smith, a "Wet" and a devout Catholic. By Smith's own choice, Roosevelt soon became the leader in his campaign. This brought him great additional political attention throughout the nation.

At the Democratic National Convention in 1924, Roosevelt was floor leader for Smith, and made the nominating speech for him. I was present—in the galleries—at Madison Square Garden in New York City during some of the days of that convention where I saw him for the first time in my life. He was on crutches, and I was filled with wonder, admiration, incredulity and a sympathy bordering on affection. His eloquent nominating speech, and the sight of this gallant man making his way on crutches to the Speaker's stand, rendered him, except for the candidates themselves, the outstanding figure of the convention.

The speech used for the first time the phrase, "Happy warrior of the political bat-
tlefield." "Happy warrior" was remembered more than the speech itself, and is still remembered by many who have forgotten that it was popularized in a Roosevelt speech. It became a political slogan. The phrase came originally from the poem by William Wordsworth, "Character of the Happy Warrior."

Whether actually written into this speech of 1924 (and again in his nominating speech of 1928) by Roosevelt himself or by someone else, it is typical of many examples which showed Roosevelt's ability to take a phrase, use it in a speech, and make it a popular byword. There were to be many others during his presidency which caught the people's imagination: "New Deal," "Nothing to fear but fear itself," "Economic Royalists," "Arsenal of Democracy," "Rendezvous with Destiny," "Four Freedoms," "Bold Experimentation," "Martin, Barton and

Fish," "One-Third of a Nation." While these famous phrases did not all come from FDR's pen, if they had been used by someone else, they would not have been long remembered.

After the McAdoo-Smith deadlock and the compromise nomination of John W. Davis, many Democrats urged Roosevelt to run for Governor that year. His reply was that he would not run for any office until he could walk again. It was a determination he would break six times.

After the debacle of the 1924 election, Roosevelt, never ready to quit, kept on trying to learn to walk. He never succeeded; but in the course of trying, he discovered and began to build up the Warm Springs resort. In politics, he continued writing and preaching and insisting that the Democratic Party must always be the party of progressiveness and liberal thought. He was to take drastic action because of this thesis several times during his presidency.

In 1928 at the next Democratic National Convention, in Houston, the delegates and press must have realized how much improvement Roosevelt's dogged efforts had produced in his legs as compared with four years before. The crutches had disappeared; instead, he had braces, a cane, and the strong arm of his son, Elliott. He appeared so firm of motion, and of such high spirits, that the general impression about his helplessness soon began to disappear.

Again, he delivered the nominating speech for Smith. By this time, radio had been developed to a high state of perfection; and through it, Roosevelt was able to broadcast his personality, warmth and impressiveness to the whole nation as he could not do four years earlier. He prepared this speech with the radio audience, rather than the convention, in mind. Again using the "Happy Warrior" phrase, it created spectacular, national enthusiasm for the speaker. Talking of Smith, he emphasized, in the resonant voice which was to become familiar to so many millions of radio listeners, the deeper understanding which comes to a man from his great struggles in life, the development of a deeper human sympathy for the afflicted, the urge to extend help to those in trouble, a feeling and sympathy for the underprivileged, and a fuller realization of the plight of those who had been unable to overcome the many obstacles in life.

This was a famous passage in the speech:

"I have described so far qualities entirely of the mind—the mental and moral equipment without which no President can successfully meet the administrative and material problems of his office. It is possible with only these qualities for a man to be a reasonably efficient President, but there is one thing more needed to make him a great President.

"It is that quality of soul which makes a man loved by little children, by dumb animals, that quality of soul which makes him a strong help to all those in sorrow or in trouble, that quality which makes him not merely admired, but loved by all people—the quality of sympathetic understanding of the human heart, of real interest in one's fellowmen. Instinctively, he senses the popular need because he himself has lived through the hardship, the labor and the sacrifice which must be endured by every man of heroic mould who struggles up to eminence from obscurity and low estate. Between him and the people is that subtle bond which makes him their champion and makes them enthusiastically trust him with their loyalty and their love."

Smith was listening to the speech in the Executive Mansion in Albany. The next morning, an editorial in the *New York Times* praised it as "a model of its kind . . . the address of a fair-minded and cultivated man, avoiding . . . usual

convention oratory . . . seldom has a political speech attained this kind of elo-
quence . . . limpid and unaffected in style, and without a single trace of fustian."
Smith clipped the editorial, and sent it to Roosevelt with a notation in the margin:
"This must be right because it brought tears in the Mansion when you spoke it."

Some people who knew Roosevelt personally in those days, and many others
who did not, have speculated that it was his crippling and painful experience
which created "that quality of soul which makes him a strong help to all those
in sorrow or in trouble," that "real interest in his fellowmen" and that unquench-
able liberalism which were part of his entire life, especially after the tragic event
of 1921.

I do not think that that is the full explanation.

Nevertheless, I've not been able to learn to my own satisfaction—in spite of
eighteen years of close personal association—the original sources of his unwavering liberalism. There was nothing in his home environment, education or early
experiences to account for it. I have tried to find that source by indirect conversations with Roosevelt himself, with his old friends and with members of his family;
I conclude that there was none of the usual outside influence. There was no need
for any. The reason was born when he was born; it was in the heart and soul of
the man, in his love of people, his own sense of social justice, his hatred of the
greedy exploitation of the weak, his contempt for the bully and the fraud—
whether it was a Hitler or a Mussolini, the owner of a sweatshop, the operator
of a bucket shop, or the employer of child labor. There was, of course, his early
and continued veneration for the older Roosevelt and for his later progressive
policies. There was his experience with that other great liberal and progressive
President, Woodrow Wilson. But neither of these had anything like FDR's keen
sense of social justice.

During that desperate period of his life when he had to remain immobile so
much of the time at home, there had come to visit him—at the suggestion of Mrs.
Roosevelt and others—many men and women of liberal thought, labor union
leaders, leaders of the Women's Trade Union League and of the League of
Women Voters. They found him a willing and absorbed listener to their liberal
ideas.

Three months after Smith was nominated for the presidency at Houston,
Roosevelt was nominated for the governorship of the State of New York at the
New York Democratic State Convention in Rochester, New York. He was
elected, then re-elected, and served, in all, four years as Governor. These four
years had as much to do with his style and thinking as President as any other
experience.

It is important that we first take a quick look at how he came to be nominated;
how the decision to accept the nomination was made by him solely in the loneliness of Warm Springs, just as so many fateful decisions were to be made by him
later in the loneliness of the White House. The decision—probably the most
important to his future political career that he ever made—showed many qualities
of the fox as well as of the lion.

After the nomination of Smith in 1928, Roosevelt continued to work as
diligently as he could for Smith's election, although there must have been a great
doubt in his mind that it could be done. There were so many things to create this
doubt: the Coolidge prosperity was booming and there was no indication that it
would one year later, under Hoover, end in a bust. Smith was a devout Catholic,
the most important Catholic layman in America, in a period of American life

disgraced by extreme religious intolerance and by a revival of the Ku Klux Klan; Smith was a "Wet" when most of rural America—where he would especially have to look for votes—was "Dry"; Smith was quite unknown to the voters outside his own state, and he refused to take Roosevelt's repeated advice to show himself sufficiently to the rest of the country; and Smith was known to be the favorite son of Tammany Hall which, in many of the rural areas of the United States, was considered the incarnation of all political evil. But if all of this gradually began to make Roosevelt despair of Smith's election in 1928, he never showed it. He continued to work, to make speeches and to write letters to prominent Democrats around the country in Smith's behalf.

Soon, Al's friends persuaded him that it would be a great help in the Presidential campaign, especially in carrying New York State, if he could induce Roosevelt to run for Governor. It would provide a popular Protestant, a "non-Wet" and a teammate politically strong throughout the state, who would undoubtedly help the Smith candidacy by his own. It also would be the only way to avoid a split between the upstate leaders and the Tammany leaders, who could not agree on any candidate for Governor but Roosevelt.

Smith said he would try to persuade Roosevelt to run—and he did try, several times. Roosevelt's answer was consistently the same: he was confident that with continued treatment at Warm Springs, he might discard one of his two braces and one of his two canes. Mrs. Roosevelt has expressed the belief that by this time —September 1928—he had recovered as much as he ever would. I did not get to know Roosevelt personally until the following month, October 1928, but after that, I did not notice any improvement. I am sure that FDR, realist that he was, was no longer too sanguine himself of further progress. Knowing him well, as I later did, I am positive that he never would have admitted this to anyone, including Mrs. Roosevelt. His consistent rejoinder to the importunities of Smith and his friends was a perfect one for a man who did not want to run—it was one which could not well be ignored or resisted.

And he definitely had decided not to run for Governor in 1928 for many reasons other than recovering greater use of his legs. He did not think that 1928 was his year. Nor did Louis Howe, who was at this time, and for many years had been, his closest political adviser. The landslide for Hoover which seemed probable would most likely carry with it a defeat for the gubernatorial candidate. And he realized very well that a smashing defeat in his own state would be an almost insurmountable roadblock on his way to Washington. It has been reported by one political writer that Howe revealed that the plan was for Roosevelt to run for Governor in 1932, and then for President in 1936. Whether this is true or not, it seems clear that Howe and Roosevelt had agreed that the race for Governor —if it really should be necessary for Roosevelt to become Governor before actively aiming at the White House—should not be in 1928. Howe did not think it would ever be necessary; he kept wiring and phoning Roosevelt in September 1928 not to yield to Smith's entreaties but to base his refusal on health alone— an unanswerable reason.

Smith, however, continued to press, Roosevelt continued to resist, and finally he dodged the phone calls. Smith then asked Mrs. Roosevelt to call him, which she did. Roosevelt did answer the call from his wife, who had told Smith that she would not try to influence her husband's decision once she had reached him on the phone. She merely handed the phone to Smith and left for the railroad station. The reason she did not wait to hear what her husband would do was that she had to catch the sleeper to New York City (this was before the airplane age) in order to reach the class she taught at Todhunter School.

A long conversation followed her departure; Smith, Herbert Lehman and Raskob, successively and often together, were on the phone in Rochester, pleading with Roosevelt in Warm Springs to run. Roosevelt's objections were talked down. Lehman was to be the candidate for Lieutenant-Governor; Roosevelt knew him and his ability to occupy his desk temporarily, if Roosevelt wanted to go back to Warm Springs from time to time to renew his treatments. Raskob even agreed to help take care of the Warm Springs project, to which Roosevelt had committed a large share of his own personal funds. There was no other candidate available who had a chance to win; Smith needed him to help carry the crucial State of New York.

Roosevelt began to yield, but not to say "yes." All he would finally promise was that if the convention nominated him in spite of his reluctance, he would reassess the situation; but he added that he did not know just what he would do if such a genuine draft took place. That was all Smith needed. The delegates were just marking time during these negotiations, waiting to do whatever Smith asked. Roosevelt was nominated by acclamation. He accepted. Howe, in New York, was dismayed; all his telegrams and phone calls, and all his efforts to dissuade Roosevelt had failed. FDR, alone in Warm Springs, had finally succumbed.

Why?

He was not one to be unduly impressed by the arguments they offered him —except, perhaps, the one which would financially guarantee continuation of Warm Springs. Personally, I believe that during the two days of these dramatic long-distance appeals, Roosevelt had plenty of time to think things through entirely by himself. I believe he had reached the conclusion that if his financial problem about developing Warm Springs could be even partially solved, it was politically advisable, if not absolutely necessary, for him to run in 1928—not only to help Smith but to advance his own political career.

Why?

Roosevelt must have felt that he had gone as far as he could since 1920 without holding public office. If he did not run in 1928, someone else would, who might be elected Governor. If so, Roosevelt's chances to use Albany as a springboard for the presidency would be blocked for four years or maybe eight. He must have realized that it would be difficult to continue to maintain his national stature for such a long period as a private citizen and then try for the presidency. Someone else might come along—a Governor or a senator—and it would be too late. As we now know, there did develop plenty of well-known prominent candidates for the nomination in 1932. It seems very improbable to me that Roosevelt, if he had still been a private citizen, could have obtained a majority on the first ballot in Chicago in 1932 against Smith, Ritchie, Baker and all the others. What gave him that majority was principally his phenomenal success as Governor and the way he had been able to use the office to get support for himself throughout the country. Without this majority, he never could have made the deal which finally gave him the necessary two-thirds. Of course, Roosevelt could not have foreseen all this, but he knew very well that a successful four years as Governor would certainly make him a strong contender in 1932 if that should become a good year to strike, or an even stronger contender in 1936 after eight years in Albany.

And so he made this most critical political decision on his own. It required courage to take such a risk of defeat which might mean the end of his White House ambition—after so brilliant a career and so many years of tireless effort. But it was also a canny, shrewd calculation, very much in line with his usual style.

Having decided to accept, he put behind him all his doubts, as was also his style. He often said that if he were 51 per cent convinced that a course was correct, he would always follow it with the same force as if he had been 100 per cent convinced. That's what he did in October 1928; he plunged into the campaign.

FDR recognized that his most important job was to dispel the idea that he was an "incurable invalid who had been sacrificed to satisfy the ambition" of his friend Smith, as many Republican newspapers and orators stated. He decided to accomplish this by undertaking a whirlwind automobile campaign all over the state, making ten or more speeches a day at remote crossroads, ending each day with a principal address in some city. Time and again he proudly called his audience's attention to the fact that he was able to do this—and that he enjoyed it.

This 1928 campaign trip was the first time I had met Mr. Roosevelt. I was asked to accompany him, because I'd become familiar with the recent legislative and political history of both parties in New York State, as a member of the legislature for five years and of the Legislative Bill Drafting Commission for three years. Since he had been out of close contact with legislative affairs in New York since 1913, it was thought that I could be of some help in bringing his knowledge up to date. I did not expect to do any speech-writing; but he soon began to have me prepare some rough first drafts.

I was with him during the whole of this campaign trip and can testify to the back-breaking pace, which seemed to tire all the young reporters—and me also, then only thirty-two years of age—much more than it did him. I saw the *extra* physical effort he had to make doing all the routine things the normal person so easily does: getting downstairs each morning in his hotel, walking to his car, getting into his car by a kind of strenuous gymnastic use of his arms and shoulders; pulling himself up to his feet to speak to a street crowd in a village from his car; getting out of his car by the same strenuous tactic when he was to attend a political luncheon; getting back in; leaving his car when it arrived in the next city; getting up to his room for a final review of his prepared speech, and for meetings with the local Democratic leaders. And then the whole process would begin all over again as he left for the meeting hall that evening and returned to the hotel. This long, tiring grind was repeated day after day.

At one meeting, I even saw him carried up the fire escape of the meeting hall, unseen by the audience, get down on his braces, straighten out his disarranged jacket, and then walk onto the platform with great dignity, in high spirits, with friendly smiles, and with no trace of the humiliation he must have felt at being carried like a baby.

He seemed to enjoy the daily ordeal, and frequently boasted to his audiences about how strenuously he was campaigning. For example, in Troy, on October 26, 1928, he recounted with obvious satisfaction—indeed, with some glee—the campaigning he had done on that one day. This is the way he put it:

"Well, I am glad to get back to the Hudson River. You know, I have been a little bit amused during the last three weeks. I understand that after the Rochester Convention took the action that it did, there was a good deal of what might be called sob stuff among the Republican editorial writers in the State of New York. They said, 'Isn't it too bad that that unfortunate man has had to be drafted for the governorship? Isn't it too bad that his health won't stand it?'

"We started off nearly two weeks ago from the City of New York, consisting of a caravan—a whole flock of people, candidates, the press, the stenographic force, etc. We started in Orange County and we went on through Sullivan, Delaware, Broome, Steuben, and so forth, out through the Southern Tier, all the way to Jamestown. One day we covered 190 miles by automobile and made seven speeches. Then we worked our way up to Buffalo and back to Rochester and Syracuse. Because we were getting into our stride, we took a little side trip up to Oswego and Watertown, and then we dropped back to Utica. We left Utica this morning, intending to have an easy day of it. We got to Herkimer, where we made speeches; then we expected to come through to Schenectady, but when we got to Fonda, there were forty or fifty automobiles in line blocking the road, and we were literally kidnapped. It threw the whole schedule out. We were told that up in that neck of the woods, Gloversville, where in the past there had been occasionally two Democrats, and sometimes three, who had gone to the polls, there were two thousand people waiting for us on the street, and that all the talk of the owners of the glove factories there could not keep them off the streets. So we changed our plans a little and went up to Gloversville. There they were, all of them going to vote the Democratic ticket. When we came on down, we were kidnapped again. We got to Amsterdam. We expected to go through Amsterdam just as fast as the traffic cops would let us, but there were sixteen hundred people in the theatre in Amsterdam, waiting. They had been waiting there two hours.

"And then, for good measure, we just dropped into Schenectady and spoke there earlier in the evening, and now here we are in Troy. Too bad about this unfortunate sick man, isn't it? . . ."[19]

For those who knew FDR well, this kind of informal homely talk—and the political shrewdness of it in overcoming rumors about his health—were very typical.

He was to do this same strenuous campaigning time and again in four Presidential campaigns. It was his style. Everyone then alive remembers particularly his full day of riding around in an open car, campaigning in New York City in November 1944 in a driving, freezing rain—a process which left the press exhausted and everybody, including him, soaking wet—winding up in a major campaign speech before the Foreign Policy Association in the evening, all because rumors had been spread by his opponents that he was practically a dying man. That one day was more effective in stopping those rumors than a dozen certificates of good health from as many doctors. Near the end of the strenuous 1928 campaign, he said to a cheering crowd in Yonkers: "If I could keep on campaigning twelve months longer, I'd throw away my crutch."

The campaign speeches of 1928 show the extent to which Roosevelt's political and social philosophy had become fixed. Nearly all of his philosophy, as then enunciated, is now almost universally accepted in America; but back in 1928 much of it was considered, as Roosevelt later put it, "socialistic" and even "bolshevistic."

In his acceptance speech of October 16, 1928, he laid down the general path he would follow: "Our state is committed to the principle of progressive government. . . . In social legislation, in education, in health, in better housing, in the care of the aged, we have gone far, but we must go further. . . ."

During the campaign, he advocated all the reforms which he submitted after his election in his first message to the legislature. But he also covered some national issues, constantly urging the election of Al Smith to the presidency. In fact, during the first few days of the campaign, he dealt exclusively with Smith's candidacy, causing his campaign manager in New York City to send me a telegram asking that I remind Roosevelt that he was a candidate for Governor, and to begin discussing state issues.

As to Smith, Roosevelt centered chiefly on the scurrilous attacks against him as a Catholic. He picked Binghamton, New York—which was then infested by active chapters of the Ku Klux Klan and a hotbed of religious hatred—as the place for a major onslaught on religious bigotry and prejudice. All during the rest of Roosevelt's life, as I knew him, the subject aroused him deeply; and he never hesitated to express his outrage about it. Typical was this passage from his speech in Buffalo on October 20, 1928. After describing very movingly the horrors of war which he had seen at close hand in Europe, he continued: "Somehow in those days people were not asking to what church those . . . American wounded boys belonged. . . .

"And I want to say to you very simply, very solemnly, that if there is any man or woman whose mind can go back ten years; if there is any man or woman who has seen the sights that I have seen, who knows what this country went through; any man or woman who knows what Germany, Poland, France, Austria, England went through—even more than we did—in those years, if any man or woman after thinking of that, can bear in his heart any motive in this year which will lead him to cast his ballot in the interest of intolerance . . . then I say solemnly to that man or woman, 'May God have mercy on your miserable soul.' "[20]

I do not believe that Roosevelt, in considering a man's suitability for appointment to office, cared any more about his religion than he did about the color of his hair. Of course, he did follow the usual political style of not appointing too many men of one religion or ethnic group to a court or to an agency, only because such appointments might give rise to suspicion that he was prejudiced against the other religions and groups. This reasoning was not only fair but good politics, and was part of his Presidential style.

Several times, I did see him emphasize religious discrimination—but always in reverse. For example, when he decided in 1942 to appoint someone to set up the American organization that would later become the international UNRRA to relieve hunger and lack of clothing in the liberated countries, he decided upon Governor Lehman of New York—a man whom he knew to be of unquestioned integrity and ability. He told me about this choice before asking Lehman to take the appointment; and he explained to me his thinking:

"As you know, he's a fine administrator and executive with experience in this kind of work. But there is another reason. After everything that Hitler has done to the Jews of Europe, I think it would be a wonderful bit of poetic justice if we could get a Jew to head the agency which is going to feed and clothe and shelter the millions of all faiths whom Hitler had robbed and starved and tortured—a member of the very group which Hitler first selected for complete extermination. It would be a fine object lesson to have a Jew head up this operation, and I think Herbert would be fine."

Herbert Lehman got the job; and he did it splendidly.

I also had several experiences with Roosevelt, myself, which showed me how deeply he felt about religious bigotry.

In 1933, at a time when FDR was receiving many foreign leaders in Washington to discuss the general international scene, Hitler's Minister of Finance, Hjalmar Schacht—who in 1946 would be put on trial at Nüremberg with the other top Nazis as one of the war criminals—came to see Roosevelt. Bowing to protocol, the President tendered him a small stag luncheon. He invited me to this lunch. I demurred, but he insisted.

After it was over, I remarked to the President: "I don't think Schacht liked my being there very much."

"I am sure that he took notice," he replied, "and the exposure is good for him. If it were not for this protocol business, I would have seated you right next to him."

Later, in 1936, when he was about to start his main campaign trip for re-election to a second term as President, he asked Mrs. Rosenman and me to accompany him; the itinerary was largely through the Midwest. I had been helping on his speech for the Democratic Convention of 1936 and was a little taken aback because I had already examined the itinerary. I said to him: "Mr. President, you know that your train is going principally through the Bible Belt. You know how bigoted a great many people are who live there. While, of course, I would be delighted to go, I don't think that two Jews should be on that train with you." (Like so many things, the "Bible Belt" has changed a great deal since 1936.)

I have seldom seen Roosevelt lose his temper but he certainly did so then.

"That's sheer nonsense! The only way to meet that sort of thing is head-on —and not to duck it. Make arrangements for you and Dorothy to come; and let's not discuss it any further."

So we went.

To return to the 1928 campaign: At Yonkers, on November 1, Roosevelt showed quite clearly what his style of democracy was going to be. He quoted from Herbert Hoover's recent book *Rugged Individualism:* "The crowd . . . has no mind of its own which can plan. . . . The crowd is credulous, it destroys, it hates and it dreams, but it never builds." He then contrasted Hoover's belief that, because of this characteristic of the "crowd," control of this country should be vested in a very limited group at the top, with Smith's conviction that the mass of Americans does think about public questions and often even originates novel and effective ideas.

Roosevelt of course could also have pointed out his own complete difference on this score from Hoover. He often said, both in Albany and in Washington, that he would rather trust the judgment of the ordinary mass of people, providing only that they were given all the facts about an issue without distortions or partisanship or prejudices, than he would the judgment of any select few. His style was always affected by that belief.

The election results justified Roosevelt's fears about Smith. Hoover carried New York State by over 100,000 and the nation by 6.5 million. However, Roosevelt's own decision to take the risk and run for Governor was also justified—but by the narrowest of margins. He received a majority of only 25,000 out of a total vote of over 4 million.

Right after Election Day, FDR returned to Warm Springs to rest and exercise. Within a few weeks, he asked the Lieutenant-Governor-elect, the Democratic leader in each House of the legislature and me to come down to Warm Springs for a few days of conference. The purpose of the meeting was twofold. First, to map a liberal and progressive program to present, and to fight for, in the coming session of the legislature which was to start in early January; second, to lay plans for strengthening and expanding the New York Democratic organization, especially upstate where it was weakest.

This was my first opportunity to observe at close hand a very typical Rooseveltian political style and strategy, intended to make sure that the Democratic Party was a liberal progressive one, but also to perfect its organization so as to provide the greatest support for its liberal policies at the polls and in the legislature. This was to be his constant dual objective as the head of the party in state and nation. He often talked about how closely these two matters were entwined, how important each was for success in elections. In Roosevelt, the shrewd practical politician and the humanitarian statesman were combined.

When he returned to Albany for the inauguration and the session of the legislature, he had done his homework—as he always would in the White House —and he was prepared. He had his program well in mind; and the process of strengthening the party upstate had already begun.

His Annual Message to the legislature on the day after his inauguration laid out the comprehensive program on which he had successfully campaigned: the relief of agriculture in New York State, and the demand that, nationally, the farmer be given what later came to be popularly known as "parity"; the development of water power "this year" by the state, and not by utility companies, with the control and title of the power site and the water to remain forever in the hands of the people of the state; reform of county and town governments; labor and social legislation of broad scope, including an eight-hour day and a forty-eight-hour week for women and children in industry, and an extension of workmen's compensation to all occupational diseases; continuation of the state parks and parkways program; immediate study by a commission of experts on old age security; the elimination of slums; a health program especially for the care and possible cure of crippled adults and children; general reform and modernization of civil and criminal procedures in the courts; and the general duty of the state to concern itself with the health, welfare, and education of all its people. In 1928, it was a pretty radical program; today it is almost everywhere accepted.

He concluded with an eloquent plea to forget partisanship and the question of who gets the credit for legislation; and to cooperate and "march shoulder to shoulder . . . toward the goal."

He must have had "tongue in cheek" about this concluding plea, because he knew that it was an impossible hope. In fact, within a matter of weeks, he and the Republican-controlled legislature were in a knockdown, drag-out fight with each other about the executive budget which Roosevelt had submitted.

Roosevelt knew that few matters are as likely to put a Governor on the front page of the newspapers as a good fight with his legislature. He was doubly blessed by the kind of legislature he was given during his four years in Albany. The first blessing was that the legislature was overwhelmingly Republican. In a fight with a legislature of the opposite party, the executive has nearly all the advantages, providing he is on the popular side of an issue; and, in nearly every Albany fight, Roosevelt was on the popular side. He becomes the hero protecting the public interest, and the legislature opposing him the villain. If he wins the fight, or even makes a decent compromise, he gets all the glory; if he loses, he still gets the glory of a valorous effort, and the legislature can be made to appear a victorious but autocratic malefactor.

His second political blessing right from the start was that the Republican leaders in the legislature were so incredibly stupid and so inept in their public relations. They had made up their minds to oppose practically everything new that he would recommend in order to prevent him from getting political credit. It never occurred to them that their opposition would only increase his credit tenfold. Although he won on many issues because of popular support, and although he was highly acclaimed even when he lost, they never seemed to learn.

The first big fight was on the executive budget. At first, it seemed to be wholly a technical matter of little interest to the average citizen until Roosevelt explained it with that remarkable ability—so much a part of his style—to make everything seem simple, no matter how complicated it was. The legislative leaders sought to get their fingers into the allocation and itemization of lump sum appropriations in the budget; in other words, after they had passed the budget—a purely legislative function—they wanted to be able to control how it was to be spent—a purely executive function. So, as Roosevelt explained it, the dispute was concerned with a highly important constitutional question: the proper separation of the powers of the executive and legislative branches. As President he would raise the same question with the Congress, and would win—as he did in Albany.

The Attorney General of the State, to whom Roosevelt would normally turn for advice and assistance, was an elected Republican who had already publicly stated that the legislature's position was legally right. Roosevelt, therefore, had to retain outside counsel. He obtained the services of one of the best-known and successful constitutional lawyers of the day, William D. Guthrie. During the controversy, Roosevelt, as was his style, several times offered to compromise without sacrificing the constitutional principle. But the Republican leaders became more and more obstinate, and public interest grew greater and greater not only in New York but in many other states where similar questions had previously arisen.

The litigation in the courts was not finally decided until the end of November 1929; the Court of Appeals, the highest state court, upheld Roosevelt's contention. This struggle, and its final result, can be said to be the first outstanding event since his election to bring the Governor—as a strong, fighting executive—nationwide attention.

While the budget dispute was going on, Roosevelt as usual jumped into action by recommending in rapid succession and specific detail the legislation which he had discussed generally in his 1928 campaign, and in his first Annual Message to the legislature. It was much like his later action during the "one hundred days" of 1933—with one major exception. In 1933, because of the extreme emergency and his willingness to assume leadership, his recommendations were enacted by the Congress in short order. In 1929, by contrast, every recommendation he made met with immediate opposition. The same kind and volume of liberal progressive legislative recommendations were submitted by the Governor in 1930, and again in 1931 and 1932—with the same kind of legislative opposition.

After Roosevelt became President, writers and commentators expressed surprise at the rapid succession of legislative proposals urged by him during the "first hundred days" in 1933. Many have written of those proposals as a new, suddenly acquired kind of political philosophy. Many have wondered where they all came from in such rapid order.

The fact is that the basic philosophy and social objectives of the New Deal proposals of 1933 and 1935 can be found in Governor Roosevelt's speeches and messages during the four years before he became President. The details are different, because the proposals in 1933 were framed for national rather than state action. But the concepts are basically the same. In his messages and speeches from

1929 through 1932 you will find proposals for state action similar to almost every one of those he later urged upon Congress. You will also find extended discussion of many of the general themes he was later to use so frequently that they came to be well known as a part of the Roosevelt philosophy: the interdependence of all groups of the population, city and rural; subsistence homesteads and the resettlement of population; agricultural parity; regional planning; bringing industry into rural areas; conservation of natural resources; and separation of legislative from executive functions.

By the time he became Governor, FDR's basic philosophy and principles had been fairly well formed; they simply grew more specific after 1928. He would explore his ideas through long hours of conversation with experts whom he invited to the Executive Mansion in Albany—usually for dinner and to spend the night. Roosevelt learned more rapidly by personal meetings and conversation than by reading memoranda. Personal conferences gave him the chance to ask questions as they arose in his own mind, to make his own suggestions and to see how they were received. By the time he was finished probing, arguing, suggesting and debating with an expert, he was well informed. He rarely took notes; he did not need them to refresh his prodigious memory.

During the Albany days there was a steady stream of visitors—politicians, technical experts, economists, political scientists, as well as friends—from all parts of the state and, indeed, from other parts of the country. The Roosevelts liked to have the guest rooms in the Executive Mansion occupied, as they did later in the White House. The occupants of those guest rooms contributed many ideas.

In Washington, some of those visits developed into virtual monologues, with the President doing the talking. Sometimes, this style was meant to put his visitor at ease; sometimes it was a kind of filibuster to prevent his visitor from giving complaints about his actions; sometimes it was to draw his visitor out; sometimes he was testing new thoughts as trial balloons; sometimes he just loved to relax, to charm and to talk.

Cass Canfield, of Harper & Row, tells of a typical example in his delightful autobiographical book, *Up and Down and Around:*

I didn't know FDR . . . I was anxious to see the President about getting access to some of his papers. . . . The morning after my arrival in Washington, the telephone rang at the Hay-Adams Hotel, and a secretary advised me that, if I came right over, the President could see me for five minutes. I rushed to the White House wondering, on the way, whether FDR would take the trouble to turn his famous charm on me, as he was reputed to do with almost anyone he met. I couldn't imagine that he would put himself out for me since I meant nothing to him in political terms.

I was shown into his study. It was my impression that Mr. Roosevelt rose to greet me, but this was, of course, impossible for him because of his paralysis. Yet he appeared to rise from his chair, and was certainly most cordial. "Hello Cass," he said. "How long is it since we last met?"

This stumped me, because I'd *never* met him; I'd seen him, maybe twice, speaking from a platform a hundred feet away.

He continued: "Now, let's see. You're the son of Augustus Cass Canfield, aren't you?" He talked on and on, seeming to recall details as he went along. He told me that he owed more to my father than to anyone he could think of because it was he who had taught him to sail a boat—the pleasure he enjoyed above all others. He talked for nearly an hour and by the end of that visit I'd learned more about my father, his outlook and entourage than I had ever known before. It was amazing.

I departed with the papers I wanted, the business part of the visit having taken only a few moments.[21]

Innumerable other accounts by many visitors exist of this loquacious propensity and spontaneous friendliness, but there is no need to rely on them; we have the President's own statement. I quote from his extemporaneous remarks in 1943, at a White House reception for the new senators and representatives:

"And so I know that you will bear with me and be lenient, if it takes any of you who want to see me about something important, a long, long time before you can get in. I am doing the best I can. I do wish to goodness that I had more time, as I did before, to see personally the members of the House and Senate.

"I think that part of it is my fault, so my secretaries tell me. When somebody comes in on a ten-minute appointment, I start to do the talking. I get enthusiastic, and the result is that at the end of ten or fifteen minutes my visitor hasn't had a chance to get in a word edgewise. And that is something I am trying to school myself to omit, to try to let the other fellow talk, instead of my doing it. And that is about the hardest thing I have to do in this life, because as some of you who have been here before know, I love to talk. It's an unfortunate characteristic.

"So I say, please bear with me, and if you do come in, say to me quite frankly, 'Now listen, before you talk, Mr. President, let me have my say.' I think it would be a grand thing."

I must add that, to the end, he never succeeded in "schooling" himself to change that "unfortunate characteristic."

All of Roosevelt's recommendations in the 1929 session were finally rejected by the legislature, except for the farm relief measures and those creating three study commissions (old age security, revision of the public service law, and judicial reform). When they had completed what Roosevelt publicly called "the holocaust" of his recommended social legislation, many parts of which were actually in their own platform of 1928, they adjourned, and went home with a feeling of satisfaction. They had yet to learn the fighting ability of the Governor, and his way of turning legislative defeats into political victories for himself.

Nothing in Roosevelt's political career showed more clearly what a shrewd and consummate politician he was than the way he handled the 1929 legislation about farm relief. "It is," he had said in his 1929 Annual Message, "of small moment who first points out the road." But on this subject of farm relief, he got busy right after the election, before the legislature could even meet, and before he took his oath of office. He took the initiative in "pointing out the road," and he held it in spite of all the efforts of the Republican leaders to take it away from him, or even to take part of the credit.

The farmers of the United States shared practically none of the national prosperity which followed World War I. Overproduction, stagnant surpluses, low prices for their products, high taxes, high cost of farm machinery and implements —all had plagued them since 1920. Their condition was attracting national attention and many conflicting proposals were made for curing their plight. Roosevelt, as Governor, could do nothing about the national problem; therefore he did not have to commit himself—and cautiously took care not to—to any one of the different plans of relief being offered by the various farm leaders and organizations. But there was something Roosevelt could do for the New York farmer. In addition to the general distress resulting from overproduction and low prices, there were the problems of sustaining an unfair burden of taxes, and the wide disparity between what the farmer received for his products and what the consumer had to pay for them; getting the products to markets over poor roads; bad soil in many regions of the state; and too many layers of taxation in the overlapping local town and county governments.

Roosevelt had discussed the troubles of the New York farmer during the campaign. He pointed out the alarming rate at which farms all over the United States, as well as in New York, were being abandoned—chiefly because "farm families cannot make both ends meet by staying on the farm."

Almost immediately after his election he appointed an unofficial Agricultural Advisory Commission of farm experts and leaders under the chairmanship of Henry Morgenthau, Jr., editor of the *American Agriculturist,* who was also his old Dutchess County friend and neighbor. Its function was to formulate a program for the relief of New York farmers. Even before the inauguration, the commission made its first recommendation to reduce the rural tax burden for highways, bridges and schools. This could be done, they suggested, by substituting a gasoline tax, a substantial portion of which should be used for highway construction and maintenance, for expansion of work to eliminate tuberculosis among dairy herds, and for increased appropriations for agricultural research. There was nothing radical about any of this, but it was concrete; and it was something which could be pushed by Roosevelt immediately. The watchword of all his gubernatorial and Presidential style continued to be what it was in his Navy days—action. Action was what he wanted, and this report allowed some action at once. The Republican legislative leaders, alarmed by the enthusiastic reception of this report by the farmers of the state, could think of nothing to do except to call a conference of their own of farm leaders, in a ridiculous scramble to get some of the credit. But their conference adopted the recommendations of the report; and the legislative leaders were never able to convince rural voters that they, and not Roosevelt, were the great friends of the farmers. The Agricultural Advisory Commission made additional recommendations from time to time all through the Roosevelt governorship; and there was nothing the legislative leaders could do in most cases but follow the recommendations. All this enabled FDR to claim with substantial justification—which he did—that for many years before 1929, when the legislative leaders had the same opportunity as he to do something to help the New York farmers, they did nothing until he "pointed the way."

On social legislation, too, Roosevelt went to work at once, refusing to accept the inaction of the 1929 legislature. The Governor, with a vast majority of the newspapers in New York State against him, turned to what was to be his favorite and most effective weapon—radio. In two radio speeches in April, he calmly showed how the Republican leaders had violated many of their own platform pledges in killing his proposals for social legislation; that they had done it only because of their fear that he would get the political credit. He did not hesitate to ask his listeners to write letters to their legislators indicating what they thought of this. They did so—by the thousands.

He made many other speeches that summer of 1929. He went across the state on the Erie Canal in a small glass-roofed yacht, *Inspector,* to inspect state institutions located near the Canal. But incidentally, and purposely, he was meeting people of all kinds, including many of the leading Republican citizens of the region. He talked personally to many farmers, explaining what he had already done for them, asking for suggestions and advice, promising additional help. He had seen to it that the Democratic State Committee set up a full-time press bureau, and statements began to issue informing farmers and others what had been done for them by Roosevelt.

My wife and I were invited along on some of these barge canal trips. They were leisurely enough to be restful, but when the little boat stopped in one of the locks or at a village, it was a big event in the neighborhood. Many people would come down to the landing place for a glimpse of the Governor. He would greet them smilingly, shake hands with as many as he could; ask how the crops were coming on; and, of course, he would find a discreet way to ask them whether they realized what had been done in Albany to help them on their taxes. He had carefully prepared an estimate on the tax savings for every county in the state and for most of the towns. He kept this estimate in his pocket, and would pull it out frequently to show to an individual or to read to an audience. As the boat pulled out, he would wave and laugh in response to their hearty applause and cheers. At some cities, there would be a parade in his honor which he was delighted to join, waving to the folks lining the sidewalks. Luncheons were given by leading citizens, to which were invited other leading citizens of both parties; they all were given plenty of opportunity to talk with the Governor and ask questions. We visited the grape-growing territory in the Finger Lakes region. FDR was very interested and delighted that New York grapes were being turned into good champagne and other wines, and enjoyed tasting the samples that the farmer had ready for us—in spite of the 90° temperature and the blistering rays of the mid-morning sun.

I shall never forget one incident which showed a great deal about Roosevelt's character as a man of compassion and human sympathy. At a stop at one of the locks, I noticed a young woman standing on the outskirts of the crowd and her young son of about nine, both staring at the braces on the Governor's legs as he sat out on deck talking to some people. The boy was wearing a brace on one leg. She finally mustered the courage to tell one of the state troopers that she would like to talk with the Governor about her boy who had just had an attack of infantile paralysis. When the Governor was informed of this, he smilingly motioned to the young woman and boy to come aboard. The boy was helped aboard by a trooper. She told the Governor that her child had recovered the use of one leg, but had to wear a brace on the other. He showed them the braces on both his own legs, and they were visibly impressed and encouraged to see that one so crippled had become the Governor of New York. We were behind schedule; but the Governor began to talk with the boy. He put his arm around him as he talked. He examined the child's brace, asked him about the treatments he was getting, pointed out how much better the boy could get around than he could, and said: "The important thing is to keep on working at your exercises, especially in the pool, as much as you can—and never get discouraged. I'm sure if you do that, your leg will get well. But even if it doesn't, don't give up; you can get along as well as your friends in everything except running and jumping." The boy seemed very much comforted and happier; and, finally, as the signal for departure came, threw his arms around the Governor, kissed him and insisted on getting off the boat without any help from anyone. As the boat pulled away, he kept waving to us until we were out of sight.

Roosevelt had *not* said to him: "Someday, you might even become Governor of the State of New York."

The three study commissions which FDR had rescued from the 1929 legislative slaughter included one to study the problem of old age security. This proposal was a very radical one in the United States in 1928; indeed, the Governor had to defend it in advance as not "socialistic." The Republican leaders tried to bury the proposal in committee, but Roosevelt kept after it. It was easy for him to rally great public support from liberal organizations. The proposal was finally passed in 1930 after long hearings and debates over the composition of the proposed commission. The Republican legislative leaders were, as usual, building Roosevelt up as a great hero, and tearing themselves down as the villains of the piece.

An example of the many proposals which the legislature did not approve in 1929 was one recommending a commission to study the development of water power by the state. This, like farm relief, was an urgent national problem as well as a New York one. Especially out west, it was the leading problem of the day —and many leaders in the movement for public power around the country were watching to see what Roosevelt would do. The big struggle everywhere was whether water power should be developed by the state or by private corporations. This dispute had deadlocked water power development in New York since the Hughes administration, and had been particularly bitter during Smith's. Roosevelt, well aware of the national as well as state interest, had many times announced—as far back as his speech accepting the nomination as Governor in October 1928—that he was in favor of development of water power by the state, and of continued ownership by the people of all water power sites.

He finally won his three-year fight with the legislature on this subject, but only after appealing time and again by radio to the people of the state.

In a radio speech announcing the legislature's final capitulation, he enumerated several reasons for his victory; then added: "But stronger than all of those put together is the influence of Mr. & Mrs. Average Voter. It may take a good many years to translate the influence of the people of the state into terms of law, but public opinion, when it understands a policy and supports it, is bound to win in the long run." This conviction influenced all his methods of operation as Governor and, later, his style as President.

In general, all the advanced social legislation which Roosevelt was able during his governorship to wrest from the legislative pigeonholes had the same general history: immediate Republican opposition, strong public protests instigated by the Governor, attempts by the legislative leaders to water down the legislation, again inspired public protests, and finally, compromise or capitulation by the legislature. Every one of these instances, of course, enhanced the stature and reputation of Roosevelt throughout the state and nation—the very result the Republican leaders were trying so hard to avoid.

The bills are too numerous to discuss here.[22] However, one additional example must be cited because it probably had more to do with making Roosevelt President of the United States than any other single piece of legislation. It came after his re-election in 1930.

On October 24, 1929, now known as "Black Thursday," Wall Street collapsed in a panic. The Great Hoover Depression began—not as a result of the stock market crash but precipitated by it. Hoover and the Republican leaders had taken the position—and maintained it stubbornly throughout the deepening Depression —that direct relief for unemployment distress was no function of the federal government, but must come exclusively from local charities, cities, counties and villages.

After waiting through the dreary winter and spring and most of the summer of 1931 for some action or some leadership from Washington, Roosevelt decided to assume leadership himself, and to provide action for the State of New York.

It happened that about this time the legislative committee which had been investigating the affairs of New York City asked the Governor to convene the legislature in extraordinary session in order to pass a technical statute which the committee thought necessary for its investigation. The Governor said that he would comply with the request, but he had in mind other matters for the legislature to consider—far more important ones. Under the New York Constitution, the legislature in an extraordinary session can consider only matters specifically submitted to it in writing by the Governor. Consequently, at the same time as he instructed me to draft the necessary message to the legislature, he added: "This is the time to get some direct state action to relieve unemployment. Suppose you take a try at a first draft of a message." He had come to the conclusion that New York should be the first state to provide relief to its great number of unemployed. Charities and local communities had tried; but the need by this time had grown far beyond their means. This kind of direct government action seems quite natural now, indeed, routine; but in 1931, it was a brand-new, extraordinary and startling proposal.

The State of New York was to be the first state to accept that responsibility —under Roosevelt's leadership as Governor; and the United States would accept it later for the first time under his leadership as President.

He told me several times during the drafting of his message that he disliked the payment of money as a dole, that he preferred that the state provide some kind of public work for its unemployed citizens; but that if no such work could be found for them by the state, then, as a last resort, those who remain unemployed through no fault of their own should be given food, clothing and shelter for themselves and their families from public funds.

"The important thing to recognize is that there is a duty on the part of government to do something about this—it just can't sit back and expect private charity or even local government to take care of it entirely."

His message was delivered to the legislature in extraordinary session, in person, on August 28, 1931. It is a landmark date in the history of governmental social thinking in the United States. It contained the first full statement of the underlying concept of the New Deal: that it is the duty of the federal government to use the combined resources of the nation to prevent distress, and to help those who are unable to help themselves because of reasons beyond their control.

The message included these words, which caught the imagination of the entire nation:

"What is the State? It is the duly constituted representative of an organized society of human beings, created by them for their mutual protection and well-being.

"One of these duties of the State is that of caring for those of its citizens who find themselves the victims of such adverse circumstances as make them unable to obtain even the necessities for mere existence without the aid of others. . . .

"The same responsibility of the State undoubtedly applies when widespread economic conditions render large numbers of men and women incapable of supporting either themselves or their families because of circumstances beyond their control which make it impossible for them to find remunerative labor. To these unfortunate citizens, aid must be extended by Government *not as a matter of charity, but as a matter of social duty.*"[23] (Emphasis added)

Pointing out that local charities and local government could no longer meet the new burdens, he recommended that the state immediately appropriate $20 million, to be raised by new taxes and administered by a special temporary emergency organization to provide useful work for the needy where possible, and where such work could not be found, "to provide them with food against starvation and with clothing and shelter against suffering."

In the State of New York, and all through the nation, the message was a breath of fresh air in the stagnant, depressing fog of inaction and indecision which had come from Washington. If there was such a thing as a Roosevelt Revolution, this was the first shot. It was heard around the nation.

It seems unbelievable, but the Republican leaders at Albany in 1931, in the face of all the distress and destitution among so many residents of New York who had looked in vain for work, decided to oppose Roosevelt even on this recommendation. He had publicly offered to let Republican legislators introduce the legislation, and, in this way, to share the political credit with him. Roosevelt, the politician, did not usually make such a noble gesture to his political opponents. His offer in 1931 showed that he wanted to avoid another of the long battles of the past three sessions—and to get relief to the hungry as quickly as possible. Intelligent—or even average—leadership in the Republican Party would have eagerly seized upon his offer; but Roosevelt's political luck and blessing in having stupid Republican legislative opposition did not fail him this time—in the politically most important recommendation of his governorship.

The Republican leaders rejected his offer of sharing the credit with them. Instead, in a fanatical attempt to stop Roosevelt's bold, far-sighted program—and his political progress—they introduced, and threatened to pass, their own bill, which provided that the administration of relief should be placed in one of the regular departments of the state which was headed by a Republican; and that instead of a direct appropriation, the state should agree merely to match any and all local grants of money for this type of relief. Of course they knew, or should have known, that the local governments neither could nor would pay out monies in substantial amounts for this purpose. In spite of almost universal dissent, even from the Republican State Chairman, they stuck to their guns; they were prepared, with their clear majority of votes, to force through their own legislation, and immediately thereafter to adjourn. Roosevelt again took to the radio. He explained the defects of their program: that it would put relief in the hands of bureaucrats, and would provide a blank check to localities which might bankrupt themselves and the state. He threatened to veto their bill if they did pass it, and stated that he would immediately call the legislature into a second extraordinary session to pass an effective bill. At the very last hour, the Republican leaders, knowing that the Governor would again provoke public outrage, capitulated.

The newspapers soon began to call this new Temporary Emergency Relief Administration by its initials, T.E.R.A. This was the first of the scores of alphabetical agencies to be set up by Roosevelt as Governor, and later as President. For the same reasons that Roosevelt refused to put the functions and duties of T.E.R.A. in one of the old-line departments of the state, he would later refuse to put the many other new alphabetical agencies in the old-line departments of the federal government. What he wanted for these separate agencies, all having new and untried powers, was men of bold imagination, infinite resourcefulness and capacity for new ideas—who would not get bogged down by the outmoded thinking of the regular bureaucratic departments. This became his regular style as he moved on to the national scene to cope with the Depression by experimental and imaginative legislation.

The message and the victory which followed in 1931 had a public impact all over the country, greater than any of the other accomplishments during his governorship. Roosevelt's lead in the race for the Democratic nomination to oppose President Hoover in 1932 was greatly widened. The contrast between Roosevelt's bold experimental action and Hoover's temporizing refusal to act at all was made dramatically clear and unmistakable by this episode in New York State to the mass of American voters as well as the Democratic political leaders. It was not merely the contrast between two methods or styles; it was the contrast between the new venturesome philosophy which became the New Deal, and the old, dying rugged individualism of Hoover and his associates.

Roosevelt's election victory in 1930, ten months before this unemployment message, was the culmination of much hard work and preparation. During the summer preceding the election campaign, he kept building up a personal New York State following to assure his re-election in November. And he also devoted much time and attention to building up the Democratic Party in upstate New York. For, although he had already been mentioned in 1930 by Senator Burton K. Wheeler and other prominent progressives as the next Presidential nominee, he knew that if he lost in 1930, the White House would be a very dim prospect.

Prohibition had become an important state issue in 1930. Roosevelt had shamelessly continued to straddle this issue in spite of all efforts to smoke him out. But during the summer of 1930, he again made trips by boat through the canal system. He discussed many issues with local leaders to learn what their constituents were thinking; the chief issues were unemployment and prohibition. On the basis of what he learned in gauging sentiment around the state on prohibition he finally broke his silence, and stopped his pussyfooting. On September 9, 1930, he came out in favor of repeal of prohibition and the enactment of a new constitutional amendment which would leave control over intoxicants with the respective states.

The timing of this statement was perfect. It was the end of a ten-year straddle; and by 1932 prohibition would lose potency as an issue. For by that time—though Roosevelt could not have foreseen it in 1930—the overpowering issue would not be what you could drink, but what you could earn to buy something to eat. As President, Roosevelt would use the same kind of style in political straddling, awaiting the proper timing for a definite decision.

As the 1930 campaign time came around, and unemployment got worse and worse, Roosevelt decided to run against the Hoover administration as well as against the reactionary Republican leaders of the state. The Republicans had elected to run against Tammany Hall. This, of course, made Tammany fight triply hard for Roosevelt to save their own skins from the United States Attorney, Charles Tuttle, Roosevelt's opponent who had already exposed a great deal of Tammany corruption.

The issue between liberalism and conservatism in New York State was even more sharply defined in the 1930 re-election campaign than it had been two years before. The bitter legislative struggles of the two sessions of 1929 and 1930 had highlighted and emphasized the differences between the two political parties. The Governor concentrated much of his fire on this issue. But he realized that, if he was to win by a substantial majority, he would have to win the votes of many hundreds of thousands of normally Republican voters. He did not want to alienate them by making attacks on "Republicans" or even on the "Republican Party," so he followed a practice that he continued through all his Albany and Washington days—centering his attack on the Republican leadership and leaders.

In his acceptance speech in 1930 FDR struck a note that was soon to grow in volume, and develop into forceful and repeated attacks upon the Hoover administration:

"Lack of leadership at Washington has brought our country face to face with serious questions of unemployment and financial depression. Each state must meet this situation as best it can. . . ."

During the campaign, he repeatedly blamed the Republican federal administration, first for not putting brakes on the speculation orgy of 1928 and 1929; second, for concealing the seriousness of the situation after the crash of October 1929, and issuing false, optimistic statements about it; and third, for failure to take quick and decisive action on it. He would say that he was making these points only to prove an old thesis of his that "No political party has any monopoly on prosperity," although the Republican Party had for many years preached, apparently successfully, that it had.

As another main thesis of the 1930 campaign, he hammered home what he had already accomplished in two short years: labor legislation, old age pensions, construction of hospitals, public works, cheap electricity, regulation of public utilities, relief for farmers, prison reform, and the other items of his program.

His knack of homely exposition—which would be prominent time and again in his style as President—enabled him to get across to the people in understandable language his ideas about complicated or technical subjects such as, for example, cheap electricity. Instead of talking about kilowatt hours and the technical machinery for developing and transmitting water power, he discussed in "one-syllable words" how little it cost a housewife in Toronto, Canada, where water power was developed publicly, to use electric appliances like a stove, refrigerator, iron, toaster, vacuum cleaner, waffle iron, and so on, and then contrasted that cost with the large sum it would cost a housewife in Syracuse or Brooklyn or Utica to use the same appliances. Graphic campaign pamphlets were prepared with pictures of the appliances and specific figures showing the great disparity of cost; they were distributed by hundreds of thousands throughout the state. The speeches and the campaign pamphlets about cheap electricity got so much attention and circulation that many newspapers began to refer to the 1930 campaign as a "waffle-iron" campaign.

His position on state issues was piling up greater support for him upstate every day, and his new stand on prohibition was giving him more than the usual Democratic strength in the large cities. The Republican administration in Washington was getting scared. If Roosevelt was to be stopped for 1932, the time to do it was in 1930. So, in their desperation, the Washington Republican leaders made the mistake that Roosevelt nearly always avoided (except for the ill-fated "purge" of 1938): they decided to send into New York some of their leading political figures to campaign against him in this state election.

Three high Cabinet officers appeared on the stump in New York: the Secretary of State, Henry L. Stimson; the Under Secretary of Treasury, Ogden L. Mills; and the Secretary of War, Patrick Hurley. Most of their attacks, especially Stimson's, were directed at the charges of Democratic corruption in New York City. The weight of these gentlemen began to be felt in the campaign.

How should this be handled? Roosevelt decided on ridicule, one of his most effective political speaking weapons, and a style to which he returned on many occasions. The speech in answer to the three Cabinet officers was the last one of the campaign. It is hardly remembered now; but in its own way, it was comparable in its use of ridicule to the use of "Martin, Barton and Fish" in the 1940 campaign[24] and to the "Fala" speech[25] of 1944:

"Before we look into the soundness of the instructions given to the people of this State by these representatives from Washington, we have a right to demand that they show their credentials. Of these three estimable gentlemen, one comes from that great State of Oklahoma, which we all respect. He has never lived in New York State; he knows nothing of the problems of New York State; he knows nothing of the situation in New York City; he knows nothing of the requirements and necessities of the twelve million people in this State. . . . And yet, he comes to us presumably only by virtue of his great office. Well may the people of New York State resent this, as would the people of Oklahoma if the tables were turned.

"The other two gentlemen of this triumvirate, the Secretary of State and the Under-Secretary of the Treasury, are both citizens of this State. The credentials that they present to the people of the State as authorizing them to give instructions are the same in both cases. Both of them have run for Governor of the State of New York in campaigns based largely on the same kind of merits as are being employed in this campaign. Both of them were defeated at the polls by the people of this State. The people did not believe in them or in their issues *then,* and they will not believe in them or in their issues *now.* . . .

"I say to these gentlemen: We shall be grateful if you will return to your posts in Washington, and bend your efforts, and spend your time solving the problems which the whole nation is bearing under your Administration. Rest assured that we of the Empire State can and will take care of ourselves and our problems."[26]

In that same final speech—and not until then—he paid some attention to the charges which had been hurled at him almost every day of the campaign about corruption and bribery in the selection of judges in New York City.

Roosevelt, in all his campaigns for Governor and later for the presidency, maintained as part of his style of campaigning a cardinal principle: that a candidate should pick his own battleground in a political campaign, just as a general does in a military campaign. By the same token, he said: "Never let your opponent pick the battleground on which to fight. If he picks one, stay off that battlefield, and let him fight it out all by himself." He recommended this style to Wilson in 1916 (see page 276) and invariably used it in his campaigns as President.

Since in this 1930 campaign the Republican strategy was to use New York City corruption as almost the sole battleground, Roosevelt spoke about everything *except* corruption in New York City. The more his opponent Charles H. Tuttle talked about New York City judges, the more Roosevelt talked about water power, cheap electricity, and old age pensions. He completely and consistently ignored both the Republican charges and the Republican candidate. Because of the monotonous daily repetition by Tuttle, these charges had slipped from the first to the obituary page. In New York City he decided to meet them once, and only once—and to meet them head-on. This is what he did. He recited everything he had done, and could have done, to uncover the facts, and to punish the criminals. He expressed resentment at the false charge that he had refused to "lift a finger to restore confidence in the courts, and punish the guilty." Then he concluded: "If there is corruption in our courts, I will use every rightful power of the office of Governor to drive it out; and I will do this regardless of whether it affects, or may affect, any Democratic or any Republican organization . . . in any one of the five counties of New York City or in any one of the fifty-seven other counties of the State. This is clear. That is unequivocal. That is simple honesty. That is justice. That is American. That is right."

The New York City speech was successful in both objectives he had in mind: to remove by ridicule the effect of the speeches of the Washington Cabinet officers, and finally to meet directly—once only—the attacks arising out of charges of New York City corruption.

The results of the 1930 campaign made new political history in New York, and sent across the nation a tidal wave of Democratic enthusiasm. Roosevelt was elected by the unprecedented plurality of 725,001 votes. The highest Democratic plurality before that had been 386,000—for Smith in 1922. Upstate New York, which for generations had been conceded to be safely Republican, gave Democratic Roosevelt, for the first time in the state's history, a plurality. It was a plurality of 167,784 votes, a plurality in forty-one of the fifty-seven upstate counties.

What were the reasons for this extraordinary outcome in 1930? It was not only the Hoover Depression. It was the style of Roosevelt, the statesman and the liberal leader: his program of help to the farmer, the laborer, the aged, the consumer, the housewife; his whole social attitude.

It was also the style of the politician and political strategist: his buildup of the Democratic Party upstate, his unflagging interest in all political details, which he discussed twice a week with the chairman of the New York State Democratic Committee, James A. Farley; his constant trips around the state; his close attention to the public relations of his office; his many radio speeches; and his ability to put complicated problems of state government into simple language which the voters could understand. Climaxing all of this was FDR's warmth, which he conveyed to the people of the state with whom he talked over the air.

All of this constituted a style which he was to continue just as successfully as Presidential candidate four different times.

Overnight, the election results—especially those upstate—made Roosevelt a powerful contender for the Democratic nomination for the presidency two years ahead.

In Roosevelt's favor, of course, there had been a number of other tangibles and intangibles. His name was still a great factor. His energy and physical stamina had practically obviated any public concern about his health. His many successful struggles with the New York legislative leaders—even his unsuccessful ones—had proven his boldness, initiative, imaginativeness, aggressiveness and spiritual leadership. His smile had become a national asset—people like a leader who can smile. He seemed to be on terms of close relationship with all the 12 million people of his state. In this respect the contrast to Hoover was dramatic.

He also knew how to talk to politicians and political leaders in their own language. When national leaders visited him at the Executive Mansion—and he saw to it that such visits were frequent—they came away impressed. They had met a reformer, true; but they had also met a practical fellow who knew their own problems as politicians, and was willing—indeed anxious—to discuss them frankly.

He had raised the level of public understanding of government issues by his frank and simple talks about them directly to the people of the state. He had also raised the level of debate in the legislature itself by his frequent meetings with Democratic legislators, encouraging, and teaching them state issues.

Very shortly after the extraordinary victory of 1930, we were embarked on another campaign. It was the campaign for the Presidential nomination.

As is customary, it was not an open campaign effort of his own; rather, it was conducted by the friends of the candidate. But FDR was always consulted on strategy and even on many details; he was kept advised of every move; no important decision was made without his prior approval; and he knew that everything he said or did from that time on would be interpreted in the light of his candidacy and would affect it.

The national political atmosphere in 1932 demanded a progressive Democrat who liked and practiced bold action—the very antithesis of Hoover. Roosevelt fitted the bill perfectly. If being a progressive means the willingness to advocate change in order to meet changing conditions, that was the very foundation of Roosevelt's political thinking. The dictum of Macaulay, "Reform if you would preserve," was one of Roosevelt's maxims, which as Governor and President he quoted frequently and observed always. That was why he was always so receptive to new ideas; why in administering affairs of state he believed so strongly in "bold, persistent experimentation."

In physical appearance, he had the dignity and the bearing that Americans like to see in their Presidents. He disdained any attempts at pretentiousness. He did not seek to impose respect toward himself on visitors or friends or servants; like all natural-born leaders, he seemed to command respect and even affection —unconsciously and without effort.

His campaigning of 1928 and 1930 had shown what a great campaigner he could become in 1932. So it was no wonder that, aided by Farley's services in corralling delegates, Roosevelt by the spring of 1932 had forged way out in front in the political race for the nomination. The story of the campaign for the nomination, of the convention itself and of the campaign for election has been told in many books; it will not be repeated here. I propose to refer only to those matters which indicate his later style as President—for the closer he came to the White House, the more clearly his style, his social philosophy and his conception of the presidency emerged.

As I contemplated the coming pre-convention campaign, I realized that Roosevelt would require help in the formulation of national policies, not only to meet the immediate crisis but for long-range reform and recovery. He had, during his governorship, called in experts on particular technical problems. But his present need was for help in the formulation of policy, rather than in merely ascertaining facts or seeking technical expertise; and it was required on a national rather than a state basis. The whole American economy was going rapidly to pieces before our eyes. Financial experts were being called down to Washington almost daily to consult with President Hoover; but things kept getting worse.

Early in 1932, I suggested to him the formation of a group, for advice on policy. He asked what I had in mind.

"Usually in a situation like this," I said, "a candidate gathers around him a group composed of some successful industrialists, some big financiers, and some national political leaders. I think we ought to steer clear of all those. They all seem to have failed to produce anything constructive to solve the mess we're in today. So why not go to the universities of the country? You have been having some good experience with college professors. I think they wouldn't be afraid to strike out on new paths just because the paths are new. They would get away from the old fuzzy thinking which certainly has failed; and that seems to me to be the most important thing."

He asked what I would have them do, and I replied:

"I don't know exactly; we'll have to kind of feel our way as we go along. My thought is that if we can get a small group together willing to give us some time, they can prepare memoranda for you about such things as the national relief of agriculture, tariffs, railroads, government debts, private credit, money, gold standard—all the matters that enter into the present crisis; the things on which you will have to take a definite stand in the campaign. You'll want to talk with them youself, and maybe out of all the talk some concrete ideas will come."

I got the green light, and proceeded at once to get a group together. Thus was born a new phrase in American political jargon: the "Brain Trust."

I have told in *Working with Roosevelt*,[27] as have others, about the composition of the group, the way it functioned and the work it did. It was the beginning of Roosevelt's style during his presidency to look frequently to university professors for advice on national problems.

He was greatly helped by the Brain Trust. He appreciated their importance and assistance, and went out of his way to say so. Three days after his inauguration, while he was waiting to see what Congress would do with his first legislative proposal on the closed banks all over the nation and when he was probably as busy and as occupied as any day during his presidency, he took the time and trouble to write me this letter (reproduced on page 308).

The letter, incidentally, also shows how wrong some writers have been in calling him a man who never showed gratitude for help and service. I have several other letters which prove my point.

The short "Forgotten Man" speech which he made by radio on April 7, 1932, threw down a liberal challenge to all his conservative rivals for the nomination. The philosophy of that speech was to govern all Roosevelt's actions and experiments in Washington: that sound prosperity depends upon plans "that rest upon the forgotten, the unorganized but indispensable units of economic power . . . that build from the bottom up, and not from the top down, that put their faith once more in the *forgotten man* at the bottom of the economic pyramid."[28] (Emphasis added) It was a complete antithesis to the philosophy which had prevailed in Washington since 1920—the "trickle-down theory," that taking care of the few at the top of the economic pyramid means their prosperity will trickle down to those at the bottom. That Washington philosophy in 1932 had definitely been proven a failure. There had been very little "trickle."

The "forgotten man" to Roosevelt was not merely an oratorical abstraction. He was a living human being—in many different capacities; he was the man without money, power or social position; he was the worker in the sweatshop; he was the small farmer who had to face the problem of a high mortgage and a low cash income; he was the little businessman struggling against ever-growing monopoly, the housewife beset with high prices and a thin pay envelope, the youngster who had to go to an inferior and impoverished local school, the child laborer, the unemployed, the destitute aged, and the handicapped. These were the people of the United States who were to receive Roosevelt's major attention and concern during his presidency.

Into this ten-minute "Forgotten Man" speech Roosevelt was able to crowd many intimations of things to come—all based on that general philosophy:

March 9, 1933.

Dear Sammy:-

I am waiting to hear what the Congress will do with my first bill. We worked until two o'clock this morning preparing it and it seemed queer to do this kind of work without you. After four years of such close association it is not easy to work with others.

I want you to know how grateful I am for the fine loyalty you have shown and for the unselfish service you gave me during the campaign. Even though you were not with me all the time I knew how hard you were working behind closed doors in smoke-filled rooms, and your contribution of Ray and Rex was probably the best that anyone made during the whole campaign.

I hardly need tell you that I want you to feel perfectly free to telephone or come to see me at any time. If I can be of help to you please let me know. I do hope that we will see you and Dorothy here in Washington often. Our contact has been too close to need constant correspondence or conversations. I just want you to know of my feeling toward you and my gratitude for all that you did.

As ever yours,

Franklin D. Roosevelt

Hon. Samuel I. Rosenman,
444 Central Park West,
New York, N. Y.

Increase the purchasing power of the half of our population who live by "farming or in small towns whose existence immediately depends on farms." The interdependence of the "city worker's employment" and the "farmer's dollar" makes this essential. (Here was the germ of the Agricultural Adjustment Act and of "parity.")

Prevent foreclosures of homes and farm mortgages. (Here were the germs of the Home Owners Loan Corporation and the Farm Credit Administration.)

Assist small local banks who lend on homes and farms as well as the giant city banks miles away. (Here was the new policy which was to govern the Reconstruction Finance Corporation after 1933.)

Reduce tariff walls in order to enable us to sell our surplus manufactures abroad, and to provide "a reciprocal exchange of goods." (Here was the germ of the Reciprocal Trade Agreements Act.)

And, foreshadowing his first Inaugural Address in which he was to say that he would not hesitate to ask Congress, if it became necessary to meet the emergency of the Depression, to give him all the powers essential to wage a war, he added: "It is high time to admit with courage that we are in the midst of an emergency at least equal to that of war. Let us mobilize to meet it." Smith, now grown conservative, called it "demagogic," echoing the cry of anguish which arose from all conservatives and devotees of the status quo.

This speech was followed a month later by another which also set an important style for Roosevelt's actions all through his presidency—experimentation. It was delivered at Oglethorpe University in Atlanta on May 22, 1932. The theme was that "the country needs . . . the country demands bold, persistent experimentation . . . it is common sense to take a method and try it. If it fails, admit it frankly and try another. But above all, try something. The millions who are in want will not stand by silently forever, while the things to satisfy their needs are within easy reach."

As we shall see, experimentation became a watchword for future New Deal programs. Roosevelt felt confident that he could finally always get a desired result by continual experimentation. Experimentation is, of course, the handmaiden of action; and it was the insistence upon action which dominated the Roosevelt presidency—in peacetime, in wartime, and in erecting the foundations for a peaceful postwar world.

As the convention drew nearer, Roosevelt had to play the fox more and more, the lion less and less. He had established his great reputation with strong, affirmative, liberal action. But this would not be enough to get the nomination. He had to look for delegates where he could find them: in the more conservative East, the progressive West, among intellectuals, and also in the unsavory political organizations of the big cities.

He often said that the only way he could put any social program of reform into effect and obtain the objectives he was seeking was first to get elected.

"A man in the Executive Mansion or in the White House is in a position to do wonders toward the kind of social justice he wants to fight for. The same man, as a private individual, can only urge and recommend, but he can take no direct action of any significant kind. The first step in any political or social crusade is to get elected to a place from which he can direct and control it."

The difficult job in 1932 was not to get elected; it was to get nominated—and in those days it was made more difficult by the fact that nomination by a Democratic National Convention required a two-thirds vote.

He could point easily and proudly to a clear-cut successful progressive domestic program as Governor. However, on foreign policy he had remained silent—especially on the vital issue of the League of Nations—as long as he could. But he was being constantly attacked for his silence by the progressive leaders on the one side, and by the far more numerous anti-Leaguers and isolationists on the other. Finally, in his efforts to hold isolationist Democrats (especially in the South and West) who were influenced by the powerful Hearst papers, and fearful of possible war by any commitment of the United States to any form of collective international security, he spoke out. He declared that he would not favor the United States now joining the League of Nations. He said that he had fought for the League in 1920, and had no apologies to make for it. But he added, quite correctly, that the League of 1932 was not the League conceived in 1919 by Woodrow Wilson—which it might have become had the United States originally entered it. This statement by Roosevelt caused consternation among most of his progressive followers, as he knew it would. But there were many millions of voters suspicious of all foreign nations and much more intimately engrossed in 1932 with the growing crisis of depression.

Another issue on which he was walking a tightrope was prohibition. He repeated his 1930 statement, which had proven successful in New York, in favor of repealing the Prohibition Amendment and returning control of alcoholic beverages to the states. The "Drys" did not like it; but the alternative choices of Smith and Ritchie, both extreme "Wets," were much worse. He was, and always would be, a practical man of politics.

During the spring and early summer while all the maneuvering for delegates to the national convention was feverishly going on, the troublesome question of Tammany Hall and New York City corruption began to reach a climax.

The Republican leaders in New York State, continuing their old efforts of 1929 and 1930 to "stop Roosevelt in 1932," were bent now on using the issues of corruption in New York City and the alleged unwillingness of Roosevelt to alienate the Tammany Hall and New York City vote by forthright action. Their setback in the 1930 election did not discourage them.

The story of their efforts in 1931 and 1932 is not strictly relevant here, because Roosevelt was to have no similar problem as President. However, it does show how adroit a politician he was—both as a lion and as a fox—in meeting this grave threat to his ultimate political ambition, and even in finally managing it to his own political advantage. It is also important in that it gave Roosevelt the opportunity to enunciate his high standard of political morality—a standard upon which he would, as President, insist. It also illustrates two personal characteristics which were to continue with him as President and influence a great deal of his style: his secretiveness and his vindictiveness.

The Republican leaders of 1931 saw Roosevelt's political dilemma as clearly as he did. The political considerations on both sides were also quite clear to every intelligent voter. Roosevelt knew that if he really waded into New York City corruption, he might destroy one of the strong organizations he needed for support in the 1932 convention. If he refused to do anything, he would give the appearance of condoning corruption for his own political advantage.

If the Republican leaders had really been interested in uncovering corruption, it would have been quite simple for them to have done in 1929 or 1930 what they finally had to do in 1931—set up a legislative committee to conduct a general investigation into the affairs of New York City. But their interests were not the "affairs of the city," or its corruption, or its grafting officials. Their only interests were Roosevelt himself—and the election of 1932. So they continued to try to put him into a political straitjacket. But as Professor Freidel has said so graphically, "The Republicans found themselves trying to pin down a drop of mercury with a blunt instrument."[29]

Roosevelt was determined not to adopt either extreme of the dilemma but to walk the slippery, "mercurial," twisting road between them. He would take action in particular cases where he had the specific legal power to investigate or remove an official, such as a sheriff or district attorney or Mayor. But he would not himself enter into any broad general investigation, because he claimed—with legal justification—that a roving investigation into the affairs of any city was not his duty or even his constitutional right, that the power rested only with the legislature. But the legislative leaders were not even slightly interested in the abstract question of legal jurisdiction and constitutional power. They knew that thousands of liberal supporters of Roosevelt wanted direct action from him— irrespective of legal jurisdiction—against Tammany Hall, all its leaders, and all the public officials which it had sponsored.

Roosevelt had indeed already taken action when specific charges, based on evidence instead of rumor, were presented to him against individuals who by law he could discipline or remove. His action in these instances was direct and forceful, but this tended to be forgotten as new acts of misfeasance were publicized.

To give the highlights of only a few actions he had taken:

1. On August 19, 1930, he had removed from the hands of the District Attorney of New York County the investigation of one city magistrate charged with buying his job from a district political leader in New York City; he had placed it in the hands of the Republican Attorney General of the state, Hamilton Ward; he had also assigned a Republican judge to a special term to supervise the investigation, with a "blue-ribbon" grand jury to carry it forward. This action was clearly within his power under a specific statute, which provided for this exact procedure whenever the Governor felt that any local official was not performing his duty satisfactorily.

2. On August 21, 1930, he had recommended to the appellate division of the Supreme Court in New York that it conduct a general investigation of all magistrates in the city, because the appellate division alone had the power to investigate, remove or discipline such magistrates.

3. On March 10, 1931, he had appointed a highly respected former judge and practicing lawyer, Hon. Samuel Seabury, to hear the charges filed with the Governor against District Attorney of New York City Thomas Crain. The Governor had the specific constitutional power to remove district attorneys and, consequently, to investigate their conduct preparatory to so doing.

4. In September 1930, sixteen district leaders in Tammany Hall, including the boss himself, John F. Curry, were subpoenaed to appear before the grand jury by Attorney General Ward, who had the power under the aforementioned authority given him by Roosevelt to subpoena them. They all refused to sign waivers of immunity. Roosevelt immediately wired the Mayor of New York, James Walker, to direct those of his subordinates who had been summoned to sign waivers or resign. Walker complied.

The charges and countercharges which continued to appear in the press, the multiplicity of requests for investigation—some of which were granted and some denied—were confusing to the ordinary voter in New York State. Many intellectuals in and outside the state, not understanding the technical provisions of New York statutes—and really having no interest in them—complained of "temporizing" and "shillyshallying." Roosevelt was firmly convinced that he was right, and stuck to his course. I too thought he was absolutely right in his interpretation of the constitution and statutes of New York, and as his counsel, I so advised him.

If Roosevelt had been willing to act in a recklessly courageous lion-like fashion, he could have ordered his own roving investigation into the affairs of New York City, and let the courts decide whether he had the constitutional power to do so. But, had he done this, how could he have avoided doing the same for many other cities in the state where charges of corruption were being made from time to time? Roosevelt's was the only statesman-like course to take; it did finally succeed. But for him it was a constant source of worry, because so many respected and intelligent people were pressing him to go ahead without regard to what they called "the legal niceties." Roosevelt, by reckless action, stood to lose not only all the votes of Tammany Hall in the forthcoming Presidential convention, but also those controlled by the political bosses of Illinois, Indiana, New Jersey and several other states, who were closely watching what he would do, and would look upon him as a potential danger to their own power.

Finally, in 1931, the Republican legislative leaders created a legislative committee controlled by Republicans and chaired by a prominent Republican senator. They invested it with full powers to conduct a roving investigation into all the affairs of New York City. And they appointed as counsel former Judge Samuel Seabury. Roosevelt had repeatedly suggested that a legislative committee was the only legal way for a general investigation; he readily signed the appropriation of $500,000 for its expenses.

The investigation began to produce daily headlines of graft and corruption throughout city offices leading up to the Mayor himself. Walker was serving his second term as Mayor. He was a brilliant man, a scintillating orator but a notorious playboy, who was more interested in nightclubs than in municipal affairs.

The first public officer named officially by Seabury in a report to the Governor as a result of this new investigation was Thomas M. Farley, a typical Tammany Hall district leader of those days—uneducated, rough, insensitive, a hero in his local district who could always deliver the votes on Election Day. He was the sheriff of New York County, a job which required little work, no thought and little time, but which was one of great political influence. The charges, based not on rumor but on proven testimony and bank records, included one that, though his total salary as sheriff for the last seven-year period was only $87,000, and though he had no other apparent source of income, his bank accounts for those years showed deposits of $396,000. His explanation of the origin of these funds was ridiculous—that they came from a wonderful little tin box he owned. This provided a new idiom in the English language, which became very popular in the newspapers and in conversation in 1932, "a little tin box."

Here, the Governor could act forcefully, for he had the legal power to remove sheriffs. He did. He received the charges on December 30, 1931, and sent them immediately to Farley for reply. The reply came on February 1, 1932. The Governor set a hearing before himself for February 16, 1932. Seabury, Farley and

Farley's lawyer appeared before the Governor. I sat alongside the Governor, as his counsel. He had done his homework, and had discussed with me all the relevant documents and testimony. At the hearing, he asked questions of the accused which showed his familiarity with the record. Farley made the same ridiculous explanation to him of the source of his funds.

On February 24, 1932, the Governor removed him, with a memorandum repeating the following significant statement which he had made during the hearing:

"As a matter of general sound public policy, I am very certain that there is a requirement that where a public official is under inquiry or investigation, especially an elected public official, and it appears that his scale of living, or the total of his bank deposits far exceeds the public salary which he is known to have received, he, the elected public official, owes a positive public duty to the community to give a reasonable and credible explanation of the sources of the deposits, or the source which enables him to maintain a scale of living beyond the amount of his salary.

"While this rule may seem to be an enlargement of any previous ruling by a Governor of this State, it is time, I believe, that the standard of the conduct of public officer be put on a plane of personal as well as official honesty and that therefore, there is a positive duty on the part of the public official to explain matters which arise on an inquiry which involve the expenditure or the depositing of large sums of money."

He added:

"The stewardship of public offices is a serious and sacred trust. They are so close to the means for private gain that in a sense not at all true of private citizens their personal possessions are invested with a public importance in the event that their stewardship is questioned. One of their deep obligations is to recognize this, not reluctantly or with resistance, but freely. It is in the true spirit of a public trust to give, when personally called upon, public proof of the nature, source and extent of their financial affairs. . . ."[30]

This was the standard of financial integrity which Roosevelt would set for all federal public officers throughout his presidency. During the twelve years he served in Washington, no scandal involving bribery or financial corruption on the part of any federal public official ever appeared. This is particularly significant when one considers the billions of dollars expended so quickly on direct relief and on public works to provide relief for the unemployed. It is even more extraordinary in the light of the many more billions of dollars spent each year in building up defenses after 1939, and in waging war after Pearl Harbor. It is true that there were a few local political scandals arising out of the way relief funds were distributed, but the amounts involved were picayune; and never was the charge made that any official of the federal government received any corrupt money in relief administration.

Early in his administration, he laid down a rule of political behavior in Washington which was closely obeyed. At a press conference on January 17, 1934, for example, he received a question which had evidently been planted:

"Q. Mr. President, quite a few of us have been writing stories about the activities of National Committeemen practicing before the Departments, and some have gone so far as to say that it is embarrassing the Administration. Have you anything to say on that?"

He answered: "I think if we can avoid reference to individuals, it is all right to talk about the general principle. I have felt all along that it is not quite in accord with the spirit of the Administration that any individual who holds a high Party position, such as National Committeeman, should earn a livelihood by practicing law, because, in a sense, he holds himself out as having access to the back door of the Administration. It just 'is not done. . . .' "[31]

This was a further advance in public morality since the Tom Farley dictum of 1932.

Finally, on June 8, 1932, less than a month before the national convention was to meet, the climax of the legislative investigation was reached—a climax which the Republican leaders had sought by so many intrigues and political machinations to bring about.

On that day, Seabury sent to the Governor what he called "the stenographic transcript of the testimony taken before the Joint Legislative Committee to Investigate the Affairs of the City of New York in so far as it relates to the conduct of the Hon. James J. Walker while he has held the office of Mayor." The transcript and an analysis of the evidence were, Seabury wrote, "presented in my individual capacity as a citizen of the State of New York and not as the representative of, or counsel to the committee," and were submitted, "not as formal charges, but for your information so that you may determine what should be done." No adequate explanation was offered—or asked for—as to: (1) Why the legislative committee itself did not take this action; (2) why the transmittal was in an individual capacity and not as counsel (except an obviously specious one that the duties of counsel had ended with the end of the hearings); and (3) why there was no request in Seabury's letter actually to remove the Mayor—in fact, not even formal charges. Obviously some kind of mysterious political reasoning was at work which neither the Governor nor anyone else could ascertain. Two other citizens separately filed formal charges against the Mayor, and did formally request his removal—all on Seabury's documents. Many people at the time linked this devious procedure in some way with the growing awareness that Seabury was still politically ambitious, and that he hoped that somehow as a result of his "individual" efforts, lightning might strike him at the forthcoming convention.

All three documents were forwarded (with a public announcement of the fact) to the Mayor on June 21, 1932, requesting an answer by him. The Mayor's answer had not arrived by the time the convention convened in Chicago.

During the voting at the convention, Mayor Walker, a delegate, made a dramatic personal announcement from the floor of his vote; it was for Smith. This was in line with the action of all the other delegates controlled by the city political leaders, except those of the Bronx under the control of Edward J. Flynn who was supporting Roosevelt. It is difficult to understand the political strategy of Tammany Hall in thus throwing down the gauntlet to the Governor, because it was clear that no matter who was nominated in Chicago, Roosevelt would still be Governor until December 31, and would still be empowered to remove the Mayor. If it was intended as a threat to Roosevelt that they would try to defeat him in New York in the election, it was a silly one. Roosevelt needed their votes only for the nomination; the election was obviously going to be easy. He would no longer need them after his nomination; indeed, he would then feel more confident about the rest of the country without Tammany Hall around his neck.

When the convention closed after nominating Roosevelt, Walker's answer had still not arrived. It did not arrive until Roosevelt had publicly expressed impatience with the delay, implying that the Mayor was stalling. Finally, on July 28,

1932, the answer came in; it was sent by the Governor to Seabury for reply; a telling reply came in promptly on August 2, 1932. The Governor thereupon directed the Mayor to appear before him in Albany for a hearing on August 11, 1932. Seabury was also notified.

The eyes of the nation were turned toward the Executive Chamber in Albany when the hearings opened. All the intrigues of the Republican legislative leaders, all the publicity emanating (sometimes surreptitiously) from the hearings before the committee, all the maneuvering of Tammany Hall and of the political bosses of New York, had succeeded in making the Walker Case and Roosevelt the center of national attention. To me, it is no mere coincidence that the date set by Roosevelt for the hearings to begin was the same date that had been previously set by President Hoover to deliver his belated acceptance speech of the Republican nomination. The two events shared the front pages.

At a time when Roosevelt should have been preparing for active campaigning for the President, he had to remain in Albany conducting the hearings for fourteen full days from August 11 through September 2, 1932.

A less shrewd fox than Roosevelt, under all these circumstances—the open defiance by Walker and Tammany Hall, and the thinly veiled threat and challenge at the convention—would have tried to assume the role of an avenging angel, excoriating Walker's misconduct in office and his evasion of questions. Not Roosevelt. He knew that every word, every action of his, would be broadcast throughout the nation; he therefore assumed the role of the most impartial of judges—courteous in spite of provocation, non-political, objective, attentive, putting questions calmly, always with a friendly smile. He even started by announcing that if the Mayor or his counsel wanted any witnesses not previously called by the legislative committee, he would entertain and give consideration to the request.

Roosevelt had prepared for these hearings with great energy and at the expense of precious time. As he continued expertly to question the Mayor, and to display the patience of a Job, respect for him grew—especially among those who had regarded his past conduct with Tammany Hall as too gentle and evasive. He was moving with great care in reaching a decision.

I feel quite confident that, as the testimony proceeded, Roosevelt was gradually concluding that he would have to remove the Mayor. But he never had to decide. We were discussing the proceedings one night in his little study in the Mansion—O'Connor, Moley, several others, and I—when a telegram came in from Walker. It was his resignation. The hearings were over; the matter was finished. We were all relieved. The resignation was hailed as the result of Roosevelt's strong stand against Tammany Hall. Just as his fight in 1911 with the Hall helped launch him on his political career, his fight in 1932 with the Hall helped win his election to the presidency.

No one knew then, or knows now, or ever learned later, how he would have decided—except only Roosevelt himself. This was a part of the style of Roosevelt which was fixed and remained unchanged: secretiveness. On many important matters, he refused, as President, to take anyone into his full confidence, keeping his own final options open for himself. And by "anyone," I mean anyone—including Mrs. Roosevelt, Louis Howe, Harry Hopkins, or anyone else. There were to be many examples of this secretiveness during his presidency, not the least of which was his decision whether or not to run for a third term.

Tammany Hall's retaliation for the Walker episode was petty. It tried to deny to Lieutenant Governor Lehman the nomination for Governor to succeed Roosevelt. This effort ended when Smith came to Lehman's support. It also denied me the nomination to the Supreme Court which ordinarily was routine after an appointment by the Governor that I had received for an unexpired term. Within a short time, Curry was deposed as leader. Walker remained for years a political exile in Europe, if not a fugitive from justice, and Tammany Hall became a weak and ineffectual organization. It still is.

I have said that the story of Walker and Tammany Hall is relevant here because it shows Roosevelt's adroitness in his relationship with party bosses. During all his presidency as party leader and as a leader in the legislative process, he recognized fully the importance of party organizations and their political leaders. They were of essential help to him in two respects. The obvious one, of course, was during election time. But he would often rely upon them and call upon them to help get votes for or against proposed legislation.

To the young voters of the seventies, it must appear rather strange that the President of the United States would call upon state and city political leaders for help. It is hard for them to realize that the political leaders they presently read about and deal with, especially in the large cities, are quite different from the political leaders in the 1930's and 1940's. With a few exceptions today, the local political bosses are weak and ineffectual. Many of them have little influence on elections, and practically none on legislation. If proof were needed of this, the 1972 Democratic National Convention in Miami provides plenty. One of the most powerful of modern-day bosses was, with his entire delegation, actually excluded from the convention. No city boss had any part in selecting the candidates, or in writing the platform. The New York City delegation did not even include a single political county leader.

Indeed, the history of politics in the larger cities over the last two decades indicates that candidates (except for strictly local offices) like to be known as independents, free from any influence by political leaders. But in the days of Roosevelt the leaders were powerful figures in the political life of the cities. The only political bosses in the United States comparable in influence and power to those of 1932 like Curry (New York) or Hague (New Jersey), or McCooey (Brooklyn) or Kelly (Chicago), are Mayor Daley of Chicago, Gilligan of Ohio, and possibly a few others. But even Daley was excluded as a delegate by the vote of the 1972 convention.

It was Roosevelt's political style and genius that he could openly cooperate with these old-time political leaders, without too much of the damaging stigma to himself which political bossism implies. These bosses of 1932, and others like them, were in control of nearly all the delegations from their respective counties or states and, together, they were able to dominate the Chicago Democratic Convention of that year. At the convention, Roosevelt displayed another example of his political style—the readiness to compromise or retreat when he saw that to push ahead might result in disaster. He had a majority of the delegates ready to vote for him on the first ballot. But in 1932, the rules of the Democratic Convention required a two-thirds vote for nomination. This had been a long-standing rule, promulgated originally to give the South a veto power of some substance. Some of the strategists in the Roosevelt camp in Chicago, with Roosevelt's knowledge, began to agitate to abolish this rule and substitute a bare majority rule. This raised an immediate howl not only from the Southern delegates, but from all the leaders supporting Roosevelt's rivals. Roosevelt, in order to stop the growing unfriendly clamor, directed an immediate halt to all such efforts. This was clearly the fox at work—more sensitive to traps and pitfalls than the lion.

Of even greater importance was the compromise he made after three ballots had failed to produce a two-thirds majority for any candidate, in order to ensure victory on the fourth ballot. Without this compromise, it is possible that a deadlock might have developed at the convention, or that Roosevelt's forces might have begun to slip away. Roosevelt knew that the political domestic philosophy of John Nance Garner, the Speaker of the House, was miles apart from his own; he knew that Garner's chief backer, William Randolph Hearst, was an extreme isolationist. Yet the deal was made, resulting in the ticket of Roosevelt and Garner.

The fact that he was willing to make this kind of compromise with Garner did not mean that he was ready to accept any of Garner's conservative ideas about legislation. He knew that most of the legislation he would propose would be distasteful to Garner and completely foreign to Garner's political, economic and social thinking; but this did not deter Roosevelt from making the deal. The deal was on candidates, not on legislation. The political compromise at Chicago was indeed an example of Roosevelt's often-expressed dictum that "If you want to bring about great reforms, the first thing you have to do is to get elected."

As soon as he was nominated, the lion embarked upon a spectacular, dramatic project—how he did love drama!—which, he said in his acceptance speech, would indicate that "the task of our party [would be] to break foolish traditions." Up to this time, as an old relic of the eighteenth century when travel was slow and uncertain and news came only by courier on horseback rather than by telegraph wires, it was still the custom for the candidate to wait a month or more, and then to receive a notification committee to be told—what he and all the world had long known—that he had been nominated. He would then deliver his acceptance speech.

Roosevelt decided to accept the nomination immediately, breaking one "foolish tradition." He also decided to go to the convention site to accept it, breaking a second "foolish tradition." In order to get from Albany to Chicago before the convention would adjourn, he would have to fly, and he did, breaking a third "foolish tradition." In all of these decisions, he established precedents which have been followed ever since by Presidential candidates. During his twelve years as President, many new precedents were to be set; and many "old traditions" were to be broken.

While it had become generally known by the press in Albany that the Governor intended to break with tradition and go to the convention to accept his nomination immediately, he insisted on maintaining much good-humored mystery about his proposed means of transportation. It was originally believed that he was going to Chicago by train before the actual balloting began, where he would wait until the nomination. Some of the rival candidates were already there when the convention opened.

But Roosevelt would have none of such prosaic arrangements. He knew the value of surprise and drama in public office, and he understood the psychology of the American people of 1932. He felt that the dismayed, disheartened and bewildered nation would welcome something new, something startling, something bold, an act bursting with energy, something to give it hope that there would be an end to stolid inaction. He wanted to let people sense that in the presidency, his approach to his duties would be new, daring and even startling; that if elected, he would be ready to act—and act fast. It was in that spirit that the airplane flight to Chicago was conceived. It was a break with tradition; but it was more than that; it was a break with inaction and procrastination and slow motion, and a symbol of fast, new and direct action.

News shortly began to spread of the presence of a tri-motored plane at the Albany airport; and the newsmen, with their uncanny ability to put two and two together, predicted that the Governor was going to fly to Chicago.

The following excerpt from the Associated Press story which went out of Albany, June 29, is typical of some of the banter which passed between the Governor and the press during these days—a style of informal repartee which he was to continue in the White House. When the press asked him whether the waiting airplane was to take him to Chicago, he neither affirmed nor denied; he only laughed. "Now, I'll tell you what I'm going to do," he said with pretended seriousness, "I'm going to bicycle out to Chicago. I'm going to get one of those quintets—you know, five bicycles in a row. Father will ride in the first seat and manage the handlebars, Jim will ride second, then Elliott, then Franklin Jr. and then John [all his sons]; Sam [Rosenman] will follow—on a tricycle."

I was a passenger on that plane. In those days long-distance flights without stops were rare, except for Lindbergh and the other pioneers. Our flight plan called for stops for refueling at Buffalo and at Cleveland. We planned to arrive at the Chicago auditorium at about 2:00 P.M. By that time, the Vice-Presidential nomination would be out of the way; and the delegates would be ready for the acceptance speech. But strong headwinds delayed us, and also made it a very rough and bumpy flight.

Shortly after the flight started, we went to work to polish the acceptance speech for delivery. We were in radio communication with the Convention Hall, and learned that the delegates were becoming impatient at the delay; some of them had started for home. We would have to cut the speech drastically. Out at the Convention Hall, all kinds of devices were improvised to keep the delegates amused until the Governor's arrival. Songwriters played the piano and sang songs; the band played overtime, and although many delegates' seats became vacant, the parts of the hall into which the public was allowed became more and more crowded as the day wore on.

With each radio report, we were falling further and further behind schedule; and more and more paragraphs came out of the speech. This lopping off of material on which we had worked so long and so hopefully was a painful process. I know that there were some jewels dropped on the airplane floor that day. It is likely, though, that the cutting process hurt us much more than it did the speech itself.

The Governor did not seem to mind the bumpy ride; as he explained to the convention in his opening extemporaneous paragraph, "I regret that I am late, but I have no control over the winds of Heaven, and could only be thankful for my Navy training."

Once, between Buffalo and Cleveland, I looked up from my work toward the Governor; and what I saw convinced me that here indeed was a man of steel nerves, who could shake off all worry, all excitement, and deliberately take his rest when necessary as he would always do in the White House. The Governor, on his bumpy way to accept a nomination that was almost tantamount to an election to the presidency of the United States—a prize for which he had struggled for so many years and over so many seemingly impossible hurdles—was sound asleep!

Here was a characteristic of Roosevelt at which I never ceased to marvel. Calm, serene, no worry or fretfulness, always confident of himself. I was to see him in many crises, where after making his decision, he would dismiss the matter completely from his mind and turn to something else—whether work, sleep, solitaire, stamps, or just ordinary conversation.

There was another—even more spectacular—display of steel nerves when we landed. A large number of prominent Democrats and friends at the airport immediately crowded around the Governor, shaking hands, whispering unsolicited advice and generally creating a scene of confusion. Raymond Moley—a central figure in the Brain Trust—who had been in Chicago during all the convention, pulled me aside and whispered in great distress that Louis Howe did not like the acceptance speech and had spent the whole night dictating a brand-new one for Roosevelt to deliver. I then saw Howe at Roosevelt's side, arguing with him and urging him to deliver the speech he was handing him—even though Roosevelt had not read a word of it. It was not Roosevelt's style to deliver *any* speech without his own careful participation in the writing. This was a most important speech, on which he had worked many hours over the last two weeks, and which he knew almost by heart. He expostulated to Howe that he could not possibly deliver a speech he had never read and would have no chance to read, because he and the entire group were just about to set out in a string of cars for the Convention Hall. Louis insisted, saying that the speech Roosevelt had brought with him was impossible.

As Moley tells the story,[32] Howe, after reading that speech (which had been dictated to his secretary over the phone from Albany), shouted: "I can see Sam Rosenman all over this speech." For Howe, who had little real sympathy with the New Deal, that exclamation was synonymous with a statement that the speech could not be worse.

Roosevelt did not want to hurt the feelings of this loyal, devoted worker who had long ago dedicated his life to the objective of seeing Roosevelt in the White House, and who at Chicago had worked around the clock in spite of agonizing asthmatic attacks. So, as I saw from a following car while the procession passed thousands of shouting people jamming the highway and streets on the way to the Convention Hall, and while he was waving his hand to acknowledge the excited applause, he calmly from time to time glanced down at Howe's draft. He saw that he could deliver the first page of it; and he substituted it for the first page of his own speech. To do this in a speeding open automobile, in the midst of all the clamor from the crowd, without showing any undue excitement, stress or impatience or even letting people know what he was doing, was a spectacular performance of strong nerves and a display of gratitude for the effort and loyalty of a devoted supporter. And, I must add, Howe's first page was better and more effective than ours.

The speeches which Roosevelt made in various parts of the country in the campaign of 1932 do not express a rounded political or economic program; nor do they attempt to set forth specifically what he intended to do if he were elected. Campaign speeches of a political sophisticate necessarily deal in generalities; Roosevelt's were no exception. What was as important as what he said was the way he said it, and the way he acted—his style as a campaigner. Full of life, energetic, humorous, even gay, vigorous in attacks upon the administration, showing and feeling a close rapport with each one of his listeners, self-confident, courageous, he was able to convey the image of a man sure of himself, with unbounded faith in the future of this nation, and concerned primarily with the welfare of the ordinary men, women and children of America. He was also able to present a picture of hope for the future and a confidence that a way could and would be found out of the Depression. There was not a trace of the fear which had spread over the whole nation. This was a style for which a weary, hopeless people was waiting.

He was unrestrained in his condemnation of those who had brought this unprecedented misery—the monopolists, the financial tycoons, and the selfish interests which had taken hold of the government itself. He railed against fear, and delay, and inaction, and optimistic misrepresentation of the true state of the emergency. He condemned the government's encouragement of speculation and overproduction, the high tariff walls which had cost us much of our foreign trade. He promised a curb on all concentration of economic power which sought control in Washington; and an end to the misuse of other people's money by banks, brokers and others, to the unregulated issuance and sale of worthless stocks and bonds, and to the abuses of vast holding companies.

He was specific on certain things, such as repeal of the Prohibition Amendment, and—much to his later discomfiture—a cut in government expenditures by 25 per cent.

No one could justly complain, however, that he concealed the general objectives of what was to become known as the New Deal. Except for the policy in gold, deficit spending, and NRA, everything the New Deal tried in 1933 and in 1935 was covered by the speeches of 1932; in general terms, perhaps, but clearly enough to be recognized in the legislation which was later proposed.

He emphasized always that since the Depression was nationwide, it had to be handled by the national government and not by the separate states. The very basis of the New Deal philosophy, as he expounded it in 1932 and practiced it in 1933 and later, was the duty of the federal government to concern itself with, and take action to relieve, the distresses of modern economic life, and to use federal power and federal resources liberally to "promote the general welfare."

Roosevelt was not trying to lay out a blueprint of future mechanisms. He was trying to get elected by showing his general attitude about what the federal government should do and would do if he were elected President. In 1932, as later in 1936, 1940 and 1944, he made it his business to formulate some special appeal to each of the major economic groups of our population—farmers, laborers, consumers and businessmen, even bankers and financiers; for he emphasized that there was a "concert of interest" or "interdependence" among them all which made the prosperity of one group dependent on the prosperity of the others. It was his fundamental thesis that no nation could long survive if it was "half-boom and half-bust."

His adroitness in all of this, combined with all the charm, self-confidence, friendliness, courage and unshakable faith in the future of true democracy in a sound United States—in a word, his style of campaigning—all combined to make him the "Old Champ" of the campaign trail, which is what Willkie in 1940 was to call him. Campaigning was for him unadultered joy.

When on March 4, 1933, Roosevelt solemnly and firmly repeated the oath of office administered to him by the Chief Justice, he had already had all of the foregoing wealth of experience in practical politics, in administration of government and in the administrative and legislative processes. It was an experience mostly of glittering success, with only an occasional dismal failure. It was an experience unequalled by any President-elect up to that time, with the possible exception of Theodore Roosevelt. He also brought with him to Washington all his great objectives of social justice, of making the life of the ordinary American citizen better than it had ever been, of improving the lot of every man, woman and child in the United States. He was just as confident that all this could be done as he was determined to do it.

For many reasons, his Inaugural Speech was one of his greatest, and one of his most important and timely. An obvious reason was that it delineated with frankness and completeness so many of the Roosevelt characteristics, so many of the fundamental beliefs that were to mold his style and methods of operation in the twelve years to come. But the principal reason was that it filled a desperate, unique need of that particular moment. The American people had been gradually beaten down by three years of depression into a state of hopelessness and panic. The fear he had seen during the campaign four months earlier had increased since then, and had spread over the whole land to people of all stations of life as the Depression gradually headed for disaster. The people were now numb with fear, aghast at what seemed to be descending upon them and their families. It was not alone the unemployed or the needy. The greatest of the American industrialists, bankers and businessmen had seen their comfortable, powerful and apparently unsinkable world sink beneath them. Whether it was fear of losing one's job, or not feeding one's family, or losing one's yacht—it was all-pervasive.

In the very first paragraph of his Inaugural Speech, Roosevelt made it clear that things were to be changed—and quickly:

"I am certain that my fellow Americans expect that on my induction into the Presidency I will address them with a candor and a decision which the present situation of our Nation impels. This is preeminently the time to speak the truth, the whole truth, frankly and boldly. Nor need we shrink from honestly facing conditions in our country today. This great nation will endure as it has endured, will revive and will prosper. So, first of all, let me assert my firm belief that the only thing we have to fear is fear itself—nameless, unreasoning, unjustified terror which paralyzes needed efforts to convert retreat into advance. In every dark hour of our national life a leadership of frankness and vigor has met with that understanding and support of the people themselves which is essential to victory. I am convinced that you will again give that support to leadership in these critical days."[33]

The voice was self-confident. Hoover had also often expressed his own confidence that things would get better and had called upon the citizens to reciprocate confidence toward their government. But there are different qualities of self-confidence. Most often, self-confidence evokes no response at all; sometimes it gives rise only to disbelief and derision; sometimes however, but only rarely, it becomes contagious and those who hear it begin to feel it and take part in it, to rejoice in it—and to return it tenfold by their own confidence.

Self-confidence was the very essence of Roosevelt's style; and it was that rare quality of self-confidence which provokes confidence in others. We shall follow this trait in Roosevelt from these first words he spoke as President until the last words he wrote in office in 1945 but could not deliver because of his death. Self-confidence made him one of the strongest of our Presidents. On some occasions, it led to disaster; but whether it was to produce success or failure, it never left him.

On this occasion, he did not rest with his declaration that confidence could dissipate paralyzing error. It had to be combined first with a change in the moral climate of America: "The money changers have fled from their high seats in the temple of our civilization. We may now restore that temple to the ancient truths. The measure of the restoration lies in the extent to which we apply social values more noble than mere monetary profit."

Then came the pledge of vigorous action:

"Restoration calls, however, not for changes in ethics alone. This Nation calls for action, and action now.

"Our greatest primary task is to put people to work. This is no unsolvable problem if we face it wisely and courageously . . . treating the task as we would treat the emergency of a war. . . . There are many ways in which it [the task] can be helped, but it can never be helped merely by talking about it. We must act and act quickly."

Action—and action quickly—was to be one of the most important foundations of Roosevelt's style. But he wanted to show to what far-reaching extent he was ready to take action to meet this crisis. If anyone was in doubt at this point about his conception of the presidency and of its powers, or of his determination to use them all if needed, this first speech as President made it clear. To our despairing citizens it was a flood of light in the darkness.

"It is to be hoped that the normal balance of Executive and Legislative authority may be wholly adequate to meet the unprecedented task before us. But it may be that an unprecedented demand and need for undelayed action may call for temporary departure from that normal balance of public procedure.

"I am prepared under my constitutional duty to recommend the measures that a stricken Nation in the midst of a stricken world may require. These measures, or such other measures as the Congress may build out of its experience and wisdom, I shall seek within my constitutional authority, to bring to speedy adoption.

"But in the event that the Congress shall fail to take one of these two courses, and in the event that the national emergency is still critical, I shall not evade the clear course of duty that will then confront me. I shall ask the Congress for the one remaining instrument to meet the crisis—broad Executive power to wage a war against the emergency, as great as the power that would be given to me if we were in fact invaded by a foreign foe."

He did not add, as he would in a later crisis during the war, that if Congress refused to give him that power, he would act anyway as though it had. I have not the slightest doubt that he would have done so.

Nor did he have any doubt that our Constitution was broad and flexible enough to warrant the exercise of such drastic powers, even though no war actually existed:

"Action in this image and to this end is feasible under the form of government which we have inherited from our ancestors. Our Constitution is so simple and practical that it is possible always to meet extraordinary needs by changes in emphasis and arrangement without loss of essential form. That is why our constitutional system has proved itself the most superbly enduring political mechanism the modern world has produced. It has met every stress of vast expansion of territory, of foreign wars, of bitter internal strife, of world relations."[34]

This entire speech was the roar of a lion; there was not a trace of the fox any place in it.

It is quite remarkable how much of his philosophy of government FDR was able to crowd into this one short address. For example, included was his idea of a "concert of interest," of the interdependence of all economic groups in the nation; labor could not long be prosperous if agriculture was so depressed that farmers did not make enough cash income from their crops to buy the goods labor produced—and vice versa. This strong conviction deeply affected his style, always. As he acted to help labor by minimum wages and maximum hours, by guaranteeing collective bargaining, and by encouraging the formation of unions, he simultaneously acted to provide greater income—hopefully "parity"—for the farmer. As he acted to prevent home foreclosures by providing cheap government credit, he acted simultaneously to give the same help on farm mortgages, to provide rural electricity and commodity credit for farmers.

In his Inaugural, he put it all very succinctly and very clearly:

"If I read the temper of our people correctly, we now realize as we have never realized before our interdependence on each other; that we cannot merely take but we must give as well; that if we are to go forward, we must move as a trained and loyal army willing to sacrifice for the good of a common discipline, because without such discipline no progress is made, no leadership becomes effective."

By this single speech Roosevelt had accomplished one of the most significant achievements of his presidency: the renewal of the courage and hope and faith of the American people. Within a week, more than a half million letters and telegrams were on their way to the White House, expressing faith in him and in his leadership.

In order to show the country that he was personally in no panic, that he had no fear himself, and that he was supremely self-confident about what to do—and although he knew that many of his assistants were even then impatiently waiting to see him to have him make many decisions—he spent the afternoon after the speech leisurely reviewing the usual inaugural parade from a stand in front of the White House. Later he presided over a social gathering of many hundreds at tea in the White House, chatting with friends, public officials, campaign workers and political leaders, laughing, joking—all as if he had all the time in the world to take up the terribly pressing problems of the day.

Of course, he knew—because he had himself directed it—that throughout Washington, and also in New York City, for the past weeks men of ideas had been gathered in hotel rooms, private offices, individual homes, working on legislation to carry into effect the various policies he was to recommend to Congress. Seldom had Washington seen this kind of excitement; it was attracting to the capital brilliant young college and law school graduates, anxious to work with this new kind of liberal leadership. He had been at the center of this activity ever since Election Day in November—in his New York City home, in Hyde Park and in Warm Springs.

Finally, when the last of the guests had left the White House in the late afternoon of March 4—the newspaper reporters marvelling at the imperturbable calmness and serenity which the new President was displaying—he swore in his Cabinet in a body. This, too, was a breaking of precedent—swearing in all the Cabinet together, and in the White House. He then called in his newly appointed Secretary of the Treasury and directed him to have an emergency banking bill ready for him to present to Congress within five days.

On the next day, Sunday, late at night, he issued a proclamation calling the Congress into an extraordinary session.

The growing fear and panic had resulted in a rush of depositors during the preceding weeks to withdraw their money from banks still open, and to hide it. The tremendous withdrawals were, of course, endangering all the banks. Some 1400 had already failed in 1932. The federal government had continued to do nothing about closing banks; the states had had to take action. On February 4, 1933, the Governor of Louisiana had declared a Bank Holiday for the banks in his state. This was followed by the Governors of twenty other states. On Saturday, March 4—Inaugural Day—the Governor of the State of New York—the bulwark of all financial soundness—finally had to declare a holiday; and on the succeeding Monday, March 6, the Governors of Illinois, Massachusetts, New Jersey and Pennsylvania all followed suit. It can be said that by March 6, every bank in the United States had been closed or placed under severe restrictions by state proclamations.

On that day, relying with doubtful validity upon an old, almost forgotten wartime measure dating from World War I, the President issued a second proclamation halting all transactions in gold and declaring a nationwide Bank Holiday ending on March 9 (later extended for five more days). Knowing that the most immediate crisis was in banking, both of these proclamations had been prepared at Roosevelt's direction before he arrived in Washington for the inauguration. The second one showed that he was already using the war powers which he had mentioned in the Inaugural Address two days previously.

On March 9, the Congress met. The President sent them his banking message. Accompanying the message was a proposed bill, ratifying what the President had already done by proclamation, giving him full control over gold, and providing for a gradual reopening of the banks found to be solvent.

The bill was passed by Congress practically sight unseen, because there were only a few copies available for the members to read. It was sent to the White House and signed by the President by 8:30 P.M. that evening. The whole process from introduction to final signature took less than eight hours. This speed was typical of the quick passage of several of Roosevelt's recommendations during that session. It has been computed that eleven of the outstanding bills of 1933 passed the House with an average of 3⅔ hours debate per measure—a fact unprecedented in American history. Some contemporary wag remarked during this performance of alacrity and compliance by Congress that Congress was not really voting on the legislation, but merely waving at it as it sailed by.

There were many progressives at the time who were hopeful that the President in March 1933 would take advantage of the banking situation to produce a real fundamental change in our banking system by nationalizing the banks before permitting them to reopen. Some of them urged this on him. There is no doubt that had he decided to do so, the opposition in Congress would have been slight. Congress was ready to do anything he asked, and happy to let him take the lead and responsibility. It was, in 1933, just as frightened as anybody else. Nothing reveals so clearly Roosevelt's continued faith in the private enterprise system as his refusal—even in banking—to change in the slightest degree our private property economy, or to curtail in any way the private enterprise system under which he had lived and America had grown.

Roosevelt originally had intended to get legislation reopening the banks on a sound basis and then have Congress adjourn, to allow time for further deliberation on additional measures. He said so in his first press conference. But his zest for action and the response of the American people to action in the White House after such a long period of inaction induced him to move ahead swiftly, and to take advantage of the obvious congressional mood of cooperation.

So the banking bill was followed by a quick succession of messages to Congress asking for legislation to carry out, in part, his pledge of a New Deal; each was accompanied by a proposed bill. It was to be a part of Roosevelt's style, in order to obtain speedy action and also to show exactly what he meant by his recommendations to Congress, to include a complete bill with his messages. If the bill did not actually accompany the message, it would be given by the White House to an important congressman willing to sponsor it, who as soon as the message was read would rise and introduce the bill. This style of sending a proposed bill along with a message had been used once before, by President Lincoln, and it had infuriated the Congress.[35] As a result, the practice had been abandoned by the Presidents who had followed Lincoln. Roosevelt reversed this style, and there was no congressional murmur of protest.

The messages that followed the banking message came rapidly and steadily:

March 10:   Legislation to effect economies in government.
March 13:   Modification of the Volstead Law to permit sale of light wines and beer.
March 16:   Legislation for relief of agriculture (AAA).
March 21:   Legislation for unemployment relief, consisting of (a) a civilian conservation corps, (b) direct federal grants to the states for unemployment relief, and (c) a program of public works.
March 29:   Legislation for the supervision of the sale of securities (SEC).
April 3:   Legislation to save farms from mortgage foreclosures by use of government cheap credit (FCA).
April 5:   Legislation to create the Civilian Conservation Corps (CCC).
April 10:   Legislation to set up a Tennessee Valley Authority (TVA).
April 13:   Legislation to save small homes from mortgage foreclosures (HOLC).
May 4:   Legislation for relief of railroads.
May 17:   Legislation to establish the National Recovery Administration (NRA).
May 20:   Legislation for relief of the oil industry.

They were all adopted.

Congress finally adjourned on June 16—"one hundred days" after it had convened. It left behind the most extraordinary legislation of reform in congressional history to that time. In addition, there was the creation of the FDIC to guarantee bank deposits, one of the most successful of the 1933 enactments.

During those hectic days, the President was active on other fronts: speeches, press conferences, fireside chats, talks with foreign heads of government, arrangement of international conferences.

The legislation presented a frontal attack on the most grievous of the evils in our economic system; it was also a concerted effort to get the economy moving into a recovery. It was all done under the direction of one man in the White House, acting as a general to point out the line of attack, as a conciliator between many different points of view, as a compromiser in order to get matters decided and enacted quickly. He personally followed very minutely the course of the recommended legislation through both houses, accepting suggested changes here, rejecting them there—but always alert to what was happening on Capitol Hill.

What this unprecedented action during these hundred days did to and for the American people is hard for one not living at the time to understand and appreciate. Not only had the people seemingly been submerged into bleak hopelessness; it appeared as though their faith in the American system of free enterprise had disappeared. Democracy for at least two years under Hoover had seemed to show that it was incapable of restorative, or even alleviating, action. Naturally and inevitably, glances were directed by some at Moscow on the one hand, and at Berlin and Rome on the other, where leadership—so far as censored news was reaching us—was at least providing food and shelter.

By the end of the first week, however, most of this dangerous mood had passed. Everybody was heaping praise on the new President, giving him full credit for the change. Even the conservatives joined in. Had he not preserved the old banking system; had he not made economies in government spending? Above all, there was not a hint of the radical or the revolutionary in anything he had thus far said or proposed. Even Walter Lippmann, who had observed with scorn and contempt the 1932 nomination of Roosevelt and his campaign speeches, wrote in May 1933: ". . . At the beginning of March, the country was in such a state of confused desperation that it would have followed almost any leader anywhere he chose to go. . . . In one week, the nation, which had lost confidence in everything and everybody, had regained confidence in the government and in itself."[36]

William Allen White, the Kansas newspaper editor whom Roosevelt, in the 1936 campaign, described as a man who was with him for three and a half years but always against him in election years, wrote to Ickes in June 1933:

"How do you account for him? Was I just fooled in him before the election, or has he developed? As Governor of New York, I thought he was a good two-legged Governor of a type that used to flourish in the first decade of the century under the influence of LaFollette and Theodore Roosevelt. We had a lot of them, but they weren't presidential size. . . .

"I thought your President was one of those. Instead of which he has developed magnitude and poise, more than all, power! I have been a voracious eater in the course of a long and happy life, and have eaten many things; but I have never had to eat my words before. I shall wait six months . . . if they are still on the plate, down they go with a gusto. And I shall smack my lips as my Adams apple bobs."[37]

People who lived through those days of 1933 could almost physically see the fog lift. This resurgence of faith and hope was even more important than the bare economic statistics—which did show that some improvement had come. By the time, for example, that the congressional session ended and Roosevelt gaily went off sailing with his sons along the New England coast, the production index had gone up substantially. The economy was already feeling the effects of the government's money going into relief spending, and into the AAA and CCC projects. Roosevelt's interest was in human beings, and if they felt more confident, more comfortable and better off, this was more important to him than the figures of production. He was to ask as the important questions for each citizen—farmer, miner, factory worker, businessman: "Are *you* better off than you were last year? Are your debts less burdensome? Is your bank account more secure? Are your working conditions better? Is your faith in your own individual future more firmly grounded?" These were the criteria by which Roosevelt measured the success or failure of his style of operations in the White House.

The resurgent confidence was reflected in, and, in turn, encouraged by the new mood of the White House. This mood, too, was an integral part of the style of the new President. I had seen nothing of the White House during the Hoover days, but many of those who had remarked on, and later some wrote of, the complete change which had occurred. The Roosevelts were as gregarious as the

Hoovers were isolated. The house was filled with the laughter of grandchildren; there was a steady, unremitting flow of overnight and weekend visitors from all parts of the world; there was gaiety amidst the serious planning sessions and conferences; there were dinners and social functions; there were newspaper pictures of a smiling, confident President—so unlike those to which Americans had been accustomed for three years of a solemn, dour, worried and frightened President. This Presidential style of Roosevelt would continue even through his own dark days of 1937 and 1938, and—more important—through the nation's darker days of 1941 and 1942. It was one of his ways of imparting to the mass of the people his own confidence in the future of America—and his own self-confidence; and it succeeded, because it had a genuineness which everybody could feel.

Indeed, the hundred days revealed a great deal about the Presidential style of Roosevelt—as a human being, as a leader in legislation, as a teacher, as a political leader, and as a national leader of all the people. When you examine more closely the product of the hundred days, you will find no coordinated plan of action, no master program. He was really playing it by ear; he later likened himself to a quarterback who waits to see what one play accomplishes before deciding on another. For Roosevelt was essentially an experimenter. He refused ever to follow blindly any economic or political dogma; he rejected them all insofar as they dictated inflexibility of action. His style was that of the pragmatist. What would work to carry out his main objective? He wrote his friend from the Wilson days, Colonel E. M. House, in May 1933 that "the situation is moving so fast that what is a problem one day is solved or superseded the next. As you will realize, snap judgments have had to be made." All during his political life he had been essentially that kind of experimenter, trying one thing, and if it did not work, discarding it and trying another. Some of the bills during the hundred days, and their method of implementation, were actually inconsistent with each other. For example, in the face of monumental projects of unprecedented cost for the relief of unemployment, there were economies to carry out the platform and campaign promises to cut the budget. Even as he handed out millions in direct relief, he cut the veterans' bonuses. The AAA provided for some tariff raising at the same time as his Secretary of State and he were engaged in transferring high tariffs into reciprocal trade agreements. But consistency of methods did not weigh nearly as strongly with Roosevelt as practical results and consistency of objectives.

As Roosevelt insisted, there were no inconsistencies in ultimate objectives. These objectives were threefold: to relieve distress, to promote recovery, and to bring about reforms—all by using the powers and affirmative action of the federal government. The important thing was that both recovery and reform were to go forward simultaneously—and all within the American system of free enterprise.

Many had urged him to get recovery started first and then begin to institute reforms. Roosevelt was too experienced a politician not to know that once recovery was under way reform would be more difficult, if not impossible. So he pressed both at the same time—with equal vigor, with action, and with experimentation. He told the Congress in a formal message in June 1934: "It is childish to speak of recovery first and reconstruction afterward. In the very nature of the process of recovery we must avoid the destructive influences of the past. We have shown the world that democracy has within it the elements necessary to its own salvation."[38]

Of course the chief causes for his unprecedented success with Congress during the hundred days were the crisis of the Depression and the outpouring of enthusiastic approval from citizens and editorial writers all over the country. But the politician in the White House knew how to add to the pressure upon Congress. He let them know that patronage—that manna from the White House upon which all congressmen like to feed—would not be considered until after Congress adjourned. No congressman experienced in the ways of Washington would be under any delusion that his votes for or against legislation approved by the White House would have no connection with the kind and amount of patronage he would ultimately receive for his constituents. It did not really shock any of them, when the President finally did turn to matters of patronage, to be asked how they had voted on some of the New Deal legislation in 1933,[39] and even how they had voted in the Chicago Convention in 1932 if they had been a delegate.

This Congress needed no additional pressure from their constitutents during the one hundred days. They were so frightened themselves, so anxious to turn responsibility over to any President who was willing to lead, so relieved to learn that this President actually welcomed responsibility—even loved responsibility—that they spent little time deliberating, and even less in voting. But, whether they needed any additional stimulus or not, they were flooded with mail from their districts, just as the White House was from the entire nation—nearly all of which showed approval of the President's course and urged cooperation with him. This was to happen many times in the future when Congress, with the pressure lifted and recovery begun, was not so anxious to give the President the legislation he was requesting. Roosevelt, relying on his many past successes in Albany in creating favorable public opinion, rallying that opinion to his support and making it felt by the lawmakers, repeated the tactics he had used as Governor. He felt very strongly that Congress was but a responsive legislative agency of the people and that, as the people thought and spoke, the Congress would act. He recognized fully that the ultimate, irresistible force in American political life was public opinion; and he acted always on that conviction.

Even though it was not necessary actively to agitate for legislation in the hundred days, Roosevelt felt then as always that one of the essential tasks of a President as national leader was to educate the American people in the problems of their government, in what it was doing to solve them and in what it intended to do in the future. Roosevelt played the role of the teacher, even at times when he was not trying to get immediate action from the people. He believed in the right of the people to know, in their right to have all the facts in order intelligently to vote or pass judgment. Acting as teacher and educator was part and parcel of his style. The dispatches from Washington during the first week of the new administration practically monopolized the newspapers. But Roosevelt was never one to rely entirely on newspapers, for they invariably would select the news they wanted the people to read. In Albany as Governor, and in 1932 as a candidate for the presidency, the vast majority of the newspapers (as distinguished from reporters) had been opposed to him. He must have anticipated that the same kind of opposition would face him as President.

He was not mistaken.

In spite of the hostility of the newspapers, however, Roosevelt considered the press conference as one of the most important instruments given to a President with which to educate the public. He was untiring in performing the role of teacher and educator. And one of the reasons for his success in that role was that there was nothing he enjoyed more—unless, possibly, political campaigning, which was also a form of education. As a result, the American public was better informed about their federal government, its problems, its objectives and its philosophies during the twelve years of Roosevelt than ever before; nor did any prior public become more interested in government—in talking about it, in debating among themselves about it, and in casting their ballots on the issues involved in it. The interest in public affairs generated during Roosevelt's tenure was so well founded that it has continued unabated through the succeeding presidencies down to this day.

In his Commonwealth Club speech in San Francisco, during the 1932 Presidential campaign, he gave expression to his conception of the part which education of the people should play in government: "Government includes the art of formulating a policy, and using the political technique to attain so much of that policy as will receive general support, persuading, leading, sacrificing, teaching always, because the greatest duty of a statesman is to educate."[40]

"Educating," "teaching"—that was high politics in Roosevelt's dictionary; for it meant assuring his leadership of the people. He enjoyed that kind of politics, and he was a master at it. He also enjoyed the other kind of politics—the low politics—the politics of pressure, of threats and promises, of the bait of patronage, of intrigue and behind-the-scenes manipulation; and he was master of that too. But he relied more on the first kind of politics to get his legislation from Congress, and his votes from the people.

Professor Charles A. Beard, the renowned historian (no admirer of Roosevelt), wrote in 1938 of him as a teacher: "He has discussed in his messages and addresses more fundamental problems of American life and society than all the other Presidents combined."[41]

"The whole fate of what the government is trying to do depends, regardless of the election, on an understanding of the program by the mass of the people," Roosevelt told the National Emergency Council. He was to learn the hard way from the reaction to his "quarantine" speech of October 1937, and by other incidents, that he could go no faster or farther than the people would let him; and that the speed of action which the people would permit him to take depended upon the speed with which they were educated in advance about what he wanted to do. Roosevelt believed, as he wrote to H. G. Wells in 1935: "Our biggest success is making people think during these past two years."

Returning from a trip through the West in 1937, for example, after the disastrous defeat of his fight against the Supreme Court, he said: "The other day I was asked to state my outstanding impression gained on this recent trip. I said that it seemed to me to be the general understanding on the part of the average citizen of the broad objectives and policies which I have just outlined.

"Five years of fierce discussion and debate, five years of information through the radio and the moving pictures, have taken the whole nation to school in the nation's business."

Roosevelt viewed leadership in public life as the ability to see what is coming around the corner, to devise the best means of meeting it, and to win the people's approval to meet it. That was his style. He sometimes failed to perform these tasks perfectly, but his successes overwhelmingly outnumbered his failures.

Roosevelt's press conferences had a style completely his own. There had been press conferences before in the White House, but none like his; and the press conferences of later Presidents were also different from his. Woodrow Wilson was the first to institute formal press conferences on a regular schedule, but he did not enjoy them; and as the pressures immediately before, during, and after World War I plagued him, he found excuses to let them lapse. Harding started them again, but quickly resorted to written questions submitted in advance; under him the "White House Spokesman" was invented to provide a source for news. Coolidge held press conferences regularly, twice a week, but also with written questions. Hoover continued the same style, but as the Depression deepened, so did his distaste for the conferences—and the number of them as well as their productiveness of news diminished.

Roosevelt, who had always had press conferences while Governor, and who had always found them useful and enjoyable, lost no time in getting them started in Washington. The first one was held four days after his inauguration. His days and his nights had been crowded to the brim during those four days; but he made time for the press and radio correspondents. He remade the ground rules: no written questions but free and easy oral give-and-take; permission would be required to attribute news to the President himself; no direct quotation of the President unless specially authorized; "background material" was to be furnished by the President to enable the reporters better to understand a problem or a policy, and to give their readers the background for certain government actions as though they had dug it up by themselves but without attributing it to the White House; and "off-the-record" material, which was not to be used in any form and was intended only for those present in the conference, not even to be reported to their papers or to absent reporters. Some few questions would not be answered either because negotiations on the subject matter were still in progress, or because the President did not know the answer, or was not ready to discuss them for various other reasons. The two categories which he invented, "off-the-record" and "background material," were to be among his most important tools for educating the public and for fashioning and promoting his own leadership. They were part of his particular style.

The general tone of the 1,011 press conferences which he held during his three terms and the four months of his fourth was set by his very first words to the first conference: "It is very good to see you all. My hope is that these conferences are going to be merely enlarged editions of the kind of very delightful family conferences I have been holding in Albany for the last four years."[42]

The conferences with from one to two hundred reporters crowding around his office desk were indeed "delightful family conferences," enjoyed by most of the reporters as much as by the President. There were informal remarks, quips, asides, with the President leaning back in his chair laughing, his cigarette holder at a jaunty angle, eyes twinkling, calling reporters by their first names.

The first conference, for example, consists of sixteen typewritten pages, and lasted about thirty minutes; I have counted five instances when the shorthand reporter indicated the word "laughter." At its conclusion, the reporters were so delighted with the new atmosphere that they gave him a prolonged ovation. Sometimes there was grimness or firmness or resentment or resolute determination written into his jaw when occasions warranted them, as for example during the actions of the Supreme Court in striking down essential New Deal legislation, or during the dark days of the war; but never any appearance of fear, panic, or sense of being lost on his way—forever calm, dignified, imperturbable. Roosevelt liked reporters personally; he liked to talk with them collectively and individually. Some of them were occasionally invited to dinner or other social events at the White House. He used to seek out their views and reactions to what he had said or done, or was about to do; frequently he profited from these contacts. He read their stories and many of the various columnists as well. Frequently, he would call the attention of his department or agency heads to a column or a newspaper story, suggesting how it should be handled.[43]

But his press conferences meant much more to him than appeared on the surface. Roosevelt knew how much he needed the press and radio in his efforts to educate and lead public opinion; he also knew how much the press and radio needed him as a principal, dramatic, ultimate source of news. So in meeting their craving for news, he served his own interests by making a majority of them grateful and friendly. Each side of the conference learned to use the other for his own purposes, and each appreciated what the conferences meant to the other. The men clustering around his desk were mostly friendly to him, as he well knew, no matter what their employers believed. Of course, there are always obvious antagonisms during a press conference. The objective of the reporters is to get news quickly and accurately; sometimes the public interest or the political interest of the President calls for withholding news until a more appropriate time. I do not refer to deception, or even to management of news. There is a proper timing for news as for all political actions; and a reporter's sense of timing may frequently be different from a political officeholder's. Roosevelt, like all Presidents, liked to spring surprises or release unexpected information; he, like the others, abhorred leaks. Nothing is more appreciated by a reporter than an opportunity to scoop or take advantage of a leak. Roosevelt was quite adept at maintaining a proper balance between his own objectives and the reporters', retaining the friendship of most of the reporters in spite of this built-in diversity of interest.

He tried to keep to a schedule of two press conferences per week, one for the morning newspapers and radio announcers and one for the afternoon. Whether he was in Washington, Hyde Park or Albany, or even on a ship or train, he could always truthfully portray himself to the readers or listeners as being the center and prime mover of all activity.

"Off-the-record" and "background" statements by Roosevelt enabled him to accomplish many things he could not have done if his words were to be recorded. He could spike rumors by giving the actual facts in complete confidence; he could explain confidentially why reporters should refrain from probing into sensitive areas of foreign affairs or military strategy. He could reveal his own thinking and motives on a proposed project long before the project came into being, so that when it did appear, the news would be more intelligently written—and more helpful to him. Trial balloons could be more easily launched—and pulled down. Roosevelt knew how to use these conferences to explain in very simple newspaper language an elaborate government policy. While a press conference was less formal than a message or a speech, or even a fireside chat, it would take place more frequently. And it, too, had its own great impact on people's knowledge and understanding, which hopefully would lead to public approval of White House policy and eventually make itself felt in the halls of the Capitol. The press conference was one important means of contact between the President and the people, and Roosevelt always did his best to keep that contact close and continuous. A democracy does not have its own newspaper or official organ; it relies upon privately owned media for that purpose.

One cannot read the transcripts of these conferences without noticing at once how completely and consistently the President held the initiative at all times without being aggressive about it, and how skillfully he could lead the discussion into the fields he wanted. No President has run a press conference with more skill and charm—or with more benefit to himself.

Frequently, as in the special conferences on the annual budget consisting of several hundred printed pages, the President was to educate the press on intricate and complex questions of international finance, monetary problems, war strategy, and an infinite variety of others. When a reporter would ask a question showing misunderstanding of a policy, he would as a "background" or "off-the-record" statement explain it very carefully. This was so much more to his own interest than to have a reporter write his story in goodwill but based upon ignorance. On many occasions reporters would voluntarily ask for "background" or "off-the-record" information. The President, no matter how rushed or tired he might be, always seized the opportunity.

The press conferences of later Presidents, which are now held in a very large hall in front of television cameras, are very different from Roosevelt's conferences —all held before the popular use of television. It now has the advantage of permitting the country actually to see the President. It does not permit the devices of background and off-the-record material. It also does not allow such frequency of conferences because of the danger of public over-exposure on television; and it prevents the informality of the Roosevelt conference.

One outstanding example of the use of a press conference to educate reporters and commentators on policy and, through their stories, the public itself, was the one on lend-lease on December 17, 1940. It contained the simple analogy between the lend-lease plan he was going to present to Congress and lending a garden hose to a neighbor whose house had caught fire, to be used to put out the fire and then to be returned. The bill itself was not introduced until January 1941 and it was not passed until March 11. He thought that this idea was something which the public should have in advance, so he authorized the reporters to attribute it to him.[44] There is no doubt that this simple and appealing presentation of the plan did much to create public understanding of what was involved.

One of the devices used in connection with press conferences—secretly, infrequently, but very effectively—was the "planted" question. The President, on occasion, preferred to have a matter raised by questions from reporters. This "planting" would ordinarily be done orally and behind the scenes by the press secretary asking a friendly reporter to put the question which Roosevelt wanted to discuss.

For many of his conferences, there would be advance discussion between Roosevelt and Stephen Early, his very able press secretary, as to what was likely to come up. Early could usually determine, by casual conversation with reporters, what they were curious about on any particular day. Sometimes preparations would include hurried phone calls for the correct answers. An example was the prior preparation for his famous press conference on December 28, 1943, on the temporary replacement of "Dr. New Deal" by "Dr. Win-the-War." Roosevelt knew that this would come up, because he had casually mentioned the idea to one reporter at the end of the preceding conference, and there had been some flurries in the newspapers about it. So, in preparation for the next conference, he asked me to prepare a full list of the New Deal legislation. He kept this list before him at the conference; and he enumerated fully the accomplishments of Dr. New Deal and the necessity of replacing him temporarily with Dr. Win-the-War. These two doctors soon became well-known practitioners. They show again

Roosevelt's style of using simple terms and homely phrases to explain complex problems.[45]

Another instrument which Roosevelt used for education of the public, for maintaining public morale during dark and trying days, for projecting his own peculiar image, for building up support for his policies, and for bringing popular influence to bear on the members of Congress, was the famous "fireside chat." In 1937 he had written: "It had been my custom as Governor to make similar reports from time to time to the public of the State, not only for the purpose of informing them of what had been done, but also to enlist their support on various occasions when a hostile Legislature declined to enact legislation for the benefit of the people."

When he carried the same practice into the White House, a broadcasting official called the speeches "fireside chats." It was a symbolic phrase characterizing the intimate, chatty, informal nature of the talk; incidentally, there was a fireplace in the White House room where they were delivered, and Roosevelt did sit in front of it as he spoke. Today, by contrast, there is a special well-equipped broadcasting room in the White House used for radio and television speeches of the President. The phrase "fireside chat" has not been used with respect to any of Roosevelt's successors. All the symbolism of Roosevelt's intimate, chatty style had disappeared, even before the actual fireplace did.

Roosevelt was not the first President to use the radio; but, with few exceptions, the radio had been used only to carry a speech which was being delivered before a live audience. Roosevelt was the first to use radio in the White House on its own, and not merely as an adjunct to a speech. Obviously, the kind of speaking ordinarily used before a responsive, live audience had to be changed when addressing a bare microphone with an unseen audience. Roosevelt brought to the White House microphone, as he did to the White House press conference, his own distinctive style.

The microphone was able to reach many millions all over the nation; on important occasions it was computed to have reached more than 50 million listeners. Not only could he reach an audience of this unprecedented size; he was able to reach his listeners without the screening and manipulation of press conference news by reporters, city editors or publishers. All the devices of unfriendly reporters or newspaper owners—quoting out of context, improper emphasis, misleading headlines—were balked on the radio. The President was talking directly to the people; the people would get his message precisely as he gave it, and they would get it before some adverse radio commentator could get on the air to criticize it.

While many of the banks of the nation were still closed in the national banking holiday declared March 6, 1933, Roosevelt took to the radio to deliver on March 12 his first, and one of his most effective, fireside chats. It was on a Sunday night; and some of the solvent banks were to be permitted to open the next morning. All of the steps of the last few days which had been taken with respect to the banks were bewildering to most Americans. As the President later wrote: "There had always been so much mystery thrown around the banking business, there was so much fear in the minds of bank depositors during these days of the banking crisis, and so much had happened during this first week, that I decided to use the radio to explain to the average men and women of the nation who had their money then tied up in some bank what we had done, and what we intended to do in the banking situation."[46]

The Treasury Department prepared a scholarly, comprehensive draft of a speech. The President saw that it would be meaningless to most people, tossed it aside without any attempt at rewriting, and proceeded to dictate his own. He dictated it in simple, ordinary language, looking for words that he would normally use in an informal conversation with one or two of his friends. He usually found the kind of language that everyone could understand. And everyone did understand that fireside chat, even—as Will Rogers, the great humorist of that day said—the bankers themselves. Confidence in the banks was restored. And in those dark days, confidence was essential, for a continued panic of bewilderment could have meant chaos and collapse. The greatest compliment to Roosevelt's radio speech is that when the banks did open the next day, instead of rushing to take their money out, people rushed to them to make deposits of the money which they had drawn out to put into hiding.

The physical arrangements in which the twenty-six fireside chats were delivered during his tenure of office bore little relationship to the quiet and secluded atmosphere generally associated with a real fireside. The President would sit before a desk on which were bunched three or four microphones, a reading light, a pitcher of water and drinking glasses. Equipment and machinery had to be brought in for the broadcast to the nation. There were some thirty uncomfortable folding chairs for those who had been invited to listen, usually friends, house guests and selected public officials. The audience was seated about 10:10 P.M. for a 10:30 broadcast (the usual hour), and the President was wheeled in about 10:20, carrying his reading-copy book, with the inevitable cigarette holder set at a jaunty angle in his mouth.

Radio announcers for the major broadcasting chains walked about, testing their microphones. The radio engineers tested their equipment, which was spread all over the floor from wall to wall, making it difficult to move around the small room, never intended or constructed for such use. There was a lot of confusion until 10:30 arrived.

The President, once seated at his desk, exchanged greetings and pleasantries for a few moments with the guests and the announcers. As 10:30 approached, the atmosphere got quiet but more tense. The President would put out his cigarette, arrange his reading copy, and take a drink of water as nervously as when he was about to address a visible audience. Then, on signal, complete silence, a nod from the chief radio engineer, the usual terse statement from each announcer that the broadcast was coming from the White House and introducing "The President of the United States"—and finally the clear resonant voice: "My friends."

The President's nervousness quickly disappeared; everyone sat back and listened; some of us followed the speech from mimeographed copies. When he had finished, we all rose as the radio stations played "The Star-Spangled Banner." Then, at the signal showing that the President was off the air, we went up to his desk to talk with him. There was a general hum of conversation, congratulations and good-nights, and the audience gradually drifted away.

The President remained behind to let the newspaper and movie photographers take pictures of him reading certain passages. He would select these passages himself as the ones he wanted to be made more prominent. When this was over, he would go upstairs to the Oval Room for a drink and a sandwich, a postmortem discussion of the speech with house guests or members of his staff who were present, the reading of some of the usual telegrams which would begin to come in almost immediately; and then to bed.

I was present at many of these fireside chats, and was always struck by the simplicity, effectiveness and homely atmosphere of it all. For Roosevelt, by his style of speaking and by the words he used, was able to create a feeling of intimacy with each of his listeners. This was natural because he actually felt that intimacy himself. As he spoke, it was obvious that he was thinking of the different kinds of people he was talking with, rather than talking to. It was as if the microphone had been removed and he was seated in the living rooms of the American families. He forgot the audience of friends in the room; he would gesture as if he were discussing crops with a farmer, or the price of food with a housewife, or rates of wages with a worker. There was no attempt at oratory; in its place were substituted deep sincerity of tone, friendliness, warmth and calmness of voice. In a word, he would "chat."

So convinced was Roosevelt of the effectiveness of radio even when it was merely an adjunct to a regular speech before a live audience, that he would often prepare his live speeches more with the radio audience in mind than the audience before him. Frequently, he went out of his way to arrange to have a scheduled speech before a live audience delivered at a time when the largest possible radio audience would be available. Sometimes this was impossible—as, for example, in the case of the Annual Message to the Congress in 1944 which had to be delivered at noon. On that occasion, he delivered verbatim over the radio later in the evening the exact message he had sent to Congress that day. He added only a short introduction: "Only a few of the newspapers can print" (he refrained from saying "would be willing to print") "this message in full, and I am very anxious that the American people be given the opportunity to hear what I have recommended to Congress for this fateful year in our history—and the reasons for those recommendations. Here is what I said."[47] Then followed a reading of the message.

Part of his skill in using the fireside chat lay in his acute sense of timing, in his ability to space them—not to talk so frequently as to wear out his welcome in the homes of his listeners, but not so seldom as to lose the potentiality of the radio appeal. He preferred periods when Congress was not in session; he was of the view that while Congress was in Washington, it was the more powerful "sounding board"; but when it was not in Washington, the President was the exclusive sounding board.[48] He would wait patiently for some logical reason for making a chat.[49]

While the direct purpose of some chats was to bring pressure in support of his proposed legislation, most of them were for the purpose of educating the public about actions the government was taking, such as the one on banking. All of them in his first two years were of this type. This was quite to be expected, because so many innovations in the American economic system were being installed and because the federal government was going into so many new fields which closely touched the lives and work of all Americans.

His style in Washington was not to try to use the same kind of hard pressure against Congress that he had used against the Republican legislative leaders in Albany. He had a greater respect for congressmen generally and for the congressional leaders than he had had for the Republican leadership in Albany. Furthermore, as Governor he could almost always count on all the Democratic members following his lead. This was not true in Washington. Many of his recommendations were initially received by a number of the Democratic members with reservations and doubts. He did not want to create additional hostility by ridicule or harsh language, at least during his first term; he did not want to divide his party if he could avoid it, and he was aware that hard-sell pressure would have that effect.

But even this soft-sell approach was a form of pressure. It was a definite feature of the Roosevelt style. He knew that understanding and approval on the part of the people would indirectly but surely have their effect in Congress; and also would produce the political advantage of associating in the public mind the social advances of the New Deal with Roosevelt personally and with the Democratic administration. For years, he would repeat, in different words, the same theme: "Are you not better off now than you were in 1932?" The answers to this question would come clear and loud in the overwhelming Democratic election victories of 1934, 1936 and 1938.

The legislation which Congress had enacted, when it adjourned after the hundred days of 1933, was essentially a conservative, down-the-middle-of-the-road combination of attempts (1) to promote recovery quickly, and (2) to remove some of the most glaring evils of the industrial and financial system. There was little of a radical nature, as we now understand the term. All the essentials of a capitalistic, private profit régime had been scrupulously retained; all that was attempted was a measure of regulation and reform of the existing traditional system.

Some of the laws which Roosevelt had so strongly recommended did not reflect his own thinking on methods—as distinguished from objectives—as much as it did the thinking of those most concerned in their operation. This was an essential part of the Roosevelt style in framing some important pieces of legislation. For example, in the months following the election of 1932, there were scores of suggested measures being discussed in Washington and elsewhere for the recovery of agriculture. He had his own ideas of what should be done. But he was fox enough to know that if he suggested one, all the proponents of the other ideas would be antagonized into opposing it when it reached Congress; and he was intent on getting something done immediately, before the planting time of 1933. He insisted that the farm organizations get together under the supervision of Henry Wallace, the new Secretary of Agriculture, and stay together until they could agree upon a bill which they would all back. That is just what he got. For the extreme liberals, it did not go far enough; for the conservatives, it was too much; but it became the law in time for spring planting. The farm leaders and the farmers were satisfied with it.

In many situations during his presidency where experts or department heads disagreed with each other he would suggest, not entirely humorously, that they "be locked in a room without dinner until they agreed."

This was essentially his style also in framing the National Industrial Recovery Act. Roosevelt in 1933 believed that the best and quickest road to industrial recovery lay through some form of cooperation between business and government, with a certain amount of self-government by business, accompanied by a fair treatment of labor. In early 1933, labor began to agitate for legislation which had been introduced by Senator Hugo Black to limit hours of work to five days a week or to six hours a day. Many different ideas were suggested by others. Consensus between labor and management seemed impossible, though deputies of the President sought mightily to reach it. What everyone did agree on, however, was that the old, competitive laissez-faire system was no longer possible, and that cooperation of industry and labor under the watchful eye of government was what was needed. What finally emerged was based on the idea of industry planning, free of antitrust laws, in a way which would help both business and labor. Labor agreed to this on the theory that a federal wage-and-hour law would otherwise not be possible in 1933; fair businessmen agreed because it would protect them from the competition of the exploiters of labor. Senator Wagner, who was to sponsor the bill, also insisted that in this scheme of things labor unions must be fully protected in their right to unionize a shop and enroll members without any restraint from management, and must be assured by law of the right to collective bargaining. In the midst of wrangling over the methods to carry out all these ideas, Roosevelt appointed a small committee to draft a bill, ordered them to lock themselves in a room, and not to come out until they were agreed on one. The committee complied. Business got the right to draft codes free from the antitrust laws; labor got the right as a matter of law to minimum wages and maximum hours, the right to unionize without interference from employers, and the right to insist on collective bargaining; and child labor was eliminated.

In both of these laws, the President was following a road "down the middle"; in both, the government was to be the broker, the conciliator. It was a system of national planning of farmer-government and business-government cooperation. This was indeed the general spirit of the so-called First New Deal. For several reasons to be discussed later, his style was to change substantially in 1935 in the so-called Second New Deal when he would turn sharply to the left. But in 1933–34, Roosevelt had the style and characteristics of a President of all the people, the harmonizer, the unifier of all interests. He sought to avoid the extremes of the right and of the left; and he rose above any considerations of party.

The style of "locking people in a room" was one which he frequently followed when he was convinced that all the parties involved were really in accord with his objectives, but in disagreement as to method. Nearly always the parties would emerge with an agreement—one with which no one was entirely happy but with which all were willing to work and try to make successful. This was particularly true of many reorganizations of government agencies, and consolidations and transfers of function from one agency to another which became necessary for increased efficiency during the war.

Roosevelt, four months before his first inauguration and only a week after his election, in an interview with the *New York Times* reported on November 13, 1933, had given his conception of the office of the President:

"The Presidency is not merely an administrative office. That is the least of it. It is pre-eminently a place of moral leadership. All of our greatest Presidents were leaders of thought at times when certain historic ideas in the life of the nation had to be clarified. . . . That is what the office is, a superb opportunity for reapplying, applying to new conditions, the simple rules of human conduct to which we always go back. Without leadership alert and sensitive to change, we are all bogged up or lose our way."

Certainly this conception was exemplified by the first hundred days. The historic idea of democracy and of the role of the mass of people in that democracy was reaffirmed. The historic idea of America as a land of free enterprise and private initiative was reaffirmed. But to the new conditions of 1933 there applied "a new version of the simple rules of human conduct," that the welfare of the people—their right to the pursuit of happiness—was to be a primary concern and activity of the federal government. "New conditions" in 1933 required the abandonment of complete laissez-faire and rugged individualism, and the intervention of government into the private enterprise system under a "leadership alert and sensitive to change." It was necessary if moral leadership was to lead a system that "had lost its way" and become "all bogged up" back to a new open road.

No President had a clearer conception of the great powers of the presidency in our democratic nation—and Roosevelt showed it during the hundred days. Lincoln had increased the conception of the presidency under the conditions of armed civil strife to the logical conclusion that there was nothing the President could not do to save the Constitution, for he had sworn to preserve it, irrespective of legal strictures.

Roosevelt had the same conception as Lincoln and practiced it from 1933; but he enlarged it to apply to situations where there was no armed strife. As he said in his first Inaugural, the economic conditions he faced warranted action as strong as that toward an actual invasion by an armed enemy. Moving on that conception he had taken the necessary steps to save the American capitalist system, which had so mismanaged its own interests that the country was on the verge of economic ruin; but he also had imposed upon it a structure of reform and had added to it basic social changes. He proved that the American political structure was strong enough to retain its private enterprise economic system, reform it, and add to it a degree of economic security for the individual—and survive the kind of economic disaster which had buried the democracy of other lands. When the Supreme Court sought to thwart this conception by its decision striking down the National Recovery Act in 1935, he was to point out in the press conferences on May 29, 1935,[50] speaking of "the legislation that was passed in April, May and June of 1917," that "a great deal of that legislation was far more violative of the strict interpretation of the Constitution than any legislation that was passed in 1933—those war acts conferred upon the Executive far greater power over human beings and over property than anything that was done in 1933. But the Supreme Court has finally ruled that *extraordinary conditions* do not create or enlarge constitutional power." (Emphasis added) He then added as a masterpiece of understatement, "It was a very interesting statement on the part of the Court." He was to do something about that statement soon; but he would fail. He was to fail because, among other reasons, the Court itself was to do something about it.

What Roosevelt did after acting on all the bills which Congress had left with him on adjournment after the hundred days has always impressed me as a significant demonstration of his psychology. He cruised up to his old summer home in Campobello.

That was where twelve years before he had been stricken with polio. He had not been willing to go back since that attack. One can understand why. But now he had thoroughly beaten the crippling effects by fighting his way up to the most exalted political position in the entire civilized world. It was a complete victory over the paralysis, the results of which were still with him. Having accomplished all this—and not before—he was ready to go back where the disaster had struck.

It had been a hard road over many hurdles and obstacles, just as his whole political life starting in 1910 had been a hard road. Looking back over it, one can better understand the depth of the self-confidence and self-assurance, which had increased and become a major part of him by 1933. He had overcome so many obstacles: his patrician birth and family wealth causing an early snobbishness and superciliousness; his successful fight with the powerful organization of Tammany Hall while he was in the State Senate; the sloth, delay and red tape he found when he became Assistant Secretary of the Navy; the crushing political defeats of 1914 and 1920; the complete paralysis which had laid him low in Campobello; the tough campaign for the governorship in 1928, an uphill battle in which Smith lost the State of New York by over 100,000 votes; the many roadblocks placed in his path by a hostile legislature in Albany; the pitfalls and political traps set for him during his governorship arising out of official corruption in New York City; the touch-and-go fight in Chicago for the Presidential nomination; the election in 1932; and finally the panic and fear and despair among the American people in March 1933.

He had overcome them all. He had, to cap it all, proposed and obtained a vast program of national reform and recovery from the Congress.

There is little wonder that he had such self-confidence and self-assurance. There is little wonder that Mrs. Roosevelt was able to write after his death: "I have never heard him say there was a problem that he thought it was impossible for human beings to solve. He recognized the difficulties, and often said that while he did not know the answer he was completely confident that there was an answer ... and that one had to try until one either found it for one's self or got it through some one else. *He never talked about his doubts. . . .* I never knew him to face life, or any problem that came up, with fear. . . ."[51]

She summed it up with the statement: "I have never known a man who gave one a greater sense of security." The nation needed this sense of security in 1933. It was to need it even more during the disastrous war days of 1942.

Roosevelt's style in 1942 was to tell the American people the blunt truth about our defeats and about the Japanese and Nazi victories. He even warned them that things would get worse before they could get better. There was no such thing as a "credibility gap" in the White House. There was only one limitation: never to reveal anything which would give information to the enemy.

But he never for a moment betrayed the slightest doubt that victory would come in the long run; for he never felt any doubt. I am sure that that self-confidence also had its effect on the Chiefs of Staff of the United States. One of the most vivid recollections I have of the days of my own service in the White House is that of General Marshall, Admiral King and General Arnold (the United States Chiefs of Staff of the Army, Navy and Air Force) coming over to the White House together almost daily to consult with the President on the strategy of the war. I remember seeing them as they left the conferences with their calm, determined, fighting faces; and I always felt certain that a great deal of that calm confidence and firm determination were reflections of the spirit of the man whom they had just left.

In 1933, Roosevelt's self-confidence and self-assurance were called upon many times to keep the American people confident and self-assured as they struggled up in recovery from the depths of 1932. The economy rose; employment increased; things were a little better by July 1933. The important fact was that panic was gone, paralyzing fear had been dissipated. Then, by October 1933, the economy fell again, and unemployment got worse. Roosevelt continued to experiment—this time with gold. He never lost courage; he never stopped trying; he never lapsed into any doubt as to some final solution. In his fourth fireside chat in October 1933, he explained his monetary policy in simple language, gave some statistics of increased employment since the beginning of the New Deal, admitted he was not satisfied; but confidently asserted: "Our troubles will not be over tomorrow, but we are on our way, and we are headed in the right direction."

In 1934, improvement continued; but it was not a real recovery. It was mostly a response to putting more purchasing power in the pockets of farmers, workers and unemployed. Even though the cold statistics of the leading economic indexes read better, Roosevelt was more interested in how human beings felt than what the statistics showed. The American people acknowledged his efforts when the mid-term 1934 congressional elections came around. To Roosevelt's own admitted surprise,[52] instead of the almost invariable loss of congressional seats in mid-term elections by the party in power, the people in 1934 elected an increased Democratic majority in both houses.

But no matter what the elections showed his popularity to be, there were continuing, ominous mutterings of opposition—and of hatred. The opposition and most of the hatred had come from both sides. It had come from the right, from those who condemned certain measures of the New Deal: spending, interference with business, support of labor, desertion of the gold standard. This opposition had culminated in the formation of the American Liberty League in August 1934. From the extreme left also came opposition: from radical leaders like Huey Long, Father Coughlin, Dr. Francis Townsend—all with panaceas of "sharing the wealth," currency inflation, nationalization of banking, and so forth. All three of these left extremists were making their mark with the American people; their plans were simple and understandable. They organized thousands of clubs throughout the nation. Reports were coming into the White House that the 1936 election was going to be imperilled by the growth of these movements from both sides of extremism.

Roosevelt's style in meeting these threats from the left was different from his usual style. Instead of action, instead of the harsh words which he used against the American Liberty League, there was only watchful waiting, biding his time. He believed that they were making a political mistake in their timing in choosing 1935 rather than 1936, the election year, for their attacks; and that by Election Day the common sense of the American people would prevail. He was proven to be right. During those days before the elections of 1934, however, Roosevelt showed very little of the lion in his style of dealing with the leftists. While he wrote to some people that he was waiting for the right time, it is my own opinion that he was not yet sure of what he wanted to do.

He was unwilling, of course, as a matter of statesmanship, to compete with the dangerous ideologies of the demagogues for he knew that the panaceas they were proposing would lead to disaster. Instead, he began to think of programs of his own for the coming year. One of them was social security; foxlike, on June 8, 1934, long before the 1934 elections, he told Congress and the American people of his plan of social security in general terms, and he appointed a high-level committee to formulate specific legislation.

In his Annual Message to Congress in 1935, he was ready to admit that he had failed to accomplish in 1933 all that he had intended. He pointed out that the old inequalities of the pre-New Deal years still existed, "little changed by past sporadic remedies." He announced that he was now ready to submit to Congress a rounded broad program designed to establish the principal factors of security which he had discussed last June in his message to Congress, including "unemployment insurance, old age insurance, benefits for children, for mothers, for handicapped, for maternity care."

Putting people to work, he explained, was in 1933 a method merely to meet destitution. "The stark fact before us," he admitted in 1935, "is that great numbers still remain unemployed," estimating that there were still 5 million unemployed, of whom only 1.5 million were unemployable. In spite of his skepticism as to what he had accomplished, he had reduced unemployment by 7 million and —more important—everybody was eating; there was none of the starvation of 1932. But he was opposed to continuing the dole for the destitute, and insisted on substituting work. "The Federal Government must and shall quit this business of relief" for the 3.5 million employables.

In accordance with this general outline, he submitted to Congress during 1935 additional recommendations of legislation embracing both recovery and reform. The activist had finally made up his mind which way he should go, and he boldly struck out on his path. He was again, after months of inactivity and indecision, flexing his muscles, experimenting in many fields, looking for the solution which he knew could be found some place. This is the way he would meet the challenge of the lunatic fringe on the left; these were the bills he submitted, with a steadiness and rapidity quite reminiscent of—though not quite equal to—the speed of the hundred days of two years earlier:

1. January 17, 1935. The social security message and proposed bill. They were based upon the report of the committee he had appointed the year before to study social security and recommend legislation.

It was quite typical of Roosevelt's style in important, novel policy matters to build up interest and discussion by means of a study committee of this type, long before the final policy was fixed and announced. The newspapers and radio commentators would follow the proceedings of the committee, write stories about it and interview its members. As a result, few were startled and many had been educated when the policy was finally formulated, no matter how novel it was in American life. He had done the same thing as Governor several times with great success.

Putting forth the general idea of social security in 1934 just before the election of 1934, then enlarging upon it in 1935 before the election of 1936, was a perfect example of Roosevelt's sense of political timing.

2. January 24, 1935. A bill on the better use of our national resources for the benefit of all the people.

3. March 12, 1935. The public utility holding companies bill, which soon became known as the "death sentence bill."

4. March 22, 1935. A pure food and drug bill.

5. June 6, 1935. Two railroad retirement bills to replace the one declared unconstitutional on May 6, 1935.

6. June 19, 1935. A drastic bill for tax revision—which was immediately labelled by its critics (those whom it hit most) the "soak-the-rich" tax bill. It called for high inheritance and gift taxes; increased income taxes on very large incomes and graduated income taxes for corporations. This tax bill was clearly and admittedly not designed for additional revenue; he had said in his budget message that year that no new taxes were needed. It was purely a social experiment for greater equality in the distribution of wealth and income.

7. June 27, 1935. A bill to invalidate gold clauses in government contracts.

In addition to this list, other bills had been introduced by individual congressmen with analogous objectives which the President had approved.

This was what has been called the "Second New Deal." Gone were the attempts at planned cooperation with business. Instead recommendations for social legislation were substituted principally for the benefit of those at the bottom of the economic pyramid, traditionally the chief concern of Roosevelt.

In addition, one of the most important—and probably the most radical—bills of this Second New Deal was enacted in 1935, the Wagner Labor Relations Act. The unions of the nation were enabled by this act to build up to their present strength, because of its provisions guaranteeing by law the right to unionize without interference from employers, and requiring employers to bargain collectively in good faith.

The history of this legislation sheds no great luster on Roosevelt; but it is a good example of his occasional foxlike and opportunistic tactics. Senator Wagner introduced his bill in February 1935. He did not get one bit of help from the White House; singlehandedly, he had brought about its passage in the Senate on May 16, 1935. On May 24, Roosevelt for the first time sensing all the political advantage of the bill from which he had inexplicably remained aloof so long, and anticipating that with the overwhelming vote for the bill in the Senate (63–12) it would certainly pass the House, jumped on the bandwagon. By June 1935, the Wagner Labor Relations Bill suddenly became one of his "must" bills. In the meantime, on May 27, 1935, the Court had declared unconstitutional the National Industrial Recovery Act, on which unionism had been thriving by reason of Section 7-A, which guaranteed collective bargaining and unhampered unionization. In spite of public appeals by the United States Chamber of Commerce and the large industrial leaders of the country—and in spite of substantial amounts of personal abuse heaped upon the President—he helped push the bill through Congress, and signed it on July 5, 1935.

Many different explanations have been offered by various writers for Roosevelt's switch in 1935 to the Second New Deal:

1. It was an effort to "steal the thunder" from Long, Coughlin and Townsend.

2. The "squeeze" he was feeling between the rabid attacks from the American Liberty League and the U.S. Chamber of Commerce on the right, and the complaints of inadequacy of his leadership by the extreme liberals in Congress and even by some of his own Cabinet.

3. Most of the conservative right was by now vehemently and vitriolically against him: big business, the press, and even some of his own 1933 advisers.

4. The failure of business to cooperate fairly with labor under the National Industrial Recovery Act (NIRA).

5. The blow from the Supreme Court on NIRA on May 27, 1935, which spelled the doom of the planned cooperation with business which he had tried in the First New Deal.

6. A final victory obtained by those around the President who believed in the Brandeis theory of "fragmentation," "atomization," small enterprise and active competition rather than big enterprise with government regulation.

In my opinion, while all of these were contributing factors—especially the desire to put an end to the share-the-wealth schemes of Huey Long—the chief reason was that his experiment in 1933 with establishing a partnership between business and government had failed even before the Supreme Court struck it down. It relied upon the goodwill and cooperation of big business; real cooperation and goodwill did not last. The measures proposed in 1935 were not something new to him as the NIRA was. The social philosophy of the 1935 program was the old Roosevelt, essentially what he had carried out as Governor and had promised in the campaign of 1932. Unemployment insurance, old age relief, utility regulation, a more equitable distribution of wealth—these were all familiar, comfortable, old clothes for Roosevelt.

"Second New Deal" is really something of a misnomer if it implies a repudiation of the First New Deal in its entirety. Most of the 1933 New Deal—in fact, all of it except AAA and NIRA—was of the same general nature as the so-called Second New Deal. It included: truth-in-securities legislation, banking reform, TVA and regional planning, relief for the needy unemployed, saving homes and farms from foreclosure by federal loans at low interest, bank deposit guarantees, the Civilian Conservation Corps. These all survived attacks in the Court, and were all continued in addition to the new measures suggested by Roosevelt in 1935. Together they added up to what we now call *the* New Deal. The policies which were dropped were the planned cooperation of business and government, and of agriculture and government.

Roosevelt proposed all this new legislation in 1935; but the Congress of 1935 was not the complaisant Congress of 1933. The national sense of crisis was gone. Congress was no longer scared. Big business and big finance had been saved. Some of the bills of 1935 received very rugged treatment in Congress. The President used all his power in phone calls and letters to congressmen, sending emissaries to the Hill, all his charm and capacity for personal persuasion. But in spite of his efforts, by August 1935, at which time the Congress seemed ready to quit and go home, many of these recommended bills had not yet been enacted. Nor did they seem likely to be.

Some members of Congress had been affected by the hatred and vituperation against Roosevelt which had begun in 1934 and had reached extravagant proportions by 1935. Much of the press had joined in. It was the "upper-class" American —Roosevelt's own "class," as they called it—who led the pack of Roosevelt haters. The most incredible and vicious stories were spread about him. He was a chronic liar, a maniac, a syphilitic, a communist. The strangest part of this phenomenon—never equalled in ferocity since the time of Andrew Jackson—was that the loudest and harshest of the Roosevelt haters were those who had benefitted most from the New Deal measures of 1933. All of the critics were better off in 1935 than they had been in 1932. Probably most of the condemnation of Roosevelt was centered on the "soak-the-rich" tax bill as the favorite target. With those who cried that he was leading the country into communism, it was fruitless to argue that by his reforms and by his relief of starvation he had probably saved the American private profit system from communism or some other form of destruction. Roosevelt's thinking from the very start and all his style of legislation had assumed that reform and all measures of social welfare could be superimposed on the traditional American capitalist system without impairing it. His policies had been based on that assumption, and he never wavered from it. In fact, a large number of the New Deal measures merely brought America up to the social standards of England and some of the western European countries. Perhaps the real basis of the hatred was the fact that Roosevelt had proven the inadequacy of the great financiers and industrialists; that he had shown that financial success was not necessarily a badge of virtue, and that it definitely should not be the source of national political power which it had been in the past before Theodore Roosevelt and after Woodrow Wilson.

But the chief reason for the recalcitrance of Congress in 1935 was a desire to assert its independence of the executive, a distaste for the rubber-stamp label continually fastened on it by those hostile to Roosevelt and all his deeds.

The results of the 1934 congressional election, however—by which many Democratic congressmen were returned to Congress and new Democrats elected as members, chiefly because of Roosevelt's hold on the American voters and because of their approval of his performance during the past two years—kept intact all of Roosevelt's self-confidence and self-assurance. What he had lost in 1935 was the control of Congress which he had possessed in such great degree in the extraordinary session of 1933.

The beginning of the 1935 session was clearly a revolt. Congress rejected his proposal to join the World Court. It tacked onto the Works Relief Bill an amendment, which Roosevelt opposed, providing for prevailing wage rates. In the lower courts, some of the New Deal statutes were being struck down, encouraging the unfriendly forces in Congress to further opposition. The President's friends on the Hill and elsewhere warned him of impending disaster in Congress, and urged him to assert his leadership and to take to the radio. Roosevelt expressed his reluctance to making further radio appeals by pointing out that "people tire of seeing the same name day after day in the important headlines of the papers, and the same voice night after night over the radio." His inaction continued to surprise and to alienate many supporters, and to encourage wider rebellion on the Hill.

In June 1935, after long deliberation on what course to follow, and apparently fixing his timing by the Supreme Court's decision on May 27 striking down the NIRA, he finally went into action. On June 4, 1935, a week after the NIRA decision, he sent a very polite note to the legislative leaders in which he enumerated those bills which were "the . . . things I must get this session from the Congress." The list of "the things" was impressive—even coming from Roosevelt. Some of them had already been the subject of vitriolic congressional debate: the public utilities holding company bill, the social security bill and the Wagner national labor relations bill. Some of them which pertained to particular industries had been made necessary by the NIRA decision: the Guffey coal bill, some AAA amendments, the oil bill. On June 19, the "soak-the-rich" tax bill went up to Congress and immediately released a further flood of denunciation. All of them soon became known as the "must bills."

When talk of early adjournment without congressional action on these bills continued, Roosevelt got tougher. He had to find a way to keep Congress in session, in spite of the members' hurry to end the long, acrimonious session and to get away from the summer heat and humidity of Washington. In the Franklin D. Roosevelt Library, there is an undated, signed memorandum which apparently had been prepared for him, showing how this could be done:

Although there has been considerable talk in both Houses of adjournment early next week, this situation can easily be controlled by holding up the conference report on the Tax Bill until all other vitally important bills are disposed of. Chairman Doughton has given his assurance that he will endeavor to arrange the conference report on the tax bill so as to keep the date of adjournment under control.

The Vice-President and Senator Robinson for the Senate, and the Speaker, Mr. Boland and Mr. Taylor for the House, have given assurances that they will cooperate to oppose any move for adjournment until the "must" bills are passed.

On this sheet of paper the President had written in longhand the bills he was thinking of insisting upon.

A dinner conference (which was also referred to in this memo) had been set at the White House with the legislative leaders for Sunday evening, August 18, 1935. In preparation for the conference, the President dictated for his own use the following revised list of the "must" bills:[53]

1. Tax Bill
2. Federal Alcohol Control Bill
3. Holding Company Bill
4. Guffey Coal Bill
5. Gold Clause Bill
6. Walsh Government Control Bill
7. World Power Conference Resolution
8. Lemke Farm Moratorium Bill
9. Railroad Bankruptcy Bill
10. Two Railroad Retirement Bills
11. TVA Bill.
12. (?) [sic] Bankhead Share Cropper Bill.

Present at the dinner were the Vice President, the Democratic leaders of the Senate and House and the Democratic chairman of Appropriations and Rules. There is no record of what went on at the dinner. But the President must have taken off his gloves and bluntly insisted on these bills. We do know that after the dinner, the leaders kept Congress in session until it had passed all of this list, except for No. 6 (passed the following year) and No. 12.

When Congress finally adjourned, it had enacted almost as many and as important domestic pieces of legislation as its predecessor Congress of 1933. Only a few months before, Roosevelt had appeared to be—as Charles A. Beard has written—at the end of his rope; but now Beard summed up the results of the 1935 session: "Seldom, if ever, in the long history of Congress had so many striking and vital measures been spread upon the law books in a single session."

It was the action of the lion which had produced this; the inactivity and watchful waiting of the fox had ended.

The presence of Congress in Washington is seldom a source of comfort and tranquility for a President. Roosevelt therefore only rarely left Washington while Congress was in session. He tried it in March 1934, for example, for a fishing trip in the Bahamas. In his absence, Congress got out of hand. Roosevelt had to hurry back, and to a group of congressmen who met his train in Washington on his return, he said pleasantly, "I have come back with all sorts of new lessons which I learned from the barracuda and sharks. I am a tough guy."[54]

But he did not often use the style toward Congress of a "tough guy" as literally as he did in behalf of the "must" legislation of 1935. He even tried to deny in a press conference—much to the amusement of the reporters—that he ever used the word "must" to Congress. He generally did use a softer style.

His constitutional power to recommend legislation to Congress, however, Roosevelt used time and time again. As we have seen, he even drafted and sent up completed bills to carry out his recommendations. In the cases of very important recommendations, he followed Wilson's example of going up to the Capitol in person to impress Congress with the importance he attached to them. He used his constitutional veto power liberally; and frequently expressed pride in the great number of bills he vetoed in each session. In a letter to the widow of Grover Cleveland, he wrote April 4, 1941: "It is to me tremendously interesting that President Cleveland and I seem to have a veto record not even approached by anyone else in the White House. Also it is significant that of the bills vetoed by

Mr. Cleveland only five ever passed over his veto and in my case only seven."[55]

But these powers granted by the Constitution do not suffice by themselves to provide control over Congress. The Roosevelt style relied more on his persuasiveness in meeting congressmen face to face, on innumerable letters to congressional leaders discussing specific pieces of legislation, on his emissaries to the Hill holding out patronage as a reward, and on threats to veto legislation if passed. He also relied greatly upon the force of public opinion, which he often appealed to directly. Particularly important was proper timing, getting his proposals to Congress when the people were really prepared for them and wanted them, as for example in the case of his social security recommendation in 1935. He knew, also, that persuasive presentation, combined with courtesy and an understanding sympathy with a legislator's problems with his own limited constituency, could often be more effective than favors or threats.

A very revealing memorandum by the President dated September 6, 1941, written to Marvin McIntyre (one of his secretaries) after eight years experience with Congress, shows his attitude better than any historian could:

"I have been disturbed about things I am hearing very frequently about the Hill. You have probably heard the same. A large number of Senators and Congressmen, who should be and usually are our friends, have been saying entirely too frequently that they get no cooperation from the White House; that no one in the White House will talk to them unless we want their votes. A new refrain is that the only way to get attention from the Administration is to vote against it a few times.

"I do not think there is too much basis for these complaints. As you well know, a large portion of the favors they ask for we cannot give them. But I do think we should create a medium for them to register their complaints—and I want you to do that job.

"I certainly do not mean that you should be a liaison man with the Hill. I know you would be 'murdered' as some of our friends have been in the past. Besides, the present leadership resents liaison men and the 'big four' conferences seem to keep them happy. But you should be the man in the White House whom Senators and Congressmen can talk to. It does not matter so much that they don't get what they want. If they can tell their colleagues and friends 'I told Marvin McIntyre at the White House so and so' that will be a psychological advantage. If they can also say 'Marvin McIntyre told me so and so,' they will soon have a feeling their advice is being listened to.

"I think the way to get this started is to do it in a very casual manner. If you could start telephoning two or three of your Congressional friends a day just to ask how they are and what they know, word will soon get around that Marvin McIntyre will listen to them. In a few weeks or so, the casual phone call will soon develop into an iron-clad system. . . ."[56]

In recent years, liaison with Congress has been recognized and formalized, with several White House assistants constantly on the Hill operating exclusively in this capacity. In Roosevelt's day, it was done informally.

Roosevelt always kept a very close watch on legislation, and got immediate reports from his assistants about what was going on in Congress. He wrote innumerable letters and memoranda to the leaders and also to individual congressmen about legislation. Sometimes he counselled compromise or delay, sometimes firmness and inflexibility, sometimes urgent action. Sometimes individual congressmen would ask the President to help them pass their own bills by talking to someone higher up in Congress. The President seldom hesitated—if he approved the bills—to seize this means of ensuring the congressman's gratitude.

There are copies of many revealing memoranda about legislation now available in the Hyde Park Library showing how actively involved the President was in the process of legislating.

To give two just examples:

First, a memorandum from Benjamin V. Cohen (a Presidential adviser) to Miss M. A. Lehand (the President's personal secretary) dated June 9, 1939, is a little surprising. It came after the fight about the Supreme Court in which Senator Wheeler was the victorious leader against the President, and was sent during the bitter controversy about the repeal of the embargo provisions of the Neutrality Law in which Senator Wheeler was prominent as a leader of the isolationist bloc in Congress. It reads: "Senator Wheeler told me that he would appreciate some help from the President to get his two railroad bills out of the House Judiciary Committee. He thought some word to Rayburn and to Chandler and McLaughlin would help."

I can find no record as to whether the President complied with this request from his arch foe of those days.

Second, a memorandum from the President to Representative Hatton Sumners (Chairman of the Judiciary Committee) dated June 28, 1935, at a time when the Congress was in full revolt against the President's leadership: "Senator Hugo L. Black is most anxious that you get the Lobby Bill out and passed. He says it is pretty weak but much better than nothing. Can you do this?"

These are only two random selections from hundreds of similar communications to and from and about the Hill.

Roosevelt was normally successful with Congress for several reasons. He was a master at getting the feel of the public at any particular time. The White House mail (4,000 letters a day by January 1934), the press conferences, memoranda showing the editorial comment of about 750 newspapers prepared for him each day by the White House staff, reports from time to time from the Institute of Public Opinion about its frequent polls; personal interviews with people from different parts of the country, editorials from five or six newspapers he personally read each day; "non-political" trips of inspection when politics was the major reason for the trip—all of these were used as instruments in collecting knowledge of public opinion. This told him when the people were ready for an innovative policy he had in mind; it gave him a gauge as to their willingness to support him in his legislative proposals. He knew when to invite key congressmen who had strayed out of line to the White House to subject them to his many varieties of persuasion: flattery, diplomacy, implied threats, promises, horse trading, intellectual arguments, charm, arguments of party loyalty, or a combination. Above all his boundless energy, sheer drive, and love of fighting kept him urging, debating, pressing day after day in every way for what he wanted—once he had really made up his mind what that was.

This personal drive and his refusal to accept defeat are admirably revealed in a very confidential letter he sent to the Speaker (with a copy to the majority leader) of the House in 1940, when he was having substantial trouble in getting some legislation passed.[57] The date is important—shortly after his third election, when he knew that very tough days lay ahead requiring very tough preparations for national defense.

December 23, 1940.

PERSONAL AND CONFIDENTIAL:

Dear Sam:

Because of our long-time friendship and intimate association, I know you will not mind if I write you in great confidence some thoughts which come to me since the failure of the Republicans, and certain Democrats, to override my veto of the Walter-Logan Bill.[58] Courage—just sheer courage—brought that about.

I know that there was much inclination on the part of Democrats—the friendly kind —the "co-operative" kind, to feel, ten days ago, that the veto would be over-ridden. When all is said and done that inclination amounted to a yielding to a probable defeat.

More courageous beliefs prevailed.

I myself must, as you know, be guided by the recommendations of the Democratic Leaders in the House, and while in no sense of the word do I want the advice of "yes men," I do want the advice of fighting leadership, with the adjective "fighting" underscored.

When I got back on Monday last, I did not quite know what to make out of this particular problem—for some of my friends were pulling long faces and gave me the feeling that the veto would be over-ridden. Others among my friends were telling me that in thirty-six hours victory could be attained by enthusiasm and team-work, to sustain the President.

You and I and John McCormack are facing a very difficult session. On the success of that session will depend the future reputation of the President and the Speaker and the Majority Leader. It will not help any of the three to meet with a series of defeats in the next Congress.

That is especially true if the three of us, or any one of the three, accepts prospective defeat tamely. Therefore, I renew my ancient feeling that it is better to be defeated while going down fighting than it is to accept defeat without fighting.

The vote last Wednesday is proof of this theory. A very large number of prospective defeats—not all—can be turned into victory by carrying on a real honest-to-goodness fight, thereby cutting down the percentage of defeats.

I know you agree and I know that John McCormack agrees.

What I want to get across to both of you before the new session begins is that good fellowship for the sake of good fellowship alone, an easy life to avoid criticism, an acceptance of defeat before an issue has been joined, make, all of them, less for Party success and for national safety than a few drag-down and knock-out fights and an unwillingness to accept defeat without a fight.

You and John have an opportunity to salvage much that would otherwise be lost in the coming session, and you and I know that this means day and night work, taking it on the chin, getting knocked down occasionally, but making a comeback before you are counted out.

I am saying this for the sake of the Party. I am saying this more greatly for the sake of the Nation.

And I know you will understand—and do your bit.

Always affectionately,
Franklin D. Roosevelt

Honorable Sam Rayburn,
Speaker of the House of Representatives
Washington, D.C.

Except on very rare occasions, Roosevelt treated Congress very courteously in his *public* statements. He would scrupulously thank Congress publicly at the end of each session; and in the Hyde Park Library there are copies of many private letters of thanks to individual congressmen for their support and help. Unfortunately, what could not be preserved for history were the innumerable daily telephone conversations he had with members of Congress. I remember suggesting to him that he put a recorder on his phone to preserve this valuable source material of history, informing the other party, of course, that the conversation was being recorded. He did not want to do this, saying that the conversation would never be a frank one under those circumstances, and he would be deprived of the open discussion and advice he wanted.

He went out of his way to keep loyal congressmen, as he would phrase it, "happy." For example, on February 18, 1936, he sent this memo to Charles West, his then liaison man with Congress—typical of many other written and oral efforts to the same effect: "I think it is time you had a talk with Sabath [chairman of the Steering Committee, responsible for party policy in the House] and the Steering Committee and see what is needed to keep them happy in the next month."[59]

Patronage was one of his obvious weapons, and he never hesitated to use it. His instructions to Farley during the Court fight of 1937 were startling, but not unusual: "We must hold up judicial appointments in states where the delegation is not going along. Where there is a division, we must give posts to those supporting us. This must apply to other appointments as well as judicial appointments."[60]

Farley as the chief dispenser of patronage under Roosevelt's close and watchful scrutiny was often sent up to the Hill to talk with reluctant congressmen; and although he has assured me in a personal interview that at no time did he make promises or threats about patronage, it is obvious that the congressmen he visited must have been impressed by the fact that the man who had so much to say about patronage had come up especially to talk to them.

A revealing glimpse of the dealings between Roosevelt and congressional leaders behind closed doors, without any witnesses to make a record, is furnished by Tugwell.[61] The President had nominated Tugwell in 1934 as Under Secretary of Agriculture. There was immediately tremendous opposition in the Senate. Tugwell's writings and speeches and conversations about national planning and government relations with business had produced, unjustly, some doubts as to whether he really believed in the American system of free enterprise. After he had been confirmed—with the assistance of Farley, whom the President had specifically assigned to the difficult job of getting confirmation—Roosevelt said privately to Tugwell: "You will never know any more about it, I hope; but today I traded you for a couple of murderers."

This, of course, was exaggeration. Tugwell added that he never learned "precisely what the deal was and with what strategic Senator." No one will ever know what other deals of a similar nature Roosevelt made; but no one who lived through those days in Washington close to his administration doubts that he made many indeed.

Another potent device was to have Farley, or someone else, telephone the state or county political leader of a particular congressman to get help in swinging the congressman's vote. The promise of patronage, trading of favors, exchange of gratitudes, was always implicit in such calls even though never expressed. At times, emissaries of Roosevelt, over-enthusiastic and over-zealous New Dealers, were sent up; sometimes their pugnaciousness and blunt talks did as much harm as good—especially where the congressman involved would later voice his grievances on the floor about the pressure and about the emissary.

Though Roosevelt's normal style of dealing with Congress had been fairly consistent during his presidency, there came an abrupt change in 1937 in connection with the fight with the Congress about the Supreme Court. After the humiliating conclusion of that fight, the unusual style continued through the attempted "purge" of 1938, which was even more of a failure.

The only possible explanation for this change in 1937 was his unprecedented victory in the election of 1936 for a second term. That election gave him the electoral votes of all the states, excepting only Maine and Vermont; it gave him almost 61 per cent of the popular vote, and a plurality of over 10 million votes. But more was involved than those cold statistics. The victory was accompanied by an emotional outpouring of people—ordinary, common people—in all parts of the country, in all walks of life. It gave him the impression that they would support anything he might attempt in their behalf. It built up his self-confidence and self-assurance to a degree of over-confidence which, even for him, was spectacular and dangerous.

All during 1935 after the NRA decision, and all during 1936, he had to think about what he could and should do about the Supreme Court. For the Court, by closely divided votes in decision after decision, was dismantling most of the structure built by the New Deal statutes. The climax of the wreckage came on June 1, 1936, when the Court struck down the New York State minimum wage law for women in industry. Since an earlier federal statute providing minimum wages for women in industry had also been declared unconstitutional in 1923, this new decision created what Roosevelt called "a no man's land," in which neither the United States nor any of the individual states had any power to promote the economic and social welfare of workers.

As the President later wrote, when the Court fight was all over: "We were stopped short and thrown back in our efforts to stabilize national agriculture, to improve conditions of labor, to safeguard business against unfair competition, to protect disorganized and chaotic interstate industries, to provide old age pensions for railroad employees, and in other ways to serve national needs."[62]

What to do about it?

Very few matters in 1936 received more attention from Washington White House advisers—official and unofficial—than this question of the Supreme Court. There were many suggestions from many sources—and there was much conflicting advice. It ranged from a constitutional amendment to legislation requiring unanimity of the Court to overrule a congressional or state statute—even to outright Court-packing by merely adding additional judges. The President listened, but did not make up his mind—so far as anyone really knows—until after the election of 1936.

This secretiveness, this reluctance to state even to his closest friends and associates all of what was going on in his mind is one of the most definite and important features of his style, and of his decision-making process. This secretiveness did not mean that the President mistrusted the discretion of the people close to him, or that he was suspicious of their loyalty. I think that it was a part of his determination to keep himself free from premature commitment to any specific course. He always wanted to keep his options open to the last minute. He was ready to discuss the question at any time privately, but he would never reveal his decision until it was firmly made and until the time was, in his view, right. Of course, sometimes it was not secretiveness at all, but merely the fact that he had not yet made up his mind.

I believe that it was this trait which led some writers—a few of whom, like

Frances Perkins and Robert Sherwood, knew him personally—to conclude that he was a complex, inscrutable, and not easily understood human being. I disagree. Once one took note of this characteristic of secretiveness, of "playing his cards close to the chest," he always seemed to be an understandable and consistent personality. What bothered many of his associates was that some day he might express a casual view of a problem to one person, and the next day express a different view to another. This led to criticism at times that the person who saw him last was the one who would prevail. The facts, however, would normally be that neither had finally convinced him, that he was not ready to be convinced, that he was listening to advice from any qualified source, weighing it in the scales with other advice, and dropping tentative remarks about his own views, primarily to encourage debate. Sometimes he would listen to the advice being given, involuntarily nodding his head—a gesture which his visitor took as a sign of approval but which was only an indication that he understood what was being said, and was adding it to the rest of the evidence or suggestions he was collecting. This kind of secretiveness does not make a man a complicated individual.

Another reason for the secretiveness was Roosevelt's delight in springing surprises, even on his close associates, some of whom really should have been informed in advance; and he would try to do it in the most dramatic setting possible. Most times there is no harm in surprises—and sometimes substantial benefit. It is always fresh news; it creates an image of activism and leadership; it also prevents the opposition from making advance preparation to meet the surprise announcement. But when the success of an action depends upon the cooperation of other people—as it did in the Supreme Court proposal of 1937— it turned out to be a mistake to spring a surprise on them. In the light of events, it is quite clear that Roosevelt should have discussed his Court proposals with at least the congressional leaders, even at the risk of a "leak." Instead, he merely gave them a polite but perfunctory hour's notice of a *fait accompli.*

Ickes has written of an occasion on which he gave vent to his bewilderment about this style:

" 'You are the most wonderful person, but you are one of the most difficult men to work with that I have ever known,' he told the President.

" 'Because I get too hard at times?' the President asked.

" 'No . . . because you won't talk frankly even with people who are loyal to you, and of whose loyalty you are fully convinced. You keep your cards close up against your belly.' "[63]

More confidence might produce advice and information which would prevent mistakes, Ickes added. This was certainly true of the appointment in 1937 to the Supreme Court of Senator Hugo Black—Roosevelt's first appointment to that Court. If he had consulted the congressional leaders, all of whom knew that Black had been in his youth a member of the Ku Klux Klan, he could have anticipated the criticism, and pointed out how liberal a person the senator had become since his youth. He might have avoided all the headaches which came from his own ignorance of the fact when he made the appointment.

In discussing the various suggestions submitted to him in 1936 about the Court, he would find some fault with each one of them, except the one he finally adopted—the one which he never mentioned to any congressional leader at any time, or to any Cabinet member except the Attorney General. For example, a constitutional amendment would take too long to be ratified by the necessary three-quarters of the states, and could too easily be defeated by pressures and lobbying in only thirteen states; statutes in any way limiting the Court's right of review or requiring unanimity of voting would themselves ultimately require the approval of the same hostile Court as to constitutionality. Above all, the need for action was immediate; any delay caused by passing a statute or an amendment might be fatal.

The Supreme Court and its anti-New Deal decisions were never specifically mentioned by Roosevelt during the entire campaign of 1936. But the platform, the acceptance speech, and all his campaign speeches made it quite clear that he had just "begun to fight" for his objectives and that he would continue to fight for them.

Writing in June 1941, Roosevelt looked back on that 1936 campaign as one in which the issue was joined without reserve, in which no punches were pulled. The issue *was a single one*—the New Deal. He might have added that the New Deal had become popularly identified and synonymous with Roosevelt himself personally, so that *he* was the issue.

Roosevelt's refusal to mention the Court in the campaign, and to indicate what he proposed to do about it—assuming he had decided what to do—was typical of his style of campaigning. He dealt mostly in generalities, in his objectives, and in what the opposition was doing to thwart them. If he had made favorable specific reference to any one method of dealing with the Supreme Court, he would have alienated all those who thought they had a better method. He was too foxy to risk a public debate during an election campaign as to specific methods. What he wanted was an overwhelming approval of general objectives and of what he had done in the past three years, and a mandate to continue to fight for them. That is what he got on Election Day 1936. But all during the fight of 1937, he would be charged with deceit and trickery for not having disclosed during the campaign exactly what he was going to do about the Court.

The message on the Judiciary was sent to Congress on February 5, 1937. The recommendation which caused all the controversy was this: When a Justice of the Supreme Court reached the age of seventy and did not take advantage of his statutory right to retire on full pay, the President could, by and with the advice and consent of the Senate, appoint an additional judge.

The reasons given by the President in the message were that additional judges were needed because of the growth of litigation and the delay in the courts; the Supreme Court was overburdened by appeals and behind in its work; court calendars were congested; there were many aged and infirm judges over seventy in the Federal Judiciary, including some on the Supreme Court; modern complexities called for a "constant infusion of new blood"—not only for new physical vigor, but because of changed conditions in society, and because "little by little, new facts become blurred through old glasses, fitted, as it were, for the needs of another generation."

What followed was six months of bitter debate in Congress, ending in complete defeat for the President. There were several reasons for this defeat:

1. The President had changed his normal style of conferring with his congressional leaders in advance of important controversial legislation, getting their suggestions, or attempting to persuade them.

2. He had just won such a telling popular election victory—in many ways a personal victory—that he was over-confident that the people would support him in any proposal he would make. He assumed he could win the Court issue on the same personal appeal which he had made in the campaign, without taking his

usual precaution to build up popular support. Over-confidence had overcome his usual foxlike circumspection before plunging into action.

3. His circuitous method of attack on the Court, claiming overwork, inefficiency and delay, instead of attacking it frontally for its reactionary thinking, was tricky, devious and too clever—even if his claims had been justified.

4. Instead of trying to meet the problem which is frequently raised by a Court at odds with the legislative program of a Congress or a President (as in the more modern situation of the "Warren Court" against the Nixon program), he sought to attack only the mental alertness and slow procedures of certain of the Justices. He admitted this original error in later years. After about a month, he shifted his gears—and his style. He stated exactly what the objective was: in his words, to make the "three-horse team" (executive, legislative and judicial branches) pull as one in the same direction, instead of having one of them (the Judiciary) plunge off in another direction. But it was too late to change from the shifty attack to a frontal attack; it did not make much impression. A few days later he tried a fireside chat. Nothing would work. The people just would not get behind him. It was one thing for them to re-elect a President who was bettering the lives of all of them; but quite another to encourage him to abandon one of the important checks and balances of the American constitutional system.

5. Three unforeseen events happened beyond his control, which rendered unnecessary the drastic provisions he had recommended. The first was a switch by Mr. Justice Roberts in March 1937, voting to sustain a state minimum wage law, although only nine months earlier he had voted to declare a similar state minimum wage law unconstitutional. This was a harbinger of a series of future liberal decisions sustaining New Deal legislation. The second was the retirement of one of the conservative "nine old men," Mr. Justice Van Devanter in June 1937, leaving a vacancy to be filled by Roosevelt which would change the 5–4 line-up against the New Deal into a 5–4 line-up in its favor. A third unforeseen event was the sudden death of Joseph T. Robinson, the Senate majority leader, who had been carrying the chief responsibility for passing the Court bill in the Senate and who because of his many close friends on the Hill could probably have obtained a compromise even at a late date, which would have fulfilled Roosevelt's immediate objective of stopping the Court's destruction of the New Deal. This was especially probable since Senator Robinson was widely reputed to be the President's first choice for one of the new places on the Court to be created by the bill. Upon his death, the possibility of a favorable compromise vanished.

Having set forth all the reasons usually given for the failure of Roosevelt's attempt, I am constrained to say that I doubt whether in any event any measure which endangered or limited the Court's co-equal power to pass on legislation under the Constitution could have been adopted. The Court was too sacred an institution in 1937, just as it is today. President Lyndon Johnson and President Nixon, within recent years, have both felt the sting of public and Senate rebuke where the sanctity and prestige of the Supreme Court were threatened, either by the prospective appointment to it of an obviously incompetent or prejudiced person, or of a man who, as a sitting judge, had tolerated a conflict of interest in his judicial conduct, or one who had carried on financial dealings with persons who were in criminal difficulties with the government. In fact, in 1969 a Supreme Court Justice was forced by public opinion to leave the Bench for such financial dealings.

The defeat of the Court proposal set the tone for all of 1937 and 1938. It was to be one congressional defeat after another for the President. Congress had finally shaken itself free.

After the smoke of the Court battle cleared, the President sought to get on top of his legislative program then pending. He tried all kinds of usual tactics to regain control; but nothing worked. There were five administration measures then awaiting action by Congress—all important ones seeking to meet the challenge of "one-third of a nation ill-housed, ill-clad, ill-nourished," which he had discussed in his Second Inaugural: Wagner's low-cost housing bill, a minimum wages and maximum hours bill, an executive branch reorganization bill, a new and expanded farm program, and a bill setting up seven regional planning agencies in the United States similar to TVA. None of them was passed in the 1937 session except the housing bill, but even its passage was due more to Wagner's efforts than to Roosevelt's.

It was little comfort to the President that the Court had now become a pro-New Deal Court. He had been deeply humiliated, and his characteristic vindictiveness was aroused. He did nothing about it publicly in 1937; but he seethed inwardly.

In September 1937, he resorted to the same device in his political style that he frequently did between congressional sessions. He took a "non-political inspection" trip all the way to the Pacific coast and back, meeting people, talking "government—not politics," trying to rally their support for his legislative program which the Congress had rejected.

To add to his troubles—and incidentally to destroy some more of his already lowered prestige with the people and with Congress—October 1937 ushered in not only a series of "sit-down strikes" which he could not adequately control, but also a "Roosevelt recession." He called the Congress into an extraordinary session to begin on November 15, 1937. To bring pressure upon them in the meantime, he delivered a fireside chat explaining what he wanted Congress to do. But it was all warmed-over stuff, the legislation which he had submitted to the regular session of 1937. The fireside chat produced no visible support. The extraordinary session treated the administration program with the same disdain as the regular session had—and adjourned.

In 1938, at the next regular session, however, Congress did pass his recommendations for an enlarged program for farmers, and a watered-down wages and hours bill—but only after a long bruising battle between him and the Southern congressmen. However, Congress decisively again rejected the executive reorganization bill amid cries of "dictatorship" and "one-man rule." Under this bill the President would have been able to create a modern, institutionalized office, regrouping executive powers, and bringing additional executive functions into the White House, such as the Bureau of the Budget, the Security Council and many others.

The recession continued, and grew worse. Roosevelt wavered, in uncharacteristic style, between balancing the budget and spending. He finally came to a decision in April 1938 in favor of spending; and he asked for $3 billion for the purpose. Congress complied. Gradually the worst of the Depression wore off during 1938. But there was no doubt that Roosevelt's prestige with the American people had by now fallen very low; with the congressional majority his prestige had almost disappeared. A public opinion poll in 1938 disclosed that barely one-half of the people would vote for him if the election were to take place that year.

This usually happens, but in a much milder degree, during the second term of every President as the end of his days of power draws closer. The style which Roosevelt had used in forcing the Second New Deal through a balky Congress in 1935 no longer worked.

He tried a new style. It was an example of his belief in action; but it was so different from his previous style of dealing with Congress, and from his style as a party leader, that it was as startling to his political friends and supporters as it was to his political adversaries.

He had never, as President, openly intervened in local political party fights before. In fact, he had made a virtue of that abstinence. Many a stalwart New Dealer had turned to the White House for help in a close local political fight; but they had all met refusal. They were told that there was an "unbreakable" rule that the President "never takes part in local elections." He told Senator Key Pittman, a friend and a warm supporter of the administration, for example, in refusing to help in a bitter local fight for renomination in Nevada that "an imposed silence in things like this is one of the many penalties of my job."[64]

Now in 1938, this political style, this "rule," were both abandoned. Roosevelt was exasperated and resentful at those congressmen who had campaigned and been elected on an "uncompromisingly" liberal platform which pledged further efforts to attain the New Deal objectives, but who now were consistently voting the other way. Some of them had completely forgotten that they had been elected literally on his coattails. He decided to undertake the "purge" of 1938. It was not only the votes in the Court fight which caused this undertaking; it was the combination of all the adverse votes in the two sessions of 1937 and in the session of 1938.

The "purge" failed—as it was bound to. It was hurriedly improvised and carried on by amateurs; the professional politicians, including Farley, while giving lip service to it, did not have their hearts in it and did nothing to help. Only extreme bitterness and vindictiveness can account for this master politician thinking for a moment that he could go to Georgia, for example, and unseat the venerable and esteemed Senator George, who had represented Georgia for many terms in the Senate to the complete satisfaction of the people of his state. The purge split the party further apart.

The election results of 1938 showed the effect upon the voters of all the events which had occurred since the sweep of 1936: The Republican representation in the House was almost doubled, and the Republican seats in the Senate were increased by eight.

His tight control of 1933—when the United States faced the great crisis of survival as a democracy—was never duplicated until Pearl Harbor—when the United States faced the greater crisis of survival as a nation. In both times of crisis, Congress was willing to let the executive take all the responsibility and the power. Even the wartime control of Congress was not as absolute, however, as it had been in 1933. There were, for example, the congressional revolts in 1944 over his veto of the tax bill "for the greedy instead of the needy," over his overseas soldiers' voting legislation, and over his national or universal service bill.

But looking back over the full tenure of the presidency as a whole (1933–45), nobody can deny that Roosevelt was one of our greatest political leaders in dealing with the Congress, and with the many diverse groups which made up the Democratic Party. He changed the traditional concept that the party consisted only of the followers of the big city bosses of the North and the political barons of the South. He expanded it to include farmers, workers, intellectuals, Negroes and other minorities—and women. In addition, he made successful appeals to independents, and even to rank-and-file Republicans. In search of new ideas, he brought many Independents and Republicans into the party (at least temporarily), like Richberg, Ickes, Hugh Johnson, Wallace, Hopkins and Jerome Frank. None of these newcomers, as Professor Burns has so well pointed out, would have even been recognized in the Convention Hall in Chicago in 1932. The 1935 New Deal cemented labor support, as the AAA of the 1933 New Deal had done with the farmers.

As a party leader, Roosevelt knew that the social objectives he was after required a party unity with a strong sense of purpose, and that creating this unity required all kinds of compromises and expediency. But his belief in party unity was not adequate to make him willing to accept any ideology of members of his party inconsistent with his own objectives.

For example, there was that night of July 18, 1940, when the Democratic National Convention in Chicago which had just nominated him for a third term was engaged in a violent and disruptive battle over Roosevelt's recommendation of Henry Wallace as his Vice-Presidential candidate. The convention was in noisy revolt and was trying to nominate a conservative Southerner instead. The debates on the floor were growing more and more acrimonious. The President sat in the Oval Room of the White House listening on the radio. There were some ten associates in the room with him. I watched his face grow grimmer as he listened, while he silently played solitaire. Finally, he asked for a pad and pencil; while we sat watching and wondering, he started writing, and kept it up for five pages. When he finished, he asked me to go to work on them, smooth them out, and get them ready for delivery—in a hurry. Then he continued silently with his game. I knew Roosevelt and his moods well enough to realize that he was in dead earnest about it, and that this was no mere sideplay. The sheets of paper were in the form of a short speech which he intended to deliver to the convention by radio, instead of his prepared acceptance speech.

What he had written, after some corrections and additions, read as follows:

July 18, 1940.

MEMBERS OF THE CONVENTION:

In the century in which we live the Democratic Party has received the support of the electorate only when the party with absolute clarity has been the champion of progressive and liberal policies and principles of government.

The party has failed consistently when through political trading and chicanery it has fallen into the control of those interests, personal and financial, which think in terms of dollars instead of in terms of human values.

The Republican Party has made nominations dictated as we all know by those who put dollars ahead of human values.

The Democratic Party, as appears clear from the events of today, is divided on this fundamental issue. Until the Democratic Party, through this Convention, makes overwhelmingly clear its stand in favor of social progress and liberalism, and shakes off all the shackles fastened upon it by the forces of conservatism, reaction and appeasement, it will not continue its march of victory.

It is without question that certain political influences pledged to reaction in domestic affairs and to appeasement in foreign affairs have been busily engaged behind the scenes in the promotion of discord since this Convention convened.

Under those circumstances, I cannot, in all honor, and will not merely for political expediency go along with the cheap bargaining and political maneuvering which have brought about party dissention in this Convention.

It is best not to straddle ideals. . . .

It would be best for America to have the fight out here and now.

I wish to give the Democratic Party the opportunity to make its historic decision . . . by declining the honor of the nomination for the presidency. I so do.[65]

He calmly tallied the vote as it came in over the radio. It was close; but Wallace won. The rejection speech was never delivered—or even made public at the time. I have no doubt that if Wallace had been defeated and if some conservative had been nominated, it would have been delivered.

He believed strongly in the two-party system, but this undelivered speech shows how strongly he also felt that there was, and always must be, a major difference between the two parties, so that the voters would have a clear choice. He insisted that the Democratic Party always be the liberal party. The Republican Party was the conservative party.

He was disturbed, therefore, about the conservative elements in his own party, especially from the South; and he was continually beset by obstacles which they put in his way. The "purge" of 1938 was an unsuccessful effort to rid the party of some of those members—and to warn others. After the "purge" had failed, there came to his desk all the problems of increased national defense, followed later by all the problems and demands of getting war supplies to Britain, and finally the war itself. All these pressing crises made it impossible for him to do anything constructive about the problems of disunity in his party. But he kept it firmly in mind all through the period 1938–44 and privately talked about it freely. The conservatism of some Democratic members added to the conservatism of practically all the Republican members caused many fights with Congress. Some were successful, as in price and inflation control in 1942; some were unsuccessful, as in soldiers' voting overseas, adequate tax laws, and universal service legislation in 1944. But he never stopped trying.

It reached a climax during the elections of 1944; Wendell Willkie, the liberal Republican, had been pushed aside by his party in 1944. Roosevelt, the liberal Democrat, was being further bedeviled by the conservatives in his own party. As final victory in the war was becoming apparent, Roosevelt, the great activist, decided to stop talking about this dichotomy in both parties and to start taking some action about it.

What he did—and what he proposed to do—were startling even to me, who had grown accustomed to decisive, drastic action by Roosevelt.

He learned one day in June 1944 from his friend Gifford Pinchot that Wendell Willkie had talked with Pinchot about the possibility of a new set-up in American politics: a realignment of the liberals in both parties against the conservatives in both parties. Roosevelt had independently arrived at the same conclusion. He wanted to rid his party of reactionaries, and attract to it the liberals in the Republican Party. He had tried, by "purge" and by other means, to change his own party, but had failed. Now he was ready to undertake this kind of realignment, and he decided to try to do it in cooperation with Willkie.

He asked me to go up to New York, and to talk very secretly with Willkie about it. I found that Willkie was enthusiastic but naturally wanted to wait until after the election of 1944. Roosevelt had already told me that he too wanted to wait until after the election. By Election Day, Willkie was dead. Five months after

Election Day, Roosevelt too died. It was a bold, decisive plan; but only two men of their stature could have brought it off.[66]

Roosevelt, as a political leader, was a firm believer in—and practitioner of—the old adage that politics is pre-eminently the art of the possible. That always influenced his style. It was clear to him, and he tried to make it clear to others, that no President, as Lincoln had also discovered to his sorrow, could get everything done at once, or could have things all his own way. For example, as early as 1928, comparing Al Smith with Theodore Roosevelt, he said: "To get what one can, to fight for it but not jeopardize it by asking for the moon, brought concrete results to both of them." Mrs. Roosevelt (who was never addicted to compromise and who, of course, never had to go to the people to be elected) has told us of his refusal to enlist actively in the support of good political causes, because of "political realities." She relates what he said on one occasion about her efforts to get him publicly to support anti-lynching and anti-poll tax bills, knowing that he was really in favor of both: "First things come first, and I cannot alienate certain votes I need for measures that are more important for the moment by pushing any measure that would entail a fight."[67]

Many historians, even those writing approvingly of the President, have criticized him for not doing more during the war to make sure of a better postwar era. I think that most of their criticisms, made long after the war, fail to give adequate weight to those two realistic mottoes which guided Roosevelt's style quite consistently: "First things first," and "The art of the possible." For example, in his third term and as much of the fourth term as he was able to serve, "Winning the war" was the number one problem. That precluded many social reforms or, as Roosevelt put it, meant letting "Dr. New Deal" go for a while, and calling in "Dr. Win-the-War." It also involved political deals with people he detested, like Darlan and Badoglio. Number two problem was the creation of the United Nations and how to get Russia to join it. That involved many things he would have preferred to avoid, like the concessions at Yalta to Russia in the Far East. It involved what he often described as "Crossing a bridge with the Devil—until you reach the other side"—walking with him along many paths, providing only they would lead ultimately to a firm peacekeeping world organization.

Politician though he was, he refused ever to put politics above the obvious interest of America. Complying, for examples, with General Eisenhower's decision to start the North African invasion just two days after the congressional elections of 1942 instead of attempting it two days before; pushing for a draft act in the midst of the campaign for a third term in 1940 although, as he wrote in August 1940, he knew it would not be popular, and might well cause his defeat in November;[68] making the deal with Churchill during the same unprecedented and difficult third-term political campaign, to give Britain fifty old destroyers in exchange for some naval bases—without even asking Congress; his refusal during his first few years as President to put forward his own old age pension plan to counteract the crackpot old age handout proposed by Dr. Townsend—all these things and many others showed that he would not risk the national welfare and security for political gain.

In 1938, "First things first" became Hitler, Mussolini and the Japanese warlords. To them, Roosevelt began to give more and more attention; and as his problems with them multiplied into war he gave them his almost undivided attention. He never changed that emphasis until the day of his death. He had to play many roles in those years all at the same time: educator and leader of public opinion in the United States; Commander-in-Chief and responsible strategist of the greatest of wars; architect of the foundations of world peace; leader of world public opinion; administrator of a vast bureaucracy, now enlarged by a constantly expanding army of civilian employees and new agencies of government operating all over the world. Each of these roles would require its own political style. And it is as Commander-in-Chief that he displayed unquestionable administrative ability.

As an administrator Roosevelt received a very low rating from the majority of his associates and subordinates. Indeed, most of them considered him an absolute failure in this role.

Hull, the Secretary of State, objected, for example, to Roosevelt's use of Sumner Welles, the Under Secretary, without consulting or even telling Hull about it; also to the use of Moley in 1933, who was then also Hull's subordinate as an assistant secretary, but whom Roosevelt used on several projects normally delegated to the head of the State Department. Welles, in turn, was upset by the fact that the President had many special representatives abroad, performing missions normally within the jurisdiction of the State Department, but about which the Department was told little or nothing; they were reporting directly to the President, completely bypassing the Department. Hull was particularly resentful that the President chose Morgenthau rather than himself to open negotiations for the recognition of Russia in 1933.

The President had cogent reasons for a great many of the instances of his bizarre administrative style. In 1933, he knew—and he also knew that the Russians knew—that many of the influential officers down the line in the State Department hated Russia, and were deeply opposed to any recognition. He felt that they would try to sabotage rather than promote the venture. He did not relish spending time and energy carefully watching the operation himself. So, he just took the simplest and most flexible course; he turned the whole matter over to Morgenthau, a man he knew was in sympathy with his objective, whom he trusted, and whom he would not have to watch.

Henry L. Stimson, who had served many years in the Cabinet of several Presidents, complained in his diary that ". . . the President is the poorest administrator I have ever worked under [this even included Taft] in respect to the orderly procedure and routine of his performance." His additional complaint (and probably the real cause of his distress) was that ". . . there are a lot of young men in Washington ambitious to increase the work of their agencies . . . who report on their duties directly to the President . . . and have better access to the President than his Cabinet Officers have."

Ickes complained in his diary about "what he [Roosevelt] does so frequently, namely, calling in members of my staff for consultation without consulting me or advising me."

Perkins called the style he used in setting up the Civilian Conservation Corps, with the Departments of Labor and the Army and the Forest Service all having a part in it, "a technique of administration which drives professors of political science almost mad."

These comments and complaints and scores of similar ones were all based on fact. As an administrator, Roosevelt had a style all his own, which was fascinating to watch at work. It was completely unorthodox; it violated every rule in the books of public administration. He also paid scant attention to many of the procedures which all trained public administrators respect so much, such as job descriptions, adherence to channels of command, and so on.

His was not an orderly mind. He would sometimes assign the same job or problem to two different people, without telling either that the other was at work on the same matter. The two men, in making the necessary factual inquiries around Washington in order to do the job, were sooner or later bound to run into each other at some point and discover the duplication. Exasperation was the result; but that was Roosevelt's way of checking, or of getting diverse recommendations from which to choose. He was just as careful in checking his own opinions.

I had several personal experiences myself, when I would run into Byrnes doing the same job to which I had been assigned. I even ran into it once in a while in speech-writing, where after submitting a draft, I found that he had asked someone else, unbeknown to me, to prepare a draft of the same speech. Sometimes he would call the authors of the two drafts together for consultation, which might be the first time each knew that the other had been at work on it. Sometimes the two drafts might have entirely different tones. For example, a draft of the acceptance speech of 1936 was submitted by Stanley High and me, which was bellicose, pugnacious, and vehement in its denunciation of the "economic royalists," and which stated Roosevelt's determination to continue to fight for all the New Deal objectives in spite of the Supreme Court. Another draft submitted by Moley and Corcoran was mild and conciliatory. After a conference with the four of us, he did not think it at all strange to say to me: "I like both drafts; just weave them together."[69]

Of course it was impossible to weave them together so as to make them consistent, as a reading of that speech will show.[70] That too did not bother him. His style would be to use fight when he thought it best, and conciliation when he thought it best—and both when he thought that was best.

He gathered information and ideas informally from many sources, and tried where possible to get them from people who did not live or work in the Washington area. The reports of the regular departments were not always taken on faith by him without being checked or augmented by talks, letters and memoranda from other sources. He could absorb information better through conversation than by reading documents; but he did a great deal of both. He was able to clarify his own ideas by talking with visitors about various subjects, even with those whose main interests lay in other fields.

He liked to get opposing opinions from different people, and have them argued out before him. He would encourage rivalry among individuals and among agencies. Though this would tend to make administration very "messy," it had its advantages too, as he told Frances Perkins during the war:

"A little rivalry is stimulating. . . . It keeps everybody going, to prove that he is a better fellow than the next man. It keeps them honest too. An awful lot of money is being handled. The fact that there is somebody else in the field who knows what you are doing is a strong incentive to strict honesty."[71]

One can almost see an expert in public administration with his hair on end, hearing such a recital. But it generally worked out very well. For example, the creation in June 1940 of a new agency headed by expert civilian scientists, later expanded into the Office of Scientific Research and Development, with Vannevar Bush as director, was a source of dismay to the regular Army and Navy personnel who had always in the past conducted research themselves for new weapons. This is what Roosevelt had called "competition" and "rivalry," but under his prodding the competitive rivals learned to cooperate. Even more rivalry was created by this OSRD bringing into the program of research for new weapons and new defenses scores of different university and institutional laboratories, working independently at times on the same project. Out of it all came the atomic bomb, the proximity fuse, improved radar and other devices for detecting submarines, and dozens of new weapons of destruction and defense which shortened and helped to win the war—and also saved many American lives. It was all confusing and unorthodox, as so many of his other administrative devices were, but fully satisfying to this improvising, experimental and pragmatic President.

I do know, however, that when he called upon me to frame many reorganizations and consolidations of government agencies and functions after the war came in Europe, resulting in reorganizations such as the Office of War Information, the Supply Priorities and Allocations Board, the National Housing Agency, the Office of Price Administration and many others, he always wanted me to make sure that every agency which was to be affected should have full opportunity to discuss it with me. He also always insisted on seeing a chart which showed just where the old agencies (if they were not abolished) were to be placed in the new one, and what all lines of authority were going to be. This was, of course, very orthodox. After he had finally approved it and signed the necessary executive order for it, he wanted it obeyed by everyone—except only himself. For he paid scant attention to the chart thereafter, if it interfered with the style he wanted to follow on any particular situation.

And although he approved of competition and rivalry among agencies and people, he objected strenuously to any dispute between the rivals breaking out in public. This was the kind of thing that a hostile press always would play up as showing incompetence at the top. He would sometimes take drastic action when that happened. In 1943, for example, Vice President Wallace and Jesse Jones were both exercising overlapping powers in obtaining strategic war materials; a bitter dispute between them erupted publicly into reckless charges and countercharges against each other. Roosevelt, by an executive order, promptly took the powers away from both and placed them elsewhere. At the same time, he addressed a public letter to the heads of all federal departments and agencies, repeating his previous admonition forbidding public airing of disputes and directing them "to be submitted to me." He added to this letter that if they felt the need, nevertheless, to submit any dispute to the press, "I ask that when you release the statement for publication, you send me at the same time a letter of resignation."

Sometimes, as in the case of Hopkins and Ickes who were fighting with each other in the field of work relief projects, he would settle the dispute privately and quietly. He took both Ickes and Hopkins on a cruise with him, and blandly announced that the feud had been buried at sea.

The New Deal was essentially a combination of new ideas in government. New ideas do not ordinarily come from old, well-established departments of government. The old civil service employee who has sat at his desk—or similar desks—from an early age through his maturing years is apt to be satisfied with the status quo which has sustained him and also the nation so well in the past. Innovations are generally regarded at such desks with skepticism or even suspicion. And even if a fresher breeze comes in with a new department head trying to rejuvenate his department, the old bureaucracy, which has seen Cabinet officers and Presidents come and go over the years, knows how to smooth out any surge of new ideas until it becomes a mere ripple.

Roosevelt was very familiar with that process from his earlier days in the Navy; and he saw more examples of it as President. At a press conference one day, in an unusual burst of confidence and candor, he said (off the record): "The Treasury is so large and far-flung that I find it almost impossible to get the action and results I want—even with Henry [Morgenthau] there. But the Treasury is not to be compared with the State Department. You should go through the experience of trying to get any change in the thinking, policy and action of the career diplomats, and then you'd know what a real problem was. But the Treasury and State Department put together are nothing as compared with the Na-a-vy [mimicking the pronunciation of some naval officers]. The admirals are really something to cope with—and I should know. To change anything in the Na-a-vy is like punching a feather bed. You punch it with your right and you punch it with your left until you are finally exhausted, and then you find the damn bed just as it was before you started punching."

Even forceful Presidents like Roosevelt and Truman were unable completely to stop the sabotage of policy which occurs down the line in a department. That explains why Roosevelt so often—especially during the war—bypassed the State Department. But, as we shall see, when it came to controlling the "Na-a-vy" (or the Army) in wartime, he succeeded in bending the admirals or generals to his own ideas of strategy, not hesitating to overrule them bluntly and peremptorily when necessary.

Roosevelt, therefore, when he started his program in 1933, often set up a new agency for each innovation. There he could place bright, tireless, eager and enthusiastic young people, anxious to respond to his own new objectives and knowing that eventually their new ideas would reach the top without having to pass through the tortuous and dark alleys of an old department bureaucracy. He was looking for initiative and imagination, for "bold experimentation" rather than orthodoxy. Each new agency he created would make administration just so much more difficult, because he would have to deal with just so many additional new people; but he never doubted that this difficulty was more than balanced by the advantages of the new enthusiasms.

He made it his business to get detailed independent information about how all his new, and his old, agencies were doing—refusing to rely entirely on the reports which came in from the agencies themselves. He had to do this, for he always reserved to himself the final decision on any important policy, and refused to delegate absolute authority to anyone. This, too, created despair among those under him trained in the ways of orthodox public administration. President Truman kept on his desk a little sign which read: "The buck stops here." Roosevelt might well have had a sign on his desk reading: "Pass the buck up here," for he always arranged to have final policy decisions come up to him. It created many additional hours of work and study, but that was his way; and he let all of his department heads know that that was his way. That was his conception of what the Constitution meant when it vested the executive power in the President. There was never any doubt by anyone in his administration, no matter how many "advisers" he had or how many "assistants to the President" there were, as to who was the Boss. And when he decided upon a policy, he expected further argument about it to stop, and that it be carried out fully.

After the fall of France in 1940 when, in rapid succession, scores of new agencies for defense were created, and were added to the scores which had been created during Roosevelt's first term in office, the demand grew for the appointment of some "czar" to administer them, with full power and responsibility. Roosevelt balked. That was not his style of administration—for two reasons. First he felt, as I have said, that this was a responsibility of the Chief Executive which he could not delegate. Secondly, he saw the danger of such a "czar" running off on his own course of policy which might be entirely inconsistent with Roosevelt's objectives—social, military, and postwar. I believe that if he had been able to find a man whose philosophy was the same as his own, it might have been different. A "czar" can very rapidly become so strong with Congress, and even with the people, that it would be difficult to remove him without great resultant conflict. I know that in 1941, he offered Justice William O. Douglas a post in full charge of all war production and distribution, with all the power that that would entail. I feel confident that if Douglas had accepted, the President would have, with full confidence, given him free rein in such a way as to fulfill the functions of a so-called czar in the field. He even spoke to Douglas of the political possibilities which such a job might open up for him in the future. But Douglas preferred to remain on the Supreme Court.

There were other characteristics of his style of administration which baffled and irritated many of his subordinates. His sense of timing and his patience in waiting for the right time often led to complaints of indecision and even lethargy. Decisionmaking in the White House always included a decision not to decide— at least for the moment, or the day, or even for the year. We have seen some instances of patient waiting, for instance, after the NRA decision in April 1935 when he decided not to decide—at least publicly—what to do about the Supreme Court until after the election of 1936, actually a wait of twenty-two months. The timing in that case was correctly aimed at not dividing the party before Election Day, and in not getting sidetracked by debates about specific methods of dealing with the Court in a general election where the issue was to be all the general objectives of his New Deal.

Timing was closely related to his passion for experimentation; and he was not discouraged at the failure of an experiment. He did not expect to be successful all the time. After only two months in office he told the American people in his second fireside chat: "I do not deny that we may make mistakes of procedure as we carry out the policy [of the New Deal]. I have no expectation of making a hit every time I come to bat. What I seek is the highest possible batting average. . . . Theodore Roosevelt once said to me: 'If I can be right 75 percent of the time I shall come up to the fullest measure of my hopes.' " And if FDR found that one thing did not work, he would change to another; he never let himself get committed irrevocably to any one specific remedy.

He sometimes—but only rarely—made a mistake in timing. Fortunately he could almost instinctively recognize his mistake, and execute a quick retreat, as he did after his speech in October 1937 suggesting an international quarantine for the aggressors of Europe.

For the distress which his kind of administrative procedures brought to Cabinet officers, he was willing and ready to pay the price by what he called "holding the hands" of any aggrieved official. Much of his valuable time was taken up in this process; but the results were always an increased loyalty and affection, improved mutual understanding and respect, and a renewed energy and enthusiasm on the part of the official to push ahead. He liked to refer to himself as "Papa," to whom subordinates could come for advice, consolation and restoration of spirit. Day-to-day routine administration he was willing to leave to department heads; but he could, at times, tell a Cabinet officer more about what was going on in his department than the officer himself. He had an extraordinary ability and willingness to pay attention to the smallest details of administration, just as he did to the details of politics, even under the workload of the defense and war years.

The Roosevelt volumes of letters (1928–45) are full of examples of this meticulous style:

(1) Memorandum to Secretary of State, April 7, 1941.

"In regard to the 3,000 tons of rubber recently unloaded (according to the French) from the S.S. Bangkok at Casablanca, why not offer to buy this rubber and pay for it with some commodity like gasoline which is much needed in French Morocco?" (p. 1140)

(2) Memorandum for Jerry Land, May 10, 1941.

"I am sending this to you personally, confidentially and unofficially. . . . In view of the unfortunate figures given out in regard to merchant ship losses, and, today, the announcement that 27 American flag ships are about to sail for the Red Sea, I make the following suggestion: etc." (p. 1152)

(3) Memo for Donald Nelson and Sidney Hillman, March 24, 1942.

"Please let me have the actual facts on the statement by Kaltenborn [an unfriendly radio commentator] that 200 more bombers could have been built during the time lost by strikes during February of this year. I am enclosing the broadcast. . . ." (p. 1302) He wanted to say something publicly to counteract the broadcast.

(4) He even found time to include in this style of vigilance over all details the following memo for the acting Secretary of State, April 11, 1942:

"I agree with you about the visit of the King of Greece. I should like to suggest that he should come not only as the King, but as the head of the Greek Armies, and that he should wear at all times a Greek service uniform as simple as possible, and with not more than one ribbon on his coat. In other words, it will be much easier if he comes as a soldier than as a monarch. . . ." (p. 1308)

There are innumerable other examples.

If there were good reason, he would not shrink from appointing men with a social or economic outlook different from his own. That was a part of the Roosevelt style as an administrator and also as a leader in legislation. For example, Joseph Kennedy, an old and experienced Wall Street hand, was made the first chairman of the SEC although he did not agree with most of the New Deal, chiefly because of his great experience and expertise in the kind of shenanigans that went on in Wall Street and which the new statute sought to outlaw. That experience enabled him to spot an evasive tactic immediately. Jesse Jones differed radically with the New Deal and the New Dealers; but he was kept in office as the head of the RFC until he became actually politically disloyal to the President, because he was so highly regarded by the business community, and also because he had an extraordinarily close association and influence with the influential members of Congress. He was frequently used by Roosevelt as a liaison with the Hill in promoting or opposing legislation. Roosevelt knew very well that Jones would drag his feet when asked to help on a policy with which he did not agree; but he used him anyway. Hull, much less conservative, was useful in the same way. As a member of Congress for twenty-four years, he was always welcome on the Hill; he could drop in at any time for lunch or social gatherings—a much more effective way of getting action than in formal appearances before congressional committees.

In the main, Roosevelt's style of appointments, except to the Supreme Court or to the head and upper secretariat of a department or agency, was about the same as that of other Presidents. There were ethnic and social groups to satisfy; geographical considerations; political recommendations. His chief failing with respect to subordinates was his reluctance to fire. He would go to great lengths either to place the official he wanted to discharge in some other and less important place, or to "kick him upstairs," or to take steps to induce a resignation.

Roosevelt's style of disregarding the orthodox theories of administration was not born of ignorance about those theories or about their application. In fact, he was the prime mover in the reorganization of the White House Executive offices to make the administrative task of the President more manageable. He had to fight Congress for more than two years to get the legislation which enabled him to do this. The message containing his recommendations for the authority to reorganize the Executive Office was based on a report of a Committee on Administrative Management, which he had appointed in March 1936, consisting of three well-known and well-trained experts in public administration. Four times he had to repeat the message and recommendations, until finally in 1939 they were passed though in a watered-down state. The Executive Office of the President was then created by Executive Order #8248 on September 8, 1939, which institutionalized and departmentalized the Office of the President, placing in it many new functions and bureaus reporting directly to the President. This form of organization has, with additions, lasted through all of the succeeding presidencies. In light of his struggle—and final success—to increase the efficiency of the office and to bring within it all the instrumentalities for national policy formation, it is a little difficult to condemn Roosevelt as a bad administrator. As Professor Clinton Rossiter in his standard text on the American presidency has said: "For some years it has been popular, even among his friends, to write off Mr. Roosevelt as a 'second-rate' administrator. In the light of Executive Order #8248, an accomplishment in public administration *superior to that of any other President,* this familiar judgment seems a trifle musty."[72] (Emphasis added)

One of the agencies brought into the new Executive Office was that of the Bureau of the Budget. Its director was Harold D. Smith, a well-recognized and highly trained and respected public administrator. I had many conferences with him in connection with administrative reorganizations which the President had assigned to me. We used to discuss the unorthodox style of the President—more in amazement at what he was able to accomplish in running the government than in criticism. We had both become accustomed to it, and were no longer surprised by any new demonstration of his style of administration.

In later years after Smith's retirement, when he had the time and the distance from the daily pressures of hectic administrative activity to think in a leisurely way about it, he had an interview with Robert Sherwood, who was then preparing his *Roosevelt and Hopkins.* Sherwood wrote:

"I know of no one whose judgment and integrity and down-right common sense the President trusted more completely [than Smith's]. In the course of a long conversation, Smith said to me: 'A few months ago, on the first anniversary of Roosevelt's death, a magazine asked me to write an article on Roosevelt as an administrator. I thought it over and decided I was not ready to make such an appraisal. I've been thinking about it ever since. When I worked with Roosevelt —for six years—I thought, as did many others, that he was a very erratic administrator. But now, when I look back, I can really begin to see the size of his programs. They were by far the largest and most complex programs that any

President ever put through. People like me who had the responsibility of watching the pennies could only see the five or six or seven percent of the programs that went wrong through inefficient organization or direction. But now I can see in perspective the ninety-three or -four or -five per cent that went right—including the winning of the biggest war in history—because of unbelievably skillful organization and direction. And if I were to write that article now, I think I'd say that Roosevelt must have been one of the greatest geniuses as an administrator that ever lived. What we couldn't appreciate at the time was the fact that he was a real artist in government.' "[73]

Marriner Eccles, who as the chairman of the Federal Reserve Board came to know Roosevelt as an administrator very well, put it a little more succinctly. He, too, had found frustrations at times in conferring with the President about the problems then uppermost in Eccles's mind. Writing in 1951, he said: "When I recall the din in which we lived as we vied for his support and attention, I marvel that he was able to see not just single administrators, but the world; that he was able to fill not just one role of the Presidency, but all its roles."

A dozen years after Roosevelt died, Sam Rayburn of Texas, Speaker of the House of Representatives, was talking to a friend. Rayburn was a hardbitten Democrat from Texas who had been in the House for many years; he was a realistic and blunt political protégé of Garner, not given to flattery or to overstatement. He, like Garner before him, reported on matters to the President "with the bark off"—just as he saw them, without any soft coating. After reminiscing about why Roosevelt was so hated by the economic royalists of his day, he said "softly but with utter conviction":

"Roosevelt was a great man. He saved the country—not once but twice."[74]

We have already discussed the first time—when in 1933 he "saved" the American system of private enterprise from the threat posed by the misery and despair of the Great Depression.

We now take up the events of the second time Roosevelt "saved" America —the war years of 1939–45. The crisis of these years was more formidable and dangerous even than that of 1933. The crisis of 1933, however, had been right in the midst of every American home. But up until the end of 1941, the 1939 crisis of the war was more than 3,000 miles away. Only a small minority of Americans were able to see the danger to the United States—so far away—in the crisis of 1939, and to understand that it was their own crisis as well as the crisis of Europe. Many of those who did see it preferred to stick their heads in the sand, to pray and hope that it would go away. Some who saw it were not too much concerned; a handful were even pleased. To these few the events of the crisis of 1939 were the "wave of the future" for the whole world; they were confident in their ability "to do business with Hitler" at any time.

The President's job in the crisis of 1939 was even more difficult than in 1933. First, he had to make Americans realize the crisis in all its ugliness. Then he had to persuade them to do all the unpleasant, costly and dangerous things necessary to meet it. He would have to repeat the process of 1933–37 which he described as "taking the whole nation to school on the nation's business," and expand it to "taking the whole nation to school on the world's business."

Starting in 1937—for Roosevelt saw the crisis coming two years before it actually erupted in 1939—he began this second round of "five years of fierce discussion and debate" to educate the American people on the dangers which the international situation presented to the very survival of the United States. It was to be a long and difficult process, much more vehemently opposed than his first five-year course of education.

Roosevelt's foreign policy announced in his Inaugural of 1933 was very simple and understandable, the policy of the Good Neighbor: "the neighbor who resolutely respects himself and . . . the rights of others—the neighbor who respects his obligations and respects the sanctity of his agreements with a world of neighbors." Roosevelt was to follow this style in all his dealings with Latin America. It was a style which was to pay off handsomely in many ways, particularly during the war.

The Good Neighbor policy represented a steady and expanding movement away from the former policies of intervention to the policy of friendly collective security. Roosevelt began to put it into practice at once by refusing to interfere by force in the internal affairs of Cuba. Such intervention had been authorized by the Platt Amendment to the United States-Cuba Treaty of 1903.

When the annual Pan American Conference convened in Montevideo in December 1933, Roosevelt asked the Secretary of State to attend. This was the first Pan American Conference which a Secretary had ever attended as a delegate —a token of the new respect of the Good Neighbor to the north for the other republics. Many international agreements were reached at Montevideo, the most important being a declaration that no state in the Western Hemisphere had the right to intervene in the affairs of another. The President then announced "that the definite policy of the United States from now on is one opposed to armed intervention." A new spirit of friendship and confidence had begun.

In May 1934, the President asked for and obtained ratification of a new treaty he had sponsored with Cuba, abrogating the Platt Amendment entirely. In January 1936, he called an Inter-American Conference at Buenos Aires to maintain peace among all the American republics. The reason for this call was the growing international discord, the violation of treaties and the building up of armaments in the rest of the world. Roosevelt thought this conference so important that he went himself, taking Secretary Hull with him. He stopped off at Rio to pay his respects to the government of Brazil, where he delivered an address to a joint session of the Congress and the Supreme Court and the President of Brazil.[75] He delivered another address to the international conference when he arrived in Buenos Aires, and a further one in Montevideo two days later. This was the style of the Good Neighbor.

The results of the Montevideo conference were far-reaching. The great majority (though not all) of the twenty-one republics agreed that if a dispute arose between any of them no hostilities would occur for six months so that all the republics could consult with the disputants and also among each other; that if an international war outside the Americas or any event anywhere might endanger the peace of the Western Hemisphere, the republics would consult together; and that they reaffirmed the policy adopted at Montevideo in 1933 against intervention in the internal or external affairs of any republic by any other republic.

As the prospects of war increased in Europe and Asia, the American republics grew closer together in collective security. The Eighth International Conference of American States met at Lima, Peru, from December 9 to 27, in 1938. The Secretary of State again headed the United States delegation. The conference, in addition to other agreements, adopted the "Declaration of Lima" which reaffirmed the republics' collaboration to defend their solidarity, and to make it effective even against any threat from abroad—by consultation and by any other measures they would agree upon as sovereign states.

When war finally came in Europe, the American republics met in their first consultation provided by these agreements. The meeting was in September 1939 at Panama. It resulted in several accords and a "Declaration of Panama" to protect their neutrality: no bases in the Western Hemisphere for belligerents; no military aircraft over their territory; all belligerents' combat vessels to be kept out of American waters by individual or collective patrols along the coasts of the entire hemisphere. The Good Neighbor policy had been made so successful by the Roosevelt style toward Latin America that it now had developed into collective neighborhood security.

When in 1940 France fell, the grave question immediately arose as to the status of her colonies in this hemisphere. Obviously if control or jurisdiction were to be transferred to Hitler or seized by him, it would be a matter of deep concern to all the American republics—and the principles of the Monroe Doctrine itself might be jeopardized. Again to consult on this common problem the Foreign Ministers of all of them convened in Havana on July 21, 1940. To meet this danger, the conference adopted two measures: (1) the "Act of Havana," setting up an emergency committee immediately with one member from each republic, to meet if any threat appeared; and (2) a formal treaty setting up (when ratified) this "Inter-american Territorial Commission" with power to organize a provisional government in any colony of a European power which had been left without its own adequate government as a result of the war.

The President in a speech on October 10, 1940, extended the policy of defending the Western Hemisphere to include "the right to peaceful use of the Atlantic and Pacific Oceans surrounding it."

In April 1941, Congress approved Roosevelt's policy of no recognition of the transfer of any geographic region in this hemisphere by one non-American power to another.

At a press conference on April 25, 1941, the President announced that patrol of these waters by the republics of the Western Hemisphere which had been started at the outbreak of war would extend "as far on the waters of the Seven Seas as may be necessary for the defense of the American Hemisphere."

One of the great wartime effects of the success of Roosevelt's Good Neighbor policy and his style toward Latin America was the formulation of treaties beginning in 1941 with the South American countries by which the United States would buy up all their exportable surpluses of certain critical war materials. The South American republics agreed in turn not to sell or export any of these critical materials to any of the Axis enemies—who were of course in great need of them. The United States, in order to bolster the economy of the South American republics, began also to buy from them all kinds of non-war materials such as wool and cotton which were piling up because of the elimination of European markets by the war.

Not all the republics gave wholehearted cooperation. Argentina was the worst. By September 1944 the infiltration into Argentina of Nazi economic influence, her pro-Nazi press and the growth of Fascist methods by the government itself had reached the point where the President made a formal statement condemning both tendencies, with a veiled threat that neutrals in the postwar world would be judged and affected by their attitudes during the war.[76]

But with the overwhelming number of American republics, this unwavering

Good Neighbor style of Roosevelt's—aided by the hard work of Hull and Welles —was one of his great successes. After the war, inter-American relations deteriorated. But, as in the case of deterioration in Russian relations, that belongs to another chapter.

It soon became obvious, however, that the Good Neighbor policy—if it was to be applied to the rest of the world—was not as acceptable in the United States. Here the President had to adopt a much more cautious style, much to his own distaste, but made necessary by public opinion. If he needed any official recognition of this public opinion, he got it in 1935. He recommended in January of that year that the United States join the World Court. Father Coughlin, the Hearst newspaper chain and Huey Long, warning that this would lead to war, produced 40,000 telegrams in opposition to the recommendation two days before the vote. In spite of the fact that the 1932 platforms of both parties had piously included adherence to the World Court, Roosevelt could not get the two-thirds vote he needed.

After this defeat he wrote to Henry L. Stimson, then a private citizen, ". . . these are not normal times; people are jumpy and very ready to run after strange gods. This is so in every other country as well as our own. I am afraid that common sense dictates no new method for the time being."[77]

He also sent a letter to Senator Robinson, the Democratic leader in the Senate, expressing his appreciation and gratitude to him and the fifty-one other "aye" voters for their personal and political courage; and he added: "As to the 36 Senators who placed themselves on record against the principle of the World Court, I am inclined to think that if they ever get to Heaven they will be doing a great deal of apologizing for a very long time—that is if God is against war— and I think He is."[78]

The mention of war in this letter in 1935 was not unfounded hysteria, but an example of his extraordinary feel for things to come. As early as June 1933, Roosevelt was getting reports from American representatives in Berlin that if Hitler did not get what he wanted, peace would no longer satisfy him. In 1934, he was told by the Embassy in Berlin that the Nazis were "building a tremendous military machine." From Ambassador Long in Rome, starting in 1934, came reports of war preparations by Mussolini. From Ambassador Grew in Tokyo, reports of Japanese preparations for the use of force, and somber warnings of Japanese intentions to disregard the treaties they had signed. Because of isolationist sentiment, although he showed his deep concern about all this in private letters, he took no public steps.

In 1935 he was trying to get his vast New Deal "must" legislation through the isolationist Congress which had just rejected his recommendation of adherence to the World Court. He had enough troubles getting his domestic program passed without agitating the congressional isolationists, of whom many progressives like Borah, Nye, LaFollette and Wheeler whose support he needed were the leaders. Isolationism and revulsion against any involvement in European conflicts increased rapidly in 1934 and 1935, as evidence of fantastic wartime profiteering in the American munitions industry, tax evasion and collusion with foreign munition makers during World War I was uncovered and published by the congressional investigating committee headed by the arch-isolationist Senator Gerald P. Nye.

There can be no doubt that Roosevelt during the mid-thirties was no lion and no educator in foreign affairs. Perhaps he feared that isolationism was too deeply rooted and too skillfully led, and that any effort would be a failure and a setback for his domestic program. He was to learn in 1937 that this fear was only too well justified.

In the January 1935 Annual Message, which was almost entirely taken up with his forthcoming program of social security, Roosevelt devoted a mere three short paragraphs to foreign affairs. After stating: "I cannot with candor tell you that general international relations outside the borders of the United States are improved," he called the attention of Congress to the "new strivings for armament and power" which "in more than one land rear their ugly heads."

Later that year, Mussolini invaded Ethiopia. Congress almost unanimously passed, and Roosevelt signed, the Neutrality Act of 1935 which made it mandatory for the President to place an embargo on all war supplies to all belligerents in a conflict. But as he signed the act, he made a warning statement with remarkable foresight even for this far-sighted man, that although "it was intended as an expression of the fixed desire of the Government and the people of the United States to avoid any action which might involve us in war . . . it is a fact that no Congress and no Executive can foresee all possible future situations that may call for some flexibility of action. . . . The inflexible provisions [making embargo on both sides mandatory] might drag us into war instead of keeping us out."[79] Roosevelt had urged Congress while it was considering the legislation to see that discretionary authority be given to the President to place the embargo only on the aggressor instead of mandatorily on both belligerents, thus providing a possible deterrent to aggression. In this he failed. The events of 1939 were to show how right the President was; but he made none of his usual moves to appeal to the people to help him. He knew how fruitless this would be, for the overwhelming majority of Americans favored strict neutrality as the best protection from being dragged into a foreign war.

The Neutrality Act of 1935 was only a formal statutory recognition of what everyone knew was the isolationism rampant in America ever since the disillusionment and cynicism following World War I. Wilson's idealism was condemned as naïve; he was charged with having yielded to profiteers. The 1935 wrangling among the Western nations in Europe about what course to follow concerning Mussolini's aggression in Ethiopia added to the determination that the United States remain aloof. The Hoare-Laval Treaty which accepted the Ethiopian conquest added an additional surge of isolationism. The Nye Committee by its propaganda had persuaded the majority of the American people that wars were made only by and for munitions manufacturers and international bankers. It is quite difficult for anyone in 1975, who has seen intervention by the United States in disputes in all parts of the globe, to visualize the atmosphere of 1935–38.

By 1936 Roosevelt was clearly doubtful of continued peace in Europe. In his Annual Message of that year, he devoted twenty paragraphs to the growing danger of conflict in Europe. In February 1936, he expressed his views privately to his Ambassador in Paris, Jesse Straus, in reply to the Ambassador's letter stating his impressions in France of moral decay, fear of Germany, venality, tax evasion and corruption among French politicians. Roosevelt answered: "The armaments race means bankruptcy or war—there is no possible out from that statement. . . . Heaven only knows that I do not want to spend more money on our Army and Navy. I am initiating nothing new unless and until increases by other nations make increases by us absolutely essential to national defense."[80]

His letter in the following month to William E. Dodd, the American Ambassador in Berlin,[81] was more blunt: "All the experts here, there and the other place say 'there will be no war.' They said the same thing all through July 1914. . . . In those days I believed the experts. Today I have my tongue in my cheek. This does not mean that I am becoming cynical; but as President I have to be ready just like a fire department."

This letter is a typical example of how the President, in his policy toward Europe and Asia from 1935 on, would draw upon his experience under Wilson in World War I to create his own style of operations before and during World War II—sometimes following Wilson and sometimes not.

In March 1936 came the momentous event which the leaders of the democratic nations might have used to stop Hitler's aggression—his occupation of the Rhineland. This was his first act of aggression. All of the leaders of the democratic nations—including Roosevelt—remained silent. A private request by the French to Roosevelt for a public denunciation of the invasion went unheeded. The election of 1936 was coming, and nothing could do more harm to Democratic chances than the expression of doubt as to the wisdom of American neutrality. Indeed, in the Chattaqua speech of August 14, 1936, the "I hate war" speech, the President was content to refer to the excellent results of the Good Neighbor policy in South America, to denounce generally the treaty violations in Europe, and to refer to his own determination to continue "thinking and planning how war may be kept from this nation." The most he could promise—in addition to maintaining neutrality with the weapons which Congress had given him (Neutrality Act of 1935)—was to prevent profiteering in the United States, and to resist the inevitable pleas of prospective profiteers who would, if war broke out abroad, attempt to "break down or evade our neutrality." So far had the effects of the Nye Committee's findings extended! The furthest he would go in this speech was a repetition of his earlier warning "that no [neutrality] laws can be provided to cover every contingency." The most effective assurance of staying out of any war, he added, would be that "those who watch and decide have a sufficiently detailed understanding of international affairs to make certain that the small decisions of each day do not lead toward war," and that "at the same time they possess the courage to say 'no' to those who selfishly or unwisely would let us go to war." Earlier in the speech he had made clear that from long experience, he himself possessed that kind of wisdom and that kind of determination.

In the election campaign of 1936, just as he never mentioned what, if anything, he intended to do about the Supreme Court, he never discussed what was happening in Europe or Asia, except for a passing reference here and there about staying out of war.

In 1937 the pace of warlike events increased. For Roosevelt it was the year of decision about his own course of action. It was also to be a year of extreme caution and patience, of advances here and retreats there—even vacillation. But he was no longer going to remain silent. Gradually he was coming to the decision that he no longer could be silent and encourage the isolationism of the American people, and that, on the contrary, he had to educate them as to what isolationism would mean to their own security. He could not, of course, get too far in advance of them. He had always appreciated this truism of democratic leadership; but it was dramatically brought home to him in October of 1937.

The year 1937 started out for Roosevelt with his Annual Message which ignored foreign affairs entirely. He was chiefly engrossed in his very private and undisclosed decisionmaking about the Supreme Court.

As the year progressed Roosevelt became more and more disturbed by the developments in the Far East as well as those in Europe. What the world obviously was waiting for was some indication that the United States was going to take a firm stand and make it clear to Germany, Italy and Japan (who were united in an anti-Comintern pact) that it would not remain indifferent to further acts of preparation for war, further aggression and further violations of treaties. The indication was not forthcoming.

In July 1937, Japan invaded China.

On October 5, 1937, Roosevelt finally put an end to his fears, doubts and vacillation. He decided to try to arouse the American people from their indifference to what was happening abroad, and at the same time to give courage to the European leaders who were seeking only to appease Hitler. In effect, he was putting on his robes as educator in foreign affairs for the first time. The speech was devoted entirely to international matters. It was a succinct factual statement of what was going on; a warning for the United States; and an unbelievably mild suggestion for action.

First, the prophetic warning: "If those things come to pass in other parts of the world, let no one imagine that America will escape, that America may expect mercy, that this Western Hemisphere will not be attacked. . . . War is a contagion whether it be declared or undeclared. We are determined to keep out of war, yet we cannot insure ourselves against the . . . dangers of involvement."

Then the suggested remedy: "If those days are not to come to pass . . . the peace-loving nations must make a concerted effort to uphold laws and principles on which alone, peace can rest secure. . . . There is no escape through mere isolation or neutrality. . . . The epidemic of world lawlessness is spreading. When an epidemic of physical disease starts to spread, the community approves and joins in a *quarantine* of the patients in order to protect the health of the community against the spread of the disease."[82] (Emphasis added)

The public response to this comparatively mild speech was immediate, violent, denunciatory—and almost unanimous. To the President, it was also shockingly surprising. He had apparently completely misjudged public opinion—one of the few instances of this kind of failure. With only a few exceptions, the "quarantine" speech was hailed in the press as saber-rattling and warmongering. Some congressmen even began to clamor for impeachment.[83] Thousands of protesting telegrams came into the White House. Here are two typical ones:

"If you 'hate war' do not try to incite it by such appeals as you made on the 5th in Chicago."

"All right if you want peace, keep the peace. No one is coming over here to attack us."

That was the America of 1937. Lord Lothian in the *Observer* (London) wrote that it "will probably mark the point at which the United States definitely began to turn away from the isolation which had been its policy since the rejection of the League of Nations in the presidential election of 1920."

There were some people who, to the President's great indignation, remained discreetly silent: Hull and certain other Cabinet officers, congressional Democratic leaders—all of whose verbal support he expected.[84] From this violent public reaction, Roosevelt realized he had made a major mistake in timing. He had tried to lead too quickly. Again, he had sprung a great surprise without substantial discussion with anyone, including his Secretary of State, his Cabinet or his congressional leaders. He had gone out "on a limb" too fast and too far. At his press conference the next day, as adroitly and quickly as a fox seeing a hunter in the distance, he climbed back to safer territory.[85]

If Roosevelt needed any confirmation about the reaction of the American people to his quarantine speech, he could have referred to a public opinion poll taken shortly afterward. In it, 69 per cent expressed greater confidence in even tighter neutrality than in giving the President discretion to act against aggressors.[86]

Although Roosevelt had bowed, temporarily, to American public opinion about his quarantine speech, he soon began his campaign to build up our national defenses. If the people and Congress failed to see what was coming, he did. He was finally, after the drifting of the last two years, going to change his style completely, and adopt one of action and teaching. But it was to take a long time for him to succeed. His first steps were in defense alone.

On December 12, 1937, almost as if to emphasize the warning of a spreading disease hitting us too, Japanese airplanes, without notice or provocation, bombed and sank the U.S. gunboat *Panay* (plainly marked) in the Yangtze River. On December 28, the President addressed a letter to the chairman of the Appropriations Committee:

... World events have caused me growing concern. I do not refer to any specific nation or to any specific threat against the United States. The fact is that in the world as a whole many nations are not only continuing but are enlarging their armament programs. I have used every conceivable effort to stop this trend, and to work toward a decrease of armaments. Facts, nevertheless, are facts, and the United States must recognize them. Will you therefore be good enough to inform the Sub-Committee on Naval Appropriations that after the next session of the Congress has met, it is possible that I may send supplementary estimates for commencing construction on a number of ships additional to the above program [already submitted, of two battleships, two light cruisers, eight destroyers and six submarines].

The language of this letter showed that Roosevelt had become convinced he had to proceed with action but with a very soft voice. This was still a very tame lion.

As 1938 dawned, the President was still deeply absorbed in domestic matters. His recommended legislation which had bogged down in the regular and extraordinary sessions of 1937 was still bogged down in 1938; the recession of 1937 had become worse in 1938; and later in 1938 there would come his disastrous "purge."

But foreign matters would not wait for the solution of domestic difficulties. The prolonged Civil War in Spain was causing criticism of the President for the embargo on both sides. Several of his own Cabinet—particularly Ickes—were urging him to lift the embargo, which was only helping the Fascists under Franco. Even some well-known isolationists surprisingly joined in this demand; in the spring of 1938 Senator Nye, one of the leading isolationists, introduced a resolution to lift it.[87] But Roosevelt did not want to risk reducing his prestige with Congress or with the people, both predominantly isolationist, any further. It was low enough after the failure of the Court fight, the failure of his legislative program and the "purge." The Loyalists in Spain were largely Communists; and Ickes, in his diary, said that Roosevelt had told him that lifting the embargo would lose "every Catholic vote" in the coming 1938 elections.[88]

Britain and France kept impressing upon our government the importance of maintaining the embargo so as to help restrict the conflict to the Spanish boundaries. Even Churchill, no great admirer of Chamberlain or his foreign policy, has written: "I was sure, however, that with all the rest they had on their hands, the British Government was right to keep out of Spain," and he wrote to the French Ambassador in London: "I am sure that an absolute rigid neutrality, with the strongest protest against any breach of it, is the only correct and safe course at the present time."[89]

Lifting the embargo would probably not have changed the result of the Civil War. But decisive action might possibly have bolstered the European democracies by showing that the United States was unwilling to sell arms to an aggressor nation. Roosevelt, however, was not at this point decisive within himself. He wavered at times toward lifting the embargo; but the divisions in Congress and among the people stayed him from making any definite proposal. His course on Spain in 1938 was far from his finest hour. Ickes claims that Roosevelt at a Cabinet meeting in January 1939, when it was too late, "very frankly stated, and this for the very first time, that the embargo had been a grave mistake."

While the Democratic leaders vacillated, temporized, hesitated, Hitler moved on—fast. In March 1938 he took Austria, and later in 1938, when Roosevelt was busy with his "purge," Hitler publicly demanded the Sudetenland of Czechoslovakia, and was allowed to move in without having to fire a single shot.

What Roosevelt did in all this was minimal. Instead of speaking out forthrightly to all the world condemning the acts of Hitler, he addressed an open telegram to Czechoslovakia, Germany, Great Britain and France on September 27, two days before Czechoslovakia was deserted by the European democracies, urging that they not break off negotiations but try to settle their dispute peacefully. In response to Hitler's answer, which was a tirade about Germany's past grievances, he sent Hitler another telegram. These were pathetically naïve gestures, without any effect.

There was some rejoicing in America that Munich had averted war, and that we would have, in Chamberlain's words, "peace in our time." Roosevelt felt that Munich had merely postponed the inevitable. He said, in a radio address to the *Herald Tribune* Forum the following month: "It is becoming increasingly clear that peace by fear has no higher or more enduring quality than peace by the sword."

With that thought in mind, he continued his actions for increasing national defense, especially in aircraft. At a press conference on November 15, 1938, almost a year before the *Blitzkrieg* in Poland, the President, in reply to a question, said: "You know we had a very large conference in here yesterday; you saw them. . . . As a result of world events in the last few years, and as a result of scientific advancement in waging war, the whole orientation of this country in relation to the continent on which we live has had to be changed. . . . The first thing we have to realize is the fact that any possible attack has been brought infinitely closer than it was five years ago . . . one of the reasons is the development in aircraft. We are therefore studying national defense and continental solidarity against possible attacks from other hemispheres. . . ."

He was then asked:

"Could you amplify the new danger which makes this continental defense necessary?" and his reply was:

"Read the newspapers for the past five years."[90]

In 1939, the President's pace in foreign affairs quickened. In his Annual Message of that year, he said that the storms abroad threatened three indispensable institutions of the American people—religion, democracy and international good faith. "There comes a time in the affairs of men, when they must prepare" to defend these institutions, as well as their homes. "We have learned . . . the old, old lesson that probability of attack is mightily decreased by the assurance of an ever-ready defense." The speed of modern attack, he pointed out, had changed defense methods—so the timing of defense preparation must also be changed. He promised to send a special message in a few days with defense recommendations. For the first time, he urged that "we have learned that an inflexible neutrality law may operate unevenly and actually give aid and encouragement to aggressors." This was the beginning of his all-out effort to change the Neutrality Act. It was one of the methods he had in mind when he added: "There are many methods short of war, but stronger and more effective than words, of bringing home to aggressor governments the aggregate sentiments of our own people." Although, as usual, he did not try to define what all the methods "short of war" were, relying on time and actions to reveal them, that phrase was to dominate and illustrate his style for the next three years.

His style for 1939 in foreign affairs was to be action as well as words: rearming on a vast scale and fighting with Congress to change the embargo laws which would clearly help the Nazis in a war against Britain. But he did not completely abandon words; words were now to be directed not only to the dictators but chiefly to the American people, words of warning, words of enlightenment as to the extent of the danger to us, words of leadership, rallying Americans to the crying need of their support of democracies all over the world—but cautious words, non-inflammatory words, not bellicose words. The people were not ready for that yet.

He would continue to press for domestic reforms during the year, with the argument that a sound, healthy economy without existing inequalities among its citizens was one of the strongest defenses possible in the event of war.

One week after the Annual Message he sent a message to the Congress asking for additional appropriations for national defense. And two weeks after that, he again asked for funds, to expand the air forces of the United States. This time, except from extreme isolationists, there were no cries of "warmonger."

Events in 1939 began to move even faster in Europe.

On April 14, after Mussolini had invaded Albania, Roosevelt made another try at peace. He sent a cable to Hitler and Mussolini, asking them directly: "Are you willing to give assurance that your armed forces will not attack or invade the territory or possessions of the following independent nations?"—and he named practically all the nations of Europe and those of the Near East. If they would, he offered to serve as "a friendly intermediary" in keeping each nation informed of the declared policies of the others.

In a press conference the next day, before Hitler's rejection, he read the cable he had sent, and explained: "The cause for this is that, for the second or third time, I feel that we in this country should leave no stone unturned to prevent war." He explained the message paragraph by paragraph to make sure that no inaccurate interpretations about it would be written. His eye was fixed on the congressional isolationists, and the newspapers, as well as on the American people. Hitler a few days later made a vitriolic and inflammatory speech which gave a definitive "No." This was the only reply.

Roosevelt's first effort to obtain repeal of the arms embargo came in a message to the Congress on July 14, 1939. In this he used a new style. His message was a short one of only ten lines;[91] but attached to it was a long, well-reasoned memorandum from Hull. The President never explained this unusual device. My own surmise is that, first, this was a way of using Hull's popularity and strength with Congress; and, secondly, it was a way of dissipating false rumors in the press that the President and Hull had disagreed on this question of neutrality.

Four days later, in a desperate effort to get repeal of the arms embargo before Congress adjourned, the President, putting all his prestige on the line, called the famous evening conference at the White House of congressional leaders of both parties. He maintained that if the act were amended to permit Britain to buy arms here, pay cash for them and transport the arms in its own ships, it might discourage Hitler, and enable us to help Britain without risking the loss of our own men and ships in any combat zone. This was the conference at which Senator Borah stated that his own private information—for which he did not deign to name the sources—was more reliable than the government's, and that there would positively be no war in Europe in 1939. By midnight, it became clear that a solid Republican opposition aided by the isolationist Democrats could and would block repeal at that time.

This was the last time the isolationist bloc in Congress actually defeated Roosevelt on any question he submitted to them. He would have to fight them in future repeatedly, and often his margin of victory would be very small. Also, he would thereafter be unwilling to submit any matters to Congress if he could possibly avoid doing so; he was fearful that another decisive defeat might adversely affect public opinion.

A week before war erupted, Hitler was making impossible demands on Poland. In this new crisis, Roosevelt made one more effort by words: an appeal to Hitler and Mussolini and President Moszicki of Poland. It was useless. Hitler, again, did not even answer. He invaded Poland on September 1, 1939. The war was on.

At the press conference on that day,[92] the President was able to engage in some humorous repartee even in the midst of this great new crisis. It had always been his style since 1929 as Governor and 1933 as President to seek some diversion from tasks facing him by stopping serious work for a few minutes, to exchange jokes or pieces of current political gossip, or pleasantly to tease someone about something, or tell some anecdote, relevant or irrelevant to the business at hand —and then to resume work. This style of breaking up the tensions of the moment was one of the things which enabled him to survive the crushing pressures of his office as long as he did. Fortunately, he did not desert it even during the war; and he certainly showed it in this conference.

The President [addressing Earl Godwin, a reporter, as the rest of the members of the press were coming in]: "What time did you get up?"

Mr. Godwin: "About 3:00 or 3:15, right after you aroused the nation [by putting the news of the war on the radio]. Felt like I belonged to the village fire department."

The President: "Yes, you were not the only one."

Mr. Godwin: "I know, I wonder if anybody got Borah up?"

The President: "Yes, where is he?"

Answer: "He went to Poland Springs, Maine."

The President: "What?"

Answer: "Poland Springs, Maine."

The President: "Oh, I thought you said *Poland.* That would have been news."

Two nights later, he was on the air in a fireside chat. That evening I was at a cottage in the Adirondacks with my family. It was in the middle of the forest, on the shore of a calm placid lake. There were no roads leading to it; access was only by boat across the water. Everything was very peaceful—an atmosphere totally incongruous with the war news. There was literally no noise except the quiet lapping of the lake on the rocks on shore; there were no lights visible except one three miles away on the other side of the lake. Along with nearly every American, we listened to the President at our radio on the porch overlooking the peaceful scene. The voice which came to us was just as calm as the mountains, the forest and the water. There was no trace of panic or even of extreme urgency. This was Roosevelt's usual style in the midst of crisis. I was to see the same style again and again—even on Pearl Harbor Day. He wanted to reassure the American people, not to frighten them, or even to hint that, in any way, he was himself frightened. But it was a firm voice; and it showed his deep concern.

He expressed determination to use every effort to keep the United States out of the war. But he warned that we could not shrug off the war as none of our business, for "every word that comes through the air, every ship that sails the seas, every battle that is fought, does affect the American future." Today this is an accepted fact. But in 1939 it was something quite new. He also said—in a conscious departure from the style of Wilson, who had urged Americans in 1914 to remain neutral in thought as well as in deed: "I cannot ask that every American remain neutral in thought. Even a neutral cannot be asked to close his mind to his conscience." It was to be a long road he would have to travel from this modest statement to his statement in 1941 that America should be the "arsenal of democracy."

Speaking in person to the extraordinary session of Congress which he had convened for September 21 to pass upon his recommendation for repeal of the arms embargo, he frankly admitted: "I regret that the Congress passed that [neutrality] Act. I regret equally that I signed that Act." It was not his usual style to admit error so categorically. In this, his first wartime message to Congress, Roosevelt began his bi-partisan style as an important part of his overall wartime strategy. He never abandoned that style either in waging the war or in seeking a postwar organization to keep the peace. "These perilous days demand cooperation among us without trace of partisanship," he said; and he added that, as the first step in the execution of this policy, he had asked the leaders of both parties in Congress to remain in Washington between this extraordinary session and the regular one which would begin in January 1940. He said that they had all agreed. "I expect to consult with them at frequent intervals in the course of events . . . and on the need for future action in this field, whether it be *executive* or *legislative* action." (Emphasis added)

What he asked for in his message was clearly designed to avoid the day-by-day incidents which he had seen under Wilson gradually drag us into war. He asked for a return to the historic principles of international law. He recommended (1) repeal of the mandatory embargo; (2) prohibition against American citizens and American ships entering zones of combat; (3) prohibition of American citizens from travelling on belligerent vessels; (4) prohibition of sales to a belligerent, except on a "cash and carry" basis, i.e., title to pass on delivery to the belligerent's vessel, the goods to be paid for in cash on delivery, and to be carried by the belligerent at its own risk; (5) no arms to be carried on American ships; and (6) prevention of war credits to belligerents. A mere enumeration of the recommendations shows how closely Roosevelt was adapting what he had learned as Assistant Secretary of the Navy. Knowing the full strength of the isolationists in Congress, however, Roosevelt put the main emphasis in the message on staying out of the war rather than helping the democracies.

He took personal leadership on the repeal legislation; he cancelled many longstanding appointments in order to keep in hourly touch with the Hill; he used all his influence in all directions, all his well-practiced devices, his cunning and his courage, to bring pressure on Congress.

It took Congress a month and a half of bitter debate to pass the legislation, but Roosevelt never let go; he never stopped fighting. Borah took to the air—still in opposition. The isolationists throughout the country flooded Congress with telegrams in opposition. When the bill was finally passed—almost by a party vote —it had been loaded down with many amendments. This was Roosevelt's first clear-cut victory over the isolationist block, and it was won by a bold frontal attack. While many of the restrictions of the old law remained on the books, many of them were going to be whittled away by him, one by one, during the next two years by more indirect methods. But it was distressingly clear, as 1939 came to an end, that the process of making the American people realize what an Axis victory would mean to *them* was not going to be an easy one or a short one.

The years 1940 and 1941 were to provide the ultimate test of the ability of Roosevelt to educate the American people before Pearl Harbor. He had to provide the leadership to teach them to realize how near the Nazi and Japanese threats were to them, to persuade them to approve the drastic steps he was taking to prepare, and to approve his sending much of our military supplies to Britain —and after June 22, 1941, to Russia—instead of keeping them all at home. His style would depend upon, and vary with, the course of events abroad, and also upon his appraisal of the thinking of the American people at the moment he acted.

During the first five months of 1940, it required no formal poll to ascertain the mood of the American people. It was clear to any intelligent observer that the prevailing sentiment in the United States was one of sympathetic aloofness. The American attitude was merely that of a very interested spectator. Roosevelt was fully aware of this; he did not delude himself. Nevertheless in 1939, before May 1, in five different messages he asked Congress for more and more appropriations for defense. Congress did comply each time—over the strong opposition, however, of the isolationist members.

When the "phony" war developed into a massive attack by the Nazis in April 1940, starting with their invasion and quick conquest of Denmark and Norway, the American people got a clearer picture of their own position. Denmark and Norway had both been neutral countries too, determined to maintain their neutrality and thereby escape the war, much like the attitude and wishful thinking in the United States. Americans realized very quickly how little "neutrality" meant to Hitler. Nor did the neutrality of Holland, Belgium and Luxembourg stop the Nazis, when they decided to overrun them the next month. In a few weeks France was overcome. Then followed the barbaric blitz upon the civilians of England who, with their Commonwealth and Empire, stood all alone in the world against the Nazi might.

The war was coming nearer to us with the fall of France. It soon came even closer; German submarines began to appear in the waters of the Western Hemisphere. Bases for possible future attacks on us which the Germans might seize next were very near in terms of the speed of aircraft—Greenland, Iceland, Dakar, the islands off the west coast of Africa. No one could tell when the Nazis would try to take them; and none of these bases had the slightest capacity to resist. The distance between our Eastern cities and the battlefields of Europe had become very small.

Roosevelt, in the face of all this danger, made two determinations of policy; and his style was framed for the next year and a half to carry them both into execution. First, there was the obvious one of rearming the United States; the second was one which he closely integrated with the first—keeping Britain supplied with as many arms as we could manufacture. For the longer we could help maintain Britain's resistance, the more time we had to convert our giant peacetime industries into the business of making weapons of war.

As France was being overrun in May 1940, the great importance of aircraft in modern war was brought home with shocking impact to the American people. The President immediately called the attention of Congress to the new speed of warfare in another message, on May 16, which as usual when matters which he deemed extremely important were involved, he delivered in person. He noted the "clear fact that the American people must recast their thinking about national protection." He enumerated the many possible bases the Nazis could take which would bring them within a few hours of our shores by plane. He began to talk in very concrete and ominous terms about all the dangers: "We stand ready not only to spend millions for defense but to give our service and even our lives for the maintenance of our American liberties." In addition to an immediate appropriation of about $1 billion for regular equipment by the Army and Navy and Marine Corps, he announced a plan to gear our production of war planes to a capacity of 50,000 per year. This bold fantastic goal of 50,000 was met by derision from many who thought it was just a "pipe" dream which could never become reality. But Roosevelt paid scant attention to the derision; he just kept on building. The fact is that a few years later we were turning out some 100,000 planes per year.

Two weeks after this message, he asked for another billion; a month and a half after that, for another $5 billion; the next year, after the passage of lend-lease, for another $7 billion. All these billions he got, but not without fighting for them.

On Sunday, May 26, as France was falling, the President went on the air in a fireside chat on national defense. After recounting what was happening to millions of civilians in France clogging highways to escape the Nazi bombing, and the machine-gunning aimed at them, he said: "Let us sit down together again, you and I, to consider our own pressing problems that confront us." That was the style of all his fireside chats though he did not often use these words to describe it. He pointed out that the fall of France had "shattered" the illusion that "we are remote and isolated and therefore secure against the dangers from which no other land is free." But in its place, he said, there had now arisen fears that we were completely defenseless. Again, after five years, he had to caution the people against fear. He urged: "Let us have done with both fears and illusions." He then recounted all the great increases in our defenses since 1933, and all the appropriations recently made for more defense; he announced the policy that private enterprise was to carry on war production rather than the government, but with the help of government; he announced the government's readiness to finance all new war plants and the enlargement of all existing ones, and to provide the initial money to get them into operation; he warned against heeding "fifth columnists" spreading rumors and fears—"undiluted poison," as he called it; he prayed for peace, but he would keep on building and building for national defense without the necessity of renouncing any of the recent social gains.

On July 29, he asked for authority to call out the National Guard.

On September 3, he informed Congress that he had transferred fifty over-age destroyers to Britain in exchange for several naval bases belonging to Britain in the waters of the Western Hemisphere.

On September 16, he announced registration day for selective service. He had announced his support for a military draft in his acceptance speech of the third-term nomination on July 19, ignoring the obvious political dangers.

All of these actions by Roosevelt and all his speeches and press conferences were having their effect on the American people. The President described his own estimate of public opinion in America in the fall of 1940.

"The year 1940 witnessed a great change in the attitude of the American people toward the course of the war that was raging in Europe and Asia. . . .

"By the Fall of 1940, the two-fold purpose of arming ourselves to the teeth, and at the same time, helping Great Britain and the other democracies, had become the aim of the vast majority of the American people. By that time, it had been made clear that Great Britain had the courage and stamina to resist the Nazi attack, with the assistance of the limited war supplies which we had been able to send to her.

"There was, however, a minority of the American people who were opposed to these twin objectives. . . .

"This group included the defeatists who preached that Hitler was invincible and could not be beaten. It included the appeasers who thought that the best way to get along in the world was to appease Hitler. It included some business men and financiers who urged that Americans could do business with Hitler. It included a small number of conscientious but misguided American citizens who thought that the way of peace was to put their heads in the sand and refuse to look at the storms abroad. It included all of the bundists, fascists and—before the war between Russia and Germany—all the subversive Communists. It also included all the groups in the United States committed to racial and religious intolerance and bigotry.

"This minority urged that the thing for the United States to do was to insist upon a negotiated peace, and thereafter to try to get along, in a business and in a diplomatic way, as well as possible, albeit humbly, with Hitler. For, according to them, Great Britain and the rest of the world were as good as conquered."[93]

It had not been easy to persuade the American people that our war production should not all be kept in the United States for the future defense of our own shores. It was even harder to persuade Congress. Even some of the top American military and naval officers were urging that we keep everything at home. It was, however, Roosevelt's conviction that every ton of war supplies he could deliver to Britain to sustain her while we were building up our war production capacity was worth many tons resting uselessly in our own arsenals. It was a courageous gamble to send practically all our small war production in 1940 to England; but he persuaded the American people to take it. He succeeded chiefly because of his style in persuading them that aid to Britain was not intended as an idealistic effort to help a democracy to resist aggression, but as a coolly reasoned step for their own immediate security and their own ultimate survival.

There could be no doubt about his disregard of the verities of politics in 1940, even while he was a candidate for a third term. In all the newspapers of the nation, photographs of the President were prominently displayed standing beside Stimson, the Secretary of War, as Stimson on October 29—just one week before Election Day—drew the first number in the draft which would send American young men to the Army or Navy or Air Force for training. It was the first peacetime draft in our entire history.

Roosevelt, again in simple language, explained to the American people the necessity ofthisextraordinaryandunprecedentedstep.Healsospoke"asCommander-in-Chief"
to the young men of the nation who had registered for the draft, in a simple moving statement of what their contribution would be to keeping the United States safe.

In one of the "non-political" speeches of his campaign for a third term, he repeated the basis of his Jeffersonian democracy and one of his deepest convictions—one which had a tremendous influence on his style: "On candidates and on election issues . . . I would rather trust the aggregate judgment of all the people in a factory—the president, all the vice-presidents, the board of directors, the managers, the foremen, plus all the laborers—rather than the judgment of the few who may have financial control at the time."[94]

A free election by all the people, he said, is the greatest safeguard for democracy:

"No dictator in history has ever dared to run the gauntlet of a really free election.

"Until the present political campaign opened, Republican leaders, in and out of the Congress shouted from the housetops that our defenses were fully adequate."

In the political arena he pulled no punches. Firing away at his opponents at Madison Square Garden on October 28, 1940, he said:

"Today they proclaim that this Administration has starved our armed forces, that our Navy is anemic, our Army puny, our air forces piteously weak.

"Yes, it is a remarkable somersault.

"I wonder if the election could have something to do with it." (This was said in a voice of sarcasm which brought great applause and cheers.)

"But . . . [the President added] the printed pages of the Congressional Record cannot be changed or suppressed at election time."

He then cited by chapter and verse the votes of the Republican members of earlier Congresses against appropriations for national defense. In working on this part of the speech, the President himself inserted a phrase that found great response in the audience, taking it from an old song which had been revived and was very popular in 1940, "The Daring Young Man on the Flying Trapeze."

"What did the Republican leaders do when they had this chance to increase our national defense almost three years ago? You would think from their present barrage of verbal pyrotechnics, that they rushed in to pass that bill, or that they even demanded a larger expansion of the Navy.

"But, ah! my friends, they were not in a national campaign for votes then.

"In those days they were trying to build up a different kind of political fence.

"In those days they thought that the way to win votes was by representing the Administration as extravagant in national defense, indeed as hysterical, and as manufacturing panics and inventing foreign dangers.

"But now, in the serious days of 1940, all is changed! Not only because they are serious days, but because they are election days as well.

"On the radio these Republican orators swing through the air with the greatest of ease, but the American people are not voting this year for the best trapeze performer. . . ."[95]

Coming to the Republican vote on repeal of the embargo, he pointed out that a majority of the Republican membership in both Houses had voted against it, including many Republican leaders. Among those leaders were three congressmen—Barton, Fish and Martin. In the first draft of the speech Bob Sherwood and I prepared, we had them listed in that order. We sat around—I remember we were writing in my apartment in New York City—working on that paragraph. Then as we read those names, we almost simultaneously hit on the more euphonious and rhythmic sequence of Martin, Barton and Fish. We said nothing about it when we handed the draft to the President, wondering whether he would catch it as he read the sentence aloud. He did. The very first time he read it, his eyes twinkled; and he grinned from ear to ear. To use one of his own favorite phrases, he was "tickled pink." He repeated it several times and indicated by swinging his finger in cadence how effective it would be with his audiences. I saw that he was going to have a lot of fun with that one. And he did.

The phrase was used several times in New York and Boston. The audience howled with laughter the first time he used it at Madison Square Garden. After the second time, they began to expect it and listen for it. The people in the Boston audiences had heard it on the radio, so they repeated the phrase in time with him and yelled "Barton and Fish" as soon as he said "Martin."

Professor Rauch, in *From Munich to Pearl Harbor,* reports: "Willkie said later: 'When I heard the President hang the isolationist votes of Martin, Barton & Fish on me, and get away with it, I knew I was licked."

Willkie had indeed met the "Champ"!

But again he wanted to make sure that he was not offending the rank-and-file Republican voters:

"Remember, I am making those charges against the responsible political leadership of the Republican party. But there are millions—millions and millions —of patriotic Republicans who have at all times been in sympathy with the efforts of this Administration to arm the nation adequately for purposes of defense."[96]

The political wisdom of this course was highlighted by the number of enthusiastic telegrams from people—who said specifically they were Republicans— that poured into the White House during October 1940.

Roosevelt won that election by a majority of about 5 million votes. His electoral vote was 449 from thirty-eight states against Willkie's 82 from ten states. The President admitted that this was more than he had expected.

Roosevelt was at one of the highest peaks of his career that election night. He had won in spite of the ancient third-term tradition; he had won in spite of all the public irritations that had inevitably accumulated in eight years of officeholding; he had won in spite of the overwhelming majority of the press; he had won in spite of the vast campaign funds against him, in spite of the pent-up hatred of conservatives and isolationists, and in spite of the violent opposition of the richest and most powerful industrialists and financiers in the United States.

He had won because the American people, in the terribly dangerous days which they all knew lay ahead, were willing to rely on him for leadership. He was now the moral leader of that entire part of the world which hated Hitler and his works, and which yearned for peace, democratic government, and decent standards of living.

What was Roosevelt's style in 1941, the first year of his third term?

The complexity of the task which faced him in January 1941 was matched only by its urgency. As the year began, Great Britain was standing virtually alone against Hitler. All of western Europe, its resources and productive capacity, were in Nazi hands. England's cities had been pounded by devastating Nazi air bombings since last September. Hitler was in a position to try the all-too-short jump across the Channel and had made plans and started preparations to do so in 1940. Fortunately he decided to abandon this project because of his lack of trust in Stalin and his fear that if he were engaged in an attack on Britain, Stalin would attack him on the Eastern front. He decided to eliminate this possibility by wiping out Russia and his old ally Stalin. Britain had only her Navy (including our fifty old destroyers) and her superb courage with which to turn him back. And it was England and her Navy and the ever-narrowing Atlantic Ocean which stood between Hitler and the United States.

President Roosevelt knew that we could do very little about this great danger unless the American people realized what they had to do, unless they recognized the extreme urgency, and were willing to do it quickly. His speeches and messages of 1941 were in the best style of the educator and the leader of public opinion. And they show also his great craving for action wherever action was needed— and possible.

From the beginning of 1941, down until Pearl Harbor took matters out of his hands, he had to walk the narrow line between increasing pressures on all sides. He was determined to follow the three objectives which he had been pursuing for a long time: (1) to build up our military and naval defenses to the highest possible level; (2) to deliver a substantial part of our war production to Britain while, at the same time, we continued to build up our war production capacity to its maximum limit; and (3) to keep his 1940 pledge of no war except in case of attack. A new objective was publicly added in 1941. It was his determination to work for an agency to keep the peace after the war—an agency in which the United States would be a party.

In the Atlantic, German submarines were sinking our vessels outside combat zones. In the Pacific, the Japanese, emboldened by the military agreements they had signed with the other Axis powers in September 1940, were accelerating aggression. He had to deal with the vast number of isolationists in the United States. The formidable isolationist leaders in Congress were to be harder to convince than the public. They were all clamoring that he do nothing, for "Britain was already defeated," and no provocation should be tendered to either the Nazis or the Japanese. On the other hand, Secretary of War Stimson and several others, as the sinkings in the Atlantic continued and increased, were urging him to go before Congress to ask for a declaration of war. Secretary Hull was equally persistent in his advice of caution. Hitler relied upon the division among the American people to help him avoid war with the United States. Roosevelt wanted to send aid to China which Japan had invaded, but wanted no war with Japan. All these pressures changed in emphasis from time to time, as the complicated events unfolded during the year.

Roosevelt was determined that the sinking of individual ships would not push him into war as it had Wilson. The American people agreed with this determination, and showed none of the hysteria which had been aroused during World War I by such sinkings. But now he was determined to get the supplies to Great Britain and to "shoot-it-out" with the submarines if that was necessary to get them there.

To do what he wanted to do would call for all the lion's courage but also for all the canny instincts of the fox. He displayed one or the other, or both, as each problem arose. It was quite clear, for example, that his 1941 style of using both was not entirely satisfactory to the interventionists and advisers like Stimson; and that it was far from satisfactory to the isolationists. But that was going to be his style until the Japanese bombs fell on Pearl Harbor.

The first event in 1941 was his enunciation of the Four Freedoms in his Annual Message to Congress to express the aspirations of all mankind for the future of the world. Then came the introduction of his lend-lease bill. It took a long debate in Congress to pass this, but when it finally was passed in March 1941, the President was able to say that the decision to sustain Britain with all we had and all that we could produce was the result of a united front on that objective. This was to prove something of an exaggeration, because the congressional isolationists who had held the Lend-Lease Bill up for so long were still determined to carry on their fight against his further steps "short of war" right down to the time of Pearl Harbor.

Lend-lease was a perfect example of the combination of the lion and the fox in the right proportions. It was in Roosevelt's most courageous style because it constituted an open defiance to all those in the United States who had opposed his policy, including many sincere millions of people—by now only a minority —who still believed in strict neutrality. At the same time, it was one of his most crafty devices. Had he proposed to Congress the sale of arms to belligerents on credit, there is no doubt that he would have been roundly defeated—even if Britain's credit at the time had been much better than it actually was. But by the simple invention of the homely, striking analogy to lending a neighbor your garden hose with which to save his burning home, and getting the hose back again after the fire was over, he circumvented any opposition to war loans of money. As he put it, "I want to eliminate the dollar sign." This was the kind of mixture of lion and fox which makes a President a great "operator" in the White House.

In the course of the preparation of his "unlimited emergency speech" of May 26, 1941, there was an incident which showed by indirection what was in Roosevelt's mind at the time about our getting into the war formally. There had been much talk among Roosevelt's military and other advisers about whether the time was ripe for the declaration by him of an unlimited emergency—a step which would call into action a number of war powers which he could then exercise. He himself had said nothing to us who were helping on the speech about putting it in. Finally, after several drafts, we inserted it on our own initiative. When Roosevelt read this he looked up, smiled wryly and asked: "Hasn't somebody been taking some liberties?" We said we had; but that we thought that that was what he really wanted to say. He reflected for a long time. "You know," he finally said, "there is only a small number of rounds of ammunition left to use unless the Congress is willing to give me more. This declaration of an unlimited emergency is one of those few rounds, and a very important one. Is this the right time to use it, or should we wait until things get worse—as they surely will?" He was really thinking out loud rather than asking us; and we remained silent. He reflected some more, and went on silently with the draft. The sentence never came out.

I believe that this incident shows—what I am sure was true—that the last thing he wanted then, or any time before Pearl Harbor, was a formal declaration of war either against, or by, Hitler or the Japanese. He was determined to get to Britain all the war supplies he could, and at the same time prepare ourselves if war should actually be forced upon us, as it finally was. He was ready to undertake any step necessary "short of war" to get those supplies to Britain, and keep the freedom of the seas intact. That was the best way to protect ourselves. He stalled Japan for more than two years—yielding a little oil and steel—because he did not want war in either ocean if it could be helped. That is why he was so wary of using his remaining weapons short of war, unless it was necessary; and one of these weapons was the declaration of an unlimited emergency.

This speech also illustrates Roosevelt's style in turning from the most serious and solemn duties to levity and relaxation. The speech was delivered in the East Room of the White House, with nationwide radio coverage, to the governing board of the Pan American Union. Afterwards, there was a small garden party for the audience. When that was over, the President and a few friends sat around and listened to Irving Berlin, who had been invited to listen to the speech, playing many of his past hits on the piano, while they joined in singing them. Forgotten, temporarily, were the tremendous pressures and problems weighing down increasingly upon him. He could make this kind of switch easily—and frequently did.

During the spring and early summer of 1941, he continued to urge speed and more speed in production for defense. He went far beyond the limits of strict old-fashioned neutrality when he declared that any waters or any base which could be the site for an easy attack on the United States were within the bounds of any legitimate action which the United States thought necessary for its safety. Following this theory, on April 10, 1941, after the fall of Denmark, American forces took possession of the Danish island of Greenland before Hitler could get there. In July he was to do the same thing in Iceland, and in the British West Indies. By a series of agreements in Lima, Panama and Havana, he had built up —as we have seen—a solidarity among all the Latin American countries against aggression or threat of aggression of any kind, to help thwart Hitler's efforts to get a foothold in the Western Hemisphere.

To make sure that there would be no curtailment of production of war supplies by strikes, he ordered the Army on three different occasions before Pearl Harbor to take over war plants which were having labor troubles.

On June 21, Hitler invaded Russia—as Roosevelt had warned Stalin he would. Roosevelt courageously stepped out ahead of the American people. He was shown a private poll of American opinion on July 1, indicating that though the people wanted Russia to win, the majority were not too anxious to send her military help; and that the effect of the invasion of Russia upon the American public, if any, was a desire for more aid to Britain.[97] But Roosevelt again ventured and decided to send all the aid possible to Russia, for Russia was by now destroying many thousands of Nazi soldiers. In doing this, he also stepped out ahead of many of his own military leaders, who thought that Russia could not resist for more than three weeks. Here again was a courageous leader, in advance of his people and even of his military. The American people did finally follow; and this venture, again, did pay off.

The isolationist bloc in Congress was not so easy to convince. The acid test of how far he could go ahead of the isolationists in Congress as distinguished from the people themselves came in August 1941, less than four months before Pearl Harbor. The test was not very encouraging. The Selective Service Act of 1940 was about to expire. Roosevelt hesitated for a moment to ask for an extension by Congress, fearing the devastating effect of a defeat on such a decisive measure. But realizing that silence on his part would be even worse, he finally did. The extension was passed—by a majority of only one vote in the House.

Bold action went on for many months in 1941 before Pearl Harbor. To get the goods to Britain and Russia, Roosevelt began convoys for American ships in August 1941, and he strengthened the existing patrols. He asked Congress for power to arm our merchant ships, and got it—but only by a narrow vote. Axis assets in the United States were frozen; Axis businessmen in South America blacklisted. Finally, after sinkings of several American ships had taken place, he issued his shoot-on-sight orders to sink all submarines—"rattlesnakes of the sea," as he called them—found in waters he had declared were necessary for our defense. In September he ordered convoys for any ships which joined an American convoy.

At home, the great defense agencies were created one by one in 1941 and began to function. Shortly before Pearl Harbor, while our ships and Nazi submarines were shooting at each other in the Atlantic and he was delaying Japan by every foxlike or lion-like act he could devise, Roosevelt said in a speech on Navy Day, October 27, 1941: "Today, in the face of this newest and greatest challenge of them all we Americans have cleared our decks and taken our battle stations."

Neither the Congress nor the people were yet ready for that ultimate step, in spite of the sinking of some of our ships. Nor was the President! Although, as the young Assistant Secretary of the Navy, he had been impatient with Wilson's reluctance to ask for a declaration of war, he would now refuse to do it though the provocation of sinkings was pretty much the same. But he would have none of Wilson's distaste for taking the first hostile step. He had already taken many —short of war—and was prepared to take more. For he had a different definition of attack from Wilson's and he was acting on the basis that we had already been "attacked," and were just repelling it.

On December 7, 1941, the war was forced upon us by an actual physical attack —the contingency for which Roosevelt had been preparing and preparing.

Roosevelt was now the Commander-in-Chief of a nation at war. He was soon to become the chief war strategist of the world. He was also soon to become the leader of the world in the formation of an organization to maintain the peace once unconditional surrender of the Axis triumvirate was achieved. These two projects were the pinnacle of Roosevelt's life. All that he had learned of domestic politics, of international relationships, of naval strategy, all of his skillful style of leadership, all of his receptiveness to new ideas (and new weapons), all of his self-confidence and self-assurance, especially in personal confrontation—all his flexibility and willingness to compromise, all of his arts of persuasion and conciliation, as well as his inflexible stubbornness when he felt sure he was right—all of his love of human beings living in the dark alleys of the world, exploited and disadvantaged, all of his past thirty years of training in public life seemed to converge into the style which this world statesman was now to adopt in order to try for his threefold objectives of victory, continued peace, and a new kind of world based on the Four Freedoms and the Atlantic Charter.

What in general was Roosevelt's style during his first year (1942) as war leader?

In the perspective of history we can see now that the Axis' great tactical success at Pearl Harbor on December 7, 1941, was a strategic failure. For nothing could have been worse for the Axis cause, in the long run, than to force America into the war as the attack was, of course, intended to do. That sneak attack did our fleet the greatest damage in its long history. But it did something else which the Axis powers should have feared more than our fleet and the British fleet combined. It created a unified, outraged and determined America.

The comfort of such historical perspective, however, was not available on January 1, 1942, as Franklin D. Roosevelt embarked on the second year of his third term. However hopeful President Roosevelt and all Americans might be of ultimate victory, the outcome in 1942 seemed uncertain. He knew that 1942 was the critical year. He knew that if the United States could hold in the Pacific, if her supply lines could be kept open, if Russia could hold back the Nazis from the heart of her country, if the Allies could survive the year and gather their full strength, ultimate victory would be inevitable. But the "ifs" were many, and large; and in that critical year, victory and defeat were in the balance. The great task of leadership which confronted Roosevelt in 1942 was to see that that balance was maintained, while strength could be gathered by the Allies to take the offensive. His style had to follow his own appraisal of the necessities of the hour. The fundamental problem which became acute with the Japanese attack on Pearl Harbor, and even more acute with the crushing defeats which rapidly followed in the Pacific, had been considered and, as far as the United States was concerned, settled in case war should come on both fronts. It was the problem of how best to allocate the resources of the United States in the global war; how much to the Pacific, how much to England, to Russia, to China, to the submarine war in the Atlantic? The decision had already been made by our government that the first target of our production of weapons had to be the Nazis. It became the great task of the President to convince the American people of the logic and wisdom of that course.

Today, in retrospect, the problem hardly seems difficult; the course seems quite obvious. It was obvious to President Roosevelt in 1942—but in 1942 not all Americans agreed with him. There were many who insisted that the Japanese were the "real enemy," that it was in the Pacific that all our energies and strength should be used. And there were still others—unreconstructed isolationists—who argued that all our ships, all our men, all our weapons and materiel should be brought back and kept in the United States. They would be needed here for defense, when the attack came upon us.

On this fundamental strategic issue, the President, in consultation with Churchill and the military leaders of both nations, did not waver. The decision was to dominate his style in 1942. In speeches and action, he soon disclosed the decision. As early as his State of the Union Address of 1942, one month after Pearl Harbor, the President said that the enemy had failed in its intent at Pearl Harbor to "terrify us to such an extent that we would divert our industrial and military strength to the Pacific area or even to our continental defense." And in the same address, the President referred to the "difficult choices" which had to be made, choices which included the hard decision not to try "to relieve the heroic and historic defenders of Wake Island . . . not to be able to land a million men in a thousand ships in the Philippine Islands."

Roosevelt also became the leading spokesman of the world in psychological warfare in the important battle of propaganda designed to weaken the fiber of the enemy and to strengthen the hearts and hopes of our Allies and of the resistance forces in the conquered countries. In 1942, propaganda was another foundation of his style.

Many of the President's speeches in 1942 were primarily intended for these propaganda purposes, and few, if any, failed to devote some time and attention to them: the promise of early heavy attacks on the enemies by land, sea and air; the statement of inevitable victory; the message of hope and cheer and faith to the people in the occupied countries; the triumphant recital of American production figures; the prospect of human freedoms throughout the postwar world—all these found expression in his words of leadership. They were broadcast and rebroadcast throughout the world; they were put in leaflets which were dropped everywhere.

Roosevelt was not always content to rely on words for propaganda. Actions spoke louder—and spoke in all languages at once. The greatest of the propaganda exploits in the dark days of 1942 was the first bomber raid over Tokyo, led by Colonel (later General) James H. Doolittle from the naval aircraft carrier *Hornet*. That feat was particularly the project of the President, who knew what a powerful effect on morale it would have for our enemies as well as our friends. And both effects were sorely needed in those days.

Hand in hand with his responsibilities as a military leader and as a world spokesman for the free world went his responsibility as the war leader on the home front. It, too, dominated his style for 1942. This responsibility was as complex as it was enormous. It involved the task of maintaining a strong America at home—strong in morale, strong in production, strong in its economic structure. Weakness at any point at home might mean disaster and loss of life thousands of miles away.

His speeches and his acts in 1942 show how the President discharged this less glamorous but more controversial responsibility of leadership at home. In 1942, many of the new great war agencies were established. In some cases their powers of control were unprecedented in our history; yet they soon became accepted during the war as part of our daily lives: the War Labor Board, the War Production Board, the War Shipping Administration, the National Housing Agency, the Alien Property Custodian, the War Relocation Authority, the War Manpower Commission, the Office of War Information, the Office of Strategic Services, the Office of Economic Stabilization, the Petroleum Administration for War.

The President, in dealing with this problem of morale at home, had to follow a style of walking on eggshells. On the one hand, Americans must realize the gravity of the war situation; on the other hand, they could not be allowed to submit to defeatism. Morale in 1942 meant two things: facing up to the serious danger of defeat; but not allowing that danger to impair our confidence in ultimate victory.

The President's style about giving the facts of the war to the American people was consistent throughout the war: the information had to be accurate but simultaneously of no use to the enemy. He wanted the American people to know in a general way and at an early date what was happening and what was planned —so general that the enemy would not be helped by the information. He decided to do this in a fireside chat on Washington's Birthday, 1942. It was illustrative of his style as a wartime leader of a free, informed and intelligent people. He had asked all the newspapers to print a map of the world. Then he explained the worldwide situation in detail and our proposed strategy. He had decided to do this so that, as he put it in talking to us, "they will understand what is going on and what the problems are and how we will try to meet them. If they do, they can take any bad news right on the chin." The speech was delivered at a time when our fortunes of war were almost at their lowest. For anyone to explain how victory was to come, at a time when stark defeat faced us, required all the skill and ingenuity and self-assurance he had. He did not conceal the dark truths; but throughout the speech he showed his confidence in the final outcome, and was able to transmit that confidence to his radio audience.

He was very proud of his title, "Commander-in-Chief." Whenever he used it, the pride he felt fairly exuded in his voice. I could hear it, for example, when he announced his policy of "shoot on sight"; he stressed: "I have so ordered as Commander-in-Chief." Hull has written about the great "relish" Roosevelt had in the title after Pearl Harbor—probably because "he felt that this position was now more essential than that of President." "At a cabinet Dinner in 1942 the President asked me before I rose to speak, 'Please try to address me as Commander-in-Chief, not as President!'"[98] He used the title time and again in his campaign speeches of 1944 with great relish and satisfaction. Even his message to the Democratic Convention in 1944 contained this sentence: "By next Spring, I shall have been President and Commander-in-Chief of the Armed Forces for twelve years." Until 1938, very few people ever had in mind that the President also bore this title of Commander-in-Chief; but Roosevelt soon made it well known. In fact, in 1944 his political campaign was pitched on that title —and it was impossible for Dewey to beat. His pride in the title had much to do with his style of exercising the office.

As Commander-in-Chief, he went further in his conception of war powers than any President before him, including Lincoln. Perhaps the best example was his message to Congress on September 7, 1942, asking for legislation authorizing the President "to stabilize the cost of living, including the prices of all farm commodities," hence curbing inflation during the war. He insisted that there was no distinction between the fighting front and the home front, that they were so intertwined with each other that there was only *one* war front. Therefore, in his message, he boldly and openly threatened as leader of the war and Commander-in-Chief: "in the event that Congress should fail to act and act adequately [to give him such authority], I shall accept the responsibility, and I will act. . . . The President has the powers, under the Constitution and under Congressional Acts, to take measures necessary to avert a disaster which would interfere with the winning of the war."

He gave the Congress until October 1, 1942, to take this action. Congress did act "adequately" and within the time limit.

He believed that to carry out his oath of office to "preserve and defend the Constitution" he not only could, but was obliged to take any step necessary to save the nation.

The year 1942 began with bitter defeat and humiliation, and ended with only slight glimmerings of victory. It was a year which provided the greatest challenges, the hardest trials, the worst problems the President was ever called upon to meet.

Of course, Roosevelt knew what responsibility and what power the Commander-in-Chief of the Army and the Navy wielded. He had his own style as Commander-in-Chief, different from our other war Presidents. In that capacity, as in all the others he exercised, he held on tightly to the reins of power, delegating details but never responsibility for top-level decisions. His knowledge of strategy, and even of many details of all that was happening, never ceased to surprise his associates. For example, when in 1940 he called Admiral Leahy back from Puerto Rico where he had been serving as Governor, in order to send him to Vichy to watch the over-aged French President Pétain, he had him first come to the White House for a conference which lasted two hours. Leahy has written of the conference: "I believe that that morning he could have given sentence by sentence the exact terms of the harsh Armistice the French had had to sign with the Axis on June 21, 1940."[99]

Admiral Leahy was later to serve as the Chief of Staff to the Commander-in-Chief of the Army and Navy of the United States. This was an office originated by Roosevelt to create liaison with the American Chiefs of Staff and with the Anglo-British Combined Chiefs of Staff; also to keep the President advised any time during the day or night of any significant events any place in the global war. Through this arrangement, Roosevelt kept constant, daily contact with all the details of the war. Leahy went with Roosevelt to all the conferences with Churchill and Stalin. He was an old-time, hard-bitten naval officer who had stipulated with Roosevelt frankly that if Roosevelt wanted him as Chief of Staff, he would have to expect to hear from Leahy only blunt truth and candid opinion. He was not a man given to flattery when, in 1950, he wrote: "From my study of American history it appears to me that Franklin Roosevelt performed this portion of his constitutional duties [Commander-in-Chief] with greater skill and ability than any preceding President. . . . He had a superb knowledge of international affairs and an almost professional knowledge of naval and military operations. . . .

"I believe history will record that he exercised greater skill in the direction of our global war effort than did his gallant and brilliant contemporary, Winston Churchill."[100]

Leahy corroborated others when he said: "Planning of the major campaigns was always done in close cooperation with the President. Frequently, we had sessions in his study. . . . The policy and broad objectives were stated by the President."

Leahy's résumé of how the war was managed was the result of many months of the most intimate association and observation:

"I may have indicated in this summary that the men who made up the Combined Chiefs of Staff were the men who ran the war. That is inaccurate. There were two men at the top who really fought out and finally agreed on the major moves that led to victory. They were Franklin Roosevelt and Winston Churchill. They really ran the war. Of course, they had to have some people like us to help them, but we were just artisans building definite patterns of strategy from the rough blue prints handed to us by our respective Commanders-in-Chief."[101]

I would suggest one amendment to this statement. Although Churchill and Roosevelt often "really fought out" the major moves, they did not always "finally agree." When they did not agree, Roosevelt's decision had to be final—and it was.

Leahy also made this significant statement: "To my knowledge, he never made a single military decision with any thought of his own personal political fortunes."

The Secretary of War, Henry L. Stimson, who had expressed his low opinion of Roosevelt as an administrator had quite a different estimate of him as Commander-in-Chief. In a note entered in his own private diary three days after Roosevelt's death, he said: "On the whole he has been a superb war President— far more so than any other President in our history. His role has not at all been merely a negative one. He has pushed for decisions of sound strategy, and carried them through against strong opposition from Churchill, for example, and others."

He had enunciated publicly the same high opinion at a Harvard commencement as early as June 1942, when things looked black for us all over the globe. "It has been my privilege to observe him [Roosevelt] in time of incessant strain and burden, of which he has cheerfully borne by far the heaviest share. . . . Only those who have been his lieutenants in the struggle can know the close personal attention with which he has vitalized every important decision. And only they can fully appreciate the courage and determination he has shown in time of threatened disaster. . . . Out of these characteristics comes the leadership which will achieve the final victory."[102]

As Commander-in-Chief, Roosevelt used to enjoy visiting troops in the fields of combat. It was his style of encouragement to the troops, and reciprocally of receiving renewed strength from seeing the American boys on the fields of battle. During conferences in the war area, he would arrange to do this whenever he could. With his love of dramatic surprise, he would take great delight in observing the look of utter amazement on the faces of American soldiers and sailors when they saw him—as in the deserts of North Africa during the Casablanca conference of 1943, or at their battle stations near Teheran during his conference there with Churchill and Stalin, or at the rails of naval vessels as he steamed into Pearl Harbor in 1944 for his meeting with Nimitz and MacArthur.

The Pearl Harbor visit was for the purpose of settling the differences between Admiral Nimitz and General MacArthur as to the strategy of obtaining the final victory over Japan. He wanted to meet with Nimitz and MacArthur personally, face to face, to hear their arguments. He wanted also to see the troops and sailors there, and to have them see him and take notice of his personal interest in their welfare. So he took Admiral Leahy, the one professional, with him, and left immediately after the Democratic National Convention had nominated him for the fourth term. It is significant to his style that none of the Joint Chiefs was there. Admiral King (one of the Joint Chiefs) has expressed the view that this was for the purpose of stressing Roosevelt's own role as Commander-in-Chief. I am inclined to agree.

I was with him on that trip. From the lawn of the house where we were lodged, I could observe Nimitz and MacArthur, Leahy and the Commander-in-Chief in discussion—a large war map unrolled and hanging on the wall. Nimitz was standing there with a long pointer indicating spots on the map; MacArthur followed him at the map with the pointer; then the four men gathered in earnest consultation. I could not hear what they were saying, but the picture through the window was an eloquent example of the extent of Roosevelt's participation in framing the strategy of the war from the very beginning. These three professional fighting men all sincerely respected the ability and style of Roosevelt, the civilian, in his capacity as Commander-in-Chief; and there appeared to be no resentment by them of his final decision. This was the essence of Roosevelt's style as Commander-in-Chief—listening to his professionals, encouraging them to full discussion, asking questions. Perhaps he would adopt conciliation or compromise—but always the final decision was his. He seemed to be part of the team rather than a civilian outsider—and the team accepted him as a member. He attained, during the war, complete rapport with the military commanders.

In Honolulu, Roosevelt showed again his personal physical courage by riding in an open automobile through the streets lined with people (many of whom were Japanese) waving and smiling, happy, as always, amidst crowds. To the consternation of the Secret Service, he had with him in his car all three of his high-ranking military advisers, MacArthur, Nimitz and Leahy. I could not help feeling aghast, as I followed in the procession of cars, at what one well-placed bomb might do to the military and civilian leadership of the United States.

He visited combat troops in amphibious training for the beach assaults to come. And he visited the hospitals for the wounded. In the paraplegic wards, there was a dramatic and moving spectacle, with Roosevelt as the star. Here again was the love of drama and surprise, as well as deep sympathy for the handicapped. He asked a Secret Service man to wheel him slowly through all the wards that were occupied by veterans who had lost one or more arms or legs. He insisted on going past each individual bed. He had known for twenty-three years what it was to be deprived of the use of both legs. He wanted to display himself and his useless legs to those boys who would have to face the same bitterness. This crippled man in the little wheelchair wanted to show them that it was possible to rise above such physical handicaps. With a cheery smile to each of them, and a pleasant word at the bedside of a score or more, this man who had risen from a bed of helplessness ultimately to become President of the United States and leader of the free world was living proof of what the human spirit could do to conquer the incapacities of the human body. I had seen him try to give the same sort of encouragement and example by cheerful conversation with young folks in Warm Springs and elsewhere who had been stricken by polio. Here, in the presence of great tragedy, he was doing it on a grand, heroic scale. The expressions of the faces on the pillows as he slowly passed by and smiled showed how effective was this display of crippled helplessness. I never saw Roosevelt with tears in his eyes; that day as he was wheeled out of the hospital, he was very close to them.

Roosevelt had begun acting as Commander-in-Chief, the leader of American might, even before Pearl Harbor. Admiral King gives a very good example of this, emphasizing Roosevelt's usual style of not taking the reports of his own military chiefs fully on faith without some check, if possible:

"As the war in Europe progressed, President Roosevelt frequently asked the General Board to consider various aspects of hemispheric defense. He conceived the idea, for example, of developing an out-lying patrol-plane base on Georges Bank, and was greatly interested in everything that he could learn about Cocos Island as a lookout point against possible Japanese air attack on the Panama Canal. Although this Costa Rican island, lying some five hundred miles to sea from the Pacific entrance of the Canal, had been in its time a favorite rendezvous of buccaneers, it was so small and heavily wooded that it scarcely had room for a foothold. The President, however, insisted that Admiral Stark send several seaplanes of different sizes to try out possible anchorages there. When the Navy finally reported that Cocos was useless as a seaplane base, the President, unconvinced, said he could find a proper anchorage himself, and on his next fishing trip cruised in the area to make sure that every possibility had been investigated."[103]

Neither did Roosevelt take the advice of the Chiefs of Staff without question. At times, he disagreed with them and said so. On at least two recorded occasions, we shall see him expressly overrule his Chiefs of Staff. Several times when Roosevelt insisted on his own strategy, he told Leahy: "Bill, I'm a pig-headed Dutchman, and I have made up my mind on this."[104]

For example, on Torch (the invasion of North Africa), which had been suggested by Churchill as an alternative in 1942 for the cross-Channel invasion (Overlord), Stimson, Marshall and King were all opposed. It was ordered by Roosevelt nevertheless—and he insisted on an early deadline for it.

As Commander-in-Chief, no matter how much he trusted his military commanders, he also retained complete control over any political decisions which had to be made within the combat area. In North Africa, the French and British wanted to take over the civil government of North Africa. Eisenhower tended to agree; but Roosevelt sent him word not to make any political decisions himself, but to refer them all to him. And we shall see how careful he was not to allow Churchill in his meetings with Stalin to try to bind the United States to any political agreements or even to any spheres of influence. This prohibition he extended even to Harriman, who was present at Churchill's request and with Stalin's acquiescence.

His style in dealing with Churchill during their Anglo-American war conferences alone, and with Churchill and Stalin in their tripartite conferences, shifted from time to time, depending upon what his own thinking was at the particular moment, on what he thought the other conferees were intent on doing, and what he wanted to get for the United States out of the conference.

On many occasions, he had to be quite blunt and stubborn with Churchill. Churchill was not easy to convince; he would yield one day but return again a few weeks later to renew the argument. These two men, in their historic, almost unique, partnership in the conduct of the war, and in their joint efforts toward a postwar peace, understood each other very well. They particularly appreciated each other's domestic political problems. They both had to face dissent at home which was freely expressed and often virulent; and each of them knew that this was true of the other. This was nothing like the relationship among the Axis, where each partner could do whatever he wanted to in his respective country without worrying about political opposition from anybody.

For example, Roosevelt, opposed to British colonialism and all other types of colonialism, tried to get Churchill to make concessions to the dissidents in India, as Japan was approaching India from the East in her course of conquest; but he did not press too hard. He knew that Churchill was himself a strong believer in the perpetuation of the Empire, and had frequently said so. He knew also that Churchill was always subject to hostile questions in the House of Commons and could not go along with Roosevelt's ideas about colonialism even if he had so wished. Nor did he, during the war, press too hard on France or Holland as to their colonies. He wanted to avoid bitter disputes among the Allies during the war. His style was to delay final confrontation on this subject until victory; then he would rely on his self-confident approach of face-to-face meetings, and on his friendship with Churchill, King George of England, and Queen Wilhelmina of Holland. But even during the war his style was to lead the way, and to set the example toward granting full independence to colonies such as the Philippines.

Churchill, on the other hand, understood the limits of Roosevelt's constitutional powers, and that the President always had to keep one eye on the Senate as he made military and political decisions during the war. There was always mutual respect, even mutual affection. Churchill appreciated that he had to rely on the immeasurably greater resources of men and material which Roosevelt could control; but there was, nevertheless, always the spirit and atmosphere of an equal partnership—except for those rare occasions when argument and discussion would have no effect on Churchill, when Roosevelt just had to make the final decision.

Much of Roosevelt's style in dealing with Stalin was based on two overriding considerations. The first was one which all the Combined Chiefs of Staff were urging on him with great force and persistence: to get Russia into the war against Japan as soon as possible. We should remember that up to the date of Roosevelt's death, we had not yet successfully exploded a nuclear device. It was not until three months after his death and until five months after Yalta that we knew we had succeeded in creating an atomic bomb. Without being able to rely, therefore, on the effects of atomic explosions over the cities of Japan, the American Joint Chiefs advised Roosevelt that victory over Japan was going to require several years and a million American casualties; and that Russian participation against Japan would reduce the time and the human cost. This estimate by his military had only recently been borne out by the great loss of American lives in taking Okinawa, and by the suicidal attacks of the fanatical Kamikaze. While we now know that this estimate was grossly over-pessimistic because of the great damage which had been done to Japanese shipping and, therefore, to Japan's ability to import or manufacture necessary war materials, the Joint Chiefs did not know it at the time of Yalta. Therefore it was essential, the Joint Chiefs advised, that Russia be brought into the war as a matter of high priority and urgency.

The second consideration in Roosevelt's mind in dealing with Stalin was to make sure that Russia joined in and supported the United Nations Organization which was to be set up after the war to keep the peace of the world. With his usual style of self-confidence in face-to-face confrontation, he twice travelled many thousands of miles to meet Stalin—at Teheran and at Yalta. He did get both of these considerations fulfilled although as it later developed, the first proved to be unnecessary. He also got agreements in writing about self-determination by free elections in the future in the liberated countries—all of which Stalin broke completely after Roosevelt died.

At the meetings of the Big Three, Roosevelt would often have to act as mediator between Churchill and Stalin, for the two of them frequently got into bitter disputes. Stalin, remembering Churchill's and Britain's long opposition to the Soviet Union, was much more suspicious of Churchill than of Roosevelt. This is not to minimize his suspicion of Roosevelt, but it was of a different intensity. He remembered Roosevelt's early recognition of the Soviet Union in 1933 during his first year as President; and, of course, as he frequently remarked, he realized that the great manufacturing capacity of the United States, which had been mobilized by Roosevelt and which, under Roosevelt's leadership and initiative, had supplied Russia with weapons of war at a time when they were most sorely needed, was what had enabled the Red Army to withstand Hitler's attack. He did not hesitate to add that, without it, the war would have been lost.

The chief disagreements as Commanders-in-Chief between Churchill and Roosevelt arose generally over four major problems: the second front by invasion across the English Channel; the landings in the south of France in August 1944; Churchill's many projects for diversionary moves in the eastern Mediterrean, particularly the Balkans; and the spheres of influence in the countries to be liberated from Hitler.

These disputes and the manner in which Roosevelt handled them give a good example of his flexible but successful style as Commander-in-Chief, and as one of the three great war leaders. It is impossible to cover all of Roosevelt's part in the war; it would take several volumes. No better illustration can be given than a detailed account of the delicate, patient, although sometimes confusing, handling of the much discussed invasions of the Balkans and "The Soft Underbelly of the Axis."

In 1951, Winston Churchill wrote: "There have been many misleading accounts of the line I took, with full agreement of the British Chiefs of Staff, at this Conference [Teheran]. It has become a legend in America that I strove to prevent the cross-Channel enterprise called 'Overlord,' and I tried vainly to lure the allies into some mass invasion of the Balkans, or a large scale campaign in the Eastern Mediterranean which would effectively kill it."[105]

How do the facts line up, and what was Roosevelt's style in dealing with British resistance to the cross-Channel invasion, and with other European invasions or suggested invasions?

The first big discussion between the British and the Americans regarding a European invasion took place when Churchill and his Chiefs of Staff met with the President and his Chiefs of Staff in Washington in December 1941 directly after Pearl Harbor (Arcadia Conference). On the night of the 22nd, Churchill suggested a landing in North Africa as an "exciting initial step in closing the ring about the territory under German control. . . . Roosevelt, to whom the project was not new, had agreed that this might be the right thing to do . . . one reason being that it would give the American people a feeling of being in the war."[106]

In the report made at the end of the conference on December 31, the military staffs had agreed, as stated in the official record: "In 1942, the methods of wearing down Germany's resistance will be . . . ever increasing air bombardment by British and American forces . . . assistance to Russia's offensive by all available means . . . [and operations] the main object [of which] will be gaining possession of the whole North African coast. . . . It does not seem likely that in 1942 any large scale offensive against Germany, except on the Russian front, will be possible . . . [but] in 1943 the way may be clear for a return to the continent across the Mediterranean, from Turkey into the Balkans, or by landings in Western Europe. Such operations will be the prelude to the final assault on Germany itself."[107]

However, "During the following period of waiting, American military judgment had come to the belief that the North African operation would be a wasteful use of combat resources, and a dangerous one."[108]

"The selection of a better course had been urgently argued in a series of discussions at the White House during March, 42. Vigorous Stimson, backed by impressive Marshall, in accord with the staff planners headed by persuasive Eisenhower, explained over and over why it was essential to avoid 'dispersion' and to concentrate on the build-up of forces in the United Kingdom for a cross-Channel assault."[109]

Toward the end of a tense meeting on March 25 the President ordered the preparation of what became known as the Marshall Memorandum, looking toward an actual entry into France on April 1, 1943 (Operation Bolero), with plans for a much smaller assault (Operation Sledgehammer) earlier in the fall of 1942. On April 1 the President approved the plan and asked Marshall and Hopkins to take it to Churchill.

On April 12, Churchill informed the President that the British Chiefs of Staff were in entire agreement *in principle* with the U.S. proposals. Marshall and Hopkins left London with a belief that a firm decision had been made. But the British began to waver and then weaken immediately thereafter. Marshall and Hopkins were over-optimistic; the British decision turned out to be only tentative.

Churchill described his thinking at that time: "The attempt to form a bridgehead at Cherbourg [Marshall Memorandum] seemed to me more difficult, less attractive, less immediately helpful or ultimately fruitful. It would be better to lay our right claw on French North Africa, tear with our left at the North Cape

[Norway], and wait a year without risking our teeth upon the German fortified front across the Channel.

"Those were my views then and I have never repented them."[110]

All of these differences of opinion are connected with the striking phrase used by Churchill which has been frequently quoted by historians and has become a stock phrase of many people in comparing the Churchill and Roosevelt strategy: "to strike at the soft underbelly of the Axis." Therefore it becomes relevant to trace the origin and the context of that phrase.

It was used by Churchill on August 12, 1942, at his first face-to-face meeting with Stalin—in Moscow. He journeyed there with the consent of Roosevelt to explain why the conditional promise, previously extended to Molotov in London and in Washington, of an Allied attempt to cross the English Channel in 1942 could not be fulfilled. Roosevelt and his military advisers had been pressing for this; but finally convinced of its impossibility, Roosevelt had accepted the alternative of an invasion of North Africa, insisting, however, that it must take place in 1942. Roosevelt in consenting to this trip by Churchill to Moscow advised the Prime Minister that "we have got always to bear in mind the personality of our ally and the very difficult and dangerous situation that confronts him . . . I think he should be told, in the first place, quite specifically that we have determined upon a course of action in 1942"[111] [Torch—the code name for the invasion of North West Africa].

To say that Churchill's mission was a difficult one is a gross understatement. He had to tell Stalin that there would be no cross-Channel invasion of France in 1942. "Roosevelt was ready to let him make the explanations, take the blame, and get the clouded credit." But Churchill sent word to the President, "I should greatly like to have your aid and countenance in my talks with Joe. Would you be able to let Averell [Harriman] come with me? I feel that things would be easier if we all seemed to be together. I have a somewhat raw job."[112]

The President sent Averell "to help in any way."

Having broken the news to Stalin, an ally and colleague who could not comprehend hesitation in the face of danger, Churchill proceeded to describe the projected invasion of North Africa which would draw German forces to its defense. He stated that "all of North Africa was to be brought under American and British military command by the end of the year; and then they could threaten Hitler's Europe from there—in conjunction with the 1943 cross-Channel invasion. The better to explain why he thought this North African operation would be a vital blow against Germany, Churchill drew the famous picture of the crocodile, and compared the Mediterranean operation to a stroke at the 'soft underbelly' to be delivered as the hard snout was also attacked. . . .

"Churchill went on to decorate the feast of possibilities. He said that the British and Americans might send combat air forces to fight on the southern end of the Soviet Eastern Front. Stalin said he would accept that help 'gratefully.' "[113]

This referred to shipment of British and American combat and transport air forces to fight with and for the Red Army on its southern front. In spite of his "gratefulness" and of several renewals of the offer by President Roosevelt, Stalin never took advantage of the offer. He wanted American war supplies but he did not desire foreign troops in Russia.

The phrase, "to strike at the underbelly of the Axis," was used again by Churchill on November 18, 1942, three months later, and may be found in the recently opened correspondence between Churchill and Roosevelt at the Roosevelt Hyde Park Library.[114] It is in a long five-page telegram. The first three pages deal with military matters in North Africa (the invasion of which had already begun) and with the Mediterranean, the projected bombing of Sicily, Sardinia and Corsica so as to procure airfields from which the Allies could bomb Naples, Rome and the Italian fleet.

The telegram then reads in part: "The paramount task before us is first, to conquer the African shores of the Mediterranean and set up there the naval and air installations which are necessary to open an effective passage through it for military traffic; and secondly, using the bases in the African shore, *to strike at the underbelly of the Axis* in effective strength and in the shortest time." (Emphasis added)

There is no mention of the Balkans until the last paragraph on the third page, and that is a surprising one. It reads: "I have received a telegram from the President containing the following paragraph: 'It is hoped that you with your Chiefs of Staff in London and I with the Combined Staff here may make a survey of the possibilities including forward movement directed against Sardinia, Sicily, Italy, Greece and other Balkan areas and including the possibility of obtaining Turkish support for an attack through the Black Sea against Germany's Flank.'

"I endorse the above conception of the President. The first part of the President's wishes are being studied by the Combined Staffs in Washington, and are the subject of the foregoing paragraphs for our discussion.

"The second part relating to Turkey is also of vital importance, though it is a slower process."

President Roosevelt had sent on November 11, 1942, the telegram to which the Prime Minister refers. The paragraph quoted was preceded by the following: "I am very happy with the latest news of your splendid campaign in Egypt, and of the success that has attended our joint landing in West and North Africa. This brings up the additional steps that should be taken when and if the South shore of the Mediterranean is cleared and under our control."[115]

Churchill had already answered the President on November 13 in a hearty but less detailed telegram in which the following words appear: "Meanwhile let me say that nothing pleases me more than to read what you say about trying to bring Turkey in. Our minds have indeed moved together on this, as in so much else."[116]

And the President had wired Churchill on November 14, 1942: "I think you and I have overlooked one very important step in relation to any operations springing from the Eastern Mediterranean. I suggest that after we have considered our preliminary studies we should send a small British American Staff group, possibly limited to two officers from each of us, to Moscow to discuss the procedure with Mr. Stalin and his staff.

"I realize this may cause some delay but one week in Moscow should suffice and from every point of view it looks wise to have closer staff cooperation the nearer we get to the Black Sea and Russia. Roosevelt."[117]

These communications effectively demonstrate President Roosevelt's styles: (1) as strategist—here, as often, with great relish dramatically releasing his own brain child of the moment, the Balkans; (2) striking for quick action as soon as an opportunity presented itself; (3) never forgetting that it was wise to bring "Uncle Joe" in on the ground floor.

Another style is also apparent—Roosevelt's adaptability. He did not cling to his Balkan plan once its feasibility was disproven. Churchill wrote, after failing to get Stalin's go ahead in the Balkans at the Teheran Conference in November 1943: "I could have gained Stalin, but the President was oppressed by the prejudices of his military advisers and drifted to and fro in argument, with the result that the whole of these subsidiary gleaming opportunities were cast aside unused. Our American friends were comforted in their obstinacy by the reflection that 'at any rate we have stopped Churchill entangling us in the Balkans!' "[118]

The war in North Africa and in Italy had not progressed as speedily as the sanguine telegrams of November 1942 had foretold. There was no rush for the Balkans. Meanwhile Roosevelt's ardor had been dampened if not entirely extinguished by the Joint Chiefs of Staff, by Turkey's refusal to respond to Allied entreaties to enter the war, by fear of being embroiled in European struggles for spheres of influence, by Stalin's lukewarm acquiescence and probably by Churchill's over-eagerness.

Admiral Leahy wrote that at the Trident Conference (U.S.-British Conference) on May 12, 1943, "Churchill made no mention of any British desire to control the Mediterranean regardless of how the war might end, which many people believed to be a cardinal principle of British national policy of long standing.

"As to the cross-Channel invasion in the near future, the Prime Minister said that adequate preparations could not be made for such an effort in the Spring of 1944, but that an invasion of Europe must be made at sometime in the future. There was no intimation that he favored the attempt in 1944 unless Germany should collapse as a result of the Russian campaign, assisted by the intensified Allied bombing attacks. . . .

"In a brief talk following the Prime Minister, President Roosevelt advocated the Channel operation at the earliest possible date and not later than 1944. He expressed disagreement with any Italian venture beyond the seizure of Sicily and Sardinia, and reiterated his frequently expressed determination to concentrate our military effort first on destruction of Nazi military power before engaging in any collateral campaigns and before exercising our full effort against Japan. . . .

"He directed our staff to look into the possibility, from a military point of view, of attacking Germany by way of Bulgaria, Romania, and Turkey and said he would study the political angle of such a move. This had been urged strongly by Churchill."[119]

It was not until July 26, 1943, after the fall of Mussolini, that the Prime Minister returned to the question of the Balkans in a long telegram outlining "my thoughts in the form in which I submitted them to the war cabinet obtaining their full approval."[120] The "thoughts" dealt with the surrender of Italy and of Italian troops then stationed in different parts of the Balkan peninsula and elsewhere in the Mediterranean.

On July 27, 1943, the President sent the following memorandum to Admiral Leahy: "The President directed that this copy of a message from the Prime Minister be given Admiral Leahy to discuss with the Joint Chiefs of Staff.

"The President noted that the Prime Minister made no reference [in his telegram] to what should happen to the troops in Albania, Yugoslavia, and Greece, and he also noted that the Prime Minister made no reference to self-determination.

"He wished the Joint Chiefs of Staff to consider his comments as well as the whole message."[121]

The President had his guard up as he sensed Churchill's growing interest in controlling political simultaneously with military events, and he was always conscious of Churchill's imperialistic background and outlook (especially toward colonialism).

The military, the State Department and the Secretary of War were also fearful of British postwar desires, and kept the President au courant of specific incidents giving credence to their suspicions.

Churchill and Roosevelt and their Chiefs of Staff met at Quebec (Quadrant Conference) from August 14 to 24, 1943. The Americans pushed for Overlord, the British stressed the Mediterranean, but finally did agree that Overlord was to be emphasized even though the Mediterranean might be denied all that was desired.

On August 9, prior to departure for Quebec, General Marshall had met with the President at the White House. The President "assured Marshall that he did not wish to have anything to do with an operation into the Balkans nor did he even intend to agree to a British expedition in that area that would cost the United States vital resources such as ships and landing craft necessary for other operations. He was in favor of securing a position in Italy to the North of Rome and taking Sardinia and Corsica, thereby posing a serious threat to southern France."[122]

Churchill after the conference went on to Washington with the President, and wrote to General Alexander on September 7, 1943: "I am waiting here with the President to judge results of 'Avalanche' [invasion of Italy at Salerno] and thereafter returning home. . . . I shall have some important things to tell you then."[123]

As the Allied armada approached the Salerno beaches on September 8, the Italians surrendered. On September 9, the Prime Minister and his staff and the President and his staff held a formal conference in the White House. Mr. Churchill writes:[124] "In preparation for this meeting, I had prepared a memorandum to the President, which I had submitted to him earlier in the day. He asked me to read it out loud, and thought it would be a basis for our discussion. It would surely be convenient . . . to take stock of the new world situation which will arise on the assumption that the present battle for Naples and Rome is successful and that the Germans retreat to the line of the Apennines or the Po."

The memo covers the entire *projected* "new world situation," so this story will excerpt from it only the parts pertinent to it. They are: "There can be no question of whittling down 'Overlord' . . . all the more important is it to bring Italian divisions into the line and our State policy should be adapted to procure this end. . . .

"We are both of us acutely conscious of the great importance of the Balkan situation. We should make sure that the Mediterranean High Command, absorbed in its present battle, does not overlook the needs of the patriot forces there. . . . On the assumption that the Italians can be drawn into the war against Germany, far-reaching possibilities seem to open. There is surely no need for us to work from the bottom of the Balkans upwards. If we can get an agreement between the patriots and the Italian troops, it should be possible to open quite soon one or more good Ports on the Dalmatian coast, enabling munitions and supplies to be sent in by ship and all forces that *will obey your orders* to be raised to good fighting condition. . . . When the defensive line across Northern Italy has been completed, it may be possible *to spare some of our own forces* assigned to the Mediterranean theatre to emphasize a movement *north* and *northwestward* from the Dalmation ports. . . . I am not satisfied that sufficient use is being made under the present conditions of the forces in the Middle East."[125] (Emphasis added)

This seems to be the first time that Churchill openly suggested that Allied troops be used in that region.[126]

Preceding the Sextant Conference held at Cairo November 22–December 7, 1943, Churchill accompanied by his military staff and Eisenhower met at Malta where they had a lengthy conference in advance of the President's arrival. General Eisenhower reports:

"Mr. Churchill, as always, was entertaining and interesting. I have never met anyone so capable at keeping a dinner gathering on its toes. His comments on events and personalities were pointed and pungent, often most amusing. He looked forward with great enthusiasm to his meeting with the President, from whom, he said, he always drew inspiration for tackling the problems of war and of the later peace. He dwelt at length on one of his favorite subjects—the importance of assailing Germany through the 'soft underbelly' of keeping up the tempo of our Italian attack and extending its scope to include much of the Northern shore of the Mediterranean. He seemed always to see great and decisive possibilities in the Mediterranean, while the project of invasion across the English Channel left him cold. How often I heard him say, in speaking of Overlord prospects, 'We must take care that the tides do not run red with the blood of American and British youth, or the beaches be choked with their bodies.'

"I could not escape a feeling that Mr. Churchill's views were unconsciously colored by two considerations that lay outside the scope of the immediate military problem. I had nothing tangible to justify such a feeling—I know, though, that I was not alone in wondering occasionally whether these considerations had some weight with him. The first of them was his concern as a political leader in the future of the Balkans."[127]

In recounting informal conversations with President Roosevelt, who arrived by ship and then took a plane to a villa on the seashore in Tunisia, he repeated a revealing sentence of the President's, "He told of instances of disagreement with Mr. Churchill, but earnestly and almost emotionally said, 'no one could have a better or sturdier ally than that old Tory.'"[128]

The events just described had been preceded by a typical Churchill-Roosevelt sharp dispute—no swords barred—with a virtual verbal embrace at the end. Churchill cabled the President: "I am much concerned with the situation developing in the Eastern Mediterranean . . . [references to Greek islands—Kos, Leros, and Rhodes].

"I believe it will be found that the Italian and Balkan Peninsulas are militarily and politically united and that it is really one theatre with which we have to deal. . . . I have never wished to send an army into the Balkans but only by agents supplies and Commandos to stimulate the intense guerilla [sic] prevailing there. This may yield results measureless in their consequences at very small cost to main operations. What I ask for is the capture of Rhodes and the other islands of the Dodecanese. The movement northward of our Middle Eastern Air Forces and their establishment in these islands and possibly on the Turkish shore which last might well be obtained would force a diversion on the enemy far greater than that required of us. . . . Rhodes is the key to all this. . . . I beg you to consider this and not let it be brushed aside. . . . Even if landing craft and assault ships on the scale of a division were withheld from the build up of Overlord for a few weeks without altering the zero date it would be worthwhile. . . ."[129]

Roosevelt replied promptly the same day.

"Reference your 438

"I do not want to force on Eisenhower diversions which limit the prospects for the early successful development of the Italian operations to a secure line North of Rome. I am opposed to any diversion which will in Eisenhower's opinion jeopardize the security of his current situation in Italy, the build up of which is exceedingly slow considering the well known characteristics of his opponent who enjoys a marked superiority in ground troops and panzer divisions.

"It is my opinion that no diversion of forces or equipment should prejudice Overlord as planned.

"The American Chiefs agree.

"I am transmitting a copy of this message to Eisenhower. Roosevelt."[130]

On October 8, Churchill wrote the President a long entreaty to send Marshall to meet with Churchill and the British Chiefs of Staff at Eisenhower's headquarters.[131] Roosevelt firmly replied:[132] ". . . With a full understanding of your difficulties in the Eastern Mediterranean, my thought in sending #379 was that no division of force from Italy should be made that would jeopardize the security of the allied armies in Italy, and that no action toward any minor objective should prejudice the success of Overlord. . . . The problem then is are we now to enter into a Balkan campaign starting with the southern tip, or is there more to be gained, and with security, by pushing rapidly to the agreed upon position North of Rome. . . .

"As to the meeting you propose for Sunday in Africa— . . . Frankly, I am not in sympathy with this procedure under the circumstances. . . . We have most of the facts and will soon have the results of the conference scheduled for tomorrow in Tunis. Roosevelt."

This frank, tough style in meeting issues even with Allies and friends was characteristically Roosevelt's.

The Prime Minister's answering telegram was graceful, cordial but in full pursuit of his objectives:

"Thank you very much for your kindness in giving so much of your time and thought to the views which I ventured to set before you. At your wish, and as you cannot send General Marshall, I have cancelled my journey which I told Harry [Hopkins] on the telephone I would never take without your blessing.

"I agree . . . that we should await the result of the conference scheduled for today in Tunis. . . .

"I am afraid, however, that your number 379 of October 8th to me, a copy of which was sent to Eisenhower, will be taken as an order from you and as closing the subject finally. This I should find very hard to accept. I hope, therefore, that you will make it clear that the conference is free to examine the whole question in all its bearings and should report their conclusions to you and me through C.C.S. I ask that the Conference shall give full, free, patient and unprejudiced consideration to the whole question after they have heard the Middle East point of view put forward by its representatives."[133]

That same day the President sent Eisenhower a telegram (and a copy to Churchill) which says, "The Prime Minister desires that it should be made clear to you that the conference scheduled for today in Tunis is free to examine the whole question in all its bearings. . . . The Prime Minister asks that the conference shall give full, free, patient and unprejudiced consideration to the whole question after having heard the Middle East point of view put forward by its representatives.

"The President directs that the foregoing desire expressed by the Prime Minister be accepted for your guidance. Roosevelt."[134]

General Eisenhower reported that: "It was the simplest, most unargumentative of any similar conferences I attended during the war. . . . Every officer present agreed emphatically with my conclusions, even though it was a great disappointment to the Middle East Commanders, while all of us knew that the decision could be a bitter one for the Prime Minister to accept."[135]

This is the Balkan background which preceded the Teheran Conference of November 28–December 1, 1943. One more fact must be added for, again, it shows Roosevelt's style of looking ahead and anticipating possible eventualities. In preparation for the meeting with Churchill and his staff which preceded the Teheran Conference, the President and his staff conferred on the S.S. *Iowa* on which they crossed the Atlantic. General Marshall said, "We have to see this Balkan matter finished up. We do not believe that the Balkans are necessary. To launch operations in this region could result in prolonging the war [in Europe] and also lengthening the war in the Pacific. . . . If the British insist on ditching Overlord for the Balkans, the Americans could reply that we will pull out and go into the Pacific with all our forces."

After Marshall had stated his case, "the President said he felt attention had to be paid to the Soviet attitude in the matter. The Russians were then only sixty miles from the Polish border and forty miles from Bessarabia and might shortly be on the point of entering Rumania. They might ask that Western Allied forces be sent up the Adriatic to the Danube to help defeat Germany. General Marshall replied that the Americans would have to be ready to explain to the Russians the implication of such a move. . . . He doubted that any troops the Allies might send to the Balkans, in line with the President's hypothesis, would have an appreciable effect on the situation."[136]

At the Cairo Conference which followed the American conferences on the *Iowa* and preceded the Teheran Conference, the Americans and British met in preparation for their meetings with the Russians. "The Prime Minister emphasized that he had not weakened or cooled toward it [Overlord]. Nevertheless, as he saw the problem, the timing would depend more on the state of the enemy than on the 'set perfection of our preparations.' He went on to say that 'Overlord remained top on the bill' but 'should not be such a tyrant as to rule out every other activity in the Mediterranean.' "[137]

Overlord, of course, was Stalin's primary objective at the Teheran Conference. When the military staffs of the three Allies gave their report to the Chiefs of State, Marshal Stalin showed the height of shrewdness. He "asked who was to be commander of Operation Overlord. When the President and the Prime Minister replied that the decision had not yet been made, Stalin immediately declared, 'Then nothing will come out of these operations!' The Prime Minister pointed out that his government had already expressed its willingness to accept an American as commander and that he agreed it was essential to appoint a commander for Overlord without delay. Such an appointment, he indicated, would be forthcoming within a fortnight.

"Again Churchill launched into a fervent plea for his Mediterranean policy. . . . Again Stalin was adamant. He wanted no postponement of Overlord, it must be executed by the limiting date. . . .

"To relieve the tension that was building up and bring the matter to some conclusion, the President, who until then had contributed little to the discussion, took a hand. . . .

"It was typical of the President at Teheran to act as arbitrator, if not judge, between the other two leaders who were as different in their methods as in the views they represented—Churchill, the master orator and debater, skilled both in words and parliamentary maneuvers, Stalin, 'the man of steel,' disdainful of the debater's artifices and diplomatic niceties, terse, blunt, and relentless in his refutation. The President did not appear completely indifferent to Churchill's eloquence and persuasiveness and to the possibilities of Mediterranean ventures, particularly in the Adriatic. But at the same time, he was under strong pressure from his military advisers that nothing must delay Overlord, and in the end be held through."[138]

This was Roosevelt the arbitrator, but it was also a vivid example of Roosevelt the fox, and explains the story that Robert Sherwood recounts in *Roosevelt and Hopkins:*

"Roosevelt surprised and disturbed Hopkins by mentioning the possibility of an operation across the Adriatic for a drive, aided by Tito's Partisans, northeastward into Rumania to effect a junction with the Red Army advancing southward from the region of Odessa. Hopkins thereupon scribbled a note to Admiral King. 'Who's promoting that Adriatic business that the President continually returns to?' To which King replied, 'As far as I know it is his own idea.' "[139]

The shrewd, secretive Roosevelt was playing a poker game close to his chest. He was pleasing Churchill, and he knew that Stalin would firmly refuse on two counts, first, because he wanted no diversion from Overlord, and second, because by then he was able to control the Eastern front himself and wanted no partners there. It was clear to Roosevelt that the suggestion he had made to Marshall on the *Iowa* as to what Stalin might want had no validity.

The Teheran Conference ended on December 1. Early in 1944 the subtle undertones of political considerations in military planning again surfaced. By January 1944 it was clear, even to the British, that Turkey would not join the Allies. "Churchill reluctantly became resigned to Turkish neutrality," but he didn't give up his cherished Balkan idea. "On February 21 the President informed his Joint Chiefs of Staff that he had refused to consider Churchill's proposal for an expedition composed of British troops under an American commanding general. The President would not even consider a 'token' U.S. force for such a project."[140]

On the same day, the President wrote to Under Secretary of State Stettinius, "I do not want the United States to have the postwar burden of reconstituting France, Italy and the Balkans. This is not our natural task at a distance of 3,500 miles or more. It is definitely a British task in which the British are far more vitally interested than we are."[141]

On February 29, 1944, the President sent "Dear Winston" a long letter which ends, "I am trying as hard as I can to simplify things—and sometimes I shudder at the thought of appointing as many new Committees and Commissions in the future as we have in the past!

"I note that in the British proposal the territory of Germany is divided up in accordance with the British plan. 'Do please don't' ask me to keep any forces in France. I just cannot do it! I would have to bring them all back home. As I suggested before, I denounce and protest the paternity of Belgium, France and

Italy. You really ought to bring up and discipline your own children. In view of the fact that they may be your bulwark in future days, you should at least pay for their schooling now!"[142]

Spheres of influence in the Balkans became a dominating subject. Churchill was worried that the Soviet government might seek to impose its will on eastern and central Europe as its armies conquered them. On May 4 Churchill wrote his Foreign Secretary Eden, "A paper should be drafted for the Cabinet, and possibly for the Imperial Conference, setting forth shortly—for that is essential—the brute issues between us and the Soviet government which are developing in Italy, in Rumania, in Bulgaria, in Yugoslavia and above all, in Greece. . . . Broadly speaking, the issue is, are we going to acquiesce in the communization of the Balkans and perhaps of Italy? . . . I am of opinion on the whole that we ought to come to a definite conclusion about it, and that if our conclusion is that we resist the Communist infusion and invasion, we should put it to them pretty plainly at the best moment that military events permit. We should, of course, have to consult the United States first."[143]

Eden had an informal talk on May 5 with the Soviet Ambassador to Britain —Mr. Gusev—mentioning "the possibility that the Soviet government might well leave Britain to manage the Greek situation while fighting was still going on there, and that Great Britain might well leave the management of the situation in Rumania to the Soviet government during the fighting there. . . . On May 18 Gusev told the Foreign Office that the Soviet government favored the idea but, before going ahead with it, would like to know if the American government had been consulted and did not mind.

"On the 30th, the British Ambassador in Washington, Lord Halifax, asked Hull how the American government would feel about such an accord," stressing the fact that it was only for the war period. Hull, not a naïve man, "foresaw that —despite assurances to the contrary—even such a temporary working accord might develop into a sphere-of-influence arrangement of the type he thought had always in the past brought conflict."[144]

Then—after a month of negotiations—on May 31, 1944, the Prime Minister wired the President: "There have recently been disquieting signs of a possible divergence of policy between ourselves and the Russians in regard to the Balkan countries and in particular towards Greece." He went on to describe the foregoing negotiations and added, "I hope you may feel able to give this proposal your blessing. . . . We feel . . . that the arrangement now proposed would be a useful device for preventing any divergence of policy between ourselves and them in the Balkans."[145] On June 2,1944, the President wired Churchill—"Referring back to . . . my telegram #457 of February seventh on this subject containing the following statements: Quote, I am unwilling to police France and possibly Italy and the Balkans as well, unquote." Churchill never replied to that telegram.[146] On June 8, Halifax handed Hull another message from Churchill—this one addressed to him. In this he added Bulgaria and Yugoslavia. "It seemed reasonable to him that the Russians deal with the Rumanians and Bulgarians, and that Britain should deal with the Greeks, who were in Britain's theater of operations and were Britain's old allies, for whom she had sacrificed 40,000 men in 1941. The same he added was true of Yugoslavia."[147]

On June 10, 1944, the President ended his disagreement with Churchill's proposition with these words: "In our opinion this would certainly result in the persistence of differences between you and the Soviets and in the division of the

Balkan region into spheres of influence despite the declared intention to limit the arrangement to military matters.

"We believe efforts should preferably be made to establish consultative machinery to dispel misunderstandings and restrain the tendency toward the development of exclusive spheres. Roosevelt."[148]

Churchill sent a plaintive cable the next day, ending: "Your telegrams to me on the recent crisis [the mutiny in Greece] worked wonders. We were entirely agreed, and the result is entirely satisfactory. Why is all this effective direction to be broken up into a committee of mediocre officials such as we are littering about the world? Why can you and I not keep this in our own hands considering how we see eye to eye about so much of it?

"To sum up, I propose that we agree that the arrangements I set forth in my number #687 may have a trial of three months, after which it must be reviewed by the three powers."[149]

Roosevelt, without consulting Hull, who was out of town, or even telling him when he returned, sent Churchill a telegram agreeing to the three-months trial, adding: "We must be careful to make it clear that we are not establishing any position of spheres of influence."[150]

Hull did not hear about the President's telegram until our Ambassador to Greece, Lincoln MacVeagh, whose Embassy was at Cairo, cabled the State Department on June 26 that his British colleague had informed him that the American government had agreed to the proposal with the provision that it should be subject to review after three months.[151]

Mr. Hull wrote the President a letter enclosing a copy of Ambassador Mac-Veagh's telegram and asked whether any changes had been made in our position. The President replied on June 30, simply sending Mr. Hull copies of the messages which had been exchanged between him and the Prime Minister. Included was a copy of a telegram that the President had sent the Prime Minister on June 22, 1944,[152] which had been drafted in the State Department. It reads: "With reference to your 687 and my 560 regarding matters in the Balkans, I am a bit worried and so is the State Department. I think I should tell you frankly that we were disturbed that your people took this matter up with us only after it had been put to the Russians and they had inquired whether we were agreeable. Your Foreign Office apparently sensed this and has now explained that the proposal 'arose out of a chance remark' which was converted by the Soviet government into a formal proposal. However, I hope matters of this importance can be prevented from developing in such a manner in the future. Roosevelt."

It is very difficult satisfactorily to explain this whole episode. But it is not entirely alien to some of the characteristics of Roosevelt's styles, which are exemplified in other actions seemingly equally inexplicable. He emphatically did not believe in spheres of influence, and he was definitely on record again and again as being in opposition to American postwar participation in anything that smacked of influence. Self-determination was his objective.

What happened? Did Churchill wear him down? Did he wish to conciliate Churchill? Or did he come to the conclusion that it was a senseless battle because the Soviet Union in the postwar period, since its armies were already in possession, would assert its influence over the countries close to its borders in spite of any agreement that might be made? He was, after all, a realist.

Why did he send the June 12 telegram while Hull was out of town, and then neglect to inform him when he returned? He hated an argument, he had made up his mind, and he knew that Hull would try to talk him out of it. He hated unpleasantness; so he didn't tell Hull himself, but let him find out in the natural course of events, as he knew he would.

And why did he send the telegram of June 22, 1944, drafted by the State Department but doubtless strengthened by his own pen? Presumably because he felt that Churchill deserved the rebuke and although slow to anger, he did not flinch from a call-down when sufficiently provoked. This too was his style throughout all his correspondence with Churchill; although most of it was a friendly and cordial exchange of views, it was frequently accompanied by protestations of distress when disagreement was felt to be necessary.

To return to military matters (so often flavored with political considerations), preparations for the cross-Channel invasion Overlord were nearing completion. A companion attack in the Mediterranean had been under discussion at the Quebec Conference (Quadrant) in August 1943, and was debated periodically thereafter. At Quebec, a diversionary landing in southern France code-named "Anvil" in the region between Toulon and Marseilles was construed to have been decided upon.[153] At the Moscow Military Conference of September and October 1943, Stalin, receiving ambiguous answers to his questions about the date for Overlord, expressed the opinion "that the Allies in Italy would be well advised to take up a defensive position north of Rome and use the rest of their forces for Overlord rather than to push through Italy into Germany; and he approved the idea of synchronizing a landing in Southern France, the better to force Hitler to disperse his forces."[154] However, this plan was continuously weighed with alternate plans sponsored by the British.

The War Department's official report states: "As the Allied armies pushed forward into northern Italy the debate reopened between the British proponents of the continuation of the Italian campaign and the American champions of Anvil. Would the prize be the occupation of all Italy, the capture of Istria [Istrian Peninsula projecting into the N. Adriatic between the gulfs of Trieste and Fiume] and Trieste, and an advance through the Ljubljana gap with all the attendant political and strategic consequences for the Balkans, or would it be the direct strengthening of Overlord and the occupation of Southern France? Broadly stated, was the final unfolding of the European war to be a matter of political or of military strategy for the West?"[155]

The successful cross-Channel invasion took place on June 6, 1944. Two days before (June 4), Rome was captured. Churchill immediately "revived the question of whether to go ahead with the projected landing on the Southern shores of France" (code named Dragoon, changed from Anvil). . . . "Could not these combat resources [landing craft no longer needed by Overlord] now be better used against Germany elsewhere and otherwise than in Dragoon?"[156]

"In late June the U.S. Joint Chiefs informed the British Chiefs that they could not see Italy as a decisive theatre, and that the delay now taking place in reaching agreement on Anvil was not in keeping with the early termination of the war."[157]

Churchill made an intense appeal in behalf of the Italian theatre in an attempt to persuade the President. That he was thinking in terms of the political end results of a major victory in Italy—especially for the Balkans—was evident. This appeal was sent in a long telegram July 1, 1944, from which the following excerpts are quoted:

". . . The splitting up of the campaign in the Mediterranean into two operations neither of which can do anything decisive, is, in my humble and respectful opinion, the first major strategic and political error for which we two have to be responsible.

"At Teheran you emphasized to me the possibilities of a move eastward when Italy was conquered[158] and mentioned particularly Istria. No one involved in these discussions has ever thought of moving armies into the Balkans.[159] But Istria and Trieste in Italy are strategic and political positions, which as you saw yourself very clearly might exercise profound and widespread reactions, especially now after the Russian advance. . . . If the momentum of my offensive is to be kept to its maximum, I must receive confirmation that Italian campaign is to be backed. . . .

"I have considered your suggestion that we should lay our respective cases before Stalin. The passage in the very nice telegram I have received from him yesterday . . . seems to suggest that he does not underrate the Italian front. I do not know what he would say if the issue was put to him to decide. On military grounds he might be greatly interested in the eastward movement of Alexander's army which, without entering the Balkans, would profoundly affect all the forces there and which, in conjunction with any attacks he may make upon Roumania or with Roumania against Hungarian Transylvania, might produce the most far reaching results. On a long-term political view, he might prefer that the British and Americans should do their share in France in the very hard fighting that is to come, and that east, middle and southern Europe should fall naturally into his control. However, it is better to settle the matter for ourselves and between ourselves. . . .

"It is with the greatest sorrow that I write to you in this sense. . . . I send you every good wish. However, we may differ on the conduct of the war, my personal gratitude to you in your kindness to me and for all you have done for the cause of freedom will never be diminished."[160]

(At this point it is interesting to read Mr. Churchill's words printed in 1950: "It is not possible in a major war to divide military from political affairs. At the summit they are one."[161] Mr. Stalin was undoubtedly of the same opinion.)

"The President would not yield. He immediately replied to Churchill unequivocally. 'The exploitation of "Overlord," our victorious advances in Italy, an early assault on Southern France, combined with the Soviet drives to the west—all as envisaged at Teheran—will most surely serve to realize our object—the unconditional surrender of Germany! Roosevelt reminded Churchill that Stalin had favored Anvil . . . [that] to conduct an operation against Istria would be to disregard two important considerations—the agreed grand strategy for an early defeat of Germany, and the time factor involved in a campaign to debouch from the Ljubljana Gap into Slovenia and Hungary. . . . 'I cannot agree,' he declared, 'to the employment of United States troops against Istria and into the Balkans, nor can I see the French agreeing to such use of French troops . . . !'

"On July 2 the President asked the Prime Minister to authorize a directive to be sent to General Wilson setting the wheels in motion for an early Anvil. 'I always think of my early geometry—a straight line is the shortest distance between two points.' "[162]

The British finally gave up. On August 15 the Seventh Army landed in southern France between Cannes and Hyères. Thus ended the ambiguous but insistent messages to and fro about the "Balkan invasion."

General Eisenhower described the British-American debate over the invasion of southern France as "one of the longest-sustained arguments that I had with

Prime Minister Churchill throughout the period of the war. This argument, beginning almost coincidentally with the break-through in late July, lasted throughout the first ten days of August. One session lasted several hours. . . .

"One of the early reasons for planning this attack was to achieve an additional port of entry through which the reinforcing divisions already prepared in America could pour rapidly into the European invasion. . . . The Prime Minister held . . . that the troops then in the Mediterranean could be brought in via Brittany, or even might better be used in prosecution of the Italian campaign with the eventual purpose of *invading the Balkans* via the head of the Adriatic. (Emphasis added)

"To any such change I was opposed. . . . I instantly became the individual against whom the Prime Minister directed all his argument. . . ."

One of the arguments was that "Our entry into the Balkans could encourage that entire region to flame into open revolt against Hitler and would permit us to carry to the resistance forces, arms and equipment which would make the efforts of these forces more effective. . . .

"In sustaining his argument the Prime Minister pictured a bloody prospect for the forces attacking from the south. He felt sure they would be involved for many weeks in attempts to reduce the coastal defenses and feared they could not advance as far northward as Lyon in less than three months. He thought we would suffer great losses and insisted the battlefield in that region would become merely another Anzio. It is possible the Prime Minister did not credit the authenticity of our Intelligence reports, but we were confident that few German forces other than largely immobile divisions remained in the South. . . .

"Although I never heard him say so, I felt that the Prime Minister's real concern was possibly of a political rather than military nature. He may have thought a postwar situation that would see the Western Allies *posted in great strength in the Balkans* (emphasis added) would be far more effective in producing a stable post-hostilities world than if the Russian armies should be the ones to occupy that region. I told him that if this were his reason *for advocating the campaign into the Balkans* (emphasis added) he should go instantly to the President and lay the facts, as well as his own conclusions, on the table. . . . But I did insist that as long as he argued the matter on military grounds alone I could not concede validity to his arguments. . . .

"He did not admit that political facts were influencing him, but I am quite certain that no experienced soldier would question the wisdom, strictly from the military point, of adhering to the plan for attacking southern France.

"As usual the Prime Minister pursued the argument up to the very moment of execution. As usual, also, the second that he saw he could not gain his own way, he threw every thing he had into support of the operation. He flew to the Mediterranean to witness the attack and I heard that he was actually on a destroyer to observe the supporting bombardment when the attack went in."[163]

Churchill's aim, "to strike at the soft underbelly of the Axis," has always been linked in the public mind in the United States with the Balkans. Actually, however, the phrase was not so restricted. Attacks on Europe's "soft underbelly" seemed to include, in Churchill's mind, the invasions of North Africa, Sicily, Italy, the Dodecanese Islands, Rhodes, and the Adriatic, including the Ljubljana Gap—indeed all the northern shores of the Mediterranean open to attacks when

North Africa was cleared of the Nazis, including also the islands as stepping stones. Although "the soft underbelly" was a broad and inclusive term, the Balkans—which were included in the phrase—appeared to be a fixed and definite objective in Churchill's mind.

Churchill, even after his changing and ever-shifting military suggestions for the Mediterranean were settled by the invasion of southern France, continued to pursue his search for some political influence in the Balkans.

It was not possible for the President to leave the United States before the November 1944 election. Churchill felt it necessary to confer with Stalin as soon as possible. He telegraphed the President on September 29, 1944, that "Anthony [Eden] and I are seriously thinking of flying there soon. . . . The two great objects that we have in mind would be, firstly, to clinch his coming in against Japan, and, secondly, to try to effect an amicable settlement with Poland. There are other points too concerning Yugoslavia and Greece which we would also discuss. . . ."[164]

Since Stalin would not travel, the Prime Minister suggested to Roosevelt that he go to Moscow, stating that "Averell's [Harriman] assistance would be welcomed by us." Nervous about the outcome of the meeting, and, on his guard, Roosevelt cabled Stalin on October 4, saying, "that in this global war there is literally no question, political or military, in which the United States is not interested. I am firmly convinced that the three of us, and only the three of us, can find solution to the still unresolved questions. In this sense, while appreciating the Prime Minister's desire for the meeting, I prefer to regard your forthcoming talks with Churchill as preliminary to a meeting of the three of us which, so far as I am concerned, can take place at any time after the election here."[165]

Then he went on to say that if it was agreeable to Stalin and Churchill, he would like Harriman to be present at their talks, but only as an observer.

"Naturally, Mr. Harriman," he continued, "would not be in a position to commit this government relative to the important matters which you and the Prime Minister will very naturally discuss."[166]

Churchill arrived in Moscow on October 9. On the 11th, he cabled the President: "We have found an extraordinary atmosphere of good will here, and we have sent you a joint message. You may be sure we shall handle everything so as not to commit you. . . . It is absolutely necessary we should try to get a common mind about the Balkans so that we may prevent civil war breaking out in several countries when you and I would be in sympathy with one side and U.J. [Uncle Joe, i.e., Stalin] with the other. I will keep you informed about this, and nothing will be settled except preliminary agreements between Britain and Russia, subject to further discussion and melting down with you. On this basis I am sure you will not mind our trying to have a full meeting of minds with the Russians. . . ."[167]

Two days before this cable was sent, i.e., on the evening of the day that Churchill arrived in Moscow, he met with Stalin. Later, in *Triumph and Tragedy,* he reported the meeting: "At ten o'clock that night we held our first important meeting in the Kremlin. There were only Stalin, Molotov, Eden and I, with Major Birse and Pavlov as interpreters. [Ambassador Harriman was not there.] . . . The moment was apt for business, so I said, 'Let us settle about our affairs in the Balkans. Your armies are in Rumania and Bulgaria. We have interests, missions, and agents there. Don't let us get at cross-purposes in small ways. So far as Britain and Russia are concerned, how would it do for you to have ninety per cent predominance in Rumania, for us to have ninety per cent of the say in Greece, and go fifty-fifty about Yugoslavia?' While this was being translated, I wrote out on a half sheet of paper:

Rumania	
Russia	90%
The others	10%
Greece	
Great Britain	90%
(in accord with U.S.A.)	
Russia	10%
Yugoslavia	50–50%
Hungary	50–50%
Bulgaria	
Russia	75%
The others	25%

"I pushed this across to Stalin, who had by then heard the translation. There was a slight pause. Then he took his blue pencil and made a large tick upon it, and passed it back to us. It was all settled in no more time than it takes to set down. . . . After this there was a long silence. The pencilled paper lay in the center of the table. At length I said, 'might it not be thought rather cynical if it seemed we had disposed of these issues, so fateful to millions of people, in such an offhand manner? Let us burn the paper.' 'No, you keep it,' said Stalin."[168]

This "generosity" must have given Stalin great satisfaction. Churchill had the paper, and with the help of the Red Army Stalin would soon have all except Greece in the palm of his hand. If it were not for American intervention in the Truman administration, he might have had Greece also.

The story of what had taken place was told to Harriman little by little. On October 10, Churchill and Stalin had sent Roosevelt a joint message in which they merely said, "We have to consider the best way of reaching an agreed policy about the Balkan countries, including Hungary and Turkey. At lunch on that day Harriman was told that in the first draft of this message to the President Churchill had included the phrase [to the best of Harriman's memory] . . . 'having regard to our own varying duties toward them.' Stalin had suggested that this phrase, which clearly implied spheres of influence, be omitted. On hearing this, Harriman said to Stalin, with Churchill listening, that he was sure that the President would be glad that the phrase had been eliminated since he thought that subject should be dealt with by the three of them. Stalin said he was pleased to hear Harriman say that and, reaching behind Churchill's back, he shook Harriman's hand."[169]

Churchill's message to the President of October 11 (already quoted) was—in light of this conversation—more explicit, and expressed a definite plea for approval. Roosevelt's answers were polite and noncommittal. Feis commented, "But since he thought it was impossible to find happy solutions for many European problems, he wanted to remain as clear of them as he could, except for those involving Germany."[170]

Again, after the election a meeting of the Big Three was under contemplation. Churchill was discouraged with the progress of the war. Roosevelt's telegram to him on December 9, 1944, was revealing: ". . . I am at Warm Springs in Georgia taking ten days off after the campaign. . . .

"Perhaps I am not close enough to the picture to feel as disappointed about the war situation as you and perhaps also because six months ago I was not as optimistic as you were on the time element.

"On the European front I always felt that the occupation of Germany up to the left bank of the Rhine would be a very stiff job. Because in the old days I bicycled over most of the Rhine terrain, I have never been so optimistic as to the ease of getting across the Rhine with our joint armies as many of the commanding officers have been. . . .

"For the time being, even if a little behind schedule, it seems to me the prosecution and outcome of the battles lie with our Field Commanders in whom I have every confidence. . . .

"As to the Italian front, Alexander's forces are doing their bit in keeping these German divisions in Italy, and we must remember that the Germans are really free to withdraw to the line of the Alps if they so decide.

"The same thing applies to their troops in the Balkans. I have never believed that we had the power to capture any large German forces in the Balkans without assistance by the Russians. . . .

"I think I can leave after Inauguration Day. . . . Roosevelt."[171]

The Commander-in-Chief—a realist—had gone back to his youth; his remarkable memory served to foresee the difficulties of the terrain that the armies would have to overcome.

At the Yalta Conference—February 4–11, 1945—attention was turned to the war in the northwest Pacific, to peace plans and to Poland. However, "In Greece a precarious tranquility," in Churchill's phrase, "had been achieved. The coalition government which had been patched together had broken up early in December as it tried to disband the guerrilla forces. The groups led by Communists had tried by tactics and strikes, disorder and terror, to take control. British forces had been engaged in severe street fighting in Athens. They had prevented an immediate upset. But General Alexander had put Churchill on notice (on December 21st) that 'the Greek problem cannot be solved by military measures. The answer must be found in the political field.' "[172] Churchill and Eden had flown to Athens on Christmas Eve and had persuaded the King to renounce his powers and appoint the Archbishop as Regent (December 30, 1944).

"The Archbishop had been installed on January 1st with the assent of all parties, including the Communists. Two days later a new government under General Plastiras had taken office. . . . But the Communist-led combatant groups could not be prevailed on to lay down their arms. A stiff campaign, mainly by British troops, had been required to drive them from Athens and Attica. Only after this had an armistice been effected (January 15th). . . . For the time being the revolutionary forces were scattered. The government in turn had promised fair elections, respect for civil rights, and amnesty.

"At Yalta, Stalin showed himself curious about what had taken place. But he assured Churchill that he meant no criticism and had no intention of meddling in the situation. Churchill expressed appreciation of this attitude."[173]

Perhaps Churchill wondered about that piece of paper which Stalin had so gallantly suggested he keep. Perhaps he wondered too about Yugoslavia, whose government was also in turmoil; British recommendations about Yugoslavia were not accepted by Stalin; Stalin's recommendations were not accepted by Churchill. In the closing rush of the conference a "compromise" agreement was reached. In fact, the Soviet prevailed.

In Romania the Soviet High Command was ruling with an iron hand. In

Bulgaria the British and American members of the Control Commission were being shunted out of any real part in its operation.

"The British and American governments took to Yalta their complaints about the way the Soviet chairmen were running the control commissions in these two countries, Romania and Bulgaria. They did not ask for equality. After all, Churchill had agreed that the Soviet Union was to have the lead in both while the war was on. But they did ask to be consulted in advance about political orders, and they would have liked to have gotten Stalin to assent to the idea that after the war was over, and military necessity was at an end, their members would attain authority equal to that of the Soviet chairman. But no time was found to deal with these requests."[174]

This was not because the American government was pursuing a policy of laissez-faire. On the contrary. Herbert Feis says: "Memos prepared for the Secretary of State and the President, found in the Briefing Book taken to Yalta, summed up the main objections to the way the situation was developing. They were (1) that the prospect that really representative democratic governments would emerge on many smaller countries of Europe was being diminished; and (2) that despite Anglo-Soviet accord about sphere of responsibility, tension and suspicion were growing. The British officials were becoming more and more of the opinion that the Russians were striving to bring into power governments that would be submissive to Communist control as far west in Europe as possible; while the Soviet officials were attributing to the British a plot to sustain along the Soviet western frontiers repudiated governments that would be hostile to the Soviet Union . . . So . . . the American government presented at Yalta . . . 'The Declaration on Liberated Europe.' "[175] It was a pious document of democratic recommendations, taken seriously by the Americans and given lip service by the Soviets and British.

Feis believed that "the effort to enthrone principle at Yalta and subsequently ought not to be dismissed as futile. The Declaration on Liberated Europe may have served to sustain the resistance of democratic elements in Central Europe. The principles which it avowed may have affected action for a while and may still survive as an inspiring guide to the future."[176]

The principles experienced hard going, and were finally repudiated by the Soviet Union in clear breach of its agreement.

Churchill denied any determination "to strike at the soft under-belly of the Axis" as it has been interpreted to mean through "the Balkans." The issue, however, is confused by several remarks such as this one made by Churchill at the conference of Dominions' Prime Ministers on May 3, 1944, on the eve of launching Overlord.

"He was bound to admit that if he had his own way the lay-out of the war would have been different. His inclination would have been in favor of rolling up Europe from the South-East, and joining hands with the Russians. However, it had proved impossible to pursuade the United States on this view. They had been determined at every stage upon the invasion of North-West Europe. He himself had opposed the opening of this campaign in 1942 and 1943; but now he was in favor of it, and all his military advisors supported him in this. Russian pressure, too, had been very severe."[177] It is certainly difficult to reconcile this "rolling up Europe" from the southeast with his later specific disclaimer of any desire to put "armies" into the Balkans. Roosevelt faced facts and therefore realized that there could be no entry through any part of Europe's "soft underbelly" unless Stalin were a party to it.

What specifically was Roosevelt's general style during the year 1943?

In 1943 the tides of war changed. We had taken the offensive in late 1942 in North Africa, and were now moving into Sicily and Italy. And we had taken the offensive at Midway, no longer on the defensive in the Pacific. Our production was picking up and approaching—in some items even surpassing—the fantastic levels Roosevelt had set in 1942 and increased in 1943. The Russians had successfully held Leningrad and Moscow, and were holding Stalingrad. During the year they began their offensive and started westward toward Berlin. The Red Army, the Russian winters and the American war production had proven—as Roosevelt had predicted—too much for the Nazis. In short, it was beginning to look as though Nazi Germany was going to be beaten. All this seemed very bright, but it raised some problems of its own, calling for a different style from the war leader.

For propaganda purposes, he would keep on telling the aggressors and their victims about our amazing production. As we assumed the initiative in the Pacific and the Mediterranean, however, he had to warn against complacency, instead of against defeatism.

For example, in his speech on Washington's Birthday in 1942 he had painted a gloomy picture of enemy successes and Allied defeats. In 1943, however, his speech on Washington's Birthday was a protest against a feeling that the war was practically won, with "thousands of Americans throwing their hats in the air proclaiming that victory is just around the corner." He would repeat this theme time and again. As early as his press conference on New Year's Day, 1943, and in his State of the Union Message of January 7, 1943, he began to talk about postwar America and the postwar world. Yet in the midst of all the talk he continued his activism as world strategist, world leader, and as Commander-in-Chief.

His State of the Union Message was typical of this 1943 style. After stating his opinion that 1942 "was perhaps the most crucial for modern civilization," he predicted that 1943 "will be filled with violent conflicts—yet with high promise of better things." He referred to our North African landings as causing diversion of Nazi troops from Russia, and publicized Churchill's phrase: "It has opened to attack what Mr. Churchill has well described as the 'under-belly of the Axis.' " He accurately predicted the clearing of all Axis troops from North Africa and further devastating action against Germany and Italy. He dwelt at length on our growing production figures and praised all the Americans responsible for it— "owners, managers, supervisors, draftsmen, engineers, workers—men and women—in factories and arsenals, shipyards and mines, and in mills and forests —on railroads and on highways"—and the farmers (he had to get them all in). He spoke of our growing armed forces. He predicted and emphasized again the growing need for sacrifice and price stabilization, "the sharp pinch of total war." Then he spoke of a postwar world under the Four Freedoms and with the United Nations remaining united for the maintenance of peace. All of this was propaganda and morale building for consumption both at home and in the conquered countries.

The President's style in 1943 also included providing examples of the proper treatment of colonies and weaker nations. On Friday, March 1, he announced a treaty with China relinquishing all "extraterritorial" rights we had in China; on March 9, he recommended that the people of Puerto Rico be permitted to elect their own Governor; on April 20, he visited Mexico to reaffirm the solidarity of the Western Hemisphere and to speak of our recognition of a "mutual interdependence of our great resources." He held talks with the President of Bolivia in May, reaffirming that "the era of exploitation in Latin America was over," in which he later told the press he had "apologized to him on behalf of the thing that happened many years ago"; on August 12, he addressed the Philippine people by radio, pointing out that the Philippines had been treated during the war as an independent ally, and pledging that they would get independence as a republic of the Philippines "the moment the power of our Japanese enemies is destroyed." He sent a message to Congress in September recommending self-government for Puerto Rico under the principle of self-determination set out in the Atlantic Charter; he requested authority from Congress in October to proclaim a free Philippines; and he sent a message to Congress in October recommending repeal of the Chinese Exclusion Laws.

The year 1943 was also one of impressive and extraordinary personal action, even for this outstanding and tireless activist: three international conferences—Casablanca, Teheran, Quebec; many trips to war plants and training camps; seizure of the bituminous coal mines because of a strike and excoriating John L. Lewis for stopping the operation of the mines; setting up a committee on fair employment practices in May to banish racial discrimination in war plants; a second seizure of the bituminous coal mines because of John L. Lewis's threat of another strike; and a seizure of the railroads of the United States because of the threat of a crippling strike.

It was also the year that marked the beginning of postwar planning. He had even earlier frequently spoken of planning for America and for the world during the war, not waiting, as did Wilson, for the war to end. He now began to take action on several fronts: United Nations, returning veterans, war criminals, demobilization, and feeding the people of devastated Europe.

In his fireside chat of July 27, he outlined plans to take care of returning veterans after the war: mustering-out pay; unemployment insurance if no job could be found; opportunities for further education, free and at the cost of the federal government; improved and generous provisions for hospitalization, rehabilitation, and medical care of veterans; and pensions for the disabled.

In October, these plans for returning veterans began to crystallize. This was almost two years before V.J. Day, and dramatically shows Roosevelt's style of planning long in advance for postwar projects. In November of 1942, he had appointed a committee of educators to study the problem of continued education for our returning veterans, men and women, after the war. Now, in October 1943, after receiving a report from this committee, he sent a message to Congress asking for legislation to provide free education or opportunity to learn a trade or to carry on special aptitudes—at government expense. This legislation came to be known as the G.I. Bill of Rights. In this message, he repeated: "It may well be said that the time to prepare for peace is at the height of war."

He also was thinking in 1943 about postwar trials of war criminals. He had already several times warned the war criminals of Germany and Japan that they would be punished after the war for their crimes. Now on July 30, he warned neutral countries against giving asylum to any of the Axis war leaders, such as Mussolini (who had resigned). He was to continue to plan for postwar action against war criminals even while the fighting was going on. On November 1, 1943, he, Stalin and Churchill joined in a statement laying down the definite policy that war criminals would be sent back after the war to the countries where their atrocities had been committed, to be tried there on the spot "by the people whom they have outraged." The statement added that "the major criminals whose offenses have no geographical localization will be punished by joint decision of the governments of the Allies." These "major" criminals included all those who were later tried at Nuremberg.

Another example of planning during the war for postwar projects was Roosevelt's creation of UNRRA to relieve some of the starvation and misery, and to provide food, clothing, medicine and fuel to the people of the devastated areas of the world. The normal devastation of war had been greatly multiplied, because the Nazis and Japanese had adopted a "scorched earth" policy as they retreated. UNRRA was to be an activity in which *all* the United Nations would join. It was in the style of Roosevelt to do this; as he said in his speech to the representatives of the different Allies who were to constitute UNRRA on November 9, 1943: "As in most of the difficult and complex things in life, Nations will learn to work together only by actually working together."

On March 30 he disclosed at a press conference that he had just had talks with Sir Anthony Eden (the British Foreign Minister) about planning for peace in the postwar world, and that such talks had been going on for some time with and among the other Allies: China, two of the South American republics, Stalin, Molotov. One is struck by the phrase used by him in this press conference: "problems that will arise on the surrender of the enemy." Nothing could be more eloquent of the change of mood from 1942 to 1943, from "if" to "when" we win. He recalled that when Armistice Day came suddenly in World War I, "there had been very little work on the post-war problem," and soon in Paris, "everybody was rushing around trying to dig up things." This time, he said, "the allies are already 95% together."

One reporter asked: "Could you tell us anything about the other 5%?"

Said the President: "Well every additional conversation eliminates a little bit more of the 5%."[178]

Roosevelt, always remembering Wilson's inability in 1919 to attain his most cherished dream, acted with caution and circumspection as he eyed the isolationists in the Senate of his own time who might have the power to defeat his own supreme ambition—to make the United States the leader in creating a worldwide peacekeeping security. He let Hull move ahead—without any fanfare or too much publicity—to lay the plans. Roosevelt was waiting for the correct timing, keeping all his options open as usual as to the nature and form of the organization. He, of course, was encouraged by the continuing proof of his theory that nations can get used to working together by actually doing so; already the theory was working with lend-lease, with the Combined Chiefs of Staff, the international food programs, the allocation of resources among the fighting Allies, scientific cooperation and, late in November, with UNRRA.

In Moscow at the meeting of the Foreign Ministers in November 1943, Hull had secured their assent to a four-power cooperation for postwar security until an international security organization could be set up. At Teheran later in 1943, Roosevelt discussed his plan generally for a security organization with Stalin himself. This plan was different from what finally evolved as the United Nations Organization (UNO), and represented Roosevelt's thinking at the time. Stalin pointed out some difficulties over certain details, but indicated no dissent from the idea of a postwar peacekeeping organization, by force if necessary, including Russia. Next year, these plans would crystallize. Roosevelt later characterized these discussions by Hull and himself with the British and Russians as discussions in an atmosphere of complete candor and harmony.[179]

What was Roosevelt's style for 1944?

Nineteen hundred forty-four was significant for increasing victories, advances in planning for the UNO, and the reversion of Roosevelt to the role of a fighting, liberal New Dealer. The military successes and the clear prospect of the defeat of all the remaining Axis powers called for a recall of "Dr. New Deal." It was quite remarkable that this turnabout came only a few weeks after his dissertation about "Dr. Win-the-War" replacing "Dr. New Deal."

He started right off in his State of the Union Message of 1944, which Professor Burns has called "the most radical speech of his life." In it he put in a plug for an end to American isolationism and in behalf of a postwar security organization, condemning the small percentage of Americans at home who were still not sharing in the sacrifices of war; and he proposed a drastic series of statutes— including a national service law—to make sure that all our resources including all human resources were dedicated to the war, and that we maintain a stable economy at home. Then came the announcement of a new bill of economic rights to supplement the old political bill of rights. He enumerated them. It was really a summation of the New Deal philosophy: that the government had the responsibility of looking after the welfare of its citizens who were willing to work, to see to it that each citizen, as a matter of right and regardless of creed or race, was entitled to a decent job at pay sufficient to provide food, clothing and recreation, with the same assurance to farmers who worked on their crops; to protection against monopolies; a decent home; medical care; protection from the economic losses of old age, sickness, unemployment and accidents; and a good education.

It should be pointed out that the succeeding liberal Democratic administrations under Truman, Kennedy and Johnson continued to pursue these same objectives of the New Deal as newly enunciated in this message, whether the current slogan was "Fair Deal," "New Frontiers" or "Great Society." In effect and in purpose, are all synonymous.

That part of the message which deals with national service—the drafting of every man and woman for civilian service if he was not eligible for military service —illustrates the extreme Roosevelt secretiveness and his desire to end argument. Civilian workers were scarce because the draft had taken so many of them into the armed forces. In late 1943 and 1944 many of the civilian workers were leaving their war jobs to return to their old occupations, on the theory that the war was over. It worried the Secretary of War; and it worried the President even more. Roosevelt changed his mind back and forth on Stimson's recommendation for an all-out conscription act involving civilian workers as well as military, for many of his advisers were strenuously objecting to it. He finally decided, when he visited the troops near Teheran, that he was going to recommend it to Congress, that he was not going to change his mind again, and that he would not even tell those who had objected that he was going to do it. He wanted to end the argument which had been going on for many months. I am sure he also relished the great, dramatic surprise he was to spring with this most drastic labor recommendation he had ever made with respect to workers.

When the President returned from Teheran, he said to Bob Sherwood and me that what he had seen at the fighting fronts, and his knowledge of the coming drives in Europe and in the Pacific, convinced him of the necessity of passing such a measure. He asked us to work on the first draft of a message to Congress. However, he warned us not to reveal these plans to *anyone*—not even to the

Director of War Mobilization, James F. Byrnes, or Byrnes's adviser, Bernard M. Baruch, who would both be intimately concerned with the administration of such a measure. The President handed us what he had dictated about national service for insertion into the State of the Union Message for 1944, and cautioned us again to preserve secrecy. We labelled this insert, humorously, "Project Q-38." It was not typed in the staff room along with the other drafts of the speech, but separately by Grace Tully, his private and confidential secretary, in order to maintain absolute secrecy. "Project Q-38" first appeared in the third draft of the State of the Union Message. It is included in all the subsequent drafts now kept at the Roosevelt Hyde Park Library, still labeled separately "Project Q-38." When the message was released, a great howl of protest arose from Roosevelt's advisers, who had been kept in the dark in spite of their prior objections; and there were threats of resignation.

Nineteen forty-four continued the same style of propaganda, preparation for postwar projects while the war was reaching its climax, struggle against inflation —and above all *action* on all fronts. There were steps to end discrimination against Negroes in the army and navy; creation of an agency to dispose of war surplus property after the war; many fights with Congress, growing conservative and recalcitrant, especially on taxes and inflation; creation of an agency to promote retraining and re-employment of returning veterans after the war; preference for veterans in civil service; setting up the War Refugee Board; extension of lend-lease; providing for the monetary conference at Bretton Woods; recommending receiving 1,000 refugees who had fled to southern Italy into the United States regardless of immigration laws; further planning at Dumbarton Oaks and elsewhere for a post-war security organization; setting up an agency to supervise and help the reconversion of industry after the war; a formal statement of the President that "the right to vote must be open to our citizens irrespective of race, color or creed without tax or artificial restriction of any kind"; attending the second Quebec Conference with Churchill; preparation for the liquidation of the war agencies after the war; setting up a training system for returning veterans who would want to go into farming after the end of the war; seizure of Montgomery Ward & Co. because of strikes caused by the company's refusal to follow the orders of the National War Labor Board.

The number of functions to be performed after the war by agencies set up during the war is quite remarkable—especially since it was generally thought that the war would last two years longer than it did.

The President always continued his style of framing economic questions and thinking about them in terms of human beings. Many times during his presidency he spoke about anonymous people, acquaintances of his, who dropped in to see him from time to time without notice or invitation—it must have been while all the guards, sentries, doorkeepers and secretaries were asleep—to discuss with him important questions affecting their pocketbooks. The following colloquy at the press conference of May 30 about price control is an example of this style, and also of the informality of his press conferences generally:

The President: "This reminds me of a friend of mine, a foreman of one of the substantial trades, who came in last January, and said to me, 'I have an awful time when I go home.' He says, 'My old lady is ready to hit me over the head with the dishpan.'

I said, "What's the trouble?"

"The cost of living."

"Well," I said, "what, for instance?"

"Well, last night I went home, and the old lady said, 'What's this? I went out to buy some asparagus, and do you see what I got? I got five sticks. There it is. A dollar and a quarter! It's an outrage!' "

Well, I looked at him, and I said, "Since when have you been buying asparagus in January—fresh asparagus?"

"Oh," he said, "I never thought of that."

"Well," I said, "tell that to the old lady, with my compliments."

Q. Mr. President, is that the same foreman you mentioned in a press conference sometime ago who bought the strawberries in the winter? (Much laughter)

The President (laughing): "It happened to be a different one, but it's all right, still makes a true story."[180]

The big military action, of course, in 1944 was the invasion across the Channel on June 6. Nine days after this invasion started, the President issued a statement about the conferences and planning for a postwar security organization which had been and were still being held in the State Department. He emphasized the bi-partisan nature of the planning, and the presence and participation of Republican senators in all the sessions.

In August, he spoke informally to the delegates from Russia, Britain and China who had been sent to attend the Dumbarton Oaks Conferences on the same subject. During the earlier summer of 1944, the four Allies—Britain, China, Russia and the United States—had exchanged tenative proposals which were to be used as a basis for discussion at Dumbarton Oaks (an estate in Georgetown). The conference lasted from August 21 to October 7, 1944. The final proposals were set out in a document entitled: "Proposals for the Establishment of a General International Organization." They were quite close to the final United Nations Organization, except that the knotty problem of voting in the Security Council was deferred. (It was not finally settled until Yalta.) The resemblance between these final proposals and the plans Roosevelt had been informally talking about for several years is quite remarkable. Roosevelt kept in intimate touch with the discussions at Dumbarton Oaks, and his forceful personality had much to do with producing agreement among all four participants.

In 1944 came Roosevelt's fourth campaign for the presidency. Dewey was his opponent. It was characterized later by the President as the "dirtiest campaign in all history." It was marked by misstatements by Dewey and other Republican leaders, by unbelievably false quotations torn by Dewey completely out of context, and by extreme and irresponsible charges of ineptitude, confusion and downright incompetence on the part of the administration in running the war. There was even a repetition of the charge of communism, accompanied by innuendoes that Roosevelt was completely subservient to Stalin. I was with Roosevelt in six political campaigns. In five of them, he had a deep respect for his adversaries even though they differed completely from his views. He even had a certain personal affection for them by the time the campaign was over—especially for Willkie and Landon. But in this sixth campaign he came to hate Dewey intensely, and to have a feeling of deep contempt for him.

The President, as he had indicated in his acceptance speech, had remained quite aloof from the campaign. But Dewey, an active, spirited and able campaigner, had begun early to make campaign trips around the country. At the start, the wise political prophets gave him a slim chance of winning. However, as the summer wore on, and as the stories continued to spread about the President's bad health, his weariness of mind and body, and his general disinterest in the political campaign, Dewey's chances brightened. From the very beginning, Dewey levelled his attack on the "tired old men" who were running the government, and on the frequent bickering among members of the administration. He argued that the "time for a change" had come, and that the affairs of government should be turned over to fresh, younger and more enthusiastic hands.

As Dewey continued vigorously to campaign and as the President continued to remain silent, the same thing began to happen among the voters that had happened in 1940. Sentiment began to rise for Dewey and to fall for the President. Again Democratic political leaders, friends and visitors at the White House urged the President to start campaigning. Many of them, even as they urged him, felt great doubt whether he was physically up to campaigning in his old style.

The President soon began to realize that it was necessary for him to get out again and fight; that it was up to him to prove that he could stand the physical and mental rigors of a political campaign. Accordingly, in August, he announced that he was going to open his campaign in a speech on September 23.

Dewey seemed to have forgotten that the President, as in 1940, had reserved the right to answer misstatements and false charges. At the President's request, I prepared a memorandum quoting his misstatements and distortions, contrasting them with the true facts.

He had to leave Washington for the second Quebec Conference with Churchill on September 16, 1944. From Quebec, he sent down to me in Washington a couple of pages of what he told me on the phone he had dictated as "just a happy thought." In those pages were included a paragraph typical of his style of ridicule in campaigns—indeed the most effective use he ever made of ridicule, and one which will be long remembered.

Some Republican congressmen had made and circulated the ridiculous and false charge that on the President's trip home from Alaska (where he had gone from Hawaii to look at our defenses and to talk to our troops) it was discovered after his ship was a few days out, that by inadvertence, his little dog Fala had been left behind; and that a destroyer had been sent back to Alaska to pick him up, at a cost to the taxpayers of some absurdly large sum of money. Silly as the story was, the anti-Roosevelt press played it up as if it were gospel truth.

The speech was delivered at a dinner of the Teamsters' Union in Washington and used from its very beginning many shafts of ridicule which had the audience in stitches of laughter. The climax came in discussing the charge about Fala. As you read it in cold print it is not so funny, but to hear it delivered—the mock tone of seriousness and of righteous indignation, the expression on his face as if he were discussing a matter of crucial international or military importance—made it seem hilarious, and the audience in wild laughter interrupted the speech to give him a standing ovation. Sherwood once remarked that Roosevelt would have made a wonderful actor; he certainly was that night, as he intoned:

"These Republican leaders have not been content with attacks on me, or my wife, or on my sons. No, not content with that, they now include my little dog, Fala. Well, of course, I don't resent attacks, and my family doesn't resent attacks, but Fala does resent them. You know, Fala is Scotch and being a Scottie, as soon as he learned that the Republican fiction writers in Congress and out had concocted a story that I had left him behind on the Aleutian Islands and had sent a destroyer back to find him—at a cost to the taxpayers of two or three, or eight or twenty million dollars—his Scotch soul was furious. He has not been the same dog since. I am accustomed to hearing malicious falsehoods about myself—such as that old, worm-eaten chestnut that I have represented myself as indispensable. But I think I have a right to resent, to object to libelous statements about my dog."[181]

Roosevelt, after the rambling and ineffective speech at Bremerton which he had made a month earlier and which encouraged rumors that the Old Champ had lost his magic and was finished, was that night at his vigorous best—taunting his opponents, ridiculing their misstatements and exaggerated charges, and also inspiring his listeners throughout the nation by his eloquent delineations of his aims for the future of the world. The speech had just the effect it was intended to have. Bremerton was forgotten; the picture of the sick old man disappeared, and the Democratic campaign forces were electrified.

Dewey foolishly picked it up and answered it himself in a fighting-mad speech, swinging widely in a way which hurt him more than it did the "Champ." Paul Porter, the then Democratic National chairman, summed it all up very aptly in a letter he sent me a few days after Roosevelt's speech: "We have a new slogan in headquarters now—the race is between Roosevelt's dog and Dewey's goat."

His style during the remainder of the 1944 campaign was about the same as the others—with two exceptions which had rarely occurred before. He once again let the opponents pick the battleground for one speech, as he had in 1936. And the subject was the same as the one in 1936, "Communism." In 1944 the charge was accentuated by the close wartime relation and cooperation between Roosevelt and Stalin. Roosevelt referred to a "statement signed by thirteen Republicans, one Senator and twelve Representatives,—3,000,000 copies of which were sent free through the mails." The document said that "the Red spectre of Communism is stalking our country from East to West, from North to South."

Roosevelt's reply was as direct as it had been in 1936 to the similar charge: "This form of fear propaganda is not new among rabble rousers and fomenters of class hatred—who seek to destroy democracy itself. It was used by Mussolini's black shirts and by Hitler's brown shirts. It has been used before in this country by the silver shirts and others on the lunatic fringe. But the sound and democratic instincts of the American people rebel against its use, particularly by their own Congressmen—and at the taxpayers' expense.

"I have never sought, and I do not welcome the support of any person or group committed to Communism, or Fascism, or any other foreign ideology which would undermine the American system of government, or the American system of free competitive enterprise and private property.

"That does not in the least interfere with the firm and friendly relationship which the Nation has in this war, and will, I hope, continue to have with the people of the Soviet Union. The kind of economy that suits the Russian people, I take it is their own affair. The American people are glad and proud to be allied with the gallant people of Russia, not only in winning this war but in laying the foundations for the world peace which I hope will follow this war—and in keeping that peace."[182]

The second departure from his regular style was even more unusual; indeed, I think it had never occurred since his senatorial campaign in 1910. Probably because the tactics of Dewey had made him angry and resentful, Roosevelt, in addition to his sarcasm and ridicule, resorted to unpleasant remarks about Dewey.

For example, in an informal talk from the back platform of his train in

Bridgeport, Connecticut, he said: "In this campaign . . . I cannot talk about my opponent the way I would like to sometimes, because I try to think that I am a Christian. I try to think that some day I will go to Heaven, and I don't believe there is anything to be gained in saying dreadful things about other people in any campaign."

And in Boston on November 4, he quoted a statement that "a Republican Candidate" (this time it was Dewey) had made in Boston. Again he interpolated, "and pardon me if I quote him correctly, that happens to be an old habit of mine."

In a speech in Philadelphia he took pains to remind the people who the Commander-in-Chief was who had led America from the dark days of 1942 to what looked like a certain victory. This was really the campaign image he succeeded in creating in 1944, and he never let it fade. He pointed out that under the Constitution it was the Commander-in-Chief who had to appoint the civilians and the military men who had immediate charge of production and fighting in the war. He could well boast of his appointments. His war experience as President was vastly different from that of Lincoln, who had to endure the heartbreaking failures of many generals before he picked the right one. From the very start Roosevelt had reached down, and without regard to seniority picked the right military commanders. He made a point of this in his speech, and he took advantage also of the great popularity of the men whom he had appointed. But like the good orator he was, he did it by understatement; he said: "I feel called upon to offer no apologies for any selection of Henry L. Stimson, the late Frank Knox, and Jim Forrestal, or of Admiral Leahy, General Marshall, Admiral King, and General Arnold."

To emphasize the great difficulties of the job was the most emphatic way of driving his point home. Not only was it the most emphatic; it was the least embarrassing. It would have been vainglorious and boastful for Roosevelt to point out directly how much more qualified he was than Dewey. But to enumerate the soul-searching responsibilities of the presidency—the awful decisions on each of which so many hundreds of thousands of lives might depend, the quick judgments in the face of crisis which called for soundness, maturity, experience and long seasoning—was to emphasize the very qualities the voters would recognize in Roosevelt and would not see in the untried Dewey.

He made only five or six major speeches in the 1944 campaign, but I am sure that a careful reading of them will convince any impartial reader that here was the champion American campaigner of all time.

Roosevelt won by an electoral vote of 432 in thirty-six states to Dewey's 99 in twelve states; the popular vote was 25,600,000 to 22,000,000. The President felt sure that he would win, but realizing that twelve years in the presidency would naturally cause dissatisfaction among many groups, was much less optimistic than those around him. A few days before election, six of us, including Roosevelt, had entered into a $5 pool on the forthcoming electoral vote. Watson had guessed 400, Hopkins 440, Early 449, Sherwood 484 and I 431. The President was not as confident even as Watson. In fact his guess was so low that as soon as he paid his bet he insisted on tearing up his slip. Since I was closest to the actual number of electoral votes, I collected the $25.

In January 1945, after sending to Congress the budget message and the Annual Message, detailing the progress of the war and again asking for a total national conscription act, he made his fourth Inaugural Address at a very simple ceremony held on the south lawn of the White House—in the interest of saving money. The military parade was also omitted. Two days after the Inaugural Address, the President secretly left for Yalta for his second and last tripartite conference. His style there has been discussed above. The events of Yalta, including Roosevelt's part in them, have been described, hailed, condemned, praised and denounced in hundreds of books, articles, and dissertations. I have myself written on the subject, and shall not repeat it all here.[183]

Roosevelt did at Yalta obtain the realization of his efforts begun as early as the Foreign Ministers' meeting at Moscow in October 1943, and continued at Teheran, Dumbarton Oaks and for the rest of 1944: the creation of a peacekeeping organization. At Yalta, agreement was reached on the voting arrangements, and on a meeting of all the United Nations to be called on April 25, 1945, at San Francisco. His great military aim, spurred on anew by the Combined Chiefs of Staff, he also realized: the agreement definitely fixing the time of the Russian entry into the war against Japan, "two or three months" after V.E. Day.

In addition to these, and to certain reciprocal military arrangements for the rest of the war, Yalta was a great success *on paper*. Stalin saw to it that it was to become a massive failure *in practice*.

For example, there was a beautiful, idealistic statement subscribed to by all three nations on what would happen in the countries liberated and to be liberated from the Nazis: destruction of all vestiges of Nazism or fascism, creation of democratic institutions of their own choice—described in the joint statement as a "principle of the Atlantic Charter—the right of all peoples to choose the form of government under which they will live." The powers also agreed, pending free elections, to form interim governments "broadly representative of all democratic elements in the population."

The agreement was practically torn up by Stalin within thirty days.

There was another beautiful idealistic statement concerning Poland, already liberated by the Red Army: "a Polish provisional government which can be more broadly based than was possible before liberation," with "the inclusion of democratic leaders from Poland itself and from Poles abroad" (meaning the Polish government group in England). After this reorganization, this provisional government "shall be pledged to the holding of free and unfettered elections as soon as possible on the basis of universal suffrage and secret ballot."

This agreement, too, Stalin tore up almost as soon as the Yalta Conference broke up.

Compromises were reached on other issues, and the decisions on some others were deferred. Russia made substantial concessions; so did the other Allies. None of these is relevant here.

Stalin had never broken his pledged word to Roosevelt until after Yalta. Roosevelt had gambled on Stalin's fidelity twice—once, in spite of those who predicted that Russia could not last more than three weeks after the invasion by the Nazis; the second time, in spite of those who predicted, as the Red Army started moving west, that as soon as the Nazi troops were pushed back out of Russian territory, Stalin would sign a separate peace. Both predictions proved untrue; both gambles paid off. He believed that Stalin would again keep his word. When he found signs of a breach, his style toward Stalin changed, and he got very tough, especially about Poland (as did Churchill) in his messages to Stalin. There had already been recriminations back and forth about the arrangements for the surrender of the German Army in Italy. This was finally straightened out.

It is hard to see how at Yalta he could have refused to take Stalin's promises.

One feature of Roosevelt's style got him into serious embarrassment shortly after his return to Washington—his secretiveness. There was no possible justification for it in this instance. In preparing his report, the President decided to keep one of the Yalta agreements secret, although it had nothing to do with military security. It was the agreement that Russia and the United States would each support a proposal granting two extra votes for the Soviet in the Assembly by treating the Ukraine and Byelorussia as separate entities. In turn, Stalin agreed to support any United States demands for three votes also. Roosevelt's decision not to disclose this was the kind of mistake he had never made before in any of his reports on international conferences, and I have never been able to understand the reason in this case. Of course, as always, military arrangements had to remain secret. That is why it was obvious that the Far Eastern agreement with the Soviet could not be mentioned or discussed. But there seemed to be no reason why the three votes arrangement should not be disclosed. The whole matter was bound to come out shortly in San Francisco when Russia would make her demand. Besides, anyone with any experience in Washington would have anticipated that the matter would soon "leak out" anyway, even before the meeting at San Francisco. But the President insisted that it must not be mentioned, and it was not.

The only reason I can assign, after asking many other people with whom the President might have discussed it, was that the President thought he might be able to talk Stalin into agreeing to drop the project, so that neither the United States nor Russia would make the demand at San Francisco for the two extra votes in the Assembly.

The matter did soon leak—long prior to the San Francisco Conference. Roosevelt was justifiably attacked for trying to keep the arrangement secret. Had he taken the American people into his confidence, he could have explained how unimportant a concession this was, especially since it was to be reciprocated. But having kept it from them, he never was able adequately to justify his action.

The President died too soon after Stalin's treachery began to be revealed to ascertain whether this new tough attitude would have made any difference. The day he died, he cabled in reply to a question from Churchill as to what he should report to the House of Commons.

"I would minimize the general Soviet problem as much as possible because these problems in one form or another seem to arise every day, and most of them straighten out as in the case of the Berne meeting [referring to the dispute which had arisen about the surrender in Italy]. We must be firm, however, and our course thus far has been correct." The "course" was the firm position he and Churchill were taking with Stalin on Poland.

Roosevelt was puzzled about what was happening. He was not yet ready to believe that Stalin had practiced pure deceit at Yalta. He was under the impression that perhaps the Politburo was responsible for the new attitude. This beginning of the break with Stalin had a depressing effect on the President, who realized how essential continued cooperation would be for world peace. The story of how this developed into the cold war belongs to the chapter on President Truman, and will be treated there in connection with the style of Truman.

I have often wondered, as have many others, whether the cold war would have come so quickly, and with such intensity, had Roosevelt lived through his fourth term. Certainly, whatever gratitude Stalin and the Russian leaders were capable of feeling would have been extended personally to Roosevelt—as it was not to

Truman. Roosevelt's style with Stalin would have also been different from Truman's, less abrupt, more patient, more understanding of the problems of the Soviet Union, and, above all, willing to meet Stalin face to face more frequently.

Certainly the concessions made by Stalin to Roosevelt at Yalta indicate that Roosevelt did retain to the end of that personal confrontation a certain capacity to influence Stalin—even though Stalin and the Red Army at that time no longer needed American lend-lease help from him. It is doubtful that any American could, after Roosevelt's death, have had the activating or even the restraining influence on Stalin that Roosevelt might have had—at least for a time.

However, the relations between the Soviet and the United States were not within the *ex parte* control of either one. It takes two to reach understanding and agreement. Either Ally could, of its own, break up the wartime collaboration which had won the war. If Stalin or the Politburo was bent on breaking it up, nothing Roosevelt or anybody else could do would have stopped either of them. Since we do not know—and never will—what was exactly in the minds of Stalin and the Politburo in opening up and continuing the cold war, we cannot say whether the continued leadership of Roosevelt would have prevented it, or delayed it, or even reduced its intensity. But I feel confident that the style of Roosevelt and his experiences with Stalin would have led him to try more vigorously, more patiently, and more understandingly than Truman.

As you skim over the multitude of matters—military, domestic and international—between 1933 and 1945 with which Roosevelt had to deal, you can get some idea of the impact of them on a man's physical constitution. By the time of the "Fala" speech in September 1944 he had reached the physical state where he had to deliver this and the subsequent speeches in a seated position, as he did his final report to Congress on the Yalta Conference on March 1, 1945. But the physical strain, tremendous as it was, was nothing compared to the mental, nervous and spiritual strain through which he had gone, especially in the five years commencing with the invasions of Norway, Denmark, Holland and France.

How can you measure the stress upon a man who decides that certain steps are essential, who takes the responsibility for doing them and for fighting for them night and day, against the opposition and denunciation of so many millions of his countrymen and so many members of Congress; the repeal of the neutrality embargo; the transfer to Britain of fifty American destroyers; the passage of a draft law which would disrupt the careers and maybe end the lives of so many young men; the responsibility and the fight for lend-lease, and for applying it for the benefit of Hitler's old ally, Stalin; the seizure of Greenland, Iceland and other neutral territory for bases; the escorting of cargoes of lend-lease supplies at the cost of so many American ships and lives; the "shoot-on-sight" order which was really undeclared warfare?

And when the war finally was forced upon us, who can measure the stress upon a man of the disaster at Pearl Harbor, costing thousands of American lives, for which he was not to blame personally but for which he had to take the responsibility; or the inward anguish and the abuse of many Americans because of his inability to come to the aid of the beleaguered starving American soldiers at Corregidor as a result of his refusal to budge from the correct policy of "Hitler first"?

Who can say what goes on in a man's soul who has personally insisted on American troops going into action in 1942, and then listens on the radio as they land on the North African beaches?

And what about the conscience of a man who had battled with Churchill for two years, demanding the cross-Channel invasion of France time and again instead of the easier, safer, but ineffective diversionary tactics Churchill preferred in other parts of the world?

I was with the President on the night of the Channel invasion and on the following day when he read the prayer; and I could see in his eyes the deep concern and the terrible sense of responsibility and the religious faith with which he prayed. But never, never, never did I see fear or panic—any more than I had at the news of Pearl Harbor. For the following few days after D-Day he eagerly followed every dispatch, and as prospects grew brighter and brighter, the tension lessened—but it had left its mark.

Add to this the same mental and spiritual stress which came almost every week in 1944, with a new landing by American troops on one Pacific island after another, with all the long casualty lists he would see. And then the tension of a political campaign in the midst of all of it—the campaign which he had called "the dirtiest . . . in all history."

How much does a man put of himself into a constant struggle for three years to get started a new peacekeeping security organization—always with the memory of the tragic failure of Wilson, and always under the jaundiced eye of the Senate of the United States?

Ask any experienced lawyer about his nervous tension before and during a trial in which the life or death of one client is involved. How must Roosevelt's nerves have felt about the trial of wits, and armed power, and horse trading, and grand global politics before and during Yalta where, he was convinced, the fate of the entire future world was involved? He carried the conferences off with an apparent nonchalance approaching gaiety, always sitting at the head of the table, conciliating, trading, insisting, yielding, intent on his main objectives but never neglecting the other objectives; but it was a trial which left its effects. I know because I came home with him on his ship and saw him each day as he sat on the top deck with his daughter Anna—thinking, wondering, planning. The buoyancy of the recent campaign, the excitement of preparing to go to Yalta had disappeared. In their place was gray fatigue—sheer mental and physical exhaustion. To add to it all, his great friend and secretary who had spent many years with him, General Edwin Watson, died on the cruiser on the way home. The President never regained his usual self until we approached the shores of the United States.

Add up all these trials and tribulations—and ponder the miracle that this one man could stand it as long as he did.

A young congressman from Texas named Lyndon B. Johnson expressed what Roosevelt had gone through physically and spiritually when he said, after Roosevelt's death, that Roosevelt was the only person he had ever known who was never afraid: "God, how he could take it for us all!"

On April 12, 1945, the President died.

All through the United States there was the same kind of public reaction; the same sense of personal loss. Millions of people in America and in the rest of the world, too, seemed to have lost a close relative or dear friend—even though they never laid eyes on him.

What was the source of this intimate contact which one man had been able to cement with so many millions of human beings in widely scattered parts of the world, of different races and religions, of different trades and occupations, of different stations in life?

As I watched those miles of mourning faces along the sidewalks of Washington while the coffin was being borne through the street, I thought about this unique phenomenon in American political life. There was something more to it than an eloquent, moving radio voice. There was something more than a smile, than friendliness, warmth—something more even than the fighting desire to bring a better life to the many who needed help.

There had been many statesmen who spent their political lives in the same kind of fight as Roosevelt in behalf of the forgotten man. Yet none of them evoked the kind of affection that I saw in those faces.

His unique appeal to all the people of the world was—again—closely connected with his style of action and courage, and particularly with his style of expression.

I think that the great reason for Roosevelt's place in the hearts and minds of people was his peculiar style of being able to make them feel that he was associating himself *personally* with each one of them in the aspirations of each person for something better in life than he had. Roosevelt did not seem to be aloof and far-removed, fighting their battles as a commanding general does in headquarters far behind the fighting itself. He did not seem to the people to be operating from the rarefied atmosphere of the White House. He was right down in the sweaty arena with them, side by side, expressing better than they could what they were thinking, doing or trying to do, what they wanted done, taking his strength and his courage from their strength and their support—making them feel that he and they were all fighting the battle for social justice together.

He could identify himself with each individual worker in the sweatshops as he led the fight to build up trade unions and brought about better working conditions, higher wages, shorter hours, and a higher dignity for labor.

The worker thought of him as a sympathetic and understanding friend who was fighting shoulder to shoulder with him against all labor baiters and exploiters.

The farmer recognized in him a warm human being to whom relief of agriculture did not mean dry statistics and economic charts. Here was a President who seemed to be personally interested in the mortgage on each farmer's farm, who was fighting to reduce his debts and raise his income so he could buy more shoes and schooling for his children; to get him rural electrification so that the farmer's wife could lead an easier life; to promote soil conservation so that the farmer would not see the fertility of his old farm run off to the river. It was in terms of all the members of the farm family, of human beings, that Roosevelt thought and talked; and he was able to make each farmer who listened to him think that he was the specific farmer the President had in mind.

Roosevelt was also able to do this with the small businessman who was looking for some protection from his monopolistic competitors; with the housewife and the older people who saw their money melting away in the increased cost of living; with the wage earner who wanted some protection against unemployment, old age and sickness.

As a war leader, and as an architect of the structure of peace, he never seemed to be talking down to the common people, enunciating theoretical principles and lofty precepts; rather, he seemed to be expressing in simple terms the unexpressed yearnings of each man, woman and child who listened to him and who wanted to live in a world without war. The Atlantic Charter and the Four Freedoms were not handed down by Roosevelt as something from on high. He spoke of them in simple terms as the desires and needs of all human beings in the world, as ideals which could be attained—and would be—and each person who heard the President talk about them could feel: "Yes, that's what I'd like to see happen myself."

And in the same way, the poorest and lowliest of the starving millions of India and China and the downtrodden colonies of Africa, the refugee in the streets of Jerusalem, the Frenchman, the Italian, the Dutchman picking his way through the rubble of his destroyed city—each person in the great masses of people all over the world—felt that here was a man who was fighting, not only *for* him but *with* him. Fighting for some peace and security for him as an individual, for some better food and shelter and clothing for him and his family, for his freedom of speech and religion, for the freedom from want and from fear of another devastating war.

How was Roosevelt able to do this? The answer is difficult. This much is sure. Roosevelt *thought* in terms of human beings rather than of abstract problems. To him every problem was defined in terms of its effect on people. And since he did think in those terms, it was not extraordinary that the people should come to realize it—to recognize him as an associate in their struggles and hopes for a better life and for a better world. And now that he was dead, it was not extraordinary that they should mourn him as a departed ally and close friend with whom they had fought shoulder to shoulder, without whom they would now have to get along somehow as best they could.

"All that is within me cries out to go back to my home on the Hudson River," he had said in 1944 in consenting to run again. He lies buried now in the rose garden of that home on the Hudson River. His tombstone is a simple one; on it are inscribed only his name and the years of his life.

There should be added the words Sam Rayburn said of him years later:

"He saved the nation, not once, but twice." And there should also be added to that: "The second time, he also saved the civilization of the world."

4

HARRY S. TRUMAN

(1884–1972)

President, April 12, 1945, to January 20, 1953

As they drove away from his first official meeting with President Harry S. Truman, General George Marshall observed to his colleagues—probably with some apprehension: "We shall not know what he is really like until the pressure begins to be felt."[1] Perhaps Molotov, the Russian Foreign Minister, could have given them an indication after he received a Presidential tongue-lashing on April 23, 1945, regarding Russian violation of the Yalta Agreement to establish free elections in Poland, and a stern warning that he expected the Russians to keep their word. Molotov is reported to have complained: "I have never been talked to like that in my life," and the President to have answered: "Carry out your agreements and you won't get talked to like that."[2] The words, possibly strengthened in the telling, reflect the peppery President's manner. Harry Truman talked straight from the shoulder—sometimes, as Speaker Rayburn complained, "straight from the hip"—and his actions were just as direct and sometimes brash.

The Republican leader of the House, Joe Martin, answered the query of anxious New Dealers after Truman—on September 6, only four days after V.J. Day—sent to Congress a twenty-one-point program on domestic legislation for the postwar world: "Now," said the ultra-conservative Martin, "nobody should have any more doubt. Not even President Roosevelt ever asked so much at one sitting. It is just a case of out-New Dealing the New Deal."[3]

A sober judgment was given by Admiral William D. Leahy at the beginning of the Potsdam Conference: "This new President is alright. He couldn't be more different from Roosevelt, but he has the necessary qualities to make a good President and Commander-in-Chief."[4] He went on to describe President Truman as a quick learner, a tremendously hard worker who had prepared meticulously for the Potsdam Conference. He had poured over the information prepared by the State Department and the Joint Chiefs of Staff during the eight-day Atlantic crossing on a cruiser and had "squeezed facts and opinions out of us all day long."[5] He added that the President was more systematic than Roosevelt and had considerably revived the morale of long-neglected government departments, especially the Department of State.

When Averell Harriman was asked why he returned to Washington immediately after President Roosevelt's death, the former Ambassador to Russia replied that he believed Truman did not know what was going on and therefore returned to brief him. When he arrived he found that Truman was an avid reader and had already read all of the messages that had gone back and forth between the three powers, knew exactly what had transpired, and had grasped the situation. His overwhelming concern was to ascertain exactly what had been in President Roosevelt's mind for, he said, "He was elected President, not I." Later, said Harriman, he acted on his own.[6]

Citizens of the world, the heads of government and their people, were taking Harry Truman's measure. Each started with the knowledge of his lack of formal education; but they little knew the years that those eyes behind thick lenses had spent reading history—history of the United States and of the countries of the world. This truly self-taught man, who never went to a university, is now linked with Woodrow Wilson, who had been the president of a university, as "the two twentieth century Presidents most sensitive to the constitutional origins of the Presidency."[7]

This homespun Midwesterner had been catapulated into the presidency at a dramatic moment when the war was nearing its end and the peace had to be made —a peace that would affect all the nations of every continent. This man of simple manner and meager speaking ability stepped into the arena which had been dominated by the charm, sophistication and facility of Franklin D. Roosevelt. Yet, at Potsdam when Lord Moran asked Churchill whether Truman had real ability, he answered: "I should think he has. At any rate, he is a man of immense determination. He takes no notice of delicate ground, he just plants his foot firmly on it."[8] And this was to be his style and his strength.

Why had this man, unrecognized by citizens who lived beyond the borders of the State of Missouri, been chosen by President Roosevelt as his Vice President in 1944? Surely there were others more prominent with whom Roosevelt was more closely affiliated; they each had desirable attributes marred in that shrewd politician's estimation by some that he considered to be a political Achilles' heel. While Truman lacked a country-wide reputation, he had the admiration and respect of the Congress where personal character must pass through difficult tests. He was loyal, hardworking, honest, conscientious and, though lacking glamor, he had a splendid record of accomplishment. He had lived down the stigma of being the protégé of Boss Pendergast, notoriously corrupt and finally sent to jail. That stigma had caused Roosevelt to support Truman's opponent in the Missouri senatorial primary of 1940; had led Roosevelt to ignore Truman in his first term, to deprive him of the legitimate patronage that was a senator's prerogative to dispense according to custom, and to give it to his adversary. Roosevelt even tried to get Truman to accept an appointment to the Interstate Commerce Commission, telling him that he didn't have a chance to be re-elected. Truman said the offer came "in a round-about way," and added, "I sent word, however, that if I received only one vote I intended to make the fight for vindication and re-election to the Senate."[9]

Make the fight he did and without funds. He had no personal funds and it was difficult to obtain campaign contributions for the word had gone out that he was a loser—just as it would again in 1948. Truman had had to fight for everything he had ever achieved in his life and he continued to fight for everything he believed in for the remainder of his life—fighting fair and square. He won the primary and he won the election. He won on a New Deal platform; indeed, he had consistently voted for New Deal measures. Therefore it was ironic that Roosevelt had ignored and opposed him and now chose him without informing him personally. Though loyal to President Roosevelt as senator, during his short vice-presidency and as President he bore an inward grievance that only intimates could very occasionally glean.

Al Smith would have asked, "What is the record?" What was Truman's record which recommended him? Before detailing the senatorial record upon which President Roosevelt based his choice, it is pertinent very briefly to review Truman's early life and its influences upon the future senator and President, which are, of course, part of the record.

He came from a sturdy stock of pioneers who settled at a junction of the Missouri River in a town that grew into Kansas City. Harry was a farm boy who experienced the vissicitudes of farm and business life, and found social bonds and executive experience when he joined Battery B of the Missouri National Guard, which was recruited into the regular Army in World War I. Truman hoped to become a section sergeant; but in those days the enlisted men elected their officers and the rookie was elected first lieutenant, then named regimental canteen officer with Eddie Jacobson of later haberdasher fame as his assistant. This was in addition to his regular Army duties. Here he first demonstrated his ability to organize; and here he demonstrated too his value of comradeship and his leadership. After his Artillery School training in France he was made captain and then adjutant to the 129th's Second Battalion and accompanied the outfit to Angers in Brittany for further training at Camp Coetquidan, which he knew from boyhood reading as an old Napoleonic artillery base.

Battery D of the 129th had made it so tough for its commanding officers that three had been forced out before Truman was put in command. One had been thrown out of the Army because of his failure to control the men; another had suffered a breakdown. The first day that Truman took command, the men staged a fake stampede of their horses. Then after taps they got into a fight among themselves, broke cots and chairs and sent four men to the infirmary. In the morning, Truman called his non-commissioned officers. "Men," he told the sergeants and corporals, "I know you've been making trouble for your previous commanders. From now on, you're going to be responsible for maintaining discipline in your squads and sections, and if there are any of you who can't, speak up right now and I'll bust you back right now."[10] He knew how to be tough when the occasion demanded, and he always would.

The 129th was with the first Army composed entirely of American divisions to face the Germans. They were in the midst of the heaviest of fighting—Captain Truman in the fore. The regiment's historian wrote: "How many of the men of the infantry, digging in on the open hillsides overhanging Charpentry and Baulny, owe their lives to the alertness, initiative and efficiency of Captain Truman and to the quick responsiveness and trained efficiency of his men at the guns!"[11] Alertness, initiative and efficiency were the traits that marked him for the vice-presidency.

Truman's Army experience was a meaningful part of his life. When we visited him in Independence a few years before he died, his conversation dwelt at length upon details of those days. It was, by chance, an Army acquaintance that made possible his political career—a career for which his longing dated back to boyhood when in 1892 his father had climbed to the roof of his house and tied an enormous 44-star flag to the weather vane in celebration of Grover Cleveland's victory. It was to Jim Pendergast, a nephew of Boss Tom Pendergast and an Army acquaintance, that Truman confided his political ambition—to run for county judge for Eastern Jackson County. The judge's duties included levying taxes and caring for roads and county buildings. Jim went to his father, Mike Pendergast, and Tom Pendergast's brother who was in charge of that area, with the suggestion that he and the other men of the Battery would like to have

Truman on the county ticket for judge of the Eastern District of Jackson County. Truman became Mike's candidate. However, the candidate was opposed by four others in the primary, one of whom was supported by the Big Boss, Tom Pendergast. Chances of winning were very slim, but his wartime buddies rallied round and the seemingly impossible was obtained. In January 1923 he became Judge Truman—a legal misnomer, for the county judge was an administrative and not a judicial post; it required no legal training.

Truman, establishing a routine he was to follow as senator, familiarized himself with every county road, hedge and viaduct, and knew down to the last detail the diet and operating expenses of the homes for the elderly and juveniles. "The roads were his biggest headache. . . . Shoddily constructed, with no attention paid to standard engineering practices, the roadbeds crumbled faster than they could be repaired. . . . [His predecessor] had also run the county into debt by more than a million dollars. Yet despite these burdens and Pendergast machine rule, Truman managed to improve some of the roads and cut his inherited county debt by almost $700,000 in about two years."[12] The Kansas City *Star*, a Republican newspaper and perennial battler against the Pendergast machine, praised Truman in an editorial when he ran for re-election,[13] and supported him in a fight which he lost. Out of a job and broke, this future President of the United States became a membership salesman for the Kansas City Automobile Club, and learned the hazards of various business ventures which did not end successfully.

In 1926, turned down by Boss Pendergast as a candidate for the $25,000 job of county collector, Truman ran successfully for the position of presiding judge of the county court of which he had been a member judge. There he distinguished himself by engaging expert engineers and floating a bond issue for the construction of 224 miles of new roads, thereby overcoming the resistance of the Big Boss. A telling characteristic is demonstrated by the reported conversation between Pendergast and Truman. "You can't do it," said Tom Pendergast. "They'll say I'm going to steal it . . . every other presiding judge [tried it] for twenty years." Truman replied with his customary style of determination and self-confidence: "I'll tell the people what I mean to do and they'll vote the bonds." Pendergast jeered: "Go tell the voters anything you want."[14] Pendergast allowed this improbable officeholder his way, never believing that he would be successful and surely not crediting him with public success that again in 1930 won the support of the people and of the Kansas City *Star*. His honest efficiency contrasted with the financial finagling of the Kansas City politicians, and in spite of his modest manner his reputation grew—much as it did later in Washington. But it had not grown sufficiently to mark him as a senatorial candidate. Chance did that. Senator Bennett Clark proclaimed that he would beat the Pendergast machine and name Missouri's next senator to join him in the Capitol. It was definitely a Democratic year and Pendergast, anger aroused, was out to maintain his supremacy. Three men turned down his offer of nomination to run against Clark's candidate, Jacob L. Milligan; then—and nobody knows why—he offered it to Harry S. Truman, whom he had previously refused to have nominated for county collector, Governor and congressman.

It became a three-sided race when John J. Cochran of St. Louis, a formidable opponent with excellent qualifications and a strong supporter of FDR as a member of the House of Representatives, announced his candidacy. He had both the public praise of President Roosevelt and the backing of the powerful St. Louis machine. It was a tough primary. In his opening speech, Truman hitched onto

Roosevelt's lapel, which each of his opponents claimed for themselves: "I follow him for his large honest intent; for his engaging democracy of thought and action; for his view that individual security is the basis of universal security."[15] The words, poorly delivered and more eloquent than was his style, were expressive of Harry Truman's credo—then and thereafter.

Truman electoral victories were always hard-won and unanticipated. This was no exception; he won the primary by a statewide plurality of 40,000 votes. The November election was a foregone conclusion; the Republican incumbent was unpopular and there was a Democratic swing throughout the nation. But Truman was to go to Washington under a cloud through which it was difficult to shine. The St. Louis *Post-Dispatch* printed an editorial which was widely circulated: "Under our political system an obscure man can be made the nominee of a major political party for the high office of United States Senator by virtue of the support given him by a city boss. County Judge Truman is the nominee of the Democratic Party because Tom Pendergast willed it so. . . ."[16] This was the stigma he had to live down in the Senate.

Typical is the recollection of Bill Helm, Washington correspondent of the Kansas City *Journal Post,* that Truman walked into his office unexpectedly shortly after he was elected, introduced himself, grinned like "two Cheshire cats" while he referred to himself as "only an humble member of the next Senate, green as grass and ignorant as a fool about practically everything worth knowing."[17]

His speech to the Kansas City Elks Club was also genuine Truman: ". . . I'll do the best I can and keep my feet on the ground. That's one of the hardest things for a Senator to do, it seems. All this precedence and other hooey accorded a Senator isn't very good for the Republic. The association with dressed-up diplomats has turned the heads of more than one Senator, I can tell you.

"My trouble is that I probably won't find a place to live. You see, I have to live on my salary, and a cubbyhole rents for a hundred and fifty dollars a month there. The ones that are fit to live in run from two hundred and fifty to five hundred a month, and, although it's hard to believe, there are some saphead Senators who pay fifteen hundred dollars a month for their apartments."[18]

When the country boy became President, he brought with him this simplicity and humility which the public first disparaged and then admired. These traits were not his because of humble origin or lack of learning. He came from good pioneering stock; sometimes his forebears were affluent; sometimes they struggled to make a living. His mother had attended the Baptist College for Women in Lexington, Missouri, and there gained her love of music which she taught Harry. His father was a mule trader, a grain trader, a politician fond of fisticuffs, a farmer at one time prosperous, who at another had to scrimp to buy a set of Shakespeare which he prized. Harry Truman was an educated man although he had not been able to go to a university. He had both culture and learning, but he often expressed himself in earthy terms which belied them to the public. Because he lacked a college education his respect for those who had one was excessive even during his presidency. In preparing for his senatorial post he was thorough as usual. Reading through the biographies of the members of the Senate he found that almost all were college graduates, and had held previously important positions. He was duly awed.

The Pendergast cloud that hung over Truman dissipated in the Senate as senators—both Republican and Democratic—came to know him and demonstrated their respect and affection. Among those who publicly demonstrated their trust were prominent senators of such diverse views as William Borah of Idaho, Arthur Vandenberg of Michigan, Sam Rayburn of Texas and Vice President Garner. The Senate "Club" rallied to him because of his sincerity, simplicity, good fellowship, dedication to his work and genuine ability. He became "one of the boys."

His record of votes is notable and included:

1935
For: Social security legislation, the Tennessee Valley Authority, death sentence for utility holding companies, Farmers' Loan Corporation, the Agricultural Adjustment Act, World Court adherence Resolution, and Wagner Labor Act.
1936
For: The Soil Conservation Act, Florida Ship Canal, and Passamaquoddy Dam.
1937
For: The Wagner-Steagal Low Cost Housing Bill, Fair Labor Standards Act, and reciprocal trade agreements.
1938
For: Cloture on anti-poll tax bill debate, Works Progress Administration Appropriation, and Naval Expansion.
1939
For: The Hatch Act listing political campaign contributions, and increased appropriations for aircraft and the Navy.
1940
For: Farm parity payments. *Against:* Proposals requiring Senate ratification of trade pacts.
1941
For: Extension of the Selective Service System and Ship Seizure Bill, strengthening U.S. preparation for war.
1942
For: The Price Control Act, renegotiation of war contracts, and cloture of the anti-poll tax bill debate which would have ended a Southern filibuster against the measure.
1943
For: Pay-as-you-go tax measures, continuing loan powers of the Federal Security Administration, and wage increases for rail workers. *Against:* Killing the National Resources Planning Board and National Youth Administration.[19]

Although the voting record demonstrates that he was a dedicated New Dealer, he was not a blind follower of President Roosevelt. He announced that he was opposed to a third term for the President. He did not support the White House veto of the tax bill which gave "relief not for the needy but for the greedy." His loyalty here was to his Senate colleagues who resented the language with which Roosevelt vetoed the bill—resented it as much as those castigated by Woodrow Wilson as "a little group of willful men." Loyalty was one of Truman's key characteristics. It is of great significance that although he had repeatedly in the past been hurt by President Roosevelt's opposition to him, he was loyal to him in the Senate, as Vice President and as President.

Another characteristic was his concern for the underprivileged who lacked influence, so well illustrated by an anecdote of his Senate secretary, Victor Messall: "One morning I brought him fifty folders of applications for appointments to West Point from Missouri boys. The folders were thick and contained recommendations from judges, state legislators, mayors, et cetera. We went through each folder methodically and finally we got down to a folder that contained no letter of recommendation—only a single-page application written in pencil on a sheet of cheap, rough paper. Truman read it and then he turned to me and ordered, 'Give him the appointment.' "[20] Perhaps he was qualified, perhaps not, but Truman knew what it was to rise without endorsements and his instantaneous reaction was for this boy.

It was in committee work that Truman distinguished himself and it was as chairman of the War Investigating Committee of World War II that he reached the pinnacle of that distinction. Assigned to the District Committee, which handled the affairs of the District of Columbia, when he first entered the Senate, modesty did not prevent him from resigning because the determined rookie senator "didn't come to the Senate to be a local alderman." The pinnacle was not reached without stepping stones, the most important of which was his service on the Interstate Commerce Committee, whose chairman was Burton K. Wheeler of Montana. There is no better example of Truman's persistent prodding to find information, to get at the root of any matter that interested him even though there was not the incentive of personal aggrandizement.

Wheeler introduced a resolution to investigate the American railroad system which was then, even as now, a "sick" industry, although at that time it did not have to compete with the airplane. Several roads were either bankrupt or on the verge of being so. Wheeler proposed to examine the financial management of this multi-million-dollar industry and introduce remedial legislation to protect stockholders and rehabilitate the carriers. In December 1936 he appointed a subcommittee to conduct the investigation. Senator Truman was so very disappointed that he was not made a member of the subcommittee that Wheeler permitted him to sit in on the hearings.

Steinberg says: "Reporters who covered the investigation said that 'for two years this inquiry plodded along through some of the dullest hearings ever recorded on Capitol Hill.' Yet Truman never missed a session. Hundreds of witnesses representing various railroads appeared to discuss and argue the complex financial matters. To gain a better understanding of what was going on, Truman began his own private study of the railroads. Often he spent evenings at the Library of Congress, scanning old newspaper files on the industry's financial morass. He also arranged for the Library to send him 50 volumes on the railroads which he read methodically. Senators who observed his strange pastime referred to him as 'eccentric.'

"When one of the Democratic members of the subcommittee finally withdrew because he found the hearings too dull, Wheeler promptly named Truman to replace him. Then, in the spring of 1937, Wheeler became one of the leaders opposing F.D.R.'s court-packing proposal and was soon so involved in the battle that he stopped attending the railroad hearings. Other committee members also got into that historic battle, and Truman found himself alone at the investigation. To maintain the status of the hearings, Wheeler elevated him to vice-chairman of the subcommittee. The promotion was swift and sudden, but from his observation of Wheeler [who was a born prosecutor, with a slashing style that wore witnesses down until they made incriminating admissions], and from his own intense reading, Truman proved himself a master investigator.

"One of the first railroad lines he looked into was the bankrupt Missouri-Pacific in his own state. Subtle threats came from railroad lobbyists, and bags of mail poured in from Missouri demanding that he call off the investigation. But Truman refused to be intimidated. 'Don't ease up on anything,' he told the subcommittee staff. 'Treat this investigation just as you do all the others.' . . . He was soon accusing the Missouri-Pacific of false book-keeping and fraudulent stock transactions and proving his points from the railroad's own financial records."[21]

One of the great by-products of this subcommittee chairmanship was his introduction to Justice Louis D. Brandeis, who became a great influence upon Truman as he had been upon Wilson. Truman was taken to one of Brandeis's weekly teas by Max Lowenthal, whom Wheeler had appointed counsel to the subcommittee. There Truman became a weekly visitor, listening to Harvard lawyers hold forth on constitutional law and to discussions of the philosophy of the New Deal, and to Brandeis who, Truman said, "would back me in a corner and pay no attention to anyone else while he talked transportation to me. . . ."[22]

On June 3, he made his first preliminary report of the railroad investigation to the Senate. It was not couched in Brandeis phrases. "Some of the country's greatest railroads have been deliberately looted by their financial agents. Speaking of the Rock Island reminds me that the first railroad robbery was committed on the Rock Island back in 1873 just east of Council Bluffs, Iowa. The man who committed that robbery used a gun and a horse and got up early in the morning. He and his gang took a chance of being killed and eventually most were. That railroad robber's name was Jesse James. The same Jesse James held up the Missouri Pacific in 1876 and took the paltry sum of seventeen thousand dollars from the express car. About thirty years after the Council Bluffs holdup, the Rock Island went through a looting by some gentlemen known as the 'Tin Plate Millionaires.' They used no guns but they ruined the railroad and got away with seventy million dollars or more. They did it by means of holding companies. Senators can see what 'pikers' Mr. James and his crowd were alongside of some real artists."[23]

The speech was probably delivered haltingly and without emphasis, but its content was pungent and contained Roosevelt's style of imagery. This was just the beginning of the battle which was to last over four years, but with the assistance of Lowenthal's drafting and Wheeler's work in affecting a satisfactory agreement with the difficult House conferees, the Transportation Act of 1940 became law.

Chance so often played into Truman's hands. Once more it did so as the Pendergast cloud again hung over his head. When informed of Pendergast's indictment in April 1939, he had told the reporter, "I am very sorry to hear it. I know nothing about the details, nor why the indictment was voted. Tom Pendergast has always been my friend and I don't desert a sinking ship." Although he was re-elected in 1940, the new Pendergast cloud was not dissipated. By 1941, new Army camps were being established through the country; defense contracts were being awarded. Senators were scrambling to get as many as possible for their constituents. Truman, however, was snubbed by the War and Navy Departments, presumably on White House orders.

About this time he received letters describing the tremendous waste in construction of Fort Leonard Wood at Rolla, Missouri. Truman decided to look into the matter himself.

"At the camp he found workers dawdling, some asleep on the job, and great confusion everywhere. Valuable equipment lay unprotected from the elements. He quizzed workers, foremen and contractors and worked up tables of costs, wages and expenditures. All of it added up to a tremendous waste of manpower, money and material.

"Before returning to Washington, he completed a tour of 30,000 miles, checking several other camps under construction as well as defense plants in a perimeter from Florida out to Texas, Oklahoma, up to Nebraska and back again through Michigan. 'The trip was an eye opener,' he said. Almost all projects were on a cost-plus basis: the higher the costs, the greater the profits. Nowhere did he see any sign of prior planning; everything was makeshift."[24]

The trip was not a chance trip; it was taken according to his style of scrutiny of details. The opportunity came when he introduced Senate Resolution 71, calling for a committee of five senators to investigate the operation of the vast defense program. In his earthy way he warned: "It won't do any good digging up dead horses after the war is over like last time. The thing to do is dig this stuff up now and correct it."[25] At the same time the rabidly anti-Roosevelt Congressman Cox of Georgia was in the process of having the House pass a resolution to investigate defense contracts. Fearing that Cox would do a hatchet job and desiring to stop any real investigation, Senator James Byrnes rushed to the Senate Chamber on March 1, 1941, and with only sixteen senators present secured unanimous consent to bring up Truman's resolution and secured its passage without debate. Consequently the House dropped Cox's proposal.

Inspired by the War and Navy Departments, who feared a repetition of the obstructive Civil War Committee, Senator James F. Byrnes hurried to have Resolution 71 passed—only in order to block the more serious threat of the Cox investigation. He had no intention of implementing the Truman Committee and therefore not only blocked an appropriation sufficient to make it operative, but also influenced the make-up of the committee so that most of the members were new senators like Truman with relatively little senatorial power. He failed, however, to take the measure of the junior senator from Missouri, who went directly to the Justice Department and asked Attorney General Robert H. Jackson for his best, hard-hitting lawyer. Hugh Fulton, who had prosecuted some of the Justice Department's major cases, cautiously asked the chairman of the Special Senate Committee to Investigate the National Defense Program whether the committee intended merely to get headlines. The answer was characteristic: "You get the facts. That's all we want. Don't show anybody any favors. We haven't any axes to grind, nor any sacred cows. This won't be whitewash or a witch-hunt."[26] It was neither.

From the $15,000 appropriation for the committee which was meant to strangle it, Fulton was paid a salary of $9,000, leaving $6,000 for all other expenses. The undaunted Truman borrowed personnel from other departments —the future Justice of the Supreme Court Tom Clark from Justice, and so on. They remained on the payroll of the department from which they were borrowed, an old Washington practice.

He borrowed a copy of the hearings of the Civil War Committee from the Library of Congress and learned not to repeat its mistakes; therefore when the Republican Senators Vandenberg, Brewster and Taft tried to influence him to conduct his committee as a Committee on the Conduct of the War, Truman, knowing its history, refused to do so. His committee never advocated changes in military strategy or in the size or disposal of the defense effort. Its sole purpose was to investigate the operation of the defense program, and to uncover graft, waste and inefficiency. It is estimated that the committee's probes and disclosures saved the government billions of dollars, and that some of these disclosures saved many lives.

There was no trifling with this chairman or its members who worked as a team. Rank did not daunt him. Opposed to the position taken by co-director of the Office of Production Management (OPM), Sidney Hillman, he reported to the Senate on October 29, 1941: "A responsible company has made a low bid. It is prepared to perform and is capable of performing if not illegally interfered with. Mr. Sidney Hillman advises that it be denied the contract and that the taxpayers pay several hundred thousands of dollars more because Mr. Hillman fears trouble from what he calls irresponsible elements in the American Federation of Labor."[27]

In January 1942, he presented the committee report to the Senate. No punches were pulled. The automobile industry was censured for failing to convert its plants to war production while continuing to produce millions of pleasure cars; the defense program was criticized for ignoring small firms, for its "golden goose" contracted arrangements, and for purchasing whatever airplane manufacturers produced instead of forcing the production of needed planes at full capacity; the problems of metal shortages and their causes were examined. Businessmen were called the "dupes of peddlers of influence"; and legislation to curb the Five and Ten Percenters was requested.

The ultimate result of the committee's first report was unforeseeable, but it had immediate repercussions which were calculable. The Senate increased the committee's appropriation from $15,000 to $100,000; the cloud that had enveloped Truman was completely dissipated in the Senate and was dissolving in the White House; he was getting a good press around the country. Although he now received many requests to speak, he was by no means a folk hero for his manner of speaking dulled his audience and he lacked the magnetism that could properly reflect his worth.

Most important to his future was the fact that President Roosevelt now looked to Truman and not to Senator Clark or Governor Stark for recommendations for Missouri appointments. One of these appointments was to play a major role in his selection as Vice President—Robert E. Hannegan. Bob Hannegan, one of the political bosses in St. Louis, had switched his support to Truman at the very end of his 1940 campaign for re-election—a switch that actually turned the tide for him. When, in 1942, the position of Collector of Internal Revenue at St. Louis became available, Harry Truman recommended the man who was instrumental in gaining his election. When the St. Louis *Globe-Democrat* heard that Truman was promoting Hannegan for Collector, it charged that Hannegan was the "most discredited boss of a discredited political machine."

Truman told reporters: "Hannegan carried St. Louis three times for the President and for me. If he is not nominated there will be no Collector at St. Louis."[28] Roosevelt felt the same way, and in June 1942, he appointed Hannegan to the post. Hannegan worked hard as Collector, attended night school to study taxation and earned for his office, which had been rated the worst in the country, the reputation as the most efficient by the Bureau in Washington. In October 1943, with Truman's help Hannegan moved to Washington as Commissioner of Internal Revenue, and on January 22, 1944, he became the chairman of the National Democratic Committee—a most influential post.

Having described Truman's style and record before he was chosen to run as Vice President, we return to the question of why President Roosevelt picked him. This can perhaps best be explained by my husband's account, written in 1951: "The President wanted to make sure above all that the candidate nominated was a liberal in complete sympathy with the New Deal and with the Administration's foreign policy and postwar program. He was considering several possibilities, which he discussed from time to time with different people. He weighed carefully not only the political philosophy of each candidate but also the potential political strength that each might add to the ticket. There was one man who seemed to combine political liberalism and political strength to a greater degree than anyone else, and the President was about ready to decide on him. He did not make up his mind definitely, however, until the close of a conference at the White House held on July 11, 1944. . . .

"Several possibilities, including Rayburn, Barkley, William O. Douglas, Byrnes, Truman and others, were discussed. As each name came up, it was appraised coldly and calmly; the merits of each were measured from the point of view of political strength and sympathy with the President's program. When discussion about one man was ended, they passed on to the next. Some of those present urged favorites of their own. Hannegan, who would be responsible for getting the man they decided on nominated by the convention, strongly favored Truman, who had befriended him; but leaned over backward to be fair to the other candidates. The President turned to each of his guests and asked him to express an opinion about each name under discussion.

"The political weaknesses of Byrnes were gone over in great detail: the fact that labor was only lukewarm, if not slightly hostile, to him; the fact that the Negroes would oppose him because of his Southern political and social background; the effect of his Catholic birth and later adoption of the Protestant faith. Some of the conferees thought that the matter of religion would not be important, but all agreed that the antipathy of the Negroes and the lack of enthusiasm on the part of labor would hurt the ticket in the larger Northern cities. These latter considerations weighed more heavily with the President than the religious one. He knew that labor had the same doubts about Byrnes' liberalism that he had.

"Everyone seemed to take for granted that Wallace was out; not much time was spent in discussing him. They all knew that Roosevelt's mind had been made up about him for several days. The President mentioned the names of John Winant and Justice Douglas as possibilities, but the conferees had no enthusiasm for either of them, feeling that neither would add any vote-getting to the ticket.

"When Truman's name came up, it seemed to find favor with everyone present. His qualifications as a candidate and as a prospective Vice-President were discussed fully and frankly and approvingly; no one could find any major disqualification. The President spoke very highly of him—of his ability and his liberalism and his loyalty.

"When all the names had been fully canvassed, the President said with an air of finality: 'It's Truman.' The conference was over—the next President of the United States had been selected."[29]

Added to this is the sound explanation of Harry Hopkins: "The President had his eye on him for a long time. The Truman Committee record was good—he'd got himself known and liked around the country and above all he was very popular in the Senate. That was the biggest consideration. The President wanted somebody that would help him when he went up there and asked them to ratify the peace."[30] Roosevelt was mindful of Wilson's difficulties.

But no one told Harry S. Truman that he was the President's choice until the following week when he was at the convention. Before Truman had left for Chicago, Jimmy Byrnes phoned him and asked him for his support for his candidacy. Truman, in ignorance of what had happened, promised Byrnes his support, and agreed to make the nominating speech for him at the convention.

Having committed himself to Byrnes, Truman loyally stuck to that commitment until Byrnes finally withdrew. President Truman always resented the fact that he had been placed in the position of seeming disloyalty to a friend. He would rightfully query, "Why didn't he tell me?"

His term as Vice President was brief and uneventful. He had never been a confidant of President Roosevelt and during the short period of his vice-presidency he did not become one. This he privately resented forever after for he was completely unprepared for the Herculean task that lay before him in foreign affairs and he realized it. In justice to President Roosevelt it must be said that he left Washington two days after inauguration for the trip to Yalta and did not return until the end of February. He left for Warm Springs on March 30, having been in Washington only thirty of the eighty-two days of his fourth term. Between Election Day and his departure for Yalta he was so occupied with military matters, preparation for the Yalta Conference, preparation for launching the United Nations and consideration of postwar problems that he was probably oblivious of the fact that there was a man named Truman who might become President if he died—an event he did not contemplate.

Although my husband and I had been with the small group of officials and their wives on the South Portico of the White House when President Truman took his oath of office as Vice President, my recollection is of the outgoing Vice President Henry Wallace and not, on that occasion, of the new Vice President. Walking home late that afternoon from the simple wartime festivities, we talked about the good sportsmanship of Henry Wallace, how well he conducted himself under the difficult circumstances. As both the Wallaces and Rosenmans had apartments at the Wardman Park Hotel, I suggested that it might be nice if we called upon the Wallaces that evening. Sam thought the idea right but he was of the opinion that all of Henry Wallace's close friends would be with him and we might be intruding. Later, he changed his mind and suggested I phone and find out whether they would like us to come over. They would. When we got there Henry was listening to his Russian language records; he and Mrs. Wallace were alone. We spent a pleasant evening. Henry Wallace had been in Washington for twelve years; he and Mrs. Wallace were alone when friends should have gathered round.

President Truman was a gregarious man; he quickly summoned friends whom he had accumulated over the years—at school, in the Army, in the Senate—to fill positions in the White House, in the agencies and in his Cabinet.

Some were able, some mediocre, some incapable but had always been loyal to him and he to them. Those who had been his buddies in World War I were the modern counterparts of Damon and Pithias. Some had had no previous government experience and of those who had, there were some who proved to be ill-fitted to the roles assigned. He leaned heavily for advice upon those members of the Roosevelt administration whom he asked to remain.

My first recollection of President Truman was one of amazement for I had never seen the President of the United States that I knew walk. Directly after the funeral service for President Roosevelt in the East Room of the White House, Sam and I along with other Roosevelt personnel had gone to the office wing. I believe we were in Admiral McIntyre's office with the door open when along the corridor walked a genial little man—President Truman. It seemed incongruous.

He was probably as ill at ease as were we. As we grew to know this President, we found a man very different from President Roosevelt—one whom we could admire, respect for his own qualities, and for whom we could have affection even as we had for Franklin D. Roosevelt.

This man was, as Admiral Leahy said, "a quick learner" and one can see the comprehension and self-confidence that he acquired in just one month by reading the five-page long-hand letter he wrote to Mrs. Roosevelt on May 10. Mrs. Roosevelt had expressed surprise in her column on that date that the Russians had delayed their announcement of the end of the war almost a day after the simultaneous announcements by Truman and Churchill,[31] and so he wrote in explanation:

THE WHITE HOUSE
Washington

May 10, 1945

Dear Mrs. Roosevelt:

You [sic] note of the 8th is most highly appreciated. The whole family were touched by your thoughtfulness.

I noticed in your good column today you expressed some surprise at the Russian attitude on the close of the European War.

I think I should explain the situation to you. On Wednesday April 25th our Minister to Sweden sent a message to me saying that Himmler wanted to surrender to Gen. Eisenhower all their troops facing the Western Front and that the Germans would continue to fight the Russians. Before our State Department could get the message deciphered the Prime Minister called me from London and read the message to me. That was the great mystery of the trip to the Pentagon Building.

The matter was discussed with our Staff and the offer was promptly refused. The Russians were notified of our joint action. Prince Bernadotte of Sweden informed our Minister that Hitler had had a brain blowup of some sort and would be dead in twenty-four hours—so Himmler had informed him. The P.M. and I decided that when the Gestapo Butcher said a man would be dead in twenty-four hours he usually made good on his promise.

Negotiations went on for two more days—we, always insisting on complete unconditional surrender on all fronts. The German idea, of course, was to split the three great powers and perhaps make things easier for themselves. Our Headquarters kept me informed all the time by almost hourly messages. We were nearly at an agreement and the famous Connolly statement came out and completely upset the applecart. Himmler was displaced by Admiral Doenitz and a new start was made.

Germans delayed and delayed trying all the time to quit only on the Western Front. They finally offered Norway, Denmark, Holland and the French ports they still held but wanted to keep resisting the Russians. Our Commanding General finally told them that he would turn loose all we had and drive them into the Russians. They finally signed at Rheims the terms of unconditional surrender effective at 12:01 midnight of May 8–9.

In the meantime Churchill, Stalin and I had agreed on a simultaneous release at 9 A.M. Washington time, 3 P.M. London and 4 P.M. Moscow time. The Germans kept fighting the Russians and Stalin informed me that he had grave doubts of the Germans carrying out the terms. There was fighting on the Eastern front right up to the last hour.

In the meantime Churchill was trying to force me to break faith with the Russians and release on the 7th, noon Washington time, 6 P.M. London, 7 P.M. Moscow. I wired Stalin and he said the Germans were still firing. I refused Churchill's request and informed Stalin of conditions here and in England and that unless I heard from him to the contrary I would release at 9 A.M. May 8th. I didn't hear so the release was made, but fighting was still in progress against the Russians. The Germans were finally informed that if they didn't cease firing as agreed they would not be treated as fighting men but as traitors and would be hanged as caught. They then ceased firing and Stalin made his announcement the 9th.

He had sent me a message stating the situation at 1 A.M. May 8th and asking postponement until May 9th. I did not get the message until 10 A.M. May 8, too late, of course, to do anything.

I have been trying very carefully to keep all my engagements with the Russians because they are touchy and suspicious of us. The difficulties with Churchill are very nearly as exasperating as they are with the Russians. But patience I think must be our watchword if we are to have World Peace. To have it we must have the whole hearted support of Russia, Great Britain and the United States.

I hope this won't bore you too much—but I thought you'd like to know the facts. Please keep it confidential until it can be officially released.

Please accept my thanks again for your good message.

Most sincerely, Harry S. Truman[32]

Again and again President Truman in these early days stressed patience. When Russian, American, British and French military commanders met in Berlin on June 5, 1945, to organize the four-power occupation of Germany, Marshal Zhukov made it clear that the Soviet Union would not allow the quadripartite control machinery to go into operation until all troops had been removed to their respective zones. Robert Murphy, political adviser to Eisenhower, informed the State Department that the Supreme Commander did not consider retention of American forces in the Soviet zone wise. Harry Hopkins warned Truman on June 8 that failure to withdraw Anglo-American troops into their assigned occupation zones "is certain to be misunderstood by Russia as well as at home." Accordingly, Truman informed Churchill on June 11 that in view of these considerations, "I am unable to delay the withdrawal of American troops from the Soviet zone in order to use pressure in the settlement of other problems." Churchill replied bitterly on the 14th: "Obviously we are obliged to conform to your decision. . . . I sincerely hope that your action will in the long run make for a lasting peace in Europe."[33]

Truman later explained that although "politically we would have been pleased to see our lines extend as far to the east as possible," there were two reasons why he could not accept Churchill's proposal. Logistical considerations made it necessary to shift American troops from Europe to the Far East as quickly as possible, thus restricting opportunities for challenging Russian policy in Europe. Moreover, Truman believed that the best way to handle the Soviet was "to stick carefully to our agreements and to try our best to make the Russians carry out their agreements." The United States, he felt, could hardly disregard the commitments on occupation zones which Roosevelt had made, while at the same time insisting that Moscow carry out to the letter the Yalta agreements on Poland.[34] He was not only reflecting Roosevelt's patience and sense of justice but his own. He was slow to anger, but provocation could only go so far; then the fur would fly.

President Truman listened well and then used his judgment in taking the advice he deemed wise. He had been tough with Molotov after Averell Harriman's warning that the Russians were reneging upon their agreements. He decided to curb his impatience with the Russians after Secretary of War Stimson cautioned that "the Russians perhaps are being more realistic than we were in regard to their own security," and "outside of the United States, with the exception of Great Britain, there were few countries that understood free elections."

Asked in June 1945 at an off-the-record press conference for background purposes what the West could do about the way the Russians were behaving in eastern Europe, the President replied: "Be as patient with them as you possibly can . . . I don't blame them for wanting to have these states around them, just as we want Mexico and Canada to be friendly with us." He agreed that the Russians had made more concessions at San Francisco than any other nation, and added, "We had damned near as many differences with the British and not so much publicity about it." Asked whether the Russians weren't excessively suspicious, he answered: "They have a right to be suspicious. They are not a bit more suspicious of us than we are of them. . . . Half the editorials in this country are suspicious of Russia." A few days later he asked the Association of News Analysts to "Help me keep a clear and peaceable approach and understanding . . . I really think the Russians want to get along with us. . . . They have always been our friends, and it is in their best interest."[35]

This shift in attitude was not a case of mouthing the words of the last person to whom he talked. It was a shift by a sincere man faced by a multitude of issues with which he had never before grappled; it was a shift by a man influenced by reason.

He was also loath to change Roosevelt's military policies in the Far East although he was being urged to reconsider the necessity for the early entrance of Russia into the Japanese war. Military experts still considered Soviet participation in the Pacific war highly desirable. It must be remembered that the atomic bomb had not yet been exploded and no one knew how effective it would be. In addition to his desire to carry out Roosevelt's Yalta Agreement, the President had such respect for the military opinion that he would not have thought of considering civilian advice on a matter of military strategy which went contrary to military advice.

While observing President Truman's determination to carry on President Roosevelt's policies, it is necessary to consider an item in his own record which reflects an attitude he carefully kept under control during this period, but which should be kept in mind for it probably influenced future decisions. President Truman was a fair man, but set convictions lurked beneath his fairness and would occasionally surface. His feelings against the Russians had been expressed before Pearl Harbor when Hitler's forces invaded the Soviet Union on June 23, 1941, in one of his opinions which he "shot from the hip." Asked his reaction at the time by reporters, he said: "If we see that Germany is winning we ought to help Russia, and if Russia is winning we ought to help Germany and that way let them kill as many as possible, although I don't want to see Hitler victorious under any circumstances. Neither of them think anything of their pledged word."[36]

This man, whose practice was to delve into facts whether for solutions to problems or simply to satisfy his own curiosity and pursuit of learning, would also often make snap decisions upon matters which he had not studied. Thus Truman's style included action based upon study and a spontaneity of judgment that sometimes proved correct and sometimes got him into "hot water."

One such occasion was the blunder of May 1945, when President Truman abruptly terminated lend-lease without notice to England or to touchy and suspicious Russia. Ambassador Harriman had, on May 9, suggested that in view of Germany's surrender, the United States should *begin* curtailing lend-lease shipments to the Soviet Union, continuing to send supplies for possible use against Japan and those countries which would further our own policies. " 'The American attitude should be one of firmness,' Harriman stressed, 'while avoiding any implication of a threat or any indication of political bargaining.' Two days later Secretary of War Stimson found Truman 'vigorously enthusiastic' about implementing 'a more realistic policy' on Russian lend-lease, a position which the President said was 'right down his alley.' "

Professor Gaddis continues: "Undersecretary of State Grew and Foreign Economic Administrator Crowley, after consulting the War and Navy departments and Ambassador Harriman, recommended to Truman on May 11 that he (1) continue lend-lease shipments destined for use against the Japanese as long as Soviet entry into the Far Eastern war was anticipated; (2) continue to ship supplies needed to complete work on industrial plants already under construction; (3) cut off all other lend-lease shipments to the Soviet Union as soon as physically practicable. No new lend-lease protocol should be negotiated to replace the one which would expire on June 30. Instead the Administration should consider Soviet requests for aid 'on the basis of reasonably accurate information regarding the essentiality of Soviet military supply requirements and in the light of all competing demands for supplies in the changing military situation.' . . . Truman approved their proposal.

"But Crowley interpreted the lend-lease curtailment directive far more literally than Truman or Harriman had intended. Acting on the assumption that the new policy was 'when in doubt hold,' instead of 'when in doubt give' Foreign Economic Administration representatives . . . insisted that ships containing Russian lend-lease material not destined for use in the Far East should turn around and return to port. Harriman later described himself as having been 'taken aback' by this development. Truman, who had never intended to cut off supplies already on the way to the Soviet Union, quickly countermanded the turn-around order. But the diplomatic damage had been done. Through a diplomatic blunder the Truman Administration . . . gave Moscow the impression that it was trying to extract political concessions through a crude form of economic pressure."[37]

Harry Hopkins went to Moscow in the latter part of May at President Truman's request to convey his assurances of continuing Roosevelt's policies and his desire for a peaceful solution to all of the problems they faced. He was also to attempt to work out agreements upon disputed matters. Needless to say, the exercised dictator took the occasion to vent his displeasure about the manner in which lend-lease had been terminated.

Robert Sherwood takes up the story. "[Stalin] said that if the United States was unable to supply the Soviet Union further under Lend Lease that was one thing but that the manner in which it had been done had been unfortunate and *even brutal.* (Emphasis added) For example, certain ships had been unloaded and while it was true this order had been cancelled the whole manner in which it had been done had caused concern to the Soviet Government. If the refusal to continue Lend Lease was designed as pressure on the Russians in order to soften them up then it was a fundamental mistake. He said he must tell Mr. Hopkins frankly on a friendly basis much could be done but that reprisals in any form would bring about the exact opposite effect."[38]

President Truman later described this as his "first bad experience in the problem of delegating authority."[39] Accounts differ as to the President's knowledge of the contents of the order which he signed. If Professor Gaddis's carefully documented account is correct, Harry Truman knew what he was signing and signed it without due consideration. The President himself wrote in 1955: "Leo

Crowley, Foreign Economic Administrator, and Joseph C. Grew, Acting Secretary of State, came into my office after the Cabinet meeting on May 8 and said that they had an important order in connection with Lend-Lease which President Roosevelt had approved but not signed. It was an order authorizing the FEA and the State Department to take joint action to cut back the volume of Lend-Lease supplies when Germany surrendered. What they told me made good sense to me; with Germany out of the war, Lend-Lease should be reduced. They asked me to sign it. I reached for my pen and, without reading the document I signed it. . . . I think Crowley and Grew taught me this lesson early in my administration —that I must always know what is in the documents I sign."[40]

The President placed himself in a less favorable position. However, both accounts demonstrate his tendency to act too quickly upon a matter that he had not previously studied. And he characteristically points out that he had learned by his error. England forgave; but Russia, sensitive to an affront, real or fancied, did not. It was a spoke in the wheel that whirled toward the cold war.

Not only did Truman assume the presidency without knowledge or experience in foreign affairs; he faced problems in that field more complex than those of any President save Roosevelt and Wilson. Moreover, most of them were in midstream, so that it was necessary for him to grasp the minutiae of the past in order to direct the present and future actions and policies. The European war would come to an end within a month of his oath as President; military and civil decisions had to be made immediately. The vexatious question of reparations was in the forefront of his Allies' minds. Plans were under way for the San Francisco meeting to organize the United Nations—no simple matter, and the date had been set. The military estimated that it would take a massive effort to win the war against Japan. There were great difficulties in and with China. The atom bomb was in the making but its effectiveness was unknown and its use—if successful —posed a weight upon Presidential decision. The nation faced stupendous postwar conversion and demobilization questions; and the revitalization of the devasted countries and peoples of Europe had to be met. There were also agonizing European political adjustments to be made and decisions as to what extent America should participate in deciding those adjustments.

With all this thrust upon him so suddenly, a lesser man would have panicked. Truman remained outwardly calm, self-assured, worked sixteen hours a day, slept soundly, and fortified himself by recalling the following Lincoln quotation which he kept in a leather portfolio upon his desk: "I do the very best I know how— the very best I can; and I mean to keep doing so to the end. If the end brings me out all right, what is said against me won't amount to anything. If the end brings me out wrong, ten angels swearing I was right won't make any difference."[41]

The majority of the American people believed in 1945 that the United Nations Organization was the answer to world peace. They were ready to accept Woodrow Wilson's idealism as a practicality. They were ready to discard isolationism and to take active participation in world affairs. President Roosevelt had appointed a bi-partisan delegation to the United Nations Conference on International Organization before he died. The conference had made a beginning—a beginning that was naturally cemented by the threads of strife woven into compromises. The political backgrounds and ambitions of each country differed. President Truman addressed the closing session, pointing out to the delegates: "The Constitution of my own country came from a Convention which—like this one—was made up of delegates with many different views. Like this Charter, our Constitution came from a free and sometimes bitter exchange of conflicting opinions. When it was adopted, no one regarded it as a perfect document. But it grew and developed and expanded. And upon it there was built a bigger, a better, a more perfect union. . . .

"Out of all the arguments and disputes, and different points of view, a way was found to agree. Here in the spotlight of full publicity, in the tradition of liberty-loving people, opinions were expressed openly and freely. The faith and the hope of fifty peaceful nations were laid before this world forum. Differences were overcome. This Charter was not the work of any single nation or group of nations, large or small. It was the result of a spirit of give-and-take, of tolerance for the views and interests of others. . . .

"In spite of the many distractions which came to you in the form of daily problems and disputes about such matters as new boundaries, control of Germany, peace settlements, reparations, war criminals, the form of government of some of the European countries—in spite of all these, you continued the task of framing this document. . . .

"You have created a great instrument for peace and security and human progress in the world. The world must now use it. . . ."[42]

President Truman wisely referred to the difficulties that the founding fathers had had in agreeing upon a Constitution for the United States. His speech expressed President Wilson's fundamental thought that a charter of United Nations was but the initial document, which must be perfected by the participating nations as issues arose and as they worked together to make it a viable instrument for maintaining world peace.

Unfortunately, as in Philadelphia in 1787, the Charter had been forged with acrimonious discussions. Agreements had been reached which caused public disillusionment and furthermore feelings of frustration that were the birth pains of the cold war. The public Russian-American confrontation at San Francisco had two effects which were significant for the future. First, as Professor Gaddis says, it exposed prominent Republicans like John Foster Dulles (who acted as adviser to the American delegation) and Senator Vandenberg (who was a member of the delegation) "to the frustrations of dealing with the Russians. Both men came away from the experience convinced that the only way to negotiate with Moscow was to take a firm position and avoid compromise." It also made clear to the American people "the depth and extent of the divisions which separated the Soviet Union and the United States. Opinion polls showed that by the middle of May, 1945, the number of Americans who doubted Russia's willingness to cooperate with the United States after the war had risen to 38 per cent of those questioned, the highest figure since March of 1942. Even more significantly, Americans for the first time attributed the difficulties in inter-Allied relations more to the Soviet Union than to Great Britain. As late as February, 1945, a majority of those dissatisfied with the extent of Big Three cooperation had held Britain responsible. But San Francisco shifted the blame to Russia, where it would stay for the rest of the Cold War."[43]

Truman himself shifted back and forth from ire to understanding. His old feelings about Russia would surface and then be suppressed. Early in May he told Elmer Benson, acting chairman of the National Citizen's Political Action Committee, that "the Russians were like bulls in a china shop. . . . We've got to teach them how to behave." But when Benson protested that there would be no peace unless Americans learned to get along with the Soviet Union, Truman admitted: "That is right." On May 13, Joseph E. Davies found the President "much disturbed" over the Russian problem. Molotov had apparently gone to San Francisco "to make trouble," Truman charged, and the newspapers—"these damn sheets"—were making it worse. But when Davies attributed much of the tension at San Francisco to the anti-Soviet bias of American officials, Truman agreed that such hostility existed and promised to change the situation. Davies left a memorandum to the President which argued that "it is . . . wrong to assume that tough language is the only language they [the Russians] can understand."[44]

The civilian who has had little or no contact with official Washington does not appreciate the influences that the men at the desks in the departments—those who carry on the day-to-day business of the departments—have upon carrying out and influencing policy. Many of them in the State Department were reactionary and were in a position to affect the course of events. That was why President Franklin D. Roosevelt so often bypassed the State Department and why Mrs. Roosevelt, in replying to President Truman's long-hand letter of May 10, 1945 (see page 440), warned the new President: "A rumor has reached me that the message from Mr. Stalin to you was really received in plenty of time to have changed the hour but it was held back from you. Those little things were done to my husband now and then. That is one of the things your Military and Naval aides ought to watch very carefully."[45]

Churchill had been pressing for a Big Three meeting, but the President delayed naming a date as he felt the need of preparation. Perhaps the wily Prime Minister would have preferred an unprepared Truman whom he could dominate, but he did not reckon with Harry Truman's determination to *act* in the capacity of President as well as to be the President of the United States; for that he required time to learn all the facts, and he refused to be pressed into a premature meeting. Another matter required his deliberation: the budget. When he was ready, he set the date—July 16—for the Big Three meeting at Potsdam. (The conference did not begin until the 17th because Stalin's arrival was delayed as a result of a slight heart attack.)

Herbert Feis takes up the story: "The President was being cautioned against Churchill's haste. He was being told by some about him, among them Leahy, Davies, and Marshall, that the great Prime Minister was often more concerned with the salvage of British interests than with world harmony. This caused him to wonder whether the chance of smoothing out our relations with the Soviet rulers might not be better if the Americans first saw and talked with them alone. Constantly he was evading Churchill's cordial invitation to come first to England, an invitation extended with the idea that they might then move on to Germany *together*. (Emphasis added) . . . He answered, 'When and if such a meeting is arranged, it appears to me that in order to avoid any suspicion of our "ganging up" it would be advantageous for us to proceed to the meeting place separately.' "[46]

However, there were vital decisions that could not be deferred. The President, who had always had great respect for Harry Hopkins and believed rightly that he had Stalin's respect, asked Hopkins to go to Moscow to talk with Stalin—who welcomed the suggestion. It is of note that the President sent Hopkins without seeking Churchill's assent.

The first of Hopkins's six conferences with Marshal Stalin was on May 26. The Polish question was of paramount importance to both. On the first evening, at the mention of Poland, the Marshal made a pointed reply. Hopkins had said that it was not easy to identify the precise reasons for the current alienation of American opinion. "But among the various incidents, the most troubling one seemed to be 'our inability to carry into effect the Yalta Agreement on Poland.' About the causes of this, he said, President Truman, as well as the American public were bewildered."

Stalin said "the reason was clear: the Soviet Union wanted to have a free Poland but the British Conservatives were trying to prevent that, since they wished to revive the restraining alliance ('cordon sanitaire') around the borders of the Soviet Union."[47]

The solution to the Polish impasse was discussed and discussed; Truman and Churchill were made aware of the details as the talks progressed. "What Hopkins obtained from Stalin was an affirmation: (1) that the Soviet government did not intend to interfere with Polish affairs; (2) that it would not oppose the inclusion of independent political elements in the Polish government; and (3) that it would join with the American and British governments in seeing to it that the reorganized Polish government held free elections and respected individual rights and liberties.

"In return, Hopkins agreed (1) that only Poles who had accepted the Yalta accord were to be invited to consult with the Commission of Three; (2) that the Soviet government retained the right to dominate the outcome, since all members of the Commission of Three would have to approve any agreement reached by the Polish Commission (and if no accord was reached, the Red Army and the subservient Warsaw regime could continue to extend their control); and (3) that the Warsaw government was to have a dominant place in the reformed government. Also, Hopkins had refrained from challenging two decisive acts that the Soviet government had taken on its own. These were the turning over of part of its zone in Germany to the Poles, and the signature of a treaty with the Warsaw regime.

"The President and the State Department were much relieved that a way out of the Polish morass had been sighted. They were pleased by reports of Stalin's amiability."[48]

Hopkins also tried to persuade Stalin to release arrested leaders of the Polish underground who were being examined as a preliminary to trial. Stalin promised only that he would give thought to the views and statements that Hopkins expressed. Feis adds, "There can be little doubt, in retrospect, that Stalin was dead set against doing anything that might spare anyone associated with the Polish government in London. He hated and feared it, and was determined to crush it out of existence."[49]

While these discussions were being held, the conference at San Francisco had come to an impasse over a voting procedure to which the Russians stood firm. Truman decided to put the issue directly to Stalin. He cabled Hopkins and Harriman, reviewing the issue, and with a tone of indignation observed: "The Soviet proposal carries the principle of the veto . . . even to the right of a single nation to prevent any consideration and discussion of a dispute. We feel that this would make a farce of the whole proposed world organization."

The message went on: "Please tell him in no uncertain words that this country could not possibly join an organization based on so unreasonable an interpretation of the provision of the great powers in the Security Council. Please tell him that we are just as anxious as he to build the organization on a foundation of complete unity but it must be unity of action in the light of a maximum of discussion. At no stage in our discussions relative to creation of the world organization at Dumbarton Oaks or at Yalta or at any other time was a provision ever contemplated which would make impossible freedom of discussion in the Council or Assembly. This is a wholly new and impossible situation."[50]

The sharp message drew immediate results. Marshal Stalin accepted the American position in regard to voting procedure.

These accomplishments must have given the new President additional confidence. He had dared and done well. He had sent a competent envoy and competent instructions. For the moment that was of great importance. That the Polish agreements frittered away later on does not detract from their accomplishment before Truman was to come face to face with Stalin at the Potsdam Conference six weeks later.

"There has been a very pleasant yielding on the part of the Russians to some of the things in which we are interested," Truman told a press conference on June 13. "I think if we keep our heads and be patient, we will arrive at a conclusion, because the Russians are just as anxious to get along with us as we are with them. And I think they have showed it very conclusively in these last negotiations."[51] Other agreements reached had been that Russia would enter the war against Japan as promised and she would scrupulously observe the independence of China; the Allied Control Council for Germany would begin work as quickly as possible, with Marshal Zhukov serving as the Soviet representative; Stalin would gladly meet Truman and Churchill in the vicinity of Berlin in mid-July.

Before going to Potsdam, Truman made important changes in his Cabinet. James F. Byrnes was appointed Secretary of State; Fred Vinson, later appointed a member of the Supreme Court, became Secretary of the Treasury. They were both old friends with long experience in Washington. Although Byrnes had many qualifications, he had never been identified with foreign policy; as a senator he had not been on the Foreign Relations Committee. He had been invited by President Roosevelt to accompany him to the Yalta Conference in order to assuage his feelings, hurt by being turned down as Roosevelt's choice for Vice President. Therefore he had a sense of the milieu, but that is not the reason that Truman chose him; he too was sensitive to the fact that he had been selected instead of Byrnes and was now the President of the United States for that reason. As the San Francisco Conference was about to convene, it was decided that Stettinius should remain Secretary of State until those proceedings had ended.

So Jimmy Byrnes went to Potsdam as Secretary of State; both the President and his Secretary were intelligent novices in foreign affairs but experienced in judging and dealing with people and issues—albeit domestic issues. It must be said that Byrnes had an impressive domestic record, having served with distinction in both houses of Congress, on the Supreme Court and as director of the Office of War Mobilization. While not experienced in foreign affairs he was an experienced negotiator. Professor Gaddis says: "Truman and Byrnes had one overriding objective at Potsdam: they wanted to clear up remaining wartime problems so that United States military and economic responsibilities in Europe could be terminated as quickly as possible. Both men were able practitioners of the art of politics, acutely sensitive to the American public's desire for a return to normalcy at home and abroad. Both tended to look upon the Russians as fellow politicians, with whom a deal could be made."[52]

Henry Morgenthau on the other hand was temperamentally unsuited to Truman's style of operating. He pressured the President, pressured him unsuccessfully to endorse the Morgenthau punitive plan for Germany with which he disagreed, and pressured him to announce before he left for Potsdam that he was asking Morgenthau to remain as Secretary of the Treasury. Truman would not suffer pressure. There is a dispute as to whether or not the President asked the Secretary to resign. He did; I know because just as President Roosevelt had asked his mild-mannered counsel (Sam Rosenman) to carry a like message to Henry Wallace, President Truman charged the same counsel, whom he had asked to remain with him, to carry the request for resignation to Henry Morgenthau. It was a difficult task and it broke their long friendship; unfortunately Henry could not realize that Rosenman was carrying out a directive of the President, who with the consideration native to him thought that an old friend could soften the blow.

President Truman and his new Secretary of State sailed for Europe on July 6, 1945. A subtle but unrecognized warning—if further warning was necessary —of the difficulty of dealing with Stalin had been given before their departure. Truman had asked for provision of free access for United States forces by air, road and rail to Berlin from Frankfurt and Bremen. Churchill made a similar reference to free ways from the British zone. Stalin, in communicating on other matters, had not made reference to these requests—allowing the belief to thrive that the right of access was taken for granted. The Russian word for "yes" is not in common usage, but the fact that "nyet" would be applied at a later date had evidently not occurred to the experienced Churchill any more than it had to the inexperienced Truman and Byrnes. It was Truman who was to deal courageously with the situation when "nyet" was voiced at a later date.

Just as President Wilson had used his trip to Europe on the *George Washington* to have daily conferences with the members of "The Inquiry," so did President Truman confer with the members of the American delegation to the conference on the cruiser *Augusta*. Separate and compact studies of all the issues and their past history had been prepared for his use. Each issue was analyzed as it appeared from the American viewpoint, and recommendations were outlined. Charles E. Bohlen, who had been the White House liaison with the State Department on Russian affairs during the Roosevelt administration (and who was to be a future Ambassador to Russia), a Soviet specialist who was also to be Truman's interpreter at the Potsdam Conference, reports that: "Truman, a newcomer as a world leader, was understandably somewhat nervous about confronting such awesome figures as Churchill and Stalin. But he took advantage of the conferences aboard the *Augusta* to absorb information and ask pertinent questions. He rarely philosophized about the future of the world; *he preferred to address himself to the practicalities of questions.* (Emphasis added) During our conferences, Truman spent little time on small talk and jokes. He stuck to business."[53]

Truman had the same ability to relax from the strains of the day as did Roosevelt; the difference between them was that Roosevelt could throw off the weight of the moment by light banter in the midst of serious discussion, while President Truman waited until the work was done. On the way to Potsdam he spent much time in informal talk with his friends, with the newspaper men who were on board, and in enjoying dinner concerts, movies and card games.

One of the main problems that had troubled the American military government was how to prevent the occupation of Germany from becoming an intolerable financial burden upon the American people. The situation, as they saw it, was that most European countries undoubtedly had legitimate claims for damages against the Nazis, and desperately needed immediate help, but that the war had been prolonged until nearly all Europe was in ruins and the accumulated capital of generations used up. Since almost every country was bankrupt except the United States, the American government might be saddled now with the entire cost of the German occupation, as well as huge reparations for Nazi victims. Posing this problem to Admiral Leahy upon his arrival at Potsdam, the diplomat Robert Murphy was reassured: "That danger is uppermost in the President's mind, too. I have heard him say that the American people foolishly made loans to Germany after the First World War, and the money was used to pay reparations. When the loans were defaulted, Americans were left holding the bag. The President says he is determined not to let that happen again." Murphy comments: "Like Truman himself, I failed to foresee how insignificant those previous loans would seem, compared with the billions of dollars the United States would soon be pouring into Germany and the countries devastated by the Nazis. . . .

"Although the two most famous men then alive—Stalin and Churchill—personally attended the plenary sessions, neither of these world celebrities attracted as much attention as the recent senator from Missouri, Harry S. Truman, who was completely unknown outside his country. . . . It had been Churchill's practice, when visiting wartime Washington, to seek out American senators who were active in foreign policy matters, but Truman had been so little concerned with foreign affairs that the British Prime Minister had never bothered to meet him. Now the former senator was in a position to help settle the grave disputes which had arisen between Churchill and Stalin."[54] How ironic! What would he do? How would he conduct himself?

Truman, being the only Chief of State present at the conference, was invited to preside at the plenary sessions, as Roosevelt had done at Yalta and Teheran and as Wilson had hoped to do at Paris. Robert Murphy says: "The new President presided with dignity and competence but at first was somewhat ill at ease in the presence of the fabulous Churchill and Stalin. He was under the great disadvantage of dealing with situations which were familiar to them but strange to him. But after a few sessions it seemed that Truman and Churchill were being drawn together as a result of Stalin's high-handed demands. The Russians had obtained at the Yalta Conference sweeping generalized benefits, and now they were insisting upon retaining these tentative concessions. One of the generalizations which had been accepted by Roosevelt and Churchill 'as a basis for discussion' was a total of twenty billion dollars for German reparations, half of this to go to Russia. The Soviet delegates at Potsdam interpreted this to mean that Russia had been definitely promised ten billions, much of which could come only from the Anglo-American zones. To allow this interpretation would have meant inevitable American underwriting of reparation payments."[55] This had been a worry to Truman.

On July 21, as Truman presided over the fourth day of plenary sessions, there was a decided change in the President's manner. He seemed more sure of himself, joined vigorously in discussions, and questioned some of Stalin's statements. And there was a similar change in Churchill's manner. That change in both statesmen was affected by their knowledge that the atom bomb had been successfully exploded in New Mexico on July 16. Secretary of War Stimson had arrived to tell President Truman of the closely—but not sufficiently closely—guarded secret.

Before the conference ended it was decided to tell Marshal Stalin that the United States had a powerful new weapon, but not to tell him that it was an atom bomb. Those in the know—including my husband, whom President Truman had summoned from Washington to be present at the conference and to return to the United States on the *Augusta* with him in order to assist in the preparation of his speech to Congress—watched President Truman with bated breath as he casually walked over to Stalin on July 24. My husband said that the expression on Stalin's face remained immobile as he reportedly replied: "That's fine, I hope you make good use of it against Japan."[56] He knew, of course, just what it was through his excellent spy system and had already put the heat upon Russian scientists to produce the Russian atomic bomb. I was in London on a housing mission when Sam was at Potsdam and received a long letter from him which gives his description of Stalin: "Stalin is quite a man—older than I thought but also more shrewd and calculating than I had imagined. He thinks fast. I think he understands English and does a lot of thinking while the interpreter is doing the interpreting."

It is not pertinent here to describe the many issues with which the Potsdam conference dealt, issues which were resolved or postponed. It is necessary, however, to point out that the President—with his great knowledge of world history and geography—had conceptions of his own which he advocated. The most dramatic was his proposal to internationalize the inland waterways—rivers, canals, straits. Probably this idea sprang from General Eisenhower's recommendation that regulation of Danubean traffic be placed on the Potsdam agenda because most boats on the Danube sought refuge from the Red Army by moving to the river's upper waters, which were controlled by Anglo-Americans. The crews refused to return to Soviet territory for fear that their boats would be seized. Revival of traffic on the Danube was desperately needed because other means of transportation were badly damaged.

Truman seized upon and widened this constructive and imaginative proposal with enthusiasm and with vision based upon his profound knowledge of geography and history. He wanted the conferees to consider permanent internationalization of all inland waterways, even the Panama and Suez canals. He introduced his proposal with a long statement at the plenary session on July 23, explaining that the immediate issues were the Danube and Rhine rivers, the Kiel Canal and the Bosphorus. He declared that his study of history convinced him that all major wars of the previous two centuries had originated in the area from the Black Sea to the Baltic, and from the eastern frontier of France to the western frontier of Russia. He said he did not want to become engaged in another war over the Dardanelles or the Danube or the Rhine. It would be the business of this conference and the coming Peace Conference, he said, to remove this source of conflict. The President mentioned how beneficial American rivers and canals had been in opening up the United States. He said he wanted the Russians, British, and everybody else to have free passage of goods and vessels along inland waterways to all the seas of the world, and he had prepared a paper on this subject which he would now circulate.

"The earnestness of the President's speech was evident. Noting his manner, Churchill expressed cordial support in general terms. But Stalin replied merely that he would read the President's paper. At a second session that day, Truman raised the question again. . . . The next day the President brought up the subject again, reiterating his keen personal interest in it . . . Stalin cut short the following discussion by saying, 'We have many more urgent problems before us.' . . .

"At the August 1 plenary session, the conference began to consider the final communique which soon would be made public. The President said that he regretted that no agreement had been possible on control of waterways, but he believed nevertheless that the communique should mention that this subject had been discussed. Attlee [who had replaced Churchill as Prime Minister of England] agreed, but Stalin objected. He said the communique already mentioned more subjects than the public could easily digest, and no more should be added. Truman then turned to Stalin and made a frank personal plea. He said, 'Marshal Stalin, I have accepted a number of compromises during this conference to conform to your views, and I make a personal request now that you yield on this point. My request is that the communique mention the fact that the waterways proposal has been referred to the Council of Foreign Ministers which we have established to prepare for peace proposals.' The President pointed out that if the communique mentioned this proposal, that would give him an opportunity to explain to the American Congress in a message he planned to deliver after his return to Washington.

"Stalin listened closely to the President's statement, which was addressed directly to him, and apparently the Soviet dictator understood most of the English words. Before the translation into Russian was finished, he broke in abruptly with the familiar Russian negative, 'Nyet.' Then, very deliberately he repeated in English, 'No, I say no.' "[57]

Truman was frustrated and flushed. There was never a chance that Stalin would have accepted his proposal, but Truman exacerbated the situation by mentioning his desire to explain his suggestion in his message to Congress. There was nothing Stalin wanted less than that exposition which could ignite the approval of the American people and its force to influence world opinion.

But, as Murphy says, "it was evident that the new President would never enjoy playing the elaborate game of power politics which so delighted Roosevelt. The proceedings at Potsdam made Truman first uneasy, then impatient, and the final curious passage with Stalin infuriated him."[58] It probably did as much as anything to influence his changing attitude which climaxed in the cold war.

Admiral Leahy, a well-tutored and tough critic, summed up the President's record at the conference: "Truman had stood up to Stalin in a manner calculated to warm the heart of every patriotic American. He refused to be bulldozed into any reparations agreement that would repeat the history of World War I, which found the American taxpayer paying for German reparations. He refused to recognize the Soviet-sponsored Polish land grab in eastern Germany . . . or to sanction U.S. diplomatic recognition of the puppet regimes set up from Moscow, in Rumania, Bulgaria and Hungary.

"Stalin was his usual courteous but plain-talking self, and we believed him to be arguing sincerely for what he thought the best interests of his government. Had he taken a more compromising attitude, 'Uncle Joe' undoubtedly would have been in trouble when he returned to Moscow.

"Truman could point to three major achievements. Formation of the Council of Foreign Ministers could prevent many mistakes, due to lack of preparation, that were made a quarter of a century earlier at Versailles. The council could pave the way for a final settling of accounts of World War II in the peace treaties.

"By and large, the major points in the American plan for political and economic policies to govern the control of Germany during the occupation period were incorporated in the Potsdam report. It was perhaps the President's greatest success.

"On the thorny and complex issue of German reparations, the Soviets finally receded from their stubborn insistence on a fixed dollar total and accepted the percentage principle. Stalin and Molotov also agreed, in theory, that Germany could not pay the Russian bill out of its current industrial production until the economy of the defeated nation was in balance. (In Paris, less than a year from the date of signing by Stalin of the Potsdam protocol, Molotov was to repudiate both of these principles.)"[59]

It is to be noted that there is no mention of a discussion of free access between zones of occupation at the conference. Stalin's failure to answer "Nyet" (see page 449) had led to the assumption that would be rudely destroyed and would be a major factor in the cold war. Hindsight places this oversight as a major error of the experienced Churchill and of Truman and his advisers, who should have been more wary of Stalin's wiles.

There were many items on the liability side and many items on which no agreement could be reached.

Although frustrating, this was not surprising. At Versailles there had been a comparable cleavage in ideas and objectives and a comparable shock to Wilson; Clemenceau, Lloyd George and Orlando did not come from countries with the Russian background of czarist or Lenin days, but their aggressiveness was just as tough. Theirs were not backward nations but their officials had an old world point of view. As we have seen, Winston Churchill still clung to the old policies of spheres of influence. Thus President Truman was confronted by the difficult task of facing the determination of one Ally who was trying to establish a new order of influence in Europe and another Ally who was attempting to perpetuate the old. Truman's directness and doggedness in pursuit of his objectives have been admired and respected although he did not achieve all of his goals and many that he did achieve were later nullified.

On August 6, 1945, President Truman, lunching with the crew of the *Augusta* in mid-ocean, was handed a message which told him that the Army Air Force had dropped an atom bomb on the Japanese shipbuilding center at Hiroshima. It is characteristic of Harry Truman that he first broke the news to the crew and then went to the wardroom where he informed the officers. His announcement to the American people, released at the White House, ended with a harsh threat to the Japanese not tempered by a softening phrase: "If they do not now accept our terms they may expect a rain of ruin from the air."[60] He minced no words and he meant what he said, for his aim was to terminate the war with Japan without a staggering loss of American lives. The President regarded the bomb as a military weapon and never had any doubt that it should be used. Throughout the war Anglo-American strategy had been to seek victory as quickly as possible through technology, not manpower. Nevertheless it took courage for Truman to order its use.

President Truman was alive to his duty as Commander-in-Chief of the armed forces. Almost three weeks before the bomb had been tested, on May 25, the Joint Chiefs of Staff had dispatched a formal directive to MacArthur, Nimitz and Arnold which included the instruction to "support further advances for the purpose of establishing the conditions favorable to the decisive invasion of the industrial heart of Japan."

Herbert Feis says: "The President was not sure that this program of bold and direct invasion of Japan was essential and sound . . . he asked Leahy to inform the Chiefs of Staff that he wished to discuss the proposed strategy with them again, explaining tactfully that he wanted to prepare for the talks with Churchill and Stalin, scheduled for mid-July. In particular, *the President wanted to know how many men and ships would be needed for an invasion of the home islands; and how long the consequent land battle would go on; and what losses we would incur if we attempted the invasion, and what they would be if we relied solely on sea and air blockade and attack; and what we wanted the Russians and other allies to do.* (Emphasis added) 'It is his intention,' Leahy informed the Chiefs of Staff on June 14th, 'to make his decisions on the campaign with the purpose of economizing to the maximum extent the loss of American lives.' "[61]

His Presidential style was exactly what it had been as senator—to pose every relevant question so as to ascertain all the facts. The facts which he obtained gave purpose to his decision to use the atom bomb. He explained to the American people in a radio address on August 9 upon his return from Potsdam: ". . . I realize the tragic significance of the Atom Bomb. . . . Its production and its use were not lightly undertaken by this Government. . . . We won the race of discovery against the Germans. . . . Having found the bomb we have used it. . . . We have used it in order to shorten the agony of war, in order to save the lives of thousands and thousands of young Americans. . . . We shall continue to use it until we completely destroy Japan's power to make war. Only Japanese surrender will stop us. . . ."[62]

On the morning of the 9th (Tokyo time) the Japanese Supreme War Direction Council received word that Russia had declared war against them; and that another atomic bomb had been dropped on Nagasaki. On Tuesday, August 14, 1945, the Japanese surrendered upon the terms specified by the United States, the United Kingdom and China in the Potsdam Declaration. Japan's surrender signalled the gradual re-emergence of Congress as a major influence on the making of foreign policy, and brought about a corresponding diminution in the freedom of action available to the Truman administration. The impetus for congressional resurgence was occasioned by the discussion in all walks of official Washington of domestic use and international control of the bomb. When President Truman sent his special message to the Congress on Atomic Energy on October 3, 1945,[63] he said: "The outcome of the discussions will be reported to the Congress as soon as possible, and any resulting agreements requiring Congressional action will be submitted to the Congress." To this Senator Vandenberg later growled to a reporter: "I should think he would be God damned glad to consult Congress before negotiating agreements. I wouldn't think any human being would take the responsibility for settling this issue."[64] Truman never shirked responsibility but he was aware of the constitutional powers of Congress and alert to the danger of infringing upon them in this very delicate matter.

Moreover, the Senate made it clear that it would influence policy by creating the Special Senate Committee on Atomic Energy in October 1945. Vandenberg, now ranking Republican on the Foreign Relations Committee, called for retaining the American atomic monopoly until there was "absolute free and untrammeled right of intimate inspection all around the globe." The Michigan Republican warned his colleagues: "There can be no dark corners in an atomic age."[65]

"Legislators on Capitol Hill reflected in general the attitudes of their constituents on the international control of atomic energy. Opinion polls showed that to a surprising extent Americans realized that their monopoly over the bomb would not last. A survey made in September 1945 revealed that 82 percent of a national sample expected other nations to develop bombs of their own sooner or later. The same poll indicated, however, that 85 percent of those questioned wanted the United States to retain exclusive possession of the weapon as long as possible. International control evoked little support: a poll taken in August, 1945, and repeated two months later, showed that more than 70 percent of the public opposed turning nuclear weapons over to the United Nations. Clearly the Truman Administration would have to overcome considerable skepticism on the part of Congress and the public if it was to implement its program of international control."[66]

The President's difficulties with the Congress and the public grew as the House Committee on Un-American Activities was revived and its powers were augmented in January 1945, under the leadership of John E. Rankin of Mississippi. In September it began its first postwar investigation of American communism. The committee wanted to find out whether the communists were still planning to destroy or overthrow the American system of government. Rankin, with a shrewd eye to publicity, added that the hearings would cover the Hollywood film industry: 'Alien elements are at work out there to overthrow our Government by means of subtle propaganda in our movies.' The inept broadsides of Rankin and his colleagues shed little light on the real relationship between the Kremlin and American Communists, but they did publicize the possibility of internal subversion at a time when Soviet-American relations were rapidly deteriorating."[67]

Our position *vis-à-vis* Russia was substantially weakened by the American public's insistence upon bringing our troops home from Europe. The public was hysterical in its vociferous demands. Congressmen found their mailboxes filled with letters from wives calling for quick return of their husbands, sometimes accompanied by baby pictures and even baby shoes. Secretary of War Patterson and Navy Secretary Forrestal warned the Cabinet as early as October 26, 1945, that the rapid pace of demobilization was threatening the American strategic position throughout the world. However, Truman lacked the strength, or thought he lacked the strength, to stem the tide. He did not appeal and explain to the people of the United States the necessity of keeping an Army in Europe at that time as President Wilson or Franklin D. Roosevelt probably would have done. He was unaccustomed to meeting a gigantic avalanche of public protest. It is unlikely that it was courage that failed this courageous man, but lack of experience in dealing with an explosive public and its congressional influence, and possibly a lack of appreciation of the extent of the impact our weakened European force would have upon Russian foreign policy.

Truman's solution was a request in October 1945 for the continuation of selective service and the institution of universal military training, a program which would require training for all physically fit eighteen-year-old men. James Reston noted early in 1946 that those congressmen who shouted loudest for a tough anti-Russian policy were the least willing to vote the money and the manpower necessary to implement such a policy.[68] The Truman administration was in an awkward position: further compromises with the Russians would be politically unpopular, but our weakened fighting strength was an open bid to Stalin to ignore our positions.

Just as President Wilson thought that the leverage of American postwar financial assistance would win the European statesmen to his objectives, so Secretary Byrnes gulled himself into the belief that he could control the Russians at the Conference of Foreign Ministers held in London in September 1945 by the knowledge that we had the atom bomb. But all attempts to validate the Yalta Agreement regarding free elections in Poland and the former German allies bordering Russia received Molotov's unchanging "Nyet." Professor Gaddis adds: "The London conference demonstrated clearly that simple possession of the atomic bomb had not made the United States omnipotent in its dealings with Moscow. . . . Molotov's studied intransigence at London [on all matters discussed] raised doubts as to whether the Russians were interested in signing peace treaties on any terms but their own. Moreover, Truman's October 3, 1945, message to Congress on atomic energy, made without consulting the absent Secretary of State, had undercut Byrnes' bargaining strategy by endorsing international control long before any European peace arrangements were in sight."[69]

The breakdown of the London Conference did not upset the even tenor of the President. His knowledge of history softened his disappointment; he thought that the differences would be worked out in time.

Secretary Byrnes, always bearing in his mind that he should have been President instead of Truman, and probably irked and self-defensive because of his failure to make any progress with the Russians, became a lone operator acting as though he had responsibility neither to the President or to the Congress. Having been a recognized leader in Congress, his action toward its members was even more difficult to understand than his independent stance toward the President. On December 12, the Secretary departed for the second meeting of the Foreign Ministers.

On the 14th, the President was confronted by actions the Secretary had taken independently which started the buildup of indignation that led to the replacement of Byrnes by General George Marshall after the completion of the peace treaties. Truman's loyalties were hard but also brittle; when they broke they shattered completely. When the President met on the 14th with Connally, Vandenberg and other members of the Foreign Relations Committee, he learned to his amazement that the State Department had drafted atomic proposals which permitted the exchange of scientific and technical information prior to the establishment of safeguards. The senators suggested that Byrnes be instructed by radio to change his plans, but Truman remained noncommittal. Probably intense anger swelled within him, but he choked it down. Vandenberg noted that the senators had at least made their protest: "We shall hold the Executive Department responsible. It is our unanimous opinion that Byrnes must be *stopped.*"[70]

The President acted quickly, ordering Acting Secretary of State Acheson to cable a full account of his meeting with the senators to Byrnes. Byrnes replied that he had never intended to make possible the exchange without safeguards. When news of the senators' confrontation with Truman and Byrnes leaked to the press on December 20, the President sent the Secretary an expression of confidence. This was a public gesture. Nevertheless the incident could not have been erased from his mind. Truman had great reverence for the office of the President of the United States, and expected not personal homage, but strict adherence to the proprieties due the man who held the office. They were not forthcoming from Byrnes.

Averell Harriman, who was Ambassador in Moscow during the meeting of the Foreign Ministers, recalled that after the first day's session he offered to help the Secretary draft the customary telegraphic summary to Washington. Byrnes replied: "I'm not going to send any daily reports. I don't trust the White House. It leaks. And I don't want any of this coming out in the papers until I get home."[71]

"Until I get home" was a significant phrase; he intended to report to the American people himself, and he intended to report to them before the President would know what had transpired—before the President could report to them himself. The first report that the Secretary sent was at the conclusion of the conference. "This message," wrote President Truman, "told me very little that the newspaper correspondents had not already reported from Moscow. This is not what I considered a proper account by a Cabinet member to the President. It was more like one partner in a business telling the other that his business trip was progressing well and not to worry.

"I was in Independence, Missouri, on December 27 when the next word from Byrnes reached me. Charles Ross, my press secretary, informed me from Washington that a message had been received from the Secretary of State. Byrnes had asked that the White House arrange for him to address the American people over all networks so that he might report on the results of the conference. What those results were I did not yet know.

"A little after ten that night the text of the State Department's communique on the Moscow conference was brought to me. It had been released in Washington by Byrnes' orders, an hour earlier."[72]

The President returned to Washington on December 28 and conferred with Senator Arthur H. Vandenberg and Under Secretary of State Dean Acheson, who helped him draft a statement for release to the press making clear his position regarding the Moscow agreement as it related to proper safeguards for atomic energy. Then, accompanied by a number of advisers, he went directly to the Presidential yacht *Williamsburg* for a cruise which was to be devoted mainly to preparing a radio address on domestic problems scheduled for January 3. They were anchored at Quantico, Virginia, the next day when Press Secretary Charles Ross received a telephone call from Byrnes. The Secretary of State had just arrived in Washington and wanted to know if everything was ready for the four-network broadcast he had requested. "The President asks me to tell you," Ross said, "that you had better come down here posthaste and make your report to the President before you do anything else."

By five o'clock that afternoon Byrnes had reached Quantico and the *Williamsburg.*

President Truman's account states: "We went into my stateroom when he arrived, and I closed the door behind us. I told him that I did not like the way in which I had been left in the dark about the Moscow conference. I told him that, as President, I intended to know what progress we were making and what we were doing in foreign negotiations. I said that it was shocking that a communique should be issued in Washington announcing a foreign policy development of major importance that I had never heard of. *I said I would not tolerate a repetition of such conduct.*"[73] (Emphasis added)

Senator Byrnes could well have complained, as Molotov is quoted to have done, "I have never been talked to like that." The President's account of this "dressing down" is not exaggerated, for his counsel was one of those sitting in the dining salon making small conversation with the others aboard as the unusual sound of Truman's raised voice would boom from the closed door; all of them had a forewarning and a rehashing of the tongue-lashing. The friendship which had been waning was at an end and the relationship terminated as soon as feasible. Harry Truman would never brook personal disloyalty or lack of respect to the President of the United States.

Aside from this interruption, the trip on the *Williamsburg* was devoted to the discussion of domestic policy, an area that had not been neglected because of war problems. In his very first address before a joint session of Congress on April 16, 1945, Truman had devoted just one paragraph which indicated his future concern: "Here in America, we have labored long and hard to achieve a social order worthy of our heritage. In our time, tremendous progress has been made toward a really democratic way of life. Let me assure the forward-looking people of America that there will be no relaxation in our efforts to improve the lot of the common people."[74]

Then came the September 6 special message to the Congress presenting a Twenty-One-Point Program for the reconversion period which sent Joe Martin, the Republican leader of the House, into a tizzy (see page 428)—and others too. It is difficult to understand why Harry Truman, with his New Deal senatorial voting record, should have been expected to be a conservative. Possibly it was because many of his old friends, like John Snyder, who were brought into the administration were conservative and were expected to exert a dominating influence. The President listened to them, but he listened to others as well and in his customary style made his decisions upon his own judgment when the facts were in; and he was basically and fundamentally a liberal. Those New Dealers who exclaimed: "My God, Truman," when he became President later uttered sentiments which could have been paraphrased: "Thank God, Truman."

These Twenty-One Points should rank in history with Woodrow Wilson's Fourteen Points. Wilson avowed his ideals and objectives for the peace to follow World War I. Truman, following the ending of World War II, asked the Congress to fulfill his ideals and objectives for the achievement of national goals which would ensure the well-being—the happiness, health and prosperity—of the people of this nation, of the nation's economy, of its future preparedness; and he also asked for assistance to the peoples of other nations. It was a demonstration of his leadership, of his thoroughness, of his broad-scale grasp of the nation's problems and of his courage in daring to present the entire picture to a Congress that was not composed of many men who would appreciate so comprehensive a presentation. Possibly President Roosevelt, with his sensitivity to the politically feasible, would have spooned out those twenty-one objectives in small lots. Harry Truman was not so geared. He dared tread forthrightly with vigor, even though it made Joe Martin and others wince to the extent that his honeymoon with Congress came to a standstill; he had to fight for every measure from then to the end of his presidency. Today, it seems a very reasonable program; but the world, although it does not always seem so, has moved on in these many years.

Graciously—and with reason—he began: ". . . The legislative branch of the Government is entitled to its full share of credit and glory for the victory of the Allied armies. I wish to take this opportunity on behalf of the Nation to congratulate you on the great victory which has been won—in which you played so important a part." Then he gave eight methods by which full peacetime production and employment could be achieved. Unequivocally he stated that those eight policies had been laid down and would be followed, and he plainly described what the government was doing to hurry "this reconversion process."[75]

His Twenty-One Points called for (1) *Unemployment Compensation,* which "is *not* intended to take the place of the permanent amendments to the unemployment compensation system which are now being studied by the Congress. It is an emergency measure designed to expand the present system without changing its principles. It is designed only to meet the immediate pressing human problems of reconversion.

"This recommendation is not to be confused with the broader question of extending, expanding, and improving our entire social security program, of which unemployment insurance is only a part. (Emphasis added) I expect to communicate with the Congress on this subject at a later date. But I sincerely urge that we do not wait for consideration of such a complex question before enacting this much needed emergency legislation."

This was not the goal of a timid, caretaker President; indeed, it startled those with such expectations. It was the prelude to the other progressive ambitions of the message, each outlining conversion measures and stating the aim for long-range legislation: ". . . I believed that the goal of a 40 cent minimum was inadequate when established. It is now become obsolete.

"Increases in the cost of living since 1938 and changes in our national wage structure, require an immediate and substantial upward revision of this minimum. Only in that way can the objectives of the Fair Labor Standards Act be realized, the national purchasing power protected, and an economy of full production and abundance preserved and maintained for the American people.

"The high prosperity which we seek in the postwar years will not be meaningful for all our people if any large proportion of our industrial wage earners receive wages as low as the minimum now sanctioned by the Fair Labor Standards Act.

"I therefore recommend [2] that the *Congress amend the Fair Labor Standards Act* by substantially increasing the minimum wage specified therein to a level which will eliminate substandards of living, and assure the maintenance of the health, efficiency, and general well-being of workers. . . . I urge that the Congress act promptly. The wage structure on which businessmen may make future plans should be settled quickly." This brought conservative political temperatures above the boiling point, but they were to mount still further as the intrepid, determined President proceeded to formulate a modern bill of rights.

(3) *Wartime Controls:* ". . . The American people are entitled to a firm assurance not only on the part of the Administration, but from the Congress itself that rents and prices of clothing, food, and other essentials will be held in line. They are also entitled to buy washing machines, vacuum cleaners, automobiles and other products at prices based on our traditional system of high output and low unit costs. . . . Let me add that in no case should rationing controls be removed if by so doing we should jeoparadize our relief shipments to Europe and other distressed war areas. We have a moral obligation to the people of these liberated areas. More than that, our own enlightened self-interest tells us that hungry people are rarely advocates of democracy. The rehabilitation of these countries, and indeed the removal of American occupational troops, may be unnecessarily delayed if we fail to meet these responsibilities during the next few months.

"During the reconversion period and as long as shortages in certain materials other than food continue, the War Production Board will have to support the stabilization program as it has done during the past four years.

"It must be in a position to take action where necessary, to increase scarce materials and facilities, break bottlenecks, channel production to most essential needs, safeguard the opportunities for small business concerns, and, above all, to control inventories so as to prevent speculative hoarding and unbalanced distribution."

With his knowledge of congressional sensitivity in requesting the Congress to extend the provisions of the Second War Powers Act, Truman stressed: "The Congress has my definite assurance that none of these war powers will be exercised by the executive branch of the Government unless they are deemed essential to the attainment of the objective of an orderly stabilized reconversion." In Point 4—*War Powers and Executive Agencies Reorganized*—he set forth procedures which illustrate his conception of the relative roles that the executive and the Congress should play. ". . . In my message dated May 24, 1945, it was recommended that permanent legislation be enacted which would authorize the President to submit to the Congress, from time to time, plans providing for the reorganization of executive agencies, each such plan to become effective unless the Congress should reject it by concurrent resolution.

". . . If proper progress is to be made, it is necessary to permit the President to lay out machinery for carrying out his responsibility for the conduct of the executive branch, subject to rejection by the two Houses of Congress. *Executive initiative, subject to congressional veto, is an effective approach to governmental organization.* (Emphasis added) The responsibility of conducting the executive branch rests upon the President. It is fair and efficient to permit him to lay out the machinery for carrying out that responsibility. . . ."

Point 5 concerns *Full Employment* and contains the statement that "A national reassertion of the right to work for every American citizen able and willing to work—a declaration of the ultimate duty of Government to use its own resources if all other methods should fail to avert fear and establish full employment. The prompt and firm acceptance of this bedrock public responsibility will reduce the need for its exercise.

"I ask that full employment legislation to provide these vital assurances be speedily enacted. Such legislation should also provide machinery for a continuous full-employment policy—to be developed and pursued in cooperation among industry, agriculture, and labor, between the Congress and the Chief Executive, between the people and their government."

Point 6 repeats the President's request to set up on a permanent basis the wartime *Fair Employment Practice Committee* to overcome prejudices which resulted in discrimination against minority groups.

Point 7 calls upon *the representatives of organized labor and industry to continue their adherence to the no-strike, no-lock-out policy,* pending the Presidential call of a conference of representatives of organized labor and industry for the purpose of working out by agreement means to minimize labor disputes.

Thus far we have only covered seven points. Yet to omit any of the remainder would destroy the magnitude of President Truman's conception, the thoroughness of his study of the nation's requirements and the comprehensive program he presented for meeting them. The presentation of this program demonstrates his leadership, his knowledge of governmental procedures, and his determination to accomplish reforms which he believed would implement the working of government and well-being of its people. Therefore it is necessary to spot the highlights in this long message representing Truman's program, which contributes to his classification as a "great" President.

Point 8. *United States Employment Service Extension:* ". . . Shortly after the declaration of war, the Government realized that the manpower of the Nation could be mobilized more efficiently if the United States Employment Service were centralized under Federal control. Hundreds of thousands of workers had to be recruited from all parts of the country. Often, they were wanted in regions far from their homes. Certain areas had surpluses of labor; others were desperately in need of more workers. This situation could be met only through a centrally operated employment service that covered the entire Nation.

"Now we are faced with this problem in reverse. Hundreds of thousands of men and women will want to seek jobs in towns and cities other than those in which they worked during the war. They may want to return home, or they may strike out in search of new opportunities in new surroundings. Millions of veterans also will be coming back in search of peacetime jobs. They will want to know where such jobs can be found, not only in their own areas, but also in other parts of the land.

"The task of helping this vast army of job seekers to fit themselves into peacetime economy is fully as difficult as the mobilization of manpower for war. To make any decided change in the machinery to handle this problem now would cause unnecessary hardship to workers and veterans. It would slow down the entire process for reconversion.

"I urgently recommend that the Congress do not yet return the Employment Service to the States. Ultimately it should be so returned. . . ."

Point 9. *Agriculture:* ". . . Strengthening the machinery for carrying out price-support commitments is the one measure necessary to safeguard farm prices. Stimulation of the export of farm commodities is another. More food is needed in the war-ravaged areas of the world. In the process of meeting relief requirements abroad, we have the opportunity of developing export markets for the future. . . .

"A well rounded crop insurance program, together with the assurance of reasonable and stable farm prices, will go a long way toward meeting basic problems which have plagued farmers in the past. . . . The Secretary of Agriculture is now re-examining existing agricultural programs in the light of peace-time needs in order that they make the fullest contribution to the welfare of farmers and the people as a whole. I hope that the Congress also, through its appropriate Committees, will give careful consideration to this problem with a view to making such adjustments as are necessary to strengthen the effectiveness of these various measures." President Truman made a partner of the Congress on every possible opportunity.

Point 10. *Selective Service:* "While the cruel lessons of war are fresh in every mind, it is fitting that we now undertake appropriate measures for the future security of the United States. . . .

"We have charted the course to a stable world peace, but that course still remains to be sailed.

". . . But we would break faith with those who won for us the victory, if we should fail at the same time to adopt an integrated and long-range program for the national security. . . .

"And in this first year after victory our people have another obligation, one which is felt in almost every American home. We owe it to those now in armed forces that they be returned to civilian life with all possible speed.

"To provide the personnel necessary to meet these immediate obligations we must obtain replacements for those veterans who have already rendered long and arduous service. . . .

". . . In view of our extensive national commitments, I am certain, as are the

War and Navy departments, that we cannot rely on voluntary recruitment as the sole method of procuring necessary replacements.

"I, therefore, urge that the Congress continue inductions to assure replacements for these veterans, in such numbers as are not supplied by volunteers. . . ."

Point 11. *Housing:* "The largest single opportunity for the rapid postwar expansion of private investment and employment lies in the field of housing, both urban and rural. The present shortage of decent homes and enforced widespread use of substandard housing indicate vital unfulfilled needs of the Nation. These needs will become more marked as veterans begin to come back and look for places to live. . . .

"Housing is high on the list of matters calling for decisive Congressional action. . . . While differing opinions may be held as to detail, these proposals for action already developed in the Congress appear to me sound and essential.

"I urgently commend that the Congress, at an early date, enact broad and comprehensive housing legislation.

"The cardinal principle underlying such legislation should be that house construction and financing for the overwhelming majority of our citizens should be done by private enterprise. . . .

". . . We must consider the redevelopment of large areas of the blighted and slum sections of our cities so that in the truly American way they may be remade to accommodate families not only of low-income groups as heretofore, but of every income group. . . .

"I recommend, also, that we quicken our rate of progress in rural housing. As a general rule, housing conditions on farms and in rural areas are relatively worse than in our cities. In housing, as well as in other benefits of the American system, farm families should enjoy equality with city dwellers.

"A decent standard of housing for all is one of the irreducible obligations of modern civilization. . . . We must begin to meet that challenge at once."

It is a sad commentary that although in the Truman administration and since vast quantities of private and public housing have been built, the nation has not kept pace with obsolescence and need.

Point 12. *Research:* "Progress in scientific research and development is an indispensable condition to the future welfare and security of the Nation. The events of the past few years are both proof and prophecy of what science can do. . . . No government adequately meets its responsibilities unless it generously and intelligently supports and encourages the work of science in university, industry, and in its own laboratories. . . .

"In order to derive the full profit in the future from what we have learned, I urge upon the Congress the early adoption of legislation for the establishment of a single Federal research agency which would discharge the following functions:

"1. Promote and support fundamental research and development projects in all matters pertaining to the defense and security of the Nation.

"2. Promote and support research in the basic sciences and in the social sciences.

"3. Promote and support research in medicine, public health, and allied fields.

"4. Provide financial assistance in the form of scholarships and grants for young men and women of proved scientific ability.

"5. Coordinate and control diverse scientific activities of the Federal Government.

"6. Make fully, freely, and publicly available to commerce, industry, agriculture, and academic institutions, the fruits of research financed by Federal funds.

"Scientific knowledge and scientific research are a complex and interrelated structure. Technological advances in one field may have great significance for another apparently unrelated. Accordingly, I urge upon the Congress the desirability of centralizing these functions in a single agency. . . .

"Our economic and industrial strength, the physical well-being of our people, the achievement of full employment and full production, the future of our security, and the preservation of our principles will be determined by the extent to which we give full and sincere support to the works of science.

"It is with these works that we can build the highroads to the future."

Point 13. *Transition Tax Revision:* "Taxes will play a vital role in attaining a prosperous peace.

"I recommend that a transitional tax bill be enacted as soon as possible to provide limited tax reductions for the calendar year 1946 . . . [aimed] principally at removing barriers to speedy reconversion and to the expansion of our peacetime economy. . . . After passage of the transitional bill, I hope the Congress will give careful consideration to the modernization of the Federal tax structure. A major objective of this modernization should be the encouragement of business incentives and expansion, and of consumer purchasing power. In this connection consideration of further tax reductions should have due regard to the level of government expenditures and the health and stability of our economy."

Point 14. *Surplus Property Disposed:* Recommends that Congress enact legislation creating a single Surplus Property Administrator in place of the board of three and states: "The sooner we can put plants and equipment to work, the sooner we can discard our wartime controls in the transition from war to peace."

Point 15. *Small Business:* ". . . Assistance should be given to small business to enable them to obtain adequate materials, private financing, technical improvements, and surplus property."

Today, small business is fast becoming a thing of the past.

Point 16. *Veterans:* This contains a long list of some of the major steps taken. Noteworthy among its recommendations is that "Favorable consideration should be given by the Congress to Federal reclamation projects as outstanding opportunities for returning veterans. The great Columbia Basin project in the Northwest, the projects in the Missouri River Basin, and others of equal significance will bring into existence many thousands of new family-size farms upon which returning veterans can secure a livelihood for themselves and their families and create new wealth for the Nation. A number of farms can be made ready for veterans who seek to develop farm homes on irrigated lands in Federal reclamation areas." This shows the detail into which the President delved in order to solve the problems of the veteran.

Point 17. *Public Works and National Resources:* "During the war years we have expended our resources—both human and natural—without stint. We have thrown into the battle for freedom everything we had.

"Thousands of our finest young men—our best human resources—have given their lives. . . .

"The depletion of our natural resources is even more startling. We have torn from the earth copper, petroleum, iron ore, tungsten, and every other mineral required to fight a war, without regard to our future supplies. We have taken what we needed. We were not able to, and we did not, take account of tomorrow. . . .

"With a few exceptions, we were forced to suspend the program to which this nation is committed of harnessing the waters of our great rivers so that they may become vehicles of commerce, beneficient producers of cheap electric power, and servants of the nation instead of instruments of destruction.

"In brief, although during this war this nation has reached the apex of its power—a peak of greatness and might which the world had never seen—our national capital account has suffered. We must proceed with all possible diligence not merely to restore these depleted resources to their prewar standards but to make them greater and richer than ever before. . . .

"We know that by the investment of Federal funds we can, within the limits of our own nation, provide for our citizens new frontiers—new territories for the development of industry, agriculture and commerce. . . . If there are among us for any period of time farmers who do not farm because there is no suitable land available to them; workers who do not work because there is no labor for their hands, we have only ourselves to blame so long as we fail to make available to them the opportunities before our very eyes.

"I hope that the Congress will proceed as rapidly as possible to authorize regional development of the natural resources of our great river valleys. . . .

"It is necessary that we proceed as speedily as possible to make an inventory of our national wealth and our basic resources, and to test the suitability of plans and proposals for public work in light of this purpose. *An agency of this sort could provide us with consistent direction toward the goal of rehabilitation and improvement of our basic national resources.*" (Emphasis added)

The President made seven recommendations in this connection and then added significantly: "Programs of internal improvements of a public character—Federal, State and local—must preserve competitive bidding, guarantee collective bargaining and good wages for labor, utilize skills of our returned veterans to the fullest extent, and effectively prevent discrimination because of race, creed or color." It was basic to the character of the man to demand these considerations.

Point 18. *Lend-Lease and Postwar Reconstruction:* ". . . In due time we must consider the settlement of the lend-lease obligations which have been incurred during the course of the war. We must recognize that it will not be possible for our Allies to pay us dollars for the overwhelming portion of the lend-lease obligations which they have incurred. But this does not mean that all lend-lease obligations are to be canceled. We shall seek under the procedure prescribed in the Lend-Lease Act and in subsequent agreements with other governments to achieve settlements of our wartime lend-lease relations which will permit generally a sound world-wide economy and will contribute to international peace and our own national security. . . .

"Further legislation is needed in connection with the United Nations Relief and Rehabilitation Administration. I recommend that the Congress fulfill the commitment already made by appropriating the remaining $550,000,000 granted by the Congress for United States participation.

"The Council Meeting of the United Nations Relief and Rehabilitation Administration has just been brought to a successful conclusion. At that meeting our delegate found the need for an additional contribution from all participating countries, to enable the United Nations Relief and Rehabilitation Administration to complete its work in Europe and Asia. On his motion, the Council voted to recommend to member countries a further contribution. Our own share will amount to approximately $1,350,000,000. I am confident that you will find this request for an additional authorization and appropriation fully justified, and I ask for prompt examination and consideration of the request. . . .

"Finally, I foresee the need for additional interim lending power to insure a rapid and successful transition to peacetime world trade. Appropriate recommendations will be made to the Congress on this matter when we have completed the exploratory conversations already begun with our associates. We wish to maintain the flow of supplies without interruption. Accordingly, I have directed the executive agencies to complete their conversations and studies at the earliest possible moment. I ask the Congress for speedy considerations of the recommendations when they are made."

Point 19. *Congressional Salaries:* ". . . We should make service in the Congress of the United States available without hardship to ordinary citizens who have to look to the salary for their sole support. . . . I sincerely hope that the Congress will take early steps to provide decent wage scales for its members and for the executive and judicial branches of the Government."

Point 20. *Sale of Ships:* ". . . It is recommended that suitable legislation to permit such sales be expedited so that the uncertainty about the disposal of our large surplus tonnage may be removed. In this way, American shipping companies may undertake commercial operation as rapidly as ships can be released from Government control, and the foreign market can also be used for selling those vessels which are in excess of the needs of our postwar American merchant marine and national defense."

Point 21. *Stock Piling of Strategic Material:* "One of the costliest lessons of our unpreparedness for this war was the great danger involved in depending upon foreign sources for supplies of raw materials necessary in times of emergency. . . . I recommend that the Congress enact legislation to bring about the acquisition and retention of stock piles of materials in which we are naturally deficient but which are necessary to supply the needs of the Nation for its defense."

The President then outlined three other noteworthy areas of social concern in which he would make recommendations to Congress in the future: "I shall shortly communicate with the Congress recommending a national health program to provide adequate medical care for all Americans and to protect them from financial loss and hardships resulting from illness and accident. I shall also communicate with the Congress with respect to expanding our social-security system, and improving our program of education for our citizens."

The message concluded:

"In this hour of victory over our enemies abroad, let us now resolve to use all our efforts and energies to build a better life here at home and a better world for generations to come.

"The Congress has played its full part in shaping the domestic and foreign policies which have won this victory and started us on the road to lasting peace.

"The Congress, I know, will continue to play its patriotic part in the difficult years ahead. We face the future together with confidence—that the job, the full job, can and will be done.

                              Harry S. Truman"[76]

Elsewhere, the President has written: "This twenty-one point message marked the beginning of the 'Fair Deal,' and September 6, 1945, is the date that symbolizes for me my assumption of the office of President in my own right. It was on that day and with this message that I first spelled out the details of the program of liberalism and progressivism which was to be the foundation of my administration. It was my opportunity as President to advocate the political principles and economic philosophy which I had expressed in the Senate and which I had followed all my political life. . . . I had given these matters considerable thought during my first four months in office, even though war matters and foreign-policy problems had occupied most of my time. I actually started work on this comprehensive program while I was on my way home from the Potsdam conference. Judge Samuel I. Rosenman, the counsel to the President, had joined me at the conference and, returning home with me, was helping me prepare my report to the Congress and to the nation on the recently adjourned Big Three Conference. One evening, in my cabin aboard the *Augusta,* as I was putting the finishing touches on my report, I said to Rosenman:

" 'Sam, one of the first things I want to do after we get home and make this report is to get busy on my domestic program. I would like to submit most of it at the same time instead of on a piecemeal basis. Ordinarily that would be done in a State of the Union message next January, but I cannot wait that long. What I think I will do is to send up a message as soon as we can get one up. Will you start to get together material and perhaps get up a rough draft?' . . .

" 'Fine,' he replied, 'What in general are the things you would like to say?' And he reached for a pencil and pad. I reviewed to him my views on the social and economic problems that had faced the nation before the collapse of the early thirties, and my views on the measures which the Roosevelt administration had taken for economic recovery and social reform. I spoke then of my own plans and policies for future legislation—the general direction in which I thought the United States ought to go in the years after the war. As we discussed these long-range policies and the legislation I was suggesting to carry them out, Rosenman leaned forward.

" 'You know, Mr. President,' he said eagerly, 'this is the most exciting and pleasant surprise I have had in a long time.'

" 'How is that?' I asked.

" 'Well,' he replied, 'I suppose I have been listening too much to rumors about what you are going to do—rumors which come from some of your conservative friends, and particularly from some of your former colleagues up on Capitol Hill. They say you are going to be quite a shock to those who followed Roosevelt— that the New Deal is as good as dead—that we are all going back to "normalcy" and that a good part of the so-called "Roosevelt nonsense" is now over. In other words, that the conservative wing of the party has now taken charge. I never really believed any of that in view of your long voting record in the Senate—on the basis of which President Roosevelt was so anxious that you become the vice presidential candidate. . . .'

" 'But this seems to settle it,' he continued. 'This really sets forth a progressive political philosophy and a liberal program of action that will fix the theme for your whole term in office. *It is one thing to vote for this kind of a program when you are following the head of a party; it is quite another to be the head of a party and recommend and fight for it.*' "[77] (Emphasis added)

The President was forced to combat his conservative friends as well as the

Congress. After the message was drafted, "he distributed drafts among his advisers, including Snyder. And there followed a real battle, which went on for a week. Snyder told him that this was a communistic message, that it was too left-wing, that he would murder himself politically, that he would lose the support of business, and so forth. This battle went on for a week with Snyder and Connolly on the one side, and on the other side Charlie Ross and I. We won. Not that I think that the President ever really wavered. I think that what he was doing in hesitating and deliberating at all was giving some satisfaction and comfort to his old friend John Snyder."[78]

When the last word was spoken his friends stood loyally by, uttering only a sigh; the Congress had memorized the Russian "Nyet."

By the end of his first year as President, Truman was to claim that Congress had given him less cooperation and more trouble than any President since Andrew Jackson. Congress refused to raise the minimum wage from 40 cents to 65 cents an hour, refused to set up a permanent Fair Employment Practices Committee, substituted the establishment of the Council of Economic Advisers to keep him informed about economic conditions for full-employment legislation which he had desired, returned the function of the U.S. Employment Service to the states instead of strengthening the service, failed to enact legislation for public housing, national health insurance or extension of Social Security benefits, and enacted an ineffective Price Control Bill.

One of President Truman's most notable contributions was in the field of civil rights. After Congress had refused to set up a permanent Fair Employment Practice Committee, the President established on December 5, 1946, the President's Committee on Civil Rights to determine "in what respect current law enforcement measures may be strengthened and improved to safeguard the civil rights of the people." The committee was also directed to include in its written report recommendations with respect to the adoption or establishment by legislation or otherwise, of more adequate and effective means and procedures for the protection of civil rights. This was the action of a man from the border state of Missouri, of a man whose mother was so hostile to Abraham Lincoln that she predicated her first visit to the White House on the promise that she would not have to sleep in the Lincoln bed. This was the action of a fair-minded man who, while serving his first term in the Senate, had joined Northern liberals by signing cloture petitions and endorsing motions to close debate on an anti-lynching bill;[79] who in 1940 supported an amendment to the Selective Service Act to prevent discrimination against members of minority groups who wished to volunteer for service in the armed forces.[80]

His senatorial record, however, was not unblemished; on August 25, 1942, he voted against an anti-poll tax amendment to the soldier's vote bill for national elections.[81] There lurked in him some of the prejudice which had surrounded him since birth; the greater part of his record shows that he submerged it.

The practical politician seeking the Negro vote—crucial to his election—spoke sincere words in opening his senatorial campaign: "I believe in the brotherhood of man; not merely the brotherhood of white men; but the brotherhood of all men before the law. I believe in the Constitution and the Declaration of Independence. In giving to the Negroes the rights that are theirs, we are acting in accord with the ideas of true democracy. If any class or race can be permanently set apart from, or pushed down below the rest in political and civil rights, so may any class or race when it shall incur the displeasure of its more powerful associates, and we may say farewell to the principles on which we commit our safety."[82]

His record as President proved that he meant these words. There had been no President of the United States preceding him since Lincoln who did so much for civil rights. But he proceeded at first with extreme caution, ever-mindful of the political realities with which he was forced to deal—the conservative Democratic-Republican coalition in the Congress. It has been said that he recalled the race difficulties which followed World War I when he established the Committee on Civil Rights in 1947.[83] His recollection of history being fabulous, this is probably true, but it took several severe incidents to nudge him into recollection and action. One was when a Negro veteran, still wearing his country's uniform, was blackjacked and blinded by a South Carolina police chief. Another took place near Monroe, Georgia, on July 25, 1946: two Negro couples in the company of a white farmer were shot to death. On July 30, 1946, fifty women carried banners which read: "Speak! Speak! Mr. President," and "Where is Democracy?"[84] Mob violence continued to grow; he declared: "As President of the United States I felt I ought to do everything within my power to find what caused such crimes and root out the causes."[85]

It was useless to make further appeals to Congress, and the Attorney General had no jurisdiction in violence contained within a state; so the President created the Committee on Civil Rights by Executive Order #9008 on December 5, 1946, to be financed by the Presidential budget. The importance of this committee, which had been under preparation for several months, was emphasized by the desertion by vast numbers of Negroes from the Democratic Party in the congressional elections of November 1946.

In addressing the first session of the commission, he suggested that he viewed the problem of civil rights as something more than a political issue; for him it was a constitutional issue as well. A very important feature of the President's style was expressed. As Berman says, "Truman firmly believed that as president of the United States he was obligated to defend the Constitution not only by upholding the laws of the land but by strengthening them as well. He understood that it was necessary to protect civil rights, if only to preserve the integrity of the law. Although he was destined to be attacked in the South and elsewhere as a dangerous innovator for his seeming disregard of local customs, Truman actually appears to be a traditionalist who decried acts of injustice because they violated what he thought constituted the American heritage of political liberty and fair play."[86] This is an apt characterization but it omits the fact that he was a courageous fighter for the achievement of these ideals. His reputation as a fighter for ideals was not yet established, but these were the seeds.

When, on June 29, 1947, the President addressed the NAACP rally in front of the Lincoln Memorial, he dealt with the new role he envisioned for the federal government in the defense of civil rights. It was the first time in the twentieth century that an American President publicly discussed the problem of racial discrimination with frankness and humanity. Having set out upon his purpose, he did not flinch from it. "We must keep moving forward with new concepts of civil rights to safeguard our heritage. The extension of civil rights today means, not protection of the people against the government, but protection of the people by the government. . . . There is much that state and local government can do in providing positive safeguards for civil rights. But we cannot, any longer, await the growth of a will to action in the slowest state or the most backward community. . . .

". . . We cannot wait another decade or another generation to remedy these evils. We must work, as never before, to cure them now. . . . Every man should have the right to a worthwhile job, the right to an equal share in making public decisions through the ballot, and the right to a fair trial in a fair court. We must insure that these rights—on equal terms—are enjoyed by every citizen."

When Truman finished, he turned to Walter White, secretary of the NAACP, and his words were so characteristic of this earnest man: "I mean every word of it—and I am going to prove that I do mean it."[87]

The August 1947 issue of *Crisis*—the monthly journal of the NAACP—referred to the speech as "the most comprehensive and forthright statement on the rights of minorities in a democracy and the duty of the government to secure safeguards that has ever been made by a President of the United States."

The report of the commission entitled *To Secure These Rights,* submitted to President Truman on October 29, 1947, went far beyond anything Truman had in mind when he commissioned the investigation and had a tremendous effect upon public opinion, including that of the courts and the Congress.

As an instance of its effect upon the courts, on May 3, 1948, the Supreme Court, with three justices having earlier disqualified themselves from participating in the cases, unanimously agreed that racially restrictive housing covenants were not enforceable. On the day after *To Secure These Rights* had been released, the Attorney General with the President's approval had announced at a press conference that the Justice Department was planning to involve itself in the restrictive covenant cases. On December 5, 1947, the Justice Department submitted a brief in one of the covenant cases—*Shelly* vs. *Kraemer.* This was the first of a series of briefs originating in the Solicitor General's office in the Truman administration that in time would profoundly affect American jurisprudence and American society. In a landmark decision speaking for the Court, Chief Justice Fred Vinson declared that the covenants were directed toward a group "defined wholly in terms of race and color"; and that "among the civil rights intended to be protected from discriminatory state action by the Fourteenth Amendment are the right to acquire, enjoy, own and dispose of property."[88]

On December 29, 1947, Henry Wallace announced that he would be the Presidential candidate of the newly formed Progressive Party; and Henry Wallace had a great following among black voters. In the South, Governor Fielding J. Wright announced in his Inaugural Address in Jackson, Mississippi, that he would not tolerate any federal action "aimed to wreck the South and our institutions"; the Mississippi state legislature then passed a resolution supporting Wright's threat.

Mindful of Wallace's potential strength with black voters and not at all intimidated by Governor Wright's rhetoric, President Truman sent the message he had been preparing to Congress on February 2, 1948. Similar in style to his earlier NAACP speech, this message "was not written to inflame passions; its language was dignified and responsible."[89] This was his undramatic style which dealt with facts as he saw them—dealt with his decisions in the manner of a man who had no divided opinion. If his text happened to be dramatic, his delivery would not make the most of it; but gradually his sincerity brought the message to his public. Once he made up his mind he never had further doubts.

Using the same theme that he had so successfully used at the NAACP rally —that the American heritage guaranteed equal rights to all citizens—he made the telling point that "there is a serious gap between our ideals and some of our practices," and "this gap must be closed." The President requested that the Congress:

1. Establish a permanent Commission on Civil Rights, a joint Congressional Committee on Civil Rights, and a Civil Rights Division in the Department of Justice.
2. Strengthen existing civil rights statutes.
3. Provide federal protection against lynching.
4. Protect more adequately the right to vote.
5. Establish a Fair Employment Practice Commission to prevent unfair discrimination in employment.
6. Prohibit discrimination in interstate transportation facilities.
7. Provide home rule and suffrage in Presidential elections for the residents of the District of Columbia.
8. Provide statehood for Hawaii and Alaska and a greater measure of self-government for our island possessions.
9. Equalize the opportunities for residents of the United States to become naturalized citizens.
10. Settle the evacuation claims of Japanese Americans.[90]

The President then announced that he was going to release an executive order "containing a comprehensive restatement of the federal non-discrimination policy, together with appropriate measures to insure compliance," and that he had instructed the Secretary of Defense to have "the remaining instances of discrimination in the armed services eliminated as rapidly as possible." He concluded his message with a cogent argument for its adoption—an argument that would have great appeal: "The position of the United States in the world today makes it especially urgent that we adopt these measures to secure for all our people their essential rights. . . . If we wish to inspire the peoples of the world whose freedom is in jeopardy, if we wish to restore hope to those who have already lost their civil liberties, if we wish to fulfill the promise that is ours, we must correct the remaining imperfections in our practice of democracy.

"We know the way. We need only the will."[91]

Bedlam broke forth in the South; the Republicans pressed for their own civil rights measure, asserting that the President's message had been ingeniously designed to appeal to the black votes of such states as New York, Pennsylvania and Illinois; Senate minority leader Alben Barkley of Kentucky refused to sponsor the bill (about which he had not been consulted, probably because Truman knew that he would attempt to dissuade him from his position).

It seems to be a trait of great Presidents that though they attempt the near-impossible they do not become discouraged. Sometimes they pull back for a bit and try to mend fences, but only temporarily. The White House announced on February 10 that "there will be absolutely no compromise on any point."[92] He refused to discuss the matter with any Southern group. On March 8 he announced that he would be a Presidential candidate in 1948. On May 10 a states' rights conference assembled in Jackson, Mississippi, to promote the aims and interests of "states' rights" Democrats. The Republicans nominated Governor Thomas E. Dewey of New York, who had a noteworthy civil rights record, and wrote a strong civil rights plank in their platform (although not as inclusive or far-reaching as Truman's February 2 message). In spite of his no-compromise statement, the President tried to reach compromise agreements with leading Southern-ers; when this leaked to the press, Henry Wallace charged him with hypocrisy on the civil rights issue.

Of noteworthy importance was the fact that the NAACP, holding its annual convention in St. Louis, Missouri, praised Truman for the stand he had taken on civil rights, while Wallace was attacked for his failure to fight discrimination or segregation during the years he had served as Vice President and Secretary of Agriculture and of Commerce. It was evident that the leadership of the NAACP preferred Truman to Dewey or Wallace.[93]

The great fight was in the committee to draft the Democratic platform; that fight would have to be resolved by the President, for any plank drafted would have to be satisfactory to him. Truman was confronted by the threatened revolt of the South and the forthright position of Senator Hubert Humphrey, who was a member of the drafting committee. Humphrey announced that he intended to fight for the inclusion of such specific civil rights recommendations as an anti-lynching law, abolition of the poll tax, an FEPC, and the abolition of segregation in the armed forces. The committee members divided into (1) those who were Southern states' rights adherents, (2) those Humphrey liberals who wanted civil rights spelled out in an exact program, and (3) those Truman liberals who were trying to keep the states' righters in the party by enunciating their objectives in broad terms instead of in specific terms. The majority of the 108-member commit-tee voted for the third position, and the chairman of the drafting committee, Senator Meyers, presented their version of the civil rights plank to the convention.

Tempers were too high for the convention's acceptance of the reported plank; a floor fight ensued in which the Southerners lost the minority resolution pre-sented by Dan Moody of Texas by a vote of 925 nays to 309 yeas, with only 11 votes outside the solid South cast for it. The liberals won by a vote of 651½ to 582½, and their plank was written into the platform largely because of the support they received from the big city bosses in New York, Illinois and Pennsyl-vania. Truman's efforts to preserve harmony failed; some Southerners walked out of the convention. Some stayed and gave their protest votes to Senator Richard Russell of Georgia instead of to Truman. On July 17, a states' rights conference met in Birmingham, Alabama, and selected Governor Strom Thurmond of South Carolina and Governor Fielding Wright of Mississippi to head a states' rights ticket. So President Truman had to thread his 1948 campaign between the popu-lar Republican Tom Dewey, the reactionary Southern-supported Strom Thur-mond and the ultra-liberal Henry Wallace.

He, however, did not choose to thread his way; he chose to give them hell; and "Give-'em-hell Harry," who expected to lose, won.

A fighter he had been and a fighter he remained. His acceptance speech attacked the record of the 80th Congress, which had a Republican majority. He was advised after the Republican Convention to call a special session of the Congress. "The Republicans are in control of the Congress. Cite this platform to them and tell them that it isn't necessary to elect a new Congress, that you hope it will pass this platform immediately in the special session and that you would sign it if it were passed." Truman thought that this was a good idea, and "he added one dramatic touch. In his acceptance speech to the Democratic conven-tion, he recited these facts, that the Republicans had passed a platform which called for an extension of social security and a great many other things, *and he announced then and there at the Convention that he was going to call a special session and offer the special session the right to pass the entire platform, saying that he would sign it. . . .* (Emphasis added)

"Of course, what happened was what everyone expected—namely that the Congress in the special session ran away from their platform; they adopted none of it. But I think it had a great deal to do with the 1948 victory in indicating to many of the liberal groups, who thought that a vote for Dewey would be a vote for this liberal platform, that this whole thing was a phoney."[94]

On the day before the special session was to convene he issued two executive orders pertaining to civil rights, orders which had been under consideration for at least six months; now he was ready to sign and release them. One authorized the creation of a review board in each department and agency of the federal executive branch to whom government employees could appeal if they felt victimized by discriminatory employment practices. The Fair Employment Board, attached to the Civil Service Commission, was designed "to coordinate the practices and procedures of the various departments and agencies, to maintain overall supervision as a final review body to hear appeals from the decision of departmental heads on complaints of discrimination."[95] The other order stated that: "It is hereby declared to be the policy of the President that there shall be equality of treatment and opportunity for all persons in the armed services without regard to race, color, religion or national origin. This policy shall be put into effect as rapidly as possible, having due regard to the time required to effectuate any necessary changes without impairing efficiency or morale."[96] This order is ranked among the most important steps taken to end racial discrimination in the history of civil rights in the United States.[97] It was no accident that both orders were issued as a curtain raiser to the special session of a Congress with a Republican majority. In layman's parlance it would be said—"See what I did; try to match it." The Republican leadership tried by bringing out of committee the anti-poll tax bill, only to have it met by Southern filibuster.

President Truman won the 1948 election, but his civil rights efforts in his second term made little headway with the 81st Congress. His greatest success was the climate he established by repeated messages, and by several executive orders. It was well summed up on January 12, 1953, by Roy Wilkins's letter to the President as he was about to leave office. After noting Truman's accomplishments in the field of civil rights, Wilkins concluded with the following observation: "Mr. President, you have been responsible through the pronouncements from your high office, for a new climate of opinion in this broad area of civil rights."[98] Note must be taken also of the fact that when the President delivered his farewell address to the American people he referred to civil rights, saying, "There has been a tremendous awakening of the American conscience on the great issue of civil rights—equal economic opportunities, equal rights of citizenship and equal educational opportunities for all our people, whatever their race, religion or status of birth."[99] This stubborn man was rightly proud of what he had done in the face of equally stubborn opposition which successfully blocked his recommended legislation but was powerless to block the progress for which he had pointed the way.

In the main, "pointing the way" was Truman's major accomplishment in all domestic phases of the Fair Deal. He carried the New Deal mantle and proposed social innovations that went beyond it and were accomplished in later years when the extreme conservatism of the postwar era had subsided. Congress not only defeated his civil rights legislation but failed to enact his recommendations on national health insurance, the Brannan Plan for agriculture, rational and humane immigration laws, federal aid to education. His major accomplishment in social legislation was the enactment of the Public Housing Act of 1949, a rise in minimum wages passed in 1949, and the enactment in 1950 of a social security measure that increased benefits and extended coverage to 10 million more Americans.

He won labor's gratitude not by enactment of legislation but by vetoing the Case Anti-Labor Bill in 1946, and by vetoing the Taft-Hartley Bill of 1947 with a fighting veto message which had as its peroration: "I have concluded that the bill is a clear threat to the successful working of our democratic society.

"One of the major lessons of recent world history is that free and vital trade unions are a strong bulwark against the growth of totalitarian governments. We must, therefore, be everlastingly alert that in striking at union abuses, we do not destroy the contribution which unions make to our democratic strength.

"This bill would go far toward weakening our trade-union movement. And it would go far toward destroying our national unity. By raising barriers between labor and management and by injecting political considerations into normal economic decisions, it would invite them to gain their ends through direct political action. I think it would be extremely dangerous to our country to develop a class basis for political action."[100] The bill was passed over his veto; the veto added to his prestige with labor and to his 1948 Presidential vote.

He took Labor Day, 1948, as the occasion to deliver one of the great fighting speeches of the campaign. His belligerency erupted as he began: "Two years ago the people of this country, and many workingmen among them, seemed to feel that they wanted a change. They elected the Republican 80th Congress—and they got their change. That Congress promptly fell into the familiar Republican pattern of aid for big business and attack on labor. The Republicans promptly voted themselves a cut in taxes and voted you a cut in freedom.

"The 80th Republican Congress failed to crack down on prices but it cracked down on labor all right!

"The Republicans failed to give the consumers of America protection against the rising cost of living, but at the same time they put a dangerous weapon into the hands of the big corporations in the shape of the Taft-Hartley law which I vetoed, but which was passed over my veto. . . .

"If the congressional elements that made the Taft-Hartley law are allowed to remain in power, and if these elements are further encouraged by the election of a Republican President, you men of labor can expect to be hit by a steady barrage of body blows. *And if you stay at home, as you did in 1946,* and keep these reactionaries in power, *you will deserve every blow you get.*"[101] (Emphasis added)

The style with which a President delivers his speech is significant because of its effect upon his audience—hence his effectiveness in getting across his message. For that reason the following account is of particular interest: "President Truman is very good at making extemporaneous speeches. He's not very good at writing or reading speeches. He would be the first to admit it. And therefore, he did not add as much to a speech as Roosevelt did. In fact, I would say that he did not contribute twenty percent of what Roosevelt did to speeches. I'm talking now about language only rather than thought. President Truman used to tell us in great detail the substance of what he wanted to follow. But after he had told us that, his participation in the actual phraseology was slight. He would go over the speech with us and make very few corrections unless it was a question of major policy.

"He used to practice the delivery of speeches at the beginning very assiduously. He used to read them to a recording machine, and then play them back to find the right place of emphasis, the right pause, and so forth. He would mark up his reading copy so as to indicate emphases, for example. After a while, he got more used to speaking and it came more easily for him. But at the beginning he used to work very hard over his speeches, until he developed a style of delivery of his own."[102]

This was his early style and sometimes used in later years, but in 1948 he adopted a method more effective. Sam says: "I was with him during the convention of 1948, and went with him to Philadelphia where he delivered his acceptance speech. That speech was delivered extemporaneously from notes. It was the first major speech which he delivered from notes and he did it very well. So after that convention he followed the practice very frequently especially on campaigns, of speaking from notes rather than reading speeches. His acceptance speech, as I say, was delivered from notes, and was very enthusiastically received. It had a certain eloquence."[103]

Not so eloquent, but very effective, were the extemporaneous speeches made at every whistle stop from the back of his campaign train. They won the heart of his audiences, who gloried in his toughness and determination, in what he aimed to do and the explicit, direct, unembellished way that he said it. "Give 'em hell, Harry" was the popular refrain. It seemed to be—even to the candidate who never publicly admitted it—a hopeless trip, but he set out to do his best. That was his style.

He had been doing his best in the baffling field of foreign affairs which had increased in complexity since the Potsdam Conference. Although when he became President he had no greater knowledge of foreign affairs than did President Wilson, he had three advantages which Wilson did not possess. He had the knowledge of President Roosevelt's experience and of his philosophy in dealing with Stalin and with Churchill, which he had decided to emulate. He had experienced foreign service personnel whose advice he could consult. And he had inherited the bi-partisan support which Roosevelt had achieved in his Cabinet and in Congress. But after the Potsdam Conference he seemed to be sinking deeper and deeper into a quagmire of dissension and discord.

It started upon Byrnes's return from the Moscow Conference of Foreign Ministers. The President's account states: "Byrnes left a collection of documents on the conference with me, and I agreed to study them at once. As I went through these papers it became abundantly clear to me that the successes of the Moscow conference were unreal. I could see that the Russians had given us no more than a general promise that they would be willing to sit down to talk again about the control of atomic energy. There was not a word in the communique to suggest that the Russians might be willing to change their ways in Iran—where the situation was rapidly becoming very serious—or anywhere else. Byrnes, I concluded after studying the entire record, had taken it upon himself to move the foreign policy of the United States in a direction to which I could not, and would not agree. Moreover, he had undertaken this on his own initiative without consulting or informing the President."[104]

How much Byrnes's high-handed assumption of authority and failure to report to and consult with his chief affected the President's change from patience to impatience with the Russians cannot be ascertained. It was perhaps one of many factors at play. There was the erosion of public trust in Russia evidenced by opinion polls which showed that 54 per cent of a national sample had been willing to trust the Russians to cooperate with the United States in the postwar world when Japan surrendered and only 44 per cent were of the same opinion two months after the failure of the London Conference. By the end of February 1946, it stood at 35 per cent.[105] There was increasing evidence that the Republicans in Congress were preparing to cease their wartime cooperation and were readying to capitalize on public disillusionment in the coming congressional elections. Byrnes had elevated Senate Republican dissatisfaction by acting like Woodrow Wilson in not consulting them; in fact, he added insult to injury by taking John Foster Dulles, the unofficial Republican spokesman on foreign affairs, to London to serve on the American delegation and then not consulting him.[106]

Republican criticism reached a climax on February 27, 1946, when Senator Vandenberg asked the Senate members: "What is Russia up to now? We ask it in Manchuria. We ask it in Eastern Europe and the Dardanelles. . . . We ask it in the Baltic and the Balkans. We ask it in Poland. . . . We ask it in Japan. We ask it sometimes even in connection with events in our own United States. What is Russia up to now?" He asserted that two rival ideologies, democracy and communism, now found themselves face to face. They could live together in harmony, but only "if the United States speaks as plainly upon all occasions as Russia does; if the United States just as vigorously sustains its own purposes and its ideals upon all occasions as Russia does; if we abandon this miserable fiction, often encouraged by our own fellow-travellers, that we somehow jeopardize the peace if our candor is firm as Russia's always is; and if we assume a moral leadership which we have too frequently allowed to lapse."[107]

Other influences were at work within the administration, and even as Vandenberg was speaking State Department speech writers were placing the finishing touches on the first public statement of the administration's new position.[108] The most important of these influences were the foreign service officials; of major influence was Ambassador Averell Harriman, who had reported as early as January 1945 that the Russians were using local Communist organizations as one means of extending their influence over neighboring countries, but at that time he interpreted this merely to be an effort to ensure the security of the Soviet Union. By April 1945 Harriman had become convinced that Communist ideology was the dominant factor.[109] In and out of Congress there was the fear which was to lead to McCarthyism that there was a well-organized effort to spread world revolution. That fear encompassed Secretary of the Navy James V. Forrestal, George F. Kennan, then counselor of the American Embassy in Moscow, and Under Secretary of State Joseph Grew.

On February 9, 1949, Joseph Stalin gave comfort to the postwar revisionists who believed that reason and compromise, mutual attempts to demonstrate understanding and goodwill, should be discarded; they feared Russian aggressiveness and advocated a get-tough policy as the only one which would influence Stalin. He "made a rare public speech in which he stressed the incompatibility of communism and capitalism. World War II had broken out, the Soviet leader asserted, because of the uneven rate of development in capitalist economies. War could have been avoided had some method existed for periodically redistributing raw materials and markets between nations according to need. No such method could exist, however, under capitalism. Stalin clearly implied that future wars were inevitable until the world economic system was reformed, that is, until communism supplanted capitalism as the prevailing form of economic organization."[110] Omitting the relevancy of Communist world power being the only effective means to control the world disposition of raw materials, one must admit the pertinence of Stalin's delineation of this problem to the problems the world faces today.

On February 16, 1946, news of the Canadian spy case broke and the world knew that Russia had obtained secret data on the bomb. Two weeks after Stalin's speech, and one week after news of the spy case broke, a long cable arrived at the State Department from George F. Kennan, then American chargé d'affaires in Moscow, analyzing the motives behind Soviet behavior. It fell upon receptive ears. On February 20, 1946, President Truman told Admiral Leahy that he was extremely unhappy with the existing policy of appeasing the Russians and was determined to assume a stronger position at once.[111]

Winston Churchill delivered his "iron curtain" speech at Fulton, Missouri, on March 5, 1946. It was the bolt that secured the change of policy. The speech emphasized the Soviets' determination to control the countries adjacent to them —some of which had been under British influence before the war. This struggle for Soviet influence and its opposition to the British "cordon sanitaire" had strained Soviet-British relations during and after the war; and it is possible that it had aggravated Russian policy, making it harsher than it might have been through fear. It must be recalled that the British Empire had been much more powerful before World War II than it is today; and it is pertinent to recall the European power struggle following World War I entailing the countries of that area at the time and the failure of President Wilson's efforts to curb spheres of influence.

The dramatic words uttered by one of the world's greatest orators at a crucial moment in Russian relations were: "From Serbia in the Baltic to Trieste in the Adriatic, an iron curtain has descended across the Continent. Behind that line lie all the capitals of the ancient states of central and eastern Europe. Warsaw, Berlin, Prague, Vienna, Budapest, Belgrade, Bucharest, and Sofia, all these famous cities and the population around them lie in the Soviet sphere and all are subject in one form or another, not only to Soviet influence but to a very high and increasing measure of control from Moscow."[112]

It is no wonder that opinion polls regarding public trust in Russia fell to 35 per cent after that speech (see page 474 and below). It is also no wonder that Russian alarm increased at Churchill's suggestion that although the United Nations offered the best hope for peace it would be ineffective unless there developed a "fraternal association of English-speaking peoples." The American public were by no means unanimous in their acceptance of Churchill's viewpoint; Mrs. Franklin D. Roosevelt publicly chided Mr. Churchill for implying that the English-speaking peoples could get along "without the far greater number of people who are not English-speaking," and when Winston Churchill spoke in New York on March 15, pickets chanted: "Winnie, Winnie, go away, UNO is here to stay."

Polls taken in March showed increased disillusionment with Russia; Truman and Byrnes adopted a new policy of "patience with firmness."[113] A few—such as Joseph E. Davies, former Ambassador to Soviet Union, Eleanor Roosevelt and Henry Wallace—were dismayed by the change; but the President's ear had been captured by others and the natural belligerency toward Russia which he had suppressed came to the fore. In addition, Russian rudeness riled Truman. Probably growing American hostility hardened Russian hostility—an easy thing to accomplish. The sword had a double edge.

There had been no attempt by the President to educate the American people respecting the reasons for what is now termed "détente." When that policy was changed, the American public did not understand that it entailed necessary steps which ran counter to their postwar wishes for keeping their sons and their money in the United States. The President, much as Wilson did, delayed a public position. Finally, in true Truman style, he asked his special counsel, Clark M. Clifford (who had succeeded Sam Rosenman), to compile a comprehensive report on American relations with the Soviet Union; research for the 100,000-word document which resulted was begun in the summer of 1946.

In the meantime crisis followed crisis. Typical was that involving Turkey and typical was Truman's reaction to it—his commitment to an uncompromising policy. "On August 7, the Russians requested a revision of the Montreux Convention to allow for joint Turkish-Soviet defense of the Dardanelles. American officials viewed this move as the culmination of a long effort by Moscow to establish naval bases in Turkey, a development which they feared might make that country a Soviet satellite.

"Truman's top military and diplomatic advisers concluded that the Soviet note clearly reflected a desire to dominate Turkey, and that if Moscow succeeded, it would be 'extremely difficult, if not impossible' for the United States to keep the Russians from gaining control in Greece and all the Near and Middle East. Only the conviction that the United States was prepared to use force would deter the Kremlin. . . . At a meeting on April 15, Truman endorsed this conclusion with such alacrity that General Eisenhower, then Army Chief of Staff, politely asked whether the Chief Executive realized that this position could lead to war if the Russians did not back down. Truman surprised Eisenhower by delivering a brief but impressive lecture on the significance of the Black Sea Straits, leaving no doubt that he understood fully the ominous implications of the memorandum he had just approved. The Administration strongly encouraged the Turks to resist the Russian demands and, to back them up, dispatched units of the American fleet in the eastern Mediterranean. One month later Secretary Forrestal announced that the Navy would henceforth maintain a permanent presence in that part of the world.

"In face of these maneuvers, the Russians dropped their demands for bases in the Dardanelles, thus averting a major confrontation."[114]

President Truman, with great courage and no hesitation, had started a strategy of "containment," but in order to implement that strategy there were the burdens which the American people would have to face—and they were not aware of them—the supply of American money and men. In fact in 1946 there was great difficulty in securing an extension of the Selective Service Act and in the following year Congress allowed it to expire. A powerful combination of religious, pacifist, educational, farm and labor organizations kept the proposal for universal military training from receiving serious consideration. "Not until Americans had suffered the repeated shocks of the Czechoslovak coup, the Berlin blockade, the Soviet atomic bomb, the fall of China, and the Korean War could they bring themselves to accept large peacetime military establishment as a normal state of affairs."[115]

Americans wanted to plow their fields, flush their economy and keep their money at home. Truman started to lead them by educating them on April 6, 1946, when he spoke of economic aid to foreign countries: "We shall help because we know that we ourselves cannot enjoy prosperity in a world of economic stagnation. We shall help because economic distress anywhere in the world, is a fertile breeding ground for violent political upheaval. And we shall help because we feel it is right to lend a hand to our friends and allies who are recovering from wounds inflicted by our common enemy."[116]

It was not until March 12, 1947, that the President in an address to Congress went so far as to say publicly that "it must be the policy of the United States to support free peoples who are resisting attempted subjugation by armed minorities or by outside pressures." Mr. Truman wrote in his memoirs that he himself had scratched out the word "should" in the State Department's draft and inserted "must." This sentence forms the foundation of the "Truman Doctrine," and the substitution of the word "must" for "should" illustrates the strength of the President's conviction and demonstrates the forcefulness with which he would act to implement his conviction.

A communication had been received on February 21 from Great Britain stating that because of internal economic difficulties she would have to suspend economic and military aid to Greece and Turkey as of March 31. In Greece a Communist-led guerrilla movement nurtured by economic distress threatened to take over the government when the British withdrew. The State Department, now headed by Secretary of State George Marshall and Under Secretary of State Dean Acheson, regarded these guerrillas as "instruments of Soviet policy" and were concerned that if they came to power a "domino" effect would propel Turkey, Iran and possibly Italy and France into a Russian sphere of influence.

On February 27, the President, preparing for action, with political wisdom invited a bi-partisan group of congressional leaders to the White House for a briefing on the Greek crisis; he knew that it was going to be difficult to obtain congressional support and therefore he consulted the leaders of both parties in advance. It was difficult to convince the leaders. Dean Acheson is credited with winning their support by a brilliant presentation. In brief he explained that aid to Turkey was not simply a matter of rescuing British chestnuts, it was a realistic effort to protect the security of the United States by strengthening the ability of free people to resist Communist aggression and subversion.

A long silence followed Acheson's scholarly presentation. "Then Arthur Vandenberg said solemnly, 'Mr. President, if you will say that to the Congress and the country, I will support you and I believe that most of its members will do the same.' Without much further talk the meeting broke up to convene again, enlarged, in a week to consider a more detailed program of action."[117] Much work of preparation was required, but when Acheson presented the agreed details to the President on March 7, he decided that he had no alternative but to go ahead; realizing that this was only a beginning, he approved a request for $250 million for Greece and $150 million for Turkey, and the message to Congress. Acheson's description which follows graphically describes Truman's style: "We then moved into the Cabinet Room, where the President laid out the whole program, which got unanimous Cabinet support, and ordered a meeting with congressional leaders for March 10 and, depending on its outcome, a presidential appearance before Congress on March 12. I came back to the Department somewhat breathless. When President Truman had made a decision, he moved fast."[118]

The large group of senators and congressmen who met in the President's office on March 10 were unresponsive. The majority of the members of Congress had been elected after a campaign for economy and against the policies of President Truman. The Democratic congressional conference had warned the administration against supporting British policies in the Mediterranean or the Greek monarchy. The Senate on March 4 had voted to cut the President's budget for the next fiscal year by $4.5 billion dollars, the House earlier having voted a cut of $6 billion. Senator Taft had expressed opposition to the President's request for an extension of the War Powers Act and the Selective Service Act.

This was the political atmosphere which prevailed when the President, in his matter-of-fact way, "laid out the need for action and the action proposed. . . . Vandenberg reiterated his insistence that the President put the crisis before Congress in its broadest setting. No one else said very much. No commitments were made."[119]

Two days later the President presented the program which became celebrated as the Truman Doctrine to the Congress. He made the ideological confrontation between the Soviet Union and the United States the central focus of his remarks: "At the present moment in world history nearly every nation must choose between alternative ways of life. The choice is too often not a free one.

"One way of life is based upon the will of the majority, and is distinguished by free institutions, representative government, free elections, guarantee of individual liberty, freedom of speech and religion, and freedom from political oppression.

"The second way of life is based upon the will of a minority forcibly imposed upon the majority. It relies upon terror and oppression, a controlled press and radio, fixed elections, and the suppression of personal freedoms.

"I believe that it must be the policy of the United States to support free people who are resisting attempted subjugation by armed minorities or by outside pressure."[120]

The gap in ideologies was clearly drawn, and the manner of implementing the "get tough policy" was delineated. "When he finished, the President received a standing ovation from both parties. This was a tribute to a brave man rather than unanimous acceptance of his policy."[121] It took two months for Congress to pass the Act to Provide for Assistance to Greece and Turkey.

Arthur Vandenberg's leadership in Congress was crucial to enactment; Truman's recognition of his old friend and Republican adversary's importance to the fruition of the program was a tribute to his sagacity and to his modesty. He wanted to have the program enacted; it was not necessary to him that he place himself to the fore; he was satisfied to have Vandenberg carry the ball, knowing that in his hands lay the power. Truman was never hungry for personal power; he was eager for accomplishment, and always prepared to encourage an official in whom he had confidence to exercise a delegation of power. He expected the President to be kept advised and consulted.

On April 28, 1947, Secretary of State Marshall returned from Moscow, where he had been attending the latest meeting of the Council of Foreign Ministers. He was greatly disturbed by economic conditions in western Europe and by Russia's changed attitude. There was no longer an attempt to cooperate, nor even to pretend to do so. It seemed to him that the Soviet leadership courted economic disaster for their former European allies in the hopes that they would then turn to communism.

The United States had already contributed nearly $3 billion in foreign relief; made a direct loan of $3.75 billion to Great Britain; taken the lead in organizing the International Bank for Reconstruction and Development and the International Monetary Fund, and had given large sums to them. What was now needed, Marshall felt, was a careful study of the situation to formulate a sustained, organized effort. From this realization there developed the Marshall Plan.

"Historically viewed, the authorship of the Marshall Plan lies, of course, squarely with General Marshall and President Truman. . . . President Truman deserves . . . credit . . . for his perception and political courage in selecting as Secretary of State one of the most experienced, most selfless, and most honorable of America's professional public servants, in giving to that man his confidence and a wide latitude of action, and then supporting him in an individual initiative which, had it misfired, could have brought embarrassment and misfortune to the administration."[122]

Not only did President Truman have confidence in his Secretary of State, but his political wisdom dictated to him that it would not be wise for him—at this moment of his unpopularity with the 80th Congress and with the public—to propose such a policy. General Marshall both at home and abroad was above partisan criticism; therefore he urged George Marshall to use the occasion of his address at the commencement exercises at Harvard University on June 5 to launch the plan, forever after called "The Marshall Plan."

Dean Acheson has written that "It was in the formation of the 'proposal' that the genius of General Marshall's statement stands out. It is comprised of six sentences, only one of which concerned what this country might do:

" 'It is already evident that, before the United States Government can proceed much further in its efforts to alleviate the situation and help start the European world on its way to recovery, there must be some agreement among the countries of Europe as to the requirements of the situation and the part these countries themselves will take in order to give proper effect to whatever action might be undertaken by the Government.

" 'It would be neither fitting nor efficacious for this Government to undertake to draw up unilaterally a program designed to place Europe on its feet economically.

" 'This is the business of Europeans.

" 'The initiative, I think, must come from Europe.

" 'The role of this country should consist of friendly aid in the drafting of a European program and of later support of such a program so far as it may be practical for us to do.' "[123]

At this time the Greek-Turkish aid bill had not yet been enacted. Though trusting the launching of the vast European aid proposal to the Secretary of State, the President even before that had busied himself with the important tactics of creating a favorable reception for it in Congress. Once more he had turned to the powerful Senator Arthur Vandenberg and the other congressional leaders, inviting them to tea, giving them a recital of the crisis in Europe and of the plans being devised for meeting it.

The President had lined up his most important support *before the battle started,* aware that Congress was dedicated to tax reduction and paring of governmental expenditures.

He was also more expansive with the press than was his usual style. This was one of the rare occasions when he used his press conference as a medium for the education of the country—as had President Roosevelt throughout his career. President Truman's style was to reply to press questions with a "yes" or "no" or brief one-sentence answers. Frequently correspondents, aware of this, couched their questions so as to elicit sensational quotes such as the famous "red herring" reference to Communists in government. He would rarely rephrase a question to suit himself before answering it. Sometimes he would give a one-sentence uninformative answer. A good example of his one-sentence answer at the press conference on February 24, 1949, almost two months before his proposal for a system of national health insurance was issued, is given by Elmer Cornwell. The President "was asked about the prospective content of the message, and said it would be confined to health. Then—

"Q. The whole national health program would be involved, rather than the —just one angle there?

"The President. That's right, the whole national health program, and it will be stated very plainly, so there won't be any argument about it."[124] The opportunity for mass education and support was not taken. And again on May 26 he rather brusquely cut off an inquiry about his support of specific bills like health insurance with "I am for all of them."[125] Such efforts as Truman made at explanation and elucidation at his press conferences were made almost invariably by a prepared statement carefully drafted in advance, which he read (amid many pleas that he slow down!) but which he would rarely expand upon in the ensuing question period. Almost invariably, when asked to comment on something that had been the subject of a speech or statement, he would tell his inquirers to go back and read the document.[126]

The Marshall Plan, however, was launched with special consideration for the education of the public by means of the press. The President did not use his regular press conferences to build support for the Marshall Plan; however, in 1947 and 1948 he held special off-the-record press conferences with various groups such as members of the American Society of Newspaper Editors and the Radio News Analysts. The first such occasion came on April 17, 1947, some five weeks after the Truman Doctrine message. The President opened the meeting of newspaper editors with a long informal discussion of administration foreign policy, which he prefaced with an expression of appreciation, and concluded with a request for cooperation.

"On April 23, 1948, three weeks after the Marshall Plan legislation had been signed, at an off-record meeting with the National Conference of Business Paper Editors, and on April 23, 1949, for the Newspaper Editors Association, the President did further educational work on behalf of the European Recovery Program, by then in operation. At all these gatherings he presented the administration's case carefully and at length."[127]

Directly after it had been presented, the British and French Foreign Ministers set a preliminary meeting of the conference of European nations to consider the Marshall Plan for July 17 in Paris. Greatly to everyone's surprise the Russian Minister for Foreign Affairs—the great wielder of "nyet"—turned up. "Nyet" was again the key word. He seemed determined to join the program although he continuously picked at details and expressed his suspicions of a dark, capitalist plot.

"On the fifth day, an aide, in obvious agitation, brought a telegram to Molotov at the conference table. An American observer who was on hand later described the tableau as follows:

" 'Molotov, you know, has a little bump in the middle of his forehead, and when he gets excited this thing swells and pulsates as though he had bumped his head. Well, when he read the telegram, the bump swelled up to half the size of a golf ball, and there was a lot of heated whispering among the Russians present. Then Molotov got up abruptly from his chair, swept up his papers, and announced that Russia was withdrawing forthwith, and the same would go for Poland and Czechoslovakia as well. And as for the Marshall Plan, he said it was nothing but a vicious American scheme for using dollars to buy its way into the internal affairs of European countries.' "[128]

This is a description of Russian rather than Truman style, but it is a graphic example of the difficulties of dealing with the Russians which augmented the President's inclination toward the cold war. Actually there had been great debate about the inclusion of the Russians; therefore it was a relief when they withdrew. Their real reason for withdrawing was that they were not in agreement with the objectives of the Marshall Plan. Their aim was not to see the European economy given life; communism could not be grown under prosperous conditions. The fact that Russia was not to be a participant aided congressional passage. It no doubt helped the Congress hurdle the prospect of the expenditure of $17 billion of U.S. tax money to finance the economic recovery of Britain and half of Europe in a commitment that would run at least four years. Never had this nation, or any other nation, been asked in peacetime to assume so great a burden. Although deemed altruistic, it was for the benefit of our own security—as the President intimated in his December 19 message to Congress: "Our deepest concern with European recovery, however, is that it is essential to the maintenance of the civilization in which the American life is rooted."

When the Marshall Plan was approved on April 2, 1948—by a House vote of 318 to 75 and by an overwhelming voice vote of the Senate—and had been signed by President Truman, Felix Belair, Jr., wrote in the New York Times: "What was to have been a measure of economic aid to Europe changed unnoticed to 'a measure short of war' to counteract Russian influence. . . . Never before in peacetime had Congress acted with such dispatch on such important legislation. But rarely ever before had there been such a threat to the world's free institutions."[129]

And rarely before had a President of the United States so quietly and smoothly guided so momentous a measure through the Congress, keeping himself in the background. The European Recovery Program, popularly known as the Marshall Plan, was the second of the great decisions he was to make in foreign affairs, and it must be emphasized that he had the courage to have it presented to the American people even before his first venture—the Truman Doctrine—had been enacted.

The dramatic success of the Berlin airlift greatly enhanced Truman's image as a leader. It will be remembered (see pages 449 and 453) that in setting up the four zones of occupation, President Truman included in his message of June 14, 1945, to Stalin the requirement that free access should be had to and from Berlin and that the answering message, which dealt with other matters in the communication, omitted any reference to this; the British had the same experience. It was assumed that omission meant acceptance. It did until conditions which were uncongenial to the Russians caused them abruptly to deny access by rail, road or waterway. There was, however, a written agreement for access by air—an agreement which the Russians must have deemed of small value in keeping the population and activity of the West Berlin population supplied with all necessities of life.

The Russians were disquieted by the prospect of the rehabilitation of the European countries and by the decision of the United States, Great Britain and France to combine their zones into a viable German entity; Russian plans for the spread of communism through lack of prosperity and well-being were threatened.

They were particularly disquieted by the possibility of the economic rejuvenation of Germany because of her proximity to Poland, through which she had tramped on her belligerent route to Russia throughout centuries. On the other hand, the United States and their European Allies were terrified lest there be starvation, lack of employment and political upheaval in Germany such as had followed World War I; in place of Hitlerism there was likely to be communism. Also considered was the German potential for recovery and development of commodities which would aid the recovery of other European countries. To comprehend this situation fully it is valuable to trace its development.

"From the very beginning, each of the occupying powers had different ideas about how Germany should be administered. The British decided very soon after Potsdam that Germany probably was permanently divided between East and West, and they proposed then that the United States and France cooperate with them in the three Western zones. But the French Government was adamant in opposing the Potsdam agreement to treat Germany as an economic unit. . . . So every time the British or Americans suggested fresh ideas for nationwide agencies to operate railways, power grids, and the like, the French Government would invoke its unique veto to block our plans. The Russians could sit back and let the French carry this ball for them."[130]

More than once General Eisenhower, while he was military governor of the American zone, had ruefully remarked that if his suggestion for retention of a SHAEF-type of organization had been used to organize the occupation problems the difficulties then faced would have been avoided. Now Americans in the military government began to consider a revised version of the recommendation that Eisenhower had made. "Along similar lines, a plan now evolved from an economic merger of the American and British zones. Because of French intransigence this seemed the most hopeful immediate prospect, but in order not to close the door on French and Russian cooperation, we again urged that all four occupying powers join in an economic merger."[131]

". . . And so it came about [just one year after the Potsdam Conference] that the Potsdam provision for administering Germany as an economic unit was applicable in only two of the four occupation zones. The resulting American-British merger—called Bizonia—was officially approved on July 30, 1946. . . . Bizonia really laid the foundation for western Europe's most powerful state, West Germany, destined to make possible a vigorous non-Communist Europe. I think the Soviet Government also failed to grasp immediately the full importance of Bizonia, because it was not until several months later that the Russians began their determined effort to obstruct this new administration in Germany."[132]

The formal discussions for drawing a German peace treaty opened in Moscow on March 10, 1947, and once again fate placed in the leading position a man who had been otherwise engaged and was thus out of touch with the ebb and flow concerning the matter to be discussed. Many months earlier President Truman had secretly asked the wartime Chief of Staff of the Army, General George C. Marshall, to become his Secretary of State as soon as Byrnes completed the minor peace treaties; there had been agreement at Potsdam that they should be negotiated first and that the United Nations should be created separately. This was done to avoid a repetition of the scramble at Versailles when everything was done simultaneously, resulting in hurried decisions, much haggling and trading. While waiting for this moment it would have been pertinent for Marshall to have been given time to prepare; however, men of wisdom, experience and ability were rare commodities, not to be held in obeyance. Marshall had been in China trying to effect agreement between Generalissimo Chiang Kai-shek and the Chinese Communists and thereby avoid a Chinese civil war.

"However," as Murphy says, "it is unlikely that any Secretary of State could have accomplished more at the 1947 Moscow Conference, because by this time the cold war was being fought openly. *Truman's misgivings about the Russians had hardened into certainties,* as a result of Stalin's behavior, and the *President was in no mood to concede anything.* (Emphasis added) The Soviet Government, for its part, finally put its German cards on the table at the Moscow Conference, leaving no doubt that Russia's goals were a direct threat to Anglo-American objectives in Germany. The Russians frankly revealed their confidence that they could thwart Western plans for Germany's economic recovery and thereby could jeopardize rehabilitation of non-communist Europe. . . .

"We had not expected to reach full agreement at this initial meeting, but neither did we suspect that an all-inclusive German peace treaty would remain uncompleted. . . . It was the Moscow Conference of 1947, I believe, which really rang down the Iron Curtain."[133]

It was not, however, until February 1948 that the Foreign Ministers of the Western Allies decided at their meeting in London "to combine their three zones, a step toward the formation of a West German government; and in a move to revive the country's economy, to revalue the mark" (which was grossly inflated and causing great economic hardship).[134] "The Soviets, expressing the fear that currency reform would lead to the dumping of worthless old marks in their zone and that the formation of a West German government would lead to a new German army responded on April 1 with temporary restrictions on military traffic between the Western zones and Berlin.

"There had been some warning signs as early as January that a blockade might be the Soviet answer to the Allied moves. Trains and truck convoys were frequently held up on the ground that the documentation did not cover certain requirements. Repairs were allegedly instituted on canals, delaying long strings of barges bearing much needed supplies for Berlin. . . ."[135]

On July 6, 1948, Secretary Marshall sent a formal protest to Russia which included the fact that: ". . . The United States Government regards these measures of blockade as a clear violation of existing agreements concerning the administration of Berlin by the four occupying powers. . . . These agreements *implied* the right of free access to Berlin. This right has long been confirmed by usage. . . ."[136] (Emphasis added)

On June 24, the Soviets imposed a total blockade on Berlin—all rail, canal and autobahn traffic between Berlin and the West was halted. Originally the blockade was met by using transport planes available in Europe, but soon it became clear that additional aircraft were essential.

Foreseeing coming events, President Truman on July 20 called a meeting of the National Security Council in the White House. With the use of armed convoys rejected because of their provocative nature, the question was whether to increase the airlift to circumvent the blockade.

"The Joint Chiefs had some doubts. They pointed out that the supply of military transport aircraft was not excessive and that if almost all of it was assigned to an airlift, there would be little left for regular military use and virtually none in the event of war. *After some discussion, the President made his decision to go ahead with the airlift and ordered the Joint Chiefs to provide the planes necessary to make the operation a success. He expressed his absolute deter-*

mination to stay in Berlin and not be driven out by any form of pressure. (Emphasis added)

"Soviet notes instituting the blockade asserted that the Allied currency reform had 'destroyed' the rights of access to Berlin. . . . The reason they did not interrupt air traffic was . . . because they correctly figured that such a step might have brought on war with the United States and the Western powers. Our plans were coordinated with the British and the French, the former contributing a considerable number of planes to the airlift."[137]

To demonstrate that, without doubt, the United States was deadly earnest, President Truman, ever courageous and determined, ordered in July sixty B-29 bombers, capable of carrying atomic bombs, to Britain. At that time we, alone, had atomic bombs. We were not going to withdraw, spoke this demonstration; we were not going to pick a fight; but if we were forced to fight the weapons were ready. It was believed at the time that the Kremlin did not want war. Events allowed the B-29 bombers to remain idle, for Russia would tantalize but not provoke war. She always pursued her objectives to the "brink."

Feis takes up the story: "On July 27th, a Sunday, the top men of the Pentagon and of the State Department were thrashing over the pros and cons of doing this, or that, or nothing. On the next day they submitted their dilemma to the President. It was one of those occasions on which Truman saw a situation in plain white and black. He was unhesitating in his decision. After the meeting the Secretary of Defense, Forrestal, recorded in his diary, 'When the specific question was discussed as to what our future policy in Germany was to be—namely, were we to stay in Berlin or not?—the President interrupted to say that there was no discussion on that point, we were going to stay, period.' When Secretary of the Army, Royall, queried whether the risk was clearly recognized, since 'we might have to fight our way into Berlin,' the President said that 'we would have to deal with the situation as it developed,' but that the essential decision was 'we were in Berlin by terms of an agreement and that the Russians had no right to get us out by either direct or indirect pressure.' "[138] The Soviets ended the blockade on May 12, 1949.

It is of major interest that when the situation reached its climax with the Russian halt of all rail, autobahn and canal traffic on June 24, President Truman only approved with reluctance the advice of the Joint Chiefs of Staff to refrain from contesting our right to access. Their estimate was that they would need eighteen months to prepare for what might happen in Berlin if the Russians were challenged there. "Truman reluctantly approved this opinion of the JCS although he said that if the JCS would put a paper before him ordering what Clay and Murphy proposed he would sign it."[139] This has special significance because it was uttered in an election year—at a time when the polls showed that he was running far behind his opponent, Tom Dewey. "If the President were to approve action in Berlin which the voters considered reckless, his election chances would diminish still further. In spite of his personal predicament, Truman was more disposed than his military advisers to take the chance."[140] He was restrained, not for political considerations, but because of his respect for military advice. He had within him the incentive to do what he considered the right thing, as did Wilson, regardless of consequences. In fact, the greater the risk the greater was his desire to proceed if he thought he was right; but not where military opinion ran counter to his. Franklin Roosevelt had overruled the military upon several occasions when their timidity was not persuasive to him.

The dimensions of the airlift are well illustrated by a humorous but relevant conversation that Murphy reports:

"A few days after Clay and I returned to Berlin from Washington, Clay telephoned to Le May in Frankfurt. Clay asked: 'Have you any planes that can carry coal?'

" 'Carry what?' asked Le May.

" 'Coal,' repeated Clay.

" 'We must have a bad phone connection,' said Le May. 'It sounds as if you are asking if we have planes for carrying coal.'

" 'Yes, that's what I said—coal.'

"Rallying quickly, Le May said stoutly, 'The Air Force can deliver anything.' "[141] And they did!

By chance, the French government completed arrangements to merge the economy of its occupation zone with that of Bizonia on the same day as Russia lifted her Berlin blockade. Now named Trizonia, the trizonal powers agreed upon an Occupation Statute for the eventual establishment of a Federal Republic of Germany; it was not until May 5, 1955, that this finally became a nation—West Germany.

To initiate and maintain the Berlin airlift was Truman's third courageous decision in foreign affairs. Simultaneously the West German state was being formed and the great Western Alliance was being created. Rekindled fears of Soviet aggression led Great Britain, France and the Benelux nations to sign a defensive alliance in mid-March 1948; they then approached the United States for support. Truman asked the Senate to "extend to the free nations the support which the situation requires." Since the alliance was militarily important, the State Department decided that the new union virtually needed American endorsement. It was, as usual, in matters of foreign affairs that the President, with wisdom, turned to Republican Senator Vandenberg for congressional leadership. Although the senator was reluctant to propose a military alliance to the 80th Congress, he offered a moderate resolution on July 11, 1948. "On this occasion Senator Vandenberg took seriously and responsibly the word 'advise' in the constitutional phrase giving the President power to enter into treaties 'with the advice and consent of the Senate.' By getting the Senate to give advice in advance of negotiations he got it to accept responsibility in advance of giving 'consent to ratify.' "[142]

Our action regarding the Atlantic Defence Pact was the result of the Berlin blockade and it was based upon the Vandenberg Resolution which was passed by a vote of 64 to 4 on June 11, 1948. This "informed the President that the sense of the Senate was that the United States Government should pursue: Progressive development of regional and other collective arrangements for individual and collective self-defense in accordance with the purposes, principles, and provisions of the Charter [of the United Nations].

"Association of the United States, by constitutional process, with such regional and other collective arrangements as are based on continuous and effective self-help and mutual aid, and as affects its national security."[143]

In his Inaugural Address on January 20, 1949, the President laid down four major guidelines for his foreign policy. The first two—support of the United Nations and continuation of the economic recovery policy—he regarded as extensions of the major achievements of his first administration. The third—strengthening of the free nations against aggression—was a political innovation based on the Vandenberg Resolution. It would, he said, be spelled out by "joint agreement designed to strengthen the security of the North Atlantic area," and "provide unmistakable proof of the joint determination of the free countries to resist armed attack from any quarter."

The fourth point made in the address was a plan to "embark on a bold new program for making the benefits of our scientific advances and industrial progress available for the improvement and growth of underdeveloped areas." The last two points, while by no means novel, required much breaking of new ground.[144] "Point Four," in brief, called for technical assistance to underdeveloped nations and became one of Truman's major objectives, for which he strove valiantly and tenaciously.

The North Atlantic Treaty Organization—NATO—was agreed upon by the State Department and the European countries involved by March 1949, signed in Washington on April 4, 1949. The treaty was approved by the Senate by a vote of 83 to 3 on July 21, and in an impressive ceremony a few days later President Truman signed the treaty ratification. Speaking at the ceremony he said that the American government had hoped to establish an international peace force under the United Nations, but that purpose had been frustrated by the Soviet Union, and consequently the members of the alliance had been compelled to band to-gether.[145] Speaking on August 22, he said: "We are not arming ourselves and our friends to start a fight with anybody. We are building defenses so that we don't have to fight."[146]

The NATO pact was primarily a military alliance. The determining provision was Article 5. "The Parties agree that an armed attack against all or more of them in Europe or North America shall be considered an attack against them all; and consequently they agree that, if such an armed attack occurs, each of them, in exercise of the right of individual or collective self-defense recognized by Article 51 of the Charter of the United Nations will assist the Party or Parties so attacked by taking forthwith, individually and in concert with the other Parties, such action as it deems necessary, including the use of armed force, to restore and maintain the security of the North Atlantic area."[147]

With amazing speed arrangements were worked out for an integrated NATO military force. Dwight Eisenhower, who had commanded the Western forces in the invasion of Germany, was named Commander. Despite the laments and warnings of political figures such as ex-President Herbert Hoover and Senator Robert Taft, President Truman maintained that he had the constitutional right to send American troops abroad in time of peace without the approval of Congress, and he did so. American troops who had first been placed in Europe to fight Hitler were going to remain there to deter or fight Soviet communism. In words used by De Gaulle in 1966: "An American protectorate was set up in Western Europe under cover of NATO."[148]

President Truman was not the first President to send troops abroad without the approval of Congress. President McKinley in 1900 sent troops to China to protect American citizens against the Boxer rebels.[149] At the time of the enactment of the Truman Doctrine, government officials, congressmen, journalists and other elements of the articulate public vigorously debated its merits and in the intervening years historians have kept the argument going. The defendants claim that it marked America's final abandonment of isolationism and acceptance of her responsibility as a world power, and that "the real commitment to contain communism everywhere originated in the events surrounding the Korean War, not the crisis in Greece and Turkey."[150]

State Department officials had gone out of their way during congressional hearings on aid to Greece and Turkey in late March to emphasize that the President's program would not automatically commit the United States to resist communism everywhere. Acheson specifically rejected any implication that the Truman Doctrine constituted a precedent for aid to other countries threatened by communism, especially China. Further requests, he said, would be evaluated individually, without reference to any general rule of policy.[151] It is consistent with Truman's style that the State Department maintained the contacts with congressional committees in presenting his policies; he did not essay the personal relationship—although he had been a member of the Senate—that Woodrow Wilson and both Roosevelts did; having made his decisions, he delegated to the State Department as he did to other departments the duty to see that they were implemented. A factor which may have been influential in this case was his veneration of the eloquence and knowledge which Acheson possessed; and of Marshall's wisdom and the respect, amounting almost to awe, which the Congress had for him. Truman thus displayed wisdom and humility in giving the ball to hands he considered more competent to achieve accomplishment.

However, when it was a matter of action, Harry Truman took the reins himself: "When the North Korean army made its surprise invasion of South Korea in the summer of 1950, President Truman had to act promptly if at all. His order to General MacArthur to use American armed force in resistance to North Korean forces was given as commander-in-chief and in compliance with obligations agreed to by Article 43 of the Charter of the United Nations. This obligation was in consequence of our ratification of the Covenant by the treaty power, and treaties are of course a part of the supreme law of the land, as the Constitution declares. In the heat of the campaign of 1952 it became a part of Republican strategy to disregard the indisputable legal basis of Truman's action in Korea and to brand him as a warmonger."[152] President Truman, fully aware of the discretionary power vested in him by the Constitution as Commander-in-Chief, had taken pride in maintaining that power unimpaired.

While diplomatic attention was focused upon Europe, political eruptions in the Far East menaced our equilibrium in that part of the world. The President's various emissaries to China failed to reconcile the National Chinese government of Generalissimo Chiang Kai-shek and the Communists led by Mao Tse-tung; the Nationalist government was forced to take refuge on the island of Formosa. Although Truman and Acheson[153] did not welcome Mao's victory, neither did they expect China, in the long run, to remain a Soviet satellite. Making efforts to maintain good relations with the Chinese Communists, our government was placed at the same time in the difficult position of giving support to its old ally on Formosa with whose policies it had never been at ease.

This was the political situation on Saturday, June 24, 1950, when President Truman received word as he was landing at Kansas City that North Korean troops had launched an all-out offensive against the Republic of Korea. Mr. Truman told Secretary of State Acheson to round up the chief State and Defense officials at 7 o'clock the evening of the 25th; meanwhile Acheson had asked the Secretary of the United Nations, Trygve Lie, to call an emergency session of the U.N. Security Council for the afternoon of the 25th. Cables were dispatched to United States Embassies all over the world telling them that this country would propose prompt action to block the aggression, with the full weight and authority of the United Nations backing up the effort; the Ambassadors were asked to obtain the support of the nations to which they were detailed.

Reminiscent of President Wilson's well-phrased admonition to reporters at the outbreak of World War I was President Truman's blunt admonition to the reporters who accompanied him on the plane back to Washington: "Don't make it alarmist. It could be dangerous, but I hope it isn't. There has been no formal declaration of war that I know of. I can't answer any more questions until I get all the facts."[154]

Facts were needed, but the germs of action had been firmly implanted. The philosophy that stimulated them was expressed years later in his memoirs: "In my generation, this was not the first occasion when the strong had attacked the weak. I recalled some earlier instances: Manchuria, Ethiopia, Austria. I remembered how each time that the democracies failed to act it had encouraged the aggressors to keep going ahead.

"Communism was acting in Korea just as Hitler, Mussolini, and the Japanese had acted ten, fifteen and twenty years earlier. If this was allowed to go unchallenged it would mean a third world war. It was also clear to me that the foundations and principles of the United Nations were at stake unless this unprovoked attack on Korea could be stopped."[155]

Well-recognized Russian tactics had unobtrusively and gradually led to the Pearl Harbor-like attack. During World War II the entire peninsula of Korea was under Japanese rule. As a part of the Yalta Agreement the Russians had assented to the Cairo understanding reached by the United States, Great Britain and China that Korea would become "free and independent." "When the surrender came, in August 1945, there were tens of thousands of Japanese troops and civilian administrators in Korea. The Russians sent an occupation force of approximately a full division across the border from Manchuria; and elements of the United States 24th Army Corps . . . landed at the southern port of Pusan for the same purpose. To simplify the problems of disarming and repatriating the enemy and of running the civilian government during those first weeks, the two allies agreed that, purely as a matter of convenience, the Russians would take care of things north of the 38th parallel and the Americans to the south. This line was chosen simply because it cut the country approximately in two, not because of any political or economic considerations.

"But what the Americans had regarded as demarcation was interpreted by the Russians as partition. It soon became evident that they had no interest in a unified Korea. They embargoed traffic across the parallel, cut off electric power and the transfer of goods southward, and set up a provisional government modeled on Communist lines. In 1947 the United States put the issue before the U.N. and the General Assembly established a special mission on the unification of Korea and on overseeing general elections there the next year. The Russians and their North Korean puppets refused to let the election commissioners cross the line into their territory, and so the election of 1948 was held only in the south. It resulted in the formation of the Republic of Korea on August 15 under the presidency of the aged and despotically inclined Syngman Rhee, no great favorite with Washington. The Communist answer was to announce, a few weeks later, the formation of the Democratic People's Republic of Korea, with Kim Il Sung, a Moscow trained revolutionary, as Premier."[156]

Protesting the United Nation's refusal to seat Communist China, the Russians had boycotted its sessions since January: therefore they were not present to exercise their right to veto the Council's 9 to 0 vote to denounce the North Korean aggression as "a breach of the peace." It called for an immediate end to hostilities and the withdrawal of the invaders beyond the 38th parallel.

After listening, as was his style, to the opinions and advice of the top brass of the State Department and of all branches of the military, the President made three decisions:

(1) General MacArthur, who was in Tokyo, was to be instructed to send the planes and ships necessary to evacuate all American civilian personnel from Korea. His fighter planes were to protect these operations from interference, staying south of the 38th parallel, if possible, but going beyond it if it became necessary.

(2) MacArthur was to get as much ammunition and other supplies into the hands of the ROK Army as possible.

(3) The 7th Fleet was to be called north from the Philippines into the Formosa Strait and instructed to prevent the spread of the conflict in that area.[157]

Giving his staff a complete account of developments and decisions the next morning he walked over to the big globe in his office, put his hand on Korea and said: "This is the Greece of the Far East. If we are tough enough now, there won't have to be any next step."[158] Unfortunately we were not militarily prepared for this step and we had not given the South Koreans offensive weapons for fear that President Rhee would try to bring about unification with North Korea by force. It was immediately apparent that more than airdrops of supplies was needed. The President ordered Navy and Air Force units under MacArthur's command to give direct tactical support to the defenders, *but only south of the 38th parallel.* This was another of Truman's momentous decisions, because it committed this government to military support of the South Korean forces. In addition, new instructions went out to the 7th Fleet to prevent any attack by the Chinese Communists on Formosa, and likewise to thwart any schemes of Chiang Kai-shek to put his Nationalists ashore on the mainland. Such a possibility was likely, and Truman wanted no resumption of the civil war in China to complicate matters. His earnest desire was that no act be committed that would lead to Chinese Communist intervention in this war.

The decision to act promptly and vigorously to check Communist aggression in Korea, and to throw in the Navy and the Air Force, drew an almost unanimous outpouring of praise for the President from Congress, the press and many countries. That night the U.N. Security Council adopted one of the strongest resolutions in its history up to that time—a call for armed intervention against an aggressor. Within a week we were in a shooting war. Things went badly; seasoned troops from Guadalcanal and Okinawa were sent to Korea; President Truman, pressing partial mobilization through Congress, authorized a call-up of Organized Reserves and some National Guard units; by the end of September, under MacArthur's leadership the U.N. forces were in control of the whole Korean peninsula south of the 38th parallel. Good work!

In Washington there was apprehension over what the Chinese would do if the fighting came too close to the borders of Manchuria. Washington was worried when MacArthur went to Formosa in July to see Chiang; he wanted nothing so much at the time as to keep Chiang quiet and to keep quiet about Chiang. And what would the Russians—just 40 miles away in Vladivostok—do if MacArthur led his troops too close? The Joint Chiefs of Staff urged caution on their vain, colorful, able but headstrong Far Eastern Commander. The President sent Averell Harriman as his emissary to explain that the objective was to *contain* an aggression without igniting new flames.

"In his report to the President, Harriman said that the General had expressed full approval of the decision to intervene in Korea, that he was convinced that he would ultimately be able to destroy the North Korean forces, and that he foresaw no likelihood that either Communist China or Russia would pitch in directly to help the NKPA. But MacArthur was not happy about Washington's attitude toward Chiang Kai-shek as a potential ally, and Harriman had gone to considerable lengths to try to elucidate this policy for the General—without much success, as he said in his report to the President: 'For reasons which are difficult to explain, I did not feel that we came to a full agreement on the way we believed things should be handled on Formosa and with the Generalissimo. He accepted the President's position and will act accordingly, but without full conviction. He has a strange idea that we should back anybody who will fight communism.' "[159]

Two weeks later President Truman was pitched into a state of "frozen anger" when the news wires carried the text of a message MacArthur had addressed to the annual encampment of the Veterans of Foreign Wars, "describing what was in the view of the State Department, a new foreign policy for the whole of the Pacific. It delineated a proposed United States defense line stretching from Vladivostok to Singapore, which, properly protected with United States air, naval and ground forces, would make the Pacific a 'peaceful lake.' He wound up by decrying as 'appeasement' the 'fallacious and threadbare argument' that to encourage the Chinese in Formosa would endanger our status in the rest of Asia. . . .

"With his Secretary of State and Defense and the members of the Joint Chiefs of Staff around him, the President asked each in turn, like a schoolmaster, if he had any advance knowledge of the MacArthur statement. Each replied that he had not. Then, turning to Secretary of Defense Louis Johnson he said: 'I want this message withdrawn and I want you to send an order to MacArthur to withdraw it and tell him it is an order from me. Do you understand that?' 'Yes, sir,' answered the Secretary.

"The MacArthur statement was, of course, already in all the papers. The General was nevertheless obliged to 'recall it.' "[160]

The President had acted calmly but firmly. "But when operations began to go north of the parallel, and when first intelligence reports came in, early in October, of the massing of Chinese troops on the Manchurian border, the President's anxiety about his head-strong field commander again came to the surface. He decided he had better have a face-to-face talk with MacArthur."[161] The President of the United States went all the way to Wake Island, accompanied by military and State Department advisers, for this historic meeting.

In brief, MacArthur said he expected the fighting to be substantially over by Thanksgiving. He thought there was very little prospect of Chinese or Soviet intervention. Even as he spoke, the Chinese had started their infiltration, crossing the Yalu River under cover of darkness. Before the Wake Island meeting, the Chinese Foreign Minister, Chou En-lai, on October 1, had called in the Indian Ambassador and gravely told him that the Chinese People's Republic would enter the war on the side of the North Koreans if United Nations forces carried their new offensive beyond the 38th parallel into North Korean territory; a week later, Chou En-lai repeated this threat over the official government radio for all the world to hear. But MacArthur's intelligence chief characterized it as being "probably in a category of diplomatic blackmail."[162]

"On November 6, an alarmed MacArthur messaged the Joint Chiefs of Staff that men and material were pouring over all bridges of the Yalu from Manchuria in such numbers as to threaten the destruction of the forces under his command. He asked immediate authority to bomb these bridges and other installations in the 'north area' supporting the enemy. . . .

"Permission to bomb the Yalu bridges was promptly forthcoming from Washington, but it was coupled with a repeated reminder to avoid targets inside Manchuria and, in particular, the Yalu dam and power installations. 'Because of the necessity of maintaining optimum position with United Nations policy and directives,' MacArthur's instructions from the Joint Chiefs read, 'and because it is vital in the National interest of the United States to localize the fighting in Korea, it is important that extreme care be taken to avoid violation of Manchurian territory and airspace.' "[163] For about two weeks all was quiet. On November 24, MacArthur flew from headquarters in Tokyo to Korea, and announced the immediate jump-off of a final offensive to end the war. More than 300,000 Chinese troops lay in wait for the United Nations advance. On the 25th they struck with devastating fury. By mid-December the Army had pulled back to a line a few miles south of the 38th parallel and main elements were being evacuated by sea, making ridiculous his declaration on November 24 that his "massive compression envelopment against new Red armies operating in North Korea is now approaching its decisive effort. . . . If successful, this effort should for all practical purposes end the war."[164]

Not only was the President faced by a war with Communist China which he had so pleaded with MacArthur to avoid, but a war that it was not possible to win and a war which neither the United States nor the United Nations desired to wage. MacArthur's thrust across the 38th parallel and on toward the Manchurian border sent chills of apprehension through the United Nations headquarters that this country might indeed, by intention or accident, be about to commit the international body to a "cataclysmic ideological war." World opinion, which had supported the United States against a simple act of aggression by the North Koreans, was turning away.

At this serious juncture the President made one of his "shoot from the hip" answers to a question for which he was not prepared. At a press conference on November 30, he implied that the atomic bomb might be used against the Chinese and that the decision to use it would be up to the commander in the field, General MacArthur. His press office quickly issued a clarifying statement, but alarm had already spread to every member state of the U.N.; Prime Minister Attlee hurried over from London the next day for a face-to-face talk.[165]

MacArthur had a talent for worsening a situation; it was in the midst of this impasse that he returned to the political offensive against his superiors in Washington. He suddenly became "highly accessible at his Tokyo headquarters for personal and cabled interviews with members of the press . . . he attributed his difficulties in Korea to the extraordinary inhibitions . . . without precedent in history which denied him the opportunity to carry the war into the 'privileged sanctuary' of the enemy."[166] This is but one of his statements. Truman has said that he should have fired him then. So he should, but another trait which Harry Truman possessed was consideration, and that explained the reason he gave—he didn't want it to appear that the General was being punished because of the failure of his offensive. Perhaps, too, knowing that MacArthur was a popular hero to the people of the United States, he considered the adverse effect it might have upon public opinion.

It must have been frightfully frustrating to him to have courteously travelled halfway around the world to emphasize his policy to this man of military might, to have been convinced that they saw eye to eye, and then to be so ungallantly treated and for the military to have so little deference to the civilian head of government.

"Every second lieutenant knows best what his platoon ought to be given to do," the former artillery captain sitting in the White House graphically said later. "He thinks the higher-ups are just blind when they don't see things his way. But General MacArthur—and rightly too—would have court-martialed any second lieutenant who gave press interviews to express disagreement." Patiently, however, Truman had the Joint Chiefs of Staff send directly to MacArthur a new directive instructing him that "no speech, press release, or public statement" should henceforth be issued in respect to foreign policy unless first cleared with the Department of State, or, in the case of military policy, with the Department of Defense.[167]

MacArthur responded with a proposal to the Joint Chiefs of Staff of a total reversal of the limited war policy of the Truman administration and the United Nations. He asked not only for the right to make war against the Chinese People's Republic, which was linked in a mutual defense treaty with the Soviet Union, but to underwrite Chiang Kai-shek in a resumption of the Chinese civil war.[168]

MacArthur expanded his political philosophy and demands; the Joint Chiefs sent message after message, and then two members went to Tokyo to further clarify the situation. The President, with patience and forebearance, itemized three goals which it was hoped might be reached by continuing *resistance* in Korea: (1) to demonstrate that Communist aggression against free people would not be tolerated; (2) to demonstrate that the U.N. was a viable and vigorous force that could not be brushed aside; and (3) to strengthen the will to resist of hard-pressed governments in Europe and the Middle East.

One of the strangest episodes occurred when the President and his advisers decided that a clear-cut victory could not be won and the time was propitious for peace negotiations. A draft of the statement was drawn and was sent on March 20 to each of the fourteen U.N. allies. A copy was also sent to MacArthur by radio with a covering letter from the Joint Chiefs of Staff telling him that his Chief was preparing to negotiate a settlement of the conflict at the highest level of diplomacy, and to ask what he needed to preserve the military status quo while these negotiations were in progress. Four days later, entirely on his own authority and with no warning to Washington, MacArthur made his own offer to negotiate with the enemy through a public statement, threatening that if the U.N. should decide "to depart from its tolerant effort to contain the war to the area of Korea," the whole of Red China would be "doomed to imminent military collapse."

"Word of MacArthur's manifesto reached Washington via the news wires late on March 23. . . . *Harry Truman is an impulsive man, but in moments of great trial he has the inner strength to control his impulses. He did on this Saturday forenoon when Acheson and [the "war cabinet"] gathered about his desk to discuss the latest affront from Tokyo.* (Emphasis added) . . . His mind was made up on this Saturday. He knew what he had to do, and he was going to do it. . . . But he wanted time to calculate each step of what could prove to be the most momentous decision he would take as President—and probably the most costly in terms of his own stature and political welfare. Moreover, he wanted time for the National Security Council to assess both the military and political consequences of so drastic an upheaval in the United Nations Far Eastern Command.

The dismissal of MacArthur had to be accomplished with the least possible backlash on the precarious *status quo* in world affairs."[169]

He deliberated; he meditated; there was no "shooting from the hip." But on Thursday, April 5, 1951, a MacArthur bombshell hit him. The General had written a letter to the minority leader of the House of Representatives, Joseph W. Martin—celebrated by Franklin D. Roosevelt in the Martin, Barton and Fish refrain. Though personally friendly to Truman, he was one of the President's most effective and implacable political foes, especially over foreign policy and the conduct of the Korean War. It was therefore with relish that Martin told the House that some weeks earlier he had written MacArthur asking his views about the administration's policy of refusing to make use of Chiang Kai-shek's Nationalist troops against the Chinese Reds; and it was with even greater relish that he read to the House the General's reply:

My views and recommendations with respect to the situation created by Red China's entry into war against us in Korea have been submitted to Washington in most complete detail. Generally those views are well known and generally understood, as they follow the conventional pattern of meeting force with maximum counterforce as we have never failed to do in the past. Your [Martin's] view with regard to the utilization of the Chinese forces on Formosa is in conflict with neither logic nor this tradition.

It seems strangely difficult for some to realize that here in Asia is where the Communist conspirators have elected to make their play for global conquest, and that we have joined the issue thus raised on the battlefield; that here we fight Europe's war with arms while the diplomats there still fight it with words; that if we lose this war to Communism in Asia the fall of Europe is inevitable; win it and Europe most probably would avoid war and yet preserve freedom.

As you point out, we must win. There is no substitute for victory.[170]

It would seem that the end had come. But the President realized the gravity of the decision and insisted that Acheson, Harriman, Marshall, Bradley and others of the "war cabinet" who met with him on Friday and Saturday search their conscience thoroughly over the weekend, and he asked General Bradley to put the matter squarely to the other Chiefs and report back to him Monday morning. The President said that the one assurance he needed was that there would be complete unanimity about what he was going to do. On Monday morning the same group gathered in the President's office. General Bradley reported that the Joint Chiefs were unanimous in their decision that MacArthur should be recalled and the whole command turned over to General Ridgway. The others present stated their agreement. The President said it had been his unaltered intention since March 24 that MacArthur would have to go, and he was pleased that no reservations about it lingered in the minds of any of them. He then directed General Bradley to prepare the official orders for an orderly and dignified change of command, and he suggested that Army Secretary Frank Pace, Jr., who was then in Korea, be instructed to deliver these orders to General MacArthur in person.

Had it been possible to follow this procedure the impact upon the public would have been softened. But the march of events quickened. Pace was flying over the battlefields and could not be reached; the White House press room got word that the Chicago *Tribune* was going to press with the news that MacArthur was to be fired; if the General heard the news before he received his official orders, Bradley said, he probably would try to beat the President to the punch by resigning. "He's not going to be allowed to quit on me," Mr. Truman exploded. "He's going to be fired!"[171]

He told Bradley to get the official notification to MacArthur in the shortest time possible and to keep the White House informed hour by hour. Shortly before midnight Tuesday, April 10, these words in scrambled code flashed from the Pentagon in Washington to the Dai Ichi Building in Tokyo Headquarters for the Far Eastern Command:

To General MacArthur from the President.

I deeply regret that it becomes my duty as President and Commander-in-Chief of the United States military forces to replace you as Supreme Commander, Allied Powers, Commander-in-Chief, Far East, and Commanding General, U.S. Army, Far East.

You will turn over your commands, effective at once, to Lieutenant General Matthew B. Ridgway. You are authorized to have issued such orders as are necessary to complete desired travel to such place as you select.

My reasons for your replacement will be made public concurrently with the delivery to you of the foregoing message.[172]

Shortly after midnight Press Secretary Short telephoned the press, summoning reporters to a 1:00 A.M. press conference in which he released a statement from the President, mimeographed copies of documents bearing upon the matter, and the announcement that the President would go on the air at 10:30 that evening to explain his action to the people.

Truman was assailed and applauded for his action. The dramatic General's friends staged a hero's welcome and Congress gave him an ovation. Emotion, however, faded during the course of Senate hearings. Meanwhile the war remained limited. In July truce talks began. Two years later these produced an armistice along a line the troops had reached by June 1951.

Of interest is our own personal experience ten years later with the Japanese reaction to President Truman's action in recalling MacArthur. We had vacationed in southern France with ex-President and Mrs. Truman in 1958. Our plan for a 1959 vacation was a trip to the Far East, during which we would spend three weeks in Japan; we asked whether the Trumans wanted to join us. The President feared that the Japanese would not look kindly upon his visit, remembering the atom bombing of Hiroshima; we thought his fear justified. While in Japan we mentioned this to well-positioned Japanese and to American representatives of leading newspaper and broadcasting networks. Their universal response was: "The Japanese would have welcomed President Truman because he demonstrated in recalling MacArthur the authority of the civilian over the military." For that reason they had great respect for him. Never having lived through the experience of military domination, the American public was slow to appreciate the significance of the glamorous General's removal by their down-to-earth President—not too popular at the time because of the many domestic crises which were confronting him and them even as foreign affairs kept pounding for attention. His popularity was at ebb tide.

Truman's domestic difficulties had begun to mount in the spring of 1946 when Congress, besieged by business lobbyists, passed a weak, ineffective extension of OPA (Office of Price Administration) authority. The President's dilemma was acute. If he signed the bill, he would be saddled with the responsibility for checking inflation, but would be deprived of the tools with which to make it work. If he did not sign it, there would be no price control and inflation would have free rein. His Cabinet—with the exception of the Secretary of Commerce Henry Wallace and the Secretary of the Interior Julius Krug—urged him to sign it as "better than nothing." Alben Barkley, his Senate majority leader, and Sam Rayburn, his close friend and Speaker of the House, urged him to sign because it was the best bill that they could get. He vetoed the bill and went on the radio to tell the people why he vetoed it. His words were remembered by the consuming public who had been hijacked by big business into the parade crying for "a return to normalcy" when inflation crippled their buying power, and they voted for him in 1948.

The economy and national tranquility was, at the same time, upset by the wave of strikes which had shut down one industry after another as workers battled management for peacetime wages to match their wartime earnings and for pensions, welfare funds, union security, and other fringe benefits. There was violence, and mass walkouts totalled 116 million man-days of work lost due to strikes.[173]

Months of fruitless negotiations between the twenty powerful rail brotherhoods and railroad management had reached a final impasse on April 18, 1946. The carriers had accepted and the unions had rejected the proposal of an arbitration board; Alvanley Johnston, chief of the Brotherhood of Locomotive Engineers, and Alexander F. Whitney, president of the Brotherhood of Railroad Trainmen, called a strike of their members to begin May 18. These two unions had been Truman's staunch backers in his tough 1940 senatorial race and supported his Vice-Presidential nomination. They resisted all efforts of settlement. On May 15, three days before the strike deadline, the President summoned the management representatives and the leaders of the twenty brotherhoods to his office. "He talked to them like a Dutch uncle, and when it was over found that leaders of eighteen of the unions were willing to settle on the basis of the arbitration award. But not Whitney and Johnston. Between them they could bring every wheel on the railroads to a stop, and that was what they proposed to do. Peering coldly through his thick glasses at his two old friends, the President said:

" 'If you think I'm going to sit here and let you tie up this whole country, you're crazy as hell.'

" 'We've got to go through with it, Mr. President,' Whitney said: 'Our men are demanding it.'

"Truman got up from his desk, ending the conference. 'All right, I'm going to give you the gun. You've got just 48 hours—until Thursday at this time—to reach a settlement. If you don't I'm going to take over the railroads in the name of the government.' "[174]

Even as the President met the heads of the two railroad unions head-on, the powerful John L. Lewis, president of the Mineworkers Union, had slowed the flow of coal to a trickle, causing a shutdown of thousands of factories. "The intrepid man from Missouri called the railroad leaders again to his office on the day of the deadline to watch—and to be on public view to the news photographers —as he signed an Executive order carrying out his threat of seizure of the railroads. . . . Whitney and Johnston . . . grudgingly agreed to postpone their strike for five days. . . . [On the night of the fifth day] they wrote the President a curt letter saying: 'We have told you many times that the present agitation among the men is extremely serious and their demands cannot be abandoned. Therefore your offer is unacceptable.' "[175]

Cabell Phillips's description of President Truman's next move is characteristic of the man and his style when pushed to righteous anger and to action in extremity: "When Harry Truman's mad is up, his eyes glint coldly behind his spectacles, his mouth is a thin, hard line pulled down at the corners, and his carriage has the brittleness of a bamboo reed. This was the image, as one remembers it, as he stalked into a specially called meeting of his Cabinet that Friday morning. In the manner of Lincoln and the Emancipation Proclamation, he had summoned them not to solicit their views but to tell them what he was going to do. He was going to Congress in person the next day and demand the stiffest labor law in history—one that would give him authority to draft strikers into the armed services without respect to age or dependency when their strike threatened to bring on a national emergency. When Attorney General Tom C. Clark raised a question about the constitutionality of such a move, the President brushed him aside peremptorily. 'We'll draft 'em first and think about the law later,' he said.

"Next, he turned to Charley Ross, his press secretary, and told him to arrange a coast-to-coast radio hookup for him that night so that he could explain to the people what he was about to do. He pulled from his pocket and slapped on the table a bundle of twelve small sheets of ruled tablet paper such as schoolchildren use. They were closely written in ink—and spleen. 'Here's what I am going to say,' he snapped, 'get it typed up. I'm going to take the hide off those so-and-so's.'

"Ross's blood pressure rocketed as he read what possibly will stand for all time as the angriest public message ever written in a President's own hand. It accused the labor leaders of having tried to sabotage the war effort while America's young men faced death on the battlefield; now they were sabotaging the peace by 'holding a gun to the head of the government.' He called on the ex-soldiers who had been his comrades in arms to help 'eliminate the Lewises, the Whitneys and the Johnstons' and to 'hang a few traitors and make our country safe for democracy.' "[176] There was no trace of the introvert in Harry Truman. What he thought, he said.

The President had let off steam; the efforts of his old friend Charley Ross and of Clark Clifford softened the blast but did not throttle it, for "the speech was one of the most emphatic indictments of a group of individuals by a President that has ever been uttered."[177]

The drama continued. The following Saturday John Steelman, White House labor consultant, was closeted at the Statler Hotel with Whitney and Johnston in a last-ditch effort to make them concede. "Clifford and Sam Rosenman, in the Cabinet room at the White House were battling both time and uncertainty trying to draft the President's speech to Congress. Would, or would not, the strike be settled by the time the President got to the Capitol? Steelman telephoned Clifford that an agreement might be signed any minute, but he couldn't be certain. . . . The President had already left for the Capitol . . . Clifford [dashed to the Capitol] only to find that the President had already entered the House Chamber and was about to begin his speech.

"Five minutes later, Clifford got a call through to Steelman at the Statler, who told him breathlessly: 'It's signed!'

"Clifford scribbled a note on a scrap of paper: 'Mr. President, agreement signed, strike over,' and gave it to Leslie Biffle the Secretary of the Senate . . . [who] thrust the note on top of the text from which the President had already begun to read. Truman halted in midsentence and then looked up with a grin: 'Gentlemen, the strike has been settled,' he said. There was a boisterous outbreak of applause and shouts from the packed Chamber."[178]

Even in the face of this victory Truman resumed his speech, demanding the right to draft workers as a guarantee against future strikes endangering national security. The House passed the bill that night by a vote of 306 to 13. Taft blocked the Senate from immediate action; after tempers had cooled, the bill was defeated. The fight had been won.

The style so differed from that of prolonged patience which President Truman pursued later in dealing with MacArthur that one must question whether experience and time tempered the President's patience. The answer must be "No," for he handled the steel strike of 1950 in much the same forthright, uninhibited manner without success. The next question that presents itself is: Had this man, taxed by frustration in meeting labor demands, become anti-labor? Again the answer must be definitely "No," and as proof it must be said that Whitney and the trainmen, though incensed at the time, strongly supported him in 1948. Possibly, in the case of MacArthur, the reason for sustained patience and forbearance lay in his sensitivity to the extreme delicacy of the milieu in which the altercation was taking place. Possibly, in the case of the railroad strike, Truman's exasperation was exhibited without inhibition because of his familiarity with the railroad situation, the precarious state of the economy, the attitude of the public and of the Congress; and backing him was a pro-labor record which freed him of the taint of bias and encouraged him openly to vent his spleen upon members of his own political family whom he thought to be in error and hindering the national economic recovery.

Truman gained stature by his victory because it solved the emergency situation and because it was so vivid a demonstration of a determined, tough fighter. It further endeared him to the public for it showed him to have the human characteristics of the average fellow. Moreover, they were as fed up as he was with the intransigence of labor although the majority believed as he did in labor justice. In fact, he fared far better with public reception to his outburst in the railroad strike situation than he did with his dignified and carefully worded cable to MacArthur.

Simultaneously, he was jousting with John L. Lewis, the heavyweight of the entire labor movement, who had been the boss of the United Mine Workers of America for thirty years. In January Lewis had presented the mine operators with a demand which would not be considered extraordinary today but presented conceptions that were new twenty-five years ago. He demanded a 10 cent royalty on every ton of coal mined to be put into a welfare fund to provide medical and old age care for the miners. He also had conventional demands—new wage and hour provisions, which could have been met. The mine operators refused even to consider the innovations; on March 30, in twenty-one states 400,000 miners went on strike.

Coal, which recently returned to importance in 1974, was then the rockbed upon which railroads (also returned to importance in 1974) and industry relied to make wheels turn in 1946. The age of oil had not reached its present significance. By May 15 the stockpiles of coal were exhausted and the President called Lewis and Charles O'Neill, the operators' representative, to the first of a long series of conferences with himself and Steelman—without success. Therefore on the very day—May 21—that Whitney and Johnston had refused to call off the railroad strike, President Truman ordered the seizure of the coal mines and put them under the direction of his Secretary of the Interior, Julius A. Krug. A week later, Krug and Lewis signed a contract that gave the miners just about everything for which they had asked except that the royalty on each ton of coal to underwrite their welfare program was reduced to 5 cents a ton. As the government then had possession of the mines, the operators had no say; the bargain remained in effect until the latter part of October, when the aggressive and ambitious Lewis announced his displeasure over a minor provision in his contract with the government concerning vacation pay and demanded that the whole contract be reopened. When Krug refused, Lewis gave his ultimatum: "No contract, no work," and ordered the strike for November 20.

Truman was not fazed by John L. Lewis, the king of labor leaders—at least not outwardly so. This great friend of labor resorted to the hated weapon of the labor injunction, prohibited from use by management by order of the Norris-LaGuardia Act of 1932, and further strengthened by the Wagner Act of 1935. "It was argued within the White House that the prohibition against injunctions applied only to disputes between a union and a private employer, and did not apply when, as in the present case, the government was the employer. But this interpretation had never been tested. Would it stand up in court? And if it did, would the miners obediently go back to digging coal? And if not, where would the President and the government be then?

"There was no certain answer to these questions . . . but President Truman had made his decision and it was going to be carried out.

"On Monday, November 18—two days before Lewis' contract cancellation was to take effect—Attorney General Tom C. Clark strode into the Washington courtroom . . . and asked that a temporary injunction be issued restraining the miners' chief from abrogating his union's contract with the government."[179] The order was issued, served upon Lewis, and disregarded; by morning every soft coal mine in the country was shut down. There followed tense and drama-filled days of court trials, court fines against Lewis personally of $10,000 and of $3.5 million against the union; of the union's move to appeal to the Supreme Court. The miners did not return to work. But the White House announced that President Truman, not waiting for the Supreme Court hearing, would go on the air in a direct appeal to the miners over their chieftain's head, urging them to go back to work. It was a desperate, last-ditch strategem with the prestige of the presidency laid squarely on the line.

The announcement that the President would go on the air was made in the morning; that afternoon Lewis capitulated, stating: ". . . All mines in all districts will resume production of coal immediately. . . . Each member is directed to return to work immediately under the wages and conditions of employment in existence on and before November 20, 1946." John L. Lewis was the ogre of the capitalist but the idol of the working man. He was a despot in his field and a rival for the dominance of all labor—a rival who sought to outshine the two other most powerful labor leaders of that era, William Green of the AFL and Philip Murray of the CIO. The defeat was therefore a bitter one for Lewis to take. It was a magnificent victory for Truman, a great demonstration of strength, determination and confidence in his ability to deal with situations pregnant with domestic strife —situations menacing to the welfare of all the people; situations which he could meet heroically even though they entailed a mass of men whose righteous cause he had previously upheld. While this man's personal loyalty to individual old friends knew no bounds even when they had betrayed his personal trust, his loyalty to his duty on matters of public interest could stand no trespassing. When he came to the conclusion that he was pursuing the proper course, he pursued it with vigor. His policy was not built upon abstract theories or ideological precepts; it was based upon the concrete facts of the moment, and it was administered by a flexible mind that acted with a fixed target in mind and with a tough approach.

In presenting the march of events in the coal strike, mere mention has been made of innovations established by the government's initial agreement to welfare provisions. This was a landmark decision upon which grew the many benefits which citizens of the United States now enjoy.

At this very same period he vetoed the Case bill which would have enacted into law anti-strike weapons less offensive than those that he had used. There was no inconsistency here, for the laws were hard and fast and would give the executive no discretion as to when they should and when they should not be used. He also vetoed the Taft bill in 1947—a bill less extreme than the Case bill. It was, however, passed over his veto.

At the end of the President's first year in office—before his action in the railroad and coal strikes and much before he removed MacArthur from command —Arthur Krock described the new man at the helm in these terms: ". . . The portrait is not thrilling, but there is much of comfort and reassurance in it, and much to admire. Here is to be seen no flaming leadership, little of what could be called scholarship and no more that is profound. *But it is very good and human and courageous. Common sense shines out of it, and political experience, the lack of which has been the downfall of Presidents.*"[180] (Emphasis added)

As we have seen, events thrilling in conception and in action followed close on. Not every attempt of the President to deal with runaway labor crises was a success. His notable failure took place when, on December 31, 1951, five months after the start of truce talks in Korea, contracts between the United Steel workers and major steel concerns expired with a stalemate in collective bargaining. At Truman's personal request the men continued work without a contract, while he referred their dispute to the Wage Stabilization Board, a body composed equally of labor, industry and public members, which had charge of wage control and allied functions during the Korean War. While the hearings were in progress, the union twice postponed a strike at the President's insistence. On March 20 the Board reached its conclusions and stated the terms—but its industry members dissented. The unions termed the Board's decision the least it would accept; the industry refused to accept it. The strike was just three weeks away. An enemy offensive in Korea was envisaged and the Pentagon feared any loss of steel production. The companies pressed for an increase agreement in advance, to which the director of Defense Mobilization was agreeable, the price director was not. Wilson, the director of Defense Mobilization, resigned and the whole matter was dumped into the lap of the White House. Each agency pulled and hauled and to express the situation adequately it can be said that Truman's mental reaction must have been "A plague on all your houses." His object was to avoid a shutdown of production and he acted as, by previous experience, one would have expected him to act. The style was not new. Truman seized the industry two hours before the strike deadline. He ordered the Secretary of Commerce to administer the mills and called upon the men to work as government employees.

The union honored Truman's call; the companies accepted government control *but* they went to court contending that his seizure was not within statutory sanction. The Taft-Hartley Act which had been passed over his veto provided orderly procedures. He had not liked them and he did not like them; so he ignored them and acted in his own way. The steel companies asserted that his seizure was illegal and so did the district judge; a strike began at once. On June 2, a majority of the Supreme Court upheld the district judge; the President returned the mills to the owners; the workers struck again. This time the mills remained shut for seven weeks until collective bargaining and the White House promises of price relief produced a settlement on July 24, a settlement a little less favorable than the wage members had proposed—and the companies gained considerably more price relief than had been offered. The third bold venture to settle a strike which impeded production necessary for the welfare of the nation had been launched in true Trumanesque style; but in using it he was shooting from the hip, for he closed his eyes to the strong, growing conservatism of the country and of many members of his own administration, as well as the fact that there was now a law on the statute books which wisdom if not preference would have led him to use. He was a stubborn, determined man—determined to do what he considered was required for the good of the country.

President Truman conceived himself to be the chief defender of the consumers in the face of a Congress which was overweighted with representatives of agrarian and industrial producers. He vetoed the bill that would have transferred offshore oil rights from federal to state jurisdiction; he vetoed the bill that would have transferred the determination of the price of gas at the producing well from the Federal Power Commission to the state utility commissions dominated by oil-state interests; he vetoed the Basing Point Bill which sought to legalize certain price fixing in the cement industry to the detriment of small business and the consumer. He had learned how to resist the pressures of special interests in Congress and he continued to resist such pressures as President. But the number of his recommendations that met defeat, and the number of his vetoes that were overridden, far outstripped his successes.

It was an uphill fight all the way. He was forced to battle an extraordinarily politically minded Congress through his entire tenure in office. Determined to see that a Republican-controlled Congress would be elected in 1946 and 1950, that a Republican President and Congress would be elected in 1948 and then in 1952, every Presidential recommendation was viewed by Republicans not as to its effect upon the public well-being but upon the well-being of the Republican Party; conservative Democrats representing conservative areas of the country had their eyes upon votes also and voted with the Republicans. A wave of conservatism swept the country. Nothing succeeds so well as success and nothing is so demeaning to the popularity of a leader as failure. As the polls reflected his ups and downs (with more periods of "down" than "up"), Truman showed no discouragement; his continued perseverence won in the end the admiration of the public. However, his popularity was brought to its all-time low by the charge that he was "soft on communism."

This charge, later made popular by Senator Joseph McCarthy, was not directed at President Truman. It was made by the U.S. Ambassador to China, Major General Patrick J. Hurley, when he resigned, charging that foreign service officers in China had been undercutting him and United States policy in China. Throughout his charges ran the note that those who differed with him were "soft on communism."[181]

Even before Hurley resigned, China had become a matter of major concern. Therefore, at President Truman's request, General Marshall went to China on December 15, 1945: (1) to effect a cessation of hostilities between the armies of the National government and the Chinese Communists and other dissident Chinese armed forces for the purpose of completing the return of all China to effective

Chinese control, including the immediate evacuation of the Japanese forces; and (2) to arrange a national conference of representatives of major political elements to develop an early solution to the present internal strife—a solution that would bring about the unification of China.[182]

By February 25, 1946, "The Basis for Military Re-organization and for the Integration of the Communist Forces into the National Army" was signed by Chiang Kai-shek's National government and the Chinese Communists led by Mao Tse-tung. Marshall left for Washington March 11 to arrange financial credits, hopeful that both the interim government and Army integration were well on their way to acceptance.

The President, in his December 15, 1945, letter to General Marshall, had written: "In your conversation with Chiang Kai-shek and other Chinese leaders you are authorized to speak with the utmost frankness. Particularly you may state, in connection with the Chinese desire for credits . . . that a China disunited and torn by civil strife could not be considered realistically as a proper place for American assistance along the lines enumerated."[183]

General Marshall, because of his own prestige in Congress and because of the President's full support, was able to take a large amount of promised assistance with him on his return to China. Of significant importance was the fact that he was given total authority to negotiate with the Chinese, replacing that previously held by civilian, Army and Navy agencies. However, in the interval between March 11 when Marshall left China and his return in April the truce had deteriorated. Fresh outbreaks of civil strife continued to occur, reaching a crisis of violence in Manchuria with the capture of Changchun by the Communists. The political agreements made in January and February were not implemented, and the various Chinese groups were not able to achieve the degree of agreement reached at the political consultative conference.

On October 1, 1946, Marshall notified the Generalissimo, who had launched an offensive toward Kalgan, that he would discontinue mediation unless a basis for agreement with the Communists was found without delay. No concessions were proposed. In December Marshall warned Chiang in person that the Communists were too strong to be defeated militarily and that negotiations offered the only way to avert the collapse of China's economy. Chiang paid no heed and Marshall informed the President that his mission had failed. He was recalled early in January 1947 to become Secretary of State.

Although the American people had no desire to be at war again, there were many among them who accused the President and the State Department of being pro-Communist because they did not come actively to the military aid of the Nationalists, and the sentiment was to grow, fanned by Joseph McCarthy and his vocal followers. McCarthy was elected to the Senate in November 1946 from Wisconsin, but his vilification of individuals and of the administration did not achieve momentum until February 1950.

On January 7, 1947, upon his return to the United States, General Marshall made a personal statement to the President which clearly delineated the obstacles he had faced in China:

"The President has recently given a summary of the developments in China during the past year and the position of the American Government toward China. Circumstances now dictate that I should supplement this with impressions gained at first hand. . . .

"In the first place, the greatest obstacle to peace has been the complete, almost overwhelming suspicion with which the Chinese Communist Party and the Kuomintang regard each other.

"On the one hand, the leaders of Government are strongly opposed to a communistic form of government. On the other, the Communists frankly state that they are Marxists and intend to work toward establishing a communistic form of government in China—though first advancing through the medium of a democratic form of government of the American or British type. . . ."

He reported that the most important factors involved in the recent breakdown of negotiations were (1) That on the side of the National government, which was in effect the Kuomintang, there was a dominant group of reactionaries who opposed almost every effort he had made to influence the formulation of a genuine coalition government. They were quite frank in publicly stating their belief that cooperation by the Chinese Communist Party in the government was inconceivable and that only a policy of force could definitely settle the issue. This group included military as well as political leaders. (2) "On the side of the Chinese Communist Party, there were liberals as well as radicals. There was a definite liberal group among the Communists, especially of young men who turned to the Communists in disgust at the corruption evident in the local governments—men who would put the interest of the Chinese people above ruthless measures to establish a Communist ideology in the immediate future. The dyed-in-the-wool Communists did not hesitate at the most drastic measures to gain their end as, for instance, the destruction of communications in order to wreck the economy of China and produce a situation that would facilitate the overthrow or collapse of the government without any regard to the immediate suffering of the people involved. They completely distrusted the leaders of the Kuomintang and were convinced that every government proposal was designed to crush the Chinese Communist Party."[184]

It is no wonder that General Joseph W. Stilwell, whose experience in China dated from 1911 through 1944, exclaimed upon watching Marshall's troubles develop: "But what did they expect? George Marshall can't walk on water."[185] He had not expected the mission to succeed, believing that once Chiang Kai-shek sensed the situation he would merely become more intransigent.

In February 1948, President Truman needed every vote he could muster in order to have the Marshall Plan for Europe enacted. Therefore, as a good Missouri horse trader, he sought the votes of the members of the China bloc in Congress by requesting a large appropriation to aid China. However, the economy-minded 80th Congress provided only $463 million, although the President had requested $570 million on February 18.

On December 8, 1949, the Nationalist government retreated to the island of Formosa. On December 30, Senator Robert A. Taft of Ohio (the leader of the Republican conservatives in Congress), Senator Knowland and former President Hoover suggested that the U.S. Navy should be used to keep Formosa out of Communist hands. President Truman promptly countered this proposal with a statement issued January 5, 1950, which is quoted in part:

"The United States has no predatory designs on Formosa or on any other Chinese territory. The United States has no desire to obtain special rights or privileges or to establish military bases on Formosa at this time. Nor does it have any intention of utilizing its armed forces to interfere in the present situation. *The United States Government will not pursue a course which will lead to involve-*

ment in the civil conflict in China. (Emphasis added)

"Similarly, the United States will not provide military aid or advise the Chinese forces on Formosa. . . . The United States proposes to continue under existing legislative authority the present . . . program of economic assistance."[186] There was no ambiguity in these words; they were crisp and unhedged.

It was after this statement that on February 9, 1950, Senator McCarthy, speaking at Wheeling, West Virginia, brought the charges of Communist influence in government to its peak. He stated unequivocally: ". . . While I cannot take the time to name all of the men in the State Department who have been named as active members of the Communist Party and members of a ring, I have here in my hand, a list of 205—a list of names that were made known to the Secretary of State as being members of the Communist Party and who nevertheless are still working and shaping policy in the State Department."[187] No such charges had been made during the years of Communist hysteria when allegations were investigated by the Un-American Activities Committee formed in 1938, by the FBI, the State Internal Security Committee, or by the Temporary Commission on Employee Loyalty set up by President Truman in November 1946 after unproven accusations were made against Harry Dexter White, an assistant secretary of the Treasury. By what arithmetic McCarthy arrived first at 205, then 57, and at another time 81 "card-carrying Communists" in the State Department is not known. Nor did he ever produce their names. Such was the tendency of the American public and the Congress to suspect widespread Communist infiltration that this unproved accusation started a massive witch-hunt. At its core was America's China policy and the issue was invigorated by the China lobby—the agents and partisans of Chiang Kai-shek.

McCarthy now put life into the phrase that Patrick Hurley had coined in 1945 —that the State Department was "soft on communism." China had been lost by the machinations of Soviet sympathizers. In that category McCarthy set John Carter Vincent, John Service, Philip C. Jessup (later to become a Justice of the International Court at The Hague), and Dr. Owen Lattimore of the Johns Hopkins University. He charged that Lattimore was "the architect of our Far Eastern policy," though Lattimore had never been connected with the State Department.

Senator Taft, who at first regarded McCarthy as reckless, now decided to give him Republican backing and help. McCarthy, he is quoted as saying, "should keep talking and if one case doesn't work out, he should proceed with another."[188] It is an old saying that politics makes strange bedfellows, but the alliance of Senator Taft with McCarthy was the strangest of strange; his complicity in inciting the fears and trepidations of the public was most reprehensible—and completely out of character. Senator Taft was to be an active candidate for the Republican nomination for President in 1952. The temper of the times may be measured by the extent to which this responsible and respected—albeit conservative—public servant demeaned himself. This man of impeccable reputation went so far as to attack "the pro-Communist group in the State Department who surrendered to every demand of Russia at Yalta and Potsdam, and promoted at every opportunity the Communist cause in China."[189]

How did Harry Truman react? As could be predicted, fire flamed from his nostrils. When, for instance, the Republicans in the House and Senate caucused and asked the President to remove Dean Acheson from office, he answered: ". . . If Communism were to prevail in the world today—as it shall not prevail —Dean Acheson would be one of the first, if not the first, to be shot by the enemies of liberty and Christianity. . . .

"It is the same sort of thing that happened to Seward. President Lincoln was asked by a group of Republicans to dismiss Secretary of State Seward. He refused. So do I refuse to dismiss Dean Acheson."[190] Again, he summoned history, but he used it to highlight his refusal, not as a prop to his action.

Asked at a press conference on March 30, 1950, whether McCarthy's charges of disloyalty in the State Department had any basis in fact, he replied with a peppery, "I think the greatest asset that the Kremlin has is Senator McCarthy." He went on to cite statistics about the loyalty program which he had instituted three years before. Out of more than two million civil servants, he said, only about two hundred resigned or were dismissed as a result of investigations. The Republicans, he continued scathingly, having failed with their charges of statism, the welfare state, and socialism in attempting to achieve control of Congress, were now making a political issue of loyalty. In order to do that, they were willing to "sabotage" the bi-partisan foreign policy. "And this fiasco which has been going on in the Senate is the very best asset that the Kremlin could have in the operation of the cold war." He was fed up, he said, with such antics.[191]

The President's surprising victory in 1948 had brought only a temporary relief to the struggle which he had been waging with the Congress over which branch of government was to manage the nation's internal security—the executive or the legislative branch. He was fully aware that if he lost this contest with Congress, bigotry and vigilantism would ride roughshod across the land. There were witch-hunts in local communities from one end of the country to the other—painful examples to be shunned by the national government.

President Truman termed the McCarran Act, introduced in 1950 by the chairman of the Senate Judiciary Committee, "just like the Alien and Sedition Act of 1798." Like a little boy sticking his tongue out in derision, he added, "and that didn't work either." He argued that it would fail in its main objective of stamping out communism by driving the Communists deeper underground, where it would be still more difficult to keep an eye on them. And he maintained that the bill was an unconstitutional invasion of the rights of freedom of speech and freedom of assembly; any infringement of these precious rights would be more harmful to the country than anything the Communists could do. He had offered legislation of his own to stiffen the espionage statutes, in which, he argued, the real weakness and the remedy lay. Chairman McCarran committed it to a dusty pigeonhole of his Judiciary Committee, where it would not compete with his own bill.[192]

The McCarran Bill was passed on September 17, by a vote of 354 to 20 in the House and 70 to 7 in the Senate. The *New York Times* reported that "Many who criticized the bill in debate voted for it in final passage. The feeling on Capitol Hill, apparently, is that it is too risky politically to vote against anti-Communist legislation in this election year."[193]

Truman not only vetoed the bill in spite of the fact that his veto would certainly be overridden, but he put up a good stiff fight to have his veto upheld. Cabell Phillips recorded: "Congress was driving impatiently for adjournment that week in late September so that members could get home and begin their re-election campaigns. The security bill was the last item on their agenda. It reached the President's desk on Wednesday, September 20. He returned it at noon, Friday with a hard-hitting and well-reasoned veto that covered nine single-spaced legal pages.

"He had also taken an unusual step. Each member of Congress found on his desk that morning a copy of the veto message along with a personal letter from the President. The President urged that the member, before casting his vote that day, read not only the full text of the McCarran bill but the President's reasons for refusing to sign as well. As an old congressional hand himself, he was pretty sure that most members had only a vague notion of what was in the bill, and that if they took the trouble to find out they might be more receptive to his reasons for rejecting it.

"The House totally ignored the President's request. Within an hour of its noon opening and without debate, it voted to override the veto 286 to 48. . . . But the Senate, in its more deliberate fashion, delayed and President Truman leaped to seize whatever advantage this might offer. He telephoned a high-spirited young first-termer, Hubert H. Humphrey (Democratic Majority Leader Scott Lucas was committed to vote to override), and asked him to muster what liberal forces he could to stave off a Senate vote until Saturday midnight. With adjournment set for that hour, such a filibuster just might succeed in sustaining the veto even if it couldn't be done with votes. In any event, Truman told Humphrey, a delay of twenty-four hours would give the press and radio time to alert the nation to what was involved in the conflict. Just possibly, this might build up a backfire at the grass roots. . . . At 4 o'clock, the Senate voted 57 to 10 to override, and the Internal Security Act of 1950 became law.

"It was a good fight, a typically Truman kind of to-hell-with-where-the-chips-may-fall fight. He had stood his ground against overwhelming odds for what he believed to be right. His enemies gloated over his defeat, but he won new respect with the more dispassionate editorial writers and columnists. And, just as he had prophesied, the McCarran Act did prove to be a legalistic and administrative monstrosity, destined to be fought over in the courts for more than a decade and adding little to the net security of the nation."[194]

This is the way Harry Truman reacted and this is the reason that his prestige grew. The future termed his causes right and his fight for them heroic. His reputation as a great President grew because of the fact that the odds were most frequently stacked against him, that he tackled them and the congressional club in which he had been a member regardless, that he didn't take the easy way out when his legislative leaders advised him to do so "because the political climate demanded it and a veto was certain." This was his style not only in this one instance but in all of his uphill efforts to improve the well-being of the people of the nation and of our foreign relations.

He was conscious of maintaining good international relations even when he became an ex-President. A small, amusing and telling incident occurred while we were in France in 1958. We stayed at an inn above Vence in the Maritime Alps where we expected that the Trumans would have privacy; but until Sam came to an agreement with the press, they followed us each day when we journeyed forth. It annoyed Mrs. Truman very much, the ex-President not at all. One day we went to the beautiful old city of Eze with the usual entourage in our wake. I joined Mrs. Truman in vocal complaints. As we went through the old gate, the President drew us to the parapet and gave us a thorough tongue-lashing. The tenor of it was: "After all the efforts I have made to make friends of these nations, you can destroy it by your actions. I want you to stop." We did. That noon, as the press and photographers waited for us to finish lunch at the Château Madrid, Sam met with them and came to an agreement that if they stopped following us the President would hold a press conference with them on board ship when we sailed. He suggested that the photographers take as many snaps as they desired then and there and then cease. They agreed. There was an orgy of picture-taking, accompanied by photos that we took of them. Occasionally we spied someone up a tree with a mini-camera; there must have been one at Les Baux because *Life* had a picture of the President and Sam in the swimming pool; and in typically French fashion *Paris Match* carried a picture of the President and me in the pool with a caption which gave the impression that we were vacationing together— no mention of our spouses.

The subject of McCarthyism cannot be dismissed without excepting from criticism Margaret Chase Smith and six other Republican senators who joined her in signing a Declaration of Conscience. On June 1, 1950, the lady from Maine in issuing the Declaration made a noteworthy speech in the Senate repudiating McCarthyism: "Mr. President, I would like to speak briefly and simply about a serious national condition. It is a national feeling of fear and frustration that could result in national suicide and the end of everything we hold dear. . . .

"The United States Senate has long enjoyed worldwide respect as the greatest deliberative body in the world. But recently that deliberative character has too often been debased to the level of a forum of hate and character assassination sheltered by the shield of congressional immunity. . . .

"I think it is high time for the United States Senate and its Members to do some real soul-searching and to weigh our consciences as to the manner in which we are performing our duty to the people of America and the manner in which we are using or abusing our individual powers and privileges.

"I think it is high time that we remember that we have sworn to uphold and defend the Constitution. I think it is high time that we remembered that the Constitution, as amended, speaks not only of the freedom of speech but also of trial by jury instead of trial by accusation. . . .

"The record of the present Administration has provided us with sufficient campaign issues without the necessity of resorting to political smears. America is rapidly losing its position as leader of the world simply because the Democratic administration has pitifully failed to provide effective leadership."[195]

Mrs. Smith was not without partisanship, but she was honorable. She also included in her speech the fact that "as a United States Senator, I am not proud of the way in which the Senate has been made a publicity platform for unresponsible sensationalism. I am not proud of the reckless abandon in which unproved charges have been hurled from this side of the aisle. I am not proud of the obviously staged, undignified counter-charges which have been attempted in retaliation from the other side of the aisle. . . ."[196]

Thus spoke the lady from Maine. The gentleman from Missouri went to the den of conservatism—an American Legion convention—on August 15, 1951, and boldly spoke his creed:

". . . When the Legion pledged itself to uphold the Constitution, and to foster 100-per cent Americanism, it pledged itself to protect the rights and liberties of all our citizens.

"Real Americanism means that we will protect freedom of speech—we will defend the right of people to say what they think, regardless of how much we may disagree with them.

"Real Americanism means freedom of religion. It means that we will not discriminate against a man because of his religious faith.

"Real Americanism means fair opportunities for all our citizens. It means that none of our citizens should be held back by unfair discrimination and prejudice.

"Real Americanism means fair play. It means that a man who is accused of a crime shall be considered innocent until he has been proved guilty. It means that people are not to be penalized and persecuted for exercising their constitutional liberties.

"Real Americanism means also that liberty is not license. There is no freedom to injure others. The Constitution does not protect free speech to the extent of permitting conspiracies to overthrow the government. Neither does the right of free speech authorize slander or character assassination. These limitations are essential to keep us working together in one great community.

"Real Americanism includes all these things. And it takes all of them together to make 100-per cent Americanism—the kind the Legion is pledged to support. . . .

"We want to protect the country against disloyalty—of course we do. We have been punishing people for disloyal acts, and we are going to keep on punishing the guilty whenever we have a case against them. But we don't want to destroy our whole system of justice in the process. We don't want to injure innocent people. And yet the scurrilous work of the scandalmongers gravely threatens the whole idea of protection for the innocent in our country today. . . ."[197]

He ended by exhorting the Legion to raise its voice against hysteria. Hysteria continued into the Eisenhower administration. McCarthy was finally discredited by his own misuse of power and machinations.

The cleavage between Democrats and Republicans was at an all-time high as the 1952 Presidential election approached; hence the Republicans were unwilling to shoulder responsibility for foreign policy. Nevertheless, the President with political prescience appointed a Republican, John Foster Dulles, to conduct the negotiations leading to the Japanese Peace Treaty, thus taking the treaty out of partisan politics and securing its overwhelming ratification in the midst of the Presidential election campaign. Where personalities did not intrude, the President's judgment in appointments was wise and shrewd. Professor Sidney Warren has written, "In appointing George C. Marshall and later Dean Acheson, the President demonstrated that he possessed a vital ingredient of leadership: the ability to select competent advisers."[198] He slipped up here and there and, unfortunately, the slips predominated in the public mind until the perspective of history permitted the air to clear.

Harry Truman was sensitive to the personalities of people and that sensitivity accounted for his likes, dislikes and indifference to appointees. Henry Wallace would, in all probability, have never been asked to resign as Secretary of Commerce if the President had had rapport with him. He never understood him; he neither liked nor disliked him, but Wallace had trodden upon the toes of the man for whom Truman had had friendship, Secretary of State Byrnes. That was the underlying reason that the contretemps over Wallace's speech on foreign affairs could not be overlooked. The President's mistaken loyalty to several of his friends remained unshaken in the face of facts.

However, in the summer of 1950, before the wave of scandals reached its peak, Secretary of the Treasury John Snyder—a World War I buddy—epitomized Truman's appraisal of his friends as, "My people are all honorable—all of them are." He had quietly started an investigation of the regional offices of the Collector of Internal Revenue. He found corruption and he dismissed the corrupt. It was not until January 1952 that Truman awakened from his trance of confidence because of disclosures of several congressional investigations which startled and infuriated him.

In spite of his former composure he had put through Congress a bill to reorganize RFC and was working on another which would clean house in the Revenue Service and put the collectors under civil service. He now proposed a special White House commission to study the question of corruption in government. His attempts to find a chairman failed; his appointment of the liberal Republican Newbold Morris, former president of the New York City Council, ended in a fiasco. Over-zealous and inept, Morris succeeded only in antagonizing all of official Washington—Republican as well as Democratic. The Republicans were eager for election and not for solution, a solution which would have to await the pressure caused by far greater scandals. Strangely enough, in view of today's public attitude, the issue which maddened all parties and caused Morris's final contretemps was his proposal that all federal employees, from Cabinet members down, list their assets and sources of income.

No one in government was ready for such a suggestion. The President felt that the questionnaire was an improper invasion of individual rights and privacy; he publicly rebuked his Attorney General Howard J. McGrath for allowing Morris to go to such lengths, but he didn't ask that the questionnaire be withdrawn.

"A few days later, boiling mad, McGrath told a congressional committee that he would not fill out such a questionnaire himself and that he would forbid its distribution to personnel of his department. When he got back to his office that afternoon, he dictated a terse note to Morris advising him 'Your appointment is hereby terminated.' When the President heard of this for the first time from the news-ticker, he picked up the telephone and told McGrath *he* was fired too— instanter."[199]

Although the scandals in the Truman administration were decidedly petty in comparison to those of Teapot Dome, Watergate and others of the Harding and Nixon administrations, they and the manner of handling them cast a decided shadow, however temporary.

Although President Truman lacked Democratic leadership of Congress during only two years (1947–49), his record of legislative achievement during his two terms in office is minimal. His greatest success was in the enactment of the Truman Doctrine, the Marshall Plan and NATO, and his Point Four Program. Only a trifling fraction of his "Fair Deal" legislation was passed, but its objectives lived on and were enacted when the temper of the country was more receptive in the years of the Kennedy and Johnson administrations. The principles he laid down and the legislation he sought were accepted in the days when the climate of public opinion had warmed to them. Though it may be conceded that Kennedy and Johnson were better salesmen of Truman's wares, it would not have been possible for them to have achieved his goals in the milieu that followed the war. He set the pace when the going was difficult and he did not shrink from voicing his goals even though he was conscious of the fact that they were probably beyond his reach. This fearlessness, courageousness and intrepidity were his hallmarks. "A sympathizer with the Fair Deal," which was an expansion of the New Deal, "will interpret it, temporary failure or no, as a political force that kept the atmosphere of political and social reform from being dissipated and heartened masses of people with solid expectations of better things at hand, whatever recalcitrant members of the Congress might say or vote."[200]

President Truman's espousal of the creation of the State of Israel has been attributed by many people to many reasons. By analyzing the beliefs of those who were close to the President beginning in 1945, it is clear that he was activated by deep conviction and spurred to accomplishment by the warmth of his feeling for the sincerity and devotion of Dr. Chaim Weitzmann. Sincerity and devotion, traits that were indigenous to Harry Truman, when possessed by others influenced him.

Dean Acheson, opposed to the creation of an Israeli state, has written: "Almost immediately upon becoming President, Mr. Truman with the best will in the world tackled that immensely difficult international puzzle—a homeland in Palestine for the Jews. . . . The fate of the Jewish victims of Hitlerism was a 'matter of deep personal concern' to him and as President he 'undertook to do something about it.' The Balfour Declaration, promising the Jews the opportunity to re-establish a homeland in Palestine, had always seemed to him 'to go hand in hand with the noble policies of Woodrow Wilson, especially the principles of self-determination.' From many years of talk with him, I know that this represented a deep conviction, in large part implanted by his close friend and former partner, Eddie Jacobson, a passionate Zionist."[201]

There is no intention here of following the details which led to Truman's support for partition of Palestine in the United Nations and his recognition of the State of Israel "twelve minutes after Britain's mandate expired."[202] They have been chronicled. It is important to his style to let the reader know that the President's convictions could be turned away by excessive pressure and retained by unpressured advocation; that he listened to trusted advisers who presented well-reasoned arguments and was weakened in his resolve because of some of those arguments; but that after all was said he came to his own conclusion, gave it leadership and fulfillment.

The constant hammering pressure of some of the leaders of Zionism like Rabbis Hillel Silver and Stephen Wise was most irritating to the President and influenced his vacillation. He returned to his purpose after talking with Chaim Weitzmann, whom he referred to as "the old doctor" or "Shaim." (No matter how many times he was told that the "C" in "Chaim" was silent, his pronunciation included it.) On their second meeting, "once again, the extraordinary current of mutual respect and sympathy which animated their first meeting dominated their conversation.

"Weitzmann did most of the talking. He pressed Truman for three things: lifting of the arms embargo, support for partition and Jewish Immigration into Palestine.

"The President told Weitzmann the State Department was considering the first point. As for immigration, his position in its favor had always been clear. It was on the second point, however, that this meeting would bear its fruit. The moving plea on behalf of his people by the half-blind Zionist leader nearing the end of his life and his forces weighed . . . heavily in the mind of Harry Truman," reinforcing, as it did, his own position. "He would keep faith with this elderly man and the thousands of his kinsmen still behind the barbed wire of Europe's displaced persons camps. The United States, he promised Weitzmann, would continue its support of Palestine."[203]

Prior to this meeting with Weitzmann, he had conferred with Secretary of State Marshall and others, including his counsel Clark Clifford. He listened attentively to his respected advisers. Opposed, though sympathetic to the Zionists, was General Marshall who believed that the projected Jewish state, being entirely surrounded by Arabs who had well-trained armies equipped with heavy arms, could not survive. Opposed also was James Forrestal, Secretary of the Navy. Added to his general opposition was one that is noteworthy now, twenty-seven years later; he was concerned with partition's effect on the United States' access to Middle East oil; he predicted that in a decade "the nation could be forced to convert to four-cylinder cars."[204] In favor of partition were his Counsel Clark Clifford and his White House staff adviser David Niles. General Marshall resented their intrusion in a matter that concerned the State Department and said so.

"Crestfallen, the President began to gather up the papers on his desk. There was no man in his Administration on whom he depended more than Marshall. However deep was his desire to recognize the state and however he longed to make this last gesture to 'the old doctor' he so esteemed, he could not do it if the price was going to be a rupture with his Secretary of State.

" 'Thank you for your contributions,' he said. 'I accept your recommendation, General. The United States will not *at this time* recognize a new Jewish state in Palestine.' "[205] Emphasis is added here because the President had not given word that his decision was irrevocable and certainly had not approved a public statement. His determined mind probably had already decided upon further talks with the General when the heat of this meeting had cooled. It is to be recalled that this meeting preceded by only a short time his talk with Weitzmann.

To his amazement, within hours after his talk with Weitzmann, Warren Austin, our Ambassador to the United Nations, delivered at the Security Council a speech which had been drafted by Loy Henderson, the State Department author of the trusteeship plan. Doubly angered because the speech had been delivered and because he was placed in the position of not being able openly to disavow it, Truman "ordered Judge Samuel Rosenman, a frequent visitor, to 'go find Chaim Weitzmann wherever he is. Tell him I mean every word of what I said . . . I promised him we would stick to our guns on partition and I meant it.' "[206]

It was gratifying to Truman that, after earnest conversation with Clark Clifford, General Marshall reconsidered his stand and recommended to the President that the United States recognize the new state. Therefore, the President could execute his decision without offending his valued Secretary of State. This procedure explains the use of "at this time." President Truman always sought a way to avoid rupture with a friend.

My husband believed that polls among historians in the near or distant future would classify President Truman among the "great" instead of the "near-great" Presidents. He so regarded him. His belief was based upon his own observations; therefore it is pertinent to reinforce his contention by citing the assessments of several of his contemporaries.

Ambassador Charles E. Bohlen has written: "He had one of the most important qualities necessary to be an effective president, a genuine power of decision. He lived up to the sign on his desk, 'The buck stops here.' Occasionally, his decisions would be too quick, but he was not hasty in foreign affairs."[207]

Thomas A. Bailey, Byrne Professor of American History at Stanford University, believes that "The primary reason why Truman is ranked with the Near Greats is that he acted decisively—he evidently enjoyed doing so—when faced with a dozen or so crises of earth-shaking significance. Among them were the decisions to drop the atomic bomb on Japan, to enunciate the Truman Doctrine for the salvation of Greece and Turkey, to support the Marshall Plan for the rehabilitation of post-war Europe, to inaugurate the airlift for beleaguered Berlin in 1948, to 'dump' China in 1949, to intervene in Korea, to go beyond the 38th parallel in Korea, to keep the secret of the atomic bomb, and to manufacture the hydrogen bomb. Although seeking counsel from his top advisers, he did not rely on staff decisions, at least not to the extent that President Eisenhower did. Perhaps he remembered the admonition of Theodore Roosevelt, 'A council of war never fights.' "[208]

It might be said, however, that President Truman was edged over the 38th parallel in Korea by General MacArthur.

Professor Sidney Warren, chairman of the Political Science Department of California Western University, wrote, "Many Americans could not comprehend the fantastically complex nature of the international situation. The Truman administration had inherited a Europe stripped of countervailing forces against the Soviet Union, the only military power which the war had left on the continent. Not even possession of the atom bomb could mitigate the danger to the United States arising out of the European vacuum. With the balance of power weighted in favor of Russia, it was vital that America maintain the allegiance of key areas in Western Europe, and win in the contest for such areas as Greece, Turkey, Iran, and China. As in a chess game, each move had to be calculated with the utmost finesse.

"Against constant, relentless Russian pressure to expand its power, Truman raised one bulwark after another. . . . By the time he left office, Truman had succeeded in achieving a partial readjustment of power balance, the first peacetime President to actively engage the nation's moral and material resources for that end. . . .

"Truman's extraordinary achievements as a world leader during the critical period in which he held office were obscured for the majority of Americans, partly as a result of the virulent Republican attacks on his administration, to some degree because he did not possess a commanding presence, and also because he lacked the genius of the President's schoolmaster role. When he had to deal with concrete situations, with tangible crises, he was effective in rallying the nation behind him. But he was unable to convey adequately a sense of the new dimensions of the age. . . . Probably no President could have completely reached a public whose past experience made them resistant to an acceptance of the revolutionary aspects of the current scene, but possibly a more dynamic leader, with an awareness of the subtleties of international life, might have made some inroads."[209]

Clinton Rossiter, John L. Senior Professor of American Institutions at Cornell University, took a close-up view of Harry Truman four years after he left office—a view which is at once picturesque and faithful:

"Harry S. Truman is a man whom history will delight to remember. Those very lapses from dignity that made him an object of scorn to millions of Republicans—the angry letters, testy press conferences, whistle stops, impossible sport shirts, and early-morning seminars on the streets of dozens of American cities—open his door to immortality. It is a rare American, even a rare Republican, who can be scornful about a man one hundred years dead, and our descendants will be chuckling over his Missouri wit and wisdom long after the 'five-percenters' have been buried and forgotten. They will read with admiration of the upset he brought off in 1948, with awe of the firing of General MacArthur, and with a sense of kinship of the way he remained more genuinely 'plain folks' than any other President. They will be moved by the simple dignity of his confession: 'There are probably a million people in this country who could do the presidential job better than I, but I've got the job and I'm doing the very best I can.' He was fascinating to watch, even when the sight hurt, and he will be fascinating to read about. The historians can be expected to do their share to fix him securely in history, for he provides a classic case study of one of their favorite themes: the President who grows in office. . . .

"The office he handed over to Eisenhower was no less magnificent than the office he inherited from Roosevelt. Looked at in the light of what took place during the term of every other man who succeeded a great President—John Adams, Madison, Van Buren, Johnson, Taft and Harding—this may well appear as Truman's most remarkable achievement. . . .

"Harry S. Truman will be a well-remembered President because he proved that an ordinary man could fill the world's most extraordinary office with devotion and high purpose. He may serve as a lasting symbol of the noble truth that gives strength and meaning to the American experiment: plain men *can* govern themselves; democracy *does* work. And his epitaph will read: He was distressingly petty in petty things; *he was gallantly big in big things.*" [210] (Emphasis added)

5

WARREN G. HARDING

(1865–1923)

President, March 4, 1921, to August 3, 1923[1]

Harry Micah Daugherty met Warren Gamaliel Harding as the thirty-four-year-old editor of the Marion *Star* was washing his boots at the school pump in Richwood, Ohio, in preparation for his appearance at the evening political rally. Daugherty was struck by his statesman-like appearance, his suavity and friendliness. Although in 1899 the young man was merely a candidate for the State Senate, it "flashed into Daugherty's mind that this man . . . looked like a President. He was possible material. The more seasoned politician expressed a hope of meeting the other again."[2]

Daugherty, now unsuccessful in attempts to obtain elected office for himself, seized upon the opportunity to be the power behind a likely candidate; a born promoter, a wheeler-dealer par excellence and an expert wire-puller, he was adept in the political milieu of the times. Fate would have it that rain constrained the politicians to the lobby and a bar of the little hotel; Daugherty's first impression was strengthened as they talked and—to the surprise of the other politicians—the political promoter suggested that the *Star* editor make the first speech of the evening. The Richwood *Gazette* editorialized: ". . . He made an able speech and pleased the immense audience by his humorous illustrations and burst of eloquence. Most of our people had been led to believe that Mr. Harding was not much of a speaker, and had been placed on the program as a sort of 'filler.' He surprised everybody present, even his most intimate friends. While he appeared a little awkward on the stage, his language was well chosen and his argument convincing. In short time we predict he will be one of the leading political orators of the state. . . ."[3]

Thus started Harding's road to the presidency. In order to achieve his objective it was necessary for Daugherty to prod the candidate every rung of his upward political path as well as promote him. The easygoing Warren was content to stay in each of his successive positions where the atmosphere of camaraderie permitted him to enjoy himself without effort—as member of the Ohio State Senate, as Republican floor leader of the State Senate, as Lieutenant Governor and as United States Senator. But the picture of Harding as President of the United States remained steadfast in Daugherty's mind. He kept prodding him on. In 1916 he maneuvered to make him the temporary chairman of the Republican National Convention. "As 'keynoter' Harding . . . could be relied upon to take direction. None of the leaders had anything to fear from him. He had made no enemies. Now he must make friends."[4]

"Gee, but he'd make a great-looking President. . . . We'll put it over some-time, Jess," said Daugherty to his friend Jesse Smith.[5]

Senator Harding had no such ambition. On October 6, 1919, he declared himself in a private letter as wishing to remain in the United States Senate, "a position far more to my liking than the Presidency could possibly be."[6] Soon thereafter the Ohio Republican State Advisory Committee tried to get him to avow his candidacy. On November 1 he declared that he desired only their support for his re-election to the Senate. This sent Daugherty poste haste to Washington. Without informing Harding he went to see Senators Penrose, Lodge, Knox and other personal friends of Harding in both houses of Congress. "Cooperation was the burden of his song; Senator Harding could be trusted to cooperate, in other words, to take orders. It was soft music to the ears of the oligarchs who had too long been under the galling discipline of obeying instead of commanding. He did some useful ground-breaking with the National Committee, practicing his best persuasions to the end that, if such members as exhibited interest could not accept the Ohio man for first choice, they should bear him in mind for second, third or even fourth."[7]

In November Daugherty decided to use his persuasive powers upon his reluctant candidate. For all his urging he could not budge Harding's unwillingness to give up a Senate seat for a long chance at something he did not want and for which he maintained he was not even fitted. Daugherty persisted. "What would you do in my place?" Harding finally asked.

Writing a dozen years later, Daugherty recalled this conversation:

"I'd go into the big circus . . ."

"And you think I'd have a fighting chance?"

"I think you have the best chance."

"How do you figure it?" he asked.

"On this line," I answered. "Neither one of the leading candidates can win. General Wood is backed by a powerful group of rich men who wish a military man in the White House. . . . But there's not enough money in the world to buy the nomination for a man who wears epaulets in 1920."

"Lowden's a power to be reckoned with," Harding suggested.

"Sure. The best man on the list, too. I like him. He'd make a fine President. But he'll never have the prize of nomination."

"Why?"

"He's too rich."

"Nonsense."

"Besides, he married Pullman's daughter. No party will name a railroad magnate to the office of President. . . ."

"Come down to brass tacks," Harding ordered. "Am I a big enough man for the race?"

"Don't make me laugh! The days of giants in the President's Chair is passed [sic]. Our so-called Great Presidents were all made by the conditions of war under which they administered the office. Greatness in the Presidential Chair is largely an illusion of the people."[8]

This is not the only occasion upon which Harding expressed doubts about his fitness. He had expressed those doubts to Senator Penrose, the powerful political boss of Pennsylvania, and in numerous letters to friends. He had no confidence in himself as a leader; he was not cut from that cloth.

In mid-December Harding announced his candidacy in a style unique but also characteristic of his lack of zeal for the leadership requisite for the office: "I venture to announce no platform, nor to emphasize any obvious policy. Men in Congress make records which speak for them. Moreover, I still believe in representative popular government through political parties, believe in party sponsorship, believe conventions representing all the Republicans of the nation should make the platforms, that nominees ought to be chosen as exponents of such platforms, and hold such declarations as inviolable covenants to the people."[9]

As President he would hold to the belief that Congress should propose and the President should dispose. Unfortunately for the country, neither the Congress nor the President would evidence an interest in proposing. When, toward the latter part of his presidency, Harding did make an effort to lead, Congress would not heed. It was an era of drift which began with the Republican Convention of 1920.

The day before balloting a New York banker, Fred W. Allen, entertained a dozen guests at luncheon, one of whom was Mark Sullivan, the dean of Washington newspaper correspondents, and "as judicious an observer as might be found at the convention. . . . His tablemates were all political sophisticates who, Sullivan felt, should have known who the nominee would be if it were possible to know. Allen, after lunch, proposed that each put a five-dollar bill in a sealed envelope together with the name of the candidate they predicted as a winner. Whoever guessed right, the total would be given to any institution he picked. Sullivan put down Harvard as his institution and Wood as his candidate. Some weeks later Allen returned Sullivan his five dollars, writing that none of his guests had picked Harding."[10]

Harding was nominated on the tenth ballot. "This year we had a lot of second raters," said Republican Senator Brandegee, who had a great deal to do with the nomination. "Harding is no world-beater. But he's the best of the lot."[11] The future President's elation was expressed in poker terms, so familiar to him. "I feel like a man who goes in on a pair of eights and comes out with aces full."[12]

Assessments of Harding lack variance in their estimations of his qualifications. David F. Houston kept a record, almost daily, of his experiences in Wilson's Cabinet, and recorded these observations following the Cabinet discussion of October 19, 1920. "If Harding is elected, the contrast will be painful. It will be somewhat tragic to have a man of Wilson's intellect and high standards succeeded by a man of Mr. Harding's mediocre mind and ordinary standards of thinking and action. At this time, particularly, the nation needs a leader, and Mr. Harding will not be a leader. He cannot be. He has never stood for any great cause. He knows very little, has no wisdom, very little sense of direction, and no independence. He was not nominated to lead. He was selected because he was colorless and pliable. If he is elected he will be the tool of such tried leaders as Lodge, Penrose, and others. He will play the game of the Senate. The Senate will be supreme. The old policies will be revived. Protection will raise its head again and raise it higher than ever. The revolt of the people against the Paine Aldrich Bill will be forgotten. This element of the Republican Party which will be in the ascendant knows exactly where it is going. It will go back where it was before 1915. What a treat it will be to have to witness Mr. Harding's effort to think and his efforts to say what he thinks."[13]

Another Democrat, William G. McAdoo, wrote at a later date: "I have always wondered and am still wondering, why the Republicans nominated Harding in 1920. He was, as everyone knows, soft and pliable and easily managed. Apparently, if one may judge from his record as President, he was ready and willing to turn over the major functions of government to 'privilege' and to give his sonorous approval to its policies. That was, of course, a desirable thing from the standpoint of vested interests; but, even so, it seems that a Republican with more stamina and a more distinguished record, who would not have brought discredit on the Administration, might have been selected. . . . Harding was a likeable person. His manner was pleasant and ingratiating; and he was 'a good fellow' in the ordinary locker room, poker-game sense of the term; far too much of a 'good fellow' in fact, to be entrusted with great authority. The possessor of an adjustable conscience, which could be altered to fit every changing circumstance, Harding went through life with good cheer and gusto, believing thoroughly that a man can get along very well if he can fool some of the people some of the time.

"He was a speech-maker; he spoke on every convenient occasion in a big bow-wow style of oratory. He would use rolling words which had no application to the topic in hand, and his speeches left the impression of an army of pompous phrases moving over the landscape in search of an idea. Sometimes these meandering words would actually capture a straggling thought and bear it triumphantly, a prisoner in their midst, until it died of servitude and overwork."[14]

As we shall see, the characterization that his opponent, James M. Cox of Dayton, Ohio, made of him was apt: "Senator Harding is the kind of man who, on his way to the legislature, would empty his pockets to some poor creature, and then vote with the conservative Republicans for a bill that would maintain the conditions making possible the sufferings of the recipient."[15]

Theodore Roosevelt's daughter, the sharp-tongued Alice Roosevelt Longworth, still smarted from the fact that Harding had secured the nomination for Governor of Ohio in 1909—a nomination which her husband, Nicholas Longworth, had desired—and that Harding had been at loggerheads with her father whose famous style, "Let's fight it out," was not akin to Harding's. She had not forgotten Harding's speech at the 1912 Republican Convention renominating President Taft instead of T.R. This excerpt from that speech is illustrative of McAdoo's description of Harding's oratorical style—full of alliterations and ambiguities—and of Harding's constant practice of carrying water on both shoulders: "Progress is not proclamation nor palaver. It is not pretense nor play on prejudice. It is not the perturbation of a people passion-wrought, nor a promise proposed. Progression is everlastingly lifting the standards that marked the end of the world's march yesterday, and planting them on new and advanced heights today. Tested by such a standard, President Taft is the greatest Progressive of the age."[16]

"Princess Alice" recalled in her book *Crowded Hours* that her dislike of President Harding began at this convention. In addition to condemning his speech "[she] condemned Harding for coming to them in the gallery and offering her husband the Governorship of Ohio. Before Longworth could answer, his wife told Harding 'that we could not accept favors from crooks.' She wrote that she thought it was 'a little raw and obtuse of Harding, to make that offer to Nick in my presence.' Longworth pleaded with Alice to apologize to Harding for calling him a crook. She declined on the ground 'that was what I meant to say.' "[17]

Thus it was not surprising that she demanded of the Harding backer, George Harvey—the same George Harvey who first proposed the college president

Woodrow Wilson for the presidency—". . . Why, if 'they' were strong enough to put Harding over, could they not have selected some 'dark horse' such as Knox who seemed to have higher qualifications for the Presidency. The reply to that [was] that Harding could be counted on to 'go along.' In other words, he could be controlled."[18]

It is important to have a picture of the temper of the public in the 1920's and of the economic and social factors which influenced that temper in order to comprehend Harding's acceptance; and to gain a knowledge of his past, which affected his attitudes and actions.

Samuel Hopkins Adams says: "It was a period of moral slump, the backswing from the idealism and sacrifices of war. Men's thoughts could not indefinitely maintain themselves on that lofty plane. Cumulative discontents blended in a savage resentment. The nation was neurotically suspicious; in a mood to blame everything upon the party in power. People felt the grind of hard times. Coal went to as much as twenty dollars a ton. All necessities were high. Pocketbooks were feeling the pinch, and when the American pocketbook is pinched, it kicks. Labor was growling at war profiteering. But Labor had been doing some fancy profiteering on its own account, in war wages. Now there was spreading unemployment. Industrialists incited the Government to repressive measures against labor organizations, under the convenient excuse of 'curbing the Reds.' People were unhappy, restless. They craved a change."[19]

These were the conditions that brought forth the call from Senator Harding for "normalcy," which was to be his campaign cry. Speaking in Boston in May 1920—in his usual alliterative style—Harding told his audience that "America's present need is not heroics but healing; not revolution but restoration . . . not surgery but serenity."[20]

By June, unemployment had climbed to over 4 million. Particularly hard-hit were the farmers; where wheat had sold for $2.15 a bushel in 1919, it now sold for 88 cents. The odds for Harding moved up from 3 to 4 to 1.[21] The American public was against those in power whom it held responsible for these conditions; it was in no mood to assess the qualifications of the candidate of the opposing party.

What were Harding's qualifications; what was his style as his position in the community grew? What was his background?

He came from a family who had to struggle for a living; whose antecedents were questioned by the citizens of the small towns in Ohio to which they moved until finally they settled in Marion; whose social equality was never recognized by the élite of those small communities so conscious of background. This probably impelled his lifelong desire to please, to belong, to be amidst those with power. Harding's first experience of "belonging" was in Marion where he played the alto horn and became the manager of the band that performed at political rallies in the area and on festive occasions. "Finesse was not their forte; nuances of expression were not for them. But they played with a virile blare and bang, and their rhythm was something to quicken the torpid blood."[22] His oratory developed in the same genre.

His boyhood gave no promise of distinction. As in later life, he manifested neither industry nor ambition. "When a corn-husking job was offered at the special rate of four bits a day—well above the regular pay for a boy, because his family were in need of money—he quit in the first hour. He hated chores, but would consider odd jobs if the money was good and the labor light."[23]

Throughout his life he sought the easy way. Upon graduation from a two-year institution known as Ohio Central College located at Iberia, he taught school but abandoned his job after the first term and later described it as "the hardest job I ever had." He then tried reading law, but decided that he had no aptitude. The next venture was selling insurance; that appealed to him because he enjoyed meeting people, and he had a knack of getting along with them—a knack which would serve him well in the future. This experience, through no fault of his, met with disastrous results. As a youngster he had played around with type in a country weekly of which his father was half-owner. At loose ends in 1884, with a few hundred dollars that one of his future partners had inherited he seized upon the opportunity of persuading two friends to join him in buying a bankrupt local newspaper in Marion, Ohio. That gave Warren Harding his start in life.

"In his maturing days, young Warren was a cheerful and attractive personality. Tall, well-proportioned, a little slouchy in posture, he was, despite the handlebar moustache of the period, a strikingly handsome specimen, with his large, liquid, friendly eyes, expansive forehead, fine, straight nose between rather prominent cheek-bones, pleasantly moulded chin, and a mouth prone to smile. The countenance was the index to his character. *He wanted to be everybody's friend.*" [24] (Emphasis added) As President-elect he confided to a newspaper man that he could not expect to be the best President the country ever had, but he did want to be the best loved. That would satisfy his highest ambition. [25]

When Harding and his two partners took over their daily newspaper, the *Star*, they were anxious to get customers from both parties, and thus announced that it would be independent politically. Although he made no enemies through this policy, he also failed to get political advertising. Later he found it expedient to make the *Star* an aggressively conservative Republican paper. It was a struggle to keep going—a struggle which did not discourage Harding for he was in a milieu which he thoroughly enjoyed. Debt didn't trouble him; he kept buying new equipment. When he installed a telephone, Warwick sold his share—which Harding bought "in a cold hand of poker." [26] The third partner, Sickel, also withdrew, making Harding the sole owner.

Debt did not trouble him even when he became President. He speculated in the market and when he died he owed the Cleveland brokerage house of Ungerleider and Company $180,000. [27]

Harding's personal relations were always generous and liberal. The *Star* plant was loyal, friendly, happy, and he always paid a bit above the going wage. Personal recognition of the worth of the individual working man contrasted with his disdain of mass recognition. He had a mental block against organized liberalism. Although Theodore Roosevelt and Woodrow Wilson were conservative in their early public life, they became liberals as they faced issues; Warren Harding had few lapses from conservatism and they occurred toward the end of his short period as President. Whether death deprived him of the opportunity to develop an interest in social progress in large terms will never be known.

The twenty-one-year-old editor of the *Star* wrote on September 1, 1886: "The Star has some knowledge of printers, both union and non-union, and while we consider them as a class a bright and intellectual body of men, we are intimately aware that a number of them are a drunken, worthless set, the majority of whom are supported by and sail under the prestige of typographical unions." [28] Later, however, he evinced no objection to his men joining a union and he himself joined the printer's union; but he opposed the Knights of Labor because of their "radicalism" and their heretical tendency to form a third party.

Adams says: "Harding was always more the printer and publisher than the editor. Writing editorials was a chore. He was far happier in the streets, in the city hall or the court house where he could mix, hear gossip, be part of the intimate, busy life of the town he loved. Personal contacts were his fad, callers were welcome at the *Star* office. All sorts of people made a habit of dropping in; businessmen, politicians, farmers from the outlying districts, visitors with axes to grind, hard-luck hopefuls. For all of them the editor had a pleasant word and smile. He had more than that for the unfortunate. At Christmas, he would fill his pockets with bills, three or four hundred dollars, go out and, with what secrecy he could manage, distribute them where they were most needed."[29] Here he dealt with people and not with the issues which concerned them.

In his searching analysis of the *Star*'s editorial content, historian Dr. Alderfer, in his thesis "The Personality and Politics of Warren G. Harding," wrote of its editor that "he gave very little attention to the issues of the day. Very few of his editorials in this period dealt with the current subjects of debate. Now and then he would quote the comment of leading Republican journals and endorse it. But when he, himself, made any excursion into the fields of tariff, regulation of railroads, or money, the result was conventional, naive, and superficial. . . . There is no evidence that he read or studied any subject well. He had no pet theories of government or economics."[30]

In the period of unemployment and economic distress of the mid-1890's Jacob S. Coxey led an army of unemployed men to Washington to demand a large-scale public works program for the unemployed—measures taken by Franklin D. Roosevelt about forty years later. Harding treated the proposal with ridicule and much boisterous front-page publicity, without any attempt to analyze or evaluate it. According to the *Star* of January 11, 1895, its supporters were mostly hoboes with "wheels in their heads."[31]

The reform movement for abolition of capital punishment found him not only unsympathetic but sordid in his demand that "If electrocution has more terrors than hanging, let the current be turned on."[32] His attitude toward lynching was expressed on August 26, 1891, when he wrote: "There are occasional lynchings of murderers now and then that do not worry the law-abiding people. In cases where there is no doubt of identity or guilt a little hasty justice doesn't shock law-abiding people and has a wholesome effect upon the tougher element. Mob law isn't commended, is indeed deplorable, but there are acceptable exceptions, so to speak."[33]

"Although Warren Harding's political opportunism was a dominant quality in his character, it does not follow that he was lacking in a certain fixity of outlook. On occasion in times of conflict of opinion, he could show himself capable of independent decisions. He could be loyal to friends who were unpopular, he could insist on party responsibility in the face of radical, though popular, attacks. He could be a stabilizing force when such was needed. But this does not rule out the fact that his ambitious nature made him more of an opportunist on his way to fame than a man of profound thought and conviction. . . . Republican bosses and businessmen with power could always count on the cooperation of Warren G. Harding."[34]

The scandals which mark the Harding administration are attributed more to the laxity he allowed his cronies than to personal dishonesty. No money is said to have stuck to his fingers and the disclosures which were mounting at his death caused him great anguish. However, throughout his life he never drew the fine line which would exclude borderline and fringe advantage. Ethical scruples were not permitted to hamper unduly the business side of the newspaper. "Competition for the public printing had become so stiff that it threatened profits. Harding entered into a private arrangement with the other Marion County publishers. One man was delegated to make a low bid for the contract, the others all bidding higher. The low figure was set so high that all the supposedly competitive bidders divided up a nice profit for the deal. Harding told William Allen White, with placid self-satisfaction over his own shrewdness, that this plan was successfully carried through year after year. That secret and collusive bidding was a form of graft on the public funds did not trouble his mind. Presumably that view did not occur to him."[35]

Nor, as the newspaper grew and manufacturing industries expanded in the area, did he refuse the gifts of big business who desired the favors of newspaper publicity. Not only did they give the *Star* their advertising, but he got $10,000 in stock from a farm implement company, as well as stock in a local brewery.[36] Apparently he never questioned favors. He accepted them also from the railroads and steamship companies; in January 1895 he and Mrs. Harding took a trip to Florida. It was the first of many such trips. "Now that he was able to leave the *Star* in competent hands for longer periods, he traveled endlessly and indiscriminately over the next two decades—to Florida, Texas, Wyoming, the Great Lakes, to New England and Nova Scotia, to the Caribbean, Hawaii, and finally Europe. These flights from himself were made possible in the early years by free railroad and steamship passes that he acquired in exchange for advertisements. Harding's *Star* correspondence is dotted with requests for additional travel passes."[37]

One of the reasons for his restless travels was health. In 1888 Harding became a delegate to the Republican State Convention and took an active part in the Presidential campaign. "Just after the election Harding suffered what he later called a nervous breakdown. On October 16 the *Star* reported that its editor was 'indisposed to such an extent that he is unable to attend any newspaper duties, being scarcely able to reach the office for half an hour each day.' Urged by his father, he left on November 7 for Battle Creek Sanitarium in Michigan. . . . After some weeks of Battle Creek's spartan regimen Harding returned early in 1890 to Marion renewed in spirit and twenty pounds lighter. This was the first of five visits that he would make to Battle Creek during the next twelve years."[38] This did not become a campaign issue as it did in the case of Senator Eagleton in 1972.

There is one more glaring example of Harding's lack of nicety in ethics, and this occurred while he was President. Twice a week there was early dinner at the White House, followed by a stiff poker game. "High the game might run; it was not stiff enough for the host. He sought an extra fillip of excitement in side-bets. Calling to see the President one evening, Louis Seibold, then a Washington correspondent . . . was complimented upon a tie-pin he was wearing.

" 'That's a nice pearl, Louis. What do you think of this one?'

"Seibold examined with interest the pearl in the Harding tie, which he guessed to be worth four or five thousand dollars. 'That's something else again, Mr. President,' he answered. 'I haven't often seen as fine a one.'

" 'Won it at the poker game Wednesday night.'

" 'You must have been holding them.'

" 'Not so good. I got this, spading with the man on my left.'[39] He took it out of his pocket and said, 'I'll put this up against a hundred dollars.' 'It looked good to me,' continued Mr. Harding, 'so I took him up. I won with a four of spades.'

"In the Wednesday night poker where the pearl pin changed hands there had participated a Cabinet official and the Chairman of a national board. Whether either of them was the man on the President's left is a matter of speculation. . . . What is fact beyond speculation is that he was receiving odds of forty or fifty to one on his side-bet."[40]

This was the moral climate set in Marion and continued in Washington. Its indulging characteristics formed the permissive base upon which knaves—who were among Harding's intimate friends—built.

"Bloviation," a word coined by Warren Harding, was what led him into politics. By it he meant public speaking in the small towns around Marion where the popular editor of the *Star*—with its vastly increased circulation—would expound upon conservative republicanism and denounce the Democratic Party and its members. "That word describes with onomatopoetic felicity the cheerful and windy expressiveness of the Harding oratory. . . . His fine presence, lush flow of verbiage, and partisan passion made a hit."[41]

His party spirit caused him to run cheerfully in the hopeless race for auditor of Marion County where the Democrats reigned supreme. When no one else would accept the nomination Harding, always game, exclaimed: "I'll do it, I'll make the run."[42] He ran and was defeated, but his horizons had broadened; his world was now the world of editors and politicians.

It was in 1898 that Harding first earned the reputation of "harmonizing" which was to become the hallmark of his future style. Ohio, at the time, was run by two powerful bosses, Mark Hanna in Cleveland and Joseph Foraker in Cincinnati, whose lieutenant was the notorious George B. Cox. They were rivals for the senatorship of the United States. "Inwardly Harding sided with Foraker, but he aimed to make no enemies in the Hanna camp. 'The *Star* has neither assailed nor opposed Senator Hanna,' Harding wrote. . . . 'It has simply declined to abuse the opposition to him.' Harding's thought, his invariable political reaction was always to get two warring factions to combine for an immediate goal. 'Harmonizing' he called it, and over the years it became his favorite expression—as verb, adjective, or noun. *Lacking the ruthless self-confidence necessary for a boss or a leader he saw himself as the affable middle-man,* the third party who brings two bargainers together, breaks the tension by the latest traveling salesman joke, suggests a compromise, and then takes the two off to have a drink."[43] (Emphasis added) His style did not contemplate a head-on approach; he met each issue either by pussyfooting, as in the issue between Foraker and Hanna, or by devious methods —neither dishonest nor straightforward.

Harding expressed his technique of "harmonizing" while President: "We all know the town meeting. Now, if I had a program that I wanted to have adopted by a town meeting, I should go to the three or four most influential men in my community. I should talk it out with them. I should make concessions to them until I had got them to agree with me. And then I should go into the town meeting, feeling perfectly confident that my plan would go through. Well, it's the same in the nation as in the town meeting, or in the world if you will. I should always go first to the three or four leading men."[44]

In this statement there is no suggestion of bringing issues to the people or of fighting for a principle or a measure; there is no mention of an attempt to persuade the citizens gathered at the town meeting. It is the statement of a politician who merely uses influence to achieve his objective.

In 1900 Harding assumed his first public office. He had won the nomination as state senator which was tantamount to election by one vote. With his election he became the leader of the Republican Party in Marion County. And with his election he became even more conservative. As editor of the *Star,* in spite of his Republican Party stance, he had espoused some progressive measures such as reforms in the Marion city government, measures that improved rather than paid off political debts; "he even praised voters who were becoming 'politically independent' in local affairs, and called this ticket-splitting tendency a safeguard against 'corruptness,' a lesson to both parties that the best man must be nominated."[45] In the State Senate Harding voted with the party—which, at that time, in the State of Ohio, meant as the bosses specified. Harding was no Theodore Roosevelt, no Franklin D. Roosevelt—both of whom gained prominence by fighting the bosses when they were members of the legislature of New York State.

Harding, voting for the "ripper" bill backed by Boss Cox that would take effective governing control of any too obstreperously progressive city and lodge it with the legislature, admitted that the bill was "against my conscience" but as a party measure he felt it was his "duty as a Republican to vote for it."[46] "He sighed one day to a newspaper friend. . . . 'Pretty raw, some of these bills. I don't like 'em. But what can I do? The Organization wants 'em.' "[47] His small fling at progressivism was over; he was now, in truth, "one of the boys." A reporter at that time covering the Capitol said of him: "It was not long before Harding was the most popular man in the legislature. He had the inestimable gift of never forgetting a man's face or name, he was a regular he-man in the sign-manual of those days, a great poker-player, and not at all averse to putting his foot on the brass rail."[48] In the State Senate he was always the harmonizer to calm flowing tempers and persuade stubborn opponents to get together and patch up differences.

His political star had risen. Contrary to Marion County custom, he was nominated and elected for a second term. In spite of the fact that there were more able men available, he was made floor leader, and by the time he had finished his term as floor leader, any notion of reform that he may have entertained had disappeared. The phrase "stand pat" which Mark Hanna coined that year became his motto and style. "In every respect except party usefulness Harding's second term was as sterile as his first. Considered as educational preparation for the United States Senate and the Presidency, the experience would appear inadequate. It measured up to the requirements of Harding's ambition. He closed his legislative course with these assets: a wide acquaintance and popularity, the easy name of a good fellow and a boon companion; the reputation of being at call for unquestioning service as a party handy-man, and a thorough working knowledge of the legislative wires and who was at the controlling end of each one. It is an interesting and significant comparison that, while his overt and official power was probably less than the undercover influence of Harry M. Daugherty, his reputation was better. He played a more open game of politics."[49]

In 1903 he was the party's successful candidate for Lieutenant Governor. His style remained unchanged. "There is little recorded of him as presiding officer of the senate. Nowhere did he leave any discernible impress upon legislation which he unquestionably could have exercised. More than ever he was the genial, suave, smiling conciliator, adjuster, compromiser; all things to all men, and, as far as might be, in both parties. On the Democratic side he was as warmly liked as on the Republican. . . ."[50]

There is no doubt that he found his popularity in the Capitol exhilarating; therefore, there is great speculation as to the reason he decided not to run for re-election. The best guess is that his interest in the prospering *Star* was greater than his interest in public life. Even when President he longed to return to his paper. As President his relations with the members of the press were fraternal. He liked reporters and they liked him. When, in 1922, Daugherty urged him to formulate plans for a campaign for a second term, Harding demurred; he wished to return to his paper. His press conferences—which he restored to the twice-a-week routine that Wilson had abandoned—were akin to the freedom of those of Franklin D. Roosevelt, though they lacked the banter and content. He answered all questions; his only qualification was that he must not be quoted directly.

After November 30, 1921, he required written questions submitted in advance in order to avoid conflicting interpretations that had been placed on Presidential refusals to answer questions in the past. In accepting from the press the gift of a chair carved from the U.S.S. *Revenge,* he said: "I am only the publisher of an interior daily paper, sometimes called a country paper. But if I had my life to live over, with all the experiences that have come to me, I would not change my profession or my occupation."[51]

Out of office by his own choice, editor Harding was by no means out of politics; in 1910 he was nominated for Governor. Caught in the fierce battle between warring Ohio political bosses, and tarred with the then public stigma of "bossism," Harding was defeated by 100,000 votes. As usual, he had sought to make no enemies and straddled every issue; the principal one was within the Republican Party and was between progressivism and reform. Harding was for the stand-pat creed of the Republican platform; however, he sought to placate the progressives with ambiguities difficult to decipher: "I have no objection to an insurgent . . . though I couldn't be one myself. I have no objection to a progressive Republican, because one must be a Republican to be progressive."[52] Muddled statements—each meant to convey all things to all men—were his style. To a man whose ambition was to be loved, this defeat came hard, and his reported comment following his defeat is indicative of his antedated philosophy: "These things will happen as long as Tom, Dick and Harry have the right to vote."[53]

This was the era of anti-bossism in Ohio. The voters recalled Harding's "harmonizing" oratory at the 1904 state convention, when he ended his speech praising the Republican "Big Four" bosses with: "And next I want to name a great big, manly, modest but grand marshal of invincible division of the grand old Republican army in Ohio. Modest, I say, but a man of ability, trusted in advice, just in judgment. We yield him our deference and devotion: George B. Cox."[54] Mr. Cox was the saloonkeeper slum boss of the Cincinnati council who was known to be living on a millionaire scale without visible funds. There were public repercussions at the time, but they did not reach full intensity until the 1910 election.

Nevertheless he was chosen to present Taft's name at the Presidential convention in 1912. Harry Daugherty now came to the fore and pressed Harding in 1914 to run in the first direct primary held for United States Senator. Harding, lacking self-confidence, was reluctant and dashed away to Florida where Daugherty pursued him and persuaded him to enter the primary race against the powerful Joseph Benson Foraker, who had not been reappointed by the legislature to the Senate when it was revealed that he had been in secret pay of the Standard Oil

Company while in the Senate. His other opponent was Ralph Cole, who came from the northwestern part of the state. Harding won both the primary and the election. The Cleveland *Plain Dealer,* which always gave Harding credit for unimpeachable personal character, did not see him measuring up to his new duties; it stigmatized him as a "Spokesman of the Past."[55]

It was fellowship that Harding enjoyed in the Senate—fellowship of the second and third raters, not of the strong men in his party. George B. Christian, Jr., President Harding's devoted secretary and friend, once surprised Samuel Hopkins Adams by saying of his chief: "He had no taste for politics. Never had."

" 'But he liked to be a Senator, didn't he?'

"Mr. Christian made a shrewd distinction. 'No, he didn't like being a Senator. He liked being in the Senate.' " [56]

Out of 245 roll calls in the first session, he answered only 112. As an unwavering conservative, he opposed the nomination of the liberal Brandeis to the United States Supreme Court and the liberal George Rublee to the Federal Trade Commission. He supported a bill which, if passed, would have undermined the government's conservation policy. He was for a tax exemption which would have favored the private water power companies. He was against a measure which would have given the government, in case of war, the power to acquire water power plants for the manufacture of nitrates, and another to provide for government manufacture of armor plate. But he upheld naval preparedness and Army increase, which the conservative Republicans were for, while voting "No" on the proposition to warn Americans against travelling on the ships of belligerent nations, which the progressive Republicans sponsored.

He did not vote for or against many important measures, including child labor, the eight-hour railroad bill, two tariff bills; he simply was not interested in such issues. "There were twenty undoubted party [Democratic] issues and on each of these Harding either voted 'No' or did not vote at all. . . . Harding recognized that the function of the minority party was to criticize and obstruct. His votes show his record that of a static conservative, supporting new measures only when fostered by his party or when demanded by public opinion."[57]

His fealty to big business was constant; his votes regarding labor number 11 unfavorable, 7 favorable, and 10 abstentions.[58] He was opposed to regulation of industry even as a war measure. His was the philosophy of many a man who has made his own way in the world; he had done it—why couldn't the other fellow do it? His employees had been satisfied—why weren't other employees satisfied? He had treated his employees fairly; therefore other businessmen surely treated their employees fairly. Labor discontent stemmed from troublemakers—labor officials. In brief, in over fifty years he had achieved no grasp of the conditions of business and labor, of economic or civil affairs that concerned the people of this nation. Certainly, he had no appreciation of the difficulties to be faced in the transition from a war to a peace economy.

Throughout his six years in the Senate his record is consistently that of a good fellow, sweet-tempered, sweet-mannered, taking part in Senate business as little as possible. Out of the total of 2,692 roll calls, he failed to answer 1,163.

The loyalty to Wilson that he usually displayed during the war without party partisanship ended with the Armistice. During the war he had, indeed, subjugated his personal inclination to that of the President of the United States. In an interview with a reporter of the *New York Times* he was quoted as saying: "I must say that [Wilson] is not my choice but the people of the country have chosen him.

... Why quibble with events which are already accomplished? Mr. Wilson is our President, duly elected. He is already by the inevitable force of events our partial dictator. Why not make him complete and supreme dictator? He will have to answer to the people and to history eventually for his stewardship. Why not give him a full and free hand, not for his sake, but for our sake?"[59] He was serious; he referred to his hero, Alexander Hamilton, who "in his matchless vision" had seen the necessity of such a crisis dictator. He was obviously happy to have the President carry the burden of responsibility and had no desire to share in it. While he objected to state and federal regulation, he supported Wilson's takeover of the railroads.

Such was Harding's inconsistency and opportunism that within nine months, speaking of the Overman bill which would give the war President unlimited power, he said: "I am not willing that Congress surrender the functions so as to create a smoke screen for the President for retreat from one established form of government to dictatorship."[60]

"The second session of the wartime Sixty-Fifth Congress ran for almost a year, from December 3, 1917, to November 21, 1918. Harding, always more conspicuous for his senatorial appearance and easy manner than for anything he ever did or said on the Senate floor, had the effect on legislature of a comma or semicolon. Silently he voted for food control, and for the war revenue bill although he opposed the 65 to 75 percent tax on war profits since 'if you strike at excess profit you reduce incomes and are likely to hinder our industrial development.' ... He called the Prohibition Amendment 'unwise, imprudent, and inconsiderate' but he voted for it 'so that this agitating question could be resolved by submitting it to ratification by the states.' "[61] He would always try to find a way to pass on responsibility.

He would never originate opposition, but he would join it. However, in the case of the League of Nations he was in a quandary. Republicans of the stature of William Howard Taft and Charles Evans Hughes were advocates. Senator Lodge, motivated by hatred for Wilson, was strongly opposed. Harding was not certain with whom he wished to stand. He wrote an old friend that he wanted "to preserve all of the League proposal which we can accept with safety to the United States, in the hope that the conscience of the Nations may be directed to perfecting a safe plan of cooperation toward maintained peace. But there will be no surrender of things essentially and vitally American."[62] It is pretty difficult to fathom just what this "bloviation" meant. Randolph Downes says: "... Harding's unanalytical mind could not encompass the international nature of the League's problem. He could only see it as a nationalist, as a patriot, as an American firster, conscious of American freedom and independence. Such an outlook did not require definition or explanation, but could have its expression in oratory and in political rhetoric, with a minimal expenditure of intellectual effort."[63] He had no conception of the inevitable interrelationships of the nations in the postwar world. He was bereft of intangible ideals.

On March 3, 1919, having come to the conclusion that he would definitely join the belligerent opposition, he signed the Lodge round robin concurred in by thirty-nine senators notifying Wilson that the signatories would not ratify the League as presented. He had decided that Senator Lodge's amendments and reservations to the Peace Treaty "echoed the conscience of the Republic."[64] And, possibly to keep him from changing his mind, Senator Lodge made Harding a member of the Foreign Relations Committee.

It is of interest, however, that having signed the round robin on March 3, 1919, he confided to Daugherty on April 4, 1919, that: "Manifestly the public mind has not been ready to accept a flat declaration against any sort of League of Nations."[65] Daugherty advised him to be reticent. One of his most telling bids for votes, when he ran in 1920 for President, was the point that in his speeches he had advocated an open mind and had encouraged the widest possible discussion on the subject of the League. The role of moderator of this widely discussed issue enabled him to receive the support of the diverse elements of Republican opinion—those who were outrightly opposed to a League, such as Hiram Johnson and William E. Borah, and those such as Taft who forthrightly supported the League. His "appearance of open-mindedness was deliberately publicized. It appeared in the Cincinnati *Enquirer* on April 11, 1919, when he was quoted as saying, 'It would not be quite fair to criticize the covenant as we hear about it today. The League of Nations, according to the articles presented, doubtless will undergo many changes before an agreement is reached.' "[66] To those who urged him to assail the League more vigorously, he counselled delay for strategic purposes; he was not going into open attack until it was expedient to do so. Meanwhile he stimulated Republican propaganda in Ohio, where there was much pro-League sentiment, to support the Root-Lodge Reservations presented on June 21, 1919.

When, in August, Senator Harding was one of four Republican members of the Foreign Relations Committee invited to confer with President Wilson in an attempt to win their support, he asked: "If there is nothing more than a moral obligation on the part of any member of the league what avails [sic] Articles 10 and 11?"[67] This was shocking to the President, who exclaimed: "Why, Senator, it is surprising that that question should be asked. If we understand an obligation we are bound in the most solemn way to carry it out."[68] When the conference ended, President Wilson commented that he was just unable to understand Senator Harding. Obviously Senator Harding could not comprehend President Wilson or his idealism.

By this time Harding was on the verge of abandoning his strategy to maintain an apparently unprejudiced mind until "we can have the treaty and the actual league of nations pact before us." He had astutely reasoned that this "leaves one in a better position to impress the public which is ready to be convinced."[69] He now decided that the public had been sufficiently prepared to accept a forthright position. By September 5, 1919, reports demonstrated a favorable trend in Ohio away from Wilson's position and in support of an "Americanized League." On September 13, 1919, he wrote: "If my correspondence is any index to the sentiment of the country, I think there has been an overwhelming change in the past sixty days and the sentiment of the country is strongly against the League covenant in the form presented."[70]

The embryonic Presidential candidate had taken a more calculated, more decisive, more active and influential role in relation to the League than he had ever evidenced in his public career.

Two days before, on September 11, Lodge had given Harding the honor of leading the debate before the final vote was taken. It was a recognition of Harding's role in educating the public to the Root-Lodge position against the Wilson League. It is a measure of the man that his pride in this speech led him to have it recorded on a phonograph record with "Beautiful Ohio" on the reverse side. The incongruity is typical of him.

"Although Harding's role in shaping the Lodge reservations was minor, his role in popularizing them was major. It consisted of his oratorical and personal ability to represent the reservations to the League covenant not as carping criticisms made by politicians against their opponents but as constructive Americanizing improvements that would save the League from destruction and assure the retention of world-security benefits that Wilson's overzealousness was losing. ... Harding's ability to blend the Lodge reservations and the League covenant into firm and inspiring Americanism was a blessing to the Republican party. The American people were ... Americans first. They were, as a whole, not averse to an American leadership in international progress as long as there was leadership and not entanglement. But they were averse to a long drawn-out effort of thinking out the pros and cons of the details of the covenant and the reservations. If someone could synthesize them all into a whole that sounded secure and reasonable, they would be satisfied. For the presentation of this kind of popularized synthesis, Harding was superbly qualified."[71]

This would not be the only example of Harding's ability to assume leadership. As President he exercised leadership upon several important occasions which were the more notable because they were exceptional. Even in 1920 Harding evidenced an interest that presaged the calling of the Washington Conference of 1921–22 for disarmament. He wrote that he had "long been convinced that we ought to make some progress in international cooperation for the prevention of war." He truly believed that the Senate Republicans were attempting "to preserve a skeleton of the Covenant ... so that the conscience of civilized nations may build upon it effectively and prudently in proper reflection and deliberation."[72]

The man who looked like a President to Harry Daugherty in 1899 became the Republican candidate in 1920. Daugherty had waited twenty-one years for the opportunity that Senator Harding feared. In the Ohio Historical Society there is a carbon copy of these words: "The only thing I really worry about is that I am going to be nominated and elected. That's an awful thing to contemplate."[73]

Yet in the very same letter to Scobey from which this excerpt is quoted, he also wrote: "Daugherty is vastly much the smartest politician in the bunch and the only one with vision and acquaintances to carry on a nationwide campaign. More than that he is the only fellow in Ohio who doesn't find his system more or less tinctured with jealousy of me.

"Things seem to be going along fine. Daugherty was here yesterday and made the most gratifying reports. More than that, reports are exceedingly good from many sections of the country."[74]

These words are dramatic examples of his styles of vacillation and recurring self-doubt. Months before they were uttered he had been working to consolidate the factions in Ohio Republican power politics so that they would be united and committed to support him. As a true poker player he aimed to keep his renomination as senator "in the kitty" in case he failed to obtain the Presidential nomination. Periodically he would continue to express his distaste for the office on grounds very real to him. At times his desire for the office and his disinclination for it were bundled into the same sentence: "I should be unhappy every hour from the time I entered the race until the thing was settled, and *I am sure I should never have any more fun or any real enjoyment in life if I should be so politically fortunate as to win a nomination and election. I had much rather retain my place in the Senate and enjoy the association of friends and some of the joys of living.*"[75] (Emphasis added) The italicized words express his enjoyment of life in the

Senate and his desire to continue in that milieu even as—in the same sentence —he says *"if I should be so politically fortunate as to win a nomination and election."*

When, after many maneuvers, he had gained control of the party machinery in Ohio he wrote on November 3, 1919: "The little bunch evidently assumed that I would assent to whatever they suggested without showing any disposition to dispute them. They have learned better and things seem quite rosy now. . . . [The situation in Ohio] leaves the way open for me to take such course as I deem best . . . I am stronger than I have been at any time in the past."[76]

On the preceding day, Daugherty—without Harding's knowledge—had started to "canvas and keep in touch with the big field" and to seek money for that "canvas."[77] There is a graphic example of the way in which Daugherty operated to make deals which Harding, as President, felt obliged to honor. On December 4, in a letter seeking to win the support of the Texas Republican machine, Daugherty wrote: "Of course, if MacGregor [the head of the Texas machine] is with us we win, he and his friends will control the patronage. The game will be played as it should be played. Harding has seen it all played often enough to know how it must be played and that the men who help must be consulted and in control."[78]

Even as convention tactics were inaugurated, Harding's friends began his enmeshment. He had poor discretion in selecting his personal friends, whom he trusted without question; most of them would plague his Presidential years. While in the Senate his political ideal and close friend was Senator Albert Fall, and while he was in Hawaii on a senatorial junket he had met and formed a friendship with Charles R. Forbes—both of whom marred his Presidential prestige by the scandals in which they were involved. And then, among others, there was the oil magnate Jake Hamon whose liberal contribution was given frankly with the objective of obtaining for himself the Cabinet post of Secretary of the Interior; unfortunately or fortunately, his mistress shot him because he was going to take his wife to the inauguration instead of her. These are but a few of Harding's supporters who would be involved in future scandals.

In view of the scandals that were to encumber the Harding administration, it is worth noting the emphasis that was placed upon honesty by the candidate and by those who urged his election. When the "unwilling" candidate was campaigning for delegates in Indianapolis on March 27, 1920, he said that we needed "more honesty in life" more than we needed a League of Nations.[79]

And the lifelong progressive Brand Whitlock wrote of Harding's nomination: "I am more and more under the opinion that for President we need not so much a brilliant man as solid, mediocre men, providing they have good sense, sound and careful judgment and good manners. All these Harding has. He is . . . more honest than McKinley, not so much a hypocrite and poser, but human and attractive personally."[80]

With Harding's ability to "bloviate," it is of particular interest that after his nomination it was decided he should confine his oratory to his front porch. It was the advice of the big Pennsylvania boss, Senator Boise Penrose, that Harding be kept at home: "Don't let him make any speeches. If he goes on a tour, somebody's sure to ask him questions, and Warren's just the sort of damn fool that'll try to answer them."[81] The "front porch" campaign was decided upon. The role assigned to the candidate was that of the modest, simple, sagacious, home-loving, home-staying statesman. He was to be "just folks."[82] This fitted Harding's style;

he liked people and he enjoyed "being folksy" with them. He didn't smile at them perfunctorily; he smiled at them because he was pleased to see them and he wanted them to be pleased with him, not just because he wanted them to vote for him but because he truly wanted them to like him. He had the same quality of personal warmth that Franklin D. Roosevelt possessed, the same love of people. Although the unsettled postwar situation demanded it, he lacked sufficient depth to think about their individual welfare except upon a strictly person to person basis.

But however much he enjoyed grasping the hand of a potential voter, there were questions with which he had to deal. Foremost was that of the League of Nations, which he must face on Notification Day, July 22, when Marion, Ohio, would be crowded with visitors awaiting his words.[83] Taft and Root, on seeing an advance copy of his speech, had begged him to make pro-League changes; but, "spurred by Lodge, he rejected even League reservations and came out flatly for a peace by declaration to be followed by a newly negotiated treaty divorced from the League. Normalcy made its by now inevitable appearance as something we must 'stabilize and strive for.' . . . Finally Harding turned almost diffident as he spoke of his awareness of his own limited abilities. But 'in a hopeful spirit and with a hymn of service' in his heart he pledged fidelity to God and country in accepting the nomination."[84]

The National Committee sent two men to steer Harding: Richard Washburn Child, a successful fiction writer with political ambitions, and editor George Harvey, the erstwhile Wilson backer. "So deftly did they employ language to conceal thought that Harding himself was befogged at times. Midway in one of his (or their) addresses, he slowed down, stumbled, retraced his course, and, then, looking up from the manuscript with a frankly baffled smile, announced to his astonished audience: 'Well, I never saw this before. I didn't read this speech and I don't believe what I just read.' "[85]

This was "honesty in life"; it was also naïve and shallow of him to have delivered the speech without reading it and without contributing his own time and thought in working on it with his "ghost writers"—a phrase that can be aptly used in this case. Use of thought was not his style, nor was use of time in pursuit of knowledge for subjects which were pertinent to policy.

His opponent, James M. Cox, came out flatly for the League of Nations, as did his running mate, Franklin D. Roosevelt. Harding, never endorsing the League, flung his words hither and yon in an effort to please those divisions within his own party and appeal to voters who might support his opponent's forthright endorsement of the League. The Republican League proponents had organized the Committee of Thirty-One, composed of such prestigious men as Charles Evans Hughes, Herbert Hoover, William Howard Taft, Harvard's President Lowell, and Columbia University's President Butler. They endorsed the League with modifications to conform to Senate requirements and the Republican Party platform.

"Harding's record would have furnished them little hope. It grew more astonishing and anomalous as the question pressed. In the Senate he had twice voted for treaty ratification with reservations. But after nomination, he promised 'complete reversal' of our foreign policy. Four days later, he hinted at an association of nations on a basis not dissimilar to the Root plan. There followed the speech, published on August 29, which heartened the pro-Leaguers and exasperated the isolationists with its design for an international association for conference. . . . Minatory growls from the irreconcilables scared Harding. For a time he avoided the touchy subject. Borah, Johnson, and their ilk proved more influential with him than the Thirty-One. He dismissed the League as a fraud, following up by the assertion that he was seeking not interpretation but rejection."[86]

His problem was difficult and he was not capable of meeting it in a straightforward manner. Therefore he and his advisers devised a counterplan which would straddle and becloud the issue: "The League of Nations would be rebuilt in conformance with its specifications, on the twin foundations of a world Court of Justice and a World Association for Conference, using the mechanism of the League where convenient."[87] The bitter enders were privately assured that Harding was with them in heart and the pro-Leaguers were given lip service. Harding, the "harmonizer," was pursuing his style of being all things to all men.

Although entertainment headquarters at Marion flowed with alcoholic refreshment and was to flow privately in the White House during these prohibition years, he stated that it was "impossible to ignore the Constitution . . . unthinkable to evade the law."[88] Harding was forced to abandon his front porch and bring his ambiguous words directly to the people as he travelled in their midst. Cox and Roosevelt were conducting a whirlwind campaign throughout the country. Cox spoke as many as twenty-six times a day. He charged the Republicans with raising a tremendous "corruption fund" from powerful interests attempting to buy control of the government. His campaign charges, unfortunately, proved to be more than oratory.

Harding sallied forth to show his warm smile and Presidential bearing in the Southwest and Midwest. Meanwhile the first "Madison Avenue" campaign technique was employed. Albert Lasker, head of the prestigious advertising firm, Lord & Thomas, set up campaign publicity headquarters in New York. With a dozen expert assistants, he used the skills upon Harding that he had employed upon Pepsodent, Puffed Wheat, Palm Olive and Lucky Strikes. His job was to "humanize Harding as an old-fashioned, sage, honest-to-the-core Middle Westerner who could be trusted never to rock the boat."[89] The boat was not rocked; it skimmed over the surface of the water. Harding was elected with a plurality of more than 7 million—at that period a record. The candidate was not the issue; postwar confusion brought forth the vote. The fact that Harding had added to the confusion of the confused was not heeded.

The President-elect, faced with making appointments, "was divided between his awe of the Presidency and his wish to reward his friends. . . . 'I am just beginning to realize what a job I have taken over,' he wrote Jennings [his friend from State Senate days]. 'The man who has a Cabinet to create has one tremendous task. I find I am called upon to be rather impersonal about it and put aside some of my very intimate views of men and give some consideration to the public estimate of available timber.' "[90] Upon reading the last sentence, the only conclusion is that the President-elect was truly a "Babe-in-the-Woods."

There were able men in Harding's Cabinet: Secretary of State Charles Evans Hughes, Secretary of Commerce Herbert Hoover, Secretary of Treasury Andrew Mellon, Secretary of Agriculture Henry C. Wallace (the father of Franklin D. Roosevelt's Secretary of Agriculture and Vice President) and Postmaster General Will Hays, chairman of the Republican National Committee. Hughes, however, was not Harding's first or second or third choice. His first choice was Nicholas Murray Butler, the president of Columbia University; his second choice was Senator Albert B. Fall, who would stigmatize the Harding administration with the Teapot Dome Scandal. "When Butler refused to consider the office, Harding remarked that the best man he could then see for the post was Senator Fall. The dismayed Butler told him Fall's reputation in Pueblo, before he ever left Colorado for New Mexico, was such that he should not be considered for the Cabinet. 'You are entirely mistaken,' Harding replied. 'You have listened to rumors circulated by jealous enemies of his. Fall is a very able man. I sat with him on the Committee on Foreign Relations and he is the best-posted man of the whole lot, particularly as to all Latin-American matters.' "[91]

The party elders had better judgment and persuaded Harding not to appoint Fall. After offering it to George Harvey, who did not feel qualified, he appointed the distinguished Charles Evans Hughes. Fall, however, would be appointed to a post more congenial to his financial machinations—Secretary of the Interior. Harding's loyalty to his friends could not be overcome by this newfound conception that he give some consideration to the public estimate of available timber. It was a matter of common knowledge that Harding wanted Harry M. Daugherty as Attorney General but was delaying the announcement because of strong objections within the party. He could not be budged, not even by such attempts at discussion as that of Myron T. Herrick whom Harding wanted in his Cabinet: "Is Harry Daugherty going to be in the Cabinet?" Herrick asked.

"Yes," was the unwavering answer.

"Then I can't accept. Harry Daugherty will wreck your Administration."[92] Herrick preferred to be Ambassador to France.

There were others who tried to persuade Harding not to appoint Harry Daugherty. To Senators New of Indiana and Wadsworth of New York, who argued that Daugherty was a politican with too many enemies, that he would be a disappointment to members of the bar who would expect something a great deal better, that the appointment would not only be a mistake but dangerous, Harding replied with deep feeling: "Harry Daugherty has been my best friend from the beginning of this whole thing. I have told him that he can have any place in my Cabinet he wants, outside of Secretary of State. He tells me that he wants to be Attorney General and by God he will be Attorney General."[93]

Loyalty to friends is an admirable trait but Harding was a poor judge of men and blind to their faults. Although he owed much to Daugherty, it is incredible that over the years he had not learned of his reputation. He had no appreciation of the fact that a President of the United States cannot afford the luxury of promiscuously appointing unqualified friends to offices of trust.

Warren Harding could not have been ignorant of the fact that Harry Daugherty had not earned his money and reputation as a lawyer, but as a lobbyist for the American Tobacco Company, Armour and Company, American Gas and Electric Company, the Western Union Telegraph Company, and the Ohio State Telephone Company.[94] "Evil report beset him early and pursued him throughout his active life. . . . First, last and all the time he was the political manipulator, the adroit fixer."[95] The touch of scandal had always enveloped him but had never caught up with him.

To Harding's credit it must be said that he withstood the pressures of Penrose and Lodge against the appointment of Hughes, and those of Borah, Johnson, Smoot, Curtis and Penrose against Herbert Hoover. He had determined that he must have such men if he were to have a great Cabinet, if his administration were to make a "seemly" mark.[96] Perhaps he was not unaware of the lack of fitness which some of his appointees had and wished to balance them with those of esteemed reputations.

Penrose was placated by the appointment as Secretary of the Treasury of Andrew W. Mellon, whose qualifications were that he came from Pennsylvania and was the second richest man in the world. John W. Weeks, a wealthy Massachusetts broker turned politician who had been defeated for re-election to the Senate, was named Secretary of War; his chief qualification was that he had made large contributions to the Republican Party and it was said that through his good offices a Boston bank in which he was interested had underwritten part of the campaign deficit.[97] It was he who recommended the wealthy but weak Edwin N. Denby as Secretary of the Navy; the appointment proved to be a major blunder, for Denby permitted himself to be the stooge for Albert B. Fall, thus contributing to the worst debacle of the Harding régime.

Even the Secretary of Labor, James J. Davis, represented big business. Although he held a union card, he was actually an affluent banker and was considered too conservative by organized labor. The *New York Herald Tribune* viewed the Cabinet as a "disappointment tempered only by Messers Hughes and Hoover."[98]

Qualifications played no part in the selection for lesser government posts of friends such as Scobey, the former Miami sheriff; Harding's boyhood friend and Marion political organizer, Dick Crissinger; his brother-in-law Haber Votaw, a former lecturer at the Adventist Missionary College; and his jovial Hawaiian acquaintance, Charlie Forbes. Harding planned to make Jesse Smith, Daugherty's man-Friday, Commissioner of Indian Affairs, and, after Western senators objected to that, even considered making him Treasurer of the United States. But Jesse was content to settle for entry to the White House and an unofficial desk of his own near Harry Daugherty's office in the Department of Justice Building.[99] These old friends would sadden Harding's last days with the scandals they evoked. Even then, he would take no action but would lament: "Some day the people will understand what some of my erstwhile friends have done to me in these critical times when I depended so much upon them."[100] There is no quote which demonstrates that he realized his lack of judgment in selecting these men as his friends and in appointing them to office.

This was a President who would pour forth his warmth for people by opening wide the doors of the White House; the Marine Band would play on the White House lawn; at 12:30 each day he would shake hands with Tom, Dick and Harry. When his secretary pointed out that these mass greetings took too much time and energy, he characteristically replied: "I *love* to meet people. It is the most pleasant thing I do; it is really the only fun I have. It does not tax me, and it seems to be a very great pleasure to them."[101]

His emphasis was ever upon pleasure. His Inaugural Address said nothing about plans to improve peoples' lives; he presented no pattern to achieve "normalcy." The genial President did not seem to recognize the problems he faced. "Due to Wilson's collapse, post-war economic complications, and the 'quarrelsome inertia' of Congress, the mechanism of government was practically stalled. Vital readjustments were necessary. Businessmen were demanding, 'What is to be done to restore good times?' The unemployed were crying, 'When do we get our jobs back?' The more decent minded of the public, now widely given over to the lawlessness of evasion, impatiently wanted to know, 'When does Prohibition begin to prohibit?' All voices joined in the wail, 'Reduce the cost of living.' More specifically, constructive action was required on waning national finances, taxation, disarmament, tariff, the peace treaties, and the League of Nations."[102] His Inaugural Address implied no awareness of these problems or of troublesome foreign questions relating to such countries as Mexico, Cuba, Russia and Japan. Indeed, it reflected the opinion that he had expressed as President-elect that "government after all, was a pretty simple business."[103]

This well-meaning but confused man, well over his depth, decried his ignorance. When on occasion he turned to able advisers, the administration profited; indeed, there were some notable accomplishments in the Harding administration. Unfortunately, he also took the counsel of those whom he had unwisely appointed. Illustrative of his confusion was his admission to one of his secretaries that "I cannot make a damn thing out of this tax problem. I listen to one side and they seem right and then—God!—I talk with the other side and they seem just as right, and here I am where I started. I know somewhere there is a book that will give the truth, but hell! I couldn't read the book."[104]

That he was confounded by the tariff question is apparent in an interview with Bruce Bliven, editor of the *New Republic,* in which he said: "The United States should adopt a protective tariff of such a character as will help the struggling industries of Europe to get on their feet." Bliven, thinking he had not heard correctly, asked the President to repeat and took down the words verbatim.[105] When Arthur S. Draper, the foreign correspondent of the *New York Herald Tribune,* called at the White House after an extended tour of Europe expecting an interview, Harding turned him over to his political secretary, Judson Welliver, saying: "I don't know anything about this European stuff. You and Jud get together and he can tell me later; he handles these things for me."[106]

Russell says: "He devoted much time to answering unsolicited private correspondence, often working late at night to reply personally to the juvenile or crackpot letters that should have been handled by some third assistant secretary. . . . Nicholas Murray Butler, coming to the White House one evening, found him in his private office staring at a huge pile of letters which he had not had time to examine and which he said with a groan that he must go through. Butler asked if he might look at some of them, and Harding told him to take any he pleased. Those Butler glanced through he found trivial, and protested that it was ridiculous for a President to spend his time answering them. . . . 'I suppose so,' Harding said, 'but I am not fit for this office and should never have been here.' "[107]

After his Inaugural Address, Harding ceased writing his speeches himself. He had been stung during the campaign by criticisms such as Mencken's characterization of the style upon which he had prided himself as "Gamalielese"; he could not change his style and he could not supply the context which the issues required. Most of his speeches were written by Welliver.

The great Presidents shouldered responsibility and assumed leadership. Harding shirked both—he looked to the Republicans in Congress to take the initiative which he would follow. However, the strong voices of Senators Lodge and Penrose had weakened with age; Republican authority in the House was divided between regulars and anti-Harding congressmen; the Congress had no leadership to guide the groping President.

Penrose had voiced the sentiment of Republican leaders who nominated Harding in saying: "We are going to put in a man who will listen." But now, divided among themselves, their advice was disjointed by internal squabbles. Listen as attentively as he would, there was no clear congressional path to follow. Turning to his Cabinet he met baffling advice.

During the campaign Harding had answered the Republican clamor for tax revision by promising heavier rates on large incomes. His wealthy Secretary of the Treasury, Andrew Mellon, believed in the protection of wealth and influenced the President to advocate the reduction of rates on high incomes. Harding, the first senator to become President, suffered his first defeat when the Midwest Republicans refused to follow him and the Congress passed a 50 per cent maximum income tax.

Fighting with Congress was uncongenial to this man who would have enjoyed being a ceremonial President who could travel the country dedicating buildings, reviewing the fleet, glowing in the admiration of the people. He loved travel; he loved to be in the public eye; that was the breadth of his horizon. However, conditions demanded that Harding call Congress into special session for early April, distasteful as it might be. "The League issue still refused to be harmonized, the voices of the irreconcilables ringing as loudly as ever. Knox was ready to by-pass the Versailles Treaty and had prepared a separate resolution that would have merely repealed the 1917 declaration of war. Hoover and Hughes and Root still continued to be hopeful of America's accepting the Treaty along with League reservations.

"In preparing his first message to Congress Harding again attempted to appease with his vague notion of 'an association of nations.' "[108] It is noteworthy of the influences that played upon him that the night before its delivery Mrs. Harding and Daugherty were able to persuade him to delete a paragraph they considered might commit the United States to the actual League by inference. The address, however, contained a spark that betokened an awakening to the powers belonging to the executive—a spark that threw into consternation those who relied upon Harding "to listen." He told the senators and congressmen that he was willing to accept Knox's peace resolution *only* if a clause about treaty making was omitted, since for the Senate "to assume the function of the Executive" in foreign affairs would be as objectionable as was "the failure of the Executive under Wilson."[109]

Although the message called in general terms for the expected Republican measures to cut expenditures, lower taxes, repeal the excess profits tax, consider permanent tariff legislation, lower railroad rates and promote agricultural interests, there were four specific deviations of note. One of his most important requests was for the creation of the national budget system, a request rejected several times in previous administrations, which was to result in the organization of the Bureau of the Budget and become the first high mark for Harding. "From Washington's to Wilson's administration the United States had never had a formal budgetary system to coordinate its haphazard and often conflicting financial activities, and Harding in his special session message demanded and received the authorization for a Bureau of the Budget. Prompting him, steering him to make this request was the Ohio banker and public utilities consolidator Charles E. Dawes, McKinley's old Controller of the Currency. . . . Knowing nothing of finance, Harding was in awe of those who did."[110] With one of his rare flares of perspicacity he succeeded in persuading Dawes to head the new Bureau. Taking a dozen dollar-a-year men with him, determined to reorganize the United States financially, this Ohioan who did not belong to the Ohio gang became the first Director of the Budget and a credit to the Harding administration.

Harding was also specific in asking Congress for a great Merchant Marine and for a Department of Public Welfare. Then, with a show of courage, this man who had been tarred from his first entrance into politics with the story that he had Negro blood called upon Congress to "wipe out the stain of barbaric lynching."

He was to show the same courage and "leadership of his party in a surprise speech that he made in Birmingham, Alabama, at the celebration of the city's semi-centennial where he dared to stand in the South and demand civil rights for Negroes. It was the first time since the Civil War that an American President had been bold enough to mention the subject below the Mason-Dixon line."[111] It is of lesser consequence that Harding was motivated by political consideration, although that is a mark of his style; the important fact is that, tainted by that ever-recurring rumor, he had the courage to speak out upon the subject. On rare and notable occasions Harding showed courage and self-confidence.

But, in general, the President was confounded by the necessity of taking positions. He had anticipated that Congress would take the leadership; as we have seen, congressional leadership had disintegrated. Ducking a confrontation with important issues, he busied himself with questions of postmasterships and such minor patronage. Daugherty and Hays were the chief patronage dispensers. Woodrow Wilson, after replacing Republican with Democratic postmasters, had placed them under civil service. By Presidential order, Harding now removed civil service restrictions from 13,000 postmasterships.[112] This created a division in the Cabinet. Hughes, Mellon, Hoover and Wallace stood for the merit system; Daugherty, Davis and Fall stood for the spoils system. Harding, the great "harmonizer," could not unify his Cabinet and therefore could only turn to its individual members; and that required that he decide to which to turn. Until Secretary Mellon threatened to resign, the Assistant Secretary of the Treasury (Mark Hanna's old secretary appointed at Daugherty's suggestion) "Hardinized" the Custom and Revenue Service. The Prohibition Department was dominated by the lobbyist for the Anti-Saloon League, who cleared all 1,500 prohibition agents and all other appointees of the department.

The Cabinet was also split on the farm issue. Backed by Secretary of Agriculture Wallace, Senators LaFollette, Norris, Kenyon and Capper organized a farm bloc of twenty-seven senators that held the balance of power in the Senate, demanding that the government come to the farmer's financial aid. Echoing Hoover and Mellon's opposition, Harding declared: "The farmer requires no special favors at the hands of the government. All he needs is a fair chance."[113] As was his style, President Harding could not sympathize with or attempt to solve the problems of masses of people. "Insurgent Westerners, denied aid for their farms, were in no mood to repeal the excess-profits tax or reduce the income surtax of the wealthy, and the tax revision was delayed again and again. A makeshift tariff bill was passed, obviously temporary; and a temporary immigration bill, obviously permanent, was enacted to cut the admission of the homeless . . . to a fraction and eliminate Orientals altogether. Harding's Department of Public Welfare and his request for an expanded merchant marine were rejected out of hand. The Congress did not even manage by the time of its vacation adjournment in August to bring an official end to the state of war with Germany and Austria-Hungary."[114]

As air rushes into a vacuum, so was Harding sucked into action which eventuated in the second noteworthy accomplishment of his administration. It seems inconsistent, but his ardent desire for the Congress to lead had one great loophole: he was jealous of the prerogatives of the presidency. When Senator Borah tacked an amendment onto the annual Naval Appropriations Bill "requesting and authorizing" the President to hold a conference with Japan and Great Britain on the subject of disarmament, his Senate colleagues adopted it unanimously. Harding, however, demanded that it be removed. Suddenly assuming the style of a President conscious of his constitutional power, he refused to accept any directive about foreign affairs from Borah or the Senate and refused to sign the bill until an innocuous substitute replaced the Borah amendment.

Approximately two months later the President informally asked the governments of Great Britain, France, Italy and Japan to participate in a "conference on the subject of limitation of armaments, in connection with which Pacific and Far Eastern questions will be discussed. . . . On August 11 Secretary of State Hughes, on behalf of the President, sent formal invitations to the four powers."[115] Although Hughes's advice probably inspired Harding's stand upon his Presidential prerogative and his call for a disarmament conference, it was Warren Harding's decision and to him goes the credit for leadership. As the conception of the conference expanded from naval disarmament to an attempt to resolve great power rivalry in the Orient, the President through Hughes sent an invitation to China "to participate in the discussion of Far-Eastern questions." Belgium, Portugal and The Netherlands, all colonial powers with pertinent interests, were also invited. There was universal approval in the United States for this tangible attempt to prevent war; even pro-League Bryan and anti-League Borah espoused it.

Harding became active and prepared for the conference with great care. He had Will Hays mobilize nationwide publicity. A State Department memorandum stated: "To a peculiar degree this conference is dependent upon atmosphere, open hope, open or warm and friendly disposition, and favorable expectations on the part of the public."[116]

President Harding reached the peak of his career, his finest hour, when he addressed the delegates assembled on November 12, 1921, dramatically following the November 11 Armistice Day burial of the American Unknown Soldier in the Arlington National Cemetery. Wisely—probably because of Wilson's error—he had appointed the irreconcilable Senator Lodge and Alabama's Democratic Senator Oscar Underwood as delegates, along with Elihu Root and Secretary Hughes. He spoke briefly and impressively. There is one sentence which was his style and was probably penned by him; he spoke of the Unknown Soldier's burial of the day before, and how "a hundred million of our people were summarizing the inexcusable causes, the incalculable cost, the unspeakable sacrifices, and the unutterable sorrows, and there was the ever-impelling question: How can humanity justify or God forgive?"[117] The concluding paragraph, probably written in the State Department, brought enthusiastic applause:

"We are met for a service to mankind. In all simplicity, in all honesty and all honor, there may be written here the avowals of a world conscience refined by the consuming fires of war, and made more sensitive by anxious aftermath. I hope for that understanding which will emphasize the guarantees of peace and for commitments of less burdens and a better order which will tranquilize the world. In such an accomplishment there will be added glory to your flags and ours, and the rejoicing of mankind will make the transcending music of all succeeding time."[118]

Russell writes: "Clamorously the gallery and the delegates applauded as he walked away, diffident, still bowing slightly and with a shy smile of appreciation."[119] One may surmise that Warren Gamaliel Harding felt that he was in truth President of the United States at that moment, and that the applause of the delegates gave him the assurance that he could be a leader. The shy smile betokened an awareness of pride in himself as President.

It was Secretary Hughes, the chairman of the conference, who created havoc among the delegates by announcing that the way to disarm was to disarm; he proposed that no more warships of any kind be built for ten years, and that Japan, England and the United States, the three great naval powers, proceed at once to cut down the fleets they already had. Then, in the midst of the consternation, he called for a weekend adjournment. When the delegates reassembled, world opinion had so crystallized that none dared challenge Hughes's proposal. After twelve weeks of deliberation England, the United States and Japan agreed to keep their naval ratio of 5:5:3 in capital ships for the next fifteen years; the French and Italian navies would remain half of that of Japan's. The Anglo-Japanese Alliance was to be replaced by a Four Power Treaty between the United States, Great Britain, Japan and France. The nine powers signed a treaty pledging fairer treatment to China, and Japan agreed to withdraw from the province of Shantung.

The Four Power Treaty was ratified in the Senate by a vote of 67 to 27 with the support of Lodge and Underwood. The treaty limiting naval armament was passed with only 1 negative vote. That the nation was favorably inclined to disarmament measures in 1921 does not detract from the astuteness with which the conference was arranged and carried to conclusion. Although Borah conceived the idea, and Hughes carried it to fruition, the President of the United States received the praise, for it was consummated under his aegis. The world basked in hopefulness.

That Harding was above the stature of those who were to disgrace his administration can be gleaned from the reasons that he gave for persistently expressing his desire for legislation limiting the Presidential term to a single one of six years. He explained "that he was tired of buying congressional support with jobs, of always having to take account of his renomination and re-election. It was only when a President was relieved of patronage responsibilities and such things that the civil service could be taken out of politics and put on a real merit basis."[120] It was Mrs. Harding, "the Duchess," who angrily demanded that he eliminate the proposal from his message to Congress.

The Duchess was always on hand attempting to influence her husband to set aside good intentions. She was not always successful; she failed to dissuade him from granting a Christmas pardon to the pacifist, Eugene Debs, and twenty-three other conscientious objectors. Not only did Harding pardon Debs, but—in his style of personal kindness—asked him to stop at the White House on his way from Atlanta. "Well," said Harding, striding toward him with outstretched hand—"I have heard so damned much about you, Mr. Debs, that now I am very glad to meet you personally."[121]

Harding, from the start of his administration, was not the easy tool that his congressional supporters had expected. At the very outset he opposed the soldiers' bonus bill, called by its active supporter, the American Legion, the Soldier's Adjustment Compensation Bill. Pledged to economy and a balanced budget, he considered the bill a hurdle to "normalcy" and announced his opposition to any bonus bill which did not definitely provide for revenue to meet it through new taxation. So strongly was he opposed that he made a personal appeal to the Senate and thereby delayed the passage for six months. For the plight of the returning soldier *en masse* he had no personal concern.

He battled Congress, vetoing the bill it passed with a message stating that: "To add one sixth of the total sum of our public debt for a distribution among less than 3,000,000 out of 110,000,000 whether inspired by grateful sentiment or political expediency, would undermine the confidence on which our credit is builded and establish the precedent of distributing funds whenever the proposals and the numbers affected made it seem politically appealing to do so."[122] Harding, however vigorously he fought with Congress, was not happy in that role; he did not enjoy the struggle for accomplishment of his objectives as did both Roosevelts, Wilson and Truman.

By September there were still no signs of "normalcy"; the Depression deepened; joblessness increased. Urged by Hoover, Harding called a Conference on Unemployment, but nothing could be accomplished with his type of leadership. "There has been vast unemployment before and there will be again. There will be depression after inflation, just as surely as the tides ebb and flow."[123] It is significant that Herbert Hoover, who had urged Harding to call the conference, was to reflect Harding's viewpoint during the Depression of his administration —the viewpoint that the federal government could do little about it, the sole responsibility being local. Harding called upon the mayors of America to act; Hoover called upon local charities, cities, counties and villages to act.

"Harmonizing" the Cabinet continued to be a trial. The anti-conservationist Fall had scarcely settled in the Interior Department before he brazenly drew up an executive order for Harding's signature that would have transferred the Forest Service and all the national forests both in the United States and Alaska to the Department of the Interior. Secretary Wallace denounced Fall in the official bulletin of the Department of Agriculture as a conspirator with big business to exploit the public lands. Conservationists such as Gifford Pinchot attacked Fall so fiercely that Fall appealed to Harding for protection against such "vicious propaganda."

"The question of the transfer of the National forests and of the natural resources of Alaska to Fall's Interior Department finally came up in a Cabinet meeting. 'A row ensued that nearly blew the roof off,' Wallace told the conservationist Senator Norris. The Secretary of Agriculture let the Cabinet and the President know that if the Forest Service transfer should take place he would resign and denounce Fall in public meetings all through the West. Harding hesitated, tried to compromise, then for the moment agreed not to make the transfer."[124] (The question of the appropriate agency would again be acrimonious in FDR's administration when the then Secretary of Agriculture Wallace would battle the "old cumudgeon" Secretary of the Interior Harold Ickes, but neither had venal motives.) This was but one of the disturbances among Cabinet members. Wallace supported Senator Norris's Farmers Export Financing Corporation which Hoover and Mellon vigorously opposed; Hughes and Hoover did not see eye to eye. Cabinet meetings were hardly convivial. In January 1922, the respected, able Postmaster General Will Hays resigned to become the head of the Motion Picture Producers and Distributors. The schism between the factions of the Cabinet grew as Fall, Daugherty and other members of the administration became suspect.

Secretary Fall had entered office with the firm belief that, with the exception of national parks, the place for public land was in private hands. As Fall's boon companion, Harding must have known this. He may or may not have known that Fall assumed his post owing the M.D. Thatcher Estates Company of Pueblo $140,500 and eight years of tax arrears,[125] but he was warned about Fall's negotiations regarding Teapot Dome. He did know that Fall had persuaded the inept Secretary of the Navy Edwin N. Denby to transfer the management of the naval oil reserves back to the Interior Department, for he had signed the executive order effecting the transfer. Even before the notorious leasing of Teapot Dome, there were rumors of it. "Early in April Walter Teagle of the Standard Oil Company of New Jersey burst in Albert Lasker's office at the Shipping Board to tell him: 'I understand the Interior Department is just to close a contract to lease Teapot Dome, and all through the industry it smells. I'm not interested in Teapot Dome. It has no interest whatsoever for Standard Oil of New Jersey, but I do feel that you should tell the President that it *smells*—that he *must* not permit it to go through.'

"That evening Lasker went to Harding to express his doubts about the leases. 'This isn't the first time this rumor has come to me,' Harding told him, 'but if Albert Fall isn't an honest man, I'm not fit to be President of the United States.' "[126] He thus showed his utter inability to judge men.

LaFollette made a fiery attack on Fall and Denby to a Senate in which most of the Republicans ostentatiously quit their seats. Although the Senate passed unanimously his resolution asking that the Secretary of the Interior be directed to send to the Senate all the facts about the leasing of naval oil reserves to private persons or corporations, they took no further action for eighteen months.

In April 1922, Fall leased the entire Teapot Dome Reserve for twenty years to Harry F. Sinclair, the head of the Sinclair Consolidated Oil Corporation and president of Mammoth Oil Company which was organized specifically for handling the lease and development of Teapot Dome. By the terms of the transfer of naval lands to the Department of the Interior, the Secretary was free to lease the oil reserves without competitive bidding. No other bids were solicited for Teapot Dome, and Fall kept the contract with Sinclair a close secret. In view of events which transpired during the Nixon administration it is very interesting to note that Fall claimed that secrecy was justified, since "to call attention to the fact that contracts providing for enormous storages for future use in a crisis of oil were being made off the coast or in certain parts of this country" involved national security.[127]

The story of the Teapot Dome scandal is a maze of bribery. Since our concern is only with the style with which President Harding met the situation, suffice it to quote that: "Whatever it cost Sinclair to silence his critics, the sums were a fraction of what he was able to realize almost at once on the Teapot Dome lease. Sinclair Consolidated Oil stock rose to 38¾ in June from a January low of 18¾. Sinclair himself through a dummy family Corporation . . . traded a third of his Mammoth shares for a quarter million shares of Sinclair Oil which he was allowed to buy at a unit price of $17 when its public price was $50, making a profit of $17,059,700 before he had even drilled a well at Teapot Dome. With the independent stock trader, Jesse L. Livermore, he then formed a syndicate to buy 400,000 Mammoth shares at $26 which Livermore was able to market to the public at from $40 to $56.50 for an additional $8 million or so profit."[128]

Harry F. Sinclair was one of Harding's poker companions,[129] and a frequenter of the famous Little House on H Street which Harry Daugherty had borrowed from Ed McLean, the husband of Evalyn Walsh McLean—one of the wealthiest women in America. Here the President frequently came for poker; here Harry Daugherty dispensed patronage.[130] The President's choice of companions could not prevent the forthcoming scandals from enmeshing him although enmeshment was only by association. When you walk in mud, some of it sticks to your shoes. Harding was mired in bad company whose companionship he relished; he obtusely refused to believe or investigate most of the information brought to him. His characteristic of mistaken loyalty brought woe upon him and his administration.

He had no social bonds with the Hugheses, Hoovers or Wallaces. He read no books. The worlds of art and classical music were unknown to him. His theater visits were confined to the Gayety Burlesque, where he watched the girls from a special box that concealed him from the public. Poker playing and travelling for the sake of restlessly being on the move was his style of enjoyment. When he travelled, his companions were selected from the visitors to the Little House on H Street where he played poker with Jesse Smith, Harry Daugherty, Albert Fall, Ned McLean, Doc Sawyer, Charlie Forbes, his new alien property custodian Thomas W. Miller, Daugherty's associate in a questionable pardon case Thomas B. Felder, Harry Sinclair, etc.—all of whom would figure in the scandals of his administration. Playing poker was not the evil; but it was the medium through which these people gained entree and could parlay their intimacy with the President of the United States to personal advantage.

One detail of Albert Fall's many negotiations later became significant to the general public. On the day following the submission of a formal offer by Fall's old mining pal, Edward Doheny, Fall telephoned him to say that he was "prepared now to receive that loan."[131] A week later Fall arrived at his ranch in New Mexico for the Christmas holidays carrying a little black bulging bag and purchased the Harris ranch which would protect the water supply on his other properties for $91,500. That "little black bulging bag" became the symbol of the graft in Harding's administration.

Most of the facts of the Teapot Dome scandal came to light only after Harding's death. During his lifetime he lulled the public and the Congress by sending to the President of the Senate on June 7, 1922, a formal letter of explanation reading in part:

. . . I am today in receipt of a letter from the Secretary of the Interior in which he advises me of his compliance with the Resolution of the Senate and in which he makes to me a full and comprehensive report . . . of the handling of all naval reserve petroleum matters up to the present date. . . .

I am sure I am correct in construing the impelling purpose of the Secretary of the Interior in making to me this report. It is not to be construed as a defense in dealing with problems incident to the handling of the naval reserves, but is designed to afford that explanation to which the Senate is entitled, and which will prove helpful to the country generally in appraising the administration of these matters of great public concern. *I think it only fair to say in this connection that the policy which has been adopted by the Secretary of the Navy and the Secretary of the Interior in dealing with these matters was submitted to me prior to the adoption thereof, and the policy decided upon and the subsequent acts have at all times had my prior approval.*[132] (Emphases added)

True to his style, he came to the defense of his friends.

At the end of his second year, Secretary Fall resigned and went openly into the oil business.[133] It was not until October 22, 1923, more than two months after Harding's death, that the Senate Committee on Public Lands began its investigation of naval oil leases. In June 1924, Fall, Sinclair, Doheny and his son were indicted in the District Court of Columbia, charged with conspiracy and bribery.[134] There followed years of indictments and trials in which Teapot Dome and "the little black bag" were featured in the press. It was not until March 1927 that Sinclair was sentenced to prison, and not until May 1929 that an ill, decrepit Fall was, in consideration of his health, sentenced to only a year and a half and $100,000 fine.

Although many scandals marred the Harding administration, that of the Teapot Dome was the most spectacular and most remembered. It is curious that—even as these words were being written at sea en route from Villa, New Hebrides, to Suva, Fiji—the news bulletin of a Norwegian vessel carried this item: "The revelations of the Watergate Trials will be compared to Teapot Dome which has been unchallenged for 50 years as a symbol of government scandal. But even Watergate, which apparently lacks the motives of personal financial gain, may not match the stench of corruption which surrounded the Administration of President Warren Gamaliel Harding, who did not live to see it exposed."[135]

He did not live to see the Teapot Dome scandal exposed, but if he was not fully aware of this one, he knew about others. He had, at the beginning of his term, removed the office of Superintendent of Federal Prisons from the civil service list by executive order and placed his brother-in-law Reverend Haber Herbert Votaw at its head. The Reverend's experience consisted of ten years' service as a Seventh Day Adventist minister in Burma.[136] Harding also consolidated the War Risk Insurance Bureau, the Federal Hospitalization Bureau and other overlapping agencies into a central Veterans' Bureau with Charles Forbes at its head—a wise move, coupled with an unfortunate appointment. One of Forbes's first acts as Veterans' Bureau director was to persuade Harding that it would be more efficient to transfer the planning and construction of all future hospitals from the Army to the bureau. Successful in obtaining this advantage, he then convinced the President that it would save much time and cut much red tape if he had charge of the purchase and disposal of veterans' supplies, then handled by the Quartermaster General's Department. With this transfer more than fifty huge government storehouses, crammed with supplies and equipment accumulated during the war, came under Forbes's control.[137] It was Harding's style to see logic in and to acquiesce automatically to his friends' requests.

The Reverend Votaw winked at the drug traffic in the federal penitentiary at Atlanta. When rumors reached Harding, he sent his trusted poker friend Forbes to investigate. Whatever Forbes's report contained, it must have reflected on the Department of Justice as well as the Superintendent of Prisons, for Daugherty shortly afterward informed the Colonel that conditions in Atlanta were none of Forbes's damned business.

Forbes made a fortune by selling the supplies stored in the warehouses without public bidding and by graft extracted through his control of hospital construction. When Dr. Sawyer, chairman of the Federal Hospitalization Board, reported to the President that 20 per cent of the medical supplies supposedly allotted to civilian government hospitals were being shipped elsewhere, Harding ordered the shipments stopped and sent for Forbes. Forbes made a glib explanation which Harding credited and then lifted his embargo on shipments, unaware that Forbes had paid no attention to the embargo from the beginning.

Within a month Dr. Sawyer had visited the warehouses, this time with Surgeon General Hugh S. Cumming of the Public Health Service, and again found the same bustle of trains and freight cars and goods in transit. He discovered towels that had cost the government 19 cents apiece being shipped to Thompson-

Kelley at 3⅜ cents, along with sheets and other items to which the Health Service had a claim and of which it was desperately short. This time Sawyer took the matter to Forbes's enemy, Daugherty, instead of the trusting President, giving him details not only of Perryville warehouses but of the collusion he believed existed in the veterans' hospital construction.

Russell takes up the story.

"The Attorney General carried the matter directly to the White House that afternoon . . . he told Harding he had an unpleasant duty to perform. 'Shoot!' Harding said. . . . Daugherty explained what he had heard about Forbes. Harding's face reddened. 'That can't be,' he said and refused to hear anything more about his merry-Andrew favorite. Still angry, Harding let his Attorney-General leave without inviting him to dinner—the first time he had omitted such an invitation. The next day, even more pointedly, Harding failed to call Daugherty on their private telephone line that he usually used from five to twenty times a day. But the next day he sent for Daugherty, put his arm around his shoulder, and asked, 'Old man, did I hurt your feelings the last time you were here?' Never since the day they met at Richwood had Harding addressed him so intimately, and Daugherty tried to shrug off his embarrassment by saying that no one could hurt his feelings. Harding admitted that he had had Forbes investigated and found the charges true. 'I am heartsick about it,' he said in a shaky voice.

"The following afternoon a visitor to the White House with an appointment to see the President was directed by mistake to the second floor. As he approached the Red Room he heard a voice hoarse with anger and on entering saw Harding throttling a man against the wall as he shouted: 'You yellow rat! You double-crossing bastard! If you ever . . .' Whirling about at the visitor's approach, Harding loosed his grip and the released man staggered away, his face blotched and distorted. 'I am sorry,' Harding said curtly to his visitor. 'You have an appointment. Come into the next room.' On leaving the White House, the visitor asked a doorman who it was who had just gone out after he had come in, and the doorman replied: 'Colonel Forbes of the Veterans Bureau.' "[138]

Did the President reveal the scandal? Did he bring charges against Forbes? No—not his style. To avoid open scandal he let Forbes go to Europe to investigate the needs of disabled veterans still abroad. When Congress got wind of the matter and the Senate passed a resolution to investigate, Forbes cabled his resignation from Paris. It is estimated that Forbes's malpractices represented a loss of $200 million to the nation. Harding's friendships were costly.[139]

Jesse Smith, Daugherty's closest friend—private secretary, majordomo, political henchman, financial manager, and so on—refused to take an office but had a desk in Daugherty's office. Subordinates took it for granted that Smith spoke for the Attorney General and possibly for the White House. "Easily he moved into the role of what would later be called an influence-peddler; a fixer; a go-between, an arranger of pardons and liquor permits, a bagman. . . . Washington he sensed as a ripe money-tree waiting for him to shake the branches. . . . He took the cash, but often let the delivery go," as some of his victims found on their way to the penitentiary. Jesse Smith was a visible sign of Washington corruption; in addition to his desk at the Department of Justice, he met his "clients" at a corner near the Shoreham Hotel and in the lobby of the Wardman Park.

Again, when word reached Harding of Smith's demagoguery, he ordered no investigation or prosecution; he told Daugherty that Jesse would not be welcome on his projected trip to Alaska and that he should leave Washington. Thereupon

Jesse bought a revolver and shot himself. Charles Cramer, general counsel for the Veterans' Bureau, had also killed himself after the Senate passed a resolution directing a committee to determine the reports of "waste, extravagance, irregularities and mismanagement."

No wonder the President moaned: "Some day the people will understand what some of my erstwhile friends have done to me in these critical times when I depended so much upon them."[140] This remark was reportedly made in November 1922; the date lends interest as it precedes any public report of the scandals. Therefore the President must have had knowledge of them but he failed to take action.

This tortured man with his ill-conceived loyalties lacked the strength to divulge the sordid facts; there is evidence that he was struggling to do so, but always gave it up. He attempted to get advice, but when the moment of consultation was at hand, he could not find the words that would betray a friend. He telephoned Nicholas Murray Butler who was about to leave for Europe, early in May 1923, begging him to come to Washington. So urgent was his plea that Butler postponed his departure and came at once. This is his graphic and telling report of that visit: "I had a most extraordinary experience at the White House. The President came to my sitting room before I had finished breakfast and from that time, until I left at half-past eleven to return to the railway station, he hardly ever let me out of his sight for a moment. Evidently, there was something very much on his mind and he was trying to bring himself to tell me what it was. Several times during the morning, afternoon and evening he seemed to be on the point of unbosoming himself, but he never did so. He came down to the porch of the White House to say farewell, as I took the automobile to the station, and even then seemed to be trying to tell me something which troubled him. I have never been able to guess what that something was."[141]

Like a little boy he decided to run away from these and other burgeoning scandals. His form of escape was to take a trip to Alaska, thus diverting the public mind and his own. He would sell the country his World Court proposal which was meeting little success in Congress; he would lay the foundation for the re-election campaign urged upon him by Daugherty, and would leave behind him the mess in Washington.

In the Senate Harding had called the League of Nations a betrayal of America, and in his Inaugural had urged "non-involvement in old-world controversies." Not the only President to have a change of mind, he now claimed that there were "rudiments of good in both the League and The Hague Tribunal." Encouraged by Hughes, Elihu Root and Hoover, he wished the United States to become a member of the Permanent Court of International Justice established at The Hague by the League of Nations. It was the successor to The Hague Tribunal. The convert, beset by trouble from his friends, turned to the counsel of more erudite advisers and sent an unexpected message to Congress recommending that the United States join the World Court. Entrance to the League was not a requisite. Up rose the isolationists, the irreconcilables, the bitter enders. All the old slogans came forth. Harding had shot his bolt when in his message he said: "Such action would add to our own consciousness of participation in the fortunate advancement of international relationship and remind the world anew that we are ready for our proper part in furthering peace and adding to stability in world affairs."[142]

The message was sent in the last week of the session which ended March 3,

1923—the week that Albert B. Fall cabled his resignation. It was evidently meant as a distraction, for the politician Harding realized that his party would not support him. In fact it was a Democrat, Senator William H. King of Utah, who introduced the resolution that the Senate sanction adherence to the World Court. Lodge buried the resolution in his Committee on Foreign Affairs, and the Senate refused to vote it out of committee. The issue, however, had been created and was the vehicle by which the awakened shrewd politician meant to appeal to the people, raising a hue and cry that would smother the odors of scandal.

The "bloviater" was showing the characteristics of a chameleon. He wrote Malcolm Jennings: "The great hubbub over the World Court was largely bunk. Most of it emanates from members of the Senate who have very little concern about the favor with which the administration is regarded, and the remainder of it come [sic] from those who are nuts either for or against the League. The League advocates have somewhat embarrassed the situation, but I do not fear the outcome. A good many people have urged me to drop the matter, but I do not find myself ready to accept that sort of a sneaking program."[143] He had become a fighter—at least on this occasion.

This determination was strengthened by the decrease in his popularity with the people and with members of his own party, some of whom were starting booms for their own candidacy in 1924. Opposition stiffened Harding's pride, caused him to drop his advocacy of a one-term presidency, and aroused him to seek vindication and leadership and a second term. After conferring with Daugherty in Florida where they were both vacationing, Daugherty—not Harding—announced to reporters: "The President will be a candidate for renomination. He will . . . be renominated and re-elected because the country will demand it."[144] The President revealed the true intent of his trip to Alaska in a letter to Jennings: "I was a little embarrassed by General Daugherty's announcement of a candidacy and have been seeking . . . to antidote the impression which that interview may have given that I would travel across the country as a candidate for renomination. I really want to speak as President, and am convinced that I can do so, and I look forward to good results both for me and for the better understanding of the country."[145] This nascent desire to assume Presidential leadership grew as he planned to use the trip, originally to be a vacation, as a vehicle for reaching the people to get their approval of the issue concerning the World Court. Perhaps the analogy to Wilson's ill-fated journey in behalf of the League of Nations escaped him; perhaps—with growing self-confidence—he felt that he could succeed where Wilson had failed. That would have been a noteworthy accomplishment!

He seemed to have suddenly assumed command. He asked Walter F. Brown, an Ohio political leader and former congressman, to help in planning the journey from Washington to Seattle to Alaska and back by way of San Francisco and Los Angeles, and to visit each scheduled city, checking upon all local arrangements. It is notable that he and not Daugherty issued the instructions: "Please make clear that the trip is in no sense a partisan one and that I would like all elements in civic life to be properly represented in public meetings whenever such arrangements are possible."

Of equal importance is the abandonment of his habitual search for pleasure. "I have found it necessary . . . to forego the acceptance of the tenders of all private or personal hospitality."[146] After two years in office, President Harding had begun to understand its significance and was setting a new course. When on June 20 he left Washington, he had the appearance of a tired man—mentally and physically. On the trip he was more than ordinarily restless, never wanting to be alone, eager to distract himself with talk or bridge. In spite of the intense heat he appeared and spoke at each whistle stop en route to St. Louis where he made his first speech on the World Court in isolationist Missouri to 10,000 Rotarians. It was a bold stroke and an anomaly; the formerly vigorous speaker with little to say and no leadership to offer had been widely acclaimed. The now restrained President offering leadership, pleading to have the United States join the Court, was heard without applause. For the first time a President's address was broadcast live by radio stations from coast to coast.

"He condemned—without mentioning the understood names of LaFollette and Borah—those who wanted the United States to live as a 'hermit nation,' while reassuring his hearers that he did not intend to enter the League by 'back door, side door, or cellar door.' Following Hughes's plan to make the World Court more acceptable to the League's enemies, he proposed a court independent of the League, self-perpetuating, with judges themselves given the authority to fill any vacancies in court personnel. His sincerity shone through his rhetoric. . . . 'My passion is for justice over force. My hope is the great court. My mind is made up. My resolution is fixed.' "[147]

The farmers of Kansas were concerned about the falling price of wheat and cared not a hoot about anything as remote as a World Court. In Denver and in Salt Lake City he departed from his prepared texts dealing with prohibition (which he claimed would never be repealed) and taxation, to plead extemporaneously for the World Court: "I want America to have something of a spiritual ideal. I am seeking American sentiment in favor of an international court of justice. I want America to play her part in helping to abolish war."[148] In Salt Lake City he received enthusiastic applause. In planning his schedule he had intended to mention the Court only twice, but as he proceeded his own enthusiasm grew and he pleaded for it in almost every speech. He had, indeed, "bloviated" himself.

The views he expressed on this trip were those of a man who had gone through a purification process. Evidently he attempted to brush away the scar on the administration's labor record and the cause of organized labor's bitter antipathy —the injunction against striking railroad workers which forbade, among other activities of the strikers, any "display of numbers or force, jeers, entreaties, arguments, persuasions, rewards" for the purpose of influencing workmen. The plea for the injunction had been argued by Attorney General Daugherty before a judge whose appointment by Harding had been recommended by Daugherty. The injunction went so far as to prohibit picketing; union officials were not permitted to issue any strike directions, employ any funds or speak any words designed to prevent a strikebreaker from substituting for a striker. The strike had been inspired by an order of the Railroad Labor Board which would cut wages by $60 million as a step toward liquidating the scale of wartime wages.[149]

Now the President stated that he hoped to lessen the conflict between labor and capital; he was opposed to any "deflation of labor and to those who held that organized labor must be crushed." In Tacoma, Washington, he said, "I should be proud, indeed, if my administration were marked by the final passage of the twelve hour working day in American life." This was not a new position, for he had tried as early as April 1922 to influence Judge Gary of the United States Steel Corporation to set an example to the rest of the industry by reducing its twelve-hour working shift to eight hours and the seven-day week to six. The following month he had invited forty-one leaders of the steel industry to dinner at the White House and told them that the twelve-hour day must go. A committee was appointed which decided that the twelve-hour day of itself had not injured their employees "physically, mentally or morally." It is ironic that on the very day of Harding's death the newspapers carried a dispatch reporting the action of the iron and steel industry to rescind its resolutions refusing to consider any reform regarding the twelve-hour day as inconsistent with the interest of the industry.

Were these changes in President Harding's style sincere? Had he recognized his errors of judgment? As an instance, after touring Yellowstone Park he announced that it was "not desirable that the West should fall into the hands of bonanza corporations seeking to exploit it for the profit of stockholders."[150] And he advocated adding 400,000 acres of public land to the Tetons. Was this the result of expediency or conviction? Did the administration loss in the November 1922 elections influence this change? Was his advocacy of the World Court sincere or an attempt to divert attention? Would he, had he lived, have become a President who would use the Presidential power for the benefit of the people or would he have lapsed into his lackadaisical style? There can be no answer to these questions; one can only hazard that, having found that he had the ability beneficially to affect the destiny of people, he would have persevered.

While Harding was on board ship on the return voyage from Alaska he received a coded message from Washington. After reading it, "he suffered something of a collapse. For the rest of the day he seemed half stunned, muttering to himself and breaking off to ask whoever was with him what a President should do when his friends were false. What the message contained not even [his secretary] Welliver was able to find out although both he and Hoover noticed the President's distress."[151]

Yes, Secretary Hoover was aboard. Instead of travelling with his poker-playing friends, the new Harding was accompanied by Secretaries Work (who had succeeded Fall), Wallace and Hoover; and the game was bridge, not poker. The fact that Daugherty was not a member of the party is not significant of any rupture in the President's trust and friendship. The day before Harding left, Daugherty had spent several hours helping him clear his desk and it was at this time, possibly with some apprehension as to his future, that the President asked Daugherty to help him draw up a new will.

It was after Harding's death that the Attorney General achieved the dubious distinction of being the first head of the Department of Justice to be subject to two congressional investigations; and after his resignation he was twice indicted for malfeasance. His trials were for accepting bribes while in office, although because of the statute of limitations he could be charged only with conspiring to defraud the United States of his "honest, impartial, and unprejudiced services and judgment" as Attorney General. At his first trial the jury failed to agree, nine jurors being in favor of convicting him. The jury at the second trial stood eleven to one, with the lone dissenter commonly believed to have been bribed.[152]

Could the message flown to Harding have contained information about the trusted Daugherty? Certainly there were many current rumors that he was deeply involved with Alien Property Custodian Thomas W. Miller in the American Metal scandal, in an Oklahoma Indian land fraud, in the protection of prohibition smugglers, and in taking money for obtaining Presidential pardons. There are certain facts which lend credibility but not proof to these rumors. Among them is that Daugherty had liabilities of $27,000 when he entered the Cabinet and taxable property of only $8,030. His share in the expenses of the Little House on H Street amounted to twice his official salary of $12,000, yet during this period he deposited nearly $75,000 from unrevealed sources in his brother's bank. When he took office he owned five hundred shares of Wright-Martin Aircraft stock. In the next year he had an additional 2,000 shares; during that period a government suit against the company involving $3.5 million was blocked by the Justice Department. And so the deals went on and on. Therefore, the speculation is raised that the message which caused President Harding's grief may have concerned Harry Daugherty; that the results of the President's permissiveness had now become apparent to him.

So depressed was Harding that when, after several days of listless speaking in Canada, the *Henderson* returning from Alaska crashed in fog into a destroyer in Puget Sound, Harding remained in bed, his hands covering his face. Even though everyone had been ordered on deck, Harding lay there, motionless. "I hope the boat sinks," he said softly, his face still hidden.[153]

When the *Henderson* reached Seattle the next morning there were thousands of people waiting to see the President. "Hoover had written the speech on Alaska that the President was to deliver at the Seattle Stadium that afternoon, although Harding had gone over the text and introduced what Hoover called his usual three-dollar words and sonorous phrases. For all its sonorities it was a surprising speech, a rebuke to Fall and his kind. Harding came out for a policy of thorough-going conservation. He would not, he said, see the territory turned over to exploiters to loot 'as the possibility of profit arises.' Undoubtedly in his own words, he declared that Americans must 'regard life in lovely, wonderful Alaska as an end and not a means.' "[154] One must once again wonder whether this was a new Harding or a Harding influenced, as he had always been, by those around him. Would this gentle but weak man have continued to take counsel with those who remained of the old gang? Would he have distinguished between able and self-serving advisers?

A visibly sick man, he faltered through two speeches in Seattle after which he complained of violent cramps and indigestion. The Portland speech was cancelled and the train sped on to San Francisco where on Sunday, July 29, a news photographer snapped a picture of "an aging, flabby-faced man with slack chin and puffy eyes, forcing himself into a half smile as he squints into the sunshine."[155]

Harry Daugherty, having kept in touch with the Presidential party daily, arrived in San Francisco on Wednesday and went directly to see Mrs. Harding, who urged him to see the President. Curiously, Daugherty declined, saying that he did not think he should see the President and burden him with unnecessary talk. One can only surmise that the "unnecessary talk" would be unpleasant. That suspicion is confirmed by President Hoover's words written twenty-eight years later: "One day after lunch, when we were a few days out, Harding asked me to come to his cabin. He plumped at me the question: 'If you knew of a great scandal in our administration, would you for the good of the country and the party expose it publicly or would you bury it?' My natural reply was, 'Publish it, and at least get credit for integrity on your side.' He remarked that this method might be politically dangerous. I asked for more particulars. He said he had received some rumors of irregularities, centering around Smith, in connection with cases in the Department of Justice. . . . Harding gave me no information about what Smith was up to. I asked what Daugherty's relations to the affair were. He abruptly dried up and never raised the question again."[156]

On Friday, August 3, President Warren Gamaliel Harding died. He had been relieved of the necessity of meeting the issue of corruption in his administration, an issue that had plagued and sorrowed him, an issue that he could not force himself to meet. He also had been relieved of exerting Presidential leadership, which had even been urged upon him by congressional leaders who were alarmed by the aggressiveness with which the insurgent Republicans under LaFollette's leadership had assumed command in the Senate. The House, too, was divided and without leadership. Perceiving the danger, the leaders had been hopeful that the President would fill the vacuum.

According to Dr. Alderfer: "They appealed to him to take a firm hold and assert his control. He was reluctant to do this on account of his promise to refrain from administrative usurpation of legislative functions. The manner most commonly suggested was a public appeal to Congress to enact legislation which the Administration endorsed. It was believed by the leaders that the President was more popular than the party in Congress and that it was possible for him to assert leadership in a fashion that would arouse the enthusiasm of the country and force the recalcitrant legislature to action. He made several attempts to accomplish this result. . . . He wrote letters to Congress committees to influence their activities. But letter-writing did not grip the public or scare the Congressmen. Something more spectacular was needed. It was necessary to emulate Roosevelt or Wilson. He conferred with leaders in Congress in the hope that sweet reasonableness and a benediction of understanding would make the initiative, direction, energy, and driving power of the White House control unnecessary."[157]

As he was attempting to fill this uncongenial role after two years in office, death took him. That it was a role for which he was not fitted is best described in William Allen White's words written shortly after Harding had completed his first year in office, detailing a conversation he had with his old friend and the President's secretary: "Lord, lord man! (Welliver told him in distress). You can't know what the President is going through. You see he doesn't understand it; he just doesn't know a thousand things he ought to know. And he realized his ignorance, and he is afraid. He has no idea where to turn. Not long ago, when the first tax bill came up, you remember where there were two theories of taxation for the administration's support, he would listen for an hour to one side, become convinced; and then the other side would get him and overwhelm him with its contentions. Some good friends would walk into the White House all cocked and primed with facts and figures to support one side and another would reach him with a counter-argument which would brush his friends' theory aside. I remember he came in here late one afternoon after a long conference, in which both sides appeared, talked at each other, wrangled over him. He was weary and confused and heartsick, for the man really wants to do the right and honest thing. But I tell you, he doesn't know. . . . I never knew a man who was having such a hard time to find the truth. How Roosevelt [Theodore] used to click into truth with the snap of his teeth! How Wilson sensed it with some engine of erudition under the hood of his cranium! But this man paws for it, wrestles for it, cries for it, and has to take the luck of the road to get it. Sometimes he doesn't and sometimes he does, and much he knows about it when it comes."[158]

President Harding died before the American people realized his shortcomings, before historians would rate him the Presidential failure of the twentieth century—in other words, a pygmy. A giant in the White House, Woodrow Wilson, attended the funeral.

Afterword

In evaluating the use of Presidential power it is timely to recall James Madison's letter to Thomas Jefferson in 1788: "Wherever the real power in a Government lies, there is the danger of oppression. In our Governments the real power lies in the majority of the Community, and the invasion of private rights is *chiefly* to be apprehended, not from acts of a government contrary to the sense of its constituents, but from acts in which the Government is the mere instrument of the major number of the constituents. This is a truth of great importance, but not yet sufficiently attended to, and is probably more strongly impressed upon my mind by facts, and reflections suggested by them, than on yours which has contemplated abuses of power issuing from a very different quarter. Wherever there is an interest and power to do wrong, wrong will generally be done, and not less readily by a powerful and interested party than by a powerful and interested prince."[1]

Appendix

The 1948 poll taken by Harvard Professor Arthur Schlesinger, Sr., asked for the views of fifty-five experts on all the Presidents from Washington through Franklin D. Roosevelt. His 1962 poll was expanded to seventy-five experts, among whom were most of the first fifty-five. On this poll, all of the Presidents through Eisenhower were listed.

The results of the two polls follow:

SCHLESINGER POLLS OF PRESIDENTIAL GREATNESS

1948 Poll	1962 Poll
(Responses from 55 experts)	*(Responses from 75 experts)*

GREAT

1948 Poll	1962 Poll
1. Abraham Lincoln	1. Abraham Lincoln
2. George Washington	2. George Washington
3. Franklin D. Roosevelt	3. Franklin D. Roosevelt
4. Woodrow Wilson	4. Woodrow Wilson
5. Thomas Jefferson	5. Thomas Jefferson
6. Andrew Jackson	

NEAR GREAT

1948 Poll	1962 Poll
7. Theodore Roosevelt	6. Andrew Jackson
8. Grover Cleveland	7. Theodore Roosevelt
9. John Adams	8. James K. Polk ⎫ tie
10. James K. Polk	9. Harry S. Truman ⎬
	10. John Adams
	11. Grover Cleveland

AVERAGE

1948 Poll	1962 Poll
11. John Quincy Adams	12. James Madison
12. James Monroe	13. John Quincy Adams
13. Rutherford B. Hayes	14. Rutherford B. Hayes
14. James Madison	15. William McKinley
15. Martin Van Buren	16. William Howard Taft
16. William Howard Taft	17. Martin Van Buren
17. Chester A. Arthur	18. James Monroe
18. William McKinley	19. Herbert Hoover
19. Andrew Johnson	20. Benjamin Harrison
20. Herbert Hoover	21. Chester A. Arthur ⎫ tie
21. Benjamin Harrison	22. Dwight D. Eisenhower ⎬
	23. Andrew Johnson

BELOW AVERAGE

22. John Tyler	24. Zachary Taylor
23. Calvin Coolidge	25. John Tyler
24. Millard Fillmore	26. Millard Fillmore
25. Zachary Taylor	27. Calvin Coolidge
26. James Buchanan	28. Franklin Pierce
27. Franklin Pierce	29. James Buchanan

FAILURE

28. Ulysses S. Grant	30. Ulysses S. Grant
29. Warren G. Harding	31. Warren G. Harding

Professor Bailey has pointed out the many possibilities of error in these polls, which are influenced by such factors as political prejudice, since most history teachers tend to be Democratic; the recent publication of a well-received and highly regarded book about a particular President, or well-publicized and courageous activities by former Presidents *after* leaving the White House (for example, Herbert Hoover); and many other reasons, some of which he enumerates.[1]

Schlesinger himself did not fully agree with the results of his own two polls. Indeed, he received many letters of protest—especially from Roosevelt haters in 1948. One New Yorker, says Bailey, wrote: "I will agree that FDR is great, if by that is meant a great liar, great faker, great traitor, great betrayer." This was written only three years after "that man in the White House" had died, and some of the anti-New Dealers were still vitriolic.

In 1962, the Roosevelt haters had quieted down considerably, perhaps as they saw how scrupulously President Eisenhower avoided even trying to tinker with, to say nothing of repealing, those New Deal and Fair Deal programs which he had inherited but which he had called "creeping socialism." Yet there was great protest to the 1962 poll for downgrading Eisenhower to a place far below Truman.

In spite of high praise from the participants in these two polls, Professor Bailey has also pointed out the many difficulties in any attempt to appraise Presidential greatness comparatively, such as the impossibility of agreeing on yardsticks, or of blotting out from one's mind what a man like Washington, Jefferson and Jackson had done before he became President. He points out weaknesses in these two polls in many other respects, too, although he admits that: "One would be hard pressed with geography in mind [i.e., representation from all sections of the country] to assemble a more distinguished panel of historical scholars."

Professor Bailey finally gets down to listing the forty-three attributes he would consider in weighing a President's greatness. It is doubtful that any President—or in fact, any mere human being—had *all* these attributes. He also gives his own appraisals of the Presidents from Washington to Johnson. They disagree markedly with some of the ratings in the Schlesinger polls, and incidentally with this author's.

At any rate, this book follows what appears to be the consensus of these two expert polls—for all their weaknesses—as to our top performers.

Another recent, more analytical poll was taken in 1968 by Gary M. Maranell, Associate Professor of Sociology in the University of Kansas, and published in the June 1970 issue of *American History*. He describes the difference between his poll and the 1948 and 1962 polls, which he considers primarily a rating in prestige:

"This essay enlarges upon the Schlesinger polls, as well as updates them. It also introduces crucial methodological changes such as the use of social-psychological scaling methods instead of a simple ranking, the inclusion of additional dimensions of evaluation, the use of a much larger and less biased sample, and the use of a single professional society as a sampling frame."

The pollees here were drawn "at random" from the membership of the Organization of American Historians. The total sample chosen was 1095. Questionnaires were sent to all these and answered by nearly 600 historians; but only 571 answers were complete enough to be included in the analysis. This is 7½ times as large as the sample in the larger Schlesinger poll; probably with Professor Bailey's criticisms in mind, the pollster adds: "it contains no clearly identifiable regional or institutional bias."

The participants were asked to rate the Presidents on seven separate scales. I have taken only five of those as significant for this book:

1. The general prestige assigned to the President at the present time.
2. The strength of the role the President played in directing the government and shaping the events of his day.

3. The approach taken by the President toward his administration, whether it was an active approach or a passive one.

4. An evaluation of the idealistic or practical nature of the official actions of the President.

5. An evaluation of the flexibility or inflexibility of the approach the President took in implementing his programs or policies.

The tables reproduced below are based upon the deviation of each President from the mean of all of them. The pluses are the Presidents above the mean, and the minuses the Presidents below. In this way, the distance between the Presidents is more accurately measured than in the Schlesinger polls. The first table is based on "Prestige":

GENERAL PRESTIGE

Abraham Lincoln	+2.10*	Herbert Hoover	− .09
George Washington	+1.78	Dwight D. Eisenhower	− .29
Franklin Roosevelt	+1.57	Andrew Johnson	− .30
Thomas Jefferson	+1.47	Martin Van Buren	− .37
Theodore Roosevelt	+1.18	William McKinley	− .39
Woodrow Wilson	+1.01	Chester A. Arthur	− .52
Harry Truman	+ .94	Rutherford B. Hayes	− .59
Andrew Jackson	+ .87	John Tyler	− .78
John Kennedy	+ .63	Benjamin Harrison	− .89
John Adams	+ .61	Zachary Taylor	− .96
James K. Polk	+ .30	Calvin Coolidge	− .99
Grover Cleveland	+ .25	Millard Fillmore	−1.19
James Madison	+ .23	James Buchanan	−1.28
James Monroe	+ .17	Franklin Pierce	−1.29
John Quincy Adams	+ .16	Ulysses S. Grant	−1.50
Lyndon Johnson	+ .06	Warren G. Harding	−1.84
William Howard Taft	− .05		

*A high positive score is high in prestige.

The next table is based on "Strength of Action" taken by the President. This is different from "Prestige," as will be shown by comparing the two tables. The difference becomes very apparent because in strength of action, Franklin D. Roosevelt, Lyndon Johnson and Andrew Jackson have moved up significantly, while Washington has dropped down from second place to ninth.

STRENGTH OF ACTION

Franklin D. Roosevelt	+1.98*	Herbert Hoover	− .23
Abraham Lincoln	+1.74	William McKinley	− .30
Andrew Jackson	+1.37	Martin Van Buren	− .34
Theodore Roosevelt	+1.36	Andrew Johnson	− .40
Woodrow Wilson	+1.35	Dwight Eisenhower	− .43
Thomas Jefferson	+1.18	Chester A. Arthur	− .68
Harry Truman	+1.06	Rutherford B. Hayes	− .69
Lyndon Johnson	+1.00	John Tyler	− .716
George Washington	+ .89	Zachary Taylor	− .72
John F. Kennedy	+ .68	Benjamin Harrison	− .97
James K. Polk	+ .55	Calvin Coolidge	−1.17
John Adams	+ .41	James Buchanan	−1.19
Grover Cleveland	+ .18	Millard Fillmore	−1.22
James Madison	+ .05	Franklin Pierce	−1.33
James Monroe	− .02	Ulysses S. Grant	−1.36
William Howard Taft	− .17	Warren G. Harding	−1.66
John Quincy Adams	− .22		

*A high positive score is strength; a high negative score is weakness.

The next table, based on "Activeness," shows results similar to the "Strength of Action" table and very different from "Prestige."

PRESIDENTIAL ACTIVENESS

Franklin D. Roosevelt	+2.06*	Herbert Hoover	− .14
Theodore Roosevelt	+1.61	William Howard Taft	− .16
Andrew Jackson	+1.51	Martin Van Buren	− .24
Lyndon Johnson	+1.39	William McKinley	− .34
Harry Truman	+1.25	John Tyler	− .56
John F. Kennedy	+1.06	Dwight D. Eisenhower	− .59
Woodrow Wilson	+1.05	Chester A. Arthur	− .69
Abraham Lincoln	+ .93	Rutherford B. Hayes	− .74
Thomas Jefferson	+ .91	Zachary Taylor	− .86
James K. Polk	+ .59	Benjamin Harrison	− .95
George Washington	+ .44	Millard Fillmore	−1.22
John Adams	+ .34	James Buchanan	−1.26
Grover Cleveland	+ .20	Franklin Pierce	−1.29
Andrew Johnson	+ .12	Ulysses S. Grant	−1.37
James Madison	+ .03	Calvin Coolidge	−1.37
John Quincy Adams	+ .01	Warren G. Harding	−1.66
James Monroe	− .06		

*A high positive score is active; a high negative score is passive.

The next table is based on "Idealism" as opposed to "Practicality." The results are entirely different from the preceding three tables. Washington, Lincoln and Franklin D. Roosevelt drop a big distance in this list and Wilson moves to the top, with Hoover up to fourth place.

IDEALISM OR PRACTICALITY

Woodrow Wilson	+4.23*	William McKinley	− .25
John Quincy Adams	+1.18	Rutherford B. Hayes	− .29
John F. Kennedy	+1.14	Benjamin Harrison	− .33
Herbert Hoover	+1.00	George Washington	− .41
Thomas Jefferson	+ .81	Harry Truman	− .44
Andrew Johnson	+ .66	Chester A. Arthur	− .45
James Madison	+ .55	Martin Van Buren	− .47
James Monroe	+ .40	Ulysses S. Grant	− .55
Millard Fillmore	+ .36	Theodore Roosevelt	− .57
Dwight D. Eisenhower	+ .13	Abraham Lincoln	− .61
John Tyler	+ .09	Franklin D. Roosevelt	− .62
Grover Cleveland	+ .08	Andrew Jackson	− .74
Zachary Taylor	+ .01	Warren G. Harding	− .81
James Buchanan	− .017	Lyndon Johnson	−1.01
John Adams	− .02	Calvin Coolidge	−1.41
William Howard Taft	− .04	James K. Polk	−1.44
Franklin Pierce	− .17		

*A high positive score is idealistic; a high negative score is practical.

The table based on "Flexibility" again differs from the preceding tables. Outstanding, for example, is the drop of #1 idealist Woodrow Wilson to last place in "Flexibility." Lincoln and Roosevelt, both low in "Idealism," are very high in "Flexibility."

FLEXIBILITY

John F. Kennedy	+ 1.61*	Franklin Pierce	+ .16
Abraham Lincoln	+ 1.50	Rutherford B. Hayes	+ .14
Thomas Jefferson	+ 1.35	James Buchanan	+ .01
Franklin D. Roosevelt	+ 1.31	William Howard Taft	+ .01
Dwight D. Eisenhower	+ 1.21	James K. Polk	− .19
Warren G. Harding	+ 1.17	Lyndon Johnson	− .47
James Monroe	+ 1.03	Zachary Taylor	− .76
Ulysses S. Grant	+ .59	Calvin Coolidge	− .83
James Madison	+ .576	John Adams	− .85
George Washington	+ .57	Grover Cleveland	− .88
William McKinley	+ .49	Herbert Hoover	−1.01
Harry Truman	+ .31	John Tyler	−1.09
Millard Fillmore	+ .27	John Quincy Adams	−1.15
Martin Van Buren	+ .19	Andrew Jackson	−1.40
Theodore Roosevelt	+ .186	Andrew Johnson	−2.18
Benjamin Harrison	+ .186	Woodrow Wilson	−2.23
Chester A. Arthur	+ .18		

*A high positive score is flexible; a high negative score is inflexible.

The last table, based on "Accomplishments," is very similar to the one on "Prestige," and shows that accomplishments form a very large part of the modern evaluation of prestige.

ACCOMPLISHMENTS OF THEIR ADMINISTRATIONS

Abraham Lincoln	+ 2.07*	John Quincy Adams	− .24
Franklin D. Roosevelt	+ 1.91	Herbert Hoover	− .29
George Washington	+ 1.72	Dwight D. Eisenhower	− .32
Thomas Jefferson	+ 1.31	Andrew Johnson	− .40
Theodore Roosevelt	+ 1.26	Martin Van Buren	− .46
Harry Truman	+ 1.12	Chester A. Arthur	− .52
Woodrow Wilson	+ 1.11	Rutherford B. Hayes	− .64
Andrew Jackson	+ .83	John Tyler	− .80
Lyndon Johnson	+ .53	Benjamin Harrison	− .86
James K. Polk	+ .50	Zachary Taylor	− .99
John Adams	+ .37	James Buchanan	−1.136
John F. Kennedy	+ .36	Millard Fillmore	−1.14
James Monroe	+ .13	Calvin Coolidge	−1.20
Grover Cleveland	+ .11	Franklin Pierce	−1.25
James Madison	+ .10	Ulysses S. Grant	−1.38
William Howard Taft	+ .01	Warren G. Harding	−1.61
William McKinley	+ .21		

*A high positive score is great accomplishment; a high negative score is little accomplishment.

All these attributes are very significant to the style of the Presidents with which we are concerned. It is quite remarkable that the tables based on "Prestige," "Strength," and "Presidential Activeness" are so similar to the ratings of "great" and "near great" by Schlesinger. Taking all three polls into consideration, the selection of the Presidents for this volume seems justified.

Notes

PREFACE

1. *American Heritage Dictionary of the English Language* (Houghton Mifflin, 1969).

CHAPTER ONE: Theodore Roosevelt

1. See Chapter Three.
2. Corinne Robinson, *My Brother Theodore Roosevelt* (Scribners, 1921), p. 50.
3. Carleton Putnam, *Theodore Roosevelt, The Formative Years* (Scribners, 1958), Vol. I (1858–1886), pp. 198–199.
4. *The Letters of Theodore Roosevelt,* selected & edited by Elting E. Morison (Harvard University Press, 1951), Vol 3., p. 178, #2178.
5. Morison, *Letters,* Vol. 3, pp. 102, 103, #2086.
6. Putnam, Vol. I, p. 239.
7. Thomas A. Bailey, *Presidential Greatness* (Prentice-Hall, 1966), p. 200.
8. *Works of Theodore Roosevelt, Autobiography,* Memorial Edition, Vol. XXII, pp. 92, 93.
9. Putnam, Vol. I, p. 306.
10. Elections for the Assembly in those days occurred annually.
11. Putnam, pp. 368–373.
12. Ibid., Vol. I, p. 409.
13. Roosevelt, "Phases of State Legislation," *Century,* April 1885, p. 829.
14. Howard Lawrence Hurwitz, *Theodore Roosevelt and Labor in New York State, 1880–1900* (Columbia University Press, 1943), p. 105.
15. *Autobiography* in *Works,* Vol. XXII, pp. 95, 96, 110, 111.
16. Hurwitz, p. 11.
17. William Henry Harbaugh, *The Life and Times of Theodore Roosevelt* (Collier Books, new rev. ed., 1963), p. 40.
18. Roosevelt, "A Judicial Experience," *Outlook,* March 13, 1909.
19. Harbaugh, pp. 41–42.
20. Hurwitz, p. 88; Roosevelt citing "A Judicial Experience."
21. Roosevelt, ibid.
22. Harbaugh, p. 44.
23. Henry F. Pringle, *Theodore Roosevelt* (A Harvest Book, Harcourt Brace Jovanovich, 1931, 1956), p. 57.
24. *Works,* Vol. XXIII, p. 43.
25. *Works,* Vol. XVI, pp. 111–125.
26. Harbaugh, p. 77.
27. Pringle, p. 81.
28. *Autobiography* in *Works,* pp. 161, 162.
29. Pringle, p. 100.
30. *Autobiography* in *Works,* Vol. XXII, p. 241.
31. The quotes from Roosevelt's writings and speeches are taken from *Works,* Vol. XVI, chapter

entitled: *The Campaign of 1896*, pp. 384–413; and from letters and newspaper reports in Hurwitz, pp. 175–186.

32. *Works*, Vol. XVI, pp. 337 ff.
33. Ibid., p. 346.
34. *Review of Reviews*, September 1896, in *Works*, Vol. XVI, p. 49.
35. *Works*, Vol. XVI, p. 377.
36. *Works*, Vol. XXII, p. 246.
37. The phrase, "lunatic fringe," is credited first to Roosevelt in William Safire's *The New Language of Politics*, p. 360. Although "mollycoddle" is credited in that book (p. 396) to John Jay Chapman in 1900, there is no doubt that it was Roosevelt who made the word a popular one.
38. *Works*, Vol. XXIII, p. 118.
39. Roosevelt in 1886 had married Edith Carow.
40. Pringle, p. 126.
41. Morison, *Letters*, Vol. 3, p. 3, #1936.
42. *Works*, Vol. XXII, p. 311.
43. Ibid., p. 312.
44. Idem.
45. *Works*, Vol. XVI, p. 441.
46. Harbaugh, p. 115.
47. *Works*, Vol. XVII, p. 4.
48. Harbaugh, pp. 116, 117.
49. *Autobiography* in *Works*, Vol. XXII, p. 346.
50. Morison, *Letters*, Vol. 2, p. 1005, #1259.
51. *Autobiography* in *Works*, Vol. XXII, p. 347.
52. *Public Papers of Theodore Roosevelt, Governor 1899* (Albany, N.Y., Brandow Printing Co., 1900), p. 65.
53. *Public Papers 1900*, pp. 99–100.
54. Hurwitz, pp. 246, 247.
55. *Works*, Vol. XVII, p. 57.
56. Harbaugh, p. 123.
57. *Autobiography* in *Works*, Vol. XXII, p. 332.
58. Wilfred E. Binkley, *The Man in the White House* (Harper Colophon Books, 1964), p. 30.
59. *Works*, Vol. XVII, pp. 60 ff.
60. *Autobiography* in *Works*, Vol. XXII, pp. 320–322.
61. Morison, *Letters*, Vol. 2, #1486.
62. *Works*, Vol. XVI, p. 508.
63. Ibid., p. 571.
64. *Works*, Vol. XXII, pp. 405 ff.
65. C. Perry Patterson, *Presidential Government in the United States* (The University of North Carolina Press, 1947), p. 133.
66. Morison, *Letters*, Vol. 4, p. 886, #3172.
67. *Works*, Vol. XVII, p. 164.
68. *Autobiography* in *Works*, Vol. XXII, p. 398.
69. Theodore Roosevelt, *An Autobiography* (Scribners, new ed., 1913), p. 282.
70. Clinton Rossiter, *The American Presidency* (A Harvest Book, Harcourt Brace Jovanovich, 1956, 2nd ed., 1960), pp. 110–111.
71. Morison, *Letters*, Vol. 5, p. 170.
72. *Uncle Joe Cannon* as told to L. White Busbey (Holt, Rinehart & Winston, 1927), Introduction, p. xxxii.
73. Ibid., pp. 217, 219.
74. Ibid., pp. 222, 223.
75. Ibid., p. 224.
76. Ibid., p. 226.
77. Morison, *Letters*, Vol. 3, p. 466, #2639.
78. Ibid., p. 472, #2644.
79. Ibid., p. 649, #2864.
80. Roosevelt to Orville Platt (one of the "Big Four" of the Senate), November 1901: *Letters*, Vol. 3, p. 198, November 18, 1901. Roosevelt to Joseph Cannon before he became Speaker, June 13, 1902: *Letters*, Vol. 3, #2360. Roosevelt to Aldrich, August 26, 1902: *Letters*, Vol. 3, p. 323. Roosevelt to Aldrich: *Letters*, Vol. 3, p. 199.
81. *Works*, Vol XXIII, pp. 395–396.

82. Elmer E. Cornwell, Jr., *Presidential Leadership of Public Opinion* (Indiana University Press, 1966), p. 14.

83. Ibid., p. 14.

84. Ibid., p. 15.

85. Harbaugh, p. 48.

86. *Autobiography* in *Works,* Vol. XXII, p. 532.

87. Morison, *Letters,* Vol. 3, p. 337, #2456.

88. *Autobiography* in *Works,* Vol. XXII, p. 536. The story of the coal strike settlement is also told in *Works,* Vol XXIII, pp. 227–253.

89. Morison, *Letters,* Vol. 4, p. 1115, #3458.

90. Pringle, p. 197.

91. *Works,* Vol. XXIII, pp. 254, 257.

92. Pringle, p. 200.

93. Morison, *Letters,* Vol. 4, p. 723, #2963.

94. *Works,* Vol. XVII, p. 299.

95. Morison, *Letters,* Vol. 3, p. 688, #2916.

96. See Speaker Joe Cannon's version of this incident on pp. 64–65, this book.

97. See, for examples, Roosevelt to Payne, July 8, 1902: *Letters,* Vol. 3, #2383. Roosevelt to Jones, July 9, 1902: *Letters,* Vol. 3, p. 286, #2384.

98. Morison, *Letters,* Vol. 4, p. 834.

99. Ibid., Vol. 3, p. 375 *n.*

100. Ibid., p. 181, #2183, including note.

101. Ibid., Vol. 4, p. 825, #3093.

102. Ibid., p. 859, #3218.

103. *Works,* Vol. XVII, p. 196.

104. Ibid., p. 289.

105. Ibid., p. 345.

106. Erwin C. Hargrove, *Presidential Leadership* (Macmillan, 1966), pp. 21–22.

107. George E. Mowry, *The Era of Theodore Roosevelt* (Harper Torchbooks, Harper & Row, 1962), p. 202.

108. Morison, *Letters,* Vol. 5, p. 642, #4293.

109. Ibid., Vol. 3, p. 23, #1961.

110. Quoted in Sidney Warren, *The President as World Leader* (Lippincott, 1964), p. 36.

111. Morison, *Letters,* Vol. 4, #1144.

112. Ibid., #1143.

113. Ibid., Vol. 5, p. 473.

114. *Works,* Vol. XVII, p. 287.

115. Warren, p. 47.

116. Harbaugh, p. 291.

117. Ibid., p. 292.

118. Pringle, p. 314.

119. *New York Times,* September 29, 1972.

120. *New York Times,* September 30, 1972.

121. Harbaugh, p. 249.

122. *Works,* Vol. XXII, p. 18.

123. *Autobiography* in *Works,* Vol. XXII, p. 113.

124. Pringle, pp. 337, 338.

125. Morison, *Letters,* Vol. 6, p. 883, #4547.

126. Holmes was at the time the Chief Justice of Massachusetts.

127. Morison, *Letters,* Vol. 3, p. 288, #2386.

128. Harbaugh, p. 336.

129. Ibid., p. 336.

130. Busbey, p. 230.

131. Ibid., pp. 231, 232.

132. Ibid., p. 234.

133. Ibid., pp. 235, 236.

134. Ibid., p. 237.

135. Ibid., pp. 237–238.

136. Ibid., pp. 239–242.

137. H. L. Mencken, *Roosevelt: A Profile* (In American Century Series, ed. by Morton Keller, 1967), pp. 59, 60.

138. *Works,* Vol. XXIV, p. 157.
139. Harbaugh, p. 176.

CHAPTER TWO: Woodrow Wilson

1. As told by William Bayard Hale in *Woodrow Wilson* (Doubleday, 1912), pp. 200, 201.
2. Ibid., p. 184.
3. Joseph P. Tumulty, *Woodrow Wilson as I Know Him* (Doubleday, 1921), p. 457.
4. Arthur Walworth, *Woodrow Wilson* (Longmans, Green, 1958), p. 14.
5. Ibid., p. 17.
6. Hale, p. 63.
7. George Creel, *The War, the World, and Wilson* (Harper & Row, 1920), p. 17.
8. Clinton Rossiter, *The American Presidency* (A Harvest Book, Harcourt Brace Jovanovich, 1960), p. 104.
9. Eleanor Wilson McAdoo, *The Woodrow Wilsons* (Macmillan, 1937), pp. 59–60.
10. William Bayard Hale, *Woodrow Wilson, The Story of His Life* (Doubleday, 1912), p. 146.
11. Ibid., p. 152.
12. James Kerney, *The Political Education of Woodrow Wilson* (Prentice-Hall, 1926), p. 10.
13. Ray Stannard Baker, *Woodrow Wilson, Life and Letters, Governor 1910–1913* (Doubleday, 1931), Vol. III, p. 12.
14. Tumulty, pp. 17, 18.
15. Baker, Vol. III, p. 79.
16. Ibid., p. 21.
17. Tumulty, p. 37.
18. Ibid., pp. 39, 40, 41.
19. Ibid., p. 45.
20. Ibid., p. 58.
21. Walworth, p. 162.
22. Tumulty, p. 132.
23. Walworth, p. 162.
24. Baker, Vol. III, pp. 173, 174.
25. Hale, p. 200.
26. Baker, Vol. III, pp. 143, 144.
27. Ibid., p. 193.
28. Ibid., pp. 138, 139.
29. Ibid., pp. 147, 148.
30. Notes for an address before the Kansas Society, New York City, January 28, 1911.
31. Walworth, p. 189.
32. Ibid., p. 192.
33. Tumulty, pp. 79, 80.
34. Baker, Vol. III, pp. 7, 8.
35. Ibid., pp. 9, 10.
36. Tumulty, pp. 83–86.
37. Baker, Vol. III, pp. 250, 251.
38. Ibid, p. 252.
39. Woodrow Wilson to Mary A. Hulbert, January 7, 1912.
40. Baker, Vol. III, p. 260.
41. Josephus Daniels in the *Saturday Evening Post,* September 5, 1925.
42. Baker, Vol. III, p. 262.
43. Idem.
44. Ibid., p. 263.
45. Ibid., p. 265.
46. Idem.
47. Tumulty, p. 98.
48. Ibid., p. 121.
49. Baker, Vol. III, p. 334.
50. Ibid., pp. 335–336.
51. Ibid., p. 336.
52. Ibid., p. 337.
53. Tumulty, p. 117.

54. Ibid., p. 118.

55. Idem.

56. William J. Bryan, *Memoirs* (Holt, Rinehart & Winston, 1925), p. 173.

57. Official Report of the Proceedings of the National Democratic Convention, p. 129.

58. Ibid., p. 131.

59. Tumulty, p. 119.

60. Ibid., p. 120.

61. Baker, Vol. III, pp. 355, 356. Quotes within quotes taken from the Official Report of the Proceedings of the Democratic Convention, pp. 232, 234–237.

62. Ibid., Vol. III, p. 361.

63. Ibid., Vol. III, p. 369.

64. Arthur S. Link, *Wilson: The New Freedom* (Princeton University Press, 1956), p. 1.

65. Tumulty, p. 125.

66. Idem.

67. Ibid., pp. 125, 126.

68. Charles Seymour, *Intimate Papers of Colonel House: Behind the Political Curtain 1912–1915* (compiled and arranged as a narrative), (Houghton Mifflin, Riverside Press, 1926), pp. 72, 73.

69. Ibid., p. 74.

70. Baker, Vol. III, p. 374.

71. Ibid., p. 213.

72. *Crowded Years: The Reminiscenses of William G. McAdoo* (Houghton Mifflin, Riverside Press, 1931).

73. Interview in the Baltimore *Sun,* October 7, 1912; Baker, Vol. III, p. 375.

74. Baker, Vol III, p. 375.

75. Ibid., p. 381. Acceptance Speech.

76. Samuel Gompers, *Seventy Years of Life and Labor* (Dutton, 1925), pp. 543–544.

77. Baker, Vol. III, p. 394.

78. Ibid., p. 398.

79. *New York Times,* November 1, 1912.

80. Baker, p. 406.

81. Ibid., p. 411.

82. Ibid., Vol. III, pp. 434–435.

83. Link, p. 37.

84. Arthur S. Link, *The Higher Realism of Woodrow Wilson* (Vanderbilt University Press, 1971), p. 59.

85. Baker, Vol. III, p. 436.

86. *The Public Papers of Woodrow Wilson* (Harper & Row, 1925), Vol. I, pp. 215–216.

87. *New York Times,* Friday, July 27, 1973, article on editorial page, by Thomas Frank and Edward Weisband.

88. Baker, Vol. III, p. 447.

89. Woodrow Wilson to A. S. Burleson, April 4, 1913, *Wilson Papers.*

90. *New York Times,* December 14, 1913.

91. Baker, Vol. III, p. 454.

92. *House Papers* (Seymour), Vol. I, p. 111.

93. Baker, Vol. III, p. 458.

94. February 10, 1913.

95. February 23, 1913.

96. *House Papers* (Seymour), February 21, 1913.

97. Link, *Wilson: The New Freedom,* p. 23.

98. Ibid., p. 24.

99. W. J. Bryan to W. Wilson, August 16, 1913, *The Public Papers of Woodrow Wilson.*

100. Ibid., W. J. Bryan to W. Wilson, June 22, 1914.

101. Ibid., W. Wilson to C. W. Eliot, September 17, 1913.

102. Link, *Wilson: The New Freedom,* p. 158.

103. Baker, Vol. IV, p. 43.

104. Ibid., p. 45.

105. Ibid., p. 46.

106. Link, *Wilson: The New Freedom,* pp. 58, 59.

107. Ibid., p. 60 (from New York *Outlook,* CIII, March 15, 1913).

108. Josephus Daniels, *The Wilson Era, Years of Peace—1910–1917* (University of North Carolina, 1944), p. 137.

109. R. S. Baker, interview with L. M. Garrison, November 30, 1928. Baker Collection; Link, *Wilson: The New Freedom*, p. 75.

110. *House Papers* (Seymour), September 6, 1913.

111. Ibid., November 14, 1914.

112. Ibid., August 27, 1916.

113. Link, *Wilson: The New Freedom*, pp. 76, 77.

114. Ibid., p. 145.

115. Ibid., p. 179.

116. *New York Times*, April 8, 1913. (Baker, Vol. IV, p. 105.)

117. Baker, Vol. IV, p. 108.

118. Ibid., p. 109.

119. *New York Times*, April 10, 1913. (Baker, Vol. IV, p. 109.)

120. *Uncle Joe Cannon*, as told to L. White Busbey (Holt, Rinehart & Winston, 1927), Introductory Note, pp. xxxix, xl.

121. Baker, Vol. IV, p. 114.

122. *The Public Papers of Woodrow Wilson*, Vol. III, p. 36.

123. Baker, Vol. IV, p. 122.

124. *The Public Papers of Woodrow Wilson*, Vol. III, p. 52 (Baker, Vol. IV, p. 128.)

125. Paul Leland Haworth, *The United States in Our Times, 1865–1924* (Scribners, rev. ed., 1924), p. 383.

126. Arthur S. Link, *Woodrow Wilson and the Progressive Era, 1910–1917* (Harper Torchbooks, Harper & Row, 1954), p. 38.

127. Quoted in Link, *Wilson: The New Freedom*, p. 197.

128. H. Parker Willis, *The Federal Reserve System: Legislation, Organization and Opinion* (Ronald Press, 1923), pp. 79–83.

129. Baker, Vol. IV, p. 138. Quotes from New York *World*, August 8, 1912, and from Willis, p. 140.

130. Ibid.

131. Carter Glass, *An Adventure in Constructive Finance* (Doubleday, 1927), pp. 81–82.

132. Ibid., p. 82.

133. Ibid., pp. 82–83.

134. Willis, p. 169.

135. Baker, Vol. IV, p. 163, footnote 1: Letter, Louis D. Brandeis to Woodrow Wilson, June 14, 1913, a letter reviewing the main points dealt with in the interview of the 11th.

136. Glass, p. 115–116.

137. Ibid., p. 115.

138. Ibid., p. 130.

139. Woodrow Wilson to Mary A. Hulbert, June 22, 1913.

140. *The Public Papers of Woodrow Wilson*, Vol. III, p. 40.

141. Link, *Woodrow Wilson and the Progressive Era*, p. 53.

142. Address at Nashville, Tennessee, February 24, 1912. *The Public Papers of Woodrow Wilson*, Vol. II, pp. 410–411.

143. *New York Times*, January 3, 1914.

144. Ibid., January 4, 1914.

145. Baker, Vol. IV., pp. 371, 372.

146. May 30, 1914.

147. Baker, Vol. IV, p. 55 (to E. G. Conklin at Princeton University).

148. Link, *Wilson: The New Freedom*, p. 279.

149. *Foreign Relations*, 1913, pp. 170–171 (Link, *Wilson: The New Freedom*, p. 285).

150. R. M. LaFollette, "Dollar Diplomacy," *LaFollette's Weekly*, V (March 29, 1913), I; Link, *Wilson: The New Freedom*, p. 286.

151. *New York Times*, March 21, 1913.

152. Link, *Woodrow Wilson and the Progressive Era*, p. 108.

153. Baker, Vol. IV, p. 250.

154. David F. Houston, *Eight Years with Wilson's Cabinet* (Doubleday, 1926), p. 44.

155. Baker, Vol. IV, p. 66.

156. Ibid., Vol. IV, p. 243.

157. Ibid., p. 245, quoted from an interview with Woodrow Wilson by Samuel G. Blythe, April 27, 1914, *Saturday Evening Post*, May 23, 1914. *The Public Papers of Woodrow Wilson*, Vol. III, p. 111.

158. Baker, Vol. IV, pp. 266, 267. From original draft among Wilson papers. See also Wilson's

address, August 27, 1913, in which these instructions were laid before Congress. *The Public Papers of Woodrow Wilson,* Vol. III, pp. 45–51.

159. *The Public Papers of Woodrow Wilson,* Vol. III, p. 51.

160. Link, *Woodrow Wilson and the Progressive Era,* p. 115.

161. Burton J. Hendrick, *The Life and Letters of Walter Hines Page* (Doubleday, 1922), Vol. I, pp. 204, 205.

162. Draft of a note in the State Department Papers. Link, *Wilson: The New Freedom,* p. 368.

163. The Secretary of State to the American Embassy, October 24, 1913, original in the Wilson Papers, copy in the Bryan Papers, Library of Congress. Link, *Wilson: The New Freedom,* p. 369.

164. Moore to Woodrow Wilson, October 28, 1913, State Department Papers, Link, *Wilson: The New Freedom,* p. 374.

165. Link, *The Higher Realism of Woodrow Wilson,* p. 76.

166. Link, *Woodrow Wilson and the Progressive Era,* p. 121.

167. Quoted in ibid., p. 124.

168. Ibid., p. 144.

169. *The Public Papers of Woodrow Wilson,* Vol. III, p. 146.

170. Tumulty, p. 159.

171. Ibid., p. 160.

172. Link, *Wilson: The New Freedom,* pp. 281, 282.

173. *New York Times,* May 10, 1913.

174. *House Papers* (Seymour), p. 238.

175. Ibid, p. 239.

176. Ibid., p. 240.

177. Ibid., p. 241.

178. Ibid., pp. 242, 243.

179. Hendrick, Vol. I, pp. 277, 278.

180. Ibid., p. 279.

181. *House Papers* (Seymour), Vol. I, p. 258.

182. Ibid, p. 274.

183. Ibid., p. 271.

184. Idem.

185. Ibid., pp. 273, 274.

186. McAdoo, pp. 290–291.

187. Baker, Vol V, p. 2, citing *New York Times,* August 4, 1914.

188. Woodrow Wilson to A. W. Trenholm, August 2, 1914 (Baker, Vol. V, p. 1).

189. Tumulty, p. 227.

190. Baker, Vol. IV, p. 477.

191. Foreign Relations of the U.S., Supplement 1914, p. 19.

192. Ibid., pp. 24–25.

193. Ibid., p. 37.

194. Hendrick, p. 310.

195. Baker, Vol. IV., pp. 395–403.

196. W. H. Page to E. M. House, August 25, 1913, in Hendrick, Vol. I, p. 247.

197. Link, *Woodrow Wilson and the Progressive Era,* p. 92 (quote from *The Public Papers of Woodrow Wilson,* "The New Democracy I," pp. 92–93).

198. Baker, Vol. IV, pp. 406, 407.

199. Woodrow Wilson to Charles H. Grasty, of the Baltimore *Sun,* March 5, 1914 (Baker, Vol. IV, p. 408).

200. Link, *Woodrow Wilson and the Progressive Era,* p. 92.

201. Baker, Vol. IV, p. 421, Professor Stockton Axson to the author.

202. Wilson to Bryan, September 11, 1914, Wilson Papers; Link, *Woodrow Wilson and the Progressive Era,* p. 148.

203. Woodrow Wilson to R. Lansing, August 22, 1914, Wilson Papers.

204. Woodrow Wilson to Frank E. Doremus, September 14, 1914. *The Public Papers of Woodrow Wilson,* Vol. III., p. 167.

205. McAdoo, p. 296.

206. Chicago *Evening Post,* August 25, 1914 (Link, *The Struggle for Neutrality 1914–1915,* Princeton University Press, 1960).

207. Link, *The Struggle for Neutrality 1914–1915,* p. 90.

208. E. Root to C. W. Wilson, Root Papers.

209. Link, *The Struggle for Neutrality 1914–1915,* p. 149.

210. H. C. Lodge to T. Roosevelt, March 1, 1915, Roosevelt Papers (Link, *The Struggle for Neutrality 1914–1915* p. 158).

211. McAdoo, p. 299.

212. Sheppard to Wilson, October, 1914, The Papers of Woodrow Wilson, Library of Congress.

213. S. G. McLendon to Woodrow Wilson, September 18, 1914. Wilson Papers.

214. *New York Times,* September 29, 1914 (Link, *The Higher Realism of Woodrow Wilson,* p. 313).

215. Link, *The Higher Realism of Woodrow Wilson,* p. 315.

216. *New York Times,* October 8, 1914.

217. Ibid., February 3, 1915.

218. Baker, Vol. V, p. 77 (reported to the author by Josephus Daniels).

219. Ibid, p. 79. Letter to Frank E. Doremus, September 4, 1914. *The Public Papers of Woodrow Wilson,* Vol. III, p. 166.

220. Woodrow Wilson to Oscar Underwood, October 17, 1914. *The Public Papers of Woodrow Wilson,* Vol. III, p. 193.

221. Baker, Vol. IV, p. 49.

222. Tumulty, p. 101.

223. *The Memoirs of William Jennings Bryan,* p. 376.

224. Foreign Relations of the U.S., Supplement 1914, p. 573, 574.

225. Creel, p. 31.

226. Link, *The Struggle for Neutrality 1914–1915,* pp. 139, 140 (from the version of this address printed in *Foreign Relations,* 1914, pp. xi–xix).

227. Ibid., p. 140.

228. Ibid., p. 139.

229. *House Papers* (Seymour), p. 297.

230. Baker, Vol. V.

231. *House Papers* (Seymour), p. 304.

232. Ibid., p. 350.

233. Link, *The Struggle for Neutrality 1914–1915,* pp. 202, 203. Quote from letter of Woodrow Wilson to H. A. Bridgman, January 6, 1913. *The Public Papers of Woodrow Wilson.*

234. Ibid., *House Papers* (Seymour), December 3, 1914.

235. Idem.

236. Recorded in *Working with Roosevelt* by Samuel I. Rosenman (Harper & Row, 1952), pp. 440–443.

237. *House Papers* (Seymour), January 13, 1915.

238. Ibid., p. 356.

239. A. Zimmermann to E. M. House, Wilson Papers.

240. *House Papers* (Seymour), February 17, 1915.

241. Woodrow Wilson to E. M. House, February 20, 1915, Baker Collection.

242. Hendrick, Vol. II, p. 2.

243. *New York Times,* May 11, 1915.

244. Frank Parker Stockbridge, undated memorandum in the Baker Collection.

245. Transcript of press conference, May 11, 1915, Severn Papers.

246. From "Memorandum of the German Government . . . ," dated February 4, 1915, *Foreign Relations,* 1915, Supplement, pp. 96–97.

247. Link, *Woodrow Wilson and the Progressive Era,* pp. 166, 167.

248. Hendrick, Vol. III, p. 245.

249. Woodrow Wilson to Mrs. Crawford Toy, May 23, 1915. Baker Collection, quoted in Baker, Vol. VI, p. 397.

250. Woodrow Wilson to William Jennings Bryan, June 2, 1915, the Lansing Papers (Department of State, Washington, D.C., 1939–1940), I, pp. 418–419.

251. From Wilson's own typed draft, which he transcribed from his shorthand notes (quoted in Link, *The Struggle for Neutrality 1914–1915,* p. 416).

252. *House Papers* (Seymour), *From Neutrality to War 1915–1917,* p. 3.

253. Ibid., June 24, 1915.

254. Houston, Vol. I, p. 141.

255. *War Memoirs of Robert Lansing, Secretary of State* (Bobbs-Merrill, 1935), p. 15.

256. *House Papers* (Seymour), 1915–1917, p. 9.

257. June 15, 1916 (quoted in Link, *The Struggle for Neutrality 1914–1915,* p. 431).

258. C. Spring Rice to E. Grey, June 23, 1915, *The Letters of Sir Cecil Spring Rice,* Vol. II, p. 274.

259. G. Harvey, "America First!" *North American Review,* ccll (August 1915), 167.

260. *Berliner Tageblatt,* July 26, 1915, quoted in Link, *The Struggle for Neutrality 1914–1915,* p. 449.

261. The Secretary of State to Ambassador Gerard, July 21, 1915, *Foreign Relations,* 1915 Supplement, pp. 480–482. (Excerpted from quotes by Link, *The Struggle for Neutrality 1914–1915,* pp. 446, 447, 448.)

262. Arthur S. Link, *Wilson the Diplomatist; A Look at His Foreign Policies* (Johns Hopkins Press, 1957), p. 21.

263. Ambassador Page to the Secretary of State, June 22, 1915, *Foreign Relations* (**212**), 1915 Supplement, pp. 443–445. Extracted from Link, *The Struggle for Neutrality 1914–1915,* p. 594.

264. Ambassador Page to Secretary of State, July 24, 1915, *Foreign Relations* (**212**), 1915 Supplement, pp. 168–171. (Ibid., Link.)

265. *House Papers* (Seymour), June 24, 1915.

266. L. M. Garrison to William E. Brooks, February 29, Brooks Papers (1) & (2), quoted in Link, *Wilson: The New Freedom,* p. 121.

267. Tumulty, p. 246.

268. Ibid., p. 243.

269. *House Papers* (Seymour), *From Neutrality to War* 1915–1917, pp. 17, 18.

270. Ibid., p. 18.

271. Link, *Woodrow Wilson and the Progressive Era,* p. 179.

272. Ibid., pp. 183, 184.

273. Kitchin to Bryan, Feb. 9, 1916, Kitchin Papers (quoted in Link, *Woodrow Wilson and the Progressive Era,* p. 196).

274. Link, *Wilson: The New Freedom,* p. 188.

275. Link, *Woodrow Wilson and the Progressive Era,* p. 234.

276. Link, *Confusion and Crises 1915–1916* (Princeton University Press, 1964), p. 324.

277. Ibid., p. 325. A. Pinchot to N. Hapgood, c. January 29, 1916, Wilson Papers.

278. Ibid, p. 326; R. M. LaFollette, "Brandeis," *LaFollette's Magazine,* **VII** (February 1916), p. 2.

279. Link, *Woodrow Wilson and the Progressive Era,* p. 233.

280. Ibid., p. 233 *n.*

281. Walter Lippmann, "The Case for Wilson," *New Republic,* **VIII** (October 14, 1916), 263–264. Quoted in Link, *Woodrow Wilson and the Progressive Era,* pp. 240–241.

282. Wilson to O'Leary, Sept. 29, 1916, *New York Times,* September 30, 1916, quoted in Link, *Woodrow Wilson and the Progressive Era,* p. 247.

283. Link, *Confusion and Crises,* p. 106.

284. Ibid., p. 102, E. M. House to E. Grey, September 3, 1915, *House Papers* (Seymour).

285. Ibid., p. 103, E. Grey to E. M. House, September 22, 1915, *House Papers* (Seymour).

286. Ibid., p. 104, E. M. House to E. Grey, October 17, 1915, *House Papers* (Seymour).

287. Link, *Woodrow Wilson and the Progressive Era,* p. 199, quote, House to Wilson, November 10, 1915, Woodrow Wilson Papers in the Library of Congress.

288. Ibid., p. 203, quotes from House to Wilson, February 3, 1916, Wilson Papers.

289. *House Papers* (Seymour), 1915–1917, p. 165.

290. Ibid., p. 178.

291. W. W. to E. M. House, December 24, 1915, *House Papers* (Seymour). Long Letter quoted Link, *Confusion and Crises,* pp. 112, 113.

292. Ibid.

293. Ibid., p. 141.

294. The word "probably" was inserted by President Wilson when approval was cabled to Sir Edward Grey.

295. *House Papers* (Seymour), 1915–1917, pp. 219, 220; quoted in Link, *Confusion and Crises,* pp. 134, 135.

296. Link, *Confusion and Crises,* p. 137.

297. *House Papers* (Seymour), 1915–1917, p. 282.

298. Link, *Confusion and Crises,* p. 142.

299. Ibid., p. 144, Woodrow Wilson to E. M. House, February 16, 1916, *The Public Papers of Woodrow Wilson.*

300. Ibid., pp. 168, 169.

301. Ibid., p. 171, W. J. Stone to Woodrow Wilson, February 24, 1916, *The Public Papers of Woodrow Wilson.*

302. Ibid., pp. 172, 173.

303. Ibid., p. 175.

304. Idem.

305. Idem.

306. *New York Times,* July 25, 1916, quoted in Link, *Campaigns for Progressivism and Peace* (Princeton University Press, 1965), p. 67.

307. Ibid., Woodrow Wilson to E. M. House, July 23, 1916 *House Papers* (Seymour).

308. Ibid., p. 68, Woodrow Wilson to E. M. House, July 27, 1916, *House Papers* (Seymour).

309. Ibid., p. 70, *New York Times,* September 1, 1916.

310. Ibid., p. 71, Woodrow Wilson to E. M. House, July 23, 1916, House Papers.

311. Lansing, *War Memoirs,* pp. 166, 167.

312. Hendrick, Vol. II, pp. 187, 188.

313. Lansing, p. 173.

314. Baker, Vol. VI, p. 382.

315. Ibid., p. 380.

316. Ibid., p. 387.

317. Link, *Campaigns for Progressivism and Peace* (Princeton University Press, 1965), pp. 187, 188.

318. Baker, Vol. VI, p. 387.

319. Lansing, pp. 183, 184.

320. Baker, Vol. VI, p. 389.

321. Houston, Vol. I, p. 219.

322. To Lady Mary Paget, Baker, Vol. VI, p. 411.

323. Baker, Vol. VI, p. 400.

324. Lansing, pp. 186–187.

325. Ibid., p. 190.

326. Link, *The Higher Realism of Woodrow Wilson,* p. 85.

327. Lansing, *War Memoirs,* p. 406, quotation from Savage, *Policy of the United States Toward Maritime Commerce in War,* Vol. II, p. 539.

328. Baker, Vol. VI, p. 409, quoting *Official German Documents,* Vol. II, p. 1087.

329. Ibid., pp. 409–410.

330. Ibid., p. 411.

331. Ibid., p. 419, spoken at Guildhall, January 11, *New York Times,* January 12, 1917.

332. *House Papers* (Seymour), Vol. II, p. 412.

333. Baker, Vol. VI, p. 414, quoting *The Public Papers of Woodrow Wilson,* Vol. IV, p. 413. From address to Congress, January 22, 1917.

334. January 25, 1917.

335. Lansing, p. 195.

336. *Selected Literary and Political Papers and Addresses of Woodrow Wilson* (Grosset & Dunlap, 1927), Vol. 2., p. 222.

337. Ibid., p. 219.

338. Link, *Campaigns for Progressivism and Peace,* pp. 268, 269.

339. Ibid., p. 269, quoting *New York Times,* January 23, 1917.

340. Ibid., January 26, 1917.

341. Ibid., January 24, 1917.

342. Ibid., p. 266.

343. Ibid., p. 275, quoting C. Spring Rice to A. J. Balfour, January 26, 1917, S. Guynn (ed.), *The Letters of Sir Cecil Spring Rice,* Vol. II, pp. 374–375.

344. Ibid., pp. 285, 286.

345. Ibid., p. 288. Quotations from the Imperial Chancellor to Ambassador Bernstorff, January 29, 1917, *Official German Documents,* pp. 1048–1050.

346. Lansing, p. 206.

347. Ibid., p. 204.

348. Ibid., pp. 138, 139.

349. Ibid., pp. 139–140.

350. Ibid., p. 140.

351. Ibid., p. 213.

352. Baker, Vol. VI, p. 455.

353. Houston, Vol. I, p. 229.

354. Ibid., p. 230.

355. *Political Papers and Addresses,* Vol. 2, p. 233.

356. Ibid., p. 232.

357. Ibid., pp. 232, 233.

358. February 4, 1917.

359. H. C. Lodge to T. Roosevelt, February 13, 1917, Roosevelt Papers.

360. H. D. Baker to L. Wood, February 3, 1917, copy in *The Public Papers of Woodrow Wilson,* (Page 309; Link 1915–1917)

361. *New York Times,* February 6, 9, 1917 (Ibid.)

362. *New York World,* February 20, 1917 (Ibid.)

363. *New York Times,* February 4, 6, 7, 21, 23, 1917 (Ibid.)

364. Ibid., Feb. 11, 12, 1917 (Ibid.)

365. James MacGregor Burns, *Roosevelt: The Soldier of Freedom* (Harcourt Brace Jovanovich, 1970) p. 104.

366. Houston, Vol. 1, p. 234.

367. Ibid., p. 237.

368. Baker, Vol. VI, p. 480, quoting *New York Times,* March 5, 1917.

369. Ibid., from Congressional Record 64–2, pp. 4988–4989. Note: Link refers to 11 votes.

370. Link, *Campaigns for Progressivism and Peace,* p. 376.

371. Ibid., p. 365.

372. March 4 was a Sunday; he took the oath privately. The inaugural ceremonies were held on the 5th.

373. Lansing, p. 233.

374. E. D. Cronon (ed.), *Cabinet Diaries of Josephus Daniels,* pp. 116–117. (Quoted in Link, *Campaigns for Progressivism and Peace,* p. 398.)

375. Link, *Campaigns for Progressivism and Peace,* pp. 398, 399, quoting John L. Heaton, "Cobb of the World." This is a condensation.

376. "Memorandum of the Cabinet Meeting: 2:30–5:00 P.M., Tuesday, March 20, 1917," Lansing Diary. Quoted in its entirety in Link, *Campaigns for Progressivism and Peace,* pp. 401–408.

377. *House Papers* (Seymour), 1916–1917, p. 468.

378. Lansing, p. 237.

379. Woodrow Wilson to J. Daniels, March 24, 1917, Daniels Papers, quoted Baker, Vol. VI, p. 409.

380. *The Public Papers of Woodrow Wilson,* Vol. 11, p. 294, quoted Baker, Vol. VI, p. 491.

381. Ambassador Page to the Secretary of State, February 11, 1917, *Foreign Relations,* Supplement I, pp. 41–44, quoted in Link, *Campaigns for Progressivism and Peace,* p. 317.

382. Jane Addams, who visited the White House with other members of the Emergency Peace Foundation on February 28, later recounted this statement of Wilson's. Jane Addams, "Peace and Bread in Time of War," p. 64, quoted in Link, *Campaigns for Progressivism and Peace,* p. 414.

383. Link, *Campaigns for Progressivism and Peace,* p. 396.

384. Note: He did not, however, recognize the Bolshevik government when it overthrew the Kerensky government.

385. Lansing, p. 240.

386. *Political Papers and Addresses,* pp. 236–238.

387. Lansing, p. 241.

388. *Political Papers and Addresses,* p. 239.

389. Ibid., pp. 240–242.

390. Ibid., p. 242.

391. Lansing, pp. 242, 243.

392. *New York Times,* April 3, 1917, quoted in Link, *Campaigns for Progressivism and Peace,* p. 426.

393. *House Papers* (Seymour), April 1917–June 1918, p. 2. House to Lord Bryce, June 10, 1917.

394. Lansing, p. 258.

395. Ibid., p. 259.

396. Ibid., pp. 269–271.

397. Walworth, p. 107.

398. John J. Pershing, *My Experience in the World War* (Frederick A. Stokes, 1931), Vol. I, p. 37.

399. Walworth, p. 108.

400. Kerney, p. 396.

401. Rossiter, p. 105.

402. Walworth, pp. 118, 119.

403. Walworth, Vol. II, p. 130, 131.

404. Ibid., note on p. 131.

405. *House Papers* (Seymour), April 1917–June 1918, pp. 48, 49, 50.

406. Arthur S. Link, *Wilson the Diplomatist* (Johns Hopkins Press, 1957), p. 99.
407. Baker, Vol. VII, p. 180.
408. *House Papers* (Seymour), "April 1917–June 1918," p. 61.
409. Ibid., pp. 168.
410. Ibid., p. 169.
411. Ibid., p. 172.
412. *Political Papers and Addresses*, Vol. 2, p. 259.
413. Ibid., p. 257.
414. *House Papers* (Seymour), "April 1917–June 1918," p. 329.
415. *Political Papers and Addresses*, Vol. 2, pp. 257, 258.
416. Walworth, Vol. II, p. 153.
417. *House Papers* (Seymour), "April 1917–June 1918," pp. 342, 343.
418. Ibid., p. 347.
419. Wilson's second note to Allied Ambassadors regarding Japanese Expedition, March 5, 1918. *House Papers* (Seymour), April 1917–June 1918, p. 419.
420. Ibid., p. 401.
421. Ibid., p. 416.
422. *Political Papers and Addresses*, Vol. 2, pp. 262–272.
423. *House Papers* (Seymour), "The Ending of the War," June 1918-August 1919, p. 88.
424. Ibid., p. 161.
425. Ibid., p. 165, 166.
426. Ibid., p. 168.
427. Ibid., p. 185.
428. Sidney Warren, *The President as World Leader* (Lippincott, 1964), p. 107.
429. Ibid., p. 108.
430. Ibid., pp. 111, 112.
431. Robert Lansing, *The Peace Negotiations* (Houghton Mifflin, 1921), p. 22.
432. Ibid., pp. 23, 24.
433. Ibid., p. 26.
434. *House Papers* (Seymour), "The Ending of the War, June 1918-August 1919," p. 209.
435. Houston, Vol. I, p. 349.
436. *House Papers* (Seymour), "June 1918-August 1919," pp. 209, 210.
437. Ibid., p. 212.
438. Ibid., pp. 213, 214.
439. Ibid., p. 215.
440. Ibid., p. 216.
441. Idem.
442. Warren, pp. 109, 110.
443. *Political Papers and Addresses*, Vol. II, p. 298.
444. Ibid., p. 296.
445. Houston, Vol. I, p. 353.
446. Link, *The Higher Realism of Woodrow Wilson*, pp. 82–83.
447. Creel, p. 159.
448. *Political Papers and Addresses*, Vol. II, pp. 312–313.
449. Warren, p. 113.
450. Ibid., p. 114, quoting David Lloyd George.
451. Ibid., p. 113.
452. Ibid., p. 114.
453. Lansing, *The Peace Negotiations* (Houghton Mifflin, 1921), p. 3.
454. Warren, p. 115, quotation in Edith Bolling Wilson, *My Memoir* (New York, 1939), pp. 245–246.
455. Walworth, Vol. II, pp. 226–227.
456. *Political Papers and Addresses*, pp. 319–321.
457. Ibid., pp. 322, 323.
458. Ibid., p. 287.
459. Ibid., pp. 290, 291.
460. Walworth, Vol. II, p. 220.
461. *House Papers* (Seymour), June 1918-August 1919, p. 285.
462. Warren, pp. 115, 116.
463. Walworth, Vol. II, p. 241.
464. Ibid., p. 242.

465. Ibid., p. 248.

466. Ibid., footnote p. 251.

467. Warren, p. 116.

468. Creel, p. 174.

469. Ibid., pp. 174, 175.

470. Ibid., p. 175.

471. Walworth, p. 270.

472. Ibid., pp. 271, 272.

473. Ibid., pp. 272, 273.

474. Warren, p. 118.

475. Idem.

476. Quoted in Warren, pp. 118, 119.

477. Baker and Dodd, *War and Peace,* Vol. I, pp. 523–524.

478. Link, *Wilson the Diplomatist,* pp. 117, 118.

479. Printed in the Congressional Record, Washington, Tuesday, October 9, 1973.

480. Walworth, p. 284.

481. Ibid., p. 286.

482. *House Papers* (Seymour), "June 1918-August 1919," p. 387, referring to letter R. S. Baker to House, March 19, 1919.

483. Lansing, *The Peace Negotiations,* pp. 215, 216.

484. *House Papers* (Seymour), "June 1918-August 1919," p. 396.

485. Ibid., p. 396 *n.*

486. Walworth, p. 341.

487. Warren, p. 124.

488. Richard B. Morris, *Great Presidential Decisions* (Lippincott, 3rd ed., 1965), p. 365.

489. Link, *Wilson the Diplomatist,* pp. 131, 132, quoting Baker and Dodd, *War and Peace,* Vol. I, pp. 548, 551–552.

490. McAdoo, p. 514.

491. Article X guaranteed the political independence and territorial integrity of every member nation throughout the world.

492. Houston, Vol. II, pp. 8–12.

493. Ibid., p. 17.

494. Walworth, p. 302.

495. Link, *Wilson the Diplomatist,* p. 130, quotation from Thomas A. Bailey, *Woodrow Wilson and the Great Betrayal* (Macmillan, 1945), p. 9.

496. Ibid., p. 131, quoted in Nicholas Murray Butler, *Across Busy Years, Recollections and Reflections,* Vol. III, pp. 197–201.

497. Ibid., pp. 132, 133.

498. Walworth, Vol. II, p. 361.

499. Ibid., p. 372.

500. Ibid., p. 373.

501. Warren, p. 132.

502. Ibid., p. 133, quoting Edith B. Wilson, pp. 296–297.

503. *House Papers* (Seymour), "June 1918-August 1919," p. 507.

504. Jacob Javits, *Who Makes War* (Morrow, 1973), pp. 208, 209.

505. Warren, p. 134, quoting Garrity, *Lodge,* p. 379.

506. Ibid., p. 135.

507. Walworth, p. 346.

508. Warren, p. 136.

509. Kerney, pp. 469–470.

510. McAdoo, p. 513.

511. Ibid., p. 523.

512. Ibid.

513. Ibid., p. 357.

514. Walworth, p. 364.

515. Ibid., pp. 364, 365.

516. Alexander L. George and Juliette L. George, *Woodrow Wilson and Colonel House, a Personality Study* (Dover Publications, 1964), p. 16.

517. Walworth, p. 123.

518. Hale, p. 223.

519. Thomas A. Bailey, *Presidential Greatness* (Prentice-Hall, 1966), p. 158.

520. He had resumed meeting regularly with the Cabinet starting October 19, 1920.

521. Houston, Vol. II, p. 148.

522. Idem.

523. Ibid., p. 149.

CHAPTER THREE: Franklin D. Roosevelt

1. Died in office.

2. As quoted by Frank Freidel, *Franklin D. Roosevelt—The Apprenticeship* (Little, Brown, 1952), p. 165.

3. Josephus Daniels, "Franklin Roosevelt as I Knew Him," *Saturday Evening Post,* September 24, 1932.

4. James MacGregor Burns, *The Lion and the Fox* (Harcourt Brace Jovanovich, 1956), p. 50.

5. Fleet Admiral Ernest J. King and Walter Muir Whitehill, *A Naval Record* (Norton, 1952), p. 101.

6. *The Public Papers and Addresses of Franklin D. Roosevelt* (Random House, 1933), p. 250.

7. *F.D.R. His Personal Letters,* 1928–1945, edited by Elliott Roosevelt (Duell, Sloan and Pearce, 1950), p. 238.

8. *F.D.R. His Personal Letters,* 1905–1928, edited by Elliott Roosevelt (Duell, Sloan and Pearce, 1948), pp. 256, 257.

9. Ibid., FDR to Howe, August 6, 1915.

10. *Letters,* 1905–1928, p. 288.

11. *Letters,* 1905–1928, p. 261.

12. Freidel, *Apprenticeship,* p. 266.

13. Ibid., p. 287.

14. *Public Papers,* 1939 (Macmillan, 1941), p. 116.

15. Ibid., p. 117.

16. *Letters,* 1905–1928, p. 363.

17. Ibid., pp. 364–367.

18. Frank Freidel, *Franklin D. Roosevelt, The Ordeal* (Little, Brown, 1954), p. 159.

19. *Public Papers,* 1928–1932 (Random House, 1938), p. 53.

20. Ibid., p. 30.

21. Cass Canfield, *Up and Down and Around* (Harper & Row, 1971), pp. 118–119.

22. They are discussed in Samuel I. Rosenman, *Working with Roosevelt* (Harper & Row, 1952), pp. 28–55.

23. *State of New York, Public Papers of Governor Franklin D. Roosevelt,* 1931, (J. B. Lyon, Printers, 1937), p. 172.

24. See p. 382, this book.

25. See pp. 419–420, this book.

26. *Public Papers,* 1928–1932, pp. 436–440.

27. See Rosenman, pp. 56–65.

28. *Public Papers,* 1928–1932, p. 625.

29. Freidel, *The Triumph,* p. 91.

30. *Public Papers,* 1928–1932, pp. 582–583.

31. *Public Papers,* 1934 (Random House), p. 55.

32. Raymond Moley, *After Seven Years* (Harper & Row, 1939), p. 33.

33. *Public Papers,* 1933 (Random House), p. 11.

34. Ibid., pp. 11–16.

35. Wilfred E. Binkley, *The President and Congress* (Knopf, 1947), p. 244.

36. *Review of Reviews,* May 1933.

37. William E. Leuchtenburg, *Franklin D. Roosevelt and the New Deal* (Harper Torchbooks, Harper & Row, 1963), p. 62.

38. *Public Papers,* 1934, p. 287.

39. Binkley, p. 246.

40. *Public Papers,* 1928–1932, p. 742.

41. *Events,* February 1938.

42. A good description of an actual conference may be found in an article by Theodore G. Joslin, former secretary to President Hoover, in the *Sunday Star,* Washington, D.C., March 4, 1934, excerpts from which appear in *Public Papers,* 1933, pp. 40 ff.

43. See, for example, his memo to the Secretary of the Treasury re: *New York Times* Column in *Letters,* 1928–1945, p. 612.

44. For the text, see *Public Papers,* 1940 (Macmillan), pp. 607–609.
45. For the text of the conference, see *Public Papers,* 1943 (Harper & Row), p. 569.
46. *Public Papers,* 1933, p. 60 *n.*
47. *Public Papers,* 1944–1945 (Harper & Row), p. 43 *n.*
48. Letter to Frank Walker, February 13, 1936, PPF 1125, Roosevelt Library.
49. Idem.
50. *Public Papers,* 1935 (Random House), p. 206.
51. *This I Remember* (Harper & Row, 1949), pp. 68, 69.
52. *Public Papers,* 1934, p. 6.
53. Roosevelt Library, PSF Box 97.
54. *Public Papers,* 1934, p. 57.
55. *Letters,* 1928–1945, p. 1139.
56. *Letters,* 1928–1945, p. 1205.
57. Roosevelt Library, PSF Box 101.
58. The bill sought to curtail the adjudicatory powers of the federal administrative agencies; it was vetoed December 18, 1940.
59. *Letters,* 1928–1945, p. 558.
60. Booth Mooney, *Roosevelt and Rayburn* (Lippincott, 1971), p. 92.
61. Rexford G. Tugwell, "The Compromising Roosevelt," *Western Political Quarterly,* Vol. VI, No. 2, June 1953.
62. *Public Papers,* 1935, p. 13.
63. Burns, p. 375.
64. *Letters,* 1928–1945, p. 416.
65. Documents reproduced in displays in, Rosenman, between pp. 336–337.
66. See Rosenman, pp. 463–470, for details, including the way Roosevelt's secretive style temporarily caused the plan to fizzle.
67. Eleanor Roosevelt, *This Is My Story* (Harper & Row, 1937), p. 162.
68. FDR to Sheley, August 21, 1940. *Letters,* 1928–1945, p. 1058.
69. Rosenman, pp. 104–105.
70. *Public Papers,* 1936 (Random House), p. 230.
71. Frances Perkins, *The Roosevelt I Knew* (Viking Press, 1946), pp. 359–360.
72. Clinton Rossiter, *The American Presidency* (A Harvest Book, Harcourt Brace Jovanovich, 1956), p. 130.
73. Robert E. Sherwood, *Roosevelt and Hopkins* (Harper & Row, 1948), pp. 72–73.
74. Mooney, pp. 215, 216.
75. *Public Papers,* 1936, pp. 604–610.
76. *Public Papers,* 1944–1945, p. 298.
77. *Letters,* 1928–1945, p. 450.
78. Ibid., pp. 449, 450.
79. *Public Papers,* 1935, p. 345.
80. *Letters,* 1928–1945, p. 555.
81. Ibid., p. 571.
82. *Public Papers,* 1937 (Macmillan), pp. 408–411.
83. Sidney Warren, *The President as World Leader* (Lippincott, 1964), p. 192.
84. See Welles's letter to this author in Rosenman, p. 167.
85. See *Public Papers,* 1937, pp. 414–425.
86. Warren, p. 193.
87. Ibid., p. 194.
88. Ickes, *Secret Diary,* Vol. II, p. 390.
89. Winston S. Churchill, *The Gathering Storm* (Houghton Mifflin, 1948), pp. 214–215.
90. *Public Papers,* 1938 (Macmillan), pp. 596–601.
91. *Public Papers,* 1939, p. 381.
92. Ibid., p. 455.
93. *Public Papers,* 1940, Introduction, pp. xxiii–xxxi.
94. Ibid., p. 437.
95. Ibid., pp. 449–510.
96. Basil Rauch, *Roosevelt, From Munich to Pearl Harbor* (Creative Age Press, 1950), p. 266.
97. James MacGregor Burns, *Roosevelt: The Soldier of Freedom* (Harcourt Brace Jovanovich, 1970), p. 112.
98. *The Memoirs of Cordell Hull* (Macmillan, 1948), P. 1111.
99. William D. Leahy, *I Was There* (Whittlesey House, McGraw-Hill, 1950), p. 8.
100. Ibid., p. 95.

101. Ibid., p. 106.

102. Henry L. Stimson and McGeorge Bundy, *On Active Service in Peace and War* (Harper & Row, 1947), pp. 665, 666.

103. King and Whitehill, p. 301.

104. Ibid., p. 136.

105. Winston S. Churchill, *Closing the Ring* (Houghton Mifflin, 1951), p. 344.

106. Herbert Feis, *Churchill Roosevelt Stalin* (Princeton University Press, 1957), p. 47.

107. Ibid., pp. 47, 48.

108. Maurice Matloff and Ervin M. Snell, *Strategic Planning for Coalition Warfare, 1941–1942* (Washington, Office of the Chief of Military History, Dept. of the Army, 1953), p. 177.

109. Feis, p. 48.

110. Winston S. Churchill, *The Hinge of Fate* (Houghton Mifflin, 1950), pp. 323, 324.

111. Ibid., pp. 271, 272.

112. Feis, p. 73.

113. Ibid., p. 75, 76.

114. Map Room, Box #3, #195, November 18, 1942, Roosevelt Library.

115. Map Room, Box #3, #210, November 11, 1942, Roosevelt Library.

116. Map Room, Box #3, #189, November 13, 1942, Roosevelt Library.

117. Map Room, Box #3, #210, November 11, 1942, Roosevelt Library.

118. Churchill, *Closing the Ring,* p. 346.

119. Fleet Admiral William D. Leahy, *I Was There* (Norton, 1952), pp. 158, 159.

120. Map Room, Box #4, #383, July 26, 1943, Roosevelt Library.

121. Idem.

122. Maurice Matloff and Ervin M. Snell, *Strategic Planning for Coalition Warfare, 1943–1944* (Washington, Office of the Chief of Military History, Dept. of the Army, 1953), p. 211.

123. Churchill, *Closing the Ring,* p. 132.

124. Ibid., p. 133.

125. Ibid., pp. 136, 137, 139.

126. Feis, p. 152.

127. Dwight D. Eisenhower, *Crusade in Europe* (Doubleday, 1948), p. 194.

128. Ibid., p. 195.

129. Map Room, Box #4, #438, October 7, 1943, Roosevelt Library.

130. Map Room, Box #4, October 7, 1943, Roosevelt Library.

131. Map Room, Box #4, October 8, 1943, Roosevelt Library.

132. Map Room, Box #4, #381, Roosevelt Library.

133. Map Room, Box #4, #445, October 9, 1943, Roosevelt Library.

134. Map Room, Box #4, #383, October 9, 1943, Roosevelt Library.

135. Eisenhower, p. 191.

136. Matloff and Snell, *Strategic Planning for Coalition Warfare, 1943–1944,* pp. 343, 344.

137. Ibid., p. 353.

138. Ibid., pp. 363, 364.

139. Sherwood, p. 780.

140. Matloff and Snell, *Strategic Planning for Coalition Warfare, 1943–1944,* p. 427

141. Map Room, Box #3, February 29, 1944, Roosevelt Library.

142. Feis, p. 340.

143. Map Room, Box #6, #549, June 2, 1944, Roosevelt Library.

144. Feis, p. 339.

145. Ibid.

146. Map Room, Box #6, #687, May 31, 1944, Roosevelt Library.

147. Hull, *Memoirs,* Vol. II, pp. 1453, 1454.

148. Map Room, Box #6, #557, June 10, 1944, Roosevelt Library.

149. Map Room, Box #6, #700, June 11, 1944, Roosevelt Library.

150. Map Room, Box #6, #560, June 12, 1944, Roosevelt Library.

151. Hull, *Memoirs,* Vol. II, p. 1456.

152. Map Room, Box #6, #565, June 22, 1944, Roosevelt Library.

153. Feis, p. 150.

154. Ibid., p. 228.

155. Matloff and Snell, *Strategic Planning for Coalition Warfare, 1943–1944,* p. 467.

156. Feis, p. 344.

157. Matloff and Snell, *Strategic Planning for Coalition Warfare, 1943–1944,* p. 471.

158. See pp. 402–403, of this book.

159. See pp. 399–402, of this book.

160. Map Room, Box #6, #721, Roosevelt Library.

161. Winston S. Churchill, *The Grand Alliance* (Houghton Mifflin, 1950), p. 28.

162. Matloff and Snell, *Strategic Planning for Coalition Warfare, 1943–1944,* pp. 471, 472.

163. Eisenhower, pp. 281–284.

164. Winston S. Churchill, *Triumph and Tragedy* (Houghton Mifflin, 1953), p. 216.

165. Feis, p. 442.

166. Churchill, *Triumph and Tragedy,* p. 219.

167. Map Room, Box #7, #795, Roosevelt Library.

168. Churchill, *Triumph and Tragedy,* pp. 226, 227, 228.

169. Feis, p. 449.

170. Ibid., p. 451.

171. Map Room, Box #7, #672, December 9, 1944, Roosevelt Library.

172. Feis, pp. 541, 542.

173. Ibid., p. 542.

174. Ibid., p. 547.

175. Ibid., pp. 549–550.

176. Ibid., p. 550.

177. John Ehrman, *Grand Strategy* (Her Majesty's Stationary Office, London, 1956–1972), Vol. 5, Appendix VI, p. 555.

178. *Public Papers,* 1943, pp. 133–134.

179. *Public Papers,* 1944–1945, p. 32.

180. Rosenman, p. 435.

181. *Public Papers,* 1944–1945, p. 284.

182. Rosenman, p. 479.

183. *Public Papers,* 1944–1945, pp. 537–548.

CHAPTER FOUR: Harry S. Truman

1. Forrest C. Pogue, *Organizer of Victory 1943–1945 George C. Marshall* (Viking Press, 1973), p. 558.

2. Harry S. Truman, *Memoirs: Year of Decision* (Doubleday, 1955), p. 82.

3. Alfred Steinberg, *The Man from Missouri* (Van Rees Press, 1962), p. 262.

4. Robert Murphy, *Diplomat Among Warriors* (Doubleday, 1964), p. 269.

5. Idem.

6. John Schrecker interviews Mr. Harriman, Channel 13 Brandeis Television Recollections, Monday, November 26, 1973.

7. Emmet John Hughes, *The Living Presidency* (Coward, McCann & Geoghegan, 1973), p. 32.

8. *Churchill, Taken from the Diaries of Lord Moran* (Houghton Mifflin, 1966), p. 393.

9. Steinberg, p. 167.

10. Ibid., p. 45.

11. Ibid., p. 50.

12. Ibid., p. 75.

13. August 3, 1924.

14. Steinberg, p. 88.

15. Ibid., p. 116.

16. Ibid., p. 120.

17. Ibid., p. 122.

18. Ibid., p. 123.

19. Executive Office of the President, Bureau of the Budget, Washington, D.C., Compilation of Information and Statements Which May Indicate or Suggest Possible Policies of President Truman, April 1945, pp. 1–2, 58–59.

20. Cited in Steinberg, p. 134.

21. Steinberg, p. 147.

22. Ibid., p. 148.

23. Ibid., p. 149.

24. Ibid., pp. 180, 181.

25. Ibid., pp. 181, 182.

26. Ibid., p. 183.

27. Ibid., p. 190.

28. Ibid., p. 195.

29. Samuel I. Rosenman, *Working with Roosevelt* (Harper & Row, 1952), pp. 443–445.

30. Robert Sherwood, *Roosevelt and Hopkins* (Harper & Row), pp. 881–882.

31. Joseph Lask, *Eleanor, The Years Alone* (Norton, 1972), p. 28.

32. Correspondence Between President Truman and Mrs. Roosevelt, Eleanor Roosevelt Papers, Hyde Park, N.Y. Box #4560. Permission to print given by Margaret Truman Daniel.

33. John Lewis Gaddis, *The United States and the Cold War* 1941–1947 (Columbia University Press, 1972), pp. 290, 210.

34. Ibid., p. 210.

35. Quotations cited in James David Barber, *The Presidential Character* (Prentice-Hall, 1972), p. 270.

36. Steinberg, p. 186.

37. Gaddis, pp. 218, 219.

38. Sherwood, p. 894.

39. Truman, p. 227.

40. Ibid., pp. 227–228.

41. Cited in Herbert Feis, *From Trust to Terror* (Norton, 1970), p. 9.

42. Truman, pp. 290, 291.

43. Gaddis, pp. 229, 230.

44. Ibid., pp. 230, 231.

45. Letter from Eleanor Roosevelt to Harry S. Truman, May 14, 1945, Roosevelt Library, Box #4560 of Eleanor Roosevelt Papers.

46. Herbert Feis, *Between War and Peace, the Potsdam Conference* (Princeton University Press, 1960), pp. 82, 83.

47. Ibid., p. 98.

48. Ibid., p. 107.

49. Ibid., p. 109.

50. Ibid., pp. 117, 118.

51. Truman press conference of June 13, 1945, Truman Public Papers, 1945, p. 123.

52. Gaddis, p. 229.

53. Charles E. Bohlen, *Witness to History 1929–1969* (Norton, 1973), p. 226.

54. Murphy, pp. 270–271.

55. Ibid., p. 272.

56. James F. Byrnes, *All in One Lifetime* (Harper & Row, 1958), p. 300.

57. Murphy, pp. 277, 278, 279.

58. Ibid., p. 279.

59. Leahy, pp. 427, 428.

60. Ibid., p. 432.

61. Herbert Feis, *Japan Subdued—The Atomic Bomb and the End of the War in the Pacific* (Princeton University Press, 1961), pp. 7, 8.

62. *Public Papers of the Presidents of the United States—Harry S. Truman, 1945* (United States Government Printing Office, 1961), p. 212.

63. Ibid., pp. 362–366.

64. Gaddis, pp. 253, 254, citing Frank McNaughton to *Time* home office, October 6, 1945, McNaughton MSS.

65. Ibid., p. 255, citing Vandenberg press statements of August 25, 1945, *New York Times,* September 9, 21, 1945.

66. Ibid., p. 257.

67. Ibid., p. 258.

68. *New York Times,* March 17, 1946.

69. Gaddis, pp. 267, 268.

70. Ibid., p. 278, citing Vandenberg Diary, December 11, 1945 (misdated).

71. Cabell Phillips, *The Truman Presidency* (Macmillan, 1966), p. 148.

72. Truman, p. 549.

73. Ibid., p. 550.

74. *Public Papers,* p. 3.

75. The quotations which follow are taken from the 16,000-word message which was the longest handed to Congress since Theodore Roosevelt's 21,000-word message of 1901. Therefore they illustrate the points which President Truman made and his stance, but are only brief excerpts from the whole piece.

76. *Public Papers,* pp. 263–309.

77. Truman, pp. 482–483.

78. Columbia University Oral History Memoir of Samuel I. Rosenman, p. 214.

79. William C. Berman, *The Politics of Civil Rights in the Truman Administration* (Ohio State University Press, 1970), citing Congressional Record, 75th Cong., 1st Sess., 1938, LXXXIII, 1166, 2007, p. 10.

80. Ibid., 76th Congress, 2nd Sess, 1940, LXXXVI, 10895.

81. Ibid., p. 16.

82. Ibid., citing Congressional Record, 76th Cong., 3rd Sess., 1940, LXXVI, Appendix 4546, pp. 11, 12.

83. Richard P. Longaker, *The Presidency and Individual Liberties* (Cornell University Press, 1961), p. 29.

84. Berman, pp. 44–47.

85. Louis W. Koenig, *The Truman Administration: Its Principles and Practices* (New York University Press, 1956), p. 118.

86. Berman, p. 62.

87. Ibid., p. 63.

88. Ibid., p. 75, quoting "Shelly v. Kraemer," 334 U.S.1 (1948).

89. Ibid., p. 83.

90. Ibid., p. 84, citing *Public Papers of the Presidents: Harry S. Truman, 1948,* p. 122.

91. Ibid., p. 85, citing ibid., 1948, p. 126.

92. Ibid., p. 89, citing *New York Times,* February 10, 1948, p. 1.

93. Ibid., p. 105.

94. Columbia University Oral History Memoir of Samuel I. Rosenman, p. 219. Note: There is an unsigned memorandum of June 29, 1948, in the Truman Library which details the advice referred to and which is attributed to Judge Rosenman.

95. Berman, p. 117.

96. Ibid., p. 118, citing *Freedom to Serve* (United States Government Printing Office, 1950) pp xi–xii.

97. Ibid., p. 118.

98. Ibid., p. 34. Roy Wilkins succeeded Walter White as executive secretary of the NAACP.

99. Ibid., p. 235, citing *Public Papers of the Presidents: Harry S. Truman 1952–1953,* p. 1202.

100. *The Truman Administration: A Documentary History,* Barton J. Bernstein and Allen J. Matusow, eds., (Harper Colophon Books, Harper & Row), p. 128.

101. Ibid., p. 131. Excerpt reprinted from Truman Papers, 1948, pp. 475–479.

102. Columbia Oral History, pp. 216, 217.

103. Ibid., p. 218.

104. Truman, p. 550.

105. Gaddis, p. 289.

106. Ibid., p. 290.

107. Ibid., p. 295, citing *New York Times,* February 26, 1946.

108. Ibid., p. 296.

109. Idem.

110. Ibid., p. 299.

111. Ibid., p. 304.

112. Churchill, quoted in ibid., p. 308.

113. Ibid., p. 315.

114. Ibid., pp. 336, 337.

115. Ibid., pp. 341, 342.

116. *Public Papers: 1946,* p. 189.

117. Dean Acheson, *Present at the Creation* (Norton, 1969), p. 219.

118. Ibid., p. 221.

119. Ibid, pp. 221, 222.

120. *Public Papers: 1947,* pp. 178–179.

121. Acheson, p. 223.

122. George F. Kennan, *Memoirs 1925–1950* (An Atlantic Monthly Press Book—Little, Brown, 1967), p. 344.

123. Acheson, pp. 233, 234.

124. Elmer E. Cornwell, Jr., *Presidential Leadership of Public Opinion* (Indiana University Press, 1966), pp. 168, 169.

125. Ibid., p. 169.

126. Ibid., p. 165, 166.

127. Ibid., pp. 166, 167.
128. Phillips, pp. 185, 186.
129. April 4, 1948.
130. Murphy, p. 303.
131. Idem.
132. Ibid., p. 304.
133. Ibid., pp. 306, 307.
134. Bohlen, p. 275.
135. Ibid., p. 275, 276.
136. Bernstein and Matusow, p. 272.
137. Ibid., pp. 277, 278.
138. Feis, *From Trust to Terror*, p. 342.
139. Murphy, p. 316.
140. Idem.
141. Ibid., p. 318.
142. Acheson, p. 266.
143. Ibid., p. 264.
144. Idem.
145. Feis, *From Trust to Terror*, p. 379.
146. Speech at Miami, Florida, August 22, 1949, cited in ibid., p. 380.
147. Feis, *From Trust to Terror*, p. 378.
148. Ibid., pp. 382, 383.
149. Wilfred E. Binkley, *The Man in the White House* (Harper Colophon Books, Harper & Row) p. 91.
150. John Lewis Gaddis, "Was The Truman Doctrine a Real Turning Point?" *Foreign Affairs*, January 1974, Vol. 52, No. 2, p. 386.
151. Ibid., p. 390.
152. Binkley, p. 91.
153. Acheson became Secretary of State upon General Marshall's retirement.
154. Phillips, p. 291.
155. Truman, *Memoirs*, Vol. 2, p. 332.
156. Phillips, pp. 292, 293.
157. Ibid., p. 295.
158. Ibid., p. 297.
159. Ibid., p. 317, citing Truman, *Memoirs*, pp. 362–363.
160. Ibid., p. 318.
161. Idem.
162. Ibid., pp. 322, 323.
163. Ibid., p. 325.
164. Ibid., p. 327.
165. Ibid., p. 330.
166. Ibid., p. 329.
167. Ibid., p. 330.
168. Ibid., p. 333.
169. Ibid., 339, 340.
170. Ibid., pp. 340, 341.
171. Ibid., pp. 341, 342, 343.
172. Ibid., pp. 343, 344.
173. Ibid., p. 113.
174. Ibid., pp. 114, 115.
175. Ibid., p. 115.
176. Ibid., pp. 115, 116.
177. Ibid., p. 117.
178. Clifford became counsel to the President upon Rosenman's resignation. However, the President, as in this case, would frequently request Rosenman to come to the White House at crucial moments. Ibid., pp. 117, 118.
179. Ibid., p. 122.
180. Arthur Krock, *New York Times Magazine*, April 7, 1946.
181. Acheson, p. 133.
182. John Robinson Beal, *Marshall in China* (Doubleday, 1970), p. 2.
183. Acheson, p. 147.

184. Bernstein and Matusow, pp. 330–332, citing United States relations with China, pp. 686–687.

185. Barbara W. Tuchman, *Stilwell and the American Experience in China 1911–45* (Macmillan, 1970), p. 327.

186. Ibid., pp. 346, 347, citing Department of State Bulletin, January 16, 1950, p. 79.

187. "State Department Employee Loyalty Investigation," Hearings before a subcommittee of the Senate Committee on Foreign Relations, 81st Congress, 2nd Sess. 1950, p. 1760.

188. Acheson, citing *The Taft Story* (Harper & Row, 1954), p. 85.

189. Ibid., citing *The United States in World Affairs* (Harper & Row, 1951), p. 57.

190. Truman, *Memoirs: Years of Trial and Hope*, Vol. 2, p. 429.

191. Sidney Warren, *The President as a World Leader* (Lippincott, 1964), pp. 346–347.

192. Phillips, p. 375.

193. Idem.

194. Ibid., pp. 376, 377.

195. Bernstein and Matusow, pp. 412–416, citing Congressional Record, 81st Congress, 2nd Sess. pp. 7894–7895.

196. Idem.

197. Ibid., pp. 417–420, citing excerpts in ibid., 82nd Congress, 1st Sess. pp. 10051–10052.

198. Warren, p. 348.

199. Phillips, p. 413.

200. Koenig, p. 94.

201. Acheson, p. 169, citing Truman, *Memoirs*, Vol. 2, Ch. 16, pp. 132–133.

202. Larry Collins and Dominique Lapierre, *O Jerusalem* (Simon and Schuster, 1972), p. 409.

203. Ibid., pp. 211, 212.

204. Ibid., p. 188.

205. Ibid., p. 320.

206. Ibid., p. 213.

207. Bohlen, p. 301.

208. Thomas A. Bailey, *Presidential Greatness* (Prentice-Hall, 1969), p. 174.

209. Warren, pp. 349, 350.

210. *The American Presidency*, pp. 157–159.

CHAPTER FIVE: Warren G. Harding

1. Died in office.

2. Samuel Hopkins Adams, *Incredible Era: The Life and Times of Warren Gamaliel Harding* (Houghton Mifflin, 1939), pp. 36, 37.

3. Francis Russell, *The Shadow of Blooming Grove: Warren G. Harding in His Times* (McGraw-Hill, 1968), p. 105.

4. Adams, p. 109.

5. Ibid., citing Mark Sullivan, *Our Times* (Scribners, 1926–1935), Vol. VI.

6. Ibid., p. 120.

7. Ibid., pp. 120, 121.

8. Russell, p. 334.

9. Adams, p. 122.

10. Russell, p. 371.

11. Adams, p. 163, citing Clinton W. Gilbert, *Mirrors of Washington* (Putnam, 1921).

12. Ibid., citing *Literary Digest*, November 27, 1920.

13. David F. Houston, *Eight Years with Wilson's Cabinet* (Doubleday, 1926), Vol. II, p. 93.

14. William G. McAdoo, *Crowded Years* (Houghton Mifflin, 1931), pp. 387, 388, 389.

15. Adams, p. 178.

16. Russell, p. 230.

17. Randolph C. Downes, *The Rise of Warren Gamaliel Harding 1865–1920* (Ohio State University Press, 1970), p. 154.

18. Russell, p. 386, citing Alice Longworth's Memoirs.

19. Adams, p. 186.

20. Russell, p. 347. In his speech Harding said "normalty" instead of "normalcy." Reporters changed this mispronunciation in their copy.

21. Ibid., p. 409.

22. Adams, p. 3.

23. Ibid., p. 5.

24. Ibid., p. 8.

25. Ibid., pp. 194, 195.

26. Russell, p. 63.

27. Adams, p. 426.

28. Downes, p. 81.

29. Adams, pp. 29, 30.

30. Ibid., p. 32, citing H. F. Alderfer, notes for *The Personality and Politics of Warren G. Harding* (Syracuse School of Citizenship and Public Affairs, 1928).

31. Downes, p. 50.

32. Ibid., citing *Star,* August 9, 1890.

33. Ibid., p. 51.

34. Ibid., p. 55.

35. Adams, pp. 32, 33.

36. Ibid, p. 46.

37. Russell, p. 96.

38. Ibid., p. 80.

39. Spading consists of betting that one's hand will contain a spade higher than his opponents'.

40. Adams, pp. 213, 214. Told to the writer by Mr. Seibold.

41. Ibid., p. 35.

42. Ibid., p. 36.

43. Russell, p. 104.

44. Adams, p. 51, citing Clinton W. Gilbert, *Mirrors of Washington.*

45. Russell, p. 131.

46. Ibid., p. 136.

47. Adams, p. 53, citing Jacob A. Meckstroth of the *Ohio State Journal.*

48. Ibid., p. 51, citing "Harding" by George McAdam in *World's Work,* September 1920.

49. Ibid., pp. 56, 57.

50. Ibid., p. 58.

51. Russell, pp. 460, 461.

52. Adams, p. 72, citing the *Plain Dealer,* September 24, 1910.

53. Ibid., p. 73.

54. Ibid., p. 59.

55. Ibid., p. 79.

56. Ibid., p. 84.

57. Ibid., p. 86, citing Alderfer.

58. Ibid., p. 91.

59. Russell, p. 295.

60. Ibid., p. 299.

61. Idem.

62. Ibid., pp. 320, 321.

63. Downes, p. 331.

64. Russell, p. 324.

65. Downes, pp. 326, 327.

66. Ibid., p. 327.

67. Ibid., p. 337.

68. Idem.

69. Ibid., p. 327, citing correspondence in Harding Papers, Ohio Historical Society, Temporary Box 4, Folder Scobey 1, No. 321074.

70. Ibid., p. 333, citing Harding to Hard, Hard Papers, September 13, 1919.

71. Downes, pp. 338, 339.

72. Ibid., p. 344, citing Harding to Magraf, November 5, 1919, Harding Papers, Temporary folder M, HO 319313.

73. Ibid., p. 345, citing Harding to F. E. Scobey, December 30, 1919.

74. Russell, p. 338.

75. Downes, p. 301, citing letter of January 14, 1919 to Frank E. Scobey.

76. Ibid., p. 311, citing Harding to Scobey, Harding Papers, Temporary Box 4, Folder 4945–2, no. 314050.

77. Ibid., p. 312.

78. Ibid., p. 313, citing Daugherty to Scobey, Scobey Papers, Box 2, no. 328.

79. Russell, p. 343.

80. Ibid., p. 405.

81. Adams, p. 170.

82. Idem.

83. It was not until 1932 that a Presidential candidate accepted his nomination directly after his nomination—at the convention.

84. Russell, pp. 400, 401.

85. Adams, p. 172, citing statement by Professor William Estabrook Chancellor.

86. Ibid., p. 176.

87. Ibid, p. 177.

88. Ibid, p. 178.

89. Russell, p. 402.

90. Ibid., p. 424.

91. Ibid., p. 425.

92. Adams, pp. 196, 197.

93. Russell, p. 427.

94. Adams, p. 38.

95. Ibid., pp. 40, 41.

96. Russell, p. 433.

97. Adams, p. 206, citing *New York Times,* February 7, 1921.

98. Ibid., p. 207.

99. Russell, p. 439.

100. Adams, p. 272, citing Joe Mitchell Chapple, *The Life and Times of Warren G. Harding, Our After War President* (Chapple Publishing, 1924).

101. Russell, p. 438.

102. Adams, p. 221.

103. Ibid., citing Willis Fletcher Johnson, *Life of Warren G. Harding.*

104. Adams, p. 222, citing William Allen White, *Masks in a Pageant* (By permission of Macmillan).

105. Ibid., p. 223, citing "The Ohio Gang" in *New Republic,* Vols. 38 & 39.

106. Russell, p. 452.

107. Ibid., p. 453.

108. Ibid., pp. 455, 456.

109. Ibid., p. 456.

110. Ibid., p. 443.

111. Ibid., p. 470.

112. Ibid., p. 457.

113. Ibid., p. 458.

114. Idem.

115. Ibid., p. 470.

116. Ibid., p. 476.

117. Ibid., p. 482.

118. Idem.

119. Idem.

120. Ibid., p. 485.

121. Ibid., p. 487.

122. Adams, p. 259.

123. Ibid., p. 473.

124. Russell, p. 469.

125. Ibid., p. 492.

126. Ibid., pp. 501, 502.

127. Ibid., p. 495.

128. Ibid., p. 504.

129. Ibid., p. 447.

130. Ibid., p. 436, 1196.

131. Ibid., p. 498.

132. Ibid., p. 506.

133. Adams, p. 303, citing *New York Times,* March 18, 1923.

134. Russell, p. 634.

135. News bulletin, M/S *Sagafjord,* March 12, 1974.

136. Adams, p. 232.

137. Russell, pp. 522, 523.

138. Ibid., pp. 557, 558.

139. Adams, p. 297.
140. Ibid., p. 272, citing Chapple.
141. Russell, pp. 566, 567.
142. Ibid., p. 560.
143. Ibid., p. 561.
144. Ibid., p. 564.
145. Ibid., p. 565.
146. Idem.
147. Ibid., pp. 575, 576.
148. Ibid., p. 577.
149. Adams, pp. 264, 265.
150. Ibid., p. 580.
151. Ibid., p. 587.
152. Russell, p. 508.
153. Ibid., p. 588.
154. Ibid., pp. 588, 589.
155. Ibid., p. 590.
156. Ibid., p. 582.
157. Adams, p. 257, citing Alderfer.
158. Russell, pp. 558, 559.

AFTERWORD

1. *Charles A. Beard, An Economic Interpretation of the Constitution of the United States* (Macmillan, 1956), p. 158.

APPENDIX

1. *Journal of American History,* published by the Organization of American Historians, Vol. LVII, No.1, June 1970.

INDEX